SYMBOLS AND LANGUAGE ABBREVIATIONS
USED IN THE ETYMOLOGIES

‡ foreign word or phrase
< derived from
? perhaps; possibly; uncertain
+ plus
& and

Abyss., Abyssinian
Afr., African
Alb., Albanian
Am., American
Am. Ind., American Indian
Am. Sp., American Spanish
Anglo-Fr., Anglo-French
Anglo-Ind., Anglo-Indian
Anglo-Ir., Anglo-Irish
Anglo-L., Anglo-Latin
Anglo-N., Anglo-Norse
Anglo-Norm., Anglo-Norman
Ar., Arabic
Aram., Aramaic
AS., Anglo-Saxon
Assyr., Assyrian

Bab., Babylonian
Beng., Bengali
Bohem., Bohemian
Braz., Brazilian
Bret., Breton
Brit., British
Bulg., Bulgarian

Canad., Canadian
Canad. Fr., Canadian French
Catal., Catalonian
Celt., Celtic
Ch., Chaldean; Chaldee
Chin., Chinese
Corn., Cornish
Cym., Cymric

D., Dutch
Dan., Danish

E.Fris., East Frisian
Egypt., Egyptian
E.Ind., East Indian
Eng., English
Esk., Eskimo
Eth., Ethiopic

Finn., Finnish
Fl., Flemish
Fr., French
Frank., Frankish
Fris., Frisian

G., German
Gael., Gaelic

Gaul., Gaulish
Gmc., Germanic
Goth., Gothic
Gr., Greek

Haw., Hawaiian
Heb., Hebrew
Hind., Hindi; Hindu; Hindustani
Hung., Hungarian

Ice., Icelandic
IE., Indo-European
Ind., Indian
Ir., Irish
Iran., Iranian
It., Italian

Japan., Japanese
Jav., Javanese

Kor., Korean

L., Latin
LG., Low German
LGr., Late Greek
Lith., Lithuanian
LL., Late Latin; Low Latin
LWS., Late West Saxon

MD., Middle Dutch
ME., Middle English
Med., Medieval
Mex., Mexican
MFl., Middle Flemish
MFr., Middle French
MGr., Medieval Greek; Middle Greek
MHG., Middle High German
MIr., Middle Irish
MIt., Middle Italian
ML., Medieval Latin
MLG., Middle Low German
MnE., Modern English
Mod., Modern
Mod. Gr., Modern Greek
Mod. L., Modern Latin
Mongol., Mongolian
MScand., Middle Scandinavian
MScot., Middle Scottish

N., Norse
Norm., Norman
Norw., Norwegian

O, Old
OAr., Old Arabic
OCelt., Old Celtic

OCym., Old Cymric
OD., Old Dutch
ODan., Old Danish
OFr., Old French
OFris., Old Frisian
OHG., Old High German
OIr., Old Irish
OIt., Old Italian
OLG., Old Low German
ON., Old Norse
ONorm.Fr., Old Norman French
OPer., Old Persian
OS., Old Saxon
OSlav., Old Slavic
OSerb., Old Serbian
OSp., Old Spanish
OW., Old Welsh

Per., Persian
Peruv., Peruvian
Phoen., Phoenician
Pid.Eng., Pidgin English
Pol., Polish
Port., Portuguese
Pr., Provençal
Prov. Eng., Provincial English
Prov. Scot., Provincial Scottish

Russ., Russian

S.Afr.D., South African Dutch
Sans., Sanskrit
Scand., Scandinavian
Scot., Scottish
Sem., Semitic
Serb., Serbian
Singh., Singhalese
Slav., Slavic; Slavonic
Sp., Spanish
Sw., Swed., Swedish
Syr., Syrian; Syriac

Tag., Tagalog
Tart., Tartar
Tibet., Tibetan
Turk., Turkish

W., Welsh
W.Afr., West African
W.Fl., West Flemish
W.Gmc., West Germanic
W.Ind., West Indian
W.S., West Saxon

Yid., Yiddish

Gallery of
OFFICIAL
PORTRAITS
of the
PRESIDENTS
of the
UNITED STATES

GEORGE WASHINGTON
1789–1797

JOHN ADAMS
1797–1801

THOMAS JEFFERSON
1801–1809

JAMES MADISON
1809–1817

JAMES MONROE
1817–1825

JOHN QUINCY ADAMS
1825–1829

ANDREW JACKSON
1829–1837

MARTIN VAN BUREN
1837–1841

WILLIAM HENRY HARRISON
1841

JOHN TYLER
1841–1845

JAMES K. POLK
1845–1849

ZACHARY TAYLOR
1849–1850

MILLARD FILLMORE
1850–1853

FRANKLIN PIERCE
1853–1857

JAMES BUCHANAN
1857–1861

ABRAHAM LINCOLN
1861–1865

ANDREW JOHNSON
1865–1869

ULYSSES S. GRANT
1869–1877

RUTHERFORD B. HAYES
1877–1881

JAMES A. GARFIELD
1881

CHESTER A. ARTHUR
1881–1885

GROVER CLEVELAND
1885–1889, 1893–1897

BENJAMIN HARRISON
1889–1893

WILLIAM MCKINLEY
1897–1901

THEODORE ROOSEVELT
1901–1909

WILLIAM H. TAFT
1909–1913

WOODROW WILSON
1913–1921

WARREN G. HARDING
1921–1923

CALVIN COOLIDGE
1923–1929

HERBERT C. HOOVER
1929–1933

FRANKLIN D. ROOSEVELT
1933–1945

HARRY S. TRUMAN
1945–1953

DWIGHT D. EISENHOWER
1953–1961

JOHN F. KENNEDY
1961–1963

LYNDON B. JOHNSON
1963–1969

RICHARD M. NIXON
1969–1974

GERALD R. FORD
1974–1977

Charles M. Rafshoon

JAMES E. CARTER
1977–

Webster's New World Dictionary
with
Student Handbook

CONCISE EDITION

THE SOUTHWESTERN COMPANY
Nashville, Tennessee

CREDITS: CONCISE EDITION

Illustration credits. Sources for the illustrations appear below. When two or more illustrations appear on a page, they are credited in the order in which they appear on the page, left to right and top to bottom.

ACKNOWLEDGMENTS: Copyrighted Materials: Pages 1, 8 © J. Allan Cash/Rapho/Photo Researchers, 18 © 1974 F. B. Grunzweig/Photo Researchers, 32 © 1975 Myron Wood/Photo Researchers, 66, 124 © Paolo Koch/Rapho/Photo Researchers, 124 © 1973 Stephen Dalton/Photo Researchers, 162 (top) © Art Bilsten/Photo Researchers, (bottom right) © John H. Gerard/National Audubon Society/Photo Researchers, 167 (bottom) © Jeanne White/Photo Researchers, 168 (top) © Allan D. Cruickshank/Photo Researchers, 208 © Louis Goldman/Rapho/Photo Researchers, 209 (top) © Des Barlett/Photo Researchers, (bottom) ©Jen and Des Barlett, 227 © Joe Munroe/Photo Researchers, 244 (right), © 1975 Jim Cartier/Photo Researchers, 285 Christopher Morrow © 1977 Stock, Boston, 287 © 1975 Tom McHugh/Photo Researchers, 295 © 1970 Robert de Gast/Rapho/Photo Researchers, 307 © Ray Ellis/Photo Researchers, 319 © SUVA/DPI, 325 Cary Wolinsky © 1977 Stock, Boston, 326 (top right) © 1975 Arthur Sirdofsky/Editorial Photocolor Archives, (center left) Peter Vandermark © 1977 Stock, Boston, 345 © Bob Combs/Rapho/Photo Researchers, 353 Owen Franken © 1977 Stock, Boston, 355 (left), ©1976 Ray Ellis/Rapho/Photo Researchers, 356 (left) © 1973 George Gardner, 357 (left), 359 (right), © Eric Kroll/Taurus Photos, 360 (right) © 1973 Ray Ellis/Rapho/Photo Researchers, 362 (right) © R. D. Ullmann/Taurus Photos, 364 (right), © 1976 Alan C. Ross/Photo Researchers, 368 (right) © Bob Houser/Rapho/Photo Researchers, 369 (left) © Peter Angelo Simon/Photo Researchers.
   Page 7 Pictorial Parade, 13 Pictorial Parade, 15 Monkmeyer, 16 Pictorial Parade, 22 Los Angeles Chamber of Congress, 24 J. P. Laffont/SYGMA, 27 The Sophia Smith Collection, 29 Wide World, 33 Editorial Photocolor Archives, 35 Culver Pictures, 38 Editorial Photocolor Archives, 40 Culver Pictures, 41 New York Public Library Collection, 42 Culver pictures, 44 Painting by H. Charles McBarron from Center for Military History, 46, 48 Culver Pictures, 50 New York Public Library Collection, 53 Fratelli Alinari/Editorial Photocolor Archives, 54 Fratelli Alinari/Editorial Photocolor Archives, 56 Sovfoto, 59 Pictorial Parade, 60 Library of Congress, 62 Culver Pictures, 63 Pictorial Parade, 67 Keystone, 69 United Nations, 70 United Nations, 81 Hugh Rogers/Monkmeyer, 145 Grant Heilman, 149 Photo Researchers, 154 American Cancer Society, 157 Charles Pfizer and Co., 160 Ann Arbor Biological Center, Inc., 161 Runk/Schoenberger/Grant Heilman, 162 (bottom left) Grant Heilman, 163 Grant Heilman, 167 (top) Grant Heilman, 168 (bottom, both) Grant Heilman, 179 Tom Cook/RCA, 182 Du Pont, 197 Pictorial Parade, 205 Eugene Luttenberg/Editorial Photocolor Archives, 207 The Bettmann Archive, 212 Martin Levick/Black Star, 216 Culver Pictures, The Bettmann Archive, 217 Culver Pictures, 223 New York Public Library, The Metropolitan Museum of Art, 224 (all except bottom left) Rand McNally & Co., 226 Pictorial Parade, NASA, 230 The Bettmann Archive, 231 The Bettmann Archive, 235 German Information Center, 237 Joseph Abeles Studio, 239 Nat Fein/Keystone, 241 Culver Pictures, 242 Culver Pictures, 244 (left) Wide World, 245 Pictorial Parade, 249 Culver Pictures, 250 Joseph Abeles Studio, 251 Pictorial Parade, 252 Culver Pictures, 253 The Bettmann Archive, 255 New York Public Library Collection, 257 Keystone, 259 The Bettmann Archive, 288 Margot Granitas/Photo Researchers, 291, 294 Laima Turnley/Editorial Photocolor Archives, 297 Laima Druskis/Editorial Photocolor Archives, 303 H. Armstrong Roberts, 306 Andrew Sacks/Editorial Photocolor Archives, 321 American Plywood Association, 326 (top left) Hugh Rogers/Monkmeyer, (center right) Hugh Rogers/Monkmeyer, (bottom left) Sybil Shackman/Monkmeyer; (bottom right) Mimi Forsyth/Monkmeyer, 328, 329 Bethlehem Steel, 332 Yoram Kahana/Peter Arnold, 333 Sandy Hill Corporation, 334 Dow Chemical Company, 335 (both) Copper Development Association, 349 Sybil Shackman/Monkmeyer, 355 (right) Andrew Sacks/Editorial Photocolor Archives, 356 (right) Dan O'Neill/Editorial Photocolor Archives, 357 (center) Jan Lukas/Editorial Photocolor Archives (right) Steven Scher/Editorial Photocolor Archives, 358 Laima Turnley/Editorial Photocolor Archives, Editorial Photocolor Archives, 359 (left) Laima Druskis/Editorial Photocolor Archives, 360 (left) Trans World Airlines, 361 Brookhaven National Laboratory, Dan O'Neill/Editorial Photocolor Archives, 362 Laima Turnley/Editorial Photocolor Archives, Daniel S. Brody/Editorial Photocolor Archives, 363 College Newsphoto/ Editorial Photocolor Archives, Brookhaven National Laboratory, 364 Columbus-Cuneo-Cabrini Medical Center, 365 C. C. Kleinsorge/ Editorial Photocolor Archives, Dell Hermann Studio, Andrew Sacks/Editorial Photocolor Archives, 366 Russell A. Thompson/Taurus Photos, Laimute E. Druskis/Editorial Photocolor Archives, 367 Brookhaven National Laboratory, Tower News Service/Editorial Photocolor Archives, 368 Andrew Sacks/Editorial Photocolor Archives, 369 (right) Andrew Sacks/Editorial Photocolor Archives, 370 NASA, Andrew Sacks/Editorial Photocolor Archives, 371 Ann Chwatsky/Editorial Photocolor Archives, Dan O'Neill/Editorial Photocolor Archives, 372 Daniel S. Brody/Editorial Photocolor Archives, Laimute E. Druskis/Editorial Photocolor Archives.

Contents

STUDENT HANDBOOK

CHEMISTRY AND PHYSICS 179–204

SOCIAL SCIENCE 205–236

Student Handbook

Editorial development of the Student Handbook was directed by
The Hudson Group, Inc., Pleasantville, New York.

EUGENE EHRLICH / *Editor-in-Chief*　　GORTON CARRUTH / *Sponsoring Editor*

Bruce Wetterau / *Managing Editor*

David H. Scott / *Senior Editor*　　Natalie Goldstein / *Picture Editor*

Associate Editors:
Lilian Brady, Renee Cohen, Nancy Hayes, Emma G. Peirce, Katherine G. Scott

Editorial Assistants:
Hayden Carruth, Edward Fields, Susan Horton

CONTRIBUTING EDITORS

Everett J. Arthur	Norma S. Ehrlich	Harold P. Menninger
Patrick Beausoleil	Gladys Hager	David Morrill
David M. Brownstone	Murray Halwer	John A. Peirce
Gerard G. Chamberland	Gene R. Hawes	Edgar M. Reilly, Jr.
Phillip Cole	Waldeck Mainville	Richard H. Sturgeon
		Ann Waterhouse

The Student Handbook was designed by Edward Aho Design Associates, Inc.,
Pleasantville, New York.

Edward Aho / *Director*

Laurel Casazza, Pam Forde
Designers / Art Directors

Assistants:　Gregory Brownstone, Deborah Hughes

ILLUSTRATION

James Barkley	Peter Loewer
Ken Marcus Daly	Diane L. Nelson
Nick Forde	Publisher's Graphics
Graphic Presentation, Inc.	Jan Pyk
Robert Handville	Michael Vivo

Composition for the Student Handbook was by Monotype Composition Company, Inc.,
Baltimore, Maryland

THE UNITED STATES

As citizens we have the responsibility of learning all we can of how our government works. This section opens with a review of the organization and operation of the federal government and goes on to present the complete United States Constitution, along with commentary and explanations. It concludes with a detailed description of how proposed legislation becomes the law of the land.

Such information is valuable for all of us, but especially for those who will play an active role in local, state, or national politics. If you are considering a career as a lawyer, or if you dream of running for public office one day, you will find this section invaluable. Our country's past depended on informed citizens; its future, even more so. With the knowledge presented here, you can begin to prepare yourself to take an active, informed role in your government.

United States Government

The form of government that the United States possesses is the result of historical accident, political necessity, and philosophical conviction. The thirteen British colonies that became the original United States had all been incorporated separately, and each had established separate governments that were of long standing at the time of independence from Britain. Because of geographical and other factors, each colony had special and distinct problems and needs. On the other hand, from the moment of the Revolution, some form of central government to deal with common problems and programs became essential. Equally important to the colonists was the preservation of the individual and political liberties for which the Revolution had been fought.

The form of government that was established in 1787, with the writing of the Constitution, was a federal republic. The original thirteen states, and all subsequent states, retained a great measure of their sovereignty (independence). By this means, the differing interests and needs of a large nation could be handled by governments relatively close to the citizens whose interests they represented. On the other hand, a national government—often called the federal government—was established to deal with needs and interests either common to the entire nation (such as foreign policy) or common to several of the states (such as interstate commerce). This federal government, too, was republican, with

the representatives elected specially to it by the citizens of the states.

The Constitution is the supreme law of the nation. It is supreme in the sense that no law, neither national nor state, may be in conflict with it. But it is not the only law. Both the national and the state governments may enact any laws not covered by the Constitution. The Constitution also prescribes the relation of the states to the federal government, and describes the composition of the federal government.

The make-up of the federal government is the result of the fear that the writers (or "framers") of the Constitution had that any large national government would become tyrannical. The Revolutionary War had been fought to escape such tyranny and thus was an important influence. This fear also explains, in part, the federal nature of the United States. By leaving the states far-reaching authority, a limit was put on the potential power of the national government. But even within the federal government, organizations and procedures were created to forestall the growth of tyranny.

The framers' primary fear was of the exercise of arbitrary power, whether by a king or by a legislature. To deal with this fear, the Constitution established a government in which power is divided among three independent branches: the legislative, the executive, and the judicial. The exercise of power requires the cooperation of all three branches, and each, therefore, operates as a "check" or "balance" on the unlawful use of authority by the others.

THE LEGISLATIVE BRANCH

Legislative power—the power to enact laws—is vested by the Constitution in the Congress of the United States. Here, too, the fears and desires of the framers are reflected in its composition.

The Congress is divided into the House of Representatives and the Senate, and because the consent of both is necessary to the enactment of a law, each acts as a check on the other. The House of Representatives, with a larger number of members, was conceived of as the popular branch, the part of Congress in closest touch with and most responsive to the citizens. The Senate, far smaller, and with members elected for longer terms of office, was conceived of as a moderating influence on the House for two reasons. First, because Senators were elected from larger constituencies, and second, because they need not face reelection so frequently, it was felt they would not be prone to the pressures either of temporary passions or of special sectional interests. And, in fact, the Senate has tended to take a more "national" view of problems and legislation, and in this respect acts as a buffer to the more locally oriented House.

The House of Representatives

There are 435 members, called Congressmen, of the House of Representatives. The members are divided among the states proportionately to the population of the states (as established every ten years by the census), with the single exception that no state shall have less than one representative. The size of constituencies varies considerably, but the average figure (as of the 1970 census) is one representative per 412,000 persons. Members of the House are elected for terms of two years.

In common with the Senate, the House proposes and enacts legislation on matters of national interest. Many of these matters are enumerated in the Constitution; others have been added through the years as the scope of federal involvement has increased. Any member of the House (or Senate) may propose a piece of legislation, called a "bill," for consideration. Recently, however, most important legislation has come to be initiated by the President, though it must be proposed to the Congress by a representative, usually a member of the President's own political party.

The Congress also enacts bills necessary for the execution of the laws, either creating agencies to administer programs or allocating funds for their operation. The special responsibility of the House is the initiation of "money" bills. Any appropriation of federal funds must be introduced first in the House. Only after it has been approved by the House can it be sent to the Senate for approval.

Organization of the House.   The most important office in the House is that of the Speaker. The Congressman who holds this office—always now a senior member of the majority party in the House—wields extensive powers. It is he who recognizes Congressmen to speak during debates. By granting or withholding recognition, he can greatly influence the course and content of the deliberations on the floor of the House.

In addition, the Speaker is the person who assigns proposed bills to committees (discussed later) and therefore exercises enormous power over new legislation. Depending on how he distributes bills to committees, he may make the passage of a bill a simple and easy matter or an almost impossible task.

The other important offices in the House are the majority and minority floor leaders and the assistant floor leaders (also called "whips"). The majority leader and majority whip are members of the majority party in the House. Both are likely to be senior Congressmen. The majority leader is the planner of strategy for the enactment of the legislation that the majority party intends to propose. He will conduct negotiations, both in his own party and with the minority party, to ensure that there will be sufficient votes to pass the bills. The job of the whip is to guarantee that all the necessary Congressmen are present to vote when needed. The minority

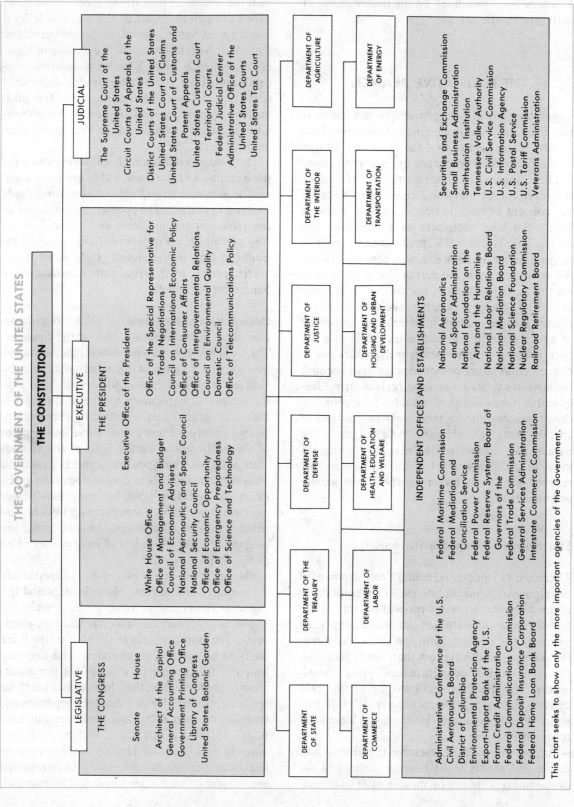

THE GOVERNMENT OF THE UNITED STATES

THE CONSTITUTION

LEGISLATIVE

THE CONGRESS

Senate   House

Architect of the Capitol
General Accounting Office
Government Printing Office
Library of Congress
United States Botanic Garden

EXECUTIVE

THE PRESIDENT

Executive Office of the President

White House Office
Office of Management and Budget
Council of Economic Advisers
National Aeronautics and Space Council
National Security Council
Office of Economic Opportunity
Office of Emergency Preparedness
Office of Science and Technology

Office of the Special Representative for
  Trade Negotiations
Council on International Economic Policy
Office of Consumer Affairs
Office of Intergovernmental Relations
Council on Environmental Quality
Domestic Council
Office of Telecommunications Policy

JUDICIAL

The Supreme Court of the
  United States
Circuit Courts of Appeals of the
  United States
District Courts of the United States
United States Court of Claims
United States Court of Customs and
  Patent Appeals
United States Customs Court
Territorial Courts
Federal Judicial Center
Administrative Office of the
  United States Courts
United States Tax Court

DEPARTMENT OF STATE

DEPARTMENT OF THE TREASURY

DEPARTMENT OF DEFENSE

DEPARTMENT OF JUSTICE

DEPARTMENT OF THE INTERIOR

DEPARTMENT OF AGRICULTURE

DEPARTMENT OF COMMERCE

DEPARTMENT OF LABOR

DEPARTMENT OF HEALTH, EDUCATION AND WELFARE

DEPARTMENT OF HOUSING AND URBAN DEVELOPMENT

DEPARTMENT OF TRANSPORTATION

DEPARTMENT OF ENERGY

INDEPENDENT OFFICES AND ESTABLISHMENTS

Administrative Conference of the U.S.
Civil Aeronautics Board
District of Columbia
Environmental Protection Agency
Export-Import Bank of the U.S.
Farm Credit Administration
Federal Communications Commission
Federal Deposit Insurance Corporation
Federal Home Loan Bank Board

Federal Maritime Commission
Federal Mediation and
  Conciliation Service
Federal Power Commission
Federal Reserve System, Board of
  Governors of the
Federal Trade Commission
General Services Administration
Interstate Commerce Commission

National Aeronautics
  and Space Administration
National Foundation on the
  Arts and the Humanities
National Labor Relations Board
National Mediation Board
National Science Foundation
Nuclear Regulatory Commission
Railroad Retirement Board

Securities and Exchange Commission
Small Business Administration
Smithsonian Institution
Tennessee Valley Authority
U.S. Civil Service Commission
U.S. Information Agency
U.S. Postal Service
U.S. Tariff Commission
Veterans Administration

This chart seeks to show only the more important agencies of the Government.

4

leader and minority whip perform comparable roles, though generally their job is to oppose and try to defeat the proposed legislation.

The Senate

The Senate of the United States is composed of one hundred Senators, two from each state, elected for terms of six years. Until 1913 Senators were elected by the legislatures of the several states, for they were conceived of as the representatives of the states to the federal government. A Constitutional amendment approved in 1913 established their popular election (though on a state-wide basis), both because their indirect election was felt to be undemocratic and because it was felt that many state legislatures were corrupt, inefficient, or controlled by special interest groups.

The primary job of the Senate, as of the House, is the proposal and enactment of legislation. Any Senator may propose a bill, and any bill except an appropriations bill may originate in the Senate. In addition to this general function, the Senate has some unique functions. All treaties with foreign nations and the appointment of all ambassadors to foreign countries must be approved by the Senate. The Senate must also approve all presidential appointments to the Supreme Court and other federal courts and to the important federal departments.

Organization of the Senate. The Constitution directs that the Vice-President of the United States be the president of the Senate. He does not vote, except in the case of a tied vote, when he can vote to break the tie. The Senate also elects one of its members president *pro tempore* ("for the time") to preside over the Senate in the absence of the Vice-President. Neither of these men, however, is influential in the Senate.

The most important political office in the Senate is that of majority floor leader. He does not have as much control over the workings of the Senate as the Speaker has in the House. In general, his job is similar to that of the majority leader in the House. The same is true of the assistant majority leader (whip), the minority leader, and assistant minority leader.

The Committee System

The most important, but often hidden, aspect of the working of Congress is the committee system. Faced with an overwhelming volume of bills to consider—bills covering a vast range of problems—Congress devised the committee structure to deal with them. There are at present fifteen Senate and twenty-two House "standing" (permanent) committees. They do the major share of work in the legislative process.

The committees were created to deal with specific areas of legislation, such as agriculture or foreign affairs. When a bill is proposed, it is sent to the appropriate committee—the one dealing with its area—where research is done on the bill and where its merits are judged. Generally, only if the committee approves of the bill, or if the committee amends or changes the bill and then approves it, does the bill come to the floor of the Congress for debate and voting. Because of the almost absolute control the committee has over the future of the bill, the chairmen of the standing committees are influential members of Congress.

The make-up of the standing committees closely represents the numerical political make-up of the Congress. The majority of the committee members will reflect the numerical majority of the majority party in that branch of Congress. The committee chairman is almost always, by custom, the senior member (in terms of service in Congress) of the majority party on that committee. The committee chairman has almost complete control over when a bill will be considered, how it will be considered, and who will speak for it or against it. Because of these powers, a sympathetic chairman can speed a bill through his committee, and an unsympathetic one can virtually kill it.

It is because committee chairmanships are assigned by seniority that the committee system has come under attack. Seniority does not necessarily reflect ability, but does tend to distribute chairmanships to representatives from "safe" districts. Consequently, certain geographical areas are disporportionately represented among chairmen—the South during Democratic majorities, the Midwest during Republican. Furthermore, chairmen are often much more conservative than the majority of the representatives.

A further problem with the committee system develops because much legislation may overlap committee responsibilities. In this case, the choice of the committee to which the bill is sent may decide its success or failure. This is another reason why the Speaker of the House is so powerful. If he favors a bill, he can send it to a committee he judges sympathetic; if he opposes it, he will do the opposite.

Representatives are assigned to committees by the caucuses of their political parties, meeting immediately before each session of Congress. Personal preference is usually the grounds for choice. A representative from a rural district will request assignment to the Agriculture Committee, while a representative from an industrial district may request the Labor Committee. In both branches of Congress, however, some committees are more influential or prestigious than the rest, and assignment to these may, again, depend on seniority.

The power of a committee may be the result of the prevailing political climate or of the committee's function. In the early years of the nation, the Agriculture committees were especially powerful, while recently the Foreign Affairs committees have come to the fore. If a presidential administration is known to be proposing a program of legislation in a particular area, those committees will receive greater prominence. On the other hand, in the House, the Ways and Means Committee has always been important, for all appropriations bills go to that committee. Similarly, the Rules Committee of the House is very powerful, for it controls when and how a bill will be debated on the floor.

Passage of a Bill

In order for a law to be enacted, it must undergo a long and complicated process. When a representative proposes a bill, a copy is printed and sent to the appropriate committee. The committee will consider it—either the whole committee or a part of it, called a subcommittee—and approve it, reject it, or amend it. If approved, the bill is "read out" of committee, that is, sent to the floor of Congress.

When a bill comes to the House floor, for example, it is given a date on the calendar of business, and then read to the House and debated. It may be passed, amended, or rejected. If passed or amended, a copy of the bill as passed is sent to the other branch of Congress, the Senate, where it goes through the same process of committee and debate. If both branches of Congress pass the same bill, it is sent to the President for his signature. If, however, the second branch passes a different version of the bill, the bill goes back to the first branch for approval. If the first branch agrees, it passes the new version and the bill is sent to the President. If it disagrees, a joint House-Senate conference committee is set up to negotiate a compromise.

When a bill reaches the President, he may do one of three things. He may sign it, in which case it becomes a law. Or he may veto it, in which case it does not, though Congress may override the veto by a two-thirds vote of both branches. Or the President may keep the bill for ten days without signing it. In this case, if the ten-day period occurs when Congress is in session, the bill automatically becomes law. If Congress adjourns during the ten-day period, the bill does not become law. This is called the "pocket veto" and is generally employed when Congress has fewer than ten days left in its session.

THE EXECUTIVE BRANCH

There are about three million civilians employed by the federal government, almost all in the executive branch. At the head of this vast force created to execute the laws and to administer the business of the United States is the President. The Constitution established a strong and effective executive branch. The President is responsible for the implementation of the laws Congress enacts, for the conduct of national foreign policy and for the appointment of federal officials. He is also commander-in-chief of the armed forces in time of war. A Vice-President is elected to replace the President should he die or become incapacitated. Both the President and Vice-President serve terms of four years, and

6

President Jimmy Carter signs the Emergency Natural Gas Bill on February 2, 1977. This was the first legislation carrying the signature of the thirty-ninth President.

may be reelected only once. The Vice-President is also the presiding officer of the Senate.

The powers of the President are theoretically checked by the legislative and judicial branches. That is, the President may not act except in accordance with the laws Congress passes; further, Congress may withhold funds from the President to make him cease a course of action he has begun. On the other hand, the twentieth century has seen the unparalleled growth—in size and influence—of the executive branch, and has seen the unparalleled centralization of political power in the office of the President.

Growth and centralization have gone together. As the federal government became responsible for more activities, more executive agencies and departments were necessary for their administration. And as the President became responsible for the increasingly extensive administration of the country—in his capacity as chief executive—so did he become more influentially connected with the enactment of legislation for the conduct of government business. In fact, most important federal legislation is now initiated or suggested by the President (rather than by Congressmen), and only spon-

sored by Congressmen on the floor of the Congress. Although the two other branches of government retain their constitutional powers of checks and balances, because of the greater size and potential for action of the executive branch, the primary source of political power in the United States is, at present, the President.

The President exercises his power both in the areas explicitly given to him by the Constitution and in his capacity as chief executive of the executive branch of government. The executive branch is composed of three distinct sorts of departments and agencies: the executive departments, the executive offices of the President, and the independent federal agencies.

The Executive Departments

The executive departments are responsible for implementation of federal law in their respective areas, and also for day-to-day conduct of business in these areas. The twelve departments are: State; Treasury; Defense; Interior; Justice; Agriculture; Commerce; Labor; Health, Education and Welfare; Housing and Urban Development; Transportation; and Energy. The Post Office used to be an executive department, but in 1971 became an independent executive agency.

The heads of these departments—all of whom are called secretaries, except the head of the Department of Justice, who is called the attorney-general—form the Cabinet of the United States, an important advisory body to the President.

The departments were created to deal with whatever business the federal government undertook. The Department of State conducts the nation's foreign policy; the Department of the Treasury manages the government's financial business, prints money, and collects taxes; the Department of Defense coordinates the armed forces, and contains within itself subdepartments of the Army, Navy, and Air Force.

The Department of Justice initiates and prosecutes all federal criminal cases. It also directs the Federal Bureau of Investigation and enforces government policies in non-criminal areas when directed to do so by Congress. In addition, the attorney-general—whose office was created in 1789, although the department was not established until much later—advises the President on the scope of his powers under the law.

The Department of the Interior carries on conservation activities, administers public lands and national parks, and is in charge of Indian affairs. The Department of Agriculture conducts scientific research and educational and economic programs to benefit the nation's farmers. The Department of Commerce (which until 1913 was combined with the Department of Labor) is a clearinghouse of information and statistics for business organizations. It also contains the Census Bureau, the Weather Bureau, and the Patent Office.

The Department of Labor collects information regarding wages and working conditions, and regulates those aspects of labor conditions that fall under federal control. The Department of Health, Education, and Welfare conducts federal social welfare programs through agencies such as the Social Security Administration and the Food and Drug Administration. The Department of Housing and Urban Development administers agencies responsible for coordination of planning for metropolitan areas. The Department of Transportation is responsible for development of coordinated policies for the expansion and improvement of all types of transportation. The Department of Energy is responsible for establishing priorities on how oil, coal, nuclear energy, solar energy and other alternative sources of energy will be produced and consumed.

The Cabinet

The Cabinet, formed of the heads of these executive departments and the Vice-President (and sometimes the ambassador to the United Nations), is a creation of custom rather than law. It is not mentioned in the Constitution. The Constitution does presume, however, that the President would have advisers, and the Cabinet grew out of the custom of the first Presidents' meetings with the departmental secretaries. Cabinet appointments must be approved by the Senate.

The President is not required to follow the advice of his Cabinet, and different Presidents have used the Cabinet in different ways. Some

Department of Justice headquarters, on Constitution Avenue, Washington, D.C. This important department is led by the Attorney General, who is the chief law enforcement officer of the United States government. One of the arms of the department is the Federal Bureau of Investigation, which occupies an entire building of its own at 9th Street and Pennsylvania Avenue, Washington, D.C.

have held meetings of the full Cabinet to conduct open discussions of policy. Others have simply met separately with secretaries on matters pertaining to the individual departments.

The Executive Offices

Beginning in 1937, a set of agencies was created by Congress to help the President perform his administrative functions more efficiently. These are called the executive offices and are specialized agencies for providing expert information and advice for the President. They include, among others: the National Security Council, the Council of Economic Advisers, the Bureau of the Budget, the Central Intelligence Agency, and the Office of Consumer Affairs.

Often these executive offices are more important than the executive departments, for the President can deal with them more easily and closely than with the large departmental bureaucracies.

Recently, the most important of all these offices has become the White House Office. This is composed of the President's closest and most trusted political and governmental advisers, as well as technical experts and even speech writers. The President deals with this office most frequently, and it may wield considerable influence and power. For some Presidents the White House Office may replace the Cabinet as the primary advisory body.

The Independent Executive Agencies

The independent agencies are of recent origin, and were created by Congress to implement laws and deal with problems. Each agency is administered by a team of commissioners or directors. These are appointed by the President, but serve terms longer than his—ranging from five to fourteen years—which gives the agencies a certain independence from the executive branch. The agencies are also independent of the executive, in that they were created by Congress and are expected to operate in accordance with policy lines laid down by Congress.

The independent agencies are of three sorts: administrative agencies, regulatory agencies, and government corporations. An example of an administrative agency is the Veterans Administration. Examples of regulatory agencies are the Interstate Commerce Commission and the National Labor Relations Board. Examples of government corporations are the United States Postal Service and the Federal Deposit Insurance Corporation.

THE JUDICIAL BRANCH

The third branch of the federal government is the judicial branch. The framers of the Constitution created a federal judiciary so that the federal laws would be interpreted uniformly throughout the nation, and so that these laws might not be obstructed or enforced prejudicially by different state authorities.

The judicial branch is composed of two types of courts. There are the courts of "general jurisdiction": the Supreme Court (which is the highest court of the entire judicial branch, and which consists of a Chief Justice and eight Associate Justices), the Federal Courts of Appeals, and the Federal District Courts. There are also courts of "special jurisdiction": the Courts of Claims, Customs, Customs and Patent Appeals, Tax, and Military Appeals.

At present there are ninety-three Federal District Courts and eleven Courts of Appeals. All federal judges are appointed by the President, but their appointments must be confirmed by the Senate. Federal judges hold their positions during good behavior (meaning virtually for life)— which is the primary way the judicial branch retains its independence from the other two branches of government. A federal judge can only be removed by impeachment and conviction by the Congress.

The federal courts have jurisdiction only over federal law. That is, a case involving a violation of a state or local law cannot be tried in a federal court. Violation of a federal law, on the other hand, cannot be tried in a state court.

Most federal cases are tried in the District Courts, which handle the greatest amount of judicial business. The decisions of the District

Courts may be appealed to the Courts of Appeals, and their decisions may be appealed to the Supreme Court. The Supreme Court is the final, or highest, court of appeals in the nation. The courts of special jurisdiction are the initial courts—or courts of "original jurisdiction"—for certain specialized cases under federal law. Their decisions may be appealed to the Supreme Court.

In addition to its role as the final appellate court, the Supreme Court is also the court of original jurisdiction for certain cases. Any case involving ambassadors and any case to which a state or the federal government is a party must be tried in the Supreme Court. Most cases reaching the Supreme Court are, however, appeals of lower decisions.

Although most of the business of the federal courts involves suits under federal law, the federal courts, in their capacity as interpreters of the federal law and the Constitution, exercise a further and more extensive power, called "judicial review." No law—federal, state or local—may be in conflict with the Constitution. A suit may be brought in a federal court when it appears that such a conflict exists. Therefore, the federal courts are sometimes called upon to rule on the constitutionality of legislative acts taken by the Congress or by state legislatures or local government bodies. If the federal courts decide that an act is in conflict with the Constitution, the courts declare the act invalid. These decisions may be appealed to higher federal courts.

Judicial review is the widest power the federal courts possess. It is this power that enables the judiciary to function as a check and balance on the actions of the other two branches of the federal government. By this power, also, the judiciary can compel the states to respect the rights of their citizens which are guaranteed by the Constitution, or it can prevent the federal government from attempting to usurp the prerogatives of the state governments.

The power of judicial review has been the source of great controversy, for it has served as a means of extending federal jurisdiction into the states. By ruling that certain areas which had previously been state controlled were to be covered by constitutional provisions, the courts have either compelled states to follow federal regulations, or have given the federal government the justification to take direct action. The parts of the Constitution most frequently used in rendering these decisions have been the "commerce clause" (Article I, Section 8.3) and the Fourteenth Amendment, which guarantees the equal protection of the laws to all United States citizens.

THE STATES

Under the Constitution, the states retain the authority over the lives of their citizens in all matters not covered by the Constitution or federal law. All states have constitutions, legislatures, an executive branch (whose chief executive is the governor), and a judicial branch. All but one of the states (Nebraska) have legislative branches which are divided into two parts, like the Congress.

Despite their constitutional retention of power, the historical trend has been towards the weakening of the states in relation to the federal government. This is the result of three processes. Most important, perhaps, is that the federal government is richer than the state governments and more capable of effectively carrying out large programs. Also important is that many state governments are comparatively inefficient. The third process has been the gradual creation of a wider feeling of national identity and a perception of the interconnection of state needs, problems, and aims. Many Americans, therefore, feel that greater numbers of matters should properly be deliberated at the national level.

Recent history, however, has demonstrated that Americans have come to feel increasingly alienated from the immense and relatively remote national government. Should these feelings continue to grow, and should the states provide their citizens with efficient and responsive governments that are significantly smaller and closer to the citizens than the federal government, it is possible that the states may reclaim much of their power and authority from the federal government.

The Constitution

In 1787 the newly written Constitution of the United States was an unusual document. Not only was it the first written national constitution since ancient times, it was also the first to set up what is called the "federal system." Under this sytem, sovereign power comes from the people. Some powers are given to the federal government, others to the states.

This system was much different from that under which the new nation had been governed since the end of the American Revolution in 1781. The Articles of Confederation left nearly all the power in the hands of the states. They could cooperate in the central government—or ignore it, if they chose.

There was considerable opposition to the new form of government, but eventually its strongest supporters, the Federalists, won out, and by 1789 the Constitution had been ratified by all thirteen states.

The full text of the Constitution, with all the amendments that have been added since 1787, is given here. Annotations in italics have been inserted from time to time as an aid to the reader.

The Constitution is divided into seven Articles. The first four Articles are the basis of the government: Article I concerns the legislative branch; Article II, the executive branch; Article III, the judicial branch; Article IV, the relationships between states and the rules for territories.

The Bill of Rights. The loss of personal and civil rights and liberties had been the original reason for rebellion against the British. Specific guarantees of these rights are given in the first ten amendments, which were added to the Constitution in 1791. A group of statesmen, led by Thomas Jefferson, felt that these rights were sufficiently important to be stated separately.

Preamble

We the People of the United States, in order to form a more perfect Union, establish justice, insure domestic tranquility, provide for the common defense, promote the general welfare, and secure the blessings of liberty to ourselves and our posterity, do ordain and establish this Constitution for the United States of America.

Article I
Legislative Branch

Section 1. All legislative powers herein granted shall be vested in a Congress of the United States, which shall consist of a Senate and House of Representatives.

Although only Congress can pass new laws, the President can veto a bill before it becomes law, and the Supreme Court can declare a law unconstitutional. The Constitution sets up many similar checks and balances on the powers of each branch of government.

Section 2.   (House of Representatives) The House of Representatives shall be composed of members chosen every second year by the people of the several States, and the electors in each State shall have the qualifications requisite for electors of the most numerous branch of the state legislature.

No person shall be a Representative who shall not have attained to the age of twenty-five years, and been seven years a citizen of the United States, and who shall not, when elected, be an inhabitant of that State in which he shall be chosen.

Representatives and direct taxes shall be apportioned among the several States which may be included within this Union, according to their respective numbers, which shall be determined by adding to the whole number of free persons, including those bound to service for a term of years, and excluding Indians not taxed, three-fifths of all other persons. The actual enumeration shall be made within three years after the first meeting of the Congress of the United States, and within every subsequent term of ten years, in such manner as they shall by law direct. The number of Representatives shall not exceed one for every thirty thousand, but each State shall have at least one Representative; and until such enumeration shall be made, the State of New Hampshire shall be entitled to choose three; Massachusetts, eight; Rhode Island and Providence Plantations, one; Connecticut, five; New York, six; New Jersey, four; Pennsylvania, eight; Delaware, one; Maryland, six; Virginia, ten; North Carolina, five; South Carolina, five; and Georgia, three.

This section set up the national census to determine how many representatives in Congress each state would have. Originally, slaves and Indians were not counted "whole persons" in the census, but the Fourteenth Amendment gave former slaves the full rights of citizenship. The number of congressmen from each state is still determined by the number of people in the state, but the total membership of the House is limited to 435.

When vacancies happen in the representation from any State, the executive authority thereof shall issue writs of election to fill such vacancies.

The House of Representatives shall choose their Speaker and other officers; and shall have the sole power of impeachment.

"Impeachment" means accusing an official of wrong conduct in office. The House of Representatives makes these charges, and the Senate acts as the court where they are tried (see Section 3).

Section 3.   (Senate) The Senate of the United States shall be composed of two Senators from each State, chosen by the legislature thereof, for six years; and each Senator shall have one vote.

Since the Seventeenth Amendment was passed in 1913, Senators are chosen by direct popular vote, not by the legislatures.

Immediately after they shall be assembled in consequence of the first election, they shall be divided as equally as may be into three classes. The seats of the Senators of the first class shall be vacated at the expiration of the second year, of the second class at the expiration of the fourth year, and of the third class at the expiration of the sixth year, so that one-third may be chosen every second year; and if vacancies happen by resignation, or otherwise, during the recess of the legislature of any State, the executive thereof may make temporary appointments until the next meeting of the legislature, which shall then fill such vacancies.

This clause set up a system of staggered elections to the Senate. All Senators now have six-year terms, but the terms expire at different times. In one election year, only one-third of the Senators are up for election; the others still have two or four more years to serve. This gives the Senate more continuity than the House, where all members are up for election every two years.

No person shall be a Senator who shall not have attained to the age of thirty years, and been nine years a citizen of the United States, and who shall not, when elected, be an inhabitant of that State for which he shall be chosen.

The Vice-President of the United States shall

be president of the Senate, but shall have no vote unless they be equally divided.

Since there are always an even number of Senators, tie votes are possible, and so the Vice-President was given the power to break ties.

The Senate shall choose their other officers, and also a president pro tempore, in the absence of the Vice-President, or when he shall exercise the office of President of the United States.

The Senate shall have the sole power to try all impeachments. When sitting for that purpose, they shall be on oath or affirmation. When the President of the United States is tried, the Chief Justice shall preside; and no person shall be convicted without the concurrence of two-thirds of the members present.

Judgment in cases of impeachment shall not extend further than to removal from office, and disqualification to hold and enjoy any office of honor, trust, or profit under the United States; but the party convicted shall nevertheless be liable and subject to indictment, trial, judgment and punishment, according to law.

Section 4. (Election of Senators and Representatives) The times, places, and manner of holding elections for Senators and Representatives shall be prescribed in each State by the legislature thereof; but the Congress may at any time by law make or alter such regulations, except as to the places of choosing Senators.

The Congress shall assemble at least once in every year, and such meeting shall be on the first Monday in December, unless they shall by law appoint a different day.

The Twentieth Amedment changed this meeting time to noon, January 3.

Section 5. (Congressional Procedures) Each House shall be the judge of the elections, returns, and qualifications of its own members, and a majority of each shall constitute a quorum to do business; but a smaller number may adjourn from day to day, and may be authorized to compel the attendance of absent members in such manner and under such penalties as each House may provide.

Each House may determine the rules of its

Powerful House Judiciary Committee, under Chairman Peter Rodino, of New Jersey, played an important role in the events that led to the resignation of President Richard Nixon in 1974. The Committee normally deals with bills affecting our court system.

proceedings, punish its members for disorderly behavior, and, with the concurrence of two-thirds, expel a member.

Each House shall keep a journal of its proceedings, and from time to time publish the same, excepting such parts as may in their judgment require secrecy; and the yeas and nays of the members of either House on any question shall, at the desire of one-fifth of those present, be entered on the journal.

In addition to the Congressional Record, which is published every day, both houses of Congress keep a record of their proceedings.

Neither House, during the session of Congress, shall, without the consent of the other, adjourn for more than three days, nor to any other place than that in which the two Houses shall be sitting.

Section 6. The Senators and Representatives shall receive a compensation for their services, to be ascertained by law, and paid out of the Treasury of the United States. They shall in all cases, except treason, felony, and breach of the peace, be privileged from arrest during their attendance at the session of their respective Houses, and in going to and returning from the same; and for any speech or debate in either house, they shall not be questioned in any other place.

These privileges are called "congressional immunity."

No Senator or Representative shall, during the time for which he was elected, be appointed to any civil office under the authority of the United States which shall have been created, or the emoluments whereof shall have been increased during such time; and no person holding any office under the United States shall be a member of either House during his continuance in office.

"Emoluments" are salaries. This section prevents federal officials from being members of Congress at the same time.

Section 7. (Passing Bills and Resolutions) All bills for raising revenue shall originate in the House of Representatives; but the Senate may propose or concur with amendments as on other bills.

Every bill which shall have passed the House of Representatives and the Senate shall, before it become a law, be presented to the President of the United States; if he approve, he shall sign it, but if not he shall return it, with his objections, to that House in which it shall have originated, who shall enter the objections at large on their journal, and proceed to reconsider it. If after such reconsideration two-thirds of that House shall agree to pass the bill, it shall be sent, together with the objections, to the other House, by which it shall likewise be reconsidered; and if approved by two-thirds of that House, it shall become a law. But in all such cases the votes of both Houses shall be determined by yeas and nays, and the names of the persons voting for and against the bill shall be entered on the journal of each House respectively. If any bill shall not be returned by the President within ten days (Sundays excepted) after it shall have been presented to him, the same shall be a law, in like manner as if he had signed it, unless the Congress by their adjournment prevent its return, in which case it shall not be a law.

This section describes the President's veto power: Even if a bill has been passed by both the Senate and the House, the President can veto it, or turn it down, instead of signing it and making it a law. However, a two-thirds vote by both houses can pass the bill over his veto. Simply holding the bill when Congress is about to adjourn is a "pocket veto."

Every order, resolution, or vote to which the concurrence of the Senate and House of Representatives may be necessary (except on a question of adjournment) shall be presented to the President of the United States; and before the same shall take effect, shall be approved by him, or being disapproved by him, shall be repassed by two-thirds of the Senate and the House of Representatives, according to the rules and limitations prescribed in the case of a bill.

Section 8. (Powers of Congress) The Congress shall have power

THE UNITED STATES

Foreign cargo ships at dockside in Newark, New Jersey. It is the responsibility of Congress to regulate commerce with foreign nations. Many times in our history, the Congress has taken steps to encourage foreign trade (free trade policy); at other times a restrictive trade policy has been followed.

To lay and collect taxes, duties, imposts and excises, to pay the debts and provide for the common defense and general welfare of the United States; but all duties, imposts, and excises shall be uniform throughout the United States;

To borrow money on the credit of the United States;

To regulate commerce with foreign nations, and among the several States, and with the Indian tribes;

To establish an uniform rule of naturalization, and uniform laws on the subject of bankruptcies throughout the United States;

To coin money, regulate the value thereof, and of foreign coin, and fix the standard of weights and measures;

To provide for the punishment of counterfeiting the securities and current coin of the United States;

To establish post offices and post roads;

To promote the progress of science and useful arts by securing for limited times to authors and inventors the exclusive rights to their respective writings and discoveries;

This section allows Congress to pass laws about patents and copyrights.

To constitute tribunals inferior to the Supreme Court;

To define and punish piracies and felonies committed on the high seas, and offences against the law of nations;

To declare war, grant letters of marque and reprisal, and make rules concerning captures on land and water;

Only Congress can declare war, but the President, as commander-in-chief, can order the armed forces to act.

To raise and support armies, but no appropriation of money to that use shall be for a longer term than two years;

To provide and maintain a navy;

To make rules for the government and regulation of the land and naval forces;

To provide for calling forth the militia to execute the laws of the Union, suppress insurrections, and repel invasions; to provide for organizing, arming, and disciplining the militia, and for governing such part of them as may be employed in the service of the United States, reserving to the States respectively, the appointment of the officers, and the authority of training the militia according to the discipline prescribed by Congress.

To exercise exclusive legislation in all cases whatsoever over such district (not exceeding ten miles square) as may, by cession of particular States and the acceptance of Congress, become the seat of government of the United States, and to exercise like authority over all places purchased by the consent of the legislature of the State in which the same shall be, for the erection of forts, magazines, arsenals, dockyards, and other needful buildings;—and

This gave Congress the authority to establish and govern the District of Columbia.

To make all laws which shall be necessary and proper for carrying into execution the foregoing powers, and all other powers vested by this Constitution in the government of the United States, or in any department or officer thereof.

This is sometimes called the "elastic clause" because it can be interpreted to give many powers not actually mentioned in the Constitution.

Section 9. (Limitations on Congressional Powers) The migration or importation of such persons as any of the States now existing shall think proper to admit, shall not be prohibited by the Congress prior to the year 1808, but a tax or duty may be imposed on such importation, not exceeding ten dollars for each person.

This paragraph set up a waiting period for action on the slave trade; Congress did abolish it in 1808.

The privilege of the writ of habeas corpus shall not be suspended, unless when in cases of rebellion or invasion the public safety may require it.

Habeas corpus *guards against unjust imprisonment by requiring a judge or court to decide whether a person may be held.*

No bill of attainder or ex post facto law shall be passed.

An ex post facto *law applies to acts committed* before *the law was passed.*

No capitation or other direct tax shall be laid,

Informal gatherings at the White House with Congressional leaders give President Carter a chance to press his position on pending legislation. Legislators, in turn, can tell the President of their constituents' concerns. Such off-the-record meetings can increase cooperation between the executive and legislative branches.

THE UNITED STATES

unless in proportion to the census or enumeration herein before directed to be taken.

The Sixteenth Amendment allowed the income tax, which is not related to the census.

No tax or duty shall be laid on articles exported from any State.

No preference shall be given by any regulation of commerce or revenue to the ports of one state over those of another: nor shall vessels bound to or from one State be obliged to enter, clear, or pay duties in another.

No money shall be drawn from the Treasury but in consequence of appropriations made by law; and a regular statement and account of the receipts and expenditures of all public money shall be published from time to time.

No title or nobility shall be granted by the United States: and no person holding any office of profit or trust under them shall, without the consent of the Congress, accept of any present, emolument, office, or title of any kind whatever from any king, prince, or foreign state.

In fact, Presidents often exchange gifts with important foreign visitors, but the gifts are considered as gifts to the country.

Section 10. (Restriction on Powers of States) No State shall enter into any treaty, alliance, or confederation; grant letters of marque and reprisal; coin money; emit bills of credit; make any thing but gold and silver coin a tender in payment of debts; pass any bill of attainder, ex post facto law, or law impairing the obligation of contracts; or grant any title of nobility.

No State shall, without the consent of the Congress, lay any imposts or duties on imports or exports, except what may be absolutely necessary for executing its inspection laws; and the net produce of all duties and imposts, laid by any state on imports or exports, shall be for the use of the Treasury of the United States; and all such laws shall be subject to the revision and control of the Congress.

No state shall, without the consent of Congress, lay any duty of tonnage, keep troops or ships of war in time of peace, enter into any agreement or compact with another State, or with a foreign power, or engage in war, unless

actually invaded, or in such imminent danger as will not admit of delay.

Article II
Executive Branch

Section 1. The executive power shall be vested in a President of the United States of America. He shall hold his office during the term of four years, and, together with the Vice-President, chosen for the same term, be elected as follows:

The system for electing the President has been changed a great deal since the Constitution was written, primarily because of the rise of political parties. The so-called "electoral college" still meets, though under the Twelfth Amendment electors vote separately for the President and Vice-President. Originally, the candidate who came in second in the presidential race became Vice-President. Since electors now are pledged to support a party's candidates, election results are actually known before the electors meet.

Each State shall appoint, in such manner as the legislature thereof may direct, a number of electors equal to the whole number of Senators and Representatives to which the State may be entitled in the Congress: but no Senator or Representative, or person holding an office of trust or profit under the United States, shall be appointed an elector.

The electors shall meet in their respective States and vote by ballot for two persons, of whom one at least shall not be an inhabitant of the same State with themselves. And they shall make a list of all the persons voted for, and of the number of votes for each; which list they shall sign and certify, and transmit sealed to the seat of the government of the United States, directed to the president of the Senate. The president of the Senate shall, in the presence of the Senate and House of Representatives, open all the certificates, and the votes shall then be counted. The person having the greatest number of votes shall be the President, if such number be a majority of the whole number of electors appointed;

The Flag of the United States, symbol of the nation, was officially created by Congress in 1777. The thirteen stripes of the flag honor the original colonies, and each star marks one state.

And if there be more than one who have such majority, and have an equal number of votes, then the House of Representatives shall immediately choose by ballot one of them for President; and if no person have a majority, then from the five highest on the list the said House shall in like manner choose the President. But in choosing the President, the vote shall be taken by States, the representation from each State having one vote; a quorum for this purpose shall consist of a member or members from two-thirds of the States, and a majority of all the States shall be necessary to a choice. In every case, after the choice of the President, the person having the greatest number of votes of the electors shall be the Vice-President. But if there should remain two or more who have equal votes, the Senate shall choose from them by ballot the Vice-President.

The Congress may determine the time of choosing the electors and the day on which they shall give their votes; which day shall be the same throughout the United States.

No person except a natural-born citizen, or a citizen of the United States at the time of the adoption of this Constitution, shall be eligible to the office of President; neither shall any person be eligible to that office who shall not have attained to the age of thirty-five years and been fourteen years a resident within the United States.

In case of the removal of the President from office, or of his death, resignation, or inability to discharge the powers and duties of the said office, the same shall devolve on the Vice-President, and the Congress may by law provide for the case of removal, death, resignation or inability, both of the President and Vice-President, declaring what officer shall then act as President, and such officer shall act accordingly, until the disability be removed, or a President shall be elected.

The Twenty-fifth Amendment (1967) makes further provisions for succession to the presidency and for cases when the President is ill.

The President shall, at stated times, receive for his services a compensation, which shall neither be increased nor diminished during the period for which he shall have been elected, and he shall not receive within that period any other emolument from the United States, or any of them.

Before he enter on the execution of his office, he shall take the following oath or affirmation:

"I do solemnly swear (or affirm) that I will faithfully execute the office of President of the United States, and will to the best of my ability, preserve, protect, and defend the Constitution of the United States."

Section 2. (Powers of the President) The President shall be Commander in Chief of the Army and Navy of the United States, and of the militia of the several States, when called into the actual service of the United States; he may require the opinion, in writing, of the principal officer in each of the executive departments upon any subject relating to the duties of their respective offices, and he shall have power to grant reprieves and pardons for offences against the United States except in cases of impeachment.

This is the only mention of the Cabinet made in the Constitution; the first three

Cabinet secretaries—State, Treasury, and War—were named in 1789.

He shall have power, by and with the advice and consent of the Senate, to make treaties, provided two-thirds of the Senators present concur; and he shall nominate, and by and with the advice and consent of the Senate, shall appoint ambassadors, other public ministers and consuls, judges of the Supreme Court, and all other officers of the United States whose appointments are not herein otherwise provided for, and which shall be established by law: but the Congress may by law vest the appointment of such inferior officers as they think proper in the President alone, in the courts of law, or in the heads of departments.

The Senate must approve presidential appointments to important posts, such as Cabinet members, ambassadors, and Supreme Court justices.

The President shall have power to fill up all vacancies that may happen during the recess of the Senate, by granting commissions which shall expire at the end of their next session.

Section 3. (Powers and Duties of the President) He shall from time to time give to the Congress information of the state of the Union, and recommend to their consideration such measures as he shall judge necessary and expedient; he may, on extraordinary occasions, convene both Houses, or either of them, and in case of disagreement between them with respect to the time of adjournment, he may adjourn them to such time as he shall think proper; he shall receive ambassadors and other public ministers; he shall take care that the laws be faithfully executed; and shall commission all the officers of the United States.

The President traditionally delivers his "State of the Union" message at the start of each session of Congress. He can suggest legislation at any time.

Section 4. (Impeachment) The President, Vice-President, and all civil officers of the United States shall be removed from office on impeachment for, and conviction of, treason, bribery, or other high crimes and misdemeanors.

Article III
Judicial Branch

Section 1. The judicial power of the United States shall be vested in one Supreme Court, and in such inferior courts as the Congress may from time to time ordain and establish. The judges, both of the Supreme and inferior courts, shall hold their offices during good behavior, and shall at stated times receive for their services a compensation, which shall not be diminished during their continuance in office.

All federal court judges are appointed for life and can be removed only by impeachment and conviction or by resigning.

Section 2. (Jurisdiction) The judicial power shall extend to all cases in law and equity arising under this Constitution, the laws of the United States, and treaties made, or which shall be made, under their authority; to all cases affecting ambassadors, other public ministers and consuls; to all cases of admiralty and maritime jurisdiction; to controversies to which the United States shall be a party; to controversies between two or more States; between a State and citizens of another State; between citizens of different States; between citizens of the same State claiming lands under grants of different States; and between a State, or the citizens thereof, and foreign states, citizens, or subjects.

In all cases affecting ambassadors, other public ministers, and consuls, and those in which a State shall be party, the Supreme Court shall have original jurisdiction. In all the other cases before mentioned the Supreme Court shall have appellate jurisdiction, both as to law and fact, with such exceptions and under such regulations as the Congress shall make.

Certain kinds of cases are taken directly to the Supreme Court. The Court can also review cases that have been tried in other federal or state courts.

The trial of all crimes, except in cases of impeachment, shall be by jury, and such trial shall be held in the State where the said crimes shall have been committed; but when not committed within any State, the trial shall be at such place or places as the Congress may by law have directed.

Section 3. (Treason) Treason against the United States shall consist only in levying war against them, or in adhering to their enemies, giving them aid and comfort. No person shall be convicted of treason unless on the testimony of two witnesses to the same overt act, or on confession in open court.

The Congress shall have power to declare the punishment of treason, but no attainder of treason shall work corruption of blood, or forfeiture except during the life of the person attainted.

Article IV
Relations Between the States

Section 1. (Recognition of Laws) Full faith and credit shall be given in each State to the public acts, records, and judicial proceedings of every other State. And the Congress may by general laws prescribe the manner in which such acts, records and proceedings shall be proved, and the effect thereof.

Contracts and other legal documents written in one state are valid in all other states; this had not been true under the Articles of Confederation, and it hampered interstate trade and business. However, it does not mean that all states have identical laws.

Section 2. The citizens of each State shall be entitled to all privileges and immunities of citizens in the several States.

A person charged in any State with treason, felony, or other crime, who shall flee from justice, and be found in another State, shall, on demand of the executive authority of the State from which he fled, be delivered up, to be removed to the State having jurisdiction of the crime.

Extradition is the process by which a fugitive from justice in one state is handed over to the state in which the crime was committed. States usually permit extradition, but they can refuse.

No person held to service or labor in one State, under the laws thereof, escaping into another, shall, in consequence of any law or regulation therein, be discharged from such service or labor, but shall be delivered up on claim of the party to whom such service or labor may be due.

This paragraph provided that runaway slaves should be returned; the Thirteenth Amendment, of course, abolished slavery.

Section 3. (New States and Territories) New States may be admitted by the Congress into this Union; but no new States shall be formed or erected within the jurisdiction of any other State, nor any State be formed by the junction of two or more States, or parts of States, without the consent of the legislatures of the States concerned as well as of the Congress.

The Congress shall have power to dispose of and make all needful rules and regulations respecting the territory or other property belonging to the United States; and nothing in this Constitution shall be so construed as to prejudice any claims of the United States, or of any particular State.

Section 4. The United States shall guarantee to every State in this Union a republican form of government, and shall protect each of them against invasion; and on application of the legislature, or of the executive (when the legislature cannot be convened) against domestic violence.

Article V
Amending the Constitution

The Congress, whenever two-thirds of both houses shall deem it necessary, shall propose amendments to this Constitution, or, on the application of the legislatures of two-thirds of the several States, shall call a convention for proposing amendments, which, in either case, shall be valid to all intents and purposes, as part of this Constitution, when ratified by the legislatures of three-fourths of the several States, or by conventions in three-fourths thereof, as the one or the other mode of ratification may be proposed by the Congress; provided that no amendment which may be made prior to the year 1808 shall in any manner affect the first and fourth clauses in the Ninth Section of the First Article; and that no State, without its consent, shall be deprived of its equal suffrage in the Senate.

Article VI
Supremacy of Federal Laws

All debts contracted and engagements entered into, before the adoption of this Constitution, shall be as valid against the United States under this Constitution, as under the Confederation.

This Constitution, and the laws of the United States which shall be made in pursuance thereof; and all treaties made, or which shall be made, under the authority of the United States, shall be the supreme law of the land; and the judges in every State shall be bound thereby, any thing in the constitution or laws of any State to the contrary notwithstanding.

> *John Marshall, the first Chief Justice, gave broad interpretations to many sections of the Constitution during his tenure from 1801 to 1835. This clause was interpreted by Marshall to mean that the Supreme Court had the power to review the consti-tutionality of acts of Congress, since, as stated here, the Constitution is the "supreme law of the land."*

The Senators and Representatives before mentioned, and the members of the several state legislatures, and all executive and judicial officers, both of the United States and of the several States, shall be bound by oath or affirmation, to support this Constitution; but no religious test shall ever be required as a qualification to any office or public trust under the United States.

Article VII
Ratification

The ratification of the conventions of nine States shall be sufficient for the establishment of this Constitution between the States so ratifying the same. Done in convention by the unanimous consent of the States present, the seventeenth day of September in the year of our Lord one thousand seven hundred and eighty-seven, and of the independence of the United States of America the twelfth. In witness whereof we have hereunto subscribed our names.

Amendments to the Constitution

THE BILL OF RIGHTS (1791)

Amendment 1
Freedom of Religion, Speech, Press, Assembly and Petition

Congress shall make no law respecting an establishment of religion, or prohibiting the free exercise thereof; or abridging the freedom of speech, or of the press, or the right of the people peaceably to assemble, and to petition the government for a redress of grievances.

> *In recent years freedom of the press has been invoked to justify publishing the so-called Pentagon Papers and material relating to Watergate. Journalists have consistently refused to reveal their sources under this amendment.*

Amendment 2
Right to Bear Arms

A well-regulated militia, being necessary to the security of a free state, the right of the people to keep and bear arms shall not be infringed.

> *This amendment is often cited as a constitutional right by those opposed to gun-control laws.*

The massive system of freeways and superhighways that crisscross the United States depends in part on the government's right to acquire private property for public use. This right of the government is known as the right of eminent domain.

Amendment 3
Quartering Soldiers

No soldier shall, in time of peace be quartered in any house, without the consent of the owner, nor in time of war, but in a manner to be prescribed by law.

Amendment 4
Searches and Seizures

The right of the people to be secure in their persons, houses, papers, and effects, against unreasonable searches and seizures, shall not be violated, and no warrants shall issue, but upon probable cause, supported by oath or affirmation, and particularly describing the place to be searched, and the persons or things to be seized.

This amendment requires police and other officials usually to have specific search warrants when they make investigations of people, homes, or private property.

Amendment 5
Rights

No person shall be held to answer for a capital, or otherwise infamous crime, unless on a presentment or indictment of a grand jury, except in cases arising in the land or naval forces, or in the militia, when in actual service in time of war or public danger; nor shall any person be subject for the same offense to be twice put in jeopardy of life or limb; nor shall be compelled in any criminal case to be a witness against himself, nor be deprived of life, liberty, or property, without due process of law; nor shall private property be taken for public use, without just compensation.

Several legal protections are included here —the need for a grand jury hearing; protection against "double jeopardy"; and the right not to testify against oneself in a trial or hearing. In a 1966 decision the Supreme Court ruled that police officers must inform suspects of these constitutional rights before questioning them. If the suspect has not been made aware of his right to refuse to testify against himself, his confession to a crime cannot be admitted as evidence in court.

The right of the government to take private property for public use is called the "right of eminent domain." If the government pays a fair price, it can take the property of individuals.

Amendment 6
Jury in Criminal Cases

In all criminal prosecutions, the accused shall enjoy the right to a speedy and public trial, by an impartial jury of the state and district wherein the crime shall have been committed, which district shall have been previously ascertained by law, and to be informed of the nature and cause of the accusation; to be confronted with the witnesses against him; to have compulsory process for obtaining witnesses in his favor, and to have the assistance of counsel for his defense.

A 1963 Supreme Court decision ruled that the basic constitutional right to legal counsel in felony cases applies whether or not the accused person can afford a lawyer. If the accused cannot, the court must appoint a lawyer.

Amendment 7
Jury in Civil Cases

In suits at common law, where the value in controversy shall exceed twenty dollars, the right of trial by jury shall be preserved, and no fact tried by a jury shall be otherwise re-examined in any court of the United States, than according to the rules of the common law.

Amendment 8
Excessive Penalties

Excessive bail shall not be required, nor excessive fines imposed, nor cruel and unusual punishments inflicted.

Amendment 9
Other Rights

The enumeration in the Constitution, of certain rights, shall not be construed to deny or disparage others retained by the people.

Amendment 10
State Powers

The powers not delegated to the United States by the Constitution, nor prohibited by it to the States, are reserved to the States respectively, or to the people.

Amendments nine and ten protected the rights of the people and the states by giving them all powers not specifically delegated to the federal government. It was a safeguard against a too-powerful federal government, which many statesmen of the 1780s and 1790s feared.

ADDITIONAL AMENDMENTS

Amendment 11
Suits Against States (1798)

The judicial power of the United States shall not be construed to extend to any suit in law or equity, commenced or prosecuted against one of the United States by citizens of another state, or by citizens or subjects of any foreign state.

Amendment 12
Presidential Elections (1804)

The electors shall meet in their respective states, and vote by ballot for President and Vice-President, one of whom, at least, shall not be an inhabitant of the same state with themselves; they shall name in their ballots the person voted for as President, and in distinct ballots the person voted for as Vice-President, and they shall make distinct lists of all persons voted for as President and of all persons voted for as Vice-President, and of the number of votes for each, which lists they shall sign and certify, and transmit sealed to the seat of the government of the United States, directed to the president of the Senate; the president of the Senate shall, in the presence of the Senate and the House of Representatives, open all the certificates and the votes shall then be counted. The person having the greatest number of votes for President shall be the President, if such a number be a majority of the whole number of electors appointed; and if no person have such majority, then from the persons having the highest numbers not exceeding three on the list of those voted for as President, the House of Representatives shall choose immediately, by ballot, the President.

But in choosing the President, the votes shall be taken by states, the representation from each state having one vote; a quorum for this purpose shall consist of a member or members from two-thirds of the states, and a majority of all the states shall be necessary to a choice. And if the House of Representatives shall not choose a President whenever the right of choice shall devolve upon them, before the fourth day of March next following, then the Vice-President shall act as President, as in the case of the death or other constitutional disability of the President. The person having the greatest number of votes as Vice-President shall be the Vice-President, if such number be a majority of the whole number of electors appointed, and if no person have a majority, then from the two high-

est numbers on the list, the Senate shall choose the Vice-President; a quorum for the purpose shall consist of two-thirds of the whole number of senators, and a majority of the whole number shall be necessary to a choice. But no person constitutionally ineligible to the office of President shall be eligible to that of Vice-President of the United States.

This amendment changed the election process so that electors voted separately for President and Vice-President.

Amendment 13
Abolition of Slavery (1865)

Section 1.   Neither slavery nor involuntary servitude, except as a punishment for crime whereof the party shall have been duly convicted, shall exist within the United States, or any place subject to their jurisdiction.

Section 2.   Congress shall have power to enforce this article by appropriate legislation.

Democratic National Convention, New York City, 1976. The national convention is an old tradition in United States political life. The Democratic Party, oldest political party in the world, was organized in 1828. The Republican Party dates from 1854. Party conventions now are viewed in most homes via television.

THE UNITED STATES

The Thirteenth and Fourteenth Amendments were added right after the Civil War. The Thirteenth was adopted in 1865 and abolished slavery in the United States. The Fourteenth, added in 1868, gave the rights of citizenship to former slaves and defined citizenship for the first time.

Amendment 14
Rights of Citizens (1868)

Section 1. All persons born or naturalized in the United States, and subject to the jurisdiction thereof, are citizens of the United States and of the state wherein they reside. No state shall make or enforce any law which shall abridge the privileges or immunities of citizens of the United States; nor shall any state deprive any person of life, liberty, or property, without due process of law; nor deny to any person within its jurisdiction the equal protection of the laws.

This is the most basic civil rights amendment. It defines who is a citizen and what every citizen's rights are.

Section 2. Representatives shall be apportioned among the several states according to their respective numbers, counting the whole number of persons in each state, excluding Indians not taxed. But when the right to vote at any election for the choice of electors for President and Vice-President of the United States, representatives in Congress, the executive and judicial officers of a state, or the members of the legislature thereof, is denied to any of the male inhabitants of such state, being twenty-one years of age, and citizens of the United States, or in any way abridged, except for participation in rebellion, or other crime, the basis of representation therein shall be reduced in the proportion which the number of such male citizens shall bear to the whole number of male citizens twenty-one years of age in such state.

Two later amendments have changed these voting rules, which gave the right to vote to black men: the Nineteenth allowed women to vote; the Twenty-sixth lowered the voting age to eighteen.

Section 3. No person shall be a Senator or Representative in Congress, or elector of President and Vice-President, or hold any office, civil or military, under the United States, or under any state, who, having previously taken an oath, as a member of Congress, or as an officer of the United States, or as a member of any state legislature, or as an executive or judicial officer of any state, to support the Constitution of the United States, shall have engaged in insurrection or rebellion against the same, or given aid or comfort to the enemies thereof. But Congress may, by a vote of two-thirds of each House, remove such disability.

The idea of this clause was to keep former Confederate officials out of the federal government. Special acts of Congress later allowed some to serve.

Section 4. The validity of the public debt of the United States, authorized by law, including debts incurred for payment of pensions and bounties for services in suppressing insurrection or rebellion, shall not be questioned. But neither the United States nor any state shall assume or pay any debt or obligation incurred in aid of insurrection or rebellion against the United States, or any claim for the loss or emancipation of any slave; but all such debts, obligations and claims shall be held illegal and void.

This clause forbade both the federal government and the states to pay any debt the Confederacy owed.

Section 5. The Congress shall have power to enforce, by appropriate legislation, the provisions of this article.

Amendment 15
Black Voting Rights (1870)

Section 1. The right of citizens of the United States to vote shall not be denied or abridged by the United States or by any state on account of race, color, or previous condition of servitude.

Section 2. The Congress shall have power to enforce this article by appropriate legislation.

This amendment was added in 1870 to strengthen the Fourteenth Amendment. The Fifteenth Amendment states specifically that the right to vote shall not be denied on account of race or color or because of former slavery.

Amendment 16
Income Taxes (1913)

The Congress shall have power to lay and collect taxes on incomes, from whatever source derived, without apportionment among the several states, and without regard to any census or enumeration.

An amendment to allow an income tax was needed because the Constitution originally did not allow any direct tax on the people (Article 1, Section 9).

Amendment 17
Senatorial Elections (1913)

Section 1. The Senate of the United States shall be composed of two Senators from each state, elected by the people thereof, for six years; and each Senator shall have one vote. The electors in each state shall have the qualifications requisite for electors of the most numerous branch of the state legislature.

Section 2. When vacancies happen in the representation of any state in the Senate, the executive authority of such state shall issue writs of election to fill such vacancies: provided, that the legislature of any state may empower the executive thereof to make temporary appointments until the people fill the vacancies by election as the legislature may direct.

Section 3. This amendment shall not be so construed as to affect the election or term of any Senator chosen before it becomes valid as part of the Constitution.

Amendment 18
Prohibition (1919)

Section 1. After one year from the ratification of this article, the manufacture, sale, or transportation of intoxicating liquors within, the importation thereof into, or the exportation thereof from the United States and all territory subject to the jurisdiction thereof for beverage purposes is hereby prohibited.

Section 2. The Congress and the several states shall have concurrent power to enforce this article by appropriate legislation.

Section 3. This article shall be inoperative unless it shall have been ratified as an amendment to the Constitution by the legislatures of the several states, as provided in the Constitution, within seven years from the date of the submission hereof to the states by the Congress.

The prohibition amendment was repealed in 1933 by the Twenty-first Amendment, after years of illegal liquor selling.

Amendment 19
Woman Suffrage (1920)

Section 1. The right of citizens of the United States to vote shall not be denied or abridged by the United States or by any states on account of sex.

Section 2. The Congress shall have power to enforce this article by appropriate legislation.

This amendment, effective in 1920, gave women the right to vote, although a few states had allowed it earlier. Reformers had been fighting for this right for nearly a century.

Amendment 20
Terms of Office (1933)

Section 1. The terms of the President and Vice-President shall end at noon on the 20th day of January, and the terms of Senators and

Suffragettes worked hard to gain women's voting rights, finally secured in the Nineteenth Amendment, 1920. Many women today support the Equal Rights Amendment, which had not yet been adopted by early 1978.

Representatives at noon on the third day of January, of the years in which such terms would have ended if this article had not been ratified; and the terms of their successors shall then begin.

Section 2. The Congress shall assemble at least once in every year, and such meetings shall begin at noon on the third day of January, unless they shall by law appoint a different day.

Section 3. If, at the time fixed for the beginning of the term of the President, the President-elect shall have died, the Vice-President-elect shall become President. If a President shall not have been chosen before the time fixed for the beginning of his term, or if the President-elect shall have failed to qualify, then the Vice-President-elect shall act as President until a President shall have qualified; and the Congress may by law provide for the case wherein neither a President-elect nor a Vice-President-elect shall have qualified, declaring who shall then act as President, or the manner in which one who is to act shall be selected, and such person shall act accordingly until a President or Vice-President shall have qualified.

Section 4. The Congress may by law provide for the case of the death of any of the persons from whom the House of Representatives may choose a President whenever the right of choice shall have devolved upon them, and for the case

of the death of any of the persons from whom the Senate may choose a Vice-President whenever the right of choice shall have devolved upon them.

Section 5. Sections 1 and 2 shall take effect on the 15th day of October following the ratification of this article.

Section 6. This article shall be inoperative unless it shall have been ratified as an amendment to the Constitution by the legislatures of three-fourths of the several states within seven years from the date of its submission.

This is known as the "lame duck" amendment because it shortened the time between congressmen's elections and the date they took office. "Lame ducks" were defeated members who, under the old system, remained in Congress long after being defeated in an election.

Amendment 21
Repeal of Prohibition (1933)

Section 1. The eighteenth article of amendment to the Constitution of the United States is hereby repealed.

Section 2. The transportation or importation into any state, territory, or possession of the

United States for delivery or use therein of intoxicating liquors, in violation of the laws thereof, is hereby prohibited.

Section 3. This article shall be inoperative unless it shall have been ratified as an amendment to the Constitution by conventions in the several states, as provided in the Constitution, within seven years from the date of the submission hereof to the states by the Congress.

Amendment 22
Presidential Terms (1951)

Section 1. No person shall be elected to the office of the President more than twice, and no person who has held the office of President, or acted as President, for more than two years of a term to which some other person was elected President shall be elected to the office of the President more than once. But this article shall not apply to any person holding the office of President when this article was proposed by the Congress, and shall not prevent any person who may be holding the office of President, or acting as President, during the term within which this article becomes operative from holding the office of President, or acting as President during the remainder of such term.

Section 2. This article shall be inoperative unless it shall have been ratified as an amendment to the Constitution by the legislatures of three-fourths of the several states within seven years from the date of its submission to the states by the Congress.
This amendment was passed after the death of Franklin D. Roosevelt, who had been elected four times. Its purpose was to prevent subsequent Presidents from serving more than two terms.

Amendment 23
District of Columbia Voting Rights (1961)

Section 1. The district constituting the seat of government of the United States shall appoint in such manner as the Congress may direct:

A number of electors of President and Vice-President equal to the whole number of Senators and Representatives in Congress to which the district would be entitled if it were a state, but in no event more than the least populous state; they shall be in addition to those appointed by the states, but they shall be considered, for the purposes of the election of President and Vice-President, to be electors appointed by a state; and they shall meet in the district and perform such duties as provided by the twelfth article of amendment.

Section 2. The Congress shall have power to enforce this article by appropriate legislation.
Before this amendment, residents of the District of Columbia could not vote.

Amendment 24
Poll Tax Prohibited (1964)

Section 1. The right of citizens of the United States to vote in any primary or other election for President or Vice-President, for electors for President or Vice-President, or for Senator or Representative in Congress, shall not be denied or abridged by the United States or any state by reason of failure to pay any poll tax or other tax.

Section 2. The Congress shall have power to enforce this article by appropriate legislation.
This amendment was passed in 1964 because poll taxes had been used in some states to prevent or discourage black voters from registering or voting.

Amendment 25
Presidential Succession (1967)

Section 1. In case of the removal of the President from office or of his death or resignation, the Vice-President shall become President.

Section 2. Whenever there is a vacancy in the office of the Vice-President, the President shall nominate a Vice-President who shall take office upon confirmation by a majority vote of both houses of Congress.

Section 3. Whenever the President transmits to the president pro tempore of the Senate and the Speaker of the House of Representatives his written declaration that he is unable to discharge the powers and duties of his office, and until he transmits to them a written declaration to the contrary, such powers and duties shall be discharged by the Vice-President as Acting President.

Section 4. Whenever the Vice-President and a majority of either the principal officers of the executive departments, or of such other body as Congress may by law provide, transmit to the president pro tempore of the Senate and the Speaker of the House of Representatives their written declaration that the President is unable to discharge the powers and duties of his office, the Vice-President shall immediately assume the powers and duties of the office as Acting President.

Thereafter, when the President transmits to the president pro tempore of the Senate and the Speaker of the House of Representatives his written declaration that no inability exists, he shall resume the powers and duties of his office unless the Vice-President and a majority of either the principal officers of the executive department, or of such other body as Congress may by law provide, transmit within four days to the president pro tempore of the Senate and the Speaker of the House of Representatives their written declaration that the President is unable to discharge the powers and duties of his office. Thereupon Congress shall decide the issue, assembling within forty-eight hours for that purpose if not in session. If the Congress, within twenty-one days after receipt of the latter written declaration, or, if Congress is not in session, within twenty-one days after Congress is required to assemble, determines by two-thirds vote of both houses that the President is unable to discharge the powers and duties of his office, the Vice-President shall continue to discharge the same as Acting President; otherwise, the President shall resume the powers and duties of his office.

Amendment 26
Voting Age (1971)

Section 1. The right of citizens of the United States, who are eighteen years of age or older, to vote shall not be denied or abridged by the United States or by any state on account of age.

Section 2. The Congress shall have power to enforce this article by appropriate legislation.

New voter learns to use voting machine. The Twenty-Sixth Amendment gave all citizens over 18 the right to vote. Despite the extension of the right to vote, only a small percentage of voters turn out for most United States elections.

How a Bill Becomes a Law

Introducing a Bill

The initial step is taken when a House member introduces a bill by handing it to the Clerk of the House or by placing it in a box called the hopper. A Senator has to go through the more formal procedure of gaining the recognition of the presiding officer to announce the introduction of a bill. If any other Senator objects, the introduction is put off until the next day. Next, in either the House or the Senate, the bill is assigned a number, referred to the appropriate committee, labeled with the sponsor's name, and sent to the Government Printing Office, where copies are made for distribution and study by other members. Often a bill is sponsored by more than one person. In the Senate it is possible to have several cosponsors and, since 1967, it has been possible in the House as well. The prefix H.R. or S. before the bill's number indicates whether the bill was initiated in the House or Senate.

The Committee's Role

Once a bill reaches a committee it is put on the committee calendar. At that point it is examined carefully and its chances of passing considered. The vast majority of bills go no further if the committee determines that passage is unlikely. The next step is for the committee to seek comments on the contents of the bill from agencies of the government that might have an interest in it. Sometimes the whole committee considers a bill; often it will be assigned to a subcommittee. Hearings are then held, and interested groups—lobbyists and others—are invited to appear personally to make a statement or respond to questions, or to submit written material. The committee then votes and reports its recommendations to the full House or Senate along with any proposed amendments. This is done in a written statement that explains the committee's reasons for supporting the bill. Members who do not agree with the majority can have their dissenting views included in the written report.

Floor Action

When the bill comes out of the committee and back to the House or Senate, it is placed on the calendar. In the House there are five different calendars intended to sort out various kinds of bills for action. The Union calendar lists bills raising revenues; the House calendar lists bills of a public nature that do not concern revenue; the Consent calendar schedules bills that are not controversial and can be passed without debate; the Private calendar is concerned with bills that represent claims against the United States; and the Discharge calendar is used when a bill's sponsor wants to get the bill considered by another committee. In the Senate there is only one legislative calendar.

BILL IS INTRODUCED

CAPITOL

| **HR 1000** | **S 900** |

REFERRED TO HOUSE COMMITTEE

REFERRED TO SENATE COMMITTEE

REFERRED TO SUBCOMMITTEE

REFERRED TO SUBCOMMITTEE

REPORTED BY FULL COMMITTEE

RULES COMMITTEE PRIORITY

REPORTED BY FULL COMMITTEE

FLOOR ACTION   **FLOOR ACTION**

HOUSE DEBATE—PASSAGE

SENATE DEBATE—PASSAGE

CONFERENCE COMPROMISES

WHITE HOUSE

VETO

SIGNED BY PRESIDENT

LEGISLATOR

LAW

PRESIDENT

THE UNITED STATES

Debate

If the bill is routine, it will be debated when its turn comes. If it is urgent its sponsor can ask for unanimous consent or a majority vote in the Senate, and in the House it takes precedence over other bills if the Rules Committee grants it a "special rule." In doing this the Rules Committee can stipulate how long the bill can be debated and whether or not it can be amended from the floor. If the bill is being debated in the House without a rule, each member is allotted one hour for debate. If an amendment is added, each member is given an additional five minutes. In the Senate, debate is usually unlimited. At various times, this has allowed members who were opposed to certain legislation the right to filibuster, or talk almost endlessly on a bill in the hope of wearing down the opposition. A filibuster can be halted by cloture —a vote that requires a three-fifths majority of the entire Senate to carry.

Voting

Both the House and the Senate can vote by voice vote or standing vote (which are not tabulated) or by roll-call vote. Electronic recording of votes has speeded up the process in recent years. Amendments to bills are voted on first, and sometimes, after this has been done, a motion may be made to send the bill back to the committee. If the motion carries, the bill goes back for further consideration.

The Opposite House

After a bill passes, it is sent to the other house. There it can be accepted as is, sent to a committee for alterations, rejected, or ignored while that house continues work on its own version of a similar bill. Conflicts are usually resolved by sending a bill to a House-Senate Conference (committee) appointed by the presiding officers of the two houses from their respective committees. When the Conference Committee has reached a decision, it prepares a report which explains the compromises arrived at; this must then be voted on in each house.

The Final Stages

After the bill has been approved in identical form by the House and the Senate, it is signed first by the Speaker of the House and then by the President of the Senate. It then goes to the President of the United States. If he approves, he so indicates on the document and adds the date and his signature. If he does not sign it within ten days when the Congress is in session, the bill becomes law without his signature. If Congress should adjourn within that ten-day period and the President has not signed the bill, it does not become law. This is known as the "pocket veto." The President can refuse to sign the bill and return it to Congress with a message stating his reasons. If no action is taken, the bill does not become law. However a two-thirds favorable vote of the members of both houses overrides his veto, and the bill becomes law without his approval.

Statue of Liberty, in New York Harbor. Gift of the French people to the United States, this great structure marks the participation of France in our revolution. Since this great statue was installed, it has served as a symbol of our welcome to new immigrants.

WORLD HISTORY

The cave drawings at Lascaux, in southern France, remind us that man's awareness of who he is and what the world around him is like dates far back to the time before man began to make written records of the events he witnessed. It is this awareness and the urge to record events that distinguish man from lower creatures. Once writing came into existence, a principal activity of life has always been that of making a complete and accurate record of what has transpired.

Beginning with ancient civilizations and moving through medieval and modern history, the following pages show us the highlights of man's time on earth. Special attention is paid to countries just emerging on the international scene, particularly to their activities in the one organization in which all countries play a part—the United Nations.

Ancient History

SUMER

Sumerian political history is divided into four periods: the Early Dynastic era (c. 3000–2300 B.C.); the Sargonid epoch (c. 2300–2150 B.C.), a period of Semitic rule; the Sumerian revival under the Third Dynasty of Ur (c. 2150–1950 B.C.); and the Old Babylonian era, memorable for the rule of Hammurabi (c. 1700 B.C.).

The Sumerians were in the forefront of early Mesopotamian political, economic, and cultural history. The material basis of Sumerian culture was founded on the struggle to control the waters of the Tigris and Euphrates and to reclaim the swamp lands for cultivation, which in turn led to the emergence of urban centers. The inhabitants of these city-states erected monumental buildings, engaged in foreign commerce, organized military campaigns, and withstood internal strife, floods, and foreign invasions. Their accomplishments included such fundamental inventions as the potter's wheel, the making of copper tools, and the wheeled vehicle. They are also credited with the development of picture writing, a lunar calendar, and the Gilgamesh epic.

EGYPT

In the same centuries that witnessed the emergence of the Sumerians, the Egyptians were developing a civilization that contributed significantly to the history of the ancient Near East and to the later societies of Greece and Rome.

The inhabitants of the Nile Valley were politically unified about 3100 B.C., when the Pharaohs of the south succeeded in conquering the north.

The long centuries of Egyptian history generally are divided into the Protodynastic stage, up to 2700 B.C.; the Old Kingdom, 2700–2200 B.C., when the famous pyramids of Gizeh were built; the First Intermediate period, 2200–2052 B.C., an era of confusion and civil strife; the Middle Kingdom, 2252–1786 B.C., a great revival of political power, prosperity, and cultural energy; the Second Intermediate period, 1786–1575 B.C., another era of disorder and the Hyksos invasion; the New Kingdom or Empire, 1575–1087 B.C., in which Egypt restored order and became a Mediterranean power and in which Pharaoh Ikhnaton preached a monotheistic religion; and the Post-Empire era, a period stretching to the Persian conquest of 525 B.C. and marked by steady decline in political power and cultural creativity. The dynasties continued until the fourth century B.C., when Egypt was conquered by Alexander the Great, the Macedonian king. Later on, following the defeat of Antony and Cleopatra, Egypt was brought under Roman control.

Few ancient civilizations surpass the Egyptian in importance to later times. Egypt contributed to mathematics, medicine, engineering, philosophy, and literature. Its scientists mapped the heavens, perfected a solar calendar, invented the sun dial, made paper and glass, and laid the basis for arithmetic and geometry.

In addition, the Egyptians developed the principle of the alphabet, amassed a large body of philosophic and religious literature, and produced many popular writings. Meanwhile, Egyptians originated architectural principles that were destined for wide use in subsequent history, such as the column, obelisk, lintel, and colonnade.

BABYLON

About 2350 B.C., the Akkadians, a Semitic people from northern Mesopotamia established control over the whole Mesopotamian valley. In addition, they extended their dominion over Assyria, reached into Asia Minor, and invaded the Zagros Mountains on the east. After many vicissitudes, the lands of Sumer and Akkad were invaded and conquered (c. 1900 B.C.) by the Amorites, another group of Semites. Under Hammurabi (1728–1686 B.C.), who made Babylon his capital, the area enjoyed stability and prosperity. During Hammurabi's reign, the laws were codified and engraved in cuneiform characters on an eight-foot column. Soon after, the

Hammurabi (*left*) receives emblems of authority from Shamash, the sun god of justice. This relief comes from the famous stele on which is engraved *The Code of Hammurabi*.

less civilized Mitanni and the Kassites gained control of Old Babylonia. In the ninth century B.C. the Assyrians established dominion over the ancient Near East. The Assyrian Empire reached its height under Sargon II (722–705 B.C.). He overpowered the Northern Kingdom of Israel and the Egyptians. Late in the seventh century B.C. the Babylonians, in alliance with the Medes and Persians, destroyed Nineveh, the Assyrian capital. Under Nebuchadnezzar (604–562 B.C.), the New Babylonian Empire reached its peak of power. Jerusalem was destroyed and many prisoners deported to Babylon (the Babylonian Captivity of Biblical history). The New Babylon fell to Persia in 538 B.C.

Despite successive invasions and rebellions, the peoples of Mesopotamia maintained a vigorous urban civilization and made advances in astronomy and mathematics. Its cultural vitality is attested not only by its art, literature, science, and law, but by its lasting influence throughout western Asia.

PERSIA

In the sixth century B.C. the Persians, under the leadership of their great ruler Cyrus (559–529 B.C.), advanced from the land to the east of Mesopotamia (now Iran) westward toward the Mediterranean, subduing the Chaldean kingdom and the Lydians. Within twenty years, Cyrus the Great established the largest empire in existence before the conquests of Alexander the Great. Only the Greeks held out against him.

Darius the Great (521–485 B.C.) determined to conquer the Greek city-states. Following the Persian defeat, the empire slowly sank into stagnation and collapsed in 330 B.C. before the armies of Alexander the Great.

Persian intellectual and artistic achievements were derived largely from the earlier civilizations of Mesopotamia and Egypt. The character of Persian culture is best represented in the palaces of Darius and Xerxes at Persepolis.

The ancient Persians established the Zoroastrian religion throughout western Asia: Shura Mazda, god of light, was said to have created the world and mankind and to be locked in endless combat with Ahriman, the god of darkness

STATUE OF ZEUS
AT OLYMPIA

HANGING GARDENS
OF BABYLON

PYRAMIDS AT GIZEH

MAUSOLEUM AT
HALICARNASSUS

LIGHTHOUSE AT ALEXANDRIA

COLOSSUS
OF RHODES

TEMPLE OF DIANA
AT EPHESUS

The man-made wonders that are known as the Seven Wonders of the World
were all constructed before the Christian Era. Of the seven, only the great
pyramids of Egypt remain.

36

and evil. Out of Zoroastrianism emerged Mithraism, Manicheism, and Gnosticism, all of which had a profound influence on the Roman world and developing Christianity.

ISRAEL

The Hebrews were primarily a Semitic people, originally nomadic, who left the deserts of Arabia about the twentieth century B.C. By 1800 B.C. Hebrews under the leadership of Abraham settled in Mesopotamia and later began to move into Palestine. Some time after 1600 B.C. a number of Hebrews migrated to Egypt, where they were enslaved by the Pharaoh. In the thirteenth century, under the leadership of Moses, the descendants of the Israelites were freed from bondage, emerged from Egypt, and began the conquest of Palestine (the Land of Canaan). Most of Palestine had been settled earlier by the Canaanites, who had an urban and sophisticated culture. The Israelites fought the Canaanites and the Philistines, who had appeared out of the islands of the Aegean Sea. Finally, the Hebrew tribes were united under Saul (c. 1120–1000 B.C.). His successor, King David (c. 1000–960 B.C.) overwhelmed the Philistines and others and established a strong kingdom from his capital at Jerusalem. Under his rule and that of his son, Solomon (c. 960–921 B.C.), the Hebrew kingdom reached its height, but it was soon weakened by civil strife.

The northern tribes set up their own kingdom, which came to be known as the Kingdom of Israel, while the southern tribes were known as the Kingdom of Judah. In 722 B.C. Israel was annexed by the Assyrians, and its people were compelled to emigrate. In 586 B.C. the people of Judah were captured by the Babylonian King Nebuchadnezzar, who destroyed Jerusalem and deported thousands of Jews to Babylon. A half a century later the Jews were liberated when Cyrus conquered the Babylonians. Gradually the Jews returned and rebuilt their capital, but the political strength and material prosperity of Solomon was never restored. From 539 to 332 B.C., Palestine was a province of the Persian Empire; in 332 B.C. it was incorporated into Alexander's Empire; and after Alexander's death, it was placed under the rule of the Ptol-

emies of Egypt. Relatively independent from 142 to 63 B.C., Palestine was conquered by Rome in 63 B.C. In A.D. 70, after a great revolt, the Romans destroyed Jerusalem, and its inhabitants were scattered throughout the empire.

The Jews distinguish themselves in religious thought, ethics, literature, law, and philosophy. They were the first of all the Eastern religions to attain monotheism, and the literature of the Hebrews, especially the Old Testament, was by far the best that the Near East produced.

PHOENICIA

The ancient Phoenicians were a Semitic people who settled along the Lebanese coast and established a commercial empire around the Mediterranean between the tenth and eighth centuries B.C. Merchants from Phoenicia carried on trade in dyestuffs, metalwork, the wood known as cedar of Lebanon, and slaves. They established trading colonies as far west as Carthage and Cadiz, and may well have circumnavigated Africa.

In the sixth century B.C. the Phoenicians submitted to the Chaldeans and then the Persians. In 332 B.C. Alexander the Great destroyed Tyre following a lengthy seige.

Phoenician civilization derived largely from Egypt and Mesopotamia, and it exhibited little original creativity in art, literature, or religion. However, the enterprising Phoenicians played an important role in diffusing civilization throughout the Mediterranean. Through them, a simplified alphabet, in which signs represent the sounds of the voice, was spread throughout the Near East and Europe.

GREECE

The beginnings of Hellenic civilization are rooted in the Homeric Age (1200–800 B.C.), so-called because Homer's *Iliad* and *Odyssey,* composed about the eighth century B.C., provide us with a vivid picture of contemporary life. The Hellenes moved down into Greece from the Danube Valley, beginning about 2000 B.C. They created institutions, notably the city-state, that survived for centuries to come.

Erechtheum on the Acropolis, Athens. A fine example of ancient architecture, the temple had sanctuaries of several gods. This Porch of the Caryatids is the temple's striking feature.

The era of colonization (800–600 B.C.) received its impetus from population growth, relatively poor soil, and land hunger; bands of colonizers began to found independent city-states around the Mediterranean and the Black Sea. The period from 600–300 B.C. is known as the Golden Age of Greece. It was marked by strife and turmoil. From 492–479 B.C. the Greek city-states entered into a life and death struggle against the Persians. The Peloponnesian War (431–404 B.C.) and invasions by Macedonian forces also occurred during this period.

Even so this age saw great artistic and intellectual contributions. The spirit of Greece, particularly in its Athenian form, was based on freedom, rationalism, individualism, democracy, and secularism. The work of Greek scientists, mathematicians, philosophers, poets, artists, dramatists, and historians surpassed the efforts of the Egyptians, Mesopotamians, Persians, and Hebrews.

After the Peloponnesian War the fortunes of Greece were determined by Philip of Macedon. Philip's son Alexander came to power in 336 B.C. and undertook the conquest of the Persian Empire. With the death of Alexander in 323,

Hellenic civilization came to an end. The new pattern of civilization that gradually emerged from the breakup of Alexander's Empire is known as the Hellenistic Age (323–31 B.C.), which lasted until the arrival of the Romans.

ROME

Italic tribesmen seem to have arrived in Italy beginning about 2000 B.C.; the Etruscans arrived about 800 B.C., and, somewhat later, Greek colonists began to settle in southern Italy and Sicily. The Etruscans successfully established their rule at Rome after 600 B.C., but the native Latins eventually began a large-scale rebellion. According to tradition, they drove out the last Etruscan ruler, Tarquin the Proud, in 509 B.C. This independent Latin city-state, called the Roman Republic (509–531 B.C.), gained control of the Italian peninsula. Meanwhile the Romans made considerable movement toward democracy.

After gaining control of Italy, the Romans entered into conflict with Carthage in the Punic Wars. The first lasted from 264–241 B.C.; the second, 218–202 B.C., was marked by the defeat of Hannibal; and, the third, 149–146 B.C., resulted in Roman control over Carthage and its colonies. Meanwhile, the Romans conquered Macedonia, Greece, and Asia Minor in the second century B.C. and, by the beginning of the first century B.C., Roman power extended throughout the Mediterranean.

The Roman Republic was soon convulsed with civil war (133–131 B.C.) which eventually led to the extinction of constitutional government and the advent of the rule of Octavian, better known as Augustus, the first emperor. For the next two hundred years, the peoples of the empire enjoyed peace and prosperity. During the succeeding three centuries, the western half of the empire gradually declined, until it was transformed by Germanic invasions.

Greco-Roman civilization continued vigorously for a thousand years in the Byzantine Empire. It profoundly influenced the Roman Church and taught Germanic invaders a civilized way of life, as well as providing much of the cultural inspiration for succeeding generations.

Medieval History

BYZANTIUM

Roman rule in the East, generally referred to as Byzantine rule, continued until the Ottoman conquest of Constantinople, the Byzantine capital, in A.D. 1453. The name Byzantine is derived from an old Greek city-state, Byzantium, which was rechristened Constantinople by the Roman Emperor Constantine, who made it his "New Rome" in A.D. 330.

During the era of barbarian invasions, the rulers at Constantinople were subjected to barbarian attack, but the state survived. Under Justinian (527–565), the regime partially recovered some lands in the Latin West, but the Byzantine state rarely was free from the threat of barbarian invasions. During the rule of Heraclius (610–641), the Lombards, Svars, and Persians menaced the borders and sometimes the capital itself. Soon the Arabs confronted Leo the Isaurian (717–740). Emperor Leo saved the Byzantine capital and, in the process, probably saved the Balkans and Western Europe from Arab conquest. Despite constant pressure on Byzantium, the Byzantines, under their Macedonian kings (867–1057), successfully maintained the most prosperous economy in the medieval Christian world and achieved a dynamic and civilized society. Other enemies later appeared, such as the Crusaders, who successfully took the capital in 1204 and maintained power until 1261. From then on, the Byzantine state decayed until Mohammed II made it the capital of the Ottoman Empire in 1453.

Throughout its long history, all aspects of Byzantine life were permeated by Christianity, but the Church was subjected to rather strict imperial control. Emperors regularly deposed patriarchs, reformed the Church, and contributed to the development of canon law. Emperors frequently were involved in theological controversies. A few of the disputes left a lasting imprint on the Church, such as the Schism of 1054, a split between Eastern and Western Christianity that continues to our own day.

Byzantine contributions to education, literature, theology, legal studies, architecture, and mosaics were outstanding. Byzantine civilization had a permanent influence on the Slavs of Eastern Europe, who looked to Constantinople for their religion, alphabet, literary and artistic modes, and much of their foreign trade. At the same time, Byzantium handed on to recovering Europe Justinian's Code and the classics of Greece and Rome.

ARABIA

Arabia is a peninsula enclosed by the Red Sea, Persian Gulf, and the Indian Ocean. It was inhabited in early times largely by nomadic tribes whose religion was polytheistic (worship of more than one god). Even before Mohammed (c. 570–632), Mecca was regarded as a holy center and possessed the Kaaba (the cube), a square temple that housed sacred relics.

Mohammed was born into the Kuraish, a trading tribe near Mecca. Orphaned at an early age, he was brought up by relatives and worked as a caravan agent for Khadijah, a wealthy widow he later married. Mohammed's prophetic mission began in his fortieth year when, according to tradition, he was named God's messenger. The Prophet called his religion Islam, which means "submission," that is, submission to the will of God. Mohammed called on his fellow Meccans to forsake belief in more than one God and to seek righteousness. He taught that the faithful would be rewarded in paradise, and the sinful would go to hell. These beliefs, together with ethical practices and ancient religious narratives, were compiled after his death into the Koran.

In 622 Mohammed left Mecca and took his followers to Medina. This exodus is known as the Hegira and marks the beginning of the Moslem calendar. In 630, after consolidating his control over Medina, Mohammed led a successful attack on Mecca and cleansed the Kaaba of all idols except a sacred black stone. By the time of his death in 632, much of Arabia had submitted to Mohammed's authority.

The Prophet's successors, called caliphs, completed the conquest of Arabia and successfully attacked the Byzantines and Persians. Under the Ommayad dynasty (660–750), they extended the empire westward into Spain and eastward to central Asia.

In the eighth century, the Abbasid family seized power from the Ommayads, and under their rule (750–1258), centered at Bagdad, the major cities of the Arab Empire experienced a golden age. Islamic civilization far surpassed western Christendom.

CAROLINGIAN EUROPE

The years from the collapse of Rome to about the tenth century have been known as the Dark Ages. Recent study reveals this time as a formative period in the development of Europe. Although much of Europe became isolated, rural, and feudal, the Carolingians of France attempted to reestablish the empire. The architect of the Carolingian Empire was Charlemagne (768–814), who conquered the Lombards of Italy, Bavaria, Saxony, part of Slavdom, and the Spanish March. Charlemagne was crowned

Charlemagne, first German emperor and first Christian emperor of the West. His ambition was to reestablish the Roman Empire in a Christian form, but his empire collapsed after his death.

emperor in 800. Accompanying these conquests was an attempt to restore education, theological studies, and art—the so-called Carolingian Renaissance. However, following the death of Charlemagne, the Carolingian Empire collapsed into feudal anarchy. In time, a more permanent recovery, generally associated with the Ottoman Renaissance, the rise of towns, and the reform of the monasteries under the leadership of the abbots of Cluny lifted Europe out of the Dark Ages and into the High Middle Ages.

ROMAN CATHOLIC CHURCH

During the decline of the Roman Empire, Christianity evolved from a despised sect to the designated state religion. In the crisis that faced Europe in the Dark Ages, the Church played a key role in fusing Germanic and Roman elements, taming the wild barbarians of northern Europe, and making possible the recovery that led to the Carolingian Empire.

In the meantime, the Church responded to the spiritual needs of the masses with elaborate rituals and ceremonies. Some of these innovations, such as the veneration of saints, as well as occasional corruption of the clergy, called forth reformers. In the tenth century, when the Papacy was controlled by Roman families, and when abuses were growing among the clergy, the Church was rescued by a monastic revival known as the Cluniac Reformation. Men trained in the Cluniac spirit revived monastic discipline, established the principle of celibacy, attacked simony, founded the College of Cardinals, and under the leadership of a reforming pope, Gregory VII, began a vigorous struggle against lay investiture.

In the twelfth century, the Cluniac movement lost its zeal and acquired wordly concerns. The Cistercian order began a pattern of reform under the inspiring leadership of St. Bernard of Clairvaux (1098–1153). As Cistercian prestige waned in the thirteenth century, and with heresy spreading through Europe, the Franciscans and Dominicans began to renew piety, mount the Inquisition, and foster scholastic studies at the universities. Meanwhile, under the leadership of Innocent III (1198–1216), the Papacy reached new heights of power and prestige. He summoned the faithful to the Fourth Crusade (1202–1204); called upon northern Frenchmen to crusade against the Albigensian heretics of southern France; repeatedly interfered in the affairs of England, France, and the Holy Roman Empire; and finally presided over the Fourth Lateran Council (1215).

The role of the Church in European affairs is nearly impossible to measure. It brought the faith to northern Europe, mediated between kings and princes, provided men with a sense of security, and fostered artistic expression and intellectual inquiry. Later in the Middle Ages, the abuse of power and the great wealth of the Church invited mounting criticism and opposition. These practices prepared the way for the Protestant Reformation.

HOLY ROMAN EMPIRE

The nation that arose in Germany during the feudal era was named the Holy Roman Empire of the German Nation. From the tenth to the thirteenth century, this principality was the most formidable state in western Europe. The fortunes of the German monarch, the long

Benedictine monks. Founded by St. Benedict in the sixth century, the Benedictine order grew rapidly in Western Europe, spreading Christianity and, especially in the Middle Ages, promoting learning.

struggle between the emperors and the Papacy, and efforts by the emperors to regain a foothold in Italy are regarded by medieval scholars as central issues in the development of western Europe.

With the collapse of the Carolingian Empire in the ninth century, the east Frankish area broke up into the duchies of Franconia, Saxony, Thuringia, Swabia, and Bavaria. This situation changed when Otto the Great (963–973), Duke of Saxony, became the monarch and was able to consolidate his authority. Otto took the offensive against the Slavic tribes to the east, defeated the Magyars (935), and checked the Vikings. Otto's rule marks a turning point in the relationship between western Christendom and the invaders from the north and east. Otto intervened in Italy and helped restore papal prestige but set in motion forces that eventually brought ruin to the empire itself.

When the Saxon dynasty expired in 1024, the crown passed to Conrad II (1024–39), Duke of Franconia, whose dynasty ruled the empire for a century. The chief development under the Franconian emperors was a dispute with the Papacy over the control of bishops. Gregory VII

(1073–85) determined to abolish lay investiture, the system of royal appointment of bishops. Emperor Henry IV depended on lay investiture, so he and Gregory soon were involved in a confrontation at Canossa (1077). Henry was forced into submission, and the controversy was settled with the Concordat of Worms (1122).

The election of Conrad III of Hohenstaufen as emperor in 1138 precipitated a dispute between the Guelfs and the Ghibellines. The Guelfs were the partisans of Henry the Proud and, in later years, allies of the Papacy. The Ghibellines supported the Hohenstaufens, Frederick I Barbarossa (1152–90) and Frederick II (1212–50). Both were determined to strengthen imperial power through domination of Italy. They met stubborn resistance from the Popes, feudal magnates of Germany, and the cities of northern Italy. After 1273, with the election of Rudolf of Hapsburg, the Holy Roman Empire was generally weakened. The unwillingness of princes to subordinate their self-interests to a national unity proved the characteristic state of affairs in Germany for centuries.

FRANCE

By the Treaty of Verdun (843), Charles the Bald, a grandson of Charlemagne, acquired control over western Frankland and styled himself king of France. The real rulers of feudal France, however, were nobles and princes.

In 987 Hugh Capet, the Count of Paris, displaced the last of the weak Carolingian kings. The descendants of Hugh were to occupy the throne from 987 to 1328. They promoted national unity by adding one fief after another to the royal domain. Fortunately, the regime was blessed with a number of worthy leaders. In particular, three Capetian kings may be considered the founders of the national monarchy in France: Philip II Augustus, Louis IX, and Philip IV, the Fair.

Philip Augustus devoted himself to the work of extending royal authority. By intrigue and combat, he annexed to France many of the Plantagenet holdings of King John of England in western France, and gained control over his many rebellious feudal lords.

The task of enlarging the royal domain was continued by Louis IX, who is known as "Saint Louis." Under his leadership, medieval France enjoyed greater prosperity than ever before, and Louis' patronage of art and learning stimulated the cultural revival of the High Middle Ages.

The reign of Philip the Fair (1285–1314) marked a further rise of royal authority. To finance his wars with Edward I of England and to pay for his staff of lawyers and officials, he expelled the Jews and Italian bankers and confiscated their property. He also debased the coinage and suppressed the wealthy order of the Knights Templars. Philip's quarrel with Pope Boniface VIII, which arose out of the king's constant need for money, led to the summoning of the first Estate General (1302), the Crime of Anagni (1303), and the Babylonian Captivity of the Papacy at Avignon (1307–78).

ENGLAND

With the departure of the Roman garrisons in the early fifth century, the British, under native leadership (possibly the legendary King Arthur), attempted to defend their homeland against the

King John signs the Magna Carta. This document, which states freemen have the right to justice and taxes must be collected by legal means, is a landmark in the history of democracy.

invading Angles and Saxons. By the end of the sixth century, the Germans had established seven principalities in the island, the so-called Anglo-Saxon Heptarchy. Following the conversion of these rough warriors to Christianity in the seventh century, the English and Irish monasteries produced a remarkable religious and cultural development.

The vitality of English cultural life was disrupted by the invasions of the Danes in the late eighth and ninth centuries. The chief organizer of defense against the Danes was Alfred the Great (871–99). Although he stopped the Danes in 878, it was not until 954 that England was finally united. Soon after the turn of the eleventh century, the Danes renewed their raids; under the command of King Canute, the ruler of Denmark, England temporarily was part of Canute's great northern Empire. Following Canute's administration, England reverted to the line of Wessex, namely to Edward the Confessor (1042–66). The relatively weak rule of Edward prepared the way for invasion by the Normans in 1066.

The Norman Conquest left a lasting imprint on English history. Although William the Conqueror respected local custom and law, he superimposed the Norman feudal system, which effectively centralized English government.

Henry II (1154–89), the first Angevin ruler of England, controlled much of western France, often referred to as the Angevin Empire. His contribution was to extend royal justice, introduce the jury system, and strengthen the administration.

The rule of King John (1199–1216) marked an attempt by his barons to transform despotic monarchy into limited monarchy. Following the French victory at the Battle of Bouvines (1214), John was compelled to agree to a list of demands at Runnymede on June 15, 1215. By this document, the Magna Carta, the king agreed to concessions that largely represented the interests of the feudal class. The Magna Carta asserted that the king was under the law and, if necessary, could be compelled to observe it.

Following Runnymede, baronial conflicts erupted anew. Henry III (1216–72) was compelled to submit to the Provisions of Oxford (1258), which further limited royal power. In 1263 Simon de Montfort led the barons in a successful attack on the king. Simon established a government based on the Provisions of Oxford and summoned an assembly of supporters that became the ancestor of the English Parliament. This precedent was continued by Edward I (1272–1307), who convened the Model Parliament in 1295. From that time on, Parliament became an essential part of government in England.

Events in Modern History

American Revolution.   The underlying causes of the Revolution were many: the struggle for survival, the immense distance that separated the colonists from Britain, and the fact that many colonists had emigrated to escape authority. All these factors caused bitter resentment.

The Stamp Act, 1765, was strongly resisted.

A few years later, the Townshend Acts, putting taxes on everyday products such as tea and paper, aroused more protest. A clash between soldiers and citizens over this act caused the Boston Massacre in 1770. All the taxes had been repealed except the one on tea, so radical patriots, dressed as Indians, dumped the tea

On June 15, 1775, General George Washington was elected Commander-in-Chief of the Continental Army, a command he held until December 23, 1783.

shipments into Boston Harbor. In revenge, the British closed the port.

In 1774 the First Continental Congress met; some leaders urged independence, and some still hoped for self-government under British rule. But many colonists were preparing for war. A British raid on a colonial weapons storehouse at Concord, Massachusetts, brought the minutemen and farmers to fight at Lexington and Concord in April 1775. Fighting broke out at various places in New England, and the strong colonial defenses against the siege of Boston (July 1775–March 1776) surprised the British forces. Meanwhile, Ethan Allen and his group captured the British fort at Ticonderoga, New York, while Benedict Arnold prevented the British troops from moving south out of Canada.

The Declaration of Independence was issued in July of 1776, just before General Sir William Howe launched his attack on New York. Fighting took place in Brooklyn, Harlem Heights, and Staten Island, and the colonial army was pushed into a retreat across New Jersey. But Washington led a sudden surprise attack on Christmas night, 1776, against the Hessian mer-

cenaries at Trenton, New Jersey, and eventually controlled northern New Jersey.

The next year the British planned an attack in which three armies would converge near Albany, New York, cutting the colonies in half. The troops coming from New York and from Canada failed to arrive, however, and General Sir John Burgoyne was forced to surrender at Saratoga on October 17, 1777, in a battle sometimes called the turning point of the war. Nevertheless, that winter was the low point of colonial morale. The ragged colonial army camped at Valley Forge, Pennsylvania, without food, shelter, or clothing.

The next year aid began to come from Britain's European enemies, notably France, whose fleet arrived off the New York coast. General Henry Clinton was settled in New York, Washington at West Point. Held to a standstill in the north, the British under General Lord Cornwallis moved steadily through the South, taking Savannah, Georgia, at the end of 1778. They soon held Georgia and the Carolinas, capturing Charleston, South Carolina in May 1780. Pockets of stubborn resistance reduced the strength of Cornwallis's army; it lost the battle of Cowpens, South Carolina, in January 1781; and in March the southern commander, General Nathanael Greene, forced Cornwallis north to Virginia.

Cornwallis fortified Yorktown, but was at last unable to withstand the combined siege by Washington's land troops and the French fleet. Surrender at Yorktown, October 19, 1781, marked the end of the war. The final peace treaty was signed at Paris in 1783.

Arab-Israeli Conflicts. A series of short wars in the Middle East, growing from Arab opposition to the establishment of an autonomous Jewish state in Palestine and from Israel's subsequent attempts to gain more land.

This first war broke out with the proclamation of the state of Israel in May 1948. Jordan, Egypt, and Iraq attacked Israel, and war continued until January 1949, with Israel occupying large portions of territory not originally allotted to it.

The second war resulted from border incidents that had occurred throughout 1956. Israel attacked Egypt on October 29, 1956, and by November 5 occupied almost the whole of the Sinai Peninsula. On November 5 and 6 French and British troops occupied the Suez Canal zone. Israel, Britain, and France were censured by the United Nations and withdrew in March 1957.

Arab refugees from the first two wars remained a constant source of tension, and Arab hostility increased, especially in early 1967. In May Egypt had United Nations peacekeeping troops withdrawn, and threatened to close the Gulf of Aqaba to Israeli shipping.

The third war, known as the Six-Day War, began on June 5, 1967. Israel attacked Egypt and Jordan, and occupied the entire Sinai Peninsula and the west bank of the Jordan River by June 8. On June 9 Israel attacked Syria and captured the strategically important Golan Heights. A cease-fire was arranged June 10.

Still another Arab-Israeli war broke out on October 6, 1973; a cease-fire was arranged the following month.

In late 1977 Egyptian President Anwar Sadat took the dramatic step of seeking and accepting an invitation to address the Israeli parliament (Knesset). This effort bridged the long-standing gap between these two states and resulted in face-to-face talks between leaders on both sides. As the year ended, prospects for peace between them appeared good.

Boer War. A conflict in 1899–1902 between Great Britain and the Boer republics of Transvaal and the Orange Free State. The war grew out of conflicts between British territorial and commercial interests in South Africa and the desire of the Boers (descendants of Dutch settlers) for independence and isolation. Cecil Rhodes, prime minister of the British Cape Colony, was eager to bring all of southern Africa under British rule; while the Boer leader Paul Kruger (''Oom Paul'') sought economic and political independence for his people.

Hostilities broke out several years later when the British refused a Boer ultimatum for the removal of British troops. The Boers were soon overwhelmed by the thousands of British reinforcements brought in from throughout the empire. The fall of Pretoria (June 1900) marked

the end of organized fighting, but the Boers resisted with guerrilla warfare. Kitchener, the new British commander, instituted civilian concentration camps and other harsh measures and eventually broke Boer resistance. The war was ended by the Treaty of Vereenigung (1902), which made the Boer republics crown colonies.

Boxer Rebellion. A revolt of the Chinese against foreign influence in China in 1899–1900. The Boxers were a Chinese secret society that began terrorizing Christian missionaries in 1899.

Officially the Boxers were denounced by their government, but they received unofficial support, including that of Tzu Hsi, the dowager empress. The terrorism reached its height in Peking on June 17, 1900, when large numbers of foreigners and Chinese Christians were slain. An expedition of French, Japanese, German, British, Russian, and American troops relieved a besieged section of the city, where foreigners were concentrated, and a peace treaty was signed on August 14, 1900.

Civil War. A conflict between the Confederate States of America and the federal government of the United States (the Union) in the years 1861–65. The main root of the conflict was slavery, which was strongly entrenched in the South.

When Abraham Lincoln, a Republican, won the election of 1860, southern leadership feared slavery would be legislated out of existence. The southern states began to secede from the Union. Hostilities began when the Southerners opened fire on Fort Sumter, South Carolina, and compelled its surrender after an extended bombardment (April 12–13, 1861).

Union war strategy was based on blockade of all southern ports, capture of Richmond, control of the Mississippi River, and destruction of southern war capacity. The opening campaign in the war was launched by Union forces with an advance toward Richmond, Virginia. On July 21, 1861, the two sides met in the first Battle of Bull Run (Manassas), which resulted in defeat for Union forces.

The Union's next move was an attack led by General McClellan in late March 1862, from Chesapeake Bay westward toward Richmond.

Union troops in the Civil War. This photograph was taken by Mathew Brady (c 1823–1896), who became famous for his pictures of President Lincoln and the war. Brady's pictures are highly prized today.

Meanwhile, Stonewall Jackson's troops were campaigning in the Shenandoah Valley. In late June, Jackson's forces joined General Lee, who was in command at Richmond, and they began the Seven Days' Battles (June 25–July 1), in which Union forces were driven back.

Lee moved his army to Maryland, where he was defeated in the Battle of Antietam on September 17. Taking advantage of this victory, President Lincoln issued the Emancipation Proclamation on September 23, 1862.

Lee crushed the Union forces at Chancellorsville on May 2, 1863. He moved northward into Pennsylvania but was intercepted at Gettysburg by General Meade's Union army, and a fierce battle took place (July 1–3).

Grant's capture of Forts Henry and Donelson in 1862 broke the Confederates' western defense line and forced them out of Kentucky and much of Tennessee. The Union captured New Orleans on April 24.

In 1863, in the West, Grant took the principal Confederate strong point, Vicksburg, Mississippi. In Tennessee, after an initial defeat at Chickamauga and victories at Lookout Mountain (Chattanooga) and Missionary Ridge, the northern forces began their advance. Atlanta was taken on September 2, 1864, and Sherman launched his "March to the Sea through Georgia."

In February 1864, Ulysses Grant was given supreme command of the Union armies. Grant fought engagements with Lee near Chancellorsville (Battle of the Wilderness), at Spotsylvania, Cold Harbor, and finally Petersburg. From August onward Grant held Lee at bay while Confederate strength was cut by hunger, disease, and desertions.

On April 2 Grant made a general advance on the Confederate lines and Lee retreated westward. Grant's forces intercepted him at Appomattox and Lee, realizing that further defense was useless, surrendered his forces on April 9, 1865. Other Confederate forces surrendered soon after, and the Civil War came to a close with over a half million casualties.

Cold War. The ideological conflict between the Soviet Union and its allies and the United States and its allies that developed out of World War II and dominated the political climate of the postwar years. Tension developed when the

Soviet Union set up communist governments in the East European countries it had occupied during the war. Between 1945 and 1948 Albania, Bulgaria, Czechoslovakia, Hungary, Poland, Rumania, and Yugoslavia came under the control of the communists.

Under the Truman Doctrine of 1947, the United States gave financial, military, and technical aid to countries threatened by communism, such as Greece and Turkey. In 1948, the Marshall Plan gave the countries of Western Europe large-scale United States financial and technological assistance to rebuild their war-shattered economies and to strengthen them against communist pressures.

In 1949 the North Atlantic Treaty Organization (NATO) was established to bring the European nations together for their common defense. The Soviet Union responded by developing cooperative economic and military programs of its own, under the Warsaw Pact.

Crimean War.   A war carried on in 1854–56 between Russia and the allied countries of Great Britain, France, and Turkey (the Ottoman Empire). Sardinia (Piedmont) and Austria joined in the diplomatic maneuverings and peace negotiations, but British and French troops bore the brunt of the fighting. Most of the war took place on the Crimean peninsula in the Black Sea, though neighboring territories were also involved. The general cause of the war was the conflict of interests between Russia and the western European nations over the territory of the weak and disorganized Ottoman Empire. Specifically, the war began when Russia demanded a protectorate over Orthodox Christians living in the Turkish empire, which the Turks considered outside intervention.

In July 1853 Russia occupied the Ottoman-held territories of Moldavia and Walachia. By the spring of 1854, Turkey, Britain, and France had declared war, and their fleets were fighting the Russians in the Black Sea. An Austrian ultimatum (June 1854) brought about Russia's withdrawal from the Danube territories, and the war moved into the Crimea itself.

The Crimean War was marked by military and diplomatic blunders on both sides and by tremendously high casualties in battle. Perhaps its most notable outcome was Florence Nightingale's establishment of a nursing hospital for the wounded. The war was ended by the Treaty of Paris, 1856; with this treaty, the European powers recognized the neutrality of the Black Sea and the territorial integrity of the Ottoman Empire.

Détente.   A new and less hostile phase in the relations between the United States and the Soviet Union. The 1970s saw the United States and the Soviet Union move from the hostility of the Cold War to a more complex phase called détente or era of negotiations. This new phase has been marked by efforts to avoid direct confrontation and to expand areas of cooperation. Its supporters argue that the Cold War represented a pessimistic approach to solving differences between the superpowers. Despite occasional strains over issues such as human rights, détente appears to be the successor to the Cold War.

European Communities.   Three organizations established in the 1950s by France, Italy, West Germany, Belgium, Luxembourg, and the Netherlands to promote economic cooperation and integration and, to a degree, political unity. The three organizations are the European Coal and Steel Community (ECSC), the European

---

MEMBERS OF THE EUROPEAN COMMUNITIES

FULL MEMBERS

Belgium	West Germany	Luxembourg
Denmark	Ireland	Netherlands
France	Italy	United Kingdom

ASSOCIATE MEMBERS*

Greece	Turkey	Morocco
Malta	Cyprus	Tunisia

*Under the Lome Convention, forty-nine other nations are affiliated with the European Economic Community (EEC), the Common Market. The EEC is one of the three organizations within European Communities.

Economic Community (EEC, or Common Market), and the European Atomic Energy Community (Euratom).

The Coal and Steel Community, established by treaty in 1951, set up a common market for coal, iron and steel. Euratom, established by the Treaty of Rome, works to develop nuclear energy for peaceful purposes.

The Common Market, established in 1957 by the Treaty of Rome, went into effect on January 1, 1958. In general, it aimed toward a complete customs union of western European nations. Great Britain, Denmark, and Ireland joined the Common Market in 1972; EEC also has associate members and special agreements with certain African and Middle Eastern states.

Franco-Prussian War.　A conflict in 1870–71 between France and the German states, led by Prussia. The war, in which Germany was the victor, completed unification of the German states and ended the second Napoleonic dynasty in France.

The war was touched off by a dispute over succession to the Spanish throne. Prussian Chancellor Otto von Bismarck supported Leopold of Hohenzollern-Sigmaringen, a Prussian prince. France, fearful of having a Prussian on the Spanish throne, demanded that Leopold repudiate his claim. Leopold refused, and France soon declared war.

Within a year the French army was defeated. France was forced to cede the province of Alsace and part of the province of Lorraine to Germany and to pay heavy reparations.

French and Indian Wars.　The overall name given to four successive wars fought by the French and the English in North America from 1689 to 1763. The wars were caused by national upheavals in Europe and conflicting claims of each country to ownership of lands in the New World. The four wars, fought in Europe for very different objectives, were to the American colonists like one great, long conflict with only short periods of respite. For three-quarters of a century French and English armies and settlers fought almost constantly for control of the eastern part of North America.

King William's War began in 1689 when the French attacked in New England, killing and capturing hundreds of English settlers. The

Death of General James Wolfe (1727–1759), at the Plains of Abraham outside old Quebec city. This British victory resulted in Canada's becoming an English possession. At night Wolfe slipped secretly down the St. Lawrence River and surprised the French forces. The battle lasted only fifteen minutes.

English retaliated with sea and land attacks on New France. But all conquests were voided by the Treaty of Ryswick, 1697, which restored the territories to their former owners.

Queen Anne's War began with an English attack on Spanish colonies in Florida, followed by counterattacks. The French, with their Algonquin Indian allies, then attacked New England. The English sent three expeditions to conquer the part of French Canada known as Acadia. They were finally successful and by the Treaty of Utrecht, 1713, were granted not only Acadia (Nova Scotia) but Newfoundland and the Hudson's Bay Territory.

In King George's War (1744) the English mounted a brilliant campaign that won them Fort Louisbourg on Cape Breton Island. The Treaty of Aix-la-Chapelle restored it to France.

The French and Indian War began in 1754 when the French drove Virginians from a strategic position at the junction of the Allegheny and Monongahela rivers. On this site the French built Fort Duquesne (now Pittsburgh), which commanded the Ohio Valley. George Washington was dispatched with another band of Virginians to expel the French. He was unsuccessful and so was the English General Braddock, who made an attempt a year later. The climactic battle was fought for Quebec on the Plains of Abraham in 1759 with English General Wolfe and French General Montcalm as the two commanders. Both were mortally wounded as Quebec fell to the English.

In 1763 the Treaty of Paris granted Canada and all land east of the Mississippi with the exception of the Louisiana Territory to England. Although France was also forced to cede Louisiana to Spain, this territory was later restored in 1800.

French Revolution. The first great European rebellion in which an established government dominated by an absolute monarch, hereditary nobility, and higher clergy was overthrown and replaced by a republic in 1789.

The cause of this struggle was the great gulf between the aristocracy and the senior clergy on the one hand and the middle class and landless peasantry on the other. The Revolution began when the latter group formed the Constituent Assembly, declaring themselves the true representatives of the French nation. The king recognized the Assembly but gathered troops to suppress it. Rumors of the king's intentions, plus serious food shortages, caused widespread unrest climaxed by the storming of the Bastille by a Paris mob on July 14, 1789. Violence spread to the provinces and, to restore calm, the Constituent Assembly abolished the feudal regime and enacted the Declaration of the Rights of Man, proclaiming the individual liberties of all. The king refused to accept these acts, whereupon the Parisians marched to Versailles and compelled the king to return with them to Paris.

The Constituent Assembly established civil equality, seized church lands to pay off the public debt, and completely reorganized the government administrative system. The Assembly attempted to grant limited powers to the king, but Louis refused and attempted to flee the country. He was captured on July 21, 1791, and returned to the Tuileries palace in Paris, a virtual prisoner.

The ideas bred by the French Revolution posed a serious threat to other absolutist states, leading to war with Austria and Prussia on April 20, 1972. In August a band of rioters broke into the Tuileries, forcing the king to seek protection from the Assembly. The Assembly imprisoned him and his family and on September 21 abolished the monarchy completely. The following January Louis XVI was tried and, with his queen Marie Antoinette, executed for treason.

In the face of French military reverses, and differences in political philosophy, a dispute broke out in the Constituent Assembly between the bourgeois Girondists and the more radical Montagnards. The Montagnards, under the leadership of Robespierre, gained the upper hand and expelled their opponents. They enacted radical laws dealing with price control, tax reform, welfare, free education, and the like. They enforced their decrees by widespread arrests and executions, which became known as the Reign of Terror. More than 300,000 arrests were made and over 17,000 persons were executed. In 1795, under the leadership of Napoleon Bonaparte, French military fortunes improved and the extremists were

English textile factory, 1850. The Industrial Revolution regimented and nearly enslaved factory workers. Of 331,000 English textile workers at that time, 9,000 were boys and 6,000 were girls under 13 years of age. Working conditions did not improve for many decades.

driven from power. Robespierre, who had directed the execution of so many, was himself guillotined. A new constitution was then created with executive power vested in a five-man Directory.

French military success continued through 1798 in campaigns against Holland, Spain, Tuscany, Great Britain, Prussia, and Austria. However, a renewed European alliance formed against France in 1799 achieved a number of rapid victories, forcing the French back to their frontiers. These defeats led to a feeling among the people that a stronger government was needed. Napoleon, taking advantage of his enormous prestige, returned to France and seized power in a coup d'état in November, 1799.

Industrial Revolution. The dramatic social and technological changes that took place when humans began relying primarily on the work of machines and on new sources of power.

The first concrete step in the revolution was the invention of machinery to replace hand tools. The introduction of power to replace the muscle of man and beasts was another giant step. Finally, factory production replaced the home industries.

The flying shuttle, invented by John Kay (1733), and the spinning jenny, developed by James Hargreaves (patented 1770), completely changed the making of cloth. Other inventions followed rapidly.

Adam Smith's support of the laissez-faire attitude toward industry in his *The Wealth of Nations* (1776) helped spread the idea of production without the strict regulation practiced so long by the guilds. New methods developed in many areas. Thomas Newcomen had invented a steam engine, and from this James Watt, a Scotsman, developed a practical model, patented in 1769. Steam power was first used in coal mining. It came into its own with the invention of the locomotive by George Stephenson (1815) and the invention of a practical steamboat by Robert Fulton (1807).

When production moved to the factory, the home workers lost a way of life. They had to leave their farms, thus converting much of England from a rural to an urban population. Men, women, and children worked long hours. Skilled workers and artisans were especially resentful of industrial regimentation, and in some factories in England riots broke out.

The man who had money to invest in a factory could make gigantic profits. Much of the profit was put back into transportation and the development of foreign trade, and an influential class of industrial capitalists arose in England.

The laissez-faire policy of the government permitted the capitalists to regulate working conditions. Workers, especially children, sometimes lived in virtual slavery. Finally, the English Parliament passed laws regulating apprenticeship. Meanwhile, the workers themselves fought fiercely for civil rights, favorable legislation, and unionization. This early labor movement was a prime catalyst in triggering the spread of democracy.

A scarcity of capital and labor slowed the development of the United States as an industrial nation. Men were primarily interested in exploring the vast lands to the west. However, much money and effort was put into overseas trade. The textile industry began the United States industrial movement in 1790 with the building of a mill on the Pawtucket River. New England used water power. Pennsylvania produced iron in charcoal furnaces. About 1810, steam-powered spinning machines were introduced in New York. After 1900, the use of electricity pushed industrial development still faster.

Korean War. An undeclared war, officially termed a "conflict" by the United States government, fought from 1950 to 1953 by South Korea and various members of the United Nations, primarily the United States, against North Korean and Chinese Communist troops, aided by the Soviet Union.

Under the terms of the 1945 Yalta agreement between the United States and the Soviet Union, Korea had been divided at the thirty-eighth parallel, with the Soviet Union in the northern part of the country and the United States in the south.

In 1948 a communist regime was established in North Korea, the Democratic People's Republic of Korea. In South Korea, elections held in 1948 resulted in the establishment of the Republic of Korea. In June 1950 North Korean troops invaded the south, and United States forces were rushed to Korea.

The United States quickly received support from the United Nations. The Security Council passed a measure authorizing a police action in Korea, made possible partly because the Soviet delegation had boycotted the meeting and so did not veto the resolution.

On July 1, 1950, United States troops under the command of General Douglas MacArthur landed in Korea. On July 7 the United Nations Security Council voted that all United Nations troops be asked to fight under a common United Nations command.

At the beginning of the war the South Korean and United Nations forces were driven southward, almost off the peninsula. In September 1950 an amphibious landing by United States troops at Inchon forced the North Koreans into retreat, and during the next seventy days North Korean forces were pushed back almost to the Yalu River, which forms the Chinese-Korean boundary.

In November 1950 a Chinese Communist army of 200,000 crossed the Yalu to counterattack. They drove the United Nations divisions steadily back, and by January 1951 Communist forces were seventy miles below the thirty-eighth parallel. The United Nations troops then began another offensive, which carried them across the thirty-eighth parallel on March 31.

The United Nations forces were not allowed to bomb airfields in Manchuria or supply depots and rail centers in other parts of China. General MacArthur repeatedly objected to these limitations, and on April 11 President Harry Truman removed him from command, replacing him with Lieutenant General Matthew Ridgway.

Thereafter, the fighting swayed back and forth, but Soviet-made MIG jet fighters were beginning to offset the former air supremacy of the United Nations. The Communists did not contest the seas, however, and United States naval units roamed the Sea of Japan, the East China Sea, and the Yellow Sea. Frequently, United Nations battleships lay offshore and gave artillery support to ground troops. Amphibious landings were highly successful, and surrounded troops were at times rescued by sea.

On July 10, 1951, the first of many armistice negotiating sessions began at Kaesong. The fighting continued while the negotiators discussed an end to the fighting. An armistice was finally signed at Panmunjom in 1953, and prisoners were exchanged. Korea remained a divided country, with the thirty-eighth parallel again serving as the boundary between north and south.

League of Nations. An international governmental organization devoted to the preservation of world peace and promotion of international cooperation. It existed from 1920 to 1946, when the league passed on its heritage to the United Nations.

The league began to function in January 1920 peace treaty with Germany. The covenant stated that members were to protect each other against aggression and submit disputes to arbitration.

The league began to function in January 1920 in Geneva, Switzerland, but was weakened by the refusal of the United States to join. The league was also weakened by the admission of such important nations as Germany, not a member until 1926, and the Soviet Union, which joined only in 1934. Moreover, three major powers withdrew—Germany in 1933, Italy in 1937, and Japan in 1933.

The league peace-keeping machinery was limited. The league had no armed forces and every member had a veto power over resolutions. The league could not agree upon a general disarmament policy and was unable to halt aggression by Japan, Italy, and Germany in the 1930s. Yet its work in social and economic affairs was considerable. Gains were made in education and public-health work, in refugee assistance, and in trade liberalization. The league also sponsored the mandate system, which placed pre-World War I colonial possessions of the defeated Central Powers under the administration of Allied nations.

Louisiana Purchase. The purchase by the United States from France, in 1803, of a large area of land lying on the west side of the Mississippi River. The negotiations were carried out shortly after Britain had defeated France at sea. For about $15 million James Monroe, representing the United States government, arranged with an agent of Napoleon to buy the western half of the Mississippi River basin—828,000 square miles extending from New Orleans to the Canadian border—thus doubling the size of the United States. Eventually the land made up the states of Arkansas, Iowa, Louisiana, Missouri, Nebraska, North Dakota, Oklahoma, and South Dakota as well as parts of Colorado, Kansas, Minnesota, Montana, and Wyoming.

Napoleonic Wars. The series of wars fought by French Emperor Napoleon during the years 1805–14. The warfare was triggered by the formation of an alliance among Russia, Austria, England, and other powers against France. Napoleon's military genius conquered most of Europe in the ensuing years.

During 1808–14, Napoleon fought Britain, Portugal, and Spanish guerrillas in the Iberian peninsula. Although generally successful, the war was extremely costly. The turning point in Napoleon's fortunes, however, was a decision to invade Russia in 1812. Forced to retreat through a severe Russian winter, his army suffered terrible losses. In 1813, at Leipzig, he confronted an alliance of European powers and was defeated at the "Battle of the Nations." Napoleon abdicated on April 11, 1814, and was exiled to the island of Elba in the Mediterranean.

He escaped and returned to France on March 1, 1815. Beginning what came to be called "the Hundred Days" of his rule, he resumed the war against the European powers. He met final defeat in June 1815 at Waterloo.

North Atlantic Treaty Organization (NATO). A mutual-defense system of the United States and Western Europe. Under the treaty, an attack on one member is to be considered an attack on all members.

NATO was established in 1949 by a treaty signed by Belgium, Canada, Denmark, France, Great Britain, Iceland, Italy, Luxembourg, the Netherlands, Norway, Portugal, and the United States. Greece and Turkey were admitted in 1952, and West Germany joined in 1955. France withdrew from the military sector of NATO in 1966.

NATO headquarters, originally in Paris, moved in 1967 to Brussels. The Council is the chief body of NATO and considers all matters pertaining to the enforcement of the treaty. It consists of a foreign minister and/or a defense minister from each country.

Reformation.   The sixteenth-century revolt against the Catholic Church that gave rise to Protestantism.

By the early 1500s the church was in a weakened condition. There was secularism in its hierarchy, ignorance among the lower clergy, and widespread abuses, such as simony (sale of church offices), pluralism (holding more than one church office), and violation of the vows of celibacy. Papal authority had been undermined, and many heresies since the 1200s, though suppressed, had left traditions that threatened the unity of the church. Competing ways of thought also raised doubts.

The matter was brought to a crisis by Martin Luther, professor of theology at the University of Wittenberg, in Germany. Luther began to question some of the teachings and practices of the church. His "revolt" began in 1517, when he posted on the Wittenberg Church door ninety-five theses, primarily concerned with the sale of indulgences (by which the Pope claimed to release souls from purgatory).

In the controversy that followed, Luther ultimately denied not only the doctrine of indulgences but the infallibility of popes and church councils. He also asserted that salvation was achieved through faith, not sacraments and works.

He denied that priests were different from laymen and rejected all the sacraments except baptism, the Lord's Supper, and, in part, confession. Regarding the Lord's Supper, he replaced the doctrine of transubstantiation with that of the Real Presence—that Christ is present in the materials of the Mass, but in spirit only.

Luther's doctrine became widely accepted. In 1520, he was excommunicated by Pope Leo X and in 1521 was put under the imperial ban by the Diet of Worms. But, protected by his prince, Frederick the Wise of Saxony, Luther

Martin Luther (1483–1546). Luther's Ninety-Five Theses, which he nailed to the door of All Saints' Church in Wittenburg, Germany, in 1517, helped initiate the Reformation.

lived, taught, and preached another twenty-five years while Lutheranism became permanently established.

Meanwhile, other Protestant groups appeared. In Zurich, Huldreich Zwingli, a priest and biblical scholar, rejected both transubstantiation and the Real Presence. He considered the Lord's Supper only a commemorative re-enactment.

Anabaptism, which had neither a uniform doctrine nor an organized church, held that the Judgment Day was near, which led some believers to try to establish the Kingdom of Heaven on earth by rebellion. The rebels took possession of the town of Münster and in 1535 were ruthlessly punished. Anabaptists were attacked savagely by both Protestants and Catholics and soon were reduced to insignificance.

John Calvin, a French theologian, broke with Catholicism in 1533 and three years later was asked to organize the Reformed Church in Geneva, Switzerland. Calvin considered the Lord's Supper central to the practice of religion, but only as a commemorative reenactment. Salvation of individuals was predestined at the time of creation, and the true church consisted only of the "elect of God." Calvinism spread rapidly to larger states, such as France and the Netherlands, where conflict was inevitable and survival a problem.

Renaissance. In the traditional sense, the term "Renaissance," which literally means rebirth, denotes the revival of classical learning and culture in Italy (the Italian Renaissance), mainly in the 1300s and 1400s, and its spread to other parts of Europe (the Northern Renaissance), mainly during the 1400s and 1500s. However, the term is often used merely as a label for the period of European history from about 1300 to about 1600.

The Renaissance was the first period in which men really considered themselves to be "modern"—that is, they believed their own age to be not only different from the preceding one but superior to it. The "Renaissance man" rejected the "barbarisms" and "corruptions" of the centuries since the decline of ancient Greece and Rome.

The Renaissance scholar was concerned with the secular side of things. Poets and philosophers concerned themselves with this world, not the next; with the world of nature, not that of theology; with man, not angels. Painters and sculptors sought to capture real people rather than general types, and individual personalities rather than universal human traits. In architecture, the heavy and complex Gothic style was thrown over for the simple classical style of straight lines and balanced proportions.

The universities not only concentrated heavily upon secular subjects but also produced large numbers of educated laymen, not just clergy. The "universal man"—one skilled in a variety of pursuits, from scholarship and poetry to the art of war—was the Renaissance ideal, concerned mainly with secular activities.

Renaissance thought still contained much that was medieval—scholastic strains as well as classical. Secular Renaissance artists portrayed religious subjects with great religiosity, differing from medieval artists in style, but not subject matter. Renaissance architects rejected much of medieval style but kept a great deal of it as well, and excelled at building churches.

Desiderius Erasmus (1466?–1536), shown in a famous Holbein portrait. His translations of Greek and Roman classics helped vitalize learning submerged during the Middle Ages.

During the classical revival, an eager search, led by Petrarch and Boccaccio, was made for early Latin manuscripts, many of which were found in monasteries. The quest for manuscripts continued for more than three generations. By studying these manuscripts, scholars and writers regained an exact knowledge of classical Latin, which had been lost during the medieval centuries.

Humanist education produced large numbers of well-lettered laymen who were much better prepared than churchmen had previously been to perform the increasingly sophisticated work of governing a modern state.

Most important of all, perhaps, the Renaissance was a period of crossfertilization in European culture, of reducing the barriers that separated various fields of knowledge.

The Renaissance in the north, starting and ending about a century later than in Italy, was in many ways native in origin and in character. Whereas Italy at the beginning of its Renaissance was becoming increasingly secular, much of northern Europe was conspicuous during the 1300s for its growing religious mysticism. Lay religion was particulary strong in the Netherlands.

Desiderius Erasmus of Rotterdam was the most respected humanist of his time. Together with Erasmus, Sir Thomas More took the lead in introducing into England the study of Greek, which was particularly important to the study of the New Testament. It is not surprising that much of the Renaissance in the north is called the "Christian Renaissance."

The Renaissance state, in many ways a forerunner of the centralized, omnipotent modern state, developed rapidly, particularly in northern Italy's cities. Medieval republican city governments, which also ruled outlying territory, gave way to rule by an individual despot in Milan and by a wealthy oligarchy in Venice. In Florence, the two were combined.

Elsewhere larger territorial states were being consolidated under strong monarchical rule, most importantly in England, France, and Spain. By the early 1500s each of these countries had achieved, in rough form, its modern boundaries. Although each developed differently, royal power was markedly increased, and the centralized institutions characteristic of modern government swiftly developed.

Restoration.   In British history, the restoration of the British monarchy after the Puritan Revolution. After the death of Oliver Cromwell in 1658, the English Puritan government no longer functioned, and the factions in the army fought among themselves. Widespread reaction to Puritan rule resulted in the dissolution of the Rump Parliament and the election of the Convention Parliament of 1660. Parliament then recalled Charles II from exile. The Restoration, which encompasses the reign of Charles II (1660–85), is noted for its literature, chiefly the works of John Dryden and the comedies of William Congreve.

Revolutions of 1848.   A series of popular revolutions that occurred throughout Europe in 1848. The first and most important took place in France. The middle class led the opposition to the increasingly oligarchic government of Louis Philippe. The bourgeoisie, devoted to nonviolence, hoped to shame the government into making concessions rather than to force a radical change.

As Louis Philippe saw the pressure mount, he made a small concession—a change of ministry in February 1848. The more cautious accepted this as a victory, but those who wished for more basic reforms manned the barricades. When a regiment of the regular army fired on a mass parade in Paris, fighting became intense. Louis Philippe fled, and the Revolution of 1848 was an accomplished fact.

The Second Republic, established as a result of the revolution, began to whittle away the revolutionary gains made by the workers. By June, the middle class was ready for a showdown and provoked the Parisian workers into rebellion. The result was a slaughter. The army moved into the working-class districts of Paris and decimated the population. The "June days" were the crucible of French working-class unity and marked the origin of socialism as an active and potent force in French politics.

In the republic's first presidential election, held in December 1851, Louis Napoleon, nephew of France's Emperor Napoleon I, won a victory based on the support of the peasantry and those weary of instability. Louis Napoleon soon declared the national legislature dissolved, and the liberal dreams of a generation were dissipated on December 2, 1852, when Louis Napoleon became by plebiscite Emperor Napoleon III.

News of the French revolt of 1848 electrified Europe, and revolutions broke out in several countries. The Hungarians broke away from Vienna; the Romans overthrew papal power; the Italians in northern Italy felt their day of liberation had come; revolution broke out even in Vienna.

The Austrian government called for aid from the Russian tsar, who was happy to help put down a revolt. The Hungarian revolution was crushed, the Vienna revolutionaries were successfully intimidated, and the Austrian army was left free to punish insurgents in other parts of the empire.

The French Revolution of 1848 also sparked a series of explosions that ran through Germany. For a while it looked as though there would be a permanent revolutionary effect. A parliament at Frankfurt debated the future of Germany. The majority at Frankfurt wanted a government that would be defined by a constitution and some form of popular participation in this government. The majority also favored German political unification. However, the Austrian government would not encourage such a move, and from then on the German states looked to Prussia for leadership.

Russian Revolution.   A revolution against the tsarist regime in Russia in 1917, during which the Bolsheviks came to power and set up the first Communist state. It was preceded by long-term agitation and unrest and a lesser revolution in 1905.

The Russian Revolution was precipitated by World War I. The Russian army was losing on the Eastern Front, discontent was rising at home, and Tsar Nicholas II's rule became less and less effectual. Workers took over St. Petersburg in February 1917, the tsar was forced to abdicate, and a moderate provisional government was set up. The various Socialist parties opposed the government and undermined it and each other. The Bolshevik faction, led by

Lenin (1870–1924) addresses troops in Red Square, Moscow, 1919. Founder of the Soviet Union, Lenin assumed power in November, 1917. After Lenin's death, Joseph Stalin became dictator.

Lenin, staged a military coup in October and took over the government, making peace with Germany.

Not all Russians went along with the Bolshevik government, and soon the Reds, or Bolsheviks, and the Whites, or anti-Bolsheviks, were involved in a bloody civil war. It ended with the triumph of the Reds and the exile of the Whites in 1920.

Seven Years' War.   A struggle fought from 1756 to 1763 by Britain, Hanover, Portugal, and Prussia against Austria, France, Russia, Sweden, Spain, and a few German principalities. It was a contest for dominance in central Europe and for control of colonies in North America and India. In America the struggle began in 1755 and was known as the French and Indian War.

The immediate cause of the war in Europe was Austria's desire to reclaim the rich territory of Silesia that it had ceded to Frederick the Great of Prussia in 1742. The war was a contest between Austria and Prussia, the two greatest German powers.

Austria allied itself with France, its traditional enemy. Austria also formed alliances with Saxony and Poland. Britain, fearing an attack on its royal province of Hanover, allied itself with Prussia. This alliance enabled Austria to win Russia as an ally and to bring France to declare war on Britain in June 1756.

Frederick the Great, aware of the Austrian moves, struck first by invading Saxony in August 1756. In January 1757 Austria declared war on Prussia in the name of the Holy Roman Empire.

During the early stages of the war, Frederick was generally successful in Europe, and Britain stripped away the French colonial empire. But after 1760 the pressure of Prussia began to tell. In 1762, however, the Russian Empress Elizabeth died and was succeeded by Peter III, who admired Frederick. Russia then withdrew from the war. This enabled Prussia to hold off the French and Austrians until 1763, when the Treaty of Hubertusburg ended the war in central Europe between Austria and Prussia. By the terms of the treaty, Prussia retained Silesia. Other European boundaries remained essentially as they were before the war. The Treaty of Paris (1763), which settled colonial matters, gave most of French North America to Britain, and forced France to leave India.

Spanish Civil War. A conflict from 1936 to 1939 between supporters of the Spanish Republic (Loyalists) and a coalition of right-wing forces (Nationalists or Insurgents). The moderately liberal Second Spanish Republic, established in 1931, was unpopular with the Roman Catholic Church and the aristocracy; the military, the monarchists, and the newly founded Falange, a fascist party, also joined in opposition to the republic and its reforms. An election victory in 1936 by the Popular Front—republicans, liberals, Socialists, and Communists—threatened conservative interests, and a right-wing rebellion broke out, led by the military. The dominant Nationalist leader was General Francisco Franco.

Soon foreign nations began to take sides despite a nonintervention pact signed in August 1936. Liberal sympathizers from the United States and other nations aided the Loyalists, as did the Soviet Union. Franco's forces, however, received large-scale aid from Nazi Germany and fascist Italy; by 1939 the Loyalists had been defeated. Franco assumed power, backed by the Falangists.

Thirty Years' War. The last of the great European wars of religion, fought throughout the northern Holy Roman Empire from 1618 to 1648.

Under the Religious Peace of Augsburg (1555), peace lasted in the empire, but old hatreds remained. Calvinism, not included in the Augsburg settlement, was now vigorous and widespread in Germany, and a revived Catholicism was gaining in strength. In 1608–09 German princes formed rival military alliances—the Protestant Union and the Catholic League. Religious and political hostility erupted into three decades of war.

Since 1526 the Austrian Hapsburg patrimony had included the kingdom of Bohemia. Because of religious oppression, the Czech nobility deposed their king Ferdinand (later Emperor Ferdinand II) and threw two royal officials out of a palace window, an act known as the Defenestration of Prague. They elected in his place Frederick V.

The rebel army was insufficiently backed by the Czechs and the Union; Ferdinand was aided by Spain and the Catholic League. In 1620, the Bohemian army was crushed at the Battle of White Mountain, and the Spanish invaded Frederick's Rhine palatinate. The Dutch-Spanish War was resumed in 1621, but by 1623 Bohemia and Frederick's own patrimony had been conquered.

In 1625, Christian IV of Denmark, a Lutheran, with the promise of English and Dutch support, revived the Protestant cause and invaded Germany. Albert Wallenstein, a wealthy Czech noble raised an army of 50,000 men for Ferdinand. Wallenstein joined forces with Count Tilly's Catholic League army to defeat the Danes at Lutter am Barenberge in 1626, and the Danes withdrew from Germany. But Ferdinand, in the Edict of Restitution of 1629, attempted to enforce restoration of all lands taken from the church since 1555, thus eliminating any hope of peace.

A new Protestant champion appeared in Gustavus Adolphus of Sweden. He was a Lutheran who combined Christian motives with territorial greed, but with more success.

Gustavus Adolphus had already made progress in turning the Baltic Sea into a "Swedish lake." With financial aid promised by France, he invaded Germany in 1630. Having gained some German allies, he defeated Count Tilly at Breitenfeld in 1631 and again in Bavaria in 1632, where Tilly was killed.

Ferdinand turned again to Wallenstein, and in 1632 Europe's two greatest generals met in battle at Lützen. The Swedes won, but Gustavus Adolphus was killed. The Protestant cause in 1634 met defeat in battle at Nördlingen, where Ferdinand disposed of the dangerously ambitious Wallenstein by assassination. In 1635 the Peace of Prague restored the disputed ecclesiastical lands to those who had held them in 1627.

The peace might have lasted had France not intervened. Cardinal Richelieu wanted to destroy Austrian and Spanish Hapsburg power, already diminished by war. Allied with Sweden, the Dutch princes, Savoy, and numerous German princes, France intentionally prolonged the war, steadily exhausting Hapsburg strength.

The war ended in Germany and the Netherlands in 1648 with the Peace of Westphalia, which gave France important territories on its German frontier and made the German states practically independent of the empire, and vulnerable to French influence. Secularized church lands were returned to their 1624 holders, and Calvinists were admitted to the privileges of the Religious Peace of Augsburg. Spain recognized the independence of the United Provinces. The war between France and Spain, however, dragged on until 1659.

Versailles, Treaty of. The most important of the treaties ending World War I. The Treaty of Versailles was framed by Britain, France, Japan, and the United States, although the United States did not ratify it.

The treaty dealt with Germany's responsibility for the war and its obligations in defeat. Among the most significant provisions were the separation of a number of territories from Germany, the requirement that Germany pay substantial reparations, and limitations on German rearmament. In addition, the treaty provided for the demilitarization of the Rhineland. One of the most significant provisions of the treaty was the establishment of the League of Nations.

Vienna, Congress of. A conference held in Vienna in 1814–15, at which the members of the coalition that had defeated Napoleon met to decide the future of Europe. The chief participants were Britain, Prussia, Russia, and Austria, though every European state including France was represented. Their primary purpose was to ensure a lasting peace and to prevent a recurrence of revolution.

The doctrine by which stability was to be regained was the balance of power. The Vienna settlement, therefore, was concerned with redrawing the map of Europe to achieve this balance.

France, the focus of revolutionary infection, was buffered by creation of the Kingdom of the Netherlands. Austria was compensated for loss of its Netherlands territory by being given

Lombardy and Venetia in Italy. Germany was organized into a confederation of thirty-nine states with a diet, or parliament, over which Austria presided, thus cushioning Austria from Prussian competition.

Prussia received territories on the Rhine and a part of Saxony. Russia agreed to give up Poland on the condition that the tsar be made king of a new kingdom of Poland. The monarchy of Sardinia was reconstituted, and a Bourbon regained the throne of Spain.

The balance of power was maintained by shuffling territories and alliances so that no one state could dominate the others. The success of the Congress of Vienna is evidenced by the fact that no major European war was fought from 1815 to 1854, a record that has never been equaled. However, despite its relative success, the congress totally ignored the vital issues of nationalism and liberalism. This shortsightedness eventually destroyed the peace.

Vietnam War. A guerilla war dating from the collapse of the French colonial empire in Southeast Asia in 1945, following World War II. Initially a nationalist struggle, the conflict grew and eventually involved both Asian and non-Asian nations.

The war in Vietnam began in 1945 as a struggle between Vietnamese nationalists seeking independence and French colonial forces attempting to reestablish French rule after the defeat of Japan, which had invaded and occupied the area during World War II.

The Viet Minh, as the Vietnamese forces were known, were led by Ho Chi Minh, an independent communist. They had great popular support. The French, realizing it could not retain the same system as before the war, came to favor a nominally independent Vietnam under a former emperor, Bao Dai.

A crucial battle in the French struggle to retain control of Vietnam was fought in 1954 at Dien Bien Phu. The Viet Minh won a decisive victory, and the French agreed to withdraw.

An international conference was held in Geneva, Switzerland, in 1954. The major participants were Britain, the People's Republic of China, the Soviet Union, and the United States. Neither the French nor the Vietnamese

Marine helicopter lands in jungle clearing, Vietnam. Helicopters were first used extensively in the Korean War.

had a significant voice in the conference, which provided for the temporary partition of Vietnam at the seventeenth parallel until elections could be held in 1956.

In spite of the terms of the Geneva agreement, the north became a communist republic led by Ho Chi Minh, and the south became a monarchy with a weak emperor, Bao Dai, and a strong prime minister, Ngo Dinh Diem. In 1955, a republic with a powerful president was established in the south. Diem served as the first president and won United States support. In 1956 Diem, backed by the United States, refused to hold the elections called for in the Geneva agreement.

In 1960 a coalition of opponents to the Diem regime, including old Viet Minh regulars, Communists, and advocates of national reunification, formed the National Liberation Front (NLF). The North Vietnamese government supported the NLF, which became known as the Viet Cong. The Viet Cong by 1965 had gained so much territory and support in the south that it was feared they would take over the country.

The Diem government was unable to cope with the problems arising from the struggle, despite United States assistance. Moreover, many Buddhist leaders strongly opposed the administration headed by Diem, who was a Roman

Catholic. Resentment against the Diem regime culminated in a bloody coup in November 1963. Diem was killed and the government was seized by a military junta.

Success of the Viet Cong prompted the United States to enter the war in early 1965. North Vietnamese army troops began fighting in the South, and the United States instituted bombing raids on North Vietnam. The bombings continued intermittently until early 1973, and well over a million tons of explosives were dropped on the north without strategic effect.

Through the early 1960s the war was conducted primarily by South Vietnamese regular troops fighting guerrillas. United States involvement increased sharply as the South Vietnamese failed to put down the Viet Cong. The Philippines, Australia, New Zealand, Thailand, and South Korea lent token military support at one time or another.

Late in January 1968 the Viet Cong launched a surprise attack on Hué, an important provincial city; Saigon, the capital city; and several smaller provincial centers. Known as the Tet offensive, the attack caused heavy loss of life and equipment in the south, and weakened morale. The Viet Cong forces were eventually expelled from the cities, but the struggle continued in the countryside.

The pressure of world opinion, the growth of United States antiwar dissension, and the obvious impossibility of a military victory led the United States to begin peace negotiations with the North Vietnamese, the Viet Cong, and the South Vietnamese in 1968. The talks dragged on until 1973, while the United States repeatedly tried and failed to win a military advantage in the South.

Early in 1973, a cease-fire agreement was reached. No political accord about the future of South Vietnam was reached, but the United States announced that it would no longer object to a communist regime, provided the takeover was peaceful.

With almost all United States troops evacuated by 1974, the United States House of Representatives voted down military aid for South Vietnam. In January 1975 President Ford's request to Congress for $300 million in further military aid for South Vietnam and $222 million for Cambodia was never authorized, for by March 1975 the North Vietnamese had launched their final offensive. The Central Highlands, Hue, and Danang fell with little resistance. Ford's plea in April for nearly a billion dollars

in aid went unheeded. In rapid order Cambodia conceded defeat, President Ford authorized the evacuation of all remaining Americans, and South Vietnam surrendered unconditionally.

The Vietnam War was one of the most costly and destructive wars in all history. It destroyed the economy, disrupted the social structure, decimated the population, and devastated the landscape of Vietnam. Its effect on the United States was also costly; it resulted in an unstable economy, worldwide condemnation of United States foreign policy, bitter internal political divisions, and widespread distrust by the people of their government's motives and credibility.

War of 1812.   A war between the United States and Great Britain. It began in 1812; a truce was made in 1814, but the last battle was fought in 1815.

The War of 1812 broke out over maritime disputes that were largely a result of the Napoleonic Wars between France and Great Britain, United States shippers, who were profiting from the wars and from their neutrality, were accused by Britain and France of violating maritime laws for wartime; the United States had already

Battle of New Orleans, War of 1812. Victorious Major General Andrew Jackson (shown on horseback) became nationally famous and a founder of the Democratic Party. In 1829 "Old Hickory" became the seventh U.S. president, the first elected by the voters instead of by Congress.

fought an undeclared war with France in 1797. The British also objected to British Navy sailors deserting to United States ships and claiming United States citizenship. British warships would stop United States merchant ships and seize any sailor suspected of being a British deserter. This practice, called impressment, was also abused by British captains whose crews were under strength. After HMS *Leopard* attacked USS *Chesapeake* in 1807, war threatened. Though maritime difficulties were being worked out, the United States frontiersmen's demand for free land west of the Alleghenies led to further agitation against Britain by "war hawks" in Congress. War was declared June 18, 1812, and at once an expedition was sent to capture Canada. It failed miserably.

In 1813, Oliver H. Perry won the Battle of Lake Erie. This enabled General William Henry Harrison to take Detroit, and the British were driven from the Northwest Territory.

In August 1814, a British force took and burned Washington, D.C., but it was stopped at Fort McHenry outside Baltimore.

New England merchants, who had been badly hurt by the war, were agitating for an end to it. Both sides agreed to negotiate at Ghent, Belgium, and a treaty was signed on Christmas Eve, 1814. However, news of the peace did not come in time to prevent the Battle of New Orleans, won by United States forces under Andrew Jackson on January 8, 1815.

The main result of the war was to open up the lands west of the Alleghenies to United States expansion.

Warsaw Pact. A military agreement signed by the Soviet Union and its East European satellites in 1955. The Warsaw Pact is essentially a mutual-defense system intended as a counterpart to the North Atlantic Treaty Organization (NATO) of the Western nations. The original members of the pact were Albania, Bulgaria, Czechoslovakia, East Germany, Hungary, Poland, Rumania, and the Soviet Union. In 1968 Albania formally withdrew.

World War I. A global conflict involving the principal powers of the world, fought from 1914 to 1918 on several widely scattered fronts. This was the first war to involve so large a number of nations, to be so costly in men and material, and to be so comprehensive and destructive.

The causes of World War I were many and reflected the state of affairs of Europe in the late 1800s and early 1900s. Chief among them were the attempts of individual nations to regulate the balance of power through alliances and counter-alliances; the resurgence of nationalism in almost every European country; and the growing power and influence of the military in government affairs.

The growth of the German Empire following the Franco-Prussian War (1870–71) made Russia in the east and Britain and France in the west afraid of German encroachments on their territory. The immediate cause of the war was the assassination in 1914 at Sarajevo, in present-day Yugoslavia, of the heir to the Austro-Hungarian throne, Archduke Francis Ferdinand, by a member of a Serbian patriotic organization. Austria presented Serbia with a humiliating ultimatum, apparently hoping to provoke a short and limited war.

At the time of the Austrian ultimatum, however, the six major powers of Europe were already divided into two groups. Austria-Hungary, Germany, and Italy were united in the Triple Alliance, and Britain, France, and Russia were allied in the Triple Entente.

Austria declared war on Serbia. Russia mobilized, and Germany followed suit. Germany then declared war on Russia, and a major conflict became inevitable.

Within three days after Germany's declaration of war, France and Britain had entered the conflict. With Russia, they were known as the Allies, while Austria-Hungary and Germany were known as the Central Powers. Japan which was allied with Britain, declared war on Germany in August 1914.

The Ottoman Empire (Turkey) came into the war in September on the side of Germany and Austria-Hungary against its old-time enemy, Russia. Bulgaria received offers from both sides in the summer of 1915 but in October declared war on Serbia. Rumania declared war on Austria-Hungary in August 1916. Greece joined the Allies in June 1917. Other countries, such as Liberia, Honduras, and Siam (Thailand), came

U.S. Army advances over trenches in World War I. Often only a hundred yards of "no-man's land" separated opposing armies. During the battle of Verdun the Germans advanced only four miles in six months. Verdun was one of the longest and bloodiest battles of World War I.

in nominally or actually against the Central Powers.

Italy in 1882 had joined Germany and Austria-Hungary in the Triple Alliance. At the beginning of the war, however, Italy declared its neutrality and demanded certain concessions from Austria as its price for continued neutrality.

The gains that Austria would not give Italy were promised by the Allies in the Treaty of London of April 1915. This brought Italy into the war against its old allies.

The United States was neutral during the early part of the war, and Woodrow Wilson was reelected President in 1916 with the campaign slogan "He kept us out of war." President Wilson hoped to make peace, but early in 1917 a German policy of unrestricted submarine warfare and effective Allied propaganda brought the United States into the war on the side of the Allies.

In the spring of 1917 Russia had practically dropped out of the war after suffering a series of defeats at the hands of the Central Powers. These defeats, coupled with internal revolution, resulted in the abdication of Tsar Nicholas II a

few weeks before the United States came into the war. In November 1917 Russia's revolutionary government sought an armistice.

The original German plan was to fight a war on two fronts, against France in the west and Russia in the east. The strategy was to overrun France quickly and then concentrate troops in the east.

The course of events defied this plan. Resistance on the western front was stronger than had been anticipated. The Balkans offered fierce resistance to German and Austro-Hungarian troops. The defection of Italy to the Allies tied down large numbers of Austrian troops on the Austro-Italian frontier. Only in Russia were the Central Powers able to win decisively.

The nature of the warfare was something previously unknown. Deep trenches kept armies battling for weeks and even months over a few feet of ground. The use of tanks and poison gas was also new.

In the war at sea the Germans had an early advantage with their submarines, which effectively destroyed shipments of supplies to the

D-Day, June 6, 1944, American troops land on the Normandy coast. This Allied invasion of France established a western front. Just under a year later, on May 7, 1945, Germany, reeling from the onslaught of the Russians in the east and the Allies in the west, surrendered.

Allies. In the early part of 1918, however, the Allied use of naval convoys effectively broke the submarine blockade.

With the arrival of troops from the American Expeditionary Force in 1918, the Allies were able to turn back a huge German offensive at the second Battle of the Marne.

Military defeats, economic disorder, and lenient peace proposals set forth in United States President Wilson's "Fourteen Points" all contributed to the German decision to seek an armistice in September 1918. A peace conference was convened in January 1919, and on June 28 the Treaty of Versailles was signed, ending the war.

World War I led to political and territorial reorganization of Europe. It resulted in the disbanding of the old German, Austro-Hungarian, Russian, and Ottoman empires; and it marked the beginning of experiments in democratic and republican government in many countries.

World War II. A global conflict fought from 1939 to 1945 on land, sea, and in the air. It was the most devastating war fought up to that time in terms of human and material losses.

The world's principal nations were divided into two groups, the Axis and the Allies. The Axis was led by Germany, Italy, and Japan. The Allies were led by Britain, France, the Soviet Union, and the United States.

The background of World War II reflects the extremely complicated circumstances of world affairs in the period following World War I. The harsh terms of the Treaty of Versailles, coupled with a worldwide economic depression in the 1930s, brought radical political groups to power in many countries. Moreover, an ideological split developed, establishing totalitarian and democratic blocs.

In Germany these factors helped to bring the Nazi (National Socialist) party, headed by Adolf Hitler, to power in 1933. Under the Nazis, Germany began to rearm. In 1936 the Germans reoccupied the Rhineland, and in 1938 they seized Austria.

During this period both Britain and France were anxious to preserve peace at any price. Both condemned Nazi actions, but did nothing to stop Germany. In 1938, at a conference held in Munich, they agreed to allow Germany to annex part of Czechoslovakia.

Italy had been under totalitarian rule since 1922, when Benito Mussolini was named premier. While Hitler ruled Germany, Italy's fascist government also followed a policy of aggression. In 1935 Italy attacked Ethiopia, and in 1939 the Italians invaded Albania.

In 1937 Germany, Italy, and Japan joined together in the Anti-Comintern Pact. Japan, eager to expand its influence in Asia, had attacked China in 1931, seizing Manchuria. In 1937 Japan launched a general invasion of China.

By 1939 war seemed inevitable, and most of the nations of Europe were speeding their armament programs. In the Soviet Union, the government led by Joseph Stalin found itself unprepared for a major conflict. The Soviet Union and Germany, which had been bitter enemies in a worldwide propaganda war, signed a nonaggression pact.

Germany, continuing its expansionist program, invaded Poland in September 1939. Britain and France, which had guaranteed Poland's borders, declared war on Germany and its allies.

The war may be divided into four major stages. The early part of the conflict was marked by sweeping German victories. Poland, Denmark, Norway, Luxembourg, the Netherlands, and Belgium quickly fell to German forces. By the summer of 1940, France had collapsed, and a puppet French government had been established in Vichy. Before the end of 1940, the Germans had pushed through the Balkans, occupying Yugoslavia and Greece.

In the west, only Britain was able to withstand the early assault. British sea and air forces were able to prevent a German invasion of the British Isles.

The second stage began in June 1941. Germany broke the terms of its treaty with the Soviet Union and invaded that country. At first it seemed that Germany would continue its military successes, but a Soviet counteroffensive, coinciding with the early arrival of a severe winter, caused a temporary setback for the Germans. The war was also being fought in Africa, the Mediterranean, and the Atlantic.

Neither side won a decisive victory in any of these theaters.

The third stage of the war began in the Pacific in December 1941, when Japan attacked the United States naval base at Pearl Harbor, in Hawaii, bringing the United States into the war. Heavy fighting in the South Pacific brought early victories to Japan, but by the spring of 1942 United States forces had regained several key islands.

The fourth stage marked the turning point of the war. By the summer of 1942, the Allies had taken the offensive on almost all fronts. The Axis powers were routed in Africa, and by the summer of 1943 Italy had surrendered. The Soviet Union mounted another offensive during the winter months, and Allied forces invaded Western Europe in June 1944.

Germany, fighting on both eastern and western fronts, had been weakened by Allied bombing raids. Moreover, the prospect of losing the long and costly war had caused internal dissension, culminating in an unsuccessful attempt to assassinate Hitler. By 1945, with Soviet troops pushing west toward Berlin and United States troops pushing east, it was evident that the Nazis were defeated. Hitler committed suicide, and on May 7 Germany surrendered.

The end of the war in Europe made it possible for the Allies to concentrate on defeating Japan. Naval battles in the Pacific broke Japanese sea power, and Allied air attacks on the Japanese home islands heralded an invasion of Japan. The final blow was an atomic-bomb attack on the cities of Hiroshima and Nagasaki in August 1945. On September 2 the Japanese surrendered, and World War II was over.

Under the terms of the surrender, Germany was partitioned, with control divided among Britain, France, the Soviet Union, and the United States. Germany also lost considerable territory in eastern Europe.

Japan was occupied following the war, with most of the troops under United States command. Italy lost its colonial conquests in Africa and some territory in Europe. The lesser Axis powers were dealt with under separate treaties.

Africa and Asia

AFRICAN INDEPENDENCE

Africa is 5000 miles long and 4500 miles wide. It has a population of over 300 million with many different cultures and languages.

By 1000 B.C. outsiders began to come as traders, then as settlers, and finally as conquerors. During the nineteenth and twentieth centuries, European powers competed with one another to colonize Africa. The two World Wars were primarily responsible for ending European dominance in Africa. From World War I came the idea that people had the right of self-determination. From World War II came a stronger commitment to end colonialism. The transition to independence was accomplished peacefully in some instances, but only after rebellion and bloodshed in others.

This map shows Africa on the eve of World War I. The colonial movement was at its height, and almost every part of Africa was staked out by European powers.

This map shows Africa today, a continent of many independent, strongly nationalistic states. Some are plagued by questions of race and white-minority rule yet to be resolved.

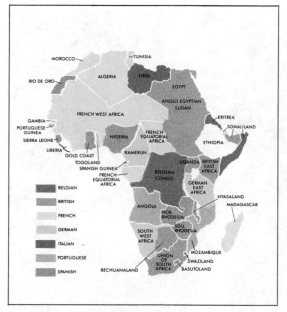

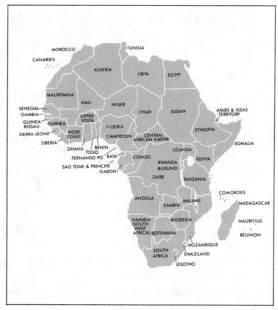

Open rebellion in German West Africa and in British Southern Rhodesia early in the twentieth century failed when confronted by superior military force. Later, using guerilla tactics, many African states were able to win independence. The slower route, which in the end proved successful, lay in educating native leaders, both at home and abroad. These leaders rallied their peoples by appealing to pride and nationalism. Among these leaders were Samuel Adjai Crowther of Sierra Leone, Jomo Kenyatta of Kenya, Ahmad Ben Bella of Algeria, Kwame Nkrumah of Ghana, and Julius Nyerere of Tanzania.

All the European colonial powers resisted the independence movement to one degree or another. Belgium and Portugal were the bitterenders. In the Congo (now Zaire), independence was declared in 1960 but lasted only five days. An armed struggle ensued involving Belgian troops and United Nations troops. It took five years more for Zaire to become independent under the strong leadership of General Joseph Mobutu. Portugal finally gave up its hold on Angola in November 1975 after fifteen years of bloody fighting. In Mozambique the independence movement succeeded in June 1975 after eleven years of guerilla warfare. The British, ultimately presided over the calm transition of many of its colonies to independence during the 1960s.

In rapid order the following colonies gained independent status: Nigeria in 1960; Sierra Leone in 1961; Uganda in 1962; Zambia, Malawi, and Zanzibar in 1964; Gambia in 1965; Botswana and Lesotho in 1966; Swaziland and Mauritius in 1968. Only Rhodesia, with its white minority government, felt compelled to act unilaterally in 1965 and declare itself independent. Like South Africa, Rhodesia has become the center of attention in the 1970s as the problem of accommodating overwhelming black majorities in the political process is addressed.

France's experience in giving up its colonial holdings was like that of Great Britain. Morocco and Togo in 1956 and Tunisia in 1957 easily gained their independence. Only in Algeria was there a violent struggle. France finally acceded to Algerian freedom in 1962.

CHINA
(PEOPLE'S REPUBLIC OF CHINA)

China has had the longest continuing civilization in the world, dating from before 2000 B.C. Throughout most of that history, Chinese leaders worked to keep outsiders from influencing Chinese culture.

Geat Wall of China meanders through the Pata Ling Hills, near Peking. Communist workmen, installing a high-power telephone line across the wall, are an emblem of the new China cast against the old.

By 1839 the British had provoked a war over opium, defeated the Chinese, and succeeded in gaining access to China for trade through so-called open ports. After World War I, China saw a continuing struggle for power among the warlords in the north and the Kuomintang, led by Chiang Kai-shek, in the south. Japan invaded Manchuria in 1931 and set up a government there.

In 1934 about 100,000 Communist troops led by Mao Tse-tung and Chou En-lai marched north some 6000 miles to avoid being encircled by the Kuomintang army. Nearly three-quarters of these troops were lost during the twelve-month march. During World War II, largely as the result of insistence by the United States, an uneasy alliance between the Communists and the Nationalists (Kuomintang) was imposed in an effort to drive the Japanese out of Manchuria. Despite the alliance, each side remained poised for the showdown—the civil war fought from 1945 until 1949, when the Communists, with the support of the peasants, routed the Nationalists. In January, 1949, the Communists captured Peking, destroying the main National-ist forces north of the Yangtze. Chiang Kai-shek and most of his troops fled to the island of Taiwan (Formosa). The People's Republic of China was proclaimed in Peking, Mao Tse-tung was installed as president, and Chou En-lai as foreign secretary.

The United States refused to recognize the People's Republic and continued to support the exiled Chiang Kai-shek and his government on Taiwan. Chinese intervention in the Korean War served to keep relations hostile between Mao and the United States. The cultural revolution in the late 1960s, in which Mao tried to reassert the old values, followed a break with the Soviet Union. By the 1970s China was exploring improved relations with the United States. In 1971 an American ping-pong team was invited to compete in China. This act was seen as an expression of a desire to improve relations between the two countries.

The United Nations General Assembly on October 25, 1971, succeeded in ousting the Taiwan delegation and seating the People's Republic delegation as the representatives of the Chinese. President Nixon, accompanied by American diplomats and the press, visited China in 1972. In 1973 the Chinese and the United States opened liaison offices in each other's capitals.

One remaining difficulty is the status of Taiwan. The People's Republic maintains that Taiwan is part of China; the Nationalists argue that they are a government in exile. Many native Taiwanese would like to be independent of both Chinas.

INDIA
(REPUBLIC OF INDIA)

India's first exposure to Europeans came in the sixteenth century, when Vasco da Gama, the Portuguese explorer, arrived in India. Portuguese conquest of Goa soon followed. For two centuries India was ruled by a Mogul dynasty and developed a large Moslem population. In the mid-1700s France and Britain became interested in India and fought one another over the right to colonize. The Treaty of Paris in 1763 gave Britain supremacy.

For one hundred years India remained under

Mohandas K. Gandhi (1886–1948). Mahatma ("Great Soul") Gandhi was shot to death by a religious fanatic months after India gained her freedom as a result of Gandhi's campaign of non-violent resistance.

the jurisdiction of the British East India Company, but in 1857 a rebellion by native employees resulted in direct rule by the British.

In 1919 Mohandas K. Gandhi, an Indian educated in England, organized the first of his many campaigns of passive resistance against British rule. Gandhi and his technique of nonviolent resistance won India's independence from the British in 1947.

Two independent nations—India and Pakistan—were created, separating Moslems from Hindus, with Pakistan providing a refuge for Moslems. Pakistan, separated by 900 miles of India in between its East and West sectors, had little to bind it together except religion.

India fought a border war with China in 1962, and subsequent relations between the two countries have been unfriendly. In 1965 India fought Pakistan over Kashmir, a still unresolved problem involving Moslem-Hindu differences.

Under its first prime minister, Jawaharlal Nehru, India pursued a postwar policy of nonalignment with major powers. Pakistan, under General Ayub Khan, joined the United States-dominated Southeast Asia Treaty Organization (SEATO). Nehru's daughter, Indira Gandhi, succeeded Lal Bahadur Shastri in 1966 and was a powerful political leader in the next five years.

After winning the election of 1971, Mrs. Gandhi's government became involved in a civil war in Pakistan by aiding the East Pakistani effort to break away from West Pakistan. India's help made the difference, but millions of East Pakistanis crossed the border into India, adding to the problems of an economy strained by rapid population growth, periodic famine, chronic unemployment, and deteriorating living conditions.

In 1975 Mrs. Gandhi suspended civil liberties and arrested hundreds of dissidents. Early in 1977 Mrs. Gandhi lifted some of the restrictions on the freedom of the press and announced that there would be an election. In March of 1977 she was soundly defeated in her bid to retain power. Victory by Moraji Desai marked the first time in the thirty years of Indian independence that the Congress Party had been out of power.

JAPAN

In 1854 Commodore Matthew C. Perry of the United States Navy sailed his fleet into Japanese harbors and opened Japan to the outside world. By 1868 a period of westernization had begun. Japan undertook an ambitious program of ship construction, railroad building, manufacturing, and a buildup of its armed forces.

Japan emerged as a world power in victories over China in the Sino-Japanese War (1894-95) and over Russia in the Russo-Japanese War (1904-05). Japan created a puppet state in Manchuria in 1931, invaded China's northern provinces in 1937, and joined Germany in a military alliance in 1940.

After its crushing defeat in World War II, Japan initiated reforms in 1946-47 during the occupation headed by United States General Douglas MacArthur. The most important were political democratization and demilitarization.

The Japanese have combined government and business in a unique way, encouraging export markets for business. As a result Japan has become a world economic power.

This economic development has been accomplished at considerable cost: crowded cities experience housing shortages and pollution; trade surpluses and protective tariffs have resulted in countermeasures by Japan's principal trading partner, the United States. Above all, Japan's economy has depended on oil, with no commitment to any other energy source, so when the OPEC (Organization of Petroleum Exporting Countries) nations raised the price of oil in 1973-74, Japan's vulnerability was exposed.

Since the 1954 treaty with the United States provided American military protection, Japan has had to maintain only minimal self-defense forces. Yet growing nationalism in Japan has led to demands that American troops be withdrawn and American bases closed. In 1971 the United States returned to Japan the Ryukyu Islands, including Okinawa, where a huge military base had been maintained. As a result the numbers of United States troops and bases on Japanese territory have been steadily reduced.

The United Nations

On June 26, 1945, fifty nations signed the charter of the United Nations, an organization planned to encourage the maintenance of international peace and security. In addition, the UN hoped to promote cooperation in solving international, social, and economic problems as well as to develop friendly relations among all nations. Its third objective was to promote respect for human rights on an international basis. To achieve these ends, the UN was divided into six principal organs: the General Assembly, the Security Council, the Economic and Social Council, the Trusteeship Council, the International Court of Justice, and the Secretariat.

GENERAL ASSEMBLY

All 149 UN member nations (as of 1977) belong to the General Assembly, in which each nation has one vote. A two-thirds majority of the members present at an Assembly meeting decide such important questions as recommendations for peace and security, election of members to other organs, trusteeship matters, and UN budgetary matters. All other questions require a majority of the members present.

The main functions of the General Assembly are to discuss issues and to make recommendations to member nations. The Assembly also elects the nonpermanent members of the Security Council. The work of the General Assembly is carried on by six major committees plus a supplementary one added to relieve the heavy burden of the first. Their concerns are as follows: the First, political and security matters; the Second, economic and financial questions; the Third, social, humanitarian and cultural issues; the Fourth, trusteeships; the Fifth, administrative and budgetary matters; and the Sixth, legal

President Jimmy Carter addresses the General Assembly. Below the UN seal sit the Secretary General, his chief assistant, and the president of the Assembly.

questions. The Special Political Committee was added to assist the work of the First Committee.

The General Assembly elects the nonpermanent members of the Trusteeship Council and the entire Economic and Social Council. The Assembly and the Security Council, voting independently, elect the members of the International Court of Justice. On the recommendation of the Security Council, the Assembly appoints the Secretary-General.

SECURITY COUNCIL

The Security Council is composed of fifteen members. The People's Republic of China, France, the Soviet Union, the United Kingdom, and the United States are permanent members. The other ten members are elected for two-year terms by the General Assembly. Each member of the Security Council has one vote. Rules for running Security Council meetings are decided by an affirmative vote of any nine members. On all other questions, the nine affirmative votes must include the five permanent members. If any permanent member *vetoes* a resolution before the Council, that resolution cannot be enacted.

The veto was intended to insure that no action would be taken without the unanimity of the great powers.

The Council may investigate any situation that might lead to international friction and recommend methods of adjustment and settlement. Such situations can be brought before the Council by UN members, by the General Assembly, by the Secretary-General, or by non-UN members who accept the obligations of settlement as outlined by the UN Charter.

ECONOMIC AND SOCIAL COUNCIL

The Economic and Social Council (ECOSOC) has fifty-four members. Every year eighteen of the members are elected to a three-year term by the General Assembly. ECOSOC promotes higher standards of living and health and the attainment of fundamental freedoms for all people.

TRUSTEESHIP COUNCIL

This council was established to supervise territories taken from former enemies after World

Meeting of the Security Council of the United Nations, October 24, 1977. At the request of the African States, the Council here resumes its deliberation of the "question of South Africa." The Council is empowered to investigate any situation that might cause international friction.

War II, former mandated territories of the League of Nations, and any other territories recommended to it. The Trusteeship Council encourages the establishment of self-government and independence for the territories it supervises. The Council has been so successful that of the eleven trust territories originally under its supervision, only the Trust Territory of the Pacific is left.

INTERNATIONAL COURT OF JUSTICE

The International Court of Justice (ICJ) is the judicial organ of the UN. It is permanently in session at The Hague, Netherlands, and is composed of fifteen judges elected to nine-year terms by the General Assembly. The Court is open to UN member nations and to nations that are parties to its statutes. Its decisions are based on international law, custom, conventions, and legal precedent.

SECRETARIAT

The Secretariat includes the Secretary-General and an international staff. The staff is appointed by the Secretary-General from as wide a geographic base as possible. The Secretary-General may convene the Security Council to consider any threat to international peace. The UN has had only four Secretaries-General in its more than thirty-year history: Trygve Lie of Norway, from 1946 to 1953; Dag Hammarskjöld of Sweden, from 1953 to 1961; U Thant of Burma, from 1961 to 1971; and Kurt Waldheim of Austria, from 1971 to the present time.

These men have played outstanding roles in maintaining world order during the difficult years that have followed World War II. Many times they have intervened successfully to calm countries troubled by the tensions arising from the economic and political turmoil of recent history.

MEMBERS OF THE UNITED NATIONS
(as of January 1978)

Afghanistan	Cape Verde	Fiji	Iran	Mauritius	Rwanda	Uganda
Albania	Central African	Finland	Iraq	Mexico	São Tomé and	Ukrainian SSR
Algeria	Empire	France	Ireland	Mongolia	Principé	Union of Socialist
Angola	Chad	Gabon	Israel	Morocco	Saudi Arabia	Soviet
Argentina	Chile	Gambia	Italy	Mozambique	Senegal	Republics
Australia	China, People's	Germany	Ivory Coast	Nepal	Seychelles	United Arab
Austria	Republic of	(Democratic	Jamaica	Netherlands	Sierra Leone	Emirates
Bahamas	Colombia	Republic)	Japan	New Zealand	Singapore	United Kingdom
Bahrain	Comoro Islands	Germany	Jordan	Nicaragua	Somalia	United States
Bangladesh	Congo	(Federal	Kenya	Niger	South Africa	Upper Volta
Barbados	Costa Rica	Republic)	Kuwait	Nigeria	Spain	Uruguay
Belgium	Cuba	Ghana	Laos	Norway	Sri Lanka	Venezuela
Benin	Cyprus	Greece	Lebanon	Oman	Sudan	Vietnam
Bhutan	Czechoslovakia	Grenada	Lesotho	Pakistan	Surinam	Western Samoa
Bolivia	Denmark	Guatemala	Liberia	Panama	Swaziland	Yemen
Botswana	Djibouti	Guinea	Libya	Papua New	Sweden	Yemen
Brazil	Dominican	Guinea-Bissau	Luxembourg	Guinea	Syria	(Southern)
Bulgaria	Republic	Guyana	Madagascar	Paraguay	Tanzania	Yugoslavia
Burma	Ecuador	Haiti	Malawi	Peru	Thailand	Zaire
Burundi	Egypt	Honduras	Malaysia	Philippines	Togo	Zambia
Byelorussian SSR	El Salvador	Hungary	Maldives	Poland	Trinidad and	
Cambodia	Equatorial	Iceland	Mali	Portugal	Tobago	
Cameroon	Guinea	India	Malta	Qatar	Tunisia	
Canada	Ethiopia	Indonesia	Mauritania	Rumania	Turkey	

Makers of world history: a time line, 600 BC to AD 2000

DARIUS THE GREAT
c. 588–486, Persian king

PYTHAGORUS
581–497, Greek philosopher, scientist

BUDDHA, GAUTAMA
c. 566–c. 480, Indian religious leader

CONFUCIUS
Chinese philosopher, teacher

AESCHYLUS
c. 525–456, Greek dramatist

PINDAR
520–447, Greek poet, composer

PHIDIAS
c. 500–c. 432, Greek sculptor

ANAXAGORAS
500–428, Greek philosopher

SOPHOCLES
c. 495–c. 406, Greek dramatist

PERICLES
c. 490–429, Athenian statesman

EMPEDOCLES
490–430, Greek philosopher

ZENO OF ELEA
490–430, Greek philosopher

HERODOTUS
c. 484–c. 425, Greek historian

EURIPIDES
c. 480–c. 406, Greek dramatist

SOCRATES
469–399, Greek philosopher

HIPPOCRATES
c. 460–c. 370, "Father of medicine"

THUCYDIDES
460–395, Greek historian

EUCLID
450–374, Greek geometrician

PARMENIDES
flourished 450, Greek philosopher

ALCIBIADES
450–404, Greek politician, general

ARISTOPHANES
c. 448–385, Greek comic playwright

XENOPHON
c. 434–c. 355, Greek historian

PLATO
427–347, Greek philosopher

ARISTOTLE
384–322, Greek philosopher

DEMOSTHENES
c. 384–322, Athenian statesman, orator

PHILIP II
382–336, Macedonian king

PTOLEMY I
367–280, Egyptian ruler

SELEUCUS I
c. 358–c. 281, Founder of Seleucid dynasty

ALEXANDER THE GREAT
356–323, Macedonian king, conqueror

PRAXITELES
flourished c. 350, Greek sculptor

EPICURUS
c. 342–c. 270, Greek philosopher

MENANDER
c. 342–291, Greek comic playwright

CHANDAGUPTA MAURYA
(ruled 322–298, King of Northern India

ASOKA
ruled c. 273–232, Ruler of India

HAMILCAR BARCA
270–228, Cathaginian general

PLAUTUS
c. 254–c. 184, Roman dramatist

HANNIBAL
247–183, Carthaginian general

CATO THE ELDER
234–149, Roman statesman

QUINTUS FABIUS PICTOR
flourished 225, first Roman historian

POLYBIUS
c. 205–123, Greek historian

500 BC	400 BC	300 BC	200 BC	100 BC

JUDAS MACCABEUS
c. 200–166, Led Maccabean revolt

TERENCE
190–c. 159, Roman dramatist

ANTIOCHUS IV EPIPHANES
ruled 175–c. 163, Syrian king

MARIUS
c. 155–86, Roman general, consul

SULLA
138–78, Roman general, dictator

MITHRIDATES THE GREAT
132–63, King of Pontus, Roman rival

POMPEY
106–48, Roman general, statesman

CICERO
106–43, Roman statesman, orator

JULIUS CAESAR
100–44, Roman general, statesman

LUCRETIUS
98–55, Roman poet, philosopher

CATO THE YOUNGER
95–46, Roman statesman, soldier

CATULLUS
c. 84–c. 54, Roman poet

MARK ANTONY
83–30, Roman soldier, politician

HEROD THE GREAT
73–4, King of Judea

VERGIL
70–19, Roman poet

CLEOPATRA
69–30, Egyptian queen

HORACE
65–8, Roman poet

AUGUSTUS CAESAR
63–AD 14, Roman emperor

STRABO
63–AD 22, Greek geographer, historian

OVID
43–AD 18, Roman poet

TIBERIUS
42–AD 37, Roman emperor

ARMINIUS
17–AD 21, German chief

JESUS CHRIST
4–AD c. 30, founder of Christianity

SENECA
4–AD 65, Roman philosopher

ST. PAUL
?–67, Christian missionary, theologian

NERO
37–68, Roman emperor

PLUTARCH
46–120, Roman biographer

TACITUS
c. 55–c. 120, Roman historian

TRAJAN
57–117, Roman emperor

EPICTETUS
c. 60–120, Greek-Roman stoic philosopher

HADRIAN
76–138, Roman emperor

MARCUS AURELIUS
121–180, Roman emperor

PTOLEMY
flourished 127–148, Alexandrian geographer

GALEN
130–200, Greek physician

ORIGEN
c. 185–c. 254, Christian theologian, teacher

DIOCLETIAN
254–313, Roman emperor

ARIUS
?–336, Priest, founder of Arianism

CONSTANTINE THE GREAT
280–337, Roman emperor

ST. ATHANASIUS
c. 296–373, Greek bishop of Alexandria

ST. JEROME
c. 340–420, Bible scholar

| 100 BC | AD 1 | AD 100 | 200 | 300 |

Roman Empire declines, 400s
Middle Ages begin,
c. 400

Knights of the
Round Table, c. 500

The Hegira, 622

ST. JOHN CHRYSOSTOM
c. 347–407, Patriarch of Constantinople

ST. AUGUSTINE
354–430, Christian theologian

ALARIC
370–410, Visigoth king

ATTILA
d. 453, King of the Huns

ST. PATRICK
385–461, Christian missionary

THEOPHILUS
385–412, Byzantine emperor

ODOACER
433–493, King of Italy

JUSTIN I
450–527, Byzantine emperor

THEODORIC
455–526, King of Italy

CLOVIS
466–511, Frankish King

ST. BENEDICT
480–543, founder of Western monasticism

BOETHIUS
c. 480–c. 524, Roman philosopher, statesman

JUSTINIAN I
483–565, Byzantine emperor

KING ARTHUR
c. 500, legendary British king

ST. COLUMBA
521–597, Irish missionary to Scotland

GREGORY THE GREAT
540–604, pope, statesman

MUHAMMAD
570–632, founder of Islam

GOGI
668–749, Korean-Japanese Buddhist priest

VENERABLE BEDE
673–735, English historian

CAEDMON
?–680, Anglo-Saxon poet

CHARLES MARTEL
688–741, Frankish leader

WANG WEI
698–759, Chinese poet, painter

LI PO
700–762, Chinese poet

Charlemagne crowned, 800

Vikings invade Europe, 800s

Feudalism established in France, 900s

Vinland discovered, c. 1000

Battle of Hastings, 1066

First Crusade, 1095

PEPIN THE SHORT
714–768, Frankish king

ALCUIN
735–804, English scholar

CHARLEMAGNE
742–814, Holy Roman emperor

HARUN AL-RASHID
766–809, caliph of Baghdad

EGBERT OF WESSEX
775–839, English king

AL-KHWARIZMI
780–850, Arab mathematician

ALFRED THE GREAT
849–889, English king

AL-FARABI
870–950, Arab philosopher

OTTO I
912–973, Holy Roman emperor

AL-BATTANI
flourished 920, Arab astronomer

BRIAN BORU
926–1014, Irish king

ROSWITHA OF GANDERSHEIM
935–c. 1000, German nun, playwright

HUGH CAPET
940–996, French king

ETHELRED II, THE "UNREADY"
960–1016, English king

ERIC THE RED
flourished 980–1000, Norwegian explorer

AVICENNA
980–1037, Arab physician, philosopher

LEIF ERICSON
flourished 1000, Norwegian explorer

CANUTE
994–1035, king of England, Denmark, Norway

GUIDO D'AREZZO
995–1050, Italian musical theorist

EDWARD THE CONFESSOR
1002–1066, king of Anglo-Saxon England

GREGORY VII
1020–1085, churchman, pope, reformer

WILLIAM THE CONQUEROR
1027–1087, Norman king of England

OMAR KHAYYAM
1027–1123, Persian poet, astronomer

ST. ANSELM
1033–1109, Archbishop of Canterbury

EL CID
1043–1099, Spanish soldier, epic hero

ABELARD
1079–1142, French philosopher, teacher

BERNARD OF CLAIRVAUX
1090–1153, French monk, mystic

IBN EZRA
1092–1167, Jewish scholar, theologian

THOMAS A BECKET
1118–1170, English prelate, saint

ELEANOR OF AQUITAINE
1122–1204, queen of France and England

FREDERICK BARBAROSSA
1123–1190, Holy Roman emperor

AVERROES
1126–1198, Moorish philosopher

HENRY II
1133–1189, king of England

MAIMONIDES
1135–1204, Spanish-Hebrew philosopher

SALADIN
1138–1193, Muslim military leader

MINAMOTO YORITOMO
1147–1199, Japanese warlord, shogun

RICHARD THE LION-HEARTED
1157–1199, king of England

INNOCENT III
1160–1216, pope, statesman

GENGHIS KHAN
1167–1227, Mongol military leader

ST. DOMINIC
1170–1221, founder of Dominican order

ST. FRANCIS
1182–1226, founder of Franciscan order

ALBERTUS MAGNUS
1200–1280, German philosopher, scientist

700 800 900 1000 1100 1200

Hanseatic League formed, 1200s
(Children's Crusade, 1212)
Magna Carta, 1215

Renaissance begins, early 1300s
Babylonian captivity of the papacy at Avignon, 1307–1878
Hundred Years' War, 1337–1453
Black Death, 1347–50

ROGER BACON
c. 1214–1294, English philosopher, scientist

KUBLAI KHAN
1215–1294, Mongol ruler, emperor of China

ALEXANDER NEVSKI
1220–1263, Russian ruler, national hero

THOMAS AQUINAS
1225–1274, Italian scholastic philosopher

MARCO POLO
1254–1324, Italian traveler, adventurer

DANTE
1265–1321, Italian poet

GIOTTO
c. 1266–1327, Florentine painter, sculptor

DUNS SCOTUS
1266–1308, Scottish theologian

ROBERT BRUCE
1274–1329, king of the Scots

WILLIAM OF OCKHAM
1290–1349, English philosopher

GUILLAUME DE MACHAUT
1300–1377, French poet, composer

PETRARCH
1304–1374, Italian poet

BOCCACCIO
1313–1375, Italian poet, writer, humanist

JOHN WYCLIFFE
c. 1324–1384, English bible translator

IBN KHALDUN
1332–1406, Arab historian

TAMERLANE
1336–1405, Mongol conqueror

GEOFFREY CHAUCER
1344–1400, English poet

JOHN HUSS
c. 1369–1415, Bohemian religious reformer

THOMAS A KEMPIS
c. 1380–1471, German mystic and author

JAN VAN EYCK
c. 1385–1440, Flemish painter

FRA ANGELICO
1387–1455, Italian painter

GUILLAUME DUFAY
1399–1474, Dutch composer

JOHANN GUTENBERG
c. 1400–c. 1468, German printer, inventor

JOAN OF ARC
1412–1431, French saint, military leader

FRANCOIS VILLON
1413–1463, French poet

WILLIAM CAXTON
1422–1491, first English printer

1200   1300   1400

Fall of Constantinople, 1453

Wars of the Roses for English throne, 1455–1485

Spanish Inquisition begins, 1480

Columbus's first voyage, 1492

Protestant Reformation, 1500s

Spanish Armada defeated, 1588

HERNAN CORTES
1485–1547, Spanish explorer, conqueror

HENRY VIII
1491–1547, king of England

IGNATIUS LOYOLA
1491–1556, founder of Jesuit order

IVAN THE GREAT
1440–1505, Russian czar

WILLIAM TYNDALE
c. 1493–1536, English bible translator

SANDRO BOTTICELLI
1444–1510, Italian painter

SULEIMAN THE MAGNIFICENT
1496–1566, Ottoman sultan

LORENZO DE'MEDICI
1449–1492, Italian prince, arts patron

CELLINI
1500–1571, Italian sculptor, metalsmith

HIERONYMUS BOSCH
1450–1516, Dutch painter

CHARLES V
1500–1558, Holy Roman emperor

HEINRICH ISAAC
1450–1517, German-Dutch composer

NOSTRADAMUS
1503–1566, French astrologer

JOSQUIN DES PREZ
1450–1521, Dutch composer

JOHN CALVIN
1509–1564, French protestant reformer

CHRISTOPHER COLUMBUS
1451–1506, Italian navigator, explorer

MERCATOR
1512–1594, Flemish geographer

LEONARDO DA VINCI
1452–1519, Italian artist, scientist, inventor

CATHERINE DE MEDICI
1519–1589, Queen of France

HENRY TUDOR
1457–1509, Henry VII of England

IVAN THE TERRIBLE
1530–1584, Russian czar

MAXIMILIAN I
1459–1519, Holy Roman emperor

ELIZABETH I
1533–1603, Queen of England

ERASMUS
1466–1536, Dutch scholar, humanist

FRANCIS DRAKE
c. 1540–1596, English navigator

VASCO DA GAMA
c. 1469–1524, Portuguese navigator

WILLIAM BYRD
1543–1623, English composer

NICCOLO MACHIAVELLI
1469–1527, Italian statesman, writer

MONTEZUMA
c. 1470–1520, Aztec emperor of Mexico

ALBRECHT DURER
1471–1528, German painter, engraver

COPERNICUS
1473–1543, Polish astronomer

MICHELANGELO
1475–1564, Italian artist, architect

FRA BARTOLOMMEO
1475–1517, Italian painter

CESARE BORGIA
1476–1507, Italian politician

TITIAN
1477–1576, Italian painter

THOMAS MORE
1478–1535, English humanist, statesman

RAPHAEL
1483–1520, Italian painter

MARTIN LUTHER
1483–1546, German protestant reformer

1400

1500

EL GRECO
c. 1545–1614, Spanish painter

MIGUEL DE CERVANTES
1547–1616, Spanish poet, novelist

BORIS GODUNOV
1551–1605, Russian czar

FRANCIS BACON
1561–1626, English philosopher, essayist

WILLIAM SHAKESPEARE
1564–1616, English dramatist, poet

GALILEO
1564–1642, Italian astronomer

CLAUDIO MONTEVERDI
1567–1643, Italian composer

JOHANNES KEPLER
1571–1630, German astronomer

PETER PAUL RUBENS
1577–1640, Flemish painter

CARDINAL RICHELIEU
1585–1642, French statesman

RENE DESCARTES
1596–1650, French philosopher

BERNINI
1598–1680, Italian sculptor, architect

OLIVER CROMWELL
1599–1658, English Lord Protector

VELASQUEZ
1599–1660, Spanish painter

PEDRO CALDERON
1600–1681, Spanish dramatist

REMBRANDT
1606–1669, Dutch painter

JOHN MILTON
1608–1674, English epic poet

BLAISE PASCAL
1623–1662, French scientist, thinker

JAN VERMEER
1632–1675, Dutch painter

JOHN LOCKE
1632–1704, English philosopher

CHRISTOPHER WREN
1632–1723, English architect

MOLIERE
1633–1673, French dramatist

LOUIS XIV
1638–1715, King of France

ISAAC NEWTON
1642–1727, English physicist

GOTTFRIED WILHELM LEIBNITZ
1646–1716, German philosopher, mathematician

EDMUND HALLEY
1656–1742, English astronomer

JONATHAN SWIFT
1667–1745, English satirist

PETER THE GREAT
1672–1725, Russian czar

JOHANN SEBASTIAN BACH
1685–1750, German composer

GEORGE BERKELEY
1685–1753, Irish philosopher

ALEXANDER POPE
1688–1744, English poet

VOLTAIRE
1694–1778, French writer, philosopher

BENJAMIN FRANKLIN
1706–1790, American statesman, scientist

LINNAEUS
1707–1778, Swedish botanist

SAMUEL JOHNSON
1709–1784, English lexicographer, critic

DAVID HUME
1711–1776, Scottish philosopher, historian

JEAN JACQUES ROUSSEAU
1712–1778, French philosopher

FREDERICK THE GREAT
1712–1786, King of Prussia

MARIA THERESA
1717–1780, Holy Roman empress

CHARLES STUART
1720–1780, pretender to the English throne

IMMANUEL KANT
1724–1804, German philosopher

THOMAS GAINSBOROUGH
1727–1788, English painter

CATHERINE THE GREAT
1729–1796, empress of Russia

GEORGE WASHINGTON
1732–1799, American general, president

THOMAS PAINE
1737–1809, American political writer

THOMAS JEFFERSON
1743–1826, American statesman, president

GOYA
1746–1828, Spanish painter

JOHANN WOLFGANG VON GOETHE
1749–1832, German poet, novelist

MARIE ANTOINETTE
1755–1793, queen of France

WOLFGANG AMADEUS MOZART
1756–1791, Austrian composer

WILLIAM BLAKE
1757–1827, English poet, artist

NAPOLEON
1769–1821, emperor of France

LUDWIG VAN BEETHOVEN
1770–1827, German composer

WILLIAM WORDSWORTH
1770–1850, English romantic poet

SIR WALTER SCOTT
1771–1832, Scottish novelist, poet

CLEMENS VON METTERNICH
1773–1859, Austrian diplomat, statesman

JANE AUSTEN
1775–1817, English novelist

SIMON BOLIVAR
1783–1830, Venezuelan soldier, statesman

LORD BYRON
1788–1824, English poet, satirist

PERCY BYSSHE SHELLEY
1792–1822, English poet

JOHN KEATS
1795–1821, English poet

ROBERT E. LEE
1807–1870, Confederate general

ABRAHAM LINCOLN
1809–1865, American president

CHARLES DICKENS
1812–1870, English novelist

CHARLES DARWIN
1812–1870, British naturalist, writer

RICHARD WAGNER
1813–1883, German composer

OTTO VON BISMARCK
1815–1898, Prussian statesman

HENRY DAVID THOREAU
1817–1862, American writer

KARL MARX
1818–1883, German economist, philosopher

FEODOR DOSTOEVSKI
1821–1881, Russian novelist

LOUIS PASTEUR
1822–1895, French chemist

LEO TOLSTOY
1828–1910, Russian writer

MARK TWAIN
1835–1910, American writer, lecturer

PAUL CEZANNE
1839–1906, French painter

PETER ILYICH TCHAIKOVSKY
1840–1893, Russian composer

THOMAS ALVA EDISON
1847–1931, American inventor

ALEXANDER GRAHAM BELL
1847–1922, American inventor

SIGMUND FREUD
1856–1939, Austrian psychoanalyst

THEODORE ROOSEVELT
1858–1919, American president

HENRY FORD
1863–1947, automotive industry pioneer

WILBUR WRIGHT
1867–1912, American aviation pioneer

FRANK LLOYD WRIGHT
1869–1959, American architect

MOHANDAS K. GANDHI
1869–1948, Indian nationalist leader

1700   1800   1900

World War I, 1914–18
Russian Revolution, 1917–20
Great Depression, 1930s
World War II, 1939–45
United Nations Charter, 1945
Vietnam War, 1945–73
Arab-Israeli Six-Day War, 1967
Man Walks on Moon, 1969

VLADIMIR ILYICH LENIN
1870–1924, Russian revolutionary, Soviet premier

ORVILLE WRIGHT
1871–1948, American aviation pioneer

BERTRAND RUSSELL
1872–1970, English philosopher, mathematician

CHAIM WEIZMANN
1874–1952, Zionist leader, president of Israel

WINSTON CHURCHILL
1874–1965, English statesman

ALBERT EINSTEIN
1879–1955, German-born American physicist

JOSEF STALIN
1879–1953, Soviet dictator

PABLO PICASSO
1881–1973, Spanish artist

POPE JOHN XXIII
1881–1963, Italian ecclesiastic, statesman

FRANKLIN DELANO ROOSEVELT
1882–1945, American president

IGOR STRAVINSKY
1882–1971, Russian composer

BENITO MUSSOLINI
1883–1945, Italian dictator

T. S. ELIOT
1888–1965, Anglo-American poet

ADOLF HITLER
1889–1945, German dictator

JAWAHARLAL NEHRU
1889–1964, prime minister of India

CHARLES DE GAULLE
1890–1970, French president, general

HO CHI MINH
1890–1969, Vietnamese revolutionary leader

FRANCISCO FRANCO
1892–1975, Spanish general, premier

MAO TSE-TUNG
1893–1976, Chinese communist leader

JOMO KENYATTA
1893–   , President of Kenya

CHOU EN-LAI
1898–1976, Chinese communist leader

CHARLES LINDBERGH
1902–1974, American aviator

WERNHER VON BRAUN
1912–1977, rocket designer

JOHN F. KENNEDY
1917–1963, American president

ANWAR EL SADAT
1918–   , President of Egypt

MARTIN LUTHER KING
1929–1968, American civil rights leader

1900   2000

MATHEMATICS

With the aid of high-speed computers, we can use our knowledge of mathematics to perform millions of calculations in the time we once took to perform a small number by hand. As a result of this development, scientists have been able to expand their knowledge of the world—far out in space and deep inside the atom. Social scientists—economists in particular—can keep track of current data and predict future trends. Except, perhaps, for the humanities, every field of study depends increasingly on mathematics.

The review that begins here deals first with arithmetic and proceeds through modern algebra, geometry, trigonometry, and calculus. If you want to learn over again some topic you missed the first time around, or if you decide to brush up on all the mathematics you once knew, here is your opportunity.

Arithmetic

INTEGERS

Numbers, Numerals

A *number* is an idea. As such, it cannot be defined, seen, written, or otherwise sensed. The group of stars that form the Big Dipper and the group of days in a week have nothing more in common than the *idea* of the *number* seven.

A *numeral* is that which represents or symbolizes a number. The number seven can be symbolized by either of the numerals 7 or VII. We manipulate these numerals in order to solve problems in arithmetic.

The *natural numbers* are the set of counting numbers 1, 2, 3, 4, . . . , where ". . ." means "continued in the same pattern indefinitely." The *whole numbers* are the natural numbers and zero. The *integers* are the whole numbers and their negatives and can be represented as . . . −3, −2, −1, 0, 1, 2, 3, ...

Factors, Primes, Composites

Factors of an integer are integers whose product gives the number. The numbers 6 and 5 are factors of 30. A number is *prime* if its only positive factors are itself and 1. The numbers 2, 3, and 5 are prime numbers and $2 \times 3 \times 5$ is a *prime factorization* of 30. The prime factorization of a number is important in many applications. A *composite number* is an integer greater than 1 that is not a prime number.

Exponents, Powers

An exponent of a number is a number that tells how many times the number is used as a factor in an expression. That is, 1000 equals the expression "10 as a factor 3 times" or $10 \times 10 \times 10$. We write $10 \times 10 \times 10$ as 10^3, which is 10 with an exponent of 3, or 10 to the third power. In general, if n is a positive integer, a^n means $\underbrace{a \times a \times a \times \cdots a}_{n \text{ factors}}$, and a^{-n} means $\frac{1}{a^n}$. By definition, a^0 is equal to 1, if a is not zero. These rules are illustrated by the powers of 10 in [1].

[1]

$$10^3 = 1000.$$
$$10^2 = 100.$$
$$10^1 = 10.$$
$$10^0 = 1.$$
$$10^{-1} = .1 = \frac{1}{10}$$
$$10^{-2} = .01 = \frac{1}{100} = \frac{1}{10^2}$$
$$\text{etc.}$$

Decimal System

In a positional number system, each digit is assigned a *place value* in addition to a quantitative value. For example, the digit 2 has a different value in each of the numbers 264, 1025, and 792. In the decimal system the positions represent successive powers of 10, starting with 10^0 on the right:

$$264 = 2 \times 10^2 + 6 \times 10^1 + 4 \times 10^0$$
$$= 200 + 60 + 4,$$

and

$$1025 = 1 \times 10^3 + 0 \times 10^2 + 2 \times 10^1 + 5 \times 10^0$$
$$= 1000 + 20 + 5.$$

Octal System

The *octal system* is base 8 because it uses 8 symbols, 0, 1, 2, 3, 4, 5, 6, and 7. The positions in an octal number represent powers of 8, not powers of 10.

To distinguish between the different numbering systems, the base of a number is usually indicated by appropriate small characters (subscripts) in the lower right corner. The base 10 number 139 can be represented as 139_{10}.

Furthermore, 139_{10} will be shown to be the same as the base 8 number 213_8. To show this, expand the 213_8 by using the meaning of place value in the *octal system*. That is:

$$213_8 = 2 \times 8^2 + 1 \times 8^1 + 3 \times 8^0$$
$$= 2 \times 64 + 1 \times 8 + 3 \times 1$$
$$= 128 + 8 + 3$$
$$= 139 = 139_{10}.$$

To change from octal to decimal, then, we expand the octal number in powers of 8 and add. From decimal to octal, the change is in the opposite direction. We look for multipliers of powers of 8 which when added give us the decimal number.

Consider the problem of changing 267_{10} to octal. We begin at the largest power of 8 contained in the given number and work to the right. It is a matter of filling in the blanks in [2].

[2]

$$267_{10} = \underline{} \times 8^3 + \underline{} \times 8^2 + \underline{} \times 8^1 + \underline{} \times 8^0.$$

There are how many 8^3s or 512s in 267? Of course there are none, so we place a 0 in the first blank. Then we see there are four 8^2s or 64s in 267; placing a 4 in the second blank takes care of 4×8^2 or 256 of the 267, leaving 11. There is one 8^1 or 8 in 11, so we put a 1 in the next blank, and this leaves $11 - 8$, or 3, units remaining. Remembering that 8^0 is one, the last blank is then the units place, so we put a 3 in the last blank and we have represented 267_{10} entirely in powers of 8.

[3]

$$267_{10} = \underline{0} \times 8^3 + \underline{4} \times 8^2 + \underline{1} \times 8^1 + \underline{3} \times 8^0.$$

We can read directly from [3] the octal number which is equal to 267_{10}; it is 0413_8 or just 413_8. The methods given here for changing bases in both directions must be understood in order to grasp the meaning of a place value system, and especially to grasp the concept of place value systems other than base 10.

A quicker way to change from decimal to octal is by successive division by 8. Divide the decimal number by 8 and record the remainder. Divide the new quotient by 8, recording the remainder; continue this procedure until the new quotient is 0. The remainders written in reverse order are the octal digits. In [4] we see

[4]

$$
\begin{array}{ccc}
33 & 4 & 0 \\
8\,)\,267 & 8\,)\,33 & 8\,)\,4 \\
\underline{24} & \underline{32} & \underline{0} \\
27 & 1 & 4 \\
\underline{24} & & \\
3 & &
\end{array}
$$

267_{10} again being changed to octal to get 413_8.

Binary System and Conversion

The binary system is the base 2 system using only the digits 0 and 1. It is just like the octal, except that powers of 2 are used in place of powers of 8. The base 2 number 1001_2 in [5] should be 9 in base 10.

[5]

$$1001_2 = 1 \times 2^3 + 0 \times 2^2 + 0 \times 2^1 + 1 \times 2^0$$
$$= 1 \times 8 + 0 \times 4 + 0 \times 2 + 1 \times 1$$
$$= 8 + 0 + 0 + 1 = 9_{10}$$

We change from base 2 to base 10 in the same fashion as from octal to decimal.

RULE: *To change from another base to base 10, expand the other base number in powers of its base and add the resulting products.*

RULE: *To change a decimal whole number to another base, divide the decimal number by the new base and record the remainder. Continue dividing each new quotient and recording the remainder until the quotient is reduced to 0. Write the remainders in reverse order.*

Counting to 9 in base 2 would go: 1_2, 10_2, 11_2, 100_2, 101_2, 110_2, 111_2, 1000_2, 1001_2. Note that there is no *digit* for 2 in base 2; it is written "10_2". Similarly, in octal counting to 9 we get: 1_8, 2_8, 3_8, 4_8, 5_8, 6_8, 7_8, 10_8, 11_8.

There is an interesting relationship between octal and binary. Consider again the octal number 413_8, which is the decimal number 267_{10}.

Changing 267_{10} to binary will give 100001011_2. Notice that if we break 100001011_2 into groups of 3 binary digits starting at the right end of the number, 100 001 011, we can read each octal digit directly from the corresponding binary group. 100_2 is a 4_8, 001_2 is a 1_8, and 011_2 is a 3_8. We can then bypass the decimal form if we change from octal to binary or vice versa as shown in [6].

[6]

$$523_8 = 101\ 010\ 011 = 101010011_2;$$
$$\text{and}\quad 011111100110_2 = 011\ 111\ 100\ 110 = 3746_8.$$

RULE: *To change octal into binary, take each octal digit and write it as three binary digits.*

RULE: *To change binary into octal, break the binary number into groups of three starting at the right and adding zeros on the left if necessary to complete the groups. Then convert each group of three binary digits into a single octal digit.* **It is important to remember that we are dealing only with integers here.**

The construction of most computers makes the binary system indispensable. The storage and arithmetic elements are designed to have two states: relays are open or closed; cores are magnetized clockwise or counterclockwise; spots on a magnetic tape are magnetized or not. In each case, one condition is chosen to represent the digit 0 and the other the digit 1. Numbers are therefore recorded by a series of magnetized cores or spots on a tape, etc. This concept can be illustrated by the series of lights in [7]. The lights are on if black, off if white. The binary number represented then is 10010_2, which is 18_{10}.

[7]

●	○	○	●	○
16s	8s	4s	2s	1s

It takes 5 lights and therefore 5 magnetic cores to represent the number 18_{10}, and thus a considerable amount of computer memory space must be devoted to storage of relatively small numbers. This inconvenience is greatly overcome by the sheer speed of the *computer operations on binary numbers* and by other means such as the *floating point*.

Because binary numbers are cumbersome, computer programmers frequently use octal coding to describe the binary numbers that the computer understands.

FRACTIONS

Types of Fractions

A *fraction* may be thought of as indicated division. Restricting ourselves momentarily to nonnegative numbers, we have four main types of fractions. A *proper fraction* is the quotient of two integers where the divisor, or denominator, is larger than the dividend, or numerator. The denominator must not be zero. An *improper fraction* can be represented as the quotient of two integers, where the numerator is equal to or greater than the denominator. A *mixed number* is a type of fraction that can be represented as a whole number and (added to) a proper fraction. A *complex fraction* is generally the quotient of two fractions or a fraction made up of fractions. *Complicated* fractions could perhaps be a better name for *complex* fractions in that *complex* numbers are not ordinarily involved.

Fundamental Theorem of Arithmetic

The fundamental theorem of arithmetic states in essence that every composite number can be expressed as a product of prime factors and that this collection of prime factors without regard to order is *unique*.

Greatest Common Divisor

The *greatest common divisor* (GCD) or *largest common factor* of a collection of positive integers is the *largest* integer that will divide into *each* of the integers of the collection without remainder. It may be found by breaking each of the numbers in the collection into its prime factors. The GCD is then the *product* of all *common factors* among the collection. If there is no common prime factor, then the GCD is 1, and the numbers in the collection are said to be relatively prime. The number 1 is always a *common divisor*, but a larger number may be the GCD.

Least Common Multiple

The *least common multiple* (LCM) of a collection of positive integers is the *smallest* integer that *each element* of the collection will divide into without remainder. To find the LCM we again factor the elements of the collection into prime factors as when finding the GCD, only here we put together the *product* of factors in which are found *all* the factors of *each* of the integers of the collection. The product of all the elements of the collection is certainly a *common multiple*, but it may not be the smallest number that will suffice.

[8]

COLLECTION	FACTORS
12	$2 \times 2 \times 3$
18	$2 \times 3 \times 3$
78	$2 \times 3 \quad \times 13$
LCM:	$2 \times 2 \times 3 \times 3 \times 13 = 468$
GCD:	$2 \times 3 = 6$

COLLECTION	FACTORS
5	1×5
14	$1 \quad \times 2 \times 7$
9	$1 \qquad \times 3 \times 3$
LCM:	$1 \times 5 \times 2 \times 7 \times 3 \times 3 = 630$
GCD:	1

Equivalent Fractions

Fractions are *equivalent* if they can be expressed so that they indicate the same quotient. We can re-express fractions by *multiplying* or *dividing* the numerators *and* denominators by the *same* non-zero number. Thus $\frac{2}{3}$ is equivalent to $\frac{4}{6}$, for we can multiply the 2 and the 3 each by 2 to get $\frac{4}{6}$. We could have shown equivalence by dividing the 4 and 6 each by 2 to get $\frac{2}{3}$.

A fraction is said to be *reduced to lowest terms* if we divide numerator and denominator by the GCD of the numerator and denominator. Fractions are *equivalent* if they *reduce* to the same fraction. $\frac{18}{24}$ and $\frac{12}{16}$ are equivalent as they both reduce to $\frac{3}{4}$.

A type of problem often given is to express $\frac{5}{6}$ as an equivalent fraction with a denominator of 24. The solution is found by noticing that if we multiply the 6 by 4, we get 24; so to get an equivalent fraction, we must also multiply the 5 by 4 and we get $\frac{20}{24}$.

To change a *mixed fraction* like $2\frac{3}{4}$ to an *improper fraction*, we multiply the 4 by the 2, then add the 3 to get 11. Putting the 11 over the 4 gives us the equivalent fraction, $\frac{11}{4}$.

Addition, Subtraction

If two or more proper or improper fractions are to be added, we find the LCM of their denominators and express each fraction as an *equivalent* fraction with the LCM as the *new denominator*. Then we *add* the numerators and put the sum over the LCM denominator. It is good practice to reduce this fraction to lowest terms.

To subtract one proper or improper fraction from another, we first, as in addition, find equivalent fractions with the LCM denominators; then we subtract the numerators and try to reduce the resulting fraction.

Now if the fractions to be added or subtracted are mixed fractions, first express them as improper fractions; then proceed as before.

Multiplication

To *multiply fractions*, we simply multiply their *numerators* to get the *numerator* of the answer and *multiply denominators* to get the *denominator* of the answer. This answer should be simplified if possible.

Division

To *divide fractions*, we multiply the *reciprocal* of the *divisor* by the *dividend*. The reciprocal of X is Y if $X \cdot Y = 1$. The division problem, $\frac{3}{4} \div \frac{7}{12}$, will be written as the multiplication problem, $\frac{3}{4} \times \frac{12}{7}$ using $\frac{12}{7}$, the reciprocal of $\frac{7}{12}$. The product is $\frac{36}{28}$ which simplifies to $\frac{9}{7}$. Some simplification could have been done prior to the multiplication by division of common factors.

[9]

$$\frac{3}{4} \div \frac{7}{12} = \frac{3}{4} \times \frac{\overset{3}{12}}{\underset{1}{7}} = \frac{9}{7}$$

Decimal, Octal, Binary Fractions

The number 129.67_{10} in expanded form is

$1 \times 100 + 2 \times 10 + 9 \times 1 + 6 \times .1 + 7 \times .01$

which is also

$1 \times 10^2 + 2 \times 10^1 + 9 \times 10^0 + 6 \times 10^{-1} + 7 \times 10^{-2}$

Note the use of negative exponents to handle the fractional parts of the decimal number. In the same manner, an octal number like 476.053_8 in expanded form is

$4 \times 8^2 + 7 \times 8^1 + 6 \times 8^0$
$\qquad\qquad + 0 \times 8^{-1} + 5 \times 8^{-2} + 3 \times 8^{-3}$

which equals

$4 \times 64 + 7 \times 8 + 6 \times 1$
$\qquad\qquad + 0 \times \frac{1}{8} + 5 \times \frac{1}{64} + 3 \times \frac{1}{512}$

and when combined gives $318\frac{43}{512}$ as the base 10 equivalent. The binary system is expanded in the same way with, of course, 2s in place of 8s in the expression.

To convert a decimal fraction to another base, multiply the decimal by the new base. As an example, we convert .6875 to binary.

$$.6875 \times 2 = 1.3750$$

Record the integer portion of the new product, 1, as the coefficient of 2^{-1}; discard the whole number and multiply the remaining decimal by 2 again.

$$.3750 \times 2 = 0.75000$$

Record the integer portion, which is 0 in this case, as the coefficient of 2^{-2} and multiply by 2 again.

$$.75000 \times 2 = 1.5000$$

Record the 1 as the coefficient of 2^{-3} and multiply the decimal part by 2 again.

$$.5000 \times 2 = 1.0000$$

Record the 1 as the coefficient of 2^{-4}. Since the decimal part is now zero, the conversion is complete and the binary fraction is exact. Thus,

$.6875_{10} = 1 \times 2^{-1} + 0 \times 2^{-2} + 1 \times 2^{-3} + 1 \times 2^{-4}$
$\qquad\quad = .1011_2$.

RULE: *To change a proper fraction in decimal form to another base, multiply the fractional part by the new base to get a product. Multiply the fractional part of this product by the new base to get a new product, etc. The digits, zero or otherwise, that appear to the left of the decimal point in each product are the digits of the fraction in the new base from left to right.*

Consider the examples: $.265625_{10}$ and $.99_{10}$ to be changed to octal. We repeatedly multiply by 8, as in [10] and in the solution

[10]

.265625	and	.99	.36
× 8		× 8	× 8
2.125000		7.92	2.88
.125000		.92	.88
× 8		× 8	× 8
1.000000		7.36	7.04

we find .265625 in decimal equals .21 in octal. The decimal .99 is shown in [10] to be multiplied four times to get .7727 in octal. However, this is not exact because the .04 could still be multiplied by 8 to carry on the process and thus add more digits to .7727.

The change from octal to binary on the fractional side is the same as with the whole number side. Change each octal digit to three binary digits, and the octal point becomes the binary point. From binary to octal, begin at the binary point separating the digits into groups of three adding zeros on each end if necessary. Change each group of three binary digits to one octal digit preserving the binary point for the octal point. For example, the octal number 2.703_8 becomes 10.111000011_2. The binary number 1101.11001_2 separates into

$$001 \quad 101.110 \quad 010$$

and becomes 15.62_8.

Computer Arithmetic

Many computer instructions, or operations, are arithmetic in nature. The following binary *addition* operation is straightforward in that it closely resembles ordinary decimal addition. The computer's arithmetic unit basically adds only two numbers at a time, place by place, and so only one of the four cases in [11] will happen as each place or column is added. The last case

[11]

$$
\begin{array}{cccc}
0 & 0 & 1 & 1 \\
+0 & +1 & +0 & +1 \\
\hline
0 & 1 & 1 & 10
\end{array}
$$

presents the only problem in that a 1 must be carried or added to the next place in the number. For example,

$$
\begin{array}{l}
\quad\quad\quad\quad 0 + 1 = 1 \\
101110 \\
+001101 \\
\hline
\quad\quad\quad 1
\end{array}
$$

$$
\begin{array}{l}
\quad\quad\quad\quad 1 + 0 = 1 \\
101110 \\
+001101 \\
\hline
\quad\quad 11
\end{array}
$$

$$
\begin{array}{l}
\quad\quad\quad\quad 1 + 1 = 10 \\
101110 \\
+001101 \quad\quad\quad \text{carry } 1 \\
\hline
\quad 011
\end{array}
$$

$$
\begin{array}{l}
\quad\quad\quad\quad 1 + 1 = 10 + 1 = 11 \\
101110 \\
+001101 \quad\quad\quad \text{carry } 1 \\
\hline
1011
\end{array}
$$

$$
\begin{array}{l}
\quad\quad\quad\quad 0 + 0 = 0 + 1 = 1 \\
101110 \\
+001101 \\
\hline
11011
\end{array}
$$

$$
\begin{array}{l}
\quad\quad\quad\quad 1 + 0 = 1 \\
101110 \\
+001101 \\
\hline
111011
\end{array}
$$

Note the carry as a result of adding two 1s in the third column from the right.

Addition in other bases causes no difficulty if we remember the following basic rule for addition:

RULE:

1. *If the sum of any column is greater than or equal to the base, subtract the base from the sum to get the final digit for the column and carry to the next column the number of times the base was subtracted.*
2. *If the sum of any column is less than the base, the base is not subtracted and there is no carry.*

For example,

$$
\begin{array}{l}
\text{Carry 8} \\
\text{eights or 1} \\
\text{sixty-four.}
\end{array}
\quad
\begin{array}{r}
\,^{1}5 \quad 2 \quad 3_8 \\
+ \quad 1 \quad 7 \quad 3_8 \\
\hline
7 \quad 9_{10}6 \\
-8 \\
\hline
1
\end{array}
$$

The answer is 736_8.

Numbers in other bases can be subtracted in a manner similar to decimal subtraction. The essential difference is that if a "borrow" is required, it is equal to the base of the number system being used.

Computer subtraction can also be performed using *two's complement* arithmetic. Assume we are working with 6-place binary numbers. The two's complement of a binary number is formed as follows:

1. Make certain that the given binary number has 6 places by adding leading zeros if necessary.
2. Replace each zero by a one and vice versa. This is known as the *one's complement* of the original binary number.
3. Add 1 to the one's complement.

$$
\begin{array}{rl}
\text{number} = & 101100_2 \\
\text{one's complement} = & 010011_2 \\
& +\ 1_2 \\
\hline
\text{two's complement} = & 010100_2
\end{array}
$$

To perform a subtraction $A - B$, add the two's complement of B to A. For example, to compute

$$
\begin{array}{r}
111001 \\
-101100 \\
\end{array}
$$

form the two's complement of 101100, which is $010011 + 1$ or 010100. Add 111001 and 010100 to get 1001101. In 6-place arithmetic the 1, if any, in the 7th place is discarded. Thus,

$$111001_2 = 57_{10}$$
$$-101100_2 = 44_{10}$$
$$001101_2 \quad 13_{10}$$

Multiplication of binary numbers can be done by repeated addition in the computer. Binary *division* is done usually by some form of repeated subtraction. *The two basic computer operations then are addition and complementation. All* of the *arithmetic operations* are derived from these.

MEASUREMENT

Definition, Error, Precision, Accuracy

A *measurement* is a comparison with a standard. There are many kinds of standards to use, depending on how an item is to be measured. We have standards of length, weight, volume, and many others. However, these standards are established by man; therefore, they are only relatively fixed and are subject to change.

When measuring, as when measuring the length of an item with a ruler, we can be correct only to the smallest unit division on the ruler. For example, if the ruler is marked in *centimeters* then our result will be correct to the *nearest centimeter*. We have to then *round* the answer we get to the nearest centimeter. Thus we lose the exactness of the result by rounding. Now any comparison with any standard will call for rounding even if it appears to be exact, and the rounding causes an error. Therefore *no measurement is exact*. All measurements involve some kind of error. There are errors other than the roundoff error, such as misreading the measuring instrument, using a faulty standard, and many more.

Consider the roundoff error in particular. This one is necessary; the others are not. *The smallest unit of measure is called the precision.* That is, on a ruler which is marked in centimeters, the precision is 1 centimeter. The roundoff error will be at *most* $\frac{1}{2}$ of a centimeter.

Thus *the greatest possible error (GPE) is one-half of the precision of the measuring device.*

A greatest possible error of 1 millimeter in measuring a diamond would make more difference to a jeweler than a GPE of 1 millimeter would make to a road builder constructing 20 kilometers of highway. Thus we have the term *relative error,* which *is the GPE divided by the measurement.* For example, if a measurement is made of the length of a box by a ruler marked in centimeters and the result is 29 centimeters, then the relative error of the measurement is $\frac{1}{2} \div 29 = \frac{1}{58}$. If we measure the diameter of a dime with the same ruler we would get 2 centimeters, to the nearest centimeter. The relative error of this measurement is $\frac{1}{2} \div 2 = \frac{1}{4}$. This is greater than the relative error of the box measurement. *The measurement with the least relative error is, by definition, the most accurate measurement.*

Rounding Off, Significant Digits

When a measurement is made and the result is to be recorded or when a number is to be rounded to a certain place, then the following rule applies:

RULE: *To round off a number, consider the amount to be dropped. If it is greater than half, round up or increase the digit to be kept by one. If the amount to be dropped is less than half, leave the digit as is. If the amount to be dropped is exactly half, make the digit to be kept an even digit.*

In [12], the top row of numbers are rounded to the hundredths place and the results are placed beneath the numbers.

[12]

10.679	3.074	21.045	16.075	1.345001
10.68	3.07	21.04	16.08	1.35

In explanation, the results are: 10.68, the 9 is over half; 3.07, the 4 is less than half; 21.04 and 16.08, make the digit even if exactly halfway;

1.35, the 1 in 5001 makes it greater than one-half.

Notice that the "make it even" rule rounds up half the time and down half the time. Thus, in general, after many roundoffs, the accumulated error is approximately zero.

If a certain lot measured 120 meters to the nearest ten meters (i.e., one dekameter), it would be written as just 120 meters. If it was 120 meters to the nearest meter, then it should be written 12<u>0</u> meters. A 120-meter measurement to the nearest tenth of a meter (i.e., decimeter) should be written 120.0 meters. To show that a zero to the left of the decimal point is part of the actual measurement and not a result of rounding off, underline the zero. Note that in any case, at most one zero will be underlined. Also, as in the 120.0 meter measurement, none of the zeros are underlined because of the fact that a zero is written to the right of the decimal indicating the measurement was carried to the tenths place and happened to be a zero.

Digits of a measurement are significant if they are necessary to tell how many of the smallest unit of measure there are. In [13] the significant digits of the first row measurements are underlined in the bottom row.

[13]

| 0.049 | 0.0490 | 20.049 | 120 | 2000 | 2000.0 |
| 0.0<u>49</u> | <u>0.0490</u> | <u>20.049</u> | <u>120</u> | <u>2000</u> | <u>2000.0</u> |

Scientific and Floating Notation

A number is in *scientific notation* if it is expressed as a product of a number between one and ten (the mantissa), and a number which is a power of ten (the characteristic or exponent). This certainly simplifies the notation for very small numbers like 0.00000000123 and very large numbers like 456,700,000,000,000 which are written 1.23×10^{-9} and 4.567×10^{14}, respectively, in scientific notation. Note that the mantissa contains only the significant digits of the number.

The FORTRAN scientific computer language has two basic kinds of numbers: integer and real. An integer number will be represented as a binary number. The real numbers are also called floating numbers because they are handled and stored in such a way that the decimal point "floats." Actually, floating notation is very similar to scientific notation, in that 1.23×10^{-9} might be written $+.123E - 8$ and -4.567×10^{14} might be $-.4567E + 15$ where the E indicates the exponent of ten. A real or floating number will be stored and manipulated separately by mantissa and by characteristic, partly because it facilitates multiplication and division.

To *multiply* two numbers in scientific notation together, *multiply* their *mantissas, add* their *characteristics,* and the results give the mantissa and characteristic of the answer in scientific notation after possibly an adjustment of decimal point and characteristic. The answer *should* contain no more significant digits than the multiplier with the least number of significant digits, thus calling frequently for rounding off the mantissa to the correct number of digits. This rounding, according to significance, is practical in scientific (slide rule) applications; however, the computer using FORTRAN generally does not adjust for significant digits. *Division* of two numbers in scientific notation is performed by *dividing* the *mantissas* and *subtracting* the *exponents.* The number of significant digits in the resulting mantissa should not exceed the number in either the divisor or the dividend. For example, 2.31×10^4 times 6.4×10^{-3} should be rounded to 1.5×10^2 for scientific notation, but left as $1.536E + 2$ on the computer. And 9.287×10^{-4} divided by 9.25×10^0 becomes 1.00×10^{-10} in scientific notation and $1.004E - 10$ on the computer.

Length, Distance

Measuring the *length* of an object, or the *distance* from one object to another, requires finding the number obtained by counting how many times some standard can be applied to successive positions on or between the objects. This includes reading the fractional part of the divisions marked on the standard, which is the *precision.*

Angle

An angle may be considered to be an amount of rotation. The first angle, [14a], shows the rotation from the *initial* side to the *terminal* side.

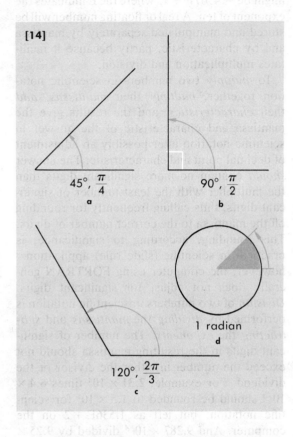

[14]

45°, $\frac{\pi}{4}$
a

90°, $\frac{\pi}{2}$
b

1 radian
d

120°, $\frac{2\pi}{3}$
c

A complete rotation or revolution is defined to be 360 degrees (°). The angle in [14a] is $\frac{1}{8}$ of a complete revolution which is $\frac{1}{8}$ of 360° or 45°. Two other angles are similarly labeled in terms of degrees. The second angle, [14b], is also called a right angle.

Another procedure for measuring angles uses the term radian. A *radian* is the angle formed by two radii of a circle fixed so that the distance around the circle from the endpoint of one radius to the endpoint of the other is one radius. (See [14d].) A radian is approximately 57.2°. Radian measure is often expressed in terms of π as in [14] where 45° = $\pi/4$ radians, 90° = $\pi/2$ radians, etc.

Area, Volume, Capacity

The area of an object is described as the amount of surface enclosed by the object. Mostly we consider areas as being on a level surface or plane. We measure area by counting how many standard units of area there are in the object. Some of the most common standards of area are square centimeters, square meters, and square kilometers. A square centimeter is just a way of referring to a square which has one centimeter sides, or a centimeter square.

Measurement of length involves measurement along one line and is called one-dimensional measure. Measure in the plane is called two-dimensional measure where measurement is in square *units* and the *unit* is one dimensional. An example of two-dimensional area is given in [15a]. Assume the little square on the left of [15a] is the standard unit of area. We want to find the area of [15a] by finding how many of the standard units will fit into [15a]. As [15a] has been sectioned already into little squares the same size as the standard unit square to the left, we just count the number of these shown and we get 32 square units as the area.

If the figure is irregularly shaped like [15b] then the problem of finding the area is toughened to the extent that fitting square units inside of [15b] will probably still leave some area uncovered. If we use smaller units, we should cover some more of the area but still not all of it. It is therefore necessary sometimes, in the case of irregularly shaped figures, to approximate the area for application.

Corresponding to area in two dimensions, we have volume in three dimensions. Here we talk about the number of standard unit cubes or cubic units of an object. Some common standard units are cubic centimeters, cubic decimeters, cubic meters, etc. To find the volume of [15c], we evaluate how many of the unit cubes on the left of [15c] are in [15c], and the sectioning shows a volume of 42 cubic units.

To find the volume of an irregularly shaped object, we will probably have to approximate as with irregular area. An approximate formula for finding the area of irregular shapes is $A \approx \square$'s inside $+\frac{1}{2}$ (□'s on boundary). With few exceptions, however, the volume of almost any shaped object in three dimensions will be measured in cubic *units* where the basic *unit* is one dimensional. Thus we can measure volume in cubic centimeters, area in square centimeters, and length in just centimeters.

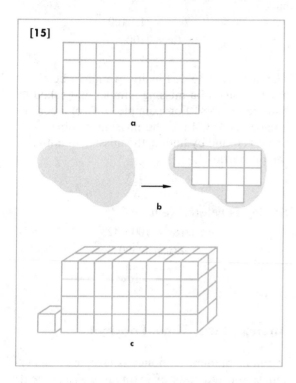

[15]

a

b

c

Capacity is the term used for the measurement of the containment of an object. We have milliliters, liters, and other standard measures of capacity. The *volume* of a basket is practically fixed, but the capacity of a basket could be 10 liters if measuring corn, but zero if measuring water as it will not *contain* water. When the capacity and volume of an object are the same amount, then conversion can be made between the systems.

Weight (Mass), Time

To *weigh* an object usually means to balance the object equally by some means with a standard mass or combination of such masses. The gram, kilogram, and ton are some of the basic standards of mass. The process of measuring "weight" is fundamentally the same as measuring length in that we can question the equality of the masses of two objects by simultaneous comparison.

Time occurs only once and is gone from grasp. Thus, of course, we cannot simultaneously compare two intervals of time. We measure time usually in terms of so many cycles, or parts thereof. We have seconds, days, years, etc., and some physical applications require milli- (thousandth), micro- (millionth), even nano- (billionth) second measurement of time.

Temperature

The Fahrenheit temperature scale measures 32° at the freezing point of water and 212° at the boiling point. The original intent, it seems, was to have 100° be the normal human body temperature. The Celsius scale is based on 0° (freezing point of water) and 100° (boiling point of water) thus making the size of a degree different for each scale.

FORMULAS AND APPLICATIONS

Ratio, Proportion

A *ratio* is a comparison of two numbers. It is often expressed as a fraction and can be reduced or simplified as such. However, we cannot add ratios as we can add fractions. As long as it is a ratio, it is two numbers and our usual operands are single numbers.

A *proportion* is two or more equal ratios. An example is: one compares to two as three compares to six. This can be written as $1:2 = 3:6$ or $\frac{1}{2} = \frac{3}{6}$.

To *solve a proportion* like $2:3 = X:9$, we find the product of the extremes, $2 \cdot 9 = 18$, and the product of the means, $3 \cdot X = 3X$, and set them equal. That is: $3X = 18$. We then divide both sides by the multiplier of X so the left side is $\frac{3X}{3}$ which is just X (three of something divided by three is just the something), and the right side is $\frac{18}{3}$ or 6. Then X on the left equals 6 on the right and we have solved the proportion by finding $X = 6$, so the proportion is $2:3 = 6:9$.

EXAMPLE:

Solve the proportion $4\frac{1}{2}:21 = \frac{6}{5}:X$.

Product of means and extremes, $4\frac{1}{2}X = 21 \cdot \frac{6}{5}$

Simplify,

$$\frac{9}{2}X = \frac{21 \cdot 6}{5}$$

Divide by $\frac{9}{2}$,

$$X = \left(\frac{21 \cdot 6}{5}\right) \div \left(\frac{9}{2}\right) = \left(\frac{21 \cdot 6}{5}\right) \cdot \left(\frac{2}{9}\right)$$

Simplify,

$$X = \frac{21 \cdot 6 \cdot 2}{5 \cdot 9} = \frac{28}{5}$$

Percent

Percent (%) means per hundred. An event which would occur 75 times out of 100 trials would occur 75 per 100 or 75 percent (75%) of the time. We can also write 75 per 100 as 0.75. Percents can be changed to decimal fractions by dividing by 100.

To change a decimal to a percent, we multiply by 100 and insert the % sign. So 1.75 becomes 175% while 0.34 becomes 34%.

There are three common types of problems involving percentage. All three of these problems are solved in the same manner. One type of problem is to find a certain percentage of a number. For example, what is 36% of 150? The result is found by finding the missing quantity in the proportion

$$\frac{36}{100} = \frac{x}{150}$$

Multiplying the means by the extremes, we get
$$100x = 36 \cdot 150$$
or
$$100x = 5400.$$
Dividing both sides by 100, we get
$$x = 54.$$

Another type of percentage problem involves finding what percent one number is of another. For example, 21 is what percent of 60? The result is found by finding the missing quantity in the proportion

$$\frac{x}{100} = \frac{21}{60}$$

Solving for x as in the previous problem, we have,
$$60x = 21 \cdot 100$$
$$60x = 2100$$
$$x = 35$$

The answer is 35%. Finally, we might be given a percentage of a missing number and asked to find the number. For example, 18% of a certain number is 423. Find the missing number. The result is found by finding the missing quantity in the proportion

$$\frac{18}{100} = \frac{423}{x}$$

Solving as before, we have
$$18x = 100 \cdot 423$$
$$18x = 42300$$
$$x = 2350$$

Interest, Rate, Time, Principal

When an amount of money is invested at a certain simple interest rate (expressed as a percent) over a length of time, it gathers more money called interest. *Interest* is the product of the amount of money (*principal*) and the interest *rate* and the length of *time* in years ($I = P \times R \times T$). Thus 700 dollars (P) invested at 5% (R) for 9 months (T) will amount to $I = P \times R \times T = \$700 \times .05 \times .75 = \$26.25$. Note that .75 is used for 9 months, which is .75 of a year.

If the problem is to find I, P, R, or T when three of the four quantities are given and one is unknown, we may employ the formulas below.

$$I = P \times R \times T \qquad R = \frac{I}{P \times T}$$

$$P = \frac{I}{R \times T} \qquad T = \frac{I}{P \times R}$$

For example, find the rate of interest if the interest is 55 dollars, the principal is 1000 dollars, and the length of time is 11 months. We use the formula

$$R = \frac{I}{P \times T}.$$

Substituting, we get

$$R = \frac{55}{1000 \times \frac{11}{12}}$$

$$R = \frac{660}{11000}$$

$$R = .06 \text{ or } 6\%.$$

The other formulas are applied in a similar manner.

Compound Interest

If an interest rate is applied periodically to a sum of money and the amounts of interest are left in order to accumulate, then the interest is compounded. That is, we will apply the interest rate at the end of a period of time to the principal, plus the interest from the previous period of time. If the interest is computed or compounded annually, the formula is

$$A = P(1 + i)^n,$$

where A is the amount (principal + interest), P is the principal, i is the interest rate per year, and n is the number of years. Then the amount resulting from $1000 invested at 1% for 4 years is

$$A = \$1000(1 + .01)^4$$
$$A = \$1000(1.01)^4$$
$$A = \$1000(1.04060)$$
$$A = \$1040.60$$

If the interest is compounded m times a year, the amount is computed as follows:

$$A = P(1 + i/m)^{n \times m}.$$

Thus the amount resulting from $2500 invested at 2% for 9 months compounded quarterly (every 3 months) is found by

$$A = \$2500\left(1 + \frac{.02}{4}\right)^{.75 \times 4}$$
$$A = \$2500(1.005)^3$$
$$A = \$2500(1.15075)$$
$$A = \$2537.69.$$

Distance, Rate, Time

Rate is usually expressed as a ratio of amount of *distance* covered per unit of *time*. One hundred kilometers per hour is a rate meaning that every hour the distance covered is one hundred kilometers. At this rate, two hundred kilometers will be covered in two hours, and fifty kilometers will be covered in one-half hour. The three formulas involved here are:

$$R = \frac{D}{T} \qquad D = R \times T \qquad T = \frac{D}{R}$$

where R = rate, D = distance, and T = time.

A train traveling at the rate of 100 kilometers per hour for 5 hours will cover a distance ($D = R \times T$) of (100 kilometers per hour) × (5 hours) or 500 kilometers. Note that the units (kilometers/hour, hours) in the problem were indicated, and the hour in the denominator of 100 kilometers per hour (100 km/hr) cancelled with the hours in 5 hours, leaving kilometers as the unit for the resulting distance.

A satellite encircles the earth at a rate of $\frac{2}{3}$ of an orbit per hour. How much time will it take for 50 orbits? We compute the time

$$\left(T = \frac{D}{R}\right)$$

as follows:

$$T = 50 \text{ orbits} \div \left(\frac{2}{3} \text{ orbits/hour}\right)$$

$$T = 50 \text{ orbits} \times \left(\frac{3}{2} \text{ hours/orbits}\right)$$

$$T = 75 \text{ hours}$$

Celsius, Fahrenheit

The formulas relating the *Fahrenheit* scale (F) to the *Celsius* scale (C) are:

$$°F = \frac{9}{5}(°C) + 32$$

$$°C = \frac{5}{9}(°F - 32)$$

Thus, to change 75°C to Fahrenheit, we use the formula

$$°F = \frac{9}{5}(°C) + 32$$

and substitute

$$°F = \frac{9}{5}(75) + 32$$

$$°F = 9(15) + 32$$
$$°F = 135 + 32$$
$$°F = 167.$$

So, $75°C = 167°F.$

To change $99°F$ to Celsius we use the formula

$$°C = \frac{5}{9}(°F - 32)$$

and substitute

$$°C = \frac{5}{9}(99 - 32)$$

$$°C = \frac{5}{9}(67)$$

$$°C = 37\frac{2}{9}$$

So, $99°F = 37\frac{2}{9}°C.$

Square Root

Finding the *square root* of a number called N means finding a positive number which multiplied by itself will equal N. For example, the square root of 9 is 3 because 3 times 3 equals 9. The symbol for the square root of a number is $\sqrt{}$, so the $\sqrt{9} = 3$. There are others that may be found by inspection, like $\sqrt{4} = 2$, $\sqrt{25} = 5$, $\sqrt{1} = 1$, etc. However, the $\sqrt{3}$ cannot be written in decimal form exactly. We usually approximate $\sqrt{3}$ and others like it by representing it in decimal form correct to as many places as are actually needed in application.

To find the square root of a number, study the example of the $\sqrt{30679}$ given in [16], which uses an algorithm that enables us to come closer and closer to the desired number.

[16]

$$\begin{array}{r} 100 \\ \sqrt{30679} \end{array}$$ $100^2 = 10,000; 200^2 = 40,000$

$$\begin{array}{r} 100 \quad -10000 \\ \hline 20679 \end{array}$$ The number is between 100 and 200.

$$\begin{array}{r} 170 \\ \sqrt{30679} \end{array}$$ $170^2 = 28,900; 180^2 = 32,400$
The number is between 170 and 180.

$$\begin{array}{r} 100 \quad -10000 \\ \hline 20679 \end{array}$$ $(100 + 70)^2$

$$\begin{array}{r} 270 \quad -18900 \\ \hline 1779 \end{array}$$

$\begin{aligned} &= 10,000 + 2 \times 100 \times 70 + 70 \times 70 \\ &= 10,000 + 70\,(200 + 70) \\ &= 10,000 + 70\,(270) \\ &= 10,000 + 18,900 \\ &= 28,900 \end{aligned}$

$$\begin{array}{r} 175 \\ \sqrt{30679} \end{array}$$ $175^2 = 30625; 176^2 = 30976$
The number is between 175 and 176.

$$\begin{array}{r} 100 \quad -10000 \\ \hline 20679 \end{array}$$

$$\begin{array}{r} 270 \quad -18900 \\ \hline 1779 \end{array}$$ $(170 + 5)^2$

$$\begin{array}{r} 345 \quad -1725 \\ \hline 54 \end{array}$$

$\begin{aligned} &= 170 \times 170 + 2 \times 170 \times 5 + 5 \times 5 \\ &= 170 \times 170 + 5\,(2 \times 170 + 5) \\ &= 170 \times 170 + 5\,(340 + 5) \\ &= 28,900 + 5\,(345) \\ &= 28,900 + 1725 \\ &= 30,625 \end{aligned}$

$$\begin{array}{r} 175.1 \\ \sqrt{30679.00} \end{array}$$ $175.1^2 = 30660.01;$
$175.2^2 = 30695.04$

$$\begin{array}{r} 100 \quad -10000.00 \\ \hline 20679.00 \end{array}$$ The number is between 175.1 and 175.2.

$$\begin{array}{r} 270 \quad -18900.00 \\ \hline 1779.00 \end{array}$$ $(175 + 0.1)^2$

$$\begin{array}{r} 345 \quad -1725.00 \\ \hline 54.00 \end{array}$$

$$\begin{array}{r} 350.1 \quad -35.01 \\ \hline 8.99 \end{array}$$

$\begin{aligned} &= 175 \times 175 + 2 \times 175 \\ &\quad \times 0.1 + 0.1 \times 0.1 \\ &= 175 \times 175 + 0.1 \\ &\quad (2 \times 175 \times 0.1) \\ &= 30625 + 0.1\,(350 + 0.1) \\ &= 30625 + 35.01 \\ &= 30660.01 \end{aligned}$

This algorithm may be continued as long as desired.

The algorithm, in its most succinct form (that is, omitting the zeros) becomes

$$\begin{array}{r} 1 \quad 7 \quad 5 \; . \; 1 \\ \sqrt{3\widehat{\,}06\widehat{\,}79\,.00} \end{array}$$

$$\begin{array}{rr} 1 & -1 \\ 27 & \overline{2\ 06} \\ & -1\ 89 \\ 345 & \overline{17\ 79} \\ & -17\ 25 \\ 350.1 & \overline{54}\ .00 \\ & -35\ .01 \\ & \overline{8}\ .99 \end{array}$$

Polygons

A *simple polygon* is a plane closed figure bounded by straight lines. By this, we mean that the lines that form the polygon lie in the same plane, and the polygon itself divides the whole plane into three distinct collections of points: those inside the polygon, on the polygon, and outside the polygon. The straight lines of the polygon are called sides; the points of intersection of the sides are called vertices.

A three-sided polygon is called a triangle; a four-sided polygon is a quadrilateral, and as the number of sides increases, we have a pentagon (5 sides), hexagon (6 sides), heptagon (7 sides), octagon (8 sides), nonagon (9 sides), decagon (10 sides), undecagon (11 sides), and dodecagon (12 sides).

Triangles. *Triangles* are classified as acute, obtuse, and right triangles. An *acute* triangle has all angles less than 90°. An *obtuse* triangle has one angle greater than 90°. A *right* triangle has one right (90°) angle. The sum of the interior angles of a triangle is 180°. Thus if we know two angles of a triangle, we can find the third by subtracting the sum of the known angles from 180°.

A triangle with two equal sides is called isosceles. With three equal sides, it is called equilateral, and in this case, it is also equiangular (equal angles).

The area of a triangle may be found if the three sides a, b, and c are known, by the formulas:

$$s = \frac{a + b + c}{2}$$
$$\text{area} = \sqrt{s(s - a)(s - b)(s - c)}$$
$$\text{area} = \frac{\text{base} \times \text{height}}{2}$$
$$= \frac{bh}{2}$$

The sides which form the 90° angle of a right triangle are called the legs. The side opposite the right angle is called the hypotenuse.

The *Pythagorean Theorem* states that the square of the hypotenuse of a right triangle is equal to the sum of the squares of the other two legs. A particular right triangle with legs of length 3 and 4 would have a hypotenuse equal to

$$\sqrt{3^2 + 4^2} = \sqrt{9 + 16} = \sqrt{25} = 5.$$

Pythagorean triples are whole numbers which can be the lengths of the sides of a right triangle. Thus, 3, 4, and 5 are Pythagorean triples as $3^2 + 4^2 = 5^2$. There are many others; in fact, we may use the following formulas to derive any number of such triples. Let a, b, and c be the sides of a right triangle such that $a^2 + b^2 = c^2$, then

$$a = 2 \cdot X \cdot Y \cdot Z \quad \text{or} \quad a = 2XYZ,$$
$$b = X(Y^2 - Z^2),$$
$$c = X(Y^2 + Z^2),$$

with these restrictions: X is any positive integer, either Y or Z is divisible by 2, and Y and Z are relatively prime (that is, Y and Z have no common prime factors between them).

Some of the triples found by this formula are: 5, 12, 13; 7, 24, 25; 9, 40, 41; and 11, 60, 61.

A right triangle with a 45° angle will have two 45° angles, and the legs will each be equal to the hypotenuse divided by the $\sqrt{2}$. A right triangle with a 30° angle will also have a 60° angle, and the side opposite the 30° angle will be one-half the hypotenuse. The other leg will be half the hypotenuse multiplied by the $\sqrt{3}$.

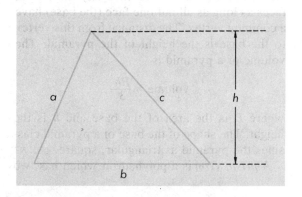

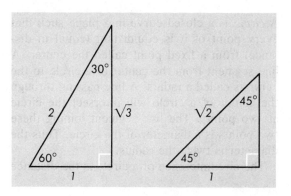

Quadrilaterals. Adjacent vertices of a quadrilateral are on the same side. The line joining nonadjacent vertices is called a diagonal. The sum of the interior angles of a quadrilateral is 360°. There are five special kinds of quadrilaterals: trapezoids, parallelograms, rhombuses, rectangles, and squares.

Trapezoids are quadrilaterals with one pair of opposite sides parallel. An isosceles trapezoid has the nonparallel sides equal. The area of a trapezoid is given by

$$\text{area} = \frac{h(a+b)}{2}$$

where a and b are the lengths of the parallel sides and h is the distance between them.

Parallelograms are quadrilaterals with both sets of opposite sides parallel. Also, the opposite sides and opposite angles are equal. The area of a parallelogram equals the length of a side times the distance from it to the opposite side. (Area equals base times height.)

Rhombuses are parallelograms which have all four sides equal. The diagonals of a rhombus form right angles (that is, they are perpendicular). The area of a rhombus is base times height.

Rectangles are parallelograms with a right interior angle. This means that all the other interior angles are right angles. The area of a rectangle is base times height.

Squares can be considered as rhombuses with right angles or as rectangles with equal sides. The diagonals are perpendicular and are equal. The area of a square is the square of one of its sides.

Circles

A *circle* is a closed curve in a plane such that every point of it is equidistant (equal in distance) from a fixed point called the center. A line segment from the center of a circle to the curve is called a radius. A line passing through the center of a circle will intersect the circle at two points. The line segment joining these two points is a diameter of the circle. Thus the diameter is twice the radius.

The circumference of a circle is the distance around the circle. The ratio of the circumference to the diameter of a circle is always a constant, no matter which circle is considered. The circumference divided by the diameter is called π and is approximately given by:

$$\pi \approx 3.141592654$$

and π may be computed to more decimal places by using this formula:

$$\pi = 4\left(1 - \frac{1}{3} + \frac{1}{5} - \frac{1}{7} + \cdots\right)$$

The formula for the circumference is

$$\text{circumference} = 2\pi r = \pi d$$

where r is the radius and d is the diameter of the circle. The area of a circle is given by

$$\text{area} = \pi r^2 = \pi d^2/4$$

When measurement is used to find r or d for these formulas, then remember to use as many decimal places for π as are used for r or d. This will give the result as many significant digits as possible.

Solids

A *solid* figure or object will lie in more than one plane. A *closed* solid figure will divide the whole space into three collections of points: the points inside the figure, the points on the figure or the ones that comprise the figure itself, and the points outside the figure.

A *polyhedron* is a closed solid which has sides or faces which are polygons. A polyhedron must have at least four faces. The intersection of two faces of a polyhedron is called an edge.

The simplest *pyramid* [17a] has four triangular faces, but a pyramid can have any number of faces as long as all but one face (the base) have a common vertex. The distance from this vertex to the base is the height of the pyramid. The volume of a pyramid is

$$\text{volume} = \frac{Bh}{3},$$

where B is the area of the base and h is the height. The shape of the base of a pyramid classifies the pyramid as triangular, square, etc.

A *prism* [17b] is a polyhedron which has two

congruent (same size and shape) polygon faces, called bases, which are parallel and have corresponding vertices joined by parallel lines. These lines are the edges of parallelogram faces and are called lateral edges. Prisms are classified by

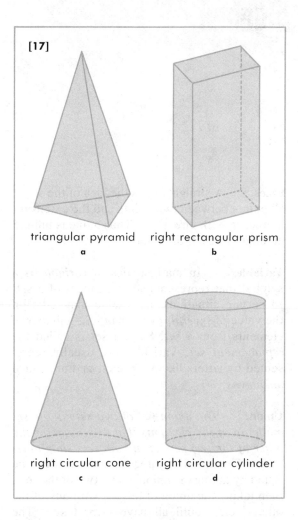

[17]

triangular pyramid
a

right rectangular prism
b

right circular cone
c

right circular cylinder
d

the shape of their bases, and are also classified as right prisms if their lateral edges are perpendicular to the bases; otherwise, they are oblique prisms.

If B is the area of a base and h is the height or distance between bases of a prism, then the volume of a prism is

$$volume = Bh$$

A special right prism is the *cube* which has squares as bases and all edges equal in length to the sides of the bases. The volume of a cube is

$$volume = S^3,$$

where S is the length of an edge.

A circular *cone* [17c] is determined by a circle (base), a point (vertex) not in the plane of the base, and the collection of all lines that connect the points on the circle to the vertex. The surface formed by these lines is called the lateral area. The volume of a circular cone is

$$volume = \frac{\pi r^2 h}{3},$$

where r is the radius of the base and h is the distance from the vertex to the base.

A circular *cylinder* [17d] is a solid figure determined by two congruent circles (bases) in parallel planes and the collection of all lines connecting the points on the circles in such a way that any two distinct lines are parallel. A right circular cylinder has each of these lines perpendicular to the bases.

The volume of a circular cylinder is

$$volume = \pi r^2 h,$$

where r is the radius of the base and h is the distance between bases.

It is worth noting that the "pointed" figures, the pyramids and the cones, have the same general formula for volume; volume equals one-third the area of the base times the height. Similarly, the prisms and cylinders have the common volume formula; volume equals area of base times height.

The *sphere* is a solid figure defined to be the collection in space of all points equidistant from a fixed point called the center. The distance from a point on the sphere to the center is a radius. A diameter of a sphere is defined similarly to the diameter of a circle. The surface area of a sphere is

$$area = 4\pi r^2,$$

and the volume of a sphere is

$$volume = \frac{4\pi r^3}{3},$$

where r is the radius of the sphere.

Modern Algebra

TERMINOLOGY

Undefined Terms. In mathematics, *undefined terms* are concepts which are usually intuitively obvious, yet cannot be flawlessly defined. Clearly we want as few undefined terms as possible.

Points. A *point* is an undefined term which represents a location only. It may be described as being infinitely thin or without thickness. The concept of point is used in one, two, three, and even higher dimensional space.

Sets, Subsets. A *set* is an undefined term that refers to a collection along with some rule which gives a means of determining whether or not some certain element is in the collection. The collection of whole numbers from 1 to 5 is a set because we have a definite means of determining whether or not a given number is in the set. This set can be written as $\{1, 2, 3, 4, 5\}$, where the brackets indicate that a *set* is enclosed. It could also be written as $\{1, 2, 3, \ldots 5\}$, where the ". . ." means to continue in the pattern. A set can be named or labeled, like $X = \{1, 2, 3\}$.

A set, S, is a subset of a set, T, if all elements in set S are also elements in set T. Every set is a subset of itself.

The *empty set,* or *null set,* $\{ \}$, is the set which contains no elements. The empty set is a subset of any set, even itself.

Lines. A straight *line* is the idea of the set of all points between two points and the extension thereof in both directions. Thus a line is infinite in length in each direction.

Variables. In mathematics, a *variable* is a symbol that represents some element of a set. In certain situations, a variable may take on the value of *several,* even an *infinite* number of elements from a set. Such a set is called the *replacement set.* Variables are usually represented by letters like X, Y, etc., and are called *unknowns.*

Union. *The union* ($\cup$) *of two sets is the set made up of the elements that are in one or the other of the two sets or in both sets simultaneously.* The union of three or more sets can be found by taking the union of any two of the sets, then taking the union of this set with any of the others, etc., until all have been taken. The union of the set $A = \{1, 2, 3\}$ with the set $B = \{3, 4\}$ gives

$$A \cup B = \{1, 2, 3\} \cup \{3, 4\} = \{1, 2, 3, 4\}.$$

Intersection. *The intersection* ($\cap$) *of two sets is the set made up only of the elements that are in both sets simultaneously.* The intersection of three or more sets is found by taking the intersection of any two of the sets, then taking the intersection of this set with any of the others, etc., until all have been taken. The intersection of the set $A = \{1, 2, 3\}$ with the set $B = \{3, 4\}$ gives

$$A \cap B = \{1, 2, 3\} \cap \{3, 4\} = \{3\}.$$

Note that the intersection of $\{1, 2\}$ with $\{3, 4\}$ is $\{\ \}$, the empty set.

Order.   We say two is greater than one and that one is greater than zero. Thus we can *order* these numbers as zero, one, and two. Any set of numbers (or their negatives) which can represent real measurements can be *ordered*. We express the order of two numbers by the greater than, $>$, the less than, $<$, or the equals, $=$, symbols. *If a set of numbers has order, then one of the three symbols ($>$, $<$, $=$) can be placed between any two numbers of the set* (Trichotomy Law). It is often helpful in the ordering of nonintegers (not whole numbers), to express them in decimal form for comparison.

For example, to order the numbers $\sqrt{22}$ and $\frac{14}{3}$, we change each to decimal form: $\sqrt{22} \approx 4.69$; $\frac{14}{3} \approx 4.66$; and as $4.69 > 4.66$, we have $\sqrt{22} > \frac{14}{3}$.

Statements, Open Sentences.   The statement $2 + 3 = 5$ is a true *statement;* $2 + 2 = 5$ is a statement, but it is false. The sentence $X + 3 = 5$ is neither true nor false. It is an *open sentence* because the value of X must be known before it becomes a statement. In mathematics, we usually say that sentences like $X + 3 = 5$ are equations. We mean by this that if a correct value is assigned to X from the replacement set, then we have *equated* both sides. That is, in $X + 3 = 5$, let the replacement set be all real numbers (see *Sets of Numbers*), then assign the value 2 to X and both sides of the equation will be equal, $2 + 3 = 5$. The open sentence, $X + 3 > 5$, is called an *inequality*. This sentence is more than just a presentation of unequalness, however, for it tells which way the unequalness is applied, in that $X + 3$ *is greater than* 5. To make a true statement of the inequality open sentence, we could replace X by 4, so that $4 + 3 > 5$, or by 10, giving $10 + 3 > 5$. There are many other values for X that would make this a true inequality statement.

Solution Sets.   A *solution set* is the set of all values in the replacement set which, when substituted for the unknown (variable) in an open sentence, make a true statement. In $X + 3 = 5$, the solution set is $\{2\}$. The statement $X + 3 > 5$ has, as a solution set, the set of all real numbers greater than 2. When we say that we solve an equation or inequality, we mean that we find the solution set.

SETS OF NUMBERS

Integers

An *integer* is a number in the set $\{\ldots -2, -1, 0, 1, 2, \ldots\}$. Here the "$\ldots$" means continued in the same pattern (without end) and thus the set of integers is infinite. The integers (positive, negative, and zero) are the natural (counting) numbers, and are sometimes called signed numbers.

Countable Sets

A set is *countable* if it can be placed into a one-to-one correspondence with the natural numbers or with a subset of the natural numbers.

For example, the set of positive even numbers can be placed into a one-to-one correspondence with the natural numbers,

1	2	3	4	5	6	. . .
↕	↕	↕	↕	↕	↕	
2	4	6	8	10	12	. . .

because for each natural number, there is a positive even integer, and for each positive even integer there is a natural number.

Rational Numbers

A number is *rational* if it can be expressed as the quotient of two integers, $\frac{a}{b}$, where b is not equal to 0. In decimal form, a rational number will terminate or repeat in a pattern. The numbers, $\frac{1}{2}$, 6, 0, .4, $7\frac{1}{2}$, .333 . . . , are all rational because respectively, they are equal to

$\frac{1}{2}$, $\frac{6}{1}$, $\frac{0}{1}$, $\frac{4}{10}$, $\frac{15}{2}$, and $\frac{1}{3}$ where each is the quotient of two integers. We say $.333\ldots = \frac{1}{3}$, because $.333\ldots$ is actually an infinite series (see *Sequences and Series*) and $\frac{1}{3}$ is the sum or limit of this infinite series.

We can show that the *rationals are countable* by considering [18]. Notice that the row number is also the numerator of the fractions in that row and the column number gives us the denominator of the fractions in that column. Thus any

[18]

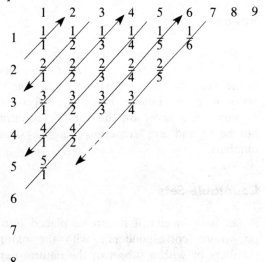

rational number will be found in the array because all possible combinations of integer numerators and denominators are given. There are some numbers repeated $\left(\frac{1}{1} = \frac{2}{2}, \frac{1}{2} = \frac{2}{4}, \text{etc.}\right)$, so the rule is to match the rational number with the corresponding fraction in the array which is in lowest terms. *The array itself can be counted* by following the arrows moving diagonally back and forth, beginning at the upper left.

The rational numbers are dense in that between any two rationals, there is another rational.

Irrational Numbers

A number is *irrational* if in decimal form it does not terminate or repeat in a pattern. An irrational number cannot be expressed as the quotient of two integers. Among the irrationals are such numbers as $\sqrt{2}$, π, and $-\sqrt{11}$.

To show that $\sqrt{2}$ is irrational, we can show that it cannot be expressed as the quotient of two integers. Euclid proved the irrationality of $\sqrt{2}$ by assuming it was rational, then showing that this reached a contradiction. So let us assume $\sqrt{2} = \frac{a}{b}$, where a and b are *relatively prime integers*. Squaring both sides, we have

$$2 = \frac{a^2}{b^2},$$

and solving for a^2,

$$2b^2 = a^2.$$

Obviously, if $a^2 = 2b^2$, then as b is an integer, b^2 is an integer, and $2b^2$ is an even integer. Thus a^2 is even and therefore *a is even*. Let $a = 2c$, where c is an integer. Then $a^2 = 4c^2$, and substituting gives

$$2b^2 = 4c^2,$$
$$b^2 = 2c^2,$$

which means *b is even*. But we assume that a and b *existed* as *relatively prime* integers (no common factors), so a and b must not exist. Note, if two numbers existed, a and b, which would do the job, $\frac{a}{b} = \sqrt{2}$, then we could make them relatively prime in the beginning. We showed that *if they exist,* no matter how many times we might reduce the fraction, $\frac{a}{b}$, there would always be a common factor of 2. Therefore, the a and b do not exist.

The irrationals are uncountable. Mathematicians prove that the irrationals are uncountable by showing that a small subset of them are uncountable. The subset usually selected is the subset of irrationals between 0 and 1. The proof generally first assumes that they *can* be counted but then shows that at least one was *not* counted.

The irrationals are also *dense,* for between any two irrationals, there is an irrational. Furthermore, between any two irrationals, there is a rational and vice versa.

Real Numbers

The *real numbers* are the set of all rational and irrational numbers. The real numbers are a dense and uncountable set since they contain the irrationals as a subset.

Imaginary Numbers

An *imaginary number* is a number that can be expressed in the form, *bi*, where *b* is a real number and $i = \sqrt{-1}$, meaning $i^2 = -1$. An imaginary number is not a real number since a real number squared is not negative.

Complex Numbers

A *complex number* is a number that can be expressed in the form $a + bi$ where *a* and *b* are real and $i = \sqrt{-1}$. If $b = 0$, then $a + bi$ is also a *real* number; if $a = 0$ and $b \neq 0$, then $a + bi$ is also a *pure imaginary* number. *Thus any number (integer, rational, irrational, or imaginary) can be expressed as a complex number.*

Order (greater than, less than) does not exist in the pure imaginary or in the complexes with nonzero imaginary parts. Mathematicians prove that the complex numbers cannot be ordered by investigating the numbers 0 and *i*. If these numbers were ordered, then we would have $0 > i$ or else $i > 0$. In both cases, with some simple calculations involving inequalities, they arrive at the surprising fact that 0 is simultaneously greater than and less than 1.

Field Properties

In order to lay a foundation for further study, we make basic assumptions in the form of equality and operation properties that we want a set, *S*, to have in order to be a *field*. It is assumed that *a*, *b*, and *c* are elements of *S*.

The *equality* properties are:

EP-1	$a = a$.	Reflexive property.
EP-2	If $a = b$, then $b = a$.	Symmetric property.
EP-3	If $a = b$ and $b = c$, then $a = c$.	Transitive property.
EP-4	If $a = b$, then *a* may be substituted for *b* in any expression.	Substitution property.

The properties are listed separately for convenience but some of them can be derived from others.

The *operation* properties are:

OP-1	$a + b$ is a unique element of *S*.	Closure of addition.
OP-2	$(a + b) + c = a + (b + c)$.	Associativity of addition.
OP-3	There is an element of *S*, called 0, such that $a + 0 = 0 + a = a$.	Additive identity element.
OP-4	For each *a* in *S*, there is an element, $-a$ (the negative of *a*), such that $a + (-a) = 0$. $(-a) + a = 0$.	Additive inverse.
OP-5	$a + b = b + a$.	Commutativity of addition.
OP-6	$a \cdot b$ is a unique element of *S*.	Closure of multiplication.
OP-7	$(a \cdot b) \cdot c = a \cdot (b \cdot c)$.	Associativity of multiplication.
OP-8	There is an element of *S*, called 1, such that $a \cdot 1 = 1 \cdot a = a$.	Multiplicative identity element.
OP-9	For each $a \neq 0$ in *S* there is an element, a^{-1} (the reciprocal of *a*), such that $a \cdot (a^{-1}) = (a^{-1}) \cdot a = 1$.	Multiplicative inverse or Reciprocal.
OP-10	$a \cdot b = b \cdot a$.	Commutativity of multiplication.
OP-11	$a \cdot (b + c) = a \cdot b + a \cdot c$, or $a(b + c) = ab + ac$.	Distributive property.

A set which has the four equality and the eleven operation properties under operations of addition and multiplication is called a field. Thus the sets of rational, real, and complex numbers each constitute a field. A set with **OP-1** through **OP-4** is a *group*.

With these field properties, we can establish some very important concepts in algebra and mathematics. As we make a statement in the proof, the justification for this step is shown on the right.

Equals added to (or subtracted from) equals are equal. If $a = b$, then $a + c = b + c$. Proof:

[19]

$$a + c = a + c \qquad \textbf{EP-1}$$
$$a = b \qquad \text{Given}$$
$$a + c = b + c \qquad \textbf{EP-4}$$

We know that equals subtracted from equals are equal, for in the proof we could use $(-c)$ instead of (c). ■ (The symbol ■ indicates the end of the proof.)

Equals multiplied (or divided) by equals are equal (except division by zero). If $a = b$, then $a \cdot c = b \cdot c$. Proof:

[20]

$$a \cdot c = a \cdot c \qquad \textbf{EP-1}$$
$$a = b \qquad \text{Given}$$
$$a \cdot c = b \cdot c \qquad \textbf{EP-4}$$

For the division part of the proof, we use (c^{-1}) instead of c. ■

Zero multiplied by any number is zero. $a \cdot 0 = 0$. Proof:

[21]

$$a + 0 = a \qquad \textbf{OP-3}$$
$$a \cdot (a + 0) = a \cdot a \qquad \textbf{[20]}$$
$$a \cdot a + a \cdot 0 = a \cdot a \qquad \textbf{OP-11}$$
$$-(a \cdot a) = -(a \cdot a) \qquad \textbf{EP-1}$$
$$a \cdot 0 = 0 \qquad \textbf{OP-4, [19]} ■$$

If the product of two numbers is zero, then one or the other or both numbers are zero. If $a \cdot b = 0$, either $a = 0$, $b = 0$, or $a = b = 0$. Proof:

[22]

Either $a = 0$ or $a \neq 0$.
If $a = 0$ we are done.
If $a \neq 0$

$$a \cdot b = 0 \qquad \text{Given}$$
$$(a^{-1}) = (a^{-1}) \qquad \textbf{EP-1}$$
$$(a^{-1}) \cdot a \cdot b = (a^{-1}) \cdot 0 \qquad \textbf{[20]}$$
$$(1) \cdot b = 0 \qquad \textbf{OP-9, [21]}$$
$$b = 0 \qquad \textbf{OP-8} ■$$

SET EQUATIONS AND INEQUALITIES

Set Notation

The expression a is an element of S is symbolized by $a \in S$. Thus, $3 \in \{3, 4\}$. A subset is designated by $\subset$, so that $\{3\} \subset \{3, 4\}$. A slash, /, denotes negation, so that $3 \notin \{1, 2\}$ and $\{1\} \not\subset \{2, 3\}$. Note that $3 \not\subset \{3, 4\}$ because a subset should be enclosed by { }. A vertical line, |, means *such that*. Let I represent the set of all integers, then the expression,

$$\{X \mid X \in I, \ X > 0\}$$

means the set of all X such that X is an integer *and* X is greater than zero. This is called *set builder* notation, and the set built here is the set of positive integers. *If the set of real numbers is represented by R,* then the set of real numbers greater than 1 and less than 3 would be

$$\{X \mid X \in R, \ 1 < X < 3\}.$$

The symbol $\geq$ means greater than or equal to; $\leq$ means less than or equal to. Then the set of real numbers greater than -3 and less than or equal to 2 is given by

$$\{X \mid X \in R, \ -3 < X \leq 2\}.$$

Number Line Graphs

The real number line (below) is a graph constructed so that for each real number there will

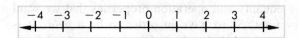

be a unique point on the line and every point on the line represents a unique real number. The arrows on each end mean that the line goes on indefinitely in each direction. Some of the points are labeled for reference.

Below are some sets given by set builder notation and shown on the number line. The color portion "covers" the set of values which X can have.

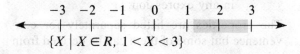

$$\{X \mid X \in R, \ 1 < X < 3\}$$

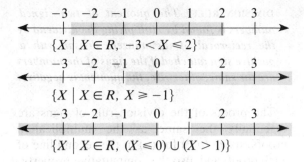

$\{X \mid X \in R, -3 < X \leqslant 2\}$

$\{X \mid X \in R, X \geqslant -1\}$

$\{X \mid X \in R, (X \leqslant 0) \cup (X > 1)\}$

Ordered Pairs

The idea of a set of *ordered pairs* of numbers is a basic concept in algebra and higher mathematics. The set of ordered pairs, $\{(3, 1), (3, 2), (3, 3), (4, 1), (4, 2), (4, 3),\}$ is the same as $\{(X, Y) \mid X, Y \in I, 3 \leqslant X \leqslant 4, 1 \leqslant Y \leqslant 3\}$, where $X, Y \in I$ means $X \in I$ and $Y \in I$. We indicate by (X, Y) that the names of the variables are X and Y, and they are ordered so that X is given first. We could write such an ordered pair, (X, Y), as $\{\{X\}, \{X, Y\}\}$ or $\{\{X, Y\}, \{X\}\}$, all meaning the same thing. The number line is not designed for number pairs so we construct two number lines in such a way that number pairs can be employed. In **[23a]**, the number lines are set at right angles at the zero (origin) point of each. Number pairs are indicated by points in this plane formed by the number lines (axes). The points shown in **[23a]** are labeled according to the units marked on each number line (axis). That is, the first number of the pair is called the X coordinate, and is read from the horizontal X axis. The second number is the Y coordinate and is read from the vertical Y axis.

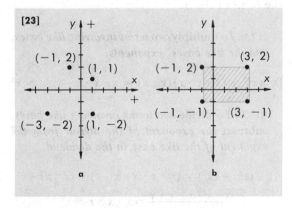

[23]

The set of ordered pairs, $\{(X, Y) \mid X, Y \in R, 3 \leqslant X \leqslant 4, 1 \leqslant Y \leqslant 3\}$, cannot be listed but is shown on the graph in **[23b]** as the shaded area.

ALGEBRAIC EXPRESSIONS

Operations

The *absolute value* of a real number is the distance from the point of the number to the origin. The absolute value of a number, X, is symbolized by $\mid X \mid$ and is computed by:

$\mid X \mid = X$, if $X \geqslant 0$;
$\mid X \mid = -X$, if $X < 0$.

Thus,

$\mid 4 \mid = 4, \mid -3 \mid = 3$, and $\mid 0 \mid = 0$.

ADDITION RULE: *To add two signed numbers with like signs, add their absolute values and insert their common sign. If their signs are unlike, then subtract their absolute values and insert the sign of the number with the larger absolute value.*

To show that the addition rule is consistent, consider the following patterns:

$$(+2) + (+2) = +4 \qquad (+2) + (-1) = +1$$
$$(+2) + (+1) = +3 \qquad (+1) + (-1) = 0$$
$$(+2) + 0 = +2 \qquad 0 + (-1) = -1$$
$$(+2) + (+1) = +1 \qquad (-1) + (-1) = -2$$
$$(+2) + (-2) = 0 \qquad (-2) + (-1) = -3$$
$$(+2) + (-3) = -1$$

The addition of positive and negative numbers is like rises and falls in temperature. If we begin at 80° and rise 20°, then fall 30°, we can compute the present temperature at $80° + 20° - 30° = 100° - 30° = 70°$.

Subtraction is performed by subtracting the *subtrahend* from the *minuend*. Thus, in $6 - 4$, the subtrahend is the 4 and the 6 is the minuend.

SUBTRACTION RULE: *To subtract one signed number (subtrahend) from another (minuend), change the sign of the subtrahend, then add the two numbers by the additon rule.*

To change the sign of a number is the same as using the additive inverse of the number. Then to subtract -10 from -8, we compute: $+10$ added to -8 and we get $+2$.

Subtraction of real numbers is the *directed distance* from the subtrahend to the minuend on the number line. So the directed distance from -3 to $+5$ is $(+5) - (-3) = (+5) + (+3) = +8$.

Multiplication of signed numbers is performed as in ordinary multiplication; only the sign of the product is given for nonzero numbers as follows:

> **MULTIPLICATION RULE:** *If the two signed numbers that form the product have* **like** *signs, then the product is* **positive.** *If they have* **unlike** *signs, the product is* **negative.**

To show that the multiplication rule is consistent, consider the following patterns:

$$(+2)(+2) = +4 \qquad (-1)(+2) = -2$$
$$(+2)(+1) = +2 \qquad (-1)(+1) = -1$$
$$(+2)\ (0) = \ \ 0 \qquad (-1)\ (0) = \ \ 0$$
$$(+2)(-1) = -2 \qquad (-1)(-1) = +1$$

To prove that a positive times a negative is negative, we again use the field properties. $(a) \times (-a) = -(a \times a)$. Proof:

[24]

$$a + (-a) = 0 \qquad \text{OP-4}$$
$$(a) \times [a + (-a)] = a \times 0 \qquad \text{[20]}$$
$$(a) \times (a) + (a) \times (-a) = 0 \qquad \text{OP-11,[22]}$$
$$a \times a + (a) \times (-a) = a \times a \qquad \text{OP-4}$$
$$+ [-(a \times a)]$$
$$(a) \times (-a) = -(a \times a) \qquad \text{[20]} \ \blacksquare$$

A negative times a negative is a positive. $(-a) \times (-a) = +a \times a$. Proof:

[25]

$$a + (-a) = 0 \qquad \text{OP-4}$$
$$(-a) \times [a + (-a)] = (-a) \times 0 \quad \text{[20]}$$
$$(-a) \times (a) + (-a) \times (-a) = 0 \qquad \text{OP-11,[21]}$$
$$-a \times a + (-a) \times (-a) = -a \times a$$
$$+ a \times a \quad \text{OP-4}$$
$$(-a) \times (-a) = +a \times a \qquad \text{[19]} \ \blacksquare$$

The division operation on signed numbers is the inverse of multiplication. The rule of signs is the same as multiplication.

> **DIVISION RULE:** *The quotient of two signed numbers is found by multiplying the dividend by the reciprocal of the nonzero divisor with a positive sign attached if the signs of the numbers are the same; otherwise, the quotient is negative.*

The proofs of the division rule of signs are essentially the same as the multiplication proofs, using (a^{-1}) for (a) in the second line of each proof, and also the commutative property. *Division by zero is a concept which is undefined in mathematics.* A point is also an undefined concept, but we have an intuitive notion about what a point is. Intuition seems to fail on all approaches to division by zero. Therefore, we carefully avoid division by zero.

Dividing zero by zero is called *indeterminant*.

Algebraic Terms

An algebraic term is made up of constant and variable *factors*. A constant, like a 2 or a -10, is sometimes written as an a or b or other letters at the beginning of the alphabet. Variables are usually denoted by letters nearer the end of the alphabet: x, y, etc. The following are algebraic terms: 2, -10, x^2, ax^2, $-3y^2$, $\dfrac{-xy}{z}$; $x + 3$ is not a term.

Coefficients, Exponents

The term $2x^3$ means x is raised to the third power and then doubled. The 2 is the constant *coefficient* of x^3; the 3 is the *exponent* of x; x is the *base* of the 3.

> **RULE:** *To* **multiply** *two terms involving like bases, add the like bases' exponents.*

$$(x^3)(x^2) = (x \cdot x \cdot x)(x \cdot x) = x \cdot x \cdot x \cdot x \cdot x = x^5$$

> **RULE:** *To* **divide** *two terms involving like bases, subtract the exponent of the divisor from the exponent of the like base in the dividend.*

$$(x^5) \div (x^2) = (x \cdot x \cdot x \cdot x \cdot x) \div (x \cdot x)$$
$$\frac{x \cdot x \cdot x \cdot x \cdot x}{x \cdot x} = x \cdot x \cdot x = x^3$$

EXAMPLES:

$$(2x^2y^3)(3xy^4) = 6x^3y^7$$

$$\frac{8x^3y}{4xy^2} = 2x^2y^{-1} = \frac{2x^2}{y}$$

$$\frac{x^2}{x^2} = x^0 = 1$$

RULE: *To raise an algebraic term to a power, multiply the exponents of the variable and constant factors of the term by the power.*

EXAMPLE:

$$(2x^3)^2(3y^{-1})^3 = (4x^6)(27y^{-3}) = 108x^6y^{-3}$$

Fractional Exponents, Radicals

We indicate by the term $x^{\frac{1}{b}}$ that x is the *base* and b is the root being taken of x. This is also written $\sqrt[b]{x}$, where the $\sqrt{}$ is called a radical. The root b of x means the number N such that $N^b = x$. Thus, $8^{\frac{1}{3}} = \sqrt[3]{8} = 2$, because $2^3 = 8$. The fractional exponent term, $x^{\frac{a}{b}}$, is the same as $\sqrt[b]{x^a}$.

$$27^{\frac{2}{3}} = \sqrt[3]{27^2} = 9$$

To simplify an nth root radical, $\sqrt[n]{}$, of a term, we reexpress it by removing the factors, which are nth powers of whole terms, and placing their nth root in front of the radical and multiplying. Then the $\sqrt{72} = \sqrt{36 \cdot 2} = 6\sqrt{2}$. Here we had the *square* root, so we found a *square* factor and removed it. The $\sqrt{20x^2y^3} = \sqrt{4 \cdot 5 \cdot x^2 \cdot y^2 \cdot y} = 2xy\sqrt{5y}$ in simplified form. On a radical like $\sqrt{2x^2 - x^3}$, we use the distributive property $\sqrt{2x^2 - x^3} = \sqrt{x^2(2-x)}$ and simplify it to $x\sqrt{2-x}$.

To simplify a radical with a denominator, we work with it until the denominator is one. The $\sqrt{3}$ is simplified; the $\sqrt{\frac{1}{3}}$ is not. We simplify it as follows:

$$\sqrt{\frac{1}{3}} = \sqrt{\frac{1}{3} \cdot \frac{3}{3}} = \sqrt{\frac{3}{9}} = \frac{1}{3}\sqrt{\frac{3}{1}} = \frac{\sqrt{3}}{3}$$

Also:

$$\sqrt{\frac{xy^2}{2x^2z}} = \frac{y}{x}\sqrt{\frac{x}{2z} \cdot \frac{2z}{2z}} = \frac{y}{x}\sqrt{\frac{2xz}{4z^2}} = \frac{y}{2xz}\sqrt{2xz}$$

Products, Factors

An algebraic term is also called a *monomial.* The sum of two terms is a *binomial,* and the sum of three terms is a *trinomial.* A *polynomial* has *any number of terms,* but the usual sense is a sum of terms involving the same variable raised to different integer powers, and with constant coefficients. For example, $x^3 + 4x^2 - 3x + 10$ is called a third degree polynomial in x.

To find the *products* of various polynomials, we employ the distributive property and simplify.

EXAMPLES:

$$2x^2(3xy^2 - yz) = 6x^3y^2 - 2x^2yz$$

$$
\begin{aligned}
(2x + y)(x - y) &= 2x(x - y) + y(x - y)\\
&= 2x^2 - 2xy + xy - y^2\\
&= 2x^2 - xy - y^2
\end{aligned}
$$

$$
\begin{aligned}
(x - 2)(x^2 - 3x + 6) &= x(x^2 - 3x + 6)\\
&\quad - 2(x^2 - 3x + 6)\\
&= x^3 - 3x^2 + 6x - 2x^2\\
&\quad + 6x - 12\\
&= x^3 - 5x^2 + 12x - 12
\end{aligned}
$$

To *factor* a polynomial, we look for lesser degree polynomials which will, when multiplied together, result in the polynomial. In practice, we try to remove, by the distributive property, first monomials, then binomials if possible.

EXAMPLES:

$$x^3 + 2x^2 - 6x = x(x^2 + 2x - 6)$$

$$x^3yz^4 - x^2yz^3 + 2xy^2z^2 = xyz^2(x^2z^3 - xz + 2y)$$

$$x^2 - 5x + 6 = (x - 2)(x - 3)$$

In explanation of the last example, to factor a trinomial into binomials:

1. Remove common monomial factors.
2. Arrange the trinomial in the descending order of a variable. That is, put the highest power on the left, etc., to the lowest power on the right. (Ascending order will work also.) Place two sets of parentheses on the right.
3. Place some *trial* factors of the first term in the left side of the parentheses. Place trial factors of the last term in the right side of the parentheses.

4. Find the product under these *trial* conditions to see if the middle term of the product agrees with the middle term of the trinomial. If yes, we have factored the trinomial. If no, go back to step 3 if there are some unused factors. If all have been tried, we say the trinomial cannot be factored with whole number factors.

EXAMPLES:

$$x^2 + 5x + 6 = (x + 2)(x + 3)$$
$$x^2 - x - 6 = (x - 3)(x + 2),$$
$$2x^2 - 15x + 18 = (2x - 3)(x - 6).$$

Some special cases of factoring follow.
Differences of two squares:

$$x^2 - y^2 = (x + y)(x - y)$$

Sum of two squares:

$$x^2 + y^2$$

The sum of two squares, $x^2 + y^2$, is *not* factorable with real numbers, but can be factored with imaginary numbers so that

$$x^2 + y^2 = (x + yi)(x - yi), \text{ where } i = \sqrt{-1}.$$

Difference of two cubes:

$$x^3 - y^3 = (x - y)(x^2 + xy + y^2)$$

Sum of two cubes:

$$x^3 + y^3 = (x + y)(x^2 - xy + y^2)$$

We may use radicals if necessary to factor some expressions. For example:

$$3x^2 - 2y^2 = (\sqrt{3}x + \sqrt{2}y)(\sqrt{3}x - \sqrt{2}y).$$

These techniques of factoring are used for many purposes in mathematics; however, we will apply them here for simplification purposes. To simplify fractions, sums, products, and quotients of polynomials (in particular trinomials), factor and divide through by common factors.

EXAMPLES:

$$\frac{x^2 + x - 6}{x^2 - 4x - 21} = \frac{(x - 2)(x + 3)}{(x + 3)(x - 7)}$$

$$= \frac{x - 2}{x - 7}$$

$$\frac{6x}{x^2 + x - 2} + \frac{1}{x + 2} - \frac{2}{x - 1}$$

$$= \frac{6x + 1(x - 1) - 2(x + 2)}{(x - 1)(x + 2)}$$

$$= \frac{6x + x - 1 - 2x - 4}{(x - 1)(x + 2)}$$

$$= \frac{5x - 5}{(x - 1)(x - 2)}$$

$$= \frac{5(x - 1)}{(x - 1)(x - 2)}$$

$$= \frac{5}{x - 2}$$

$$\left(\frac{x + 1}{x - 1}\right)\left(\frac{x^2 - 2x + 1}{x^2 - 1}\right) = \frac{(x + 1)(x - 1)(x - 1)}{(x - 1)(x + 1)(x - 1)}$$

$$= 1$$

$$\frac{x^2 - x - 2}{x^2 - 4x - 5} \div \frac{x^2 + x - 6}{x^2 - 3x - 18}$$

$$= \frac{x^2 - x - 2}{x^3 - 4x - 5} \cdot \frac{x^2 - 3x - 18}{x^2 + x - 6}$$

$$= \frac{(x - 2)(x + 1)(x - 6)(x + 3)}{(x - 5)(x + 1)(x + 3)(x - 2)}$$

$$= \frac{x - 6}{x - 5}$$

The radical expression

$$\frac{1 + \sqrt{x}}{1 - \sqrt{x}}$$

is simplified by using the radical *conjugate* as follows:

$$\frac{1 + \sqrt{x}}{1 - \sqrt{x}} = \left(\frac{1 + \sqrt{x}}{1 - \sqrt{x}}\right)\left(\frac{1 + \sqrt{x}}{1 + \sqrt{x}}\right)$$

$$= \frac{1 + 2\sqrt{x} + x}{1 - x}$$

Logarithms

A *logarithm is an exponent.* If $a^b = c$, then we can also write $\log_a c = b$, which means the logarithm to the base a of c is b. Thus, $3^2 = 9$ and $\log_3 9 = 2$. Also $10^{1.2304} = 17$, so $\log_{10} 17 = 1.2304$. The *characteristic* is 1 and the *mantissa* is .2304 of the base 10 log of 17. Ten is the *common* logarithm base.

To find the common logarithm of a number, we put the number into scientific notation. We find the mantissa of the logarithm by looking in the log table for the log which corresponds to the part of the number in scientific notation between 1 and 10. We insert the characteristic of the logarithm by adding the exponent of the number in scientific notation.

In particular, the log of 351 is computed as follows: $351 = 3.51 \times 10^2$. The 3.51 is found in the log table to correspond to .5453. We add the characteristic, 2, to .5453 so that log $351 = 2.5453$. We compute log .906 by $.906 = 9.06 \times 10^{-1}$; looking up 9.06, we get .9571. We then add the -1 and write the sum as $.9571 - 1$ or $9.9571 - 10$.

If the logarithm of a number is given, we can find the number or *antilog* by the reverse process. We find the number that is associated with the mantissa in the log table and multiply it by 10 raised to the characteristic power.

For example, if $\log_{10} 4 = 0.6021$, then 4 is the antilog of 0.6021. The antilog of $8.7938 - 10$ is found by looking up .7938 in the log table. The corresponding number is 6.22, so we multiply 6.22 by 10 to the power represented by $8 - 10$ or -2 which gives $6.22 \times 10^{-2} = .0622$.

We use *interpolation* when we want the log of an N or more place number from an N-1 place table. For example, in a three-place table we must interpolate to find the log of a four-place number. We also *interpolate* when we want the antilog of a logarithm which is found between two logarithms in the table. Examples of these are:

1. The log of 2.876 is found by noting that 2.876 is between 2.870 and 2.880; therefore, its logarithm will be between the logs of these numbers, .4579 and .4594, respectively. We set up a proportion relating distances between numbers and distances between logarithms. Thus $.006:.010 = x:.0015$, and solving the proportion we get $x = .0009$, so we add the .0009 to the .4579 and get .4588 as the desired logarithm.

2. The antilog of .9530 is found by setting up a similar proportion. We have .9530 between .9528 and .9533, which have corresponding numbers of 8.97 and 8.98. We solve the proportion, $x:.010 = .002:.0005$, and get $x = .004$ which makes our desired number $.004 + 8.97 = 8.974$.

Logarithms may be applied to multiplication, division, raising to powers, and extracting roots.

RULE: *To multiply two numbers, add their logs, then the antilog of the sum is the product of the numbers.*

RULE: *To divide two numbers, subtract the log of the divisor from the log of the dividend, then the antilog of the difference is the quotient of the numbers.*

RULE: *To raise a number to a power, multiply its logarithm by the power, then the antilog of the product is the number raised to the power.*

RULE: *To extract a root of a number, divide its logarithm by the root, then the antilog of the quotient is the extracted root of the number.*

EXAMPLE:

To find
$$\frac{(1.2)(6.7)^2}{\sqrt[4]{.35}}$$

$$\log \frac{(1.2)(6.7)^2}{\sqrt[4]{.35}}$$

$$= \log (1.2) + 2 \log (6.7) - \frac{1}{4} \log .35$$

$$= .0792 + 2(.8261) - \frac{1}{4}(7.5441 - 8)$$

$$= .0792 + 1.6522 - 1.8860 + 2$$

$$= 1.8454$$

Antilog $(1.8454) = 7.01$, approximately.

Functions

A function is a set of ordered pairs of elements such that no two different ordered pairs have the same first element. Thus several different first elements may be paired with the same second element.

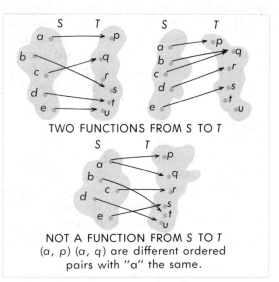

TWO FUNCTIONS FROM S TO T

NOT A FUNCTION FROM S TO T
(a, p) (a, q) are different ordered pairs with "a" the same.

The set of first elements is called the *domain* of the function. The set of second elements is called the *range*. A function is said to *map* the domain into the range.

If Y is the range and X is the domain of a function, we often symbolize this as: $y = f(x)$, meaning that to get an element of the range, y, the function, f, maps an element, x, from the domain. For example, if the function is defined by $y = f(x) = x^2 - 2$, then a *subset* of the set of function values is $\{(0, -2), (1, -1), (2, 2)\}$.

If a function, f, is such that no two ordered pairs with different first elements have the same second element, then the inverse function, f^{-1}, exists and is the set of ordered pairs formed by interchanging first and second elements of the ordered pairs of f. For example,

if $f = \{(1, 2), (4, 5), (-1, 3)\}$,
then $f^{-1} = \{(2, 1), (5, 4), (3, -1)\}$.

ALGEBRAIC EQUATIONS

Linear Equations

A polynomial equation is termed *linear* if it is of the form

$$ax + b = 0,$$

where a and b are real numbers and $a \neq 0$. It is called a *first degree* equation in x as the highest power of x is 1. The solution is $x = -b/a$.

The equation, $w = 2x^2 + 7y - 1$, is not a linear equation, but w is a *linear combination* of x^2 and y. Let y be a linear combination of x, like $y = 2x - 2$ in [26a]. Then in the x, y plane, if the set of number pairs which satisfy the equation are plotted as points on the graph, they form a straight line. Thus, y is a *linear function* of x.

Slope

The *slope* is the amount of steepness of a line. It is measured as the rise over the run or the change of y divided by the change in x by going from one point to another on the line in the x, y plane. If a line goes through the points, (x_1, y_1) and (x_2, y_2), then the slope, m, is given by

$$m = \frac{y_2 - y_1}{x_2 - x_1}.$$

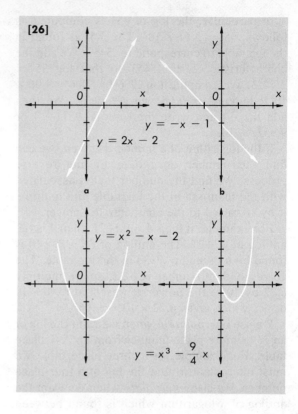

[26]

$y = -x - 1$
$y = 2x - 2$

$y = x^2 - x - 2$

$y = x^3 - \dfrac{9}{4} x$

In [26a], two points on the line are $(0, -2)$ and $(1, 0)$ and the slope is

$$m = \frac{0 - (-2)}{1 - (0)} = \frac{2}{1} = 2.$$

Using the same formula, we find the slope of the line in [26b], passing through $(-1, 0)$ and $(0, -1)$, to be -1. The equation for [26b] is also considered as a linear equation in x and y.

The equation of a non-vertical straight line in the x, y plane is

$$(y - y_1) = m (x - x_1),$$

where (x_1, y_1) is a point on the line and m is the slope.

The *intercepts* of a line are the values of x and y where the line crosses the x and y axes respectively. Thus, in [26a] the x-intercept is 1 and the y-intercept is -2. Then

$$y = mx + b$$

is the equation of a line of slope m and y-intercept b. A vertical line has no slope.

Distance Between Points

The distance between two points in the x, y plane which have coordinates, (x_1, y_1) and (x_2, y_2) is

$$d = \sqrt{(x_1 - x_2)^2 + (y_1 - y_2)^2}.$$

Quadratic Equations

A *quadratic* or *second degree* polynomial equation in x can be written in the form

$$ax^2 + bx + c = 0,$$

where a, b, and c are real numbers ($a \neq 0$). The solution to the equation is called the *quadratic formula* and is given by

$$x = \frac{-b \pm \sqrt{b^2 - 4ac}}{2a},$$

where the "$\pm$" means there are two elements (roots) in the solution set, the value computed by using the $+$ sign alone and the value computed by using the $-$ sign alone. Even though a, b, and c are real, x may be imaginary or complex. This is determined by the *discriminant*,

$$b^2 - 4ac.$$

If the discriminant is positive the roots are real and unequal. If it is zero, the roots are real and equal. If it is negative, the roots are imaginary or complex.

A quadratic function is of the form

$$y = ax^2 + bx + c.$$

The graph of this function is called a parabola, and a typical one is shown in [26c]. The point with x coordinate, $-b/2a$, is a *maximum* or *minimum* point of the quadratic function depending on whether a is negative or positive.

Polynomial Equations

A polynomial equation of the third degree is called a *cubic equation*. The general form is

$$ax^3 + bx^2 + cx + d = 0.$$

At least one of the three roots is real. A cubic function is shown in [26d].

The general *nth degree polynomial equation* is of the form

$$a_n x^n + a_{n-1} x^{n-1} + \cdots + a_1 x + a_0 = 0,$$

where a_n, a_{n-1}, etc., are real constants. There is no general formula for finding the roots of an nth degree equation. Often the closest we can come to computing the roots is by approximation procedures.

The Fundamental Theorem of Algebra

We are assured by the fundamental theorem of algebra that *a polynomial equation of degree n will have n real or complex roots*. If the degree of the equation is odd, then there is at least one real root.

Exponential Equations

If an equation has constant bases, and exponents which are variables, then we say it is an exponential equation. A frequently applied exponential equation is the compound interest equation,

$$A = P(1 + r)^n,$$

when we are given A, P, and r, thus to solve for n. If $A = 500$, $P = 120$, and $r = .04$, the equation becomes

$$500 = 120(1.04)^n$$

and we can solve for n by taking the log of both sides.

$$
\begin{aligned}
\log 500 &= \log (120(1.04)^n) \\
&= \log 120 + n \log 1.04 \\
2.6990 &= 2.0792 + n(.0170) \\
n &= \frac{2.6990 - 2.0792}{.0170} \\
&= \frac{.6198}{.0170} \\
&= 36.5.
\end{aligned}
$$

This means 37 years in actuality.

An exponential function is shown in [27a]. The x-axis ($y = 0$) is called an asymptote, meaning that the function approaches this line as a limit (here as x approaches negative infinity, y approaches zero).

Logarithmic Equations

An equation involving logarithms is a logarithmic equation. For example, $\log_{10} x = 3$ has

$x = 1000$ as the solution. The expression $y = \log_{10} x$ is a logarithmic function. See [27b] for the graph. Note that $y = \log_{10} x$ can be stated as $x = 10^y$, but is still different from $y = 10^x$, which is an exponential function. In [27b] the y-axis ($x = 0$) is an asymptote. The growth rate of most animals is a form of the logarithmic curve shown in [27b].

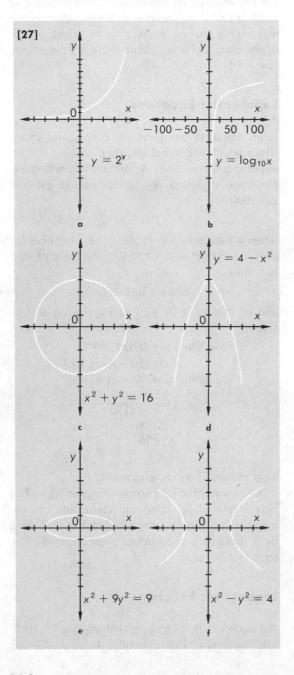

[27]

$y = 2^x$

a

$y = \log_{10} x$

b

$y = 4 - x^2$

$x^2 + y^2 = 16$

c

d

$x^2 + 9y^2 = 9$

e

$x^2 - y^2 = 4$

f

Conic Sections

A conic section is formed by the intersection of a plane and the figure made by two identical cones which share only the vertex and line of symmetry. The point and line are special cases of conic sections. The circle and parabola have been mentioned earlier; however, we now study them as well as the ellipse and hyperbola in regard to conic sections.

The *circle* with center at (h, k) and radius of c has a general equation of

$$(x - h)^2 + (y - k)^2 = c^2.$$

See [27c]

The *parabola* has a general equation of

$$(y - k) = c(x - h)^2$$

where (h, k) is the vertex and is the minimum point if $c > 0$ and a maximum point if $c < 0$. See [27d].

The *ellipse* is generally given by the equation

$$\frac{(x - h)^2}{a^2} + \frac{(y - k)^2}{b^2} = 1$$

where (h, k) is the center of the ellipse, with $2a$ and $2b$ the lengths of the axes of symmetry. See [27e].

The *hyperbola,* which is centered about the point, (h, k), and has asymptotes, $y = \pm (b/a)(x - h) + k$, is shown in [27f] and given by the equation

$$\frac{(x - h)^2}{a^2} + \frac{(y - k)^2}{b^2} = 1.$$

The theory behind conic sections is applied all the way from the minute orbits of electrons about the nucleus of an atom, to the giant movements of the heavenly bodies of outer space. In particular, circles, ellipses, and hyperbolas are employed in the lunar and interplanetary space travel program.

SIMULTANEOUS EQUATIONS

Dependence, Consistency

Two equations are said to be *dependent* if the information of one of them can be derived from the other. For example, $x + y = 3$ and $2x + 2y = 6$ are dependent equations, for we can multiply both sides of the first one by 2 to get the second one. They represent the same set of points (number pairs) and, if they are graphed, they are the same line.

Equations like $x + y = 4$ and $x + z = 6$ are called *independent* as we cannot derive one equation from the other. The equations $x + y = 4$ and $2x - y = 5$, are independent, but they are also *consistent* in that if these two equations are graphed simultaneously, they share the point, $(3, 1)$. The locating of number pairs (or triples, etc.) which consistent equations share is called the solution of the simultaneous equations.

If no solution exists, as in $x + y = 3$ and $x + y = 4$, then the equations are called *inconsistent*. Graphically speaking, this means the lines or curves do not intersect. These particular lines are parallel.

Graphical Solution

To find the solution of two equations in two unknowns, we graph both equations on the same coordinate axes; the point(s) of intersection is the solution. For example, to solve

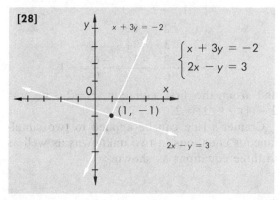

[28]
$$\begin{cases} x + 3y = -2 \\ 2x - y = 3 \end{cases}$$

We plot the graphs in [28] and get the point of intersection to be $(1, -1)$.

Algebraic Solutions

We may solve simultaneous systems of two or more equations by means of *algebraic* manipulation if the solution is nonempty. The two most common approaches are *addition* and *substitution*.

We can employ the *addition* method to the equations in [28] by multiplying both sides of $x + 3y = -2$ by -2.

$$\begin{cases} -2x - 6y = 4 \\ 2x - y = 3. \end{cases}$$

We now add equals to equals and the x terms drop out leaving $-7y = 7$, and thus $y = -1$. Knowing that $y = -1$, we insert a -1 for y in $x + 3y = -2$, and get $x + 3(-1) = -2$; from this we know that $x - 3 = -2$, so $x = -2 + 3 = +1$.

The same problem may be solved by *substitution*. Noting that $x + 3y = -2$ can be stated as $x = -2 - 3y$, we substitute the $-2 - 3y$ for x in the other equation getting an equation involving y only which we can solve.

$$2(-2 - 3y) - y = 3$$
$$-4 - 6y - y = 3$$
$$-7y = 7$$
$$y = -1$$

So again, as $x = -2 - 3y$, $y = -1$ means that $x = -2 - 3(-1) = -2 + 3 = 1$.

Cramer's Rule

A *matrix* is a rectangular array of numbers. We use subscripts to denote the elements of a matrix. That is, the matrix is arranged in rows and columns as below,

$$\begin{bmatrix} 5 & 7 & 0 \\ 3 & -2 & 4 \end{bmatrix}$$

so that the first row first column element is 5, the first row second column element is 7 and so on. We represent a 2×3, (2 by 3), matrix by

$$\begin{bmatrix} a_{11} & a_{12} & a_{13} \\ a_{21} & a_{22} & a_{23} \end{bmatrix}$$

where the subscripts indicate the row and column, respectively, of the elements.

Associated with every square matrix of real numbers is a real number called the *determinant* of the matrix. The determinant of a 2×2 matrix (call the matrix M) is symbolized as

$$\det(M) \quad \text{or} \quad \det\begin{bmatrix} a_{11} & a_{12} \\ a_{21} & a_{22} \end{bmatrix} \quad \text{or} \quad \begin{vmatrix} a_{11} & a_{12} \\ a_{21} & a_{22} \end{vmatrix}$$

and is equal to $a_{11}a_{22} - a_{12}a_{21}$. Thus we compute

$$\det \begin{bmatrix} 1 & 2 \\ 4 & -3 \end{bmatrix} = 1(-3) - 2(4) = -3 - 8 = -11.$$

The determinant of a 3×3 matrix can be found as follows: Repeat the first two columns and draw

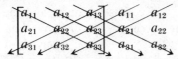

arrows as shown; form the six products of the numbers crossed by each arrow; the products indicated by the three arrows pointing to the right are added to the negatives of the remaining three products to get the value of the determinant.

EXAMPLE:

To find

$$\det \begin{bmatrix} 1 & 4 & 2 \\ -1 & 0 & 3 \\ -2 & -1 & 3 \end{bmatrix},$$

compute

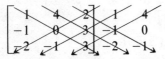

which gives

$$-(2)(0)(-2) - (1)(3)(-1)$$
$$- (4)(-1)(3) + (1)(0)(3)$$
$$+ (4)(3)(-2) + (2)(-1)(-1)$$
$$= 0 + 3 + 12 + 0 - 24 + 2$$
$$= -7.$$

When Cramer's rule is applied to the following three simultaneous equations:

$$a_1x + b_1y + c_1z = d_1$$
$$a_2x + b_2y + c_2z = d_2$$
$$a_3x + b_3y + c_3z = d_3,$$

where the a's, b's, c's, and d's are constants, then the solution, the values of x, y, and z which satisfy all three equations, is computed by

$$x = \frac{\begin{vmatrix} d_1 & b_1 & c_1 \\ d_2 & b_2 & c_2 \\ d_3 & b_3 & c_3 \end{vmatrix}}{\begin{vmatrix} a_1 & b_1 & c_1 \\ a_2 & b_2 & c_2 \\ a_3 & b_3 & c_3 \end{vmatrix}}, \quad y = \frac{\begin{vmatrix} a_1 & d_1 & c_1 \\ a_2 & d_2 & c_2 \\ a_3 & d_3 & c_3 \end{vmatrix}}{\begin{vmatrix} a_1 & b_1 & c_1 \\ a_2 & b_2 & c_2 \\ a_3 & b_3 & c_3 \end{vmatrix}},$$

$$z = \frac{\begin{vmatrix} a_1 & b_1 & d_1 \\ a_2 & b_2 & d_2 \\ a_3 & b_3 & d_3 \end{vmatrix}}{\begin{vmatrix} a_1 & b_1 & c_1 \\ a_2 & b_2 & c_2 \\ a_3 & b_3 & c_3 \end{vmatrix}}.$$

Note that the denominators are the same and that the numerators differ only by the placement of the column of d's in the column of the coefficients of the unknown that is being computed. Thus, there are only four determinants to evaluate and perhaps even fewer if we, for example, substitute the computed values of x and y in an equation and solve for z.

EXAMPLE:

Solve
$$\begin{cases} x + y + z = 2 \\ 2x - y = 3 \\ x - 2y - 3z = -3 \end{cases}$$

SOLUTION:

$$x = \frac{\begin{vmatrix} 2 & 1 & 1 \\ 3 & -1 & 0 \\ -3 & -2 & -3 \end{vmatrix}}{\begin{vmatrix} 1 & 1 & 1 \\ 2 & -1 & 0 \\ 1 & -2 & -3 \end{vmatrix}} = \frac{6}{6} = 1,$$

$$y = \frac{\begin{vmatrix} 1 & 2 & 1 \\ 2 & 3 & 0 \\ 1 & -3 & -3 \end{vmatrix}}{6} = \frac{-6}{6} = -1$$

and from the first equation, $z = 2 - x - y = 2 - (1) - (-1) = 2$.

Cramer's rule can be applied to two simultaneous equations in two unknowns as well as to three equations as shown.

SEQUENCES AND SERIES

A sequence is a set of numbers that are arranged in a one-to-one correspondence with a subset of the natural numbers. There is a first number, a second, etc., throughout the set. For example, 1, 3, 5, 7 is a sequence and so is $-2, 0, 2, 4, 6, \ldots$, where the dots mean continued in the same pattern, indicating that the set has an infinite number of elements or *terms*. If all of the terms of a sequence are not given then there must be a *pattern*, or *rule*, given to identify a particular sequence.

A *series is the indicated sum of a sequence.* Thus, $-2 + 0 + 2 + 4 + 6$ is a series and the sum is 10. The series $10 + 20 + 30 + \cdots$ is an *infinite series*.

Arithmetic Sequence

An *arithmetic sequence* is a sequence of terms such that the *difference* between any two consecutive terms is a constant. The first term of an arithmetic sequence is called a, and the difference is called d. Thus, the terms of an arithmetic sequence are given by

$$a, a + d, a + 2d, a + 3d, \ldots,$$

and the nth term of the sequence is denoted by

$$t_n = a + (n - 1)d.$$

For example, to find the 20th term of -3, 1, 5, . . . , we have $a = -3$, $d = 4$, $n = 20$, so that

$$t_{20} = -3 + (20 - 1)4 = -3 + 19(4) = 73.$$

Arithmetic Series

The sum of the terms of an arithmetic sequence is an *arithmetic series*. The sum of n terms of an arithmetic series is computed by the formula

$$s_n = \frac{n}{2}(a + t_n)$$

$$= \frac{n}{2}(a + a + (n - 1)d)$$

$$= \frac{n}{2}(2a + (n - 1)d)$$

So to find the sum of 15 terms of the series $\frac{1}{2} + \frac{3}{2} + \frac{5}{2} + \cdots$, we have $a = \frac{1}{2}$, $d = 1$, $n = 15$, and then

$$s_{15} = \frac{15}{2}(1 + (15 - 1)1) = \frac{15}{2}(15) = \frac{225}{2}$$

Geometric Sequence

A *geometric sequence* is a sequence of terms such that if a certain constant (called r, the ratio) is multiplied by any term of the sequence, the product is the following term. The first term of a geometric sequence is called a. For example, the series $\frac{1}{3}$, 1, 3, 9, 27, . . . is a geometric sequence with $a = \frac{1}{3}$ and $r = 3$.

The terms of a geometric sequence are then

$$a, ar, ar^2, ar^3, \ldots,$$

and the nth term is given by

$$t_n = ar^{n-1}$$

So to find the 7th term of the sequence 10, 5, 2.5, . . . , we have $a = 10$, $r = \frac{1}{2}$, $n = 7$, and

$$t_7 = 10\left(\frac{1}{2}\right)^6 = 10\left(\frac{1}{64}\right) = \frac{10}{64}.$$

Geometric Series

The sum of a geometric sequence is a *geometric series*. The sum of n terms of a geometric series is

$$s_n = \frac{a - ar^n}{1 - r} = \frac{a(1 - r^n)}{1 - r}, \quad \text{where } r \neq 1.$$

Thus r can be positive, negative, or zero, but not one. If $r = 1$, the series is arithmetic. As an example, to find the sum of 7 terms of $\frac{3}{4} - \frac{3}{8} + \frac{3}{16} - \frac{3}{32} + \cdots$, we note that $\frac{3}{4}\left(-\frac{1}{2}\right) = -\frac{3}{8}$, and $\left(-\frac{3}{8}\right)\left(-\frac{1}{2}\right) = \frac{3}{16}$, so $r = -\frac{1}{2}$, $a = \frac{3}{4}$, and $n = 7$.

$$s_n = \frac{\frac{3}{4}\left[1 - \left(-\frac{1}{2}\right)^7\right]}{1 - \left(-\frac{1}{2}\right)}$$

$$= \frac{\frac{3}{4}\left[1 - \left(-\frac{1}{128}\right)\right]}{\frac{3}{2}}$$

$$= \frac{1}{2}\left(\frac{129}{128}\right)$$

$$= \frac{129}{256}$$

If $|r| < 1$ in an infinite geometric series, then we can find the limit of the infinite series (called the *sum of the infinite series* and symbolized by S_∞) by noting that

$$s_n = \frac{a - ar^n}{1 - r} = \frac{a}{1 - r} - \frac{ar^n}{1 - r}$$

and that r^n in the second term approaches 0 as n gets larger with $|r| < 1$. Therefore the sum of an infinite series with $|r| < 1$ is

$$S_\infty = \frac{a}{1 - r}$$

To find the sum of the infinite series $1 + \frac{1}{2} + \frac{1}{4} + \cdots$, we use $a = 1$, $r = \frac{1}{2}$ and get

$$s_\infty = \frac{1}{1 - \frac{1}{2}} = \frac{1}{\frac{1}{2}} = 2.$$

Σ, !, Π, **Notations**

We often represent a series with the aid of the Σ symbol. The series $1 + 2 + 3 + \cdots + 10$ would be symbolized as in [29a].

[29]

$$\sum_{i=1}^{10} i \qquad \sum_{i=1}^{n} x_i \qquad \sum_{i=1}^{n} (m - x_i)^2$$

$$\text{(a)} \qquad\qquad \text{(b)} \qquad\qquad \text{(c)}$$

In [29b] we have the summation of the n terms $x_1 + x_2 + x_3 + \cdots + x_n$. To symbolize the statistical series $(m - x_1)^2 + (m - x_2)^2 + \cdots + (m - x_n)^2$ we use [29c].

If c is a constant, then we have the formulas

$$\sum_{i=1}^{n} c = nc, \qquad \sum_{i=1}^{n} cx_i = c \sum_{i=1}^{n} x_i,$$

$$\sum_{i=1}^{n} (x_i + y_i) = \sum_{i=1}^{n} x_i + \sum_{i=1}^{n} y_i$$

If n is a positive integer then $n!$ (read n factorial) is the product of n and all positive integers less than n. Thus $3! = 3 \cdot 2 \cdot 1 = 6$, $5! = 5 \cdot 4 \cdot 3 \cdot 2 \cdot 1 = 120$ and in general $n! = n(n - 1)(n - 2) \ldots 3 \cdot 2 \cdot 1$.

The symbol Π indicates the product of the elements of a given set. If the dimensions of a rectangular solid are length $= x_1$, width $= x_2$, and height $= x_3$, then the volume is given in [30a]. For $n!$ we use Π as in [30b].

[30]

$$V = \prod_{i=1}^{3} x_i \qquad\qquad n! = \prod_{i=1}^{n} i$$

$$\text{(a)} \qquad\qquad\qquad \text{(b)}$$

Mathematical Induction

Many times we may think, perhaps intuitively, that a certain formula holds for all natural numbers. We may have arrived at the formula by accident and we may have tried a few (or a million) cases and it worked every time. However, we may have still not actually proved the formula. If we are able to prove the formula by mathematical induction, then it is proved for all cases.

Mathematical induction is a method of proof which employs an axiom used by mathematicians to develop the system of natural numbers (that is, the set of natural numbers, the operations of addition and multiplication, and the relevant properties of these operations). The axiom assumes that if a certain property holds for the natural number 1 and if, while holding for given natural number k, it also holds for the successor (next number) of that number, $k + 1$, *then the property holds for all natural numbers*. It is similar to proving that one can climb a ladder. If we can get on the first step of the ladder, and if being on any step means that we can climb to the next step, then we can climb the ladder.

To illustrate how the axiom is used in mathematical induction, consider the following property about the sum of the first n even numbers.

$$2 + 4 + 6 + 8 + \cdots + 2n = n(n + 1)$$

It is easy to see that the property holds for the first natural number 1:

$$2 = 2(1) = 1(1 + 1)$$

"Climbing the ladder," let us suppose the property held for a certain natural number k. That is, $2 + 4 + 6 + 8 + \cdots + 2k$ did equal $k(k + 1)$. Will the property hold for the successor, which is $k + 1$?

$$(2 + 4 + 6 + 8 + \cdots + 2k) + 2(k + 1)$$
$$= k(k + 1) + 2(k + 1)$$
$$= (k + 2)(k + 1)$$
$$= (k + 1)(k + 2)$$

The property does hold. At this point the axiom is used; we assume via the axiom that the property will hold for all natural numbers. A complete proof by mathematical induction requires the steps above plus the reference to the axiom.

APPLICATIONS

In the next few sections, selected application problems are discussed and solved by using algebra.

Work Problems

Suppose Fred can complete a project in 6 days, Jack can complete the same project in 5 days, and David takes 4 days, then how many days will it take if all three work together?

Consider the condition of the project after one day. Fred will have completed $\frac{1}{6}$ of the project, Jack will have done $\frac{1}{5}$, and David will have finished $\frac{1}{4}$ of the project. We also know that if we let x be the number of days required to do the project together then $\frac{1}{x}$ of the project will be done after one day, $\frac{2}{x}$ of the project will be finished after two days, and so on until x days elapse and the whole $\left(\frac{x}{x} = 1\right)$ project is done. Individually, $\frac{x}{6}$ of the project will be completed by Fred after x days, $\frac{x}{5}$ will be done by Jack, and $\frac{x}{4}$ by David. The sum of their work is *one* project; therefore, we can write

$$\frac{x}{6} + \frac{x}{5} + \frac{x}{4} = 1$$

as the equation that we wish to solve. Multiplying both sides by the least common denominator, 60, gives

$$10x + 12x + 15x = 60$$
$$37x = 60$$
$$x = \frac{60}{37} = 1\frac{30}{37} \text{ (days)}$$

Mixture Problems

Assume that candy selling for 29¢ a kilogram is to be mixed with candy which sells for 39¢ a kilogram. If we want five kilograms of the mixture to sell for 36¢ a kilogram, then how many kilograms of each kind of candy should be mixed?

Let x and y be the number of kilograms of the 29¢ and the 39¢ candy, respectively, that go into the mixture. Then the value of the candies put in will be $.29x$ for the 29¢ and $.39y$ for the 39¢ candy. We write first the equation based on *mass*, and second the equation based on *value*.

$$x + y = 5$$
$$.29x + .39y = .36(5)$$

These simultaneous equations can be solved for x and y to give: $x = 1\frac{1}{2}$ (kilograms), $y = 3\frac{1}{2}$ (kilograms).

In another application, suppose a radiator system is full of 12 liters of a mixture of 30% antifreeze in water. How much should be drained and replaced by an 80% antifreeze solution to bring the antifreeze content of the 12-liter system to 60%?

Let x be the number of gallons drained and replaced in the radiator. If we write an equation based on amounts of antifreeze, we get

$$.30(12 - x) + .80x = .60(12),$$

which interpreted is: $.30(12 - x)$ means we have 30% antifreeze of what is left after taking out x liters; to this we have added some antifreeze which is 80% of the x liters replaced, and all of this adds to make 60% antifreeze of the 12-liter radiator. Completing the solution we have

$$3.60 - .30x + .80x = 7.20$$
$$.50x = 7.20 - 3.60$$
$$.50x = 3.60$$
$$x = \frac{3.60}{.50}$$
$$x = 7.2 \text{ (liters)}$$

Apportionment Problem

If a $12,000 inheritance is to be divided among three heirs in the proportion of $\frac{1}{2}$, $\frac{3}{4}$, and $\frac{5}{6}$, then how much does each receive?

We notice that the fractions do not add up to one, so we get a common denominator of 24 and express each fraction with this denominator.

$$\frac{1}{2} = \frac{12}{24}, \qquad \frac{3}{4} = \frac{18}{24}, \qquad \frac{5}{6} = \frac{20}{24}.$$

We then add the numerators, $12 + 18 + 20 = 50$, and 50 becomes the new denominator. We divide the inheritance into parts of:

$$\frac{12}{50}, \qquad \frac{18}{50}, \qquad \frac{20}{50}.$$

Multiplying \$12,000 by each of these fractions yields \$2880, \$4320, and \$4800, respectively.

Distance, Rate, Time Problems

Two trains traveled towards each other from points 200 kilometers apart. If one train is traveling at 50 kilometers per hour and the other at 60 kilometers per hour, when and where will they meet if they begin at the same time?

We set up our equation on the basis of the equal *times* that the trains traveled. We know $D = RT$ and so $T = D/R$. Letting D be the distance traveled by the 50 kilometer per hour train and $200 - D$ be the distance of the other train, the equal time equation with solution is given.

$$\frac{D}{50} = \frac{200 - D}{60}$$
$$60D = 50(200 - D)$$
$$60D + 50D = 10000$$
$$D = \frac{10000}{110}$$
$$D = 91$$

Thus the trains meet 91 kilometers from the starting point of the 50 kilometer per hour train. The length of time is

$$T = \frac{D}{R} = \frac{91}{50} = 1.8 \text{ (hours)}$$

Consecutive Integer Problems

Find two consecutive odd integers such that their product is 143.

Let the first integer be x, then the second integer is $x + 2$. The equation is

$$x(x + 2) = 143,$$

and the solution is found by grouping and applying the quadratic formula.

$$x^2 + 2x - 143 = 0$$
$$x = \frac{-2 \pm \sqrt{4 - 4(-143)}}{2}$$
$$= \frac{-2 \pm \sqrt{576}}{2}$$
$$= \frac{-2 \pm 24}{2}$$
$$x = \frac{22}{2} = 11$$

and $\qquad x = -\frac{26}{2} = -13$

The solution is 11 and 13, and also $-13, -11$.

Quadratic Max-Min Problems

A farmer's field borders a straight river bank. He wants to enclose three sides of a rectangular field with 100 meters of fencing and let the fourth side be the river bank. If he wants maximum area, what should be the dimensions?

Let x be the length of the side bordering the river bank. The opposite side then has length x, and the other two sides are each equal to $\frac{1}{2}(100 - x)$. The area (length times width) is given by

$$A = x\left(\frac{1}{2}\right)(100 - x) = -\frac{1}{2}x^2 + 50x$$

The graph of this quadratic function has a maximum point and no minimum point. We want to find the maximum of this function. The x value for maximum A is $-b/(2a)$, where $a = -\frac{1}{2}$, and $b = 50$. Therefore, the x value wanted is

$$x = \frac{-b}{2a}$$
$$x = \frac{-(50)}{(2)\left(-\frac{1}{2}\right)}$$
$$x = \frac{-50}{-1}$$
$$x = 50$$

The dimensions of the field are:

$$\text{length} = 50 \text{ (meters)}$$
$$\text{width} = \frac{1}{2}(100 - x)$$
$$= \frac{1}{2}(100 - 50)$$
$$= 25 \text{ (meters)}$$

The Hare and Tortoise

A hare and a tortoise engaged in a race. The hare, being 10 times faster, agreed to give the tortoise a head start of 100 meters. Will the hare catch the tortoise and if so, where?

Someone might conjecture the opinion that the hare will never catch the tortoise. They could say that when the hare covers the first 100 meters the tortoise has moved ahead by 10 meters. When the hare covers this 10 meters, the tortoise stays ahead by 1 meter, and so on, the tortoise always slowly staying just ahead, and the hare feverishly closing the gap but always in second place.

From the mathematical point of view, the hare and tortoise situation is an infinite geometric series with $r = \frac{1}{10}$ and $a = 100$. The sum of this series is

$$\frac{a}{1-r} = \frac{100}{1 - \frac{1}{10}} = \frac{100}{.90} = 111\frac{1}{9}$$

Thus we know that the hare *did* catch the tortoise at the distance of $111\frac{1}{9}$ meters.

Geometry

TERMINOLOGY

Undefined Terms

The undefined terms used in algebra remain undefined in geometry. We introduce other undefined terms to provide the foundation for geometry. Two common approaches to this foundation are used, one called the measurement (metric) approach because it uses a distance axiom to determine the length of segments and a measure axiom to find an angle's size. The other approach is called the nonmeasurement (synthetic) approach because ruler-and-protractor measurement is not used.

The interrelationships among these undefined and defined terms are provided by way of axioms (basic statements about the undefined and defined terms) and by way of theorems (statements which are proved from the axioms and previously proved theorems).

Defined Terms

Most of the terms commonly used in geometry are defined. We can define a segment with endpoints A and B as the set of points A and B and all points C between A and B (written A-C-B). A ray AB is the union of segment AB and all points of C of line AB such that A-B-C. The point A is called the endpoint of the ray AB. Angle BAC is the union of ray AB and ray AC, which have the common endpoint A, called the vertex. If one ray of an angle is rotated about A it will eventually coincide (that is, share all points in common) with the other ray. The amount of rotation is the measure (size) of the angle.

If two rays coincide and one is rotated in a counterclockwise fashion until they coincide again, the amount of the angle (complete rotation) formed is called 360°. One-fourth of such a rotation is thus 90°. A 90° angle is called a *right*

GEOMETRIC TERMS	METRIC APPROACH	SYNTHETIC APPROACH
point, line, plane, space	undefined	undefined
distance (length of segment)	undefined	not used
measure (size of angle)	undefined	not used
betweenness	defined	undefined
congruence (segments)	defined	undefined
congruence (angles)	defined	undefined
congruence (triangles)	defined	undefined
properties of congruence	proved as theorems	given as axioms

angle and the lines which form a 90° angle are said to be *perpendicular*. The shortest distance from a point, *A*, to a line, *l*, is along the perpendicular to the line, *l*, through point *A*.

The angle between two planes which intersect is the same as the angle formed by two rays, one in each plane, which are each perpendicular to the line of intersection of the planes at the same point. A line and a plane are perpendicular at point *A*, if the line is perpendicular to each of two distinct lines in the plane which contain *A*.

When two lines intersect, there are four angles formed by the four rays from the point of intersection. Opposite or nonadjacent (not sharing a side) angles of these four are called *vertical* angles. The smallest angle of the four is generally called the angle between the lines.

A *straight* angle has rays which extend oppositely about the vertex to form a line. A straight angle has a measure of 180°.

An *acute* angle has a measure greater than 0° and less than 90°. An *obtuse* angle is greater than 90° and less than 180°.

The sum of the measures of two right angles is a straight angle.

Complementary angles are two angles the sum of whose measures is 90°. *Supplementary* angles are two angles with a total measure of 180°. If two angles are complementary or supplementary, then each angle is called the complement or supplement, respectively, of the other.

Two angles are congruent if they have the same measure. Their measures are equal. Common usage, however, permits the interchange of these words. Thus we often say that all right angles are equal, complements of equal angles are equal, supplements of equal angles are equal, etc.

In [31a] we have a 30° angle indicating a rotation from initial side to terminal side of $\frac{1}{12}$ of 360°. The angle in [31b] can be referred to by any of the following: ∠*A* (which means angle *A*), ∠*BAC*, ∠*CAB*, ∠1.

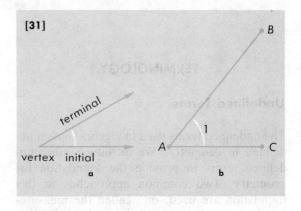

[31]

Parallel

If two lines in a plane are each perpendicular to the same line then the lines are *parallel*. In *Euclidean* geometry, through a point, *P*, not on a line, *l*, one and only one line can be passed which is parallel to *l*. Other (*non-Euclidean*) geometries are: *Hyperbolic* Geometry, where more than one line can be passed through point *P* parallel to line *l*; *Elliptic* geometry, where all lines in a plane meet in at least one point.

If two distinct planes are each perpendicular to the same line, then the planes are parallel. Planes perpendicular to the same plane are not necessarily parallel. For example, two adjacent walls of a room may each be perpendicular to the floor, yet not parallel to each other.

Incommensurable Segments

Two line segments are said to be *commensurable* if the quotient of their lengths equals a rational number. If their quotient is irrational then the line segments are *incommensurable*.

EQUALITY AND PROOF

Equality

The following properties constitute an equivalence relation:

reflexive, $a = a$, for all a.

symmetric, If $a = b$, then $b = a$.

transitive, If $a = b$ and $b = c$, then $a = c$.

Two line segments are congruent if they have the same length. Their lengths are equal. Common usage, however, permits the interchange of these words. Thus we often say that all four sides of a square are equal. The relation of congruence (equals) on line segments satisfies the above properties.

Proof

The nature of proof in geometry is *reason by precise deduction*. Deductive reasoning is usually made in the form of "if-then" statements. For example, *if* the numbers we are adding are 2 and 3, *then* the sum will be 5. *If* same size and shape, *then* congruent. In general,

if hypothesis, then conclusion

is the pattern we want to follow. A proof is considered correct, and therefore the conclusion is true, if (1) by previous agreements (definitions, other proofs, etc.) we know that if the hypothesis is met then the conclusion is true, and (2) we know that the terms or conditions of our hypothesis are satisfied by what we have established.

If A and B are statements, then the statement, "If A, then B" is also given as "A implies B" and is often symbolized as $A \Rightarrow B$. The statement $A \Rightarrow B$ is called a *theorem*. A theorem can be true or false. In geometry we are mainly interested in true theorems.

If $A \Rightarrow B$ is the theorem, then the *converse* is $B \Rightarrow A$ and is read "B implies A." If the theorem is, "If the figure is a square, then it is a rectangle.", then the converse is, "If the figure is a rectangle, then it is a square.". We know this theorem is true but the converse is false.

Let A' mean not A, then the *opposite* of the theorem $A \Rightarrow B$ is $A' \Rightarrow B'$. The converse and the opposite are *always* either both true or both false. The opposite of the preceding theorem is, "If the figure is not a square, then it is not a rectangle," which is false.

$B' \Rightarrow A'$ is called the *contrapositive* and is true or false exactly as the theorem is true or false. Thus the contrapositive of the given theorem is, "If the figure is not a rectangle, then it is not a square.", which is true.

If the theorem and its converse are true then the opposite and contrapositive are true. Thus we have in this case $A \Rightarrow B$, $B \Rightarrow A$, $A' \Rightarrow B'$, and $B' \Rightarrow A'$, all of which can be symbolized by $A \Leftrightarrow B$. Also, there are other equivalent word expressions for $A \Leftrightarrow B$ so that all of the following have the same effect:

A implies B and B implies A.

A if and only if B (A iff B).

A is necessary and sufficient for B.

If we prove that the contrapositive is true, then this makes the theorem true. It is often easier to prove (true) the contrapositive than the theorem. Hereafter, *proving* a statement will be the same as proving a statement to be true.

BASIC CONSTRUCTIONS

Bisecting Line Segments

To bisect the line segment AB in [32a], we set the point of the compass at point A and, with radius greater than one-half AB, we draw a small arc above and below AB. With the same radius, we draw two arcs with the compass point at *B* so that each of the first arcs is crossed. We then join the two points of intersection of the arcs, *C* and *D*, with a straight line and where this line *CD* crosses the line *AB* is the point *E* which bisects *AB*. Note that *CD* is actually perpendicular to *AB*; thus, it is called the perpendicular bisector of *AB*. Notice also that we could have made both sets of arcs above the line to get points *C* and *F* from which the line *CF* will also bisect *AB* at *E*.

[32]

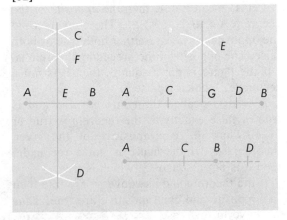

Perpendiculars

If we want to construct a perpendicular to the line *AB* at a point *G* in **[32b]**, we set the point of the compass at *G* and draw equal arcs at *C* and *D* on *AB*. With a larger radius, set the compass point at *C* and draw an arc above *AB*, then with the same radius, draw an arc with the compass point at *D*, crossing the other arc, locating point *E*. Connect *E* and *G*; *EG* is perpendicular to *AB* at *G*. If we want a perpendicular to *AB* at point *B*, then we extend *AB* as shown by the dotted segment in **[32c]**. We now set the compass point at *B*, strike arcs at *C* and *D*, and then proceed as in **[32b]**.

Equal Angles

To construct an angle equal to a given angle *A* in **[33a]**, we draw a base line *XY* in **[33b]**, set the compass point at *X* and draw an arc through *Z*. We strike the same arc with the compass point at *A* to intersect at *B* and *C* in **[33a]**. We set the

[33]

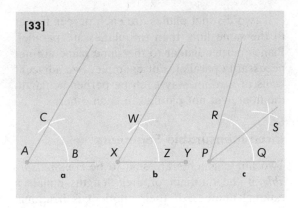

compass point at *B* and draw an arc through *C* and use this same arc with the compass point at *Z* to locate point *W*. Drawing the line *XW* completes angle *X* equal to angle *A*.

Bisecting Angles

In **[33c]** we bisect angle *P* by drawing an arc with the compass point at *P* to get points *Q* and *R*. With a sufficiently large radius we set the compass point at *Q* and strike an arc, then set the compass point at *R* and with the same radius intersect the other arc to get point *S*. The line *PS* is the bisector of angle *P*.

[34]

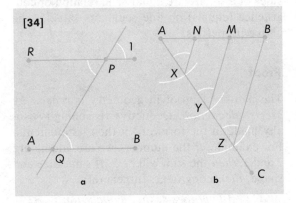

Parallel Lines

We construct a line through point *P* in **[34a]** parallel to line *AB* by drawing any line, *PQ*, through *P* intersecting *AB*. At point *P* we construct an angle *RPQ* equal to angle *PQB*. The line *RP* is parallel to line *AB*. We also could

MATHEMATICS

have constructed angle 1 equal to angle PQB and had RP parallel to AB.

Dividing a Segment

In [34b] we want to divide line segment AB into three equal parts. We proceed by drawing an auxiliary line AC and with the compass point at A, we mark point X. With the same radius we set the compass point at X and mark point Y, and similarly we get point Z. Drawing line ZB we form angle AZB. We now construct angles at Y and at X, each equal to angle AZB. The new lines drawn at X and Y strike the line AB at N and M so that $AN = NM = MB$. Note that we could have divided AB into any number of (say n) equal parts by making n marks on AC (extending AC if necessary) and proceeding as before.

Internal, External Division

We divide the line segment AB *internally* in [35a] in the ratio of $p:q$ by: drawing the line AC and locating point D so that $AD = p$; from D we locate point E so that $DE = q$; we draw ED and duplicate angle DEB at point D to get line DF; then F is the point which divides AB internally in the ratio $p:q$. Thus $AF:FB = p:q$.

[35]

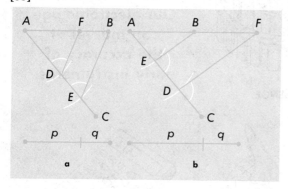

We may divide *externally* the line AB in [35b] in the ratio $p:q$ by: drawing the line AC and locating the points D and E so that $p = AD$ and $q = DE$; we then draw EB and duplicate angle DEB at point D to get line DF which intersects the extended line AB at F. Point F divides AB externally so that $AF:BF = p:q$.

Fourth Proportional

Given three line segments, a, b, and c, if we wish to find a fourth segment, d, so that $a:b = c:d$, then using [35a]: we let $a = AD$, $b = DE$, and $c = AF$; after drawing DF, we construct a line parallel to DF through E which intersects the extended line AF at point B. The line segment FB has the length d which is the fourth proportional.

Mean Proportional

If we are given two line segments, a and b, and we wish to find the mean proportional segment, m, such that $p:m = m:q$, then in [36a] we do the following: we form the line segment ABC so that $AB = p$ and $BC = q$;

[36]

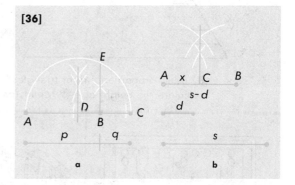

bisecting AC at point D, we draw a semicircle with center at D and radius $AD = DC$; we erect a perpendicular to AC at B which meets the semicircle at E. Segment BE is the desired mean proportional m of p and q. Here we have $p:m = m:q$ or $m^2 = p \cdot q$ which indicates the method of constructing a square, of side m, equal in area to a rectangle of length p and width q.

Sum, Difference

Knowing the sum, s, and difference, d, of two line segments in [36b], we can find the unknown segments, x and y, by: drawing segment AB equal to s-d; bisecting AB at C which gives $AC = CB = x$ which is the smaller of the segments we are seeking; adding d to x gives us y, the larger segment.

COMPUTING THROUGH THE AGES

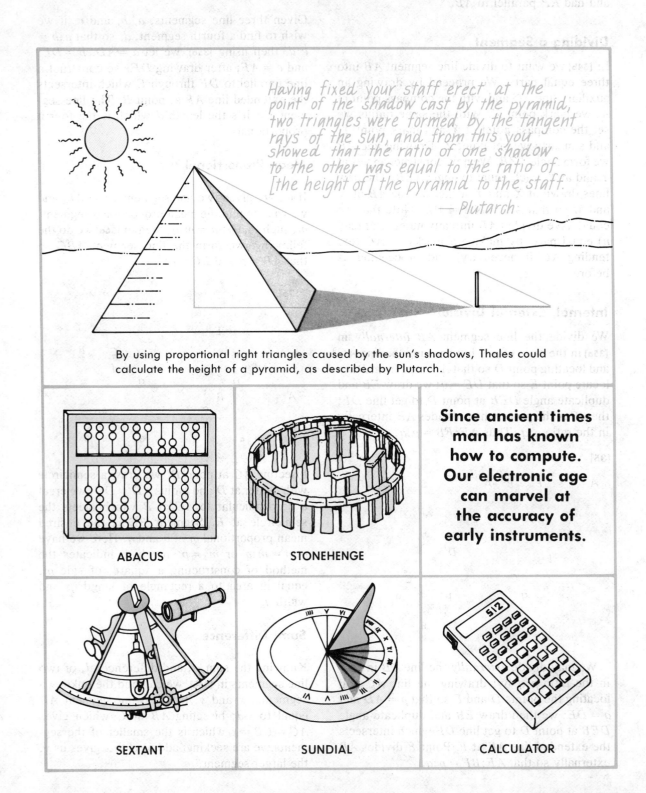

Having fixed your staff erect at the point of the shadow cast by the pyramid, two triangles were formed by the tangent rays of the sun, and from this you showed that the ratio of one shadow to the other was equal to the ratio of [the height of] the pyramid to the staff.

— Plutarch

By using proportional right triangles caused by the sun's shadows, Thales could calculate the height of a pyramid, as described by Plutarch.

ABACUS

STONEHENGE

Since ancient times man has known how to compute. Our electronic age can marvel at the accuracy of early instruments.

SEXTANT

SUNDIAL

CALCULATOR

TRIANGLES

Definitions

Two triangles are congruent if corresponding sides and corresponding angles are congruent. In everyday usage corresponding sides and corresponding angles are also said to be equal.

The *altitude* of a side of a triangle is the perpendicular segment from the side to the opposite vertex. The three *altitudes* of a triangle meet at a point called the *orthocenter*. The *median* of a triangle is the segment drawn from a vertex to the midpoint of the opposite side. The three medians of a triangle meet at a point called the *centroid*. The perpendicular bisectors of the sides of a triangle meet in a point called the *circumcenter*. The bisectors of the angles of a triangle meet in a point called the *incenter*.

The next few paragraphs illustrate basic constructions relating to triangles.

Three Sides

To construct a triangle given the three sides, *a*, *b*, and *c*, in [37a]: we draw side *c* and with the radius of the compass equal to side *b* we make an arc with the compass point at *A;* we then set the radius of the compass to the length of *a* and make an arc with the compass point at *B* which intersects the first arc at point *C*. Drawing *AC* and *CB* gives us the required triangle.

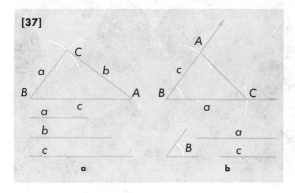

Two Sides, Angle

If we know two sides and the included angle of a triangle in [37b] we may construct the triangle by drawing the angle *B* and marking off the lengths of *a* and *c* on the sides of *B* to locate points *A* and *C*, respectively. We then draw segment *AC* to complete the required triangle.

Two Angles, Side

To construct a triangle given two angles, *A* and *B*, and the included side, *c*, we can draw the side *c* horizontally and construct the two angles on opposite ends of *c* so that the sides of the angles intersect above side *c* to locate point *C*. We then have the required triangle.

Hypotenuse, Leg

Knowing the hypotenuse, *c*, and a leg, *b*, we can in [38a] construct the triangle by: drawing the leg *b* thus locating points *A* and *C*; constructing a perpendicular at *C*; setting the compass point at *A* with radius of *c* and making an arc on the perpendicular to locate point *B*. We then draw *AB* to complete the required triangle.

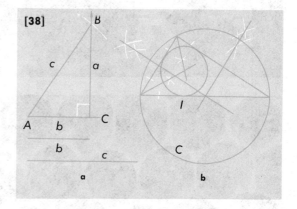

Circumscribed, Inscribed Circle

We construct the *circumscribed circle*, *C*, of a triangle in [38b] by using the circumcenter as the center, and the distance from the circumcenter to a vertex as the radius (*circumradius*). This circle intersects *all* vertices of the triangle.

The *inscribed circle*, *I*, in [38b] is drawn by using the incenter as the center, and the perpendicular distance from the incenter to a side as the radius. This circle lies within the triangle and is tangent to each side.

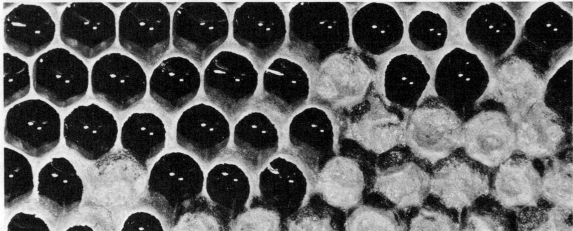

United States Pavilion, Expo 67, Montreal, Canada, is a geodesic dome.
Easy-to-construct, strong, and economical, such domes combine properties of
the sphere and tetrahedron. The hexagonal structure of the honeycomb is also
economical and strong, since it requires relatively little wax and supports
the weight of honey.

MATHEMATICS

Triangle Theorems

Two triangles are congruent if any of the following conditions are true:

S.S.S., three corresponding sides are equal.

S.A.S., two corresponding sides and included angle are equal.

A.S.A., two corresponding angles and included side are equal.

A.A.S., two corresponding angles and side not included are equal.

Hyp.L., they are right triangles and corresponding hypotenuse and leg are equal.

The *converses* of S.S.S., S.A.S., and A.S.A. are true. The converse of Hyp.L. would state that if two *right* triangles are congruent, then corresponding hypotenuse and leg are equal.

If a triangle has two equal sides, then the angles opposite these sides are equal and conversely. A triangle with three equal sides has three equal angles and conversely. If two angles of a triangle are correspondingly equal to two angles of another triangle, then the third angles are equal.

A line segment joining the midpoints of two sides of a triangle is parallel to the third side and one-half the length of the third side. Also a line which is parallel to one side of a triangle, and bisects a second side will bisect the third side. If a side of a triangle is extended, then the exterior angle formed will be equal to the sum of the two opposite interior angles.

The distance of the centroid from a vertex is two-thirds of the median drawn to that vertex. The *centroid* is also the *center of gravity* of a triangle. The *centroid, circumcenter,* and *orthocenter* of a triangle are *co-linear* (fall in a line).

Nine Point Circle

An *Euler point* is the midpoint of the line segment joining the orthocenter of a triangle to its vertex. In a triangle the Euler points, the midpoints of the sides, and the feet of the altitudes all lie on the same circle. This circle is called the *nine point circle* and it has a radius of one-half of the circumradius and the center is midway between the circumcenter and orthocenter.

POLYGONS

Definitions

A *simple* polygon is shown in [39a], and one which is *not* simple in [39b]. The simple polygon in [39c] can also be called *convex* in that it is simple and every interior angle is less than 180°.

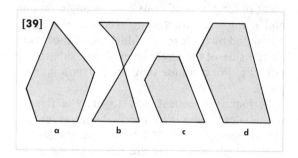

Polygons are *similar* if they have corresponding angles equal and corresponding sides proportional. See [39c, d]. A polygon is regular if it has all sides and angles equal, thus it is both equilateral and equiangular (see [40a]).

The following are basic polygonal constructions.

Parallelograms

We construct a parallelogram when given two sides and an angle in [40b] by the following: we draw the given angle B and lay off one given side, BA, to locate point A; at A we construct a line parallel to the other side of angle B; we then locate C on this parallel line by making the distance from A to C equal to the given line AC; we lay off the same distance on the parallel side of angle B to get point D. Drawing CD then completes the required parallelogram.

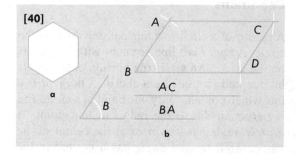

Polygon Construction

We can construct any regular polygon of n sides by using a protractor and the formula,

$$A = \frac{n-2}{n}(180°)$$

where A is the size of an interior angle. If each side is to have a length of x, then we draw a segment of length x and construct an angle on one end using a protractor to establish the angle computed by the formula. Marking off the length on the side of the angle gives a new side to the polygon. We continue until the polygon is complete.

Perhaps the easiest way to draw a regular polygon of n sides is to inscribe it in a given circle. We simply divide 360° by n to get the central angle which cuts off an arc whose chord is the length of a side. The compass can then be used to duplicate this chord around the circle completing the required inscribed polygon.

Polygon Theorems

The sum of the interior angles of a polygon of n sides is $(n-2)180°$. If one side of each angle of a polygon is extended, *the sum of these exterior angles* is 360°.

A quadrilateral is a parallelogram if any of the following is true:

O.S.E., *opposite sides* are *equal*.
O.A.E., *opposite angles* are *equal*.
D.B., *diagonals bisect* each other.
P.E.P., one *pair* of opposite sides are *equal* and *parallel*.

CIRCLES

Definitions

A *secant* of a circle is a line passing through the circle. A *chord* is a line segment with endpoints on the circle. An *arc* is the portion of the circle intercepted (cut off) by a chord. A *tangent* is a line which contains only one point of a circle and is perpendicular to the radius at that point. A *central angle* has its vertex at the center of the circle. An *inscribed angle* has a vertex on the circle and intersects the circle at two other points. A *semicircle* is half a circle. One-fourth of a circle is a *quadrant*.

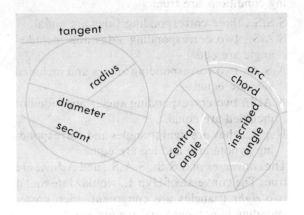

Circle, Given Three Points

If we are given three points, A, B, and C, and we want to construct the circle containing these points, then we draw the perpendicular bisector of two lines connecting the points, say AB and BC. Then the point of intersection of the bisectors is the center, O, of the circle and the radius is the distance from O to A.

Tangent From Point

To construct the tangents to a circle from a point, P, outside the circle, in **[41a]** we execute the following: we connect the center of the circle, O, to point P and bisect OP getting point M; with the compass point at M and radius MO we draw an arc intersecting the circle at T and T'. The lines PT and PT' are the required tangents.

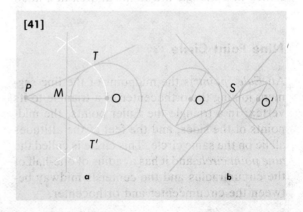

[41]

MATHEMATICS

Internal Tangents

We construct the internal (common) tangents to two given circles as follows: in [41b], we draw a diameter in circle O and a parallel diameter in circle O'; we then connect opposite ends of the diameters locating point S, the *internal center* of *similitude;* the internal tangents to both circles pass through S, therefore we construct the tangents to circle O through S and these lines will be tangent to O'.

External Tangents

The external tangents to two given circles can be formed in [42a], by connecting the corresponding ends of parallel diameters to locate point S, the *external center* of *similitude*. Then as with internal tangents, we construct tangents to one circle through S and they will also be tangent to the other circle.

[42]

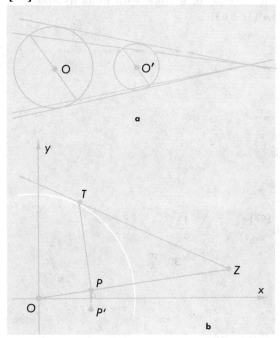

Circle Theorems

If two arcs of a circle are equal then their chords are equal and conversely. A diameter of a circle perpendicular to a chord bisects the chord and the corresponding arc. The perpendicular bisector of a chord goes through the center of the circle. The tangents drawn from an external point are equal.

An angle inscribed in a semicircle is a right angle and conversely. Inscribed angles intercepting equal arcs are equal and conversely. The angle formed by two secants or tangents meeting outside the circle will be one-half the difference of the intercepted arcs. An inscribed angle is one-half the central angle intercepting the same arc. If two chords intersect at a point in a circle, then the product of the segments of one chord equals the product of the segments of the other chord.

Inverse Points

A complex number can be represented as a point in the plane so that the number $a + bi$ would correspond to the point (a,b). The multiplicative inverse of the complex number $a + bi$ is the number $c + di$ if and only if

$$(a + bi)(c + di) = 1 + 0i = 1.$$

We may find the multiplicative inverse of a complex number $Z = a + bi$ by representing it in the plane then constructing its *inverse point* geometrically. The procedure for computing the inverse point of the complex number Z is shown in [42b] and may be described as follows:

1. Draw a line from the origin, O, to the point Z, and draw a circle about the origin of radius 1 unit.
2. Construct a tangent line from Z to the circle and locate point T.
3. Drop a perpendicular from T to the line OZ getting point P.
4. Reflect point P about the x-axis by drawing a line segment PP' through P crossing the x-axis perpendicularly, and making the x-axis bisect PP'. P' is then the inverse point of Z, so that $P' = 1/Z$.

If the point Z is found inside the unit circle then we reflect it, draw line OZ' to the origin, construct the perpendicular at Z' which intersects the circle at point T. The extended line OZ' and the tangent line at point T meet at the inverse point, P', which is $1/Z$.

SPHERICAL GEOMETRY

Definitions

A *great circle* of a sphere is the intersection of a sphere and a plane passing through the center of the sphere. Two points on a great circle, which are not ends of the same diameter, intercept two arcs which according to length are the *major* and *minor* arcs. The *distance* between two points on a sphere is the length of the minor arc of their common great circle.

A *spherical angle* is the figure formed by intersecting great circles. Their point of intersection is the *vertex,* and the *measure* of the spherical angle is the same as the measure of the angle between tangent lines to the great circles at the vertex. If three distinct arcs of great circles share endpoints and form a figure in such a way that the sphere is divided into three distinct regions (inside the figure, on the figure, and outside the figure), then the figure is called a *spherical triangle. Spherical polygons* are similarly defined.

A *spherical degree* is the area of a spherical triangle with two right angles and a 1° angle. Each of the four areas formed by two great circles (which always intersect) on a sphere are called *lines.* When parallel planes intersect a sphere the portion of the sphere between the planes is called a *zone.* The *spherical excess* of a triangle is the amount by which the sum of the angles of a spherical triangle exceeds 180°.

Spherical Theorems

A *line* of x degrees has an area of $\dfrac{\pi r^2 x}{90}$, where r is the radius. The *sum of the angles* of a spherical triangle exceeds 180°. The *area of a spherical triangle* is the number of degrees in the spherical excess. The *area* in spherical degrees of a *spherical polygon* of n sides with the sum of its angles, S, is given by $(S - (n - 2)180°)r^3$, where r is the radius of the sphere. The *area of a zone* of height h, radius of sphere, r, is $2\pi rh$. The *volume* of a *zone* with units as above is $\pi h^2(3r-h)/3$.

Trigonometry

TERMINOLOGY

Angles

An angle is said to be represented in *standard position* in the *xy* coordinate system if its vertex is at the origin and its initial side is on the positive *x*-axis. If the terminal side of the angle is measured as a counterclockwise rotation from the initial side, then the angle is *positive.* If measured clockwise, the angle is *negative* (see [43a]). If the terminal side coincides with an axis then the angle is called a *quadrantal* angle.

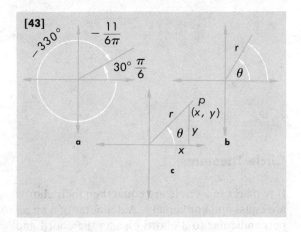

Measures

Angles are measured in degrees, radians, and mils. A *degree* is the measure of the central angle which subtends an arc equal to $\frac{1}{360}$ of the circumference of the circle. A *radian* is the measure of a central angle which subtends an arc equal to the radius of the circle. A *mil* is the measure of the central angle subtending an arc of $\frac{1}{6400}$ of the circumference of the circle. Thus $360° = 2\pi$ radians = 6400 mils and

$$1 \text{ degree} = \frac{\pi}{180} \text{ radians}$$
$$= 0.01745 \text{ radians}$$
$$= 17.778 \text{ mils}$$

$$1 \text{ radian} = \frac{180}{\pi} \text{ degrees}$$
$$= 57.29578 \text{ degrees}$$
$$= 1018.6 \text{ mils}$$

$$1 \text{ mil} = \frac{1}{1000} \text{ radian}$$
$$= 0.00098 \text{ radians}$$
$$= .05625 \text{ degrees, approximately}$$

There are 60 minutes (') in a degree and 60 seconds (") in a minute. This nearly makes 1 radian = 57°17′45″.

The *length of arc* of a circle is given by

$$s = r\theta$$

where r is the radius and θ is the central angle in radians (see [43b]). So on a circle of radius 10 centimeters the length of arc subtended by a central angle of 2 radians is 10(2) = 20 (centimeters). On a 5 centimeter circle, a central angle of 30° subtends an arc of length:

$$5(30)\left(\frac{\pi}{180}\right) = \frac{5}{6}\pi \text{ (centimeters)}$$

Trigonometric Functions

If θ is an angle in standard position, see [43c], and p is a distinct point on the terminal side with coordinates x (ordinate) and y (abscissa), and r is the positive distance between point p and the origin, then the six *trigonometric functions* of angle θ are defined as follows:

$$\text{sine } \theta = \frac{y}{r}$$
$$\text{cosine } \theta = \frac{x}{r}$$
$$\text{tangent } \theta = \frac{y}{x}$$
$$\text{cotangent } \theta = \frac{x}{y}$$
$$\text{secant } \theta = \frac{r}{x}$$
$$\text{cosecant } \theta = \frac{r}{y}$$

These functions are abbreviated respectively as sin θ, cos θ, tan θ, cot θ, sec θ, and csc θ.

The four quadrants and typical angles are shown in [44a]. In [44b] the six trigonometric functions are given with regard to their sign in a particular quadrant.

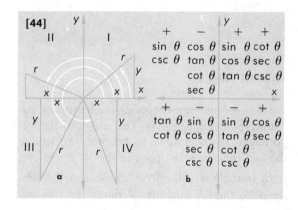

For example, in [45a], the angle in standard position has:

$$\sin \theta = \frac{3}{5} \qquad \cot \theta = \frac{4}{3}$$
$$\cos \theta = \frac{4}{5} \qquad \sec \theta = \frac{5}{4}$$
$$\tan \theta = \frac{3}{4} \qquad \csc \theta = \frac{5}{3}$$

In [45b]:

$$\sin \theta = \frac{-5}{13} \qquad \cot \theta = \frac{12}{5}$$
$$\cos \theta = \frac{-12}{13} \qquad \sec \theta = \frac{13}{-12}$$
$$\tan \theta = \frac{5}{12} \qquad \csc \theta = \frac{13}{-5}$$

Note that any point, except the origin, on the terminal side of an angle can be used to determine the six functions. Thus in [45a], the point $P = (8, 6)$ is on line OP extended and we would get the same function values by using the 6, 8, and hypotenuse of 10 as we would with 3, 4, and 5.

[45]

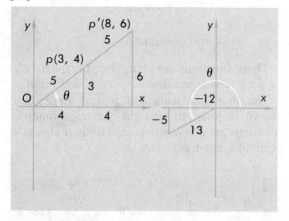

Special Angles

We find in [46] some special angles often encountered in applications. The length of the hypotenuse is understood to be one. We utilize the fact that the side opposite the 30° angle in a right triangle is $\frac{1}{2}$ the hypotenuse and the side opposite the 60° angle is $\frac{\sqrt{3}}{2}$ times the hypotenuse. We also use the fact that the side opposite the 45° angle in a right triangle is $\frac{\sqrt{2}}{2}$ times the hypotenuse. A dash means the function is undefined for that angle (division by zero).

[46]

ANGLE	SIN	COS	TAN	COT	SEC	CSC
0°	0	1	0	—	1	—
30°	$\frac{1}{2}$	$\frac{\sqrt{3}}{2}$	$\frac{\sqrt{3}}{3}$	$\sqrt{3}$	$\frac{2\sqrt{3}}{3}$	2
45°	$\frac{\sqrt{2}}{2}$	$\frac{\sqrt{2}}{2}$	1	1	$\sqrt{2}$	$\sqrt{2}$
60°	$\frac{\sqrt{3}}{2}$	$\frac{1}{2}$	$\sqrt{3}$	$\frac{\sqrt{3}}{3}$	2	$\frac{2\sqrt{3}}{3}$
90°	1	0	—	0	—	1
180°	0	−1	0	—	−1	—
270°	−1	0	—	0	—	−1

The reciprocal relationships among the functions are:

$$\sin \theta = 1/\csc \theta, \qquad \cos \theta = 1/\sec \theta,$$
$$\tan \theta = 1/\cot \theta.$$

Sine θ and *co*sine θ are called *cofunctions*. Similarly, tangent θ and *co*tangent θ, and also secant θ and *co*secant θ are cofunctions. The *complimentary* relationship of cofunctions is:

$$\sin \theta = \cos (90° - \theta), \qquad \tan \theta = \cot (90° - \theta),$$
$$\sec \theta = \csc (90° - \theta), \quad \text{where } 0° < \theta < 90°.$$

Use of Tables

Cotangent, secant, and cosecant are not listed in tables of logarithms, but can be computed by the reciprocal relationships of the trigonometric functions. The cotangent can also be found by the complement relationship with tangent. So, from the table, sin 84° = .9945, cos 50° = .6428, tan 6° = .1051, and cot 10° = tan (90° − 10°) = tan 80° = 5.6713. Notice that tan 90° is undefined.

If a function of an angle *between* what is listed in the table is desired, then *interpolation* can be employed. For example, to find sin 39°42′, we note that 39°42′ is between 39° and 40°, and in particular, it is 42/60 of the way from 39° to 40°. Therefore, we find the corresponding values in the table, sin 39° = .6293 and sin 40° = .6428, and multiply the difference between them, .6428 − .6293 = .0135, by 42/60 to get (42/60)(.0135) = .0096. We note from the table that sin θ increases as θ increases (up to 90°), so we must *add* .0096 to sin 39° giving .6293 + .0096 = .6389 = sin 39°42′.

Applications

We may employ the trigonometry of the right triangle by finding the distance across a river without crossing the river. For example, in [47a], a man stood at point A on one side of a river and noted a small tree, point B, across the river. He turned 90° to the right, walked 100 meters to point C, and then found the angle of the line of sight of the tree and his line of walk to be 63°. The distance AB can now be found from the right triangle ABC knowing tan $C =$ AB/AC; but $C = 63°$ and $AC = 100$ so that tan 63° = $AB/100$. We find tan 63° in the table to be 1.9626, making the equation read 1.9626 = $AB/100$, which has the solution $AB = 196$ (meters).

[47]

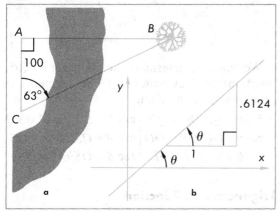

In another example, we find the angle θ that a line makes with the x axis if its slope is .6124 by realizing that slope is the y distance over the x distance or the tangent of the angle. Thus in [47b] slope = tan θ = .6124, which means the angle is between 31° and 32° according to the table. We interpolate by observing that tan 31° = .6009 and tan 32° = .6249, and their difference is .0240. Now the difference between tan θ = .6124 and tan 31° = .6009 is .0115, so the angle desired is .0115/.0240 of the way from 31° to 32°. We multiply, $\left(\frac{115}{240}\right)(60) = 28.75$, and get for our answer $\theta = 31°29'$. Note that we should not make our answer read 31°28'45", because we used a four-place table which should be interpolated only to the nearest minute.

Period

If n is an integer, positive, negative, or zero, then we have:

$\sin (\theta + n360°) = \sin \theta$ | $\cot (\theta + n360°) = \cot \theta$
$\cos (\theta + n360°) = \cos \theta$ | $\sec (\theta + n360°) = \sec \theta$
$\tan (\theta + n360°) = \tan \theta$ | $\csc (\theta + n360°) = \csc \theta$

which shows that all trigonometric functions

are periodic and repeat functional values at least every 360°. We also have

$\tan (\theta + n180°) = \tan \theta \quad \cot (\theta + n180°) = \cot \theta$

revealing that tangent and cotangent repeat functional values every 180°. The distance between repeated functional values is the *period* of the function. Thus the period of the sine, cosine, secant, and cosecant functions is 360° or 2π radians. The period of the tangent and cotangent functions is 180° or π radians.

Amplitude

As noted in [46], all trigonometric functions except sine and cosine are undefined for a certain angle, θ. So we discuss *amplitude,* meaning peak or maximum y value, only for sine and cosine functions. The functions $y = \sin x$ and $y = \cos x$ have amplitudes of 1.

In general, y = a *sin* bx *and* y = a *cos* bx *have the period 2π/b and amplitude a, where a and b are positive.*

Negative Angle

The functions of the negative angles are

$\sin (-\theta) = -\sin \theta \qquad \cot (-\theta) = -\cot \theta$
$\cos (-\theta) = \cos \theta \qquad \sec (-\theta) = \sec \theta$
$\tan (-\theta) = -\tan \theta \qquad \csc (-\theta) = -\csc \theta$

so that $\sin (-30°) = -\sin 30 = -\frac{1}{2}$, and cos $(-30°) = \cos 30° = \frac{\sqrt{3}}{2}$.

GRAPHS

Circular Functions

In [48] we have θ, an acute angle in standard position. A circle of radius one unit, centered at the origin, intersects the terminal side of θ at P. PQ is perpendicular to the x axis. ST and $S'T'$ are tangents to the circle and intersect line OP at S and S' respectively. We note that triangle OPQ is similar to triangle OST, and angle $\theta =$ angle $T'S'O$.

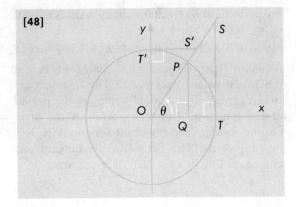

[48]

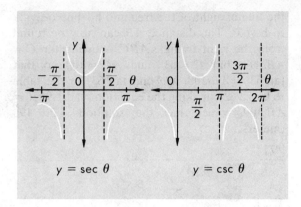

$y = \sec\theta$ $y = \csc\theta$

We can now determine the six trigonometric functions of θ as lengths of line segments in relationship to the circle.

$\sin\theta = QP/OP = QP$ $\cot\theta = S'T'/OT' = S'T'$
$\cos\theta = OQ/OP = OQ$ $\csc\theta = OS'/OT' = OS'$
$\tan\theta = ST/OT = ST$ $\sec\theta = OS/OT = OS$

Trigonometric Functions

By plotting angle values in radians with the corresponding function values we get the graphs of the trigonometric functions. The vertical dotted lines are the asymptotes of the given functions.

Special Graphs

In [49] we have $y = \frac{3}{4}\sin 2\theta$, with a period of π and amplitude of $\frac{3}{4}$, shown as the solid line. The dotted line is $y = \frac{1}{3}\sin\theta/2$, with period 4π and amplitude $\frac{1}{3}$.

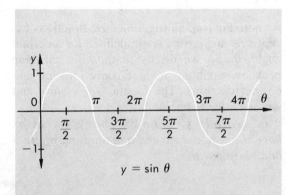

$y = \sin\theta$

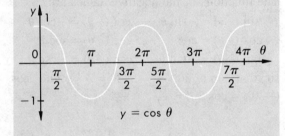

$y = \cos\theta$

[49]

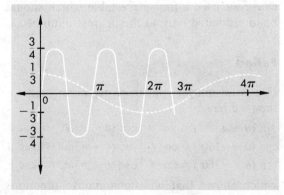

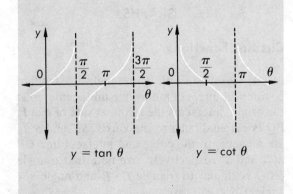

$y = \tan\theta$ $y = \cot\theta$

The sum of two trigonometric functions is illustrated in [50a]. The resulting graphs can be sketched by drawing each of the curves on the same set of axes, then "adding" corresponding y values. The sine and cosine waves are the dotted curves and their sum is the solid curve.

[50]

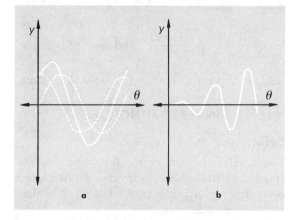

a   b

In [50b] the product function, $y = \theta \sin \theta$, is shown with the unstable characteristic of amplitude increasing without limit. It is sketched by first drawing the guide lines $y = \theta$ and $y = -\theta$, then letting the periodic "peaks" of the sine wave be tangent to the guide lines.

IDENTITIES

One-Angle Identities

If a statement involving the relationship of trigonometric functions of the same angle is true for *all* defined values of that angle then the statement is called an *identity*. The *fundamental identities* are:

$$\sin \alpha = 1/\csc \alpha, \qquad \csc \alpha = 1/\sin \alpha$$
$$\cos \alpha = 1/\sec \alpha, \qquad \sec \alpha = 1/\cos \alpha$$
$$\tan \alpha = 1/\cot \alpha = \sin \alpha/\cos \alpha,$$
$$\tan \alpha \cos \alpha = \sin \alpha$$
$$\cot \alpha = 1/\tan \alpha = \cos \alpha/\sin \alpha,$$
$$\cot \alpha \sin \alpha = \cos \alpha$$
$$\sin^2 \alpha + \cos^2 \alpha = 1, \qquad 1 - \sin^2 \alpha = \cos^2 \alpha$$
$$\sec^2 \alpha - \tan^2 \alpha = 1, \qquad 1 + \tan^2 \alpha = \sec^2 \alpha$$
$$\csc^2 \alpha - \cot^2 \alpha = 1, \qquad 1 + \cot^2 \alpha = \csc^2 \alpha$$

The notation $\sin^2 \alpha$ means $(\sin \alpha)^2$.

The verification of an identity, sometimes called proving an identity, is the process of verifying that a statement is true for all defined values of an angle by using algebraic *factoring* and *simplification*, and *substitution* of the given *fundamental identities*. We either transform one side of the identity into the other or reduce both sides to an expression in which it is obvious that all defined values are true. We can operate on both sides of an identity simultaneously (like adding $\sin \alpha$ to both sides), as long as the operation is reversible and yields an equivalent expression (that is, an expression with the same solution). We usually then work with the more complicated side first.

It may be helpful to change *both* sides to sines and cosines before attempting the transformation. A good exercise is the changing of every trigonometric function into terms of $\sin \alpha$.

$$\sin \alpha = \sin \alpha$$
$$\cos \alpha = \pm \sqrt{1 - \sin^2 \alpha}$$
$$\tan \alpha = \frac{\sin \alpha}{\cos \alpha} = \pm \frac{\sin \alpha}{\sqrt{1 - \sin^2 \alpha}}$$
$$\cot \alpha = \frac{1}{\tan \alpha} = \pm \frac{\sqrt{1 - \sin^2 \alpha}}{\sin \alpha}$$
$$\sec \alpha = \frac{1}{\cos \alpha} = \pm \frac{1}{\sqrt{1 - \sin^2 \alpha}}$$
$$\csc \alpha = \frac{1}{\sin \alpha}$$

The appropriate $\pm$ sign is used according to the quadrant of the angle.

To verify the identity, $\sin \alpha (1 + \cot^2 \alpha) = \csc \alpha$, we proceed as follows:

$$\sin \alpha (1 + \cot^2 \alpha) = \csc \alpha$$
$$\sin \alpha (\csc^2 \alpha) = \csc \alpha$$
$$\sin \alpha \left(\frac{1}{\sin^2 \alpha}\right) = \frac{1}{\sin \alpha}$$
$$\frac{1}{\sin \alpha} = \frac{1}{\sin \alpha}$$

Alternately,
$$\csc \alpha [\sin \alpha (1 + \cot^2 \alpha)] = \csc \alpha (\csc \alpha)$$
$$(\csc \alpha \sin \alpha)(1 + \cot^2 \alpha) = \csc^2 \alpha$$
$$1 + \cot^2 \alpha = \csc^2 \alpha$$

which is true for all defined values of α.

The verification of $\dfrac{\sin x + \tan x}{\cot x + \csc x} = \sin x \tan x$

is:

$$\frac{\sin x + \tan x}{\cot x + \csc x} = \sin x \tan x$$

$$\frac{\sin x + \dfrac{\sin x}{\cos x}}{\dfrac{\cos x}{\sin x} + \dfrac{1}{\sin x}} = \sin x \, \frac{\sin x}{\cos x}$$

$$\frac{\sin x \cos x + \sin x}{\cos x} \div \frac{\cos x + 1}{\sin x} = \frac{\sin^2 x}{\cos x}$$

$$\frac{\sin x \,(\cos x + 1)}{\cos x} \cdot \frac{\sin x}{\cos x + 1} = \frac{\sin^2 x}{\cos x}$$

$$\frac{\sin^2 x}{\cos x} = \frac{\sin^2 x}{\cos x}$$

Multiple Angle Identities

If α and β are two given angles, then we have:

$$\sin (\alpha + \beta) = \sin \alpha \cos \beta + \cos \alpha \sin \beta$$
$$\cos (\alpha + \beta) = \cos \alpha \cos \beta - \sin \alpha \sin \beta$$
$$\tan (\alpha + \beta) = \frac{\tan \alpha + \tan \beta}{1 - \tan \alpha \tan \beta}$$
$$\sin (\alpha - \beta) = \sin \alpha \cos \beta - \cos \alpha \sin \beta$$
$$\cos (\alpha - \beta) = \cos \alpha \cos \beta + \sin \alpha \sin \beta$$
$$\sin 2\alpha = 2 \sin \alpha \cos \alpha$$
$$\cos 2\alpha = \cos^2 \alpha - \sin^2 \alpha$$
$$\tan 2\alpha = \frac{2 \tan \alpha}{1 - \tan^2 \alpha}$$
$$\sin 3\alpha = 3 \sin \alpha - 4 \sin^3 \alpha$$
$$\cos 3\alpha = 4 \cos^3 \alpha - 3 \cos \alpha$$
$$\sin \frac{\alpha}{2} = \pm \sqrt{\frac{1 - \cos \alpha}{2}}$$
$$\cos \frac{\alpha}{2} = \pm \sqrt{\frac{1 + \cos \alpha}{2}}$$
$$\tan \frac{\alpha}{2} = \pm \sqrt{\frac{1 - \cos \alpha}{1 + \cos \alpha}}$$
$$\sin \alpha + \sin \beta = 2 \sin \frac{\alpha + \beta}{2} \cos \frac{\alpha - \beta}{2}$$
$$\sin \alpha - \sin \beta = 2 \sin \frac{\alpha - \beta}{2} \cos \frac{\alpha + \beta}{2}$$
$$\cos \alpha + \cos \beta = 2 \cos \frac{\alpha - \beta}{2} \cos \frac{\alpha + \beta}{2}$$
$$\cos \alpha - \cos \beta = -2 \sin \frac{\alpha + \beta}{2} \sin \frac{\alpha - \beta}{2}$$
$$\sin \alpha \sin \beta = \frac{1}{2} [\cos (\alpha - \beta) - \cos (\alpha + \beta)]$$
$$\cos \alpha \cos \beta = \frac{1}{2} [\cos (\alpha - \beta) + \cos (\alpha + \beta)]$$
$$\sin \alpha \cos \beta = \frac{1}{2} [\sin (\alpha + \beta) + \sin (\alpha - \beta)]$$

If A, B, and C are angles and a, b, and c are the opposite sides respectively of a triangle, then we have:

the *law of sines,* $\dfrac{a}{\sin A} = \dfrac{b}{\sin B} = \dfrac{c}{\sin C}$, and the *law of cosines,* $a^2 = b^2 + c^2 - 2bc \cos A$.

The law of cosines is similarly true for angles B and C also. If $s = \dfrac{(a + b + c)}{2}$ then

$$\cos \frac{A}{2} = \sqrt{\frac{s(s - a)}{bc}}$$, and *area of triangle*

$$ABC = \sqrt{s(s - a)(s - b)(s - c)} = \tfrac{1}{2} ab \sin C.$$

INVERSE FUNCTIONS

Definitions

The *inverse trigonometric functions* will be given in this manner: $y =$ inverse sin of angle x is written $y =$ arc sin x or $y = \sin^{-1} x$. The definitions are as follows:

If $x = \sin y$, then $y =$ arc sin x, $\dfrac{-\pi}{2} \leqslant y \leqslant \dfrac{\pi}{2}$.

If $x = \cos y$, then $y =$ arc cos x, $0 \leqslant y \leqslant \pi$.

If $x = \tan y$, then $y =$ arc tan x, $\dfrac{-\pi}{2} \leqslant y \leqslant \dfrac{\pi}{2}$.

The other three functions are similarly defined but are less often used. The symbol "$y = \sin^{-1} x$" means "y is the angle whose sine is x," and therefore $\sin^{-1} x$ does not equal $\dfrac{1}{\sin x}$ or $(\sin x)^{-1}$. The restrictions on angle y keep its range in *principal values.* That is, $y =$ arc sin x has $\dfrac{-\pi}{2} \leqslant y \leqslant \dfrac{\pi}{2}$ so the principal values of y go from $\dfrac{-\pi}{2}$ to $\dfrac{\pi}{2}$, making y a (single-valued) function of x. We know then that $\sin (\sin^{-1} x) = x$.

For example, $y = \sin^{-1} .5$ means the angle whose sine is .5. Thus $y = \dfrac{\pi}{6}$ or 30°. $\mathrm{Tan} \left(\cos^{-1} \dfrac{4}{5} \right)$ can be found by realizing that if $\cos \theta = \dfrac{4}{5}$ then the right triangle containing θ must have sides of 4, 5, and $\sqrt{5^2 - 4^2}$ or 3. $\mathrm{Tan} \left(\cos^{-1} \dfrac{4}{5} \right) = \dfrac{3}{4}$. Compute π by $\pi = 4 \tan^{-1} 1$.

Graphs

The principal values of arc sin x, arc cos x, and arc tan x are graphed in [51].

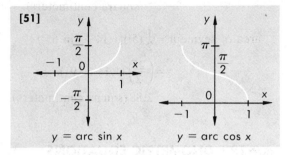

$y = \text{arc sin } x$ $y = \text{arc cos } x$

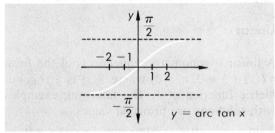

$y = \text{arc tan } x$

APPLICATIONS

Identity

If A, B, and C are the angles of a triangle, show that $\tan A + \tan B + \tan C = \tan A \tan B \tan C$. We know that $C = 180° - (A + B)$ and also that the tangent is periodic so that $\tan x = \tan (x - 180°)$. But $\tan (-x) = -\tan x$ so we have $\tan (180° - x) = -\tan x$. Thus $\tan C = \tan (180° - (A + B)) = -\tan (A + B)$. We proceed as follows:

$\tan A + \tan B + \tan C$

$= \tan A + \tan B - \tan (A + B)$

$= \tan A + \tan B - \dfrac{\tan A + \tan B}{1 - \tan A \tan B}$

$= (\tan A + \tan B)\left(1 - \dfrac{1}{1 - \tan A \tan B} \right)$

$= (\tan A + \tan B)\left(\dfrac{1 - \tan A \tan B - 1}{1 - \tan A \tan B} \right)$

$= \tan A \tan B \left(-\dfrac{\tan A + \tan B}{1 - \tan A \tan B} \right)$

$= \tan A \tan B \, (-\tan (A + B))$

$= \tan A \tan B \tan C.$

Oblique Triangles

An *oblique triangle* does not contain a right angle. We may apply trigonometry to oblique triangles as follows:

In [52a], two observation posts, A and B, spot the flash of an enemy gun, G, at angles of 40° and 76° respectively. It is required to find the distance, BG, to the gun from post B if A and B are three kilometers apart. We note that angle AGB must be 64°, and we use the law of sines to get

$$\frac{BG}{\sin 40°} = \frac{3}{\sin 64°} \quad \text{or} \quad BG = 3(\sin 40°)/\sin 64°,$$

which thus gives $BG = 3(.6428)/(.8988) = 2.15$ (kilometers).

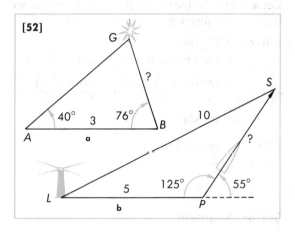

[52]

A ship sails from port, P in [52b], on a bearing of N35°E at a rate of 12 kilometers per hour. In what length of time will the ship be 10 kilometers from a lighthouse which is 5 kilometers due west from the port? The answer is computed by using the following facts: angle P is 125° and $\cos 125° = -\cos 55° = -.5736$; the law of cosines should be employed as one angle and two sides are involved. We have then,

$$LS^2 = LP^2 + PS^2 - 2(LP)(PS) \cos P,$$
$$10^2 = 5^2 + PS^2 - 2(5)(PS)(-.5736),$$

and $PS^2 + 5.736 \, PS - 75 = 0$. Using the quadratic formula we get PS = 6.2 and $PS = -11.9$. We reject the negative, so $PS = 6.2$. This means at 12 kilometers per hour, the ship will take $6.2/12 = .52$ (hours) to reach the designated location.

MATHEMATICS

Area of Triangle

To find the area of a triangle ABC given $a = 20$ cm, $b = 15$ cm, and $C = 37°$, we use area $= \frac{1}{2} ab \sin C$ to get

$$\text{area} = \frac{1}{2}(20)(15) \sin 37°$$

$$= \frac{1}{2}(20)(15)(.6018)$$

$$= 90 \text{ (square centimeters)}$$

Inverse Function

We show that arc sin $1/\sqrt{10}$ + arc sin $3/\sqrt{10}$ = $\pi/2$ by the following:

Let α = arc sin $1/\sqrt{10}$ and β = arc sin $3/\sqrt{10}$ so that the left member is just $\alpha + \beta$. Now

$$\alpha + \beta = \text{arc sin } (\sin(\alpha + \beta))$$

$$= \text{arc sin } (\sin \alpha \cos \beta + \cos \alpha \sin \beta)$$

$$= \text{arc sin } \left(\frac{1}{\sqrt{10}} \frac{1}{\sqrt{10}} + \frac{3}{\sqrt{10}} \frac{3}{\sqrt{10}} \right)$$

$$= \text{arc sin } \left(\frac{1}{10} + \frac{9}{10} \right)$$

$$= \text{arc sin } (1)$$

$$= \frac{\pi}{2}$$

Sector, Segment

A *circular sector* is the set of points covered by a radius of a circle which is rotated by some angle α. The figure formed is intuitively shaped like a piece of pie. A sector has an area given by

$$\text{area of sector} = \frac{1}{2} r^2 \alpha,$$

where α is in radians and r is the radius. A *circular segment* is the part of the sector left when the triangle, formed by the two radii on each side of the sector and the chord connecting the endpoints of the radii, is removed. The area of a segment subtended by a central angle of α in radians, with a radius of r is:

$$\text{area of segment} = \frac{1}{2} r^2 (\alpha - \sin \alpha).$$

For example, we compute the area of the circular sector and segment of a central angle of 65° in a circle of radius 5 centimeters by first changing 65° to radians, $65° = 65\pi/180$ radians = 1.14 radians, then applying the formulas:

$$\text{area of sector} = \frac{1}{2}(5)^2(1.14) = 14.2$$
$$\text{(square centimeters).}$$

$$\text{area of segment} = \frac{1}{2}(5^2)(1.14 - \sin 65°)$$

$$= \left(\frac{25}{2} \right)(1.14 - .91)$$

$$= 2.88 \text{ (square centimeters).}$$

TRIGONOMETRIC EQUATIONS

Linear

A linear trigonometric equation is of the form $aT(x) + b = 0$, $a \neq 0$, where $T(x)$ is a trigonometric function of x. The following examples with solutions use principal values.

$$2 \sin x - 1 = 0 \qquad \sin x \cos x - \cos x = 0$$
$$2 \sin x = 1 \qquad \cos x (\sin x - 1) = 0$$
$$\sin x = \frac{1}{2} \qquad \cos x = 0$$
$$x = \pi/6 \qquad \sin x - 1 = 0$$
$$\sin x = 1$$
$$x = \pi/2$$

The equation $\cos x = 2$ has no solution as $-1 \leqslant \cos x \leqslant 1$ for all real x.

Quadratic

A quadratic trigonometric equation is of the form $aT(x)^2 + bT(x) + c = 0$, $a \neq 0$. We obtain solutions by factoring or using the quadratic formula. Examples:

$$\sin^2 x + 3 \sin x + 2 = 0 \quad \cos^2 x + 3 \cos x - 3 = 0$$

Factoring: By the formula:

$$(\sin x + 2)(\sin x + 1) = 0 \; \cos x = \frac{-3 \pm \sqrt{9 + 12}}{2}$$

$$\sin x + 2 = 0$$
$$\sin x = -2 \text{ No solution} \quad \cos x = -3.8 \text{ and } 0.8$$
$$\sin x + 1 = 0 \qquad\qquad \text{the only solution is}$$
$$\sin x = -1 \qquad\qquad \cos x = 0.8$$
$$x = -\pi/2 \qquad x = 36.5° = .64 \text{ radians}$$

Special

Some special equations and their solutions will now be given. As the sine of the angle and the cosine of twice the angle must be equal in the second example, the first quadrant angle is the only solution.

$$\sin 2x = \cos 3x$$
$$\sin 2x = \sin\left(\frac{\pi}{2} - 3x\right)$$
$$2x = \frac{\pi}{2} - 3x$$

$$5x = \frac{\pi}{2}$$

$$x = \frac{\pi}{10}$$

$$\text{arc cos } 2x = \text{arc sin } x,$$

taking cosine of both sides

$$2x = \cos(\text{arc sin } x)$$
$$= \sqrt{1 - x^2},$$

squaring both sides,

$$4x^2 = 1 - x^2,$$
$$5x^2 = 1$$

$$x = \frac{1}{\sqrt{5}}$$

Calculus

The branch of mathematics called *calculus* (or *the calculus*) is customarily divided into two parts, *differential* and *integral* calculus. Each introduces an operation not found in more elementary mathematics, namely *differentiation* and *integration*. In general, differentiation is used to determine instantaneous rate of change in one variable with respect to another, and integration is used to obtain an exact sum of an infinite number of parts. Most major theorems of calculus, and the techniques for applying its operations to problem-solving, are based upon the concept of the limit of a function and upon the analysis of the graphs of functions and relations.

TERMINOLOGY

Relation.   Any set of ordered pairs is a *relation*. Thus $\{(-3, 4), (4, 4), (5, 9)\}$, $\{(0, -2), (0, 0), (.5, 2), (1, 6)\}$, and $\{(x, y) \mid x^2 + y^2 = 25\}$ are all relations.

Function.   A relation in which each different first element is paired with a single second element is a *function*. Thus, the first relation above is a function. The other relations are not functions, since at least one first element is paired with different second elements. If the pairs in a function have the order (x, y) it is said that y is a function of x, often written $y = f(x)$, and that x and y are the *independent* and *dependent* variables, respectively. In functional notation, $f(k)$ equals the value of $f(x)$ when $x = k$.

Domain and Range.   The set of all first elements of the pairs in a relation is the *domain* of the relation. The set of second elements is the *range* of the relation. In calculus, the set of all real number values of x that are paired with real number values of y forms the *natural domain* of a function $y = f(x)$. In this discussion, all work with functions will be restricted to use of the natural domain or arbitrarily chosen subsets of the natural domain.

Limit of a Function.   If $f(x)$ has a finite real number value for all $x \neq c$ in an interval containing c, then the *limit* as x approaches c, $\lim_{x \to c} f(x) = L$ if, and only if, for any $\epsilon > 0$ there exists $\delta > 0$ such that when $0 < |x - c| < \delta$, then $|f(x) - L| < \epsilon$. In effect, the definition says that the number L is the limit if the value of y can be shown to be within any challenged closeness of L when x is chosen close enough to c. These relationships are represented in [53].

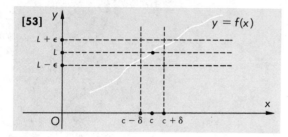

[53]

Some limit values are immediately obvious. $\lim_{x \to 1/2} 2x + 1 = 2$, since $2x$ is ever closer to 1 as x approaches $\frac{1}{2}$ from either side. It is not so obvious that $\lim_{x \to 1/2} \frac{4x^2 - 1}{2x - 1} = 2$ since $\frac{1}{2}$ is not in the domain. In a more complete treatment of limits in any standard textbook on calculus, it is shown that 2 satisfies the definition of limit in either case. When $x \neq \frac{1}{2}$, $\frac{4x^2 - 1}{2x - 1} = 2x + 1$ so the graphs of the two functions are identical except for a "hole" instead of the point $\left(\frac{1}{2}, 2\right)$ on the second graph.

Continuity.   A function, $y = f(x)$, is *continuous* at $x = c$ if $f(c)$ is defined and $\lim_{x \to c} f(x) = f(c)$. A function is continuous over an interval from $x = a$ to $x = b$ if it is continuous at all x in $a < x < b$.

DIFFERENTIAL CALCULUS

Basic Concepts

Limit Theorems.   If $\lim_{x \to c} f(x) = L_1$ and $\lim_{x \to c} g(x) = L_2$, then each of the following satisfies the definition of limit:

1. $\lim_{x \to c} k = k$, where k is any real constant.
2. $\lim_{x \to c} k \cdot f(x) = k \cdot \lim_{x \to c} f(x) = kL_1$
3. $\lim_{x \to c} [f(x) + g(x)] = L_1 + L_2$
4. $\lim_{x \to c} [f(x) - g(x)] = L_1 - L_2$
5. $\lim_{x \to c} [f(x) \cdot g(x)] = L_1 \cdot L_2$
6. $\lim_{x \to c} [f(x)/g(x)] = L_1/L_2$, when $L_2 \neq 0$.

The Derivative.   Given a function $y = f(x)$, the derivative

$$\frac{dy}{dx} = \lim_{\Delta x \to 0} \frac{\Delta y}{\Delta x} = \lim_{\Delta x \to 0} \frac{f(x + \Delta x) - f(x)}{\Delta x},$$

where Δx and Δy represent the change in x and y values between any two ordered pairs in f. (Other names used for the derivative are $f'(x)$ and y'.) The process of finding derivatives is called *differentiation*. In the event that f is a linear function, $\frac{\Delta y}{\Delta x}$ is a constant, say m, and the derivative is equal to m for all x. The reader should recognize this result as the slope of the nonvertical line $y = f(x)$. For other functions, the derivative is interpreted graphically as the slope of the tangent line at a point. In [54], P and Q are points on the graph of $y = f(x)$. Thus $\frac{\Delta y}{\Delta x}$ is the slope of line PQ. As Q is chosen closer to $P(\Delta x \to 0)$, the limiting position for line PQ is the tangent line at P. In more general terms, $\frac{dy}{dx}$ is defined as the *rate of change* in y with respect to x.

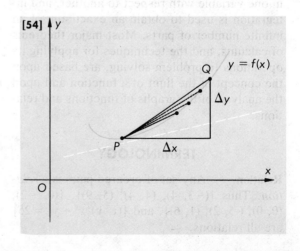

[54]

Derivative Formulas. Formulas for differentiating most types of functions have been derived through application of the limit theorems to the definition of derivative. In the frequently used formulas listed here, u and v are *functions* of x; k and n are real number constants.

1. If $y = k$, $\dfrac{dy}{dx} = 0$

2. If $y = kx^n$, $\dfrac{dy}{dx} = nkx^{n-1}$

3. If $y = u + v$, $\dfrac{dy}{dx} = \dfrac{du}{dx} + \dfrac{dv}{dx}$

4. If $y = u^n$, $\dfrac{dy}{dx} = nu^{n-1}\left(\dfrac{du}{dx}\right)$

5. If $y = uv$, $\dfrac{dy}{dx} = u\left(\dfrac{dv}{dx}\right) + v\left(\dfrac{du}{dx}\right)$

6. If $y = \dfrac{u}{v}$, $\dfrac{dy}{dx} = \dfrac{v(du/dx) - u(dv/dx)}{v^2}$

7. If $y = \sin u$, $\dfrac{dy}{dx} = \cos u\left(\dfrac{du}{dx}\right)$

8. If $y = \cos u$, $\dfrac{dy}{dx} = -\sin u\left(\dfrac{du}{dx}\right)$

As a brief illustration of using derivative formulas, consider $y = (x^2 - 1)(x^2 + x)^{1/2}$. The overall pattern is a product (**5**) with one factor a sum (**3, 2**) and the other a power of a function (**4, 3, 2**). That is, $y = uv^{1/2}$. Thus

$$\dfrac{dy}{dx} = u \cdot \dfrac{1}{2} \cdot v^{-1/2}\left(\dfrac{dv}{dx}\right) + v^{1/2}\left(\dfrac{du}{dx}\right)$$

$$= \dfrac{1}{2}(x^2 - 1)(x^2 + x)^{-1/2}(2x + 1) + 2x(x^2 + x)^{1/2}.$$

It is seldom necessary to perform extensive algebraic simplification, as the user most often wishes to compute the value of $\dfrac{dy}{dx}$ for a particular value of x.

Implicit Differentiation. To obtain $\dfrac{dy}{dx}$ in a relation which is not a function, consider that y implicitly represents one or more functions of x, and differentiate each side of the equation with respect to x. For example, if $x^2 + y^2 = 25$, then

$$2x + 2y\left(\dfrac{dy}{dx}\right) = 0 \text{ and } \dfrac{dy}{dx} = \dfrac{x}{y} \text{ or } \dfrac{x}{\pm(25 - x^2)^{1/2}}.$$

If the relation had been separated into the two functions $f(x) = (25 - x^2)^{1/2}$ and $g(x) =$ $-(25 - x^2)^{1/2}$, it is easily verified that at any point in f or g the value of $\dfrac{dy}{dx}$ obtained implicitly is equal to the value of the derivative of the appropriate explicit function. It is often cumbersome, if not impossible, to divide a relation into functions.

The Chain Rule. If x and y are given as functions of a third variable t, $\dfrac{dy}{dx}$ may be obtained from the rule

$$\dfrac{dy}{dx} = \dfrac{dy/dt}{dx/dt}$$

For example, if $x = 3\cos t$ and $y = 3\sin t$, then

$$\dfrac{dy}{dx} = \dfrac{3\cos t}{-3\sin t} = \dfrac{-\cos t}{\sin t} = -\dfrac{x}{y}.$$

Second Derivative. If $\dfrac{dy}{dx}$ is differentiated, the resulting expression is the *second derivative* of y with respect to x and is designated $\dfrac{d^2y}{dx^2}$ or $f''(x)$ or y''. Thus $\dfrac{d^2y}{dx^2}$ is the rate of change in $\dfrac{dy}{dx}$ with respect to x. It gives the rate at which the slope of the graph of $y = f(x)$ is changing at any point.

Differentials. For some purposes, it is convenient to separate the name $\dfrac{dy}{dx}$ into *differentials dy and dx*. This is particularly important for the notation employed in integral calculus. Given $y = f(x)$, then $\dfrac{dy}{dx} = f'(x)$ and the differentials are *defined* by $dy = f'(x)\,dx$.

Applications of Derivatives

Graphing. Where $y = f(x)$ is continuous, its graph is rising when $\dfrac{dy}{dx} > 0$, falling when $\dfrac{dy}{dx} < 0$, and at a *turning point* with horizontal tangent when $\dfrac{dy}{dx} = 0$. The slope is increasing when $\dfrac{d^2y}{dx^2} > 0$ and decreasing when $\dfrac{d^2y}{dx^2} < 0$. The graph has a *point of inflection* (between upward and downward concavity) when $\frac{d^2y}{dx^2} = 0$. A turning point is a *relative maximum* (highest point in an interval) if $\frac{dy}{dx} = 0$ and $\frac{d^2y}{dx^2} < 0$, and a *relative minimum* if $\frac{dy}{dx} = 0$ and $\frac{d^2y}{dx^2} > 0$. The graph of a function often can be accurately sketched by dividing the domain into intervals of rising and falling and increasing and decreasing slope, identifying relative maximum and minimum points and points of inflection, and marking other points with coordinates easily obtained from the equation.

Motion.   If the *position* of an object in linear motion is given as a function of time, $s = f(t)$, then $v = \frac{ds}{dt}$ is its velocity and $a = \frac{dv}{dt} = \frac{d^2s}{dt^2}$ is its acceleration. The motion is in a positive direction (upward, to the right, etc.), changing direction, or in a negative direction according to whether v is positive, zero, or negative. Similarly, v is increasing, changing, or decreasing according to the sign of a.

PROBLEM:
After t seconds, the altitude of a projectile fired vertically from a platform is given in meters as $h = 10 + 200t - 4.9t^2$. Write the velocity and acceleration functions, and find the maximum altitude reached, as well as the initial velocity and altitude.

SOLUTION:

$$v = \frac{ds}{dt} = 200 - 9.8t \text{ m/sec.}$$

$$a = \frac{dv}{dt} = -9.8 \text{ m/sec}^2$$

(the approximate effect of gravity).

If $v = 0, t = \frac{200}{9.8} \approx 20.4$ sec. The change from rising to falling is at $t \approx 20.4$ and $h \approx 2050$ meters. At $t = 0$, $s = 10$ and $v = 200$. Thus the initial velocity was 200 m/sec. and the platform height was 10 meters.

Related Rates.   To find the instantaneous rate of change of a variable with respect to time,

when the known conditions are in terms of other variables, write the equations relating variables and differentiate with respect to time. Then substitute in the conditions at the required instant.

PROBLEM:
Oil is pumped into a conical tank (vertex down) at the constant rate of two cubic meters per minute. The tank is eight meters high, and the radius of its circular top is six meters. At what rate is the oil level rising when its depth is two meters?

SOLUTION:
Let the filled portion have altitude $= h$ and radius $= r$. By similar triangles (see [55]) $\frac{h}{r} = \frac{4}{3}$. For all t,

$$\frac{dV}{dt} = 2, \qquad r = \frac{3h}{4}, \qquad V = \frac{\pi r^2 h}{3} \text{ or } \frac{3\pi h^3}{16}$$

Thus,

$$\frac{dV}{dt} = 9\pi h^2 \frac{dh/dt}{16} = 2$$

for all t. For $h = 2$,

$$\frac{dh}{dt} = \frac{32}{36\pi} = \frac{8}{9\pi} \text{ m/min.}$$

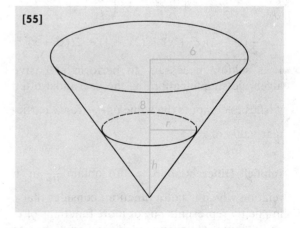

[55]

Maximum, Minimum.   If the domain of $y = f(x)$ is the set of all real numbers, the actual maximum (minimum) value of y occurs at a turning point or is undefined (infinite). When the domain is a finite interval, the actual maximum (minimum) occurs at a turning point or at an end of the interval. The process for solving maximum, minimum problems involves writing an expression for the quantity to be maximized (minimized) and using its derivative to locate relative extreme points as discussed earlier.

PROBLEM:

A manufacturer finds that his plant can produce up to 600 units of a certain product per week. For n units, the production cost $c = 10n + 40$ dollars and the expected sales income $I = n(30 - .02n)$ dollars. For what production level should profit be maximum?

SOLUTION:

Let p = profit,

$$p = I - c = 20n - .02n^2 - 40.$$

Then

$$\frac{dp}{dn} = 20 - .04n.$$

When $n = 500$,

$$\frac{dp}{dn} = 0 \quad \text{and} \quad \frac{d^2p}{dn^2} = -.04.$$

A relative maximum occurs at $n = 500$, and should be compared with the ends of the interval, $n = 0$ and $n = 600$.

$$p(0) = -40, \quad p(500) = 4960, \quad p(600) = 4760.$$

Therefore, production of 500 units per week yields maximum profit.

INTEGRAL CALCULUS

Indefinite Integration

Introduction. Indefinite integration, which might be more properly called antidifferentiation, involves solving the problem of determining a function whose derivative is known. For example, if $g'(x) = 2x$, it could be true that $g(x) = x^2$. However, it is also true that $g'(x) = 2x$ when $g(x) = x^2 + 117$, since the derivative of a constant is 0. Thus, the solution can only be given as $g(x) = x^2 + C$, where C is an unidentified constant.

Notation. Given $\frac{dy}{dx} = f(x)$ or $dy = f(x) \, dx$ (see *Differential Calculus, Differentials*), the *indefinite integral* denoted, $\int$, is defined by $y = \int dy = \int f(x) \, dx = F(x) + C$ where $F'(x) = f(x)$ and C is an unidentified *constant of integration*. Hence, above, $\int 2x \, dx = x^2 + C$. The expression to be integrated is called the *integrand*.

Formulas. Antidifferentiation yields the following basic integration formulas. Additional formulas are developed in later sections. Here, u and v are functions, while k and n are constants.

1. $\int du = u + C$
2. $\int k \, du = k \int du = ku + C$
3. $\int (du + dv) = \int du + \int dv = u + v + C$
4. $\int u^n \, du = \dfrac{u^{n+1}}{n+1} + C, \quad \text{for } n \neq -1$
5. $\int \sin u \, du = -\cos u + C$
6. $\int \cos u \, du = \sin u + C$

It is important to note that a *constant* factor may be written in the integrand or outside. To illustrate the use of integration formulas, consider the problem $\int x^2(x^3 - 5)^7 \, dx$. Let $u = x^3 - 5$. Then $du = 3x^2dx$ and a factor 3 is needed to form u^7du. This is accomplished by using a factor of 3 inside and $\frac{1}{3}$ outside (in effect, multiplying by 1). The form is then

$$\frac{1}{3}\int (x^3 - 5)^7(3x^2dx) \quad \text{or} \quad \frac{1}{3}\int u^7 \, du.$$

Thus the result is $\dfrac{u^8}{24} + C$ or $\dfrac{(x^3 - 5)^8}{24} + C$.

Application to Motion. An object in motion with position s given as a function of time has the velocity $v = \dfrac{ds}{dt}$ and acceleration $a = \dfrac{dv}{dt}$. It follows that $v = \int a \, dt$ and that $s = \int v \, dt$. For example, given $a = 9.8$ m/sec.^{2}, $v = \int 9.8 \, dt = 9.8t + C_1$ and $s = \int (9.8t + C_1) \, dt = 4.9t^2 + C_1t + C_2$. Identification of the constants of integration requires further information about v, s, and/or the motion.

Definite Integration

Definition. The *definite integral* is a *number* defined by

$$\int_a^b f(x)\,dx = F(b) - F(a)$$

when $\int f(x)\,dx = F(x) + C$ and a and b are in a continuous interval of f. For example,

$$\int_3^5 2x\,dx = x^2\Big]_3^5 = 25 - 9 = 16.$$

The Fundamental Theorem. Let f be a continuous function over an interval $a \leqslant x \leqslant b$. Partition the interval into n subintervals, each with length $\Delta x = \dfrac{b-a}{n}$, and let c_i be any value of x in the ith subinterval. Then

$$\lim_{n\to\infty} \sum_{i=1}^{n} f(c_i)\,\Delta x = \int_a^b f(x)\,dx.$$

This is the *Fundamental Theorem of Calculus* which, in effect, establishes that the definite integral provides the value of the sum of an infinite number of parts of a particular type.

Area Under a Curve. A graphic interpretation of $\int_a^b f(x)\,dx$ may be obtained by examining the problem of finding the area of a region bounded by the graph of $y = f(x)$, the vertical lines $x = a$ and $x = b$, and the x axis. An approximation can be made by constructing n rectangles with equal base length $\Delta x = \dfrac{b-a}{n}$. Any scheme may be used to choose a value $x = c_i$ in each base. (For example, the left endpoint of each subinterval could be used. See [56].) Then $f(c_i)$ is the height of the ith rectangle, and its area is $f(c_i)\,\Delta x$. All rectangles may be too small or too large, or some too small and some too large, but the sum of their areas is an approximation of the required area. It is obvious that if more and more rectangles were used, they would come closer and closer to "filling up the space" and that the limit as $n \to \infty$ is the required area. But each rectangular area is a product of the form specified in the Fundamental Theorem and the area $A_a^b = \int_a^b f(x)\,dx$. If the region is below the x axis, the value of $\int_a^b f(x)\,dx$ is nega-

tive and the actual amount of surface is the absolute value. If the graph crosses the x axis at one or more points in the interval, then $\int_a^b f(x)\,dx$ is an algebraic sum of positive and negative regions, and the actual area is computed by using subintervals and absolute values. For example, the area enclosed between $y = \sin x$ and the x axis from $x = 0$ to $x = 2\pi$ is

$$\int_0^\pi \sin x\,dx + \left|\int_\pi^{2\pi} \sin x\,dx\right|$$

$$= -\cos x\Big]_0^\pi + \left|-\cos x\Big]_\pi^{2\pi}\right|$$

$$= 1 - (-1) + |-1 - 1|$$

$$= 2 + 2 = 4 \text{ square units.}$$

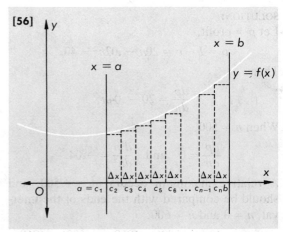

[56]

The Natural Logarithm. Note that $\int_a^b \dfrac{1}{x}\,dx$ cannot be evaluated by any previous formula since it is in the form $\int u^{-1}\,du$. By advanced methods, it is found that for $a, b > 0$ $\int_1^b \dfrac{1}{x}\,dx = \log_e b$ (also written $\ln b$) and $\int_a^b \dfrac{1}{x}\,dx = \ln b - \ln a$. That is, $\int u^{-1}\,du = \ln u + C$, $u > 0$. The number e is a transcendental number with approximate value 2.7183. A logarithm, base e, is called a *natural logarithm*.

Trigonometric Substitution. An integral can sometimes be evaluated by a change in variable. Consider the problem $\int (1 - x^2)^{-1/2}\,dx$. This cannot be converted to the form $\int u^n\,du$ since the factor needed is not a constant. Let $x = \sin\theta$, $dx = \cos\theta\,d\theta$. Then

$$\int (1-x^2)^{-1/2}\, dx = \int (1-\sin^2\theta)^{-1/2}\cos\theta\, d\theta$$
$$= \int (\cos^2\theta)^{-1/2}\cos\theta\, d\theta$$
$$= \int d\theta$$
$$= \theta + C$$
$$= \sin^{-1} x + C$$

' (see *Trigonometry, Inverse Functions*). By this and other advanced techniques, additional derivative and integration formulas may be derived.

Formulas. Related derivative and integration formulas not previously listed are shown below. A more complete list may be found in a standard textbook of calculus. Differential notation is used for convenience.

1. $d(\ln u) = \dfrac{1}{u}\, du$ $\quad \int \dfrac{1}{u}\, du = \ln u + C$

2. $d(e^u) = e^u\, du$ $\quad \int e^u\, du = e^u + C$

3. $d(\tan u) = \sec^2 u\, du$
   $\int \sec^2 u\, du = \tan u + C$

4. $d(\cot u) = -\csc^2 u\, du$
   $\int \csc^2 u\, du = -\cot u + C$

5. $d(\sec u) = \sec u \tan u\, du$
   $\int \sec u \tan u\, du = \sec u + C$

6. $d(\csc u) = -\csc u \cot u\, du$
   $\int \csc u \cot u\, du = -\csc u + C$

7. $d(\sin^{-1} u) = (1-u^2)^{-1/2}\, du$
   $\int (1-u^2)^{-1/2}\, du = \sin^{-1} u + C$
   or $-\cos^{-1} u + C$

8. $d(\cos^{-1} u) = -(1-u^2)^{-1/2}\, du$

9. $d(\tan^{-1} u) = \dfrac{du}{1+u^2}$
   $\int (1+u^2)^{-1}\, du = \tan^{-1} u + C$
   or $-\cot^{-1} u + C$

10. $d(\cot^{-1} u) = -\dfrac{du}{1+u^2}$

Integration by Parts. Since $d(uv) = u\, dv + v\, du$, $u\, dv = d(uv) - v\, du$. Integrating on both sides gives $\int u\, dv = uv - \int v\, du$. It is often possible to integrate a product by use of this result as a formula. For example, consider the problem $\int xe^{2x}\, dx$. Let $u = x$, $dv = e^{2x}\, dx$. Then

$$du = dx,$$
$$v = \int e^{2x}\, dx$$
$$= \frac{1}{2}\int e^{2x}(2\, dx)$$
$$= \frac{1}{2} e^{2x}.$$

Thus

$$\int xe^{2x}\, dx = \frac{1}{2} xe^{2x} - \int \frac{1}{2} e^{2x}\, dx$$
$$= \frac{1}{2} e^{2x} - \frac{1}{4} e^{2x} + C.$$

Applications

Volume. Suppose that the region pictured in [57] is rotated about the x axis to form a solid. Its volume may be found by the *slice method*. Divide the interval from a to b into n subintervals, form rectangles, and choose some $x = c_i$ in each subinterval, as was done in the discussion of area. Rotating the ith rectangle about the x axis forms a cylinder with radius $= f(c_i)$ and length (thickness) $= \Delta x$. Its volume is $\pi[f(c_i)]^2\, \Delta x$ and this approximates the volume of a slice of the solid. Then

$$\lim_{n\to\infty} \sum_{i=1}^{n} \pi[f(c_i)]^2\, \Delta x = V = \int_a^b \pi y^2\, dx.$$

[57]

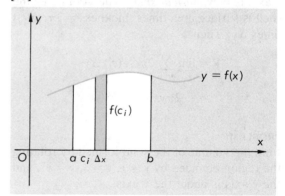

PROBLEM:
Find the volume of the solid formed by rotating the region bounded by $x = 1$, $x = 3$, $y = x^2$, and the x axis about the x axis.

SOLUTION:

$$V = \int_1^3 \pi y^2 \, dx$$

$$= \int_1^3 \pi x^4 \, dx$$

$$= \frac{\pi}{5} x^5 \bigg]_1^3$$

$$= \frac{\pi}{5}(243 - 1)$$

$$= \frac{242\pi}{5} \text{ cubic units.}$$

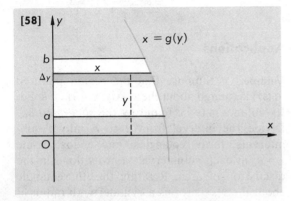

[58]

The slice method is not always appropriate. Suppose a solid is formed by rotating the region bounded by $y = a$, $y = b$, $x = g(y)$, and the y axis about the x axis. (See [58].) Divide the y interval into subintervals and form rectangles horizontally with length $= g(c_i)$ and thickness $= \Delta y$. The rotation of the ith rectangle about the x axis is a *cylindrical shell*. The volume of the shell is surface area times thickness $= 2\pi c_i g(c_i)$ times Δy. Then

$$V = \lim_{n \to \infty} \sum_{i=1}^{n} 2\pi c_i g(c_i) \, \Delta y$$

$$= \int_a^b 2\pi y x \, dy.$$

PROBLEM:

Find the volume of the solid formed by rotating the region bounded by $y = 1$, $y = 3$, $x = y^2$, and the y axis is about the x axis.

SOLUTION:

$$V = \int_1^3 2\pi y x \, dy$$

$$= \int_1^3 2\pi y^3 \, dy$$

$$= \frac{1}{2} \pi y^4 \bigg]_1^3$$

$$= \frac{1}{2} \pi(81 - 1)$$

$$= 40\pi \text{ cubic units.}$$

Length of Curve. If $P(a, b)$ and $Q(c, d)$ are points on the graph of a continuous function $y = f(x)$, the distance *along the graph* from P to Q is $\int_a^c \big(1 + [f'(x)]^2\big)^{1/2} \, dx$.

PROBLEM:

Find the length of $y = \frac{1}{3}(4x^2 + 1)^{3/2}$ from $x = 1$ to $x = 3$.

SOLUTION:

$$f'(x) = 4x(4x^2 + 1)^{1/2}$$

$$1 + [f'(x)]^2 = 64x^4 + 16x^2 + 1$$

$$= (8x^2 + 1)^2.$$

$$L = \int_1^3 8x^2 + 1 \, dx$$

$$= \frac{8x^3}{3} + x \bigg]_1^3$$

$$= 75 - \frac{11}{3}$$

$$= \frac{214}{3} \text{ units.}$$

Other Applications. Most other applications of integral calculus are at a level beyond the scope of this book, or involve the need for technical knowledge of another subject. For example, in science, integration is applied to problems involving center of gravity, work, voltage drop, battery power leakage, etc. The reader may find such applications in textbooks on the subject matter of interest.

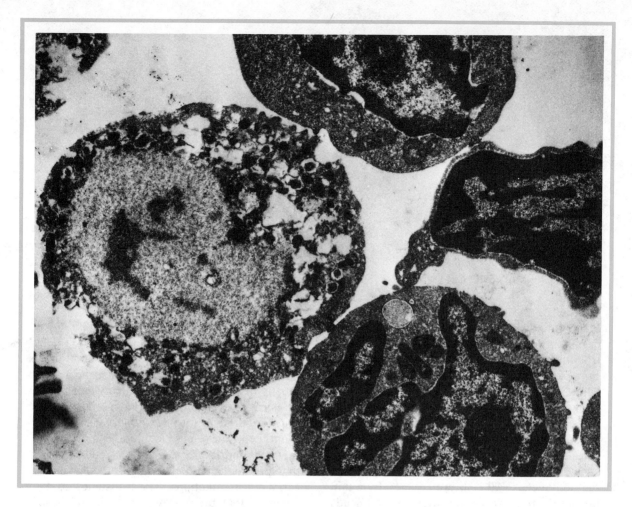

BIOLOGY

In recent years there has been a dramatic increase in knowledge of how organisms grow, multiply, and die. Through development of the electron microscope, improved x-ray machines, and a great battery of diagnostic and therapeutic machines, medical and biological scientists have probed deeply into the smallest units of life. They have learned much about the genetic code that determines our physical make-up and health, and progress has been so great that biological engineering is fast becoming the reality predicted by science fiction writers.

You may anticipate playing an active role in the biological sciences or you may merely be curious about it. Whatever your interest, the following pages offer information on the structure and variety of living things to help you understand this keystone science.

The Structure of Life

THE CELL

The cell is the basic unit of all living things. Plants and animals may consist of a single cell or of many cells; man is made up of more than a trillion cells. Almost all cells are microscopic. For example, one square inch of human skin contains over a million cells.

The cell is a living thing that is always active. Cells divide to replace worn-out tissue; they constantly carry out chemical reactions; and certain specialized cells produce substances, such as hormones, enzymes, and proteins, that the body needs. All cells are covered by a thin membrane that allows only what the cell needs to pass through. This membrane encloses the cytoplasm, which itself contains many structures. All cells contain chromosomal material (nuclear plasm), and in most cells this material is enclosed in a nucleus.

The Nucleus. The structure that controls all activity in the cell is the nucleus. It is usually located near the center of the cell. A nuclear membrane surrounds the nucleus and keeps it separate from the cytoplasm. Two main structures lie inside the membrane: chromatin and nucleoli.

Chromatin is made up of strands of DNA (deoxyribonucleic acid) and proteins. DNA is the substance that controls the hereditary characteristics of all living things. It also directs the production of proteins, which make up almost all of the cell. The nucleoli are small round bodies that contain RNA (ribonucleic acid). RNA also plays a role in heredity and, with DNA, helps in protein production.

Cytoplasm. All cell material outside the nucleus and enclosed by the cell membrane is called the cytoplasm. The cytoplasm is made up mostly of water and contains many small structures called organelles. The main organelles are mitochondria, lysosomes, endoplasmic reticulum, centrioles, and Golgi bodies.

Mitochondria are sausage-shaped structures that provide all the energy the cell needs to carry out its functions. The lysosomes contain enzymes that break down the cell and its organelles; it is thought that the lysosome may dissolve the cell when the cell dies. Endoplasmic reticulum looks like strands or canals winding their way through the cytoplasm. There are many tiny round bodies lining the walls of the endoplasmic reticulum. These structures, called ribosomes, manufacture the protein needed by the cell. The endoplasmic reticulum connects with the cell nucleus and with the cell membrane. The two centrioles, which look like bundles of rods, are located near the nucleus. The centrioles play a role in cell division.

The cell membrane, which we have mentioned before, holds the cell together. Most cell membranes are made up of four layers. Two layers are made of a fatty substance and are layered between two layers of protein. Only the materials needed by the cell can enter through the membrane. The Golgi bodies look like

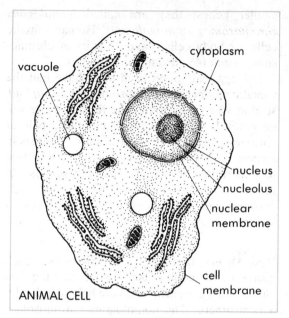

An animal cell is composed essentially of a nucleus, the surrounding cytoplasm, and a cell membrane. The nucleus controls the life of the cell.

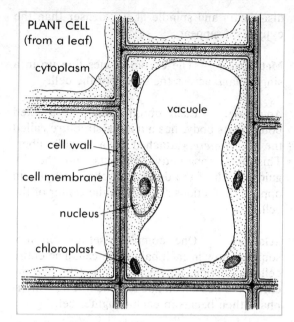

A plant cell, like an animal cell, is composed essentially of a nucleus, cytoplasm, and membrane. It has chloroplasts containing chlorophyll.

stacks of thin plates. Scientists are not sure what their function is, but it is thought they may play a part in cell secretion.

Plant Cells.   Plant cells are much like animal cells except that they have a cell wall and chloroplasts. The cell wall surrounds the cell membrane and is made up of cellulose that is made by the cell. It is the cellulose in plants that makes their stems and branches rigid. The chloroplasts look like small green bundles. They contain chlorophyll, with which the plant cell carries out photosynthesis.

CELL DIVISION

All cells are derived from other cells by a process called cell division. There are three types of cell division: amitosis, mitosis, and meiosis. Amitosis, or fission, occurs in primitive plants like bacteria and in certain animal cells. In this method of division, a cell seems to pinch in half to form two new cells. Mitosis is the process by which animal and plant embryos grow from fertilized eggs, and by which worn-out cells of plants and animals are replaced. Meiosis is a

special process involving two nuclear divisions that results in half the original number of chromosomes. It is sometimes referred to as "reduction division." Meiosis occurs in the formation of germ cells, such as ova and sperm.

Mitosis

Chromosomes are accurately reproduced and transmitted in a precise process that ensures that each new cell formed will receive one of each chromosome. The number of chromosomes characteristic of each species remains constant. That is, every normal somatic cell in a human being has 46 chromosomes; in the fruit fly, 8; in the garden pea, 14.

Although mitosis is a continuous process, it is described in terms of five phases.

Interphase.   Chromosomes are usually not individually distinguishable; they are stretched out in long, diffuse threads. In this phase, each chromosome copies itself.

Prophase.   The chromosomes coil up and become short and thick. The nuclear membrane disappears and spindle fibers, denser than the cytoplasm, appear.

Metaphase.   The chromosomes line up in a single plane across the center of the cell.

Anaphase.   Each chromosome, at a fixed point on its body, has a minute structure called the *centromere,* attached to a spindle fiber. This fiber apparently contracts and thereby guides each of the duplicated chromosomes in opposite directions away from the center of the cell.

Telophase.   One complete set of chromosomes is now in each half of the cell. The entire cell then divides between the two sets, and the chromosomes uncoil and lengthen. A new interphase then begins in each daughter cell.

Meiosis

The chromosomes in each cell occur in pairs, one from the mother and one from the father. Each member of the chromosomal pair has similar genes; they are called *homologous chromosomes,* or *homologues.* Human somatic cells, or body cells, have 23 pairs of chromosomes each (46 chromosomes in all).

The egg and sperm each must have half the somatic number of chromosomes, or be *haploid,* so that when they unite, the fertilized egg will be *diploid,* that is, have a complete pair of chromosomes. The number of chromosomes in somatic cells remains constant from generation to generation of the species; the process of meiosis ensures that one member of each chromosome pair is in each germ cell. Meiosis has two stages.

First Meiotic Division.   In this phase, each chromosome copies itself once, creating two *chromatids;* the chromatids are held together by a centromere. The homologous chromosomes move toward each other and pair tightly, so that similar genes, or *alleles,* lie alongside each other. This makes a bundle of four chromatids and two centromeres. During this time the partner, or matching, strands twist around each other, break, and then reunite. As a result,

Mitosis, the division of a nucleus, is part of the process by which all living things grow or replace worn-out cells. In lower forms of life, mitosis reproduces new living forms. Meiosis, a specialized kind of nuclear division, is the beginning of the process by which higher forms of life reproduce themselves.

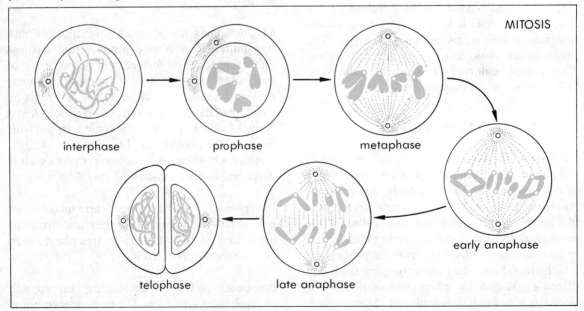

MITOSIS

interphase   prophase   metaphase   early anaphase   late anaphase   telophase

chromosomes consist of parts from both paternal and maternal chromosomes. The centromere of each of the homologous chromosomes, attached to the spindle fiber and to the chromosome, is pulled to an opposite pole of the cell. The cell divides. Each new cell now has the haploid chromosome number (in humans, 23), with either a maternally or paternally derived member of each chromosomal pair. Whether the chromosome comes from the mother or the father depends on chance and on the random attachment of each centromere to the spindle fibers.

Second Meiotic Division.   In this phase, the centromeres divide so that each chromatid separates from its duplicate. Another division follows that is much like ordinary mitosis—two duplicate cells are formed.

Because of the two meiotic divisions, four cells are formed from the original cell; each has a haploid number of chromosomes, one of each homologous pair.

GENETICS

The study of the inheritance of biological characteristics in living things—characteristics that are passed from generation to the next—is called genetics. What is inherited is a code message in the genetic material (*genes*) of egg and sperm. The code directs embryonic development and organization of cells into tissues and organs; in addition, it directs the function of each tissue and organ. This development is also influenced by the external and internal environment. Thus an organism is the product of interaction between genetic material and environment.

Mendelian Genetics

Gregor Johann Mendel (1822–1884), an Austrian monk, analyzed the basic laws of inheritance in 1866. The results were lost until 1900, when investigators in Holland, Germany, and Austria each rediscovered the Mendelian concept.

Mendel had proved hereditary traits are transmitted by pairs of distinct units, later called

Drosophila, a tiny fruit fly, is used in genetic experiments. Its life cycle is about a week and its mutations and hereditary changes are easy to see.

genes, which reshuffle, segregate, and redistribute, rather than blend, in the offspring.

Mendel used garden peas in his experiments because they hybridize easily. When a purebred tall plant was crossed with a purebred short plant, all hybrid offspring were tall, no matter which type was the mother and which the father. The hybrids self-fertilized. Mendel counted the offspring and found 787 tall and 277 short plants, a ratio of about 3 to 1. When the short plants self-fertilized, they produced only short offspring, but when the tall plants self-fertilized, there were two types of offspring: one-third had only tall offspring, and two-thirds produced both tall and short in a ratio of 3 to 1. Mendel crossed six other characters: round and wrinkled peas, colored and uncolored flowers, and yellow and green peas. He had approximately the same results.

Mendel then formulated the *law of segregation*. Today this principle states that hereditary traits (such as tallness or shortness of peas) are transmitted by *zygotes* (fertilized eggs). One member of each pair of traits comes from the female parent; the other, from the male. In the

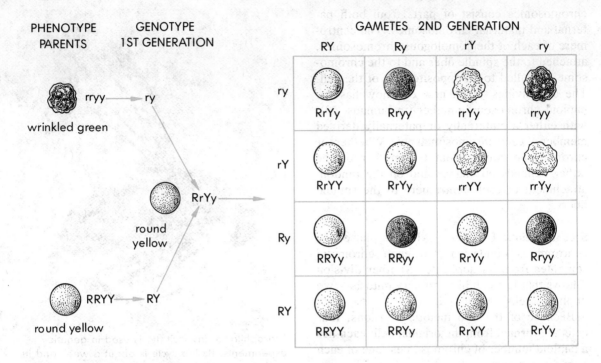

| | | GAMETES 2ND GENERATION | | |

PHENOTYPE PARENTS | GENOTYPE 1ST GENERATION

GAMETES 2ND GENERATION

	RY	Ry	rY	ry
ry	RrYy	Rryy	rrYy	rryy
rY	RrYY	RrYy	rrYY	rrYy
Ry	RRYy	RRyy	RrYy	Rryy
RY	RRYY	RRYy	RrYY	RrYy

The Mendelian Square represents diagrammatically the various combinations that occur in two generations of hybrid peas. A similar pattern occurs in the sexual reproduction of all plants and animals. Sometimes the inherited traits, however, are intermediate, instead of purely dominant or recessive.

mature plant, these paired genes segregate during the formation of *gametes* (sperm and egg cells) so that just one of the pair is transmitted by a particular gamete. The gamete has only one gene from each pair and is called haploid. When the male and female gametes unite to form the zygote, it is called double or diploid.

Mendel's studies showed the *principle of dominance.* For instance, in garden peas the trait of tallness is dominant over shortness; when there is a gene for tallness and one for shortness, all peas are tall. The opposite, unexpressed factor is *recessive.*

To a geneticist, an individual with unlike paired genes is represented as *Tt. T* represents the dominant gene for tallness; *t*, the recessive gene for shortness. Such an individual is called a *heterozygote.* If both genes are alike (*tt* or *TT*) the individual is a *homozygote.*

The genetic makeup is called the *genotype;* the character determined by this genotype and expressed in the individual is called the *pheno-type.* If the genotype is *TT,* for instance, the phenotype is tallness, but a different genotype —*Tt*—can also give the phenotype tallness. The alternative forms of a gene are called *alleles.*

Mendel concluded that dominant and recessive genes do not affect each other; gametes are haploid and have only one of a pair of genes; each type of gamete is produced in equal numbers by a hybrid parent; and combination between gametes depends on chance—the frequency of each class of offspring depends on the frequency of the gametes produced by each parent.

Mendel next determined how two or more pairs of genes would behave in crosses. He crossed plants with round yellow seeds with those with wrinkled green seeds. He knew a cross between round (*R*) and wrinkled (*r*) seeds produced round seeds in the F_1, or first, generation and three round to one wrinkled seed in the F_2, or second generation, plants. He knew crossing yellow (*Y*) with green (*y*) produced all yellow in the F₁ and three yellow to one green seed in the F₂ generation. This showed the dominance of roundness and yellowness over their respective contrasting alleles. Thus, when Mendel crossed round yellow with wrinkled green, the first generation (F₁) produced all round yellow seeds.

In the second generation (F₂), a more complicated assortment of differing seed types resulted:

Type	Proportion
Round yellow	9/16
Round green	3/16
Wrinkled yellow	3/16
Wrinkled green	1/16

Two combinations, round green and wrinkled yellow, not present in either the parents or the first generation, have appeared. This result can be explained by Mendel's *law of independent assortment,* which states that members of one pair of genes segregate independently of other pairs.

Mendel also tested his F₂ (second generation) plants to determine whether all of a single phenotype class, such as round yellow, were alike in genotype. According to his hypothesis, there should be four different genotypes in this group: *RR, YY; RR, Yy; Rr, YY;* and *Rr, Yy.* When F₂ plants self-fertilized, he found four classes of round yellow seeded plants; the ratios fitted expectations. The breeding behavior of the F₂ round green, wrinkled yellow, and wrinkled green seeded plants also fitted the hypothesis that each pair of genes segregates independently from other pairs of genes and is transmitted independently to the next generation.

Mendel's inheritance rules were later found to apply in other plants and in animals. More information explained the seeming exceptions.

In all characteristics studied by Mendel, the heterozygote was phenotypically identical with the homozygote dominant. In some cases studied later, however, the heterozygote was intermediate. This is true in the color of the flower known as the "four o'clock." If a red parent is crossed with a white, all F₁ hybrids are intermediate in color, while one-quarter of the F₂ offspring are red, one-quarter white, and one-half intermediate. In some cases, both

Genetic inheritance. Two *recessive* b genes occurring together: offspring have blue eyes; one *dominant* B gene: brown eyes; two *recessive* y genes: blond hair; one dominant Y gene: dark hair. Other genes may alter eye color inheritance, so parents of one eye color may have children of another eye color.

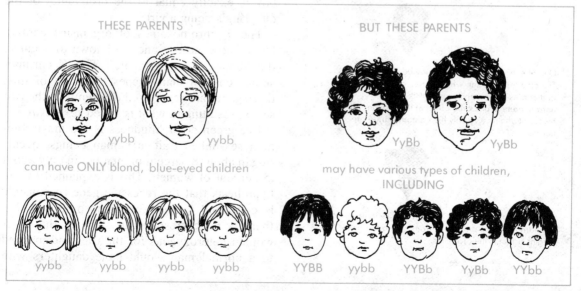

alleles are equally "dominant," for example, those that determine the *MN* factors in blood. If one parent is *M* and the other *N*, all children will be *MN*. If both parents are *M*, or both *N*, all children will be *MM* or *NN*, respectively. If both parents are *MN*, one-quarter of the children are *M*, one-quarter *N*, and one-half *MN*.

Sex-Linkage

Chromosomes occur in pairs, one from the mother, one from the father. All but one pair are identical in both sexes. In one sex (the male in most species) there is one pair of unidentical chromosomes—*X* and *Y*. In the human male, there are 22 pairs of identical (nonsex) chromosomes called *autosomes*, and 1 unmatched pair—*X* and *Y*. The female has 22 pairs of autosomes and 1 pair of *X* chromosomes. The *X* and *Y* chromosomes are the *sex chromosomes*. If an egg is fertilized by a sperm bearing an *X* chromosome, it becomes female (*XX*). If it is fertilized by a sperm carrying a *Y* chromosome, it becomes male (*XY*). Thus, sex determination occurs at the moment of fertilization. Since segregation of the sex chromosomes takes place randomly during meiosis exactly as does segregation of the other chromosomes, the chance is even that any sperm will contain a *Y* chromosome. Since all eggs contain one *X* chromosome, the probability of the offspring's being a boy is exactly equal to the probability of the offspring's being a girl.

The *Y* chromosomes of organisms contain few or no genes. (None are known to occur in the human *Y* chromosome.) The *X* chromosomes contain many genes. Because of this, these genes are segregated differently in the two sexes, resulting in what is called *sex-linkage*.

Red-green color blindness is the most common sex-linked trait in human beings, occurring in about 8 percent of men but in only about .5 percent of women. This is explained by the hypothesis that the recessive gene responsible is contained in the *X* chromosome and that there is no corresponding allele in the *Y*. A woman heterozygous for the trait and married to a normal man would have daughters with

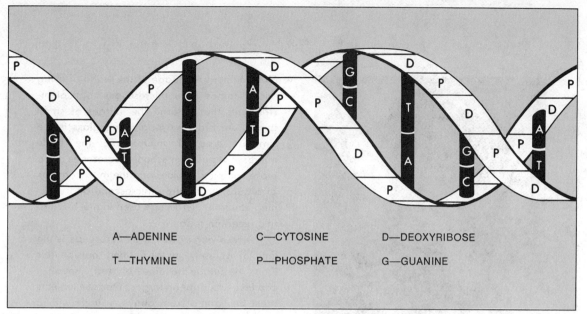

The double helix model represents the simple molecules that are linked together in various repeating combinations—sugar-phosphate backbones, or ribbons, twist about the four base pairs—to form the giant DNA molecule. You can see how the double helix model resembles a twisted ladder.

normal vision but half of her sons would probably be color-blind. The children of a homozygous (for normal vision) woman married to a color-blind man would all be normal, but half the daughers would probably be heterozygous and would transmit the trait to half their sons.

CHEMICAL BASIS OF GENETICS

Modern study of genetics has focused on a unique material called DNA, or *deoxyribonucleic acid,* which is found only in the chromosomes of the cell. The amount of DNA is remarkably constant from cell to cell within an organism and within a single species. Only the egg cells and sperm cells contain a different amount: half the normal amount of DNA (and half the number of chromosomes) found in other body cells.

Proteins and ribonucleic acid (RNA), which are also found in the chromosomes, vary considerably in the amounts found in different tissues within a species. However, they are associated with DNA in carrying and transferring genetic information.

The Watson-Crick Model

DNA is a polymer with a high molecular weight—a giant molecule formed from a few simple molecules linked repeatedly by chemical bonds. The repeating units that form the molecule are *nucleotides,* each built from similar components: a phosphate group; a 5-carbon sugar, deoxyribose; and a nitrogenous base. The base may be any one of four—either the *purines* adenine (A) or guanine (G) or the *pyrimidines* cytosine (C) and thymine (T). The nucleotides are connected by a bond between the phosphate group of one and the adjacent sugar (deoxyribose) of the next.

Various studies, including X-ray diffraction analyses by Maurice Wilkins, led James Watson and F. H. C. Crick to propose in 1953 the double helix structure of the DNA molecule. A double helix is something like a twisted ladder or zipper; the sides are made of the linked sugar-

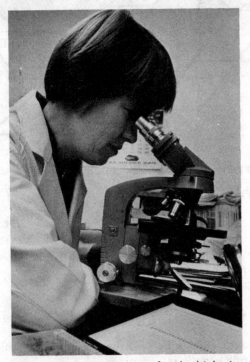

Microscopes are important for the biologist, chemist, and medical researcher. About 1590 the Dutch optician Janseen developed the compound microscope, which uses two lenses. Except for important technological improvements in making lenses, microscopes did not change much until invention of the electron microscope in 1937. While ordinary microscopes can magnify by as much as 2500 times, electron microscopes magnify by as much as 600,000 times.

Much of our knowledge of the world of living things comes from microscopes, optical instruments that enlarge the images of small things. An ordinary magnifying glass is the simplest type of microscope; the table microscopes used in school laboratories are a more complex version; and the most complex of all are the electron microscope and scanning electron microscope used in much scientific research today.

The resolving power of a *microscope* is the limit of its useful magnification; outside this limit, the image becomes blurred, though it continues to appear larger. Opaque objects must be lighted from above, usually with a light source built into the microscope tube and focused through the objective lens system.

The *electron microscope* uses electrons to form an image. This microscope is an evacuated tube with an electron gun at one end; the gun accelerates a beam of freed electrons which is directed by electromagnetic and electrostatic fields (acting as lenses) onto the specimen. The electrons interact with the atoms of the specimen and enter other lenses, finally hitting a screen or photographic emulsion where they form an image. Magnifications up to 600,000 × and resolution down to a few Ångstroms are possible with the electron microscope. It is widely used in hospitals and research laboratories and in such varied fields as polymer chemistry and solid state physics.

The *scanning electron microscope* moves a beam of electrons over the surface of the subject, producing an effect something like that of a television camera. The magnification range is about 1,400 to 200,000 ×. Pictures taken with the scanning microscope have a life-like quality because the microscope has a large depth of focus.

phosphate backbone, and the rungs are the bases (purines or pyrimidines). The sequence of bases in one strand determines the base sequence in the complementary strand—A matches with T, C matches with G. These bases are held together by weak hydrogen bonds, making the "ladder" firm but still able to separate during mitosis.

With this model (for which Watson, Crick, and Wilkins won the Nobel Prize in 1962), it is possible to explain how genetic information is duplicated and transmitted. When the strands of the double helix "unzip," or separate, each strand becomes a mold, or template, that governs the replication of its new complementary stand. The result is two DNA molecules, each identical with the original because each new strand has been formed in accordance with a specified pattern.

The Genetic Code

DNA, according to this model, carries the genetic information in a kind of code, which depends on the varying sequence of the four bases in relation to each other—in effect, a four-letter alphabet. Since there are ten base pairs in each complete turn of the double helix (which is only a small part of the entire large molecule), the theoretical number of possible combinations in a turn is 4^{10} or 1,048,576. Thus the storage potential for different items of genetic information is vast, even with only four bases to work with.

The information carried by DNA must be translated into the formation of proteins, for DNA itself is inactive in the metabolic processes of the cell. So the DNA "message" carrying the coded instructions is given to the RNA within the nucleus. Messenger-RNA then transmits the information to the place in the cytoplasm where proteins are synthesized. These protein-producing areas, in the ribosomes, are another form of RNA; there a model, or template, is formed according to the coded instructions.

Proteins themselves are long chains of amino acids hooked together by peptide bonds in which the 20-odd basic amino acids are repeated

several times and arranged in different orders. Even the smallest protein is a chain of 124 amino acids. The protein chains (polypeptides) form a helix that folds into a definite shape, determined by the sequence of amino acids in the chain.

For proteins to be synthesized on the RNA model in the ribosome, another kind of RNA (transfer-RNA or S-RNA) must pick up the right amino acid and fit it to the right place in the template. When the amino acid sequence has been established, peptide bonds are formed, and the new protein "unzips" from the template to carry out its functions in the cell.

RNA Structure

Not as much is known of the structure of RNA as of that of DNA, though RNA plays a vital role in carrying the information from the DNA and in translating the message into protein structure. Like DNA, RNA is a long-chain giant molecule (a polymer); its components are similar except that the sugar in RNA is ribose (not deoxyribose) and one of the pyrimidine bases that form the nucleotides is uracil (U) instead of thymine.

Studies of RNA have concluded that its code is read in groups of three bases (triplets or trinucleotides), with each triplet (say, GUU or AUC) coding the formation of a given amino acid. Experiments have also been done to discover which triplet combinations govern the formation of which amino acids; it has also been found that several different triplets may code the same amino acid.

Evidence also suggests that the genetic code is universal—more or less the same code governs genetic information and protein building in all animal species. Interest is building in the possibility of *cloning,* an asexual reproduction achieved by transplanting the nucleus of a donor's cell into a fertile egg cell, whose nucleus has been removed. The cloned offspring develops as a genetically identical copy of the individual supplying the donor cell. Cloning has been accomplished in frogs, but not in mammals as yet.

Variety of Living Things

About four million kinds of plants and animals live on the earth today. Only about forty percent of these have been described and catalogued; very few of even the known species bear common names. We could just file these names aphabetically and forget them, but people are orderly, inquisitive creatures. In order to satisfy our curiosity, the plants and animals bearing the names must be arranged according to some system. After much trial and error, the system of classification devised by the great Swedish naturalist Linnaeus in the 1700s was finally adopted.

To be most useful, the system must avoid the confusion of using popular names, which of course differ from one language to another and from one area to another even when the language is the same. The system needs to be based on the most stable characteristics, such as basic anatomy and structure. It must organize the large numbers of species into readily recognized groups and then divide each group into smaller units until a single unit, the species, is reached. Fortunately, there are two languages, Latin and Greek, which are not widely or commonly spoken today but which contain many useful words that are not easily confused with "common tongue" names. These two languages are the source for most of the plant and animal names in the Linnaean system. The Linnaean system has proven successful; scientists can communicate with each other all over the world about the animal *Equus caballus* without having to translate the name into any other language

(*Equus caballus* is also known, by its English common name, as the horse).

The largest divisions established by Linnaeus are the *Kingdoms;* there are the plant, or vegetable, kingdom and the animal kingdom. Some scientists believe we should recognize a sort of in-between kingdom, the Protists, and others believe we should create another kingdom for microscopic life that does not depend on oxygen. Though we can recognize most *visible* forms of life as either plant or animal, we might have difficulty sorting our plant or animal into the next categories. They are the *Phyla* (botanists sometimes use "Division" in place of, or above, Phylum); the *Classes,* with each Class subdivided into *Orders;* the Orders, with each order divided into *Families;* and finally, the Families, divided into *Genera* and *Species.* By cataloguing the different kinds of plants and animals in this taxonomic (systematic classification) manner, we place like with like; and we are able to study the biotic (living) world in an easier, more orderly manner. Thus, the classification for Man would be:

Kingdom:	Animal
Phylum:	Chordata
Class:	Mammalia
Order:	Primata
Family:	Hominidae
Genus:	*Homo*
Species:	*sapiens*

The species name is *sapiens.* Because there may be another *sapiens* in another genus, the names of the genus and species are always given together: *Homo sapiens*. There is no other such combination in zoological nomenclature. (Words in a language different from that of the main text are printed in a different type, usually italic; *Homo sapiens* is the Latin for "wise man.")

There is no single book cataloguing all the species of plants and animals known to man. There are books describing all the known birds of the world, and others describe all the known mammals. Still other books cover molluscs, reptiles, amphibians, etc.; but these are never completely up-to-date because new species are constantly being discovered and new knowledge changes their relationships to each other. Even a tiny insect requires many words to describe it, so we are not surprised to learn that the more than 800,000 known insects can be catalogued most easily only by continent or by family. The following classification list, covering the major,

or prominent, groups, gives us a glimpse of the great variety of life on earth.

We start with the viruses which, because they are incapable of independent life, can increase only within the cells of a host. Some biologists do not consider viruses true life, but viruses do show some true biologic activities and are described without being placed either in the plant or animal kingdoms.

VIRUSES

Viruses are the smallest of the microorganisms and are not as complex in structure as a cell. Viruses are said to be parasitic. The presence of a virus in a host usually causes changes recognizable as a disease, although animal viruses have been found that cause no recognizable symptoms in the host.

DISEASES CAUSED BY VIRUSES

Animal and human diseases caused by viruses include influenza, measles, mumps, distemper, warts, and the common cold. These diseases are transmitted in several ways—by carriers such as the mosquito that carries yellow fever, by direct contact, or by contact with infected material. There is also evidence that some types of human cancer may be caused by viruses. Viruses can be cultivated in chicken embryos and laboratory tissue cultures, making possible new ways of immunization against viral diseases.

Plants may also be infected with viral diseases; among these plant diseases are the mosaics, including tobacco mosaic, studies of which have yielded much information about the behavior of viruses.

The electron microscope makes it possible to examine viruses closely, as shown in the photograph of the virus that causes leukemia in rats. Because scientists see a connection between viruses and cancer, such studies are particularly promising.

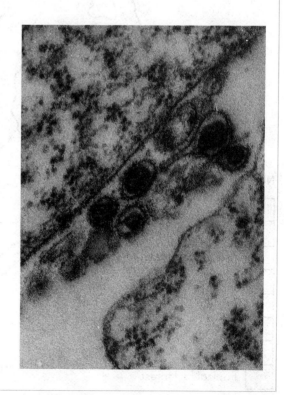

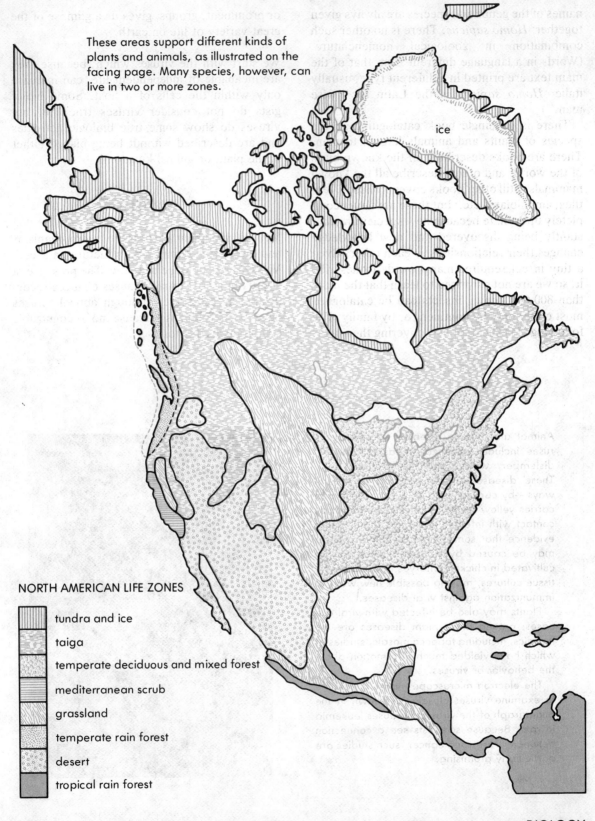

These areas support different kinds of plants and animals, as illustrated on the facing page. Many species, however, can live in two or more zones.

ice

NORTH AMERICAN LIFE ZONES

	tundra and ice
	taiga
	temperate deciduous and mixed forest
	mediterranean scrub
	grassland
	temperate rain forest
	desert
	tropical rain forest

lichen
polar bear
snow goose
reindeer
arctic poppy
crowberry

jack pine
white spruce
birch
willow ptarmigan
ermine

white-tailed deer
red-tailed hawk
meadow mouse
trillium
hemlock
downy woodpecker

California laurel
ringtail
foxtail barley
prairie dog
bobolink
buffalo grass

gila monster
coati
yucca
roadrunner
cactus

toucan
orchid
banana
liana
tapir
jaguar

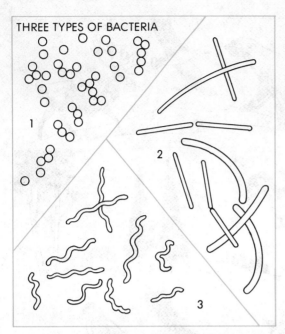

THREE TYPES OF BACTERIA

1

2

3

Bacteria—single-celled plants either (1) round, (2) rod-shaped, or (3) spiral—are found in nearly all natural environments, including ocean depths, hot springs, arctic ice, the stratosphere, and plants and animals.

Blue-green mold Penicillium. From it is extracted penicillin, the first successful antibiotic, discovered in 1928 by Alexander Fleming. Note the spores growing at the tips of the filaments.

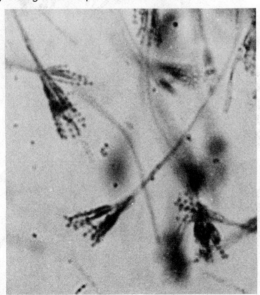

PLANT KINGDOM

Phylum Schizomycetes: Bacteria

Bacteria are single-celled plants, without the typical nucleus of higher plants and animals. They multiply by cell division. There are an estimated 150,000 species, many of which cause diseases or disorders in humans, such as tuberculosis, cholera, typhoid fever, and tetanus. They are found in three basic shapes: round, rod-shaped, and spiral; this characteristic aids in their classification.

Phylum Myxophyta: Blue-green Algae

By structure and chemical composition, these algae are more closely related to bacteria than to algae. Like bacteria they have no true nucleus. There are an estimated 45,000 species, which live in open waters and the soil.

Phylum Chlorophyta: Green Algae
Phylum Chrysophyta: Yellow-green and
  Golden-brown Algae
Phylum Phaeophyta: Brown Algae
Phylum Rhodophyta: Red Algae

The above four phyla are often referred to as the true algae. They are the simplest of the plants, producing their own food by means of various pigments. All of them also contain the chlorophylls found in higher plants. There are perhaps 50,000 species throughout the world, including the predominately one-celled diatoms of open waters. The diatoms of the oceans produce great amounts of the oxygen found in our atmosphere. The large prominent sea weeds, as well as the tiny forms, are algae.

Phylum Mycophyta: Fungi

The fungi are divided into three classes: the Phycomycetes, or tube fungi, which include

Liverworts. These small green plants, which are closely related to mosses, are often shaped like the human liver. They grow in damp, darkish places, usually on rocks or beneath bark. The umbrella-like stalks carry eggs that eventually produce spores from which new plants grow.

some bread molds, rusts, and mildews; the Ascomycetes, or sac fungi, which include *Penicillium,* yeasts, bread molds, blue-green molds, powder mildews, cup fungi, and morels (delicious edible mushrooms); and Basidomycetes, which include the more common mushrooms, bracket fungi, smuts, and rusts. It is estimated that there are about 200,000 species in this phylum. Without the fungi we would have no cheese or the drug penicillin. Fungi are the principal decay agents of the fields and forests, breaking down the bodies of dead plants and animals and returning their chemical constituents to the soil.

Lichens should be mentioned here since there are many "species," each of which is composed of one species of algae and one species of fungus living as a single organism. The fungus forms a framework within which the algae live and are supported and contained. Some lichens are crustlike (*crustose*); others are leaflike (*foliose*); others are branching (*fructicose*). In some instances the individual species may grow separately thus creating a puzzle for the classi-fiers. How do you give a formal scientific name to such a mixture?

Phylum Bryophyta: Liverworts, Hornworts, and Mosses

Liverworts, small, flat-leaved plants confined to wet or moist places form the Class Hepaticae, and the somewhat similar hornworts compose the Class Anthocerotae. The better-known and more common mosses form the Class Musci. There may be as many as 20,000 species in this Phylum.

All the above phyla form the Division Thallophyta of about 475,000 species.

Phylum Tracheophyta (equals Pteridophyta plus Spermatophyta): Vascular Plants

All the rest of the plants on earth, from the ferns and buttercups to the giant sequoias and tall oaks, are placed in this phylum. They all

Bristlecone pine, the oldest known living tree. Some are more than 4000 years old. This specimen has been twisted in one direction by continual high winds.

Sugar maple, one of our most beautiful and important trees. A mature tree produces 20 gallons of sap, which reduces to one-half gallon of good syrup, prized for its natural sweetness.

have specialized cells forming long bundles that transport nutritional substances as well as other substances to various parts of the plant. The phylum is divided into several classes, of which the following three are most familiar to us:

Class Filineae, or ferns

Class Gymnospermae, or seed ferns, ginkgo trees, and coniferous trees, such as pine, hemlock, spruce, cedar, and redwoods

Class Angiospermae, or the flowering plants

The flowering plants are divided into two main groups: the dicots, with the seed cotyledon consisting of two parts, and the monocots, which have only one cotyledon in the seed. The dicots include oaks, maples, elms, beeches, blackberries, mustards, dandelions, and many others; the grasses, lilies, orchids, palms, and others make up the monocots. The flowers may be tiny and inconspicuous in many of these plants. Some plants bear male flowers, with the female flowers appearing either on the same plant or on separate plants; other plants have flowers with both the pistil (female) and the stamen (male) in the same blossom. The great variety of these plants is evident all about us in the forests and fields and never so evident as when in flower. There may be as many as 500,000 species of flowering plants spread throughout our planet.

Pasture rose, one of the prettiest of our eastern flowering plants. The pasture rose provides cover and food for birds and other animals.

ANIMAL KINGDOM

Phylum Mastigophora: Flagellates
Phylum Sarcodina: Rhizopods (the
Amoeba and Foraminifera) and
Radiolarians
Phylum Ciliophora: Ciliates

These three phyla are all one-celled animals; they are often placed in a separate kingdom called the Protista. They are abundant in fresh and marine waters throughout the world. The Foraminifera were once so abundant in shallow seas that their remains formed thick deposits on the sea bottoms; the chalk cliffs of Dover, England, are such a deposit lifted above sea level. The Ciliophora include such well-known genera of one-celled protozoans as *Stentor* and *Paramecium*. In all three phyla, formerly listed as protozoa, there are probably 30,000 species.

Phylum Porifera: Sponges

There are horny sponges, chalky sponges, and glass or silica sponges; there are even some sponges found in fresh water. Sponges are groups of animal cells bound together in various shapes and sizes as colonies of individuals, each cell semi-independent, yet often specialized, and performing particular functions for the good of the whole animal. There are perhaps 4,000 species.

Phylum Coelenterata: Hydras,
Jellyfishes, Corals, and Sea Anemones

These are organized, multicellular animals that consist of a sac-like digestive cavity surrounded by special organs, such as tentacles, about the single opening to the cavity; these organs draw in food matter. Other organs are composed of special cells for protection and digestion. In reef-forming coral, individual polyps live in the chalky exoskeleton, connected to one another through tunnels left in the surface layer. There are about 12,000 species, mainly marine.

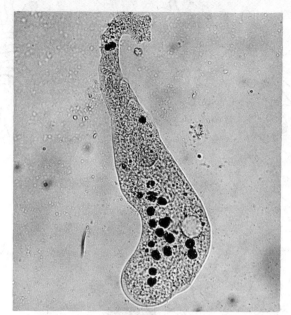

Amoeba, a one-celled animal that moves with the help of pseudopodia, or false feet. Amoeba live in salt and fresh water, and in the bodies of animals. In humans, they may cause amoebic dysentery.

Phylum Platyhelminthes: Planarians,
Flukes, Tapeworms
Phylum Nemertea: Ribbon Worms
Phylum Nematoda: Round Worms

The above phyla and five others are all worm-like animals differing enough anatomically so that they are placed in separate major divisions. Together they include about 25,000 species.

Phylum Entoprocta (equals Bryozoa):
Sea Mosses, Moss Animals

Found in marine and freshwater habitats, this relatively small phylum of animals superficially resembles the mosses or small fan corals. There are only about 4,000 species.

Phylum Brachiopoda: Lampshells

This phylum contained the most abundant shell species for millions of years and is best known

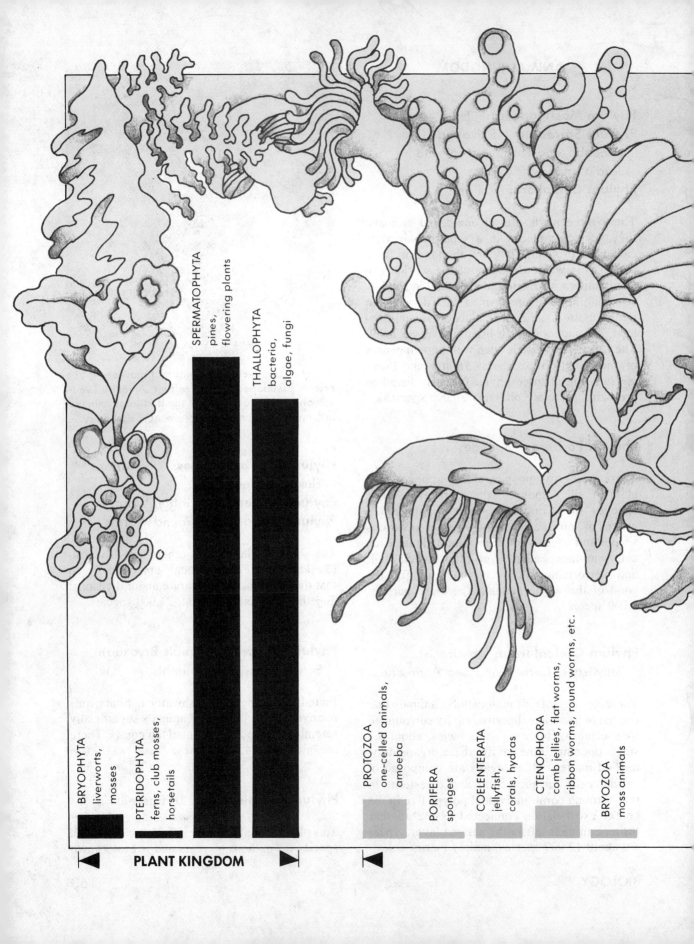

SPERMATOPHYTA
pines,
flowering plants

THALLOPHYTA
bacteria,
algae, fungi

BRYOPHYTA
liverworts,
mosses

PTERIDOPHYTA
ferns, club mosses,
horsetails

PROTOZOA
one-celled animals,
amoeba

PORIFERA
sponges

COELENTERATA
jellyfish,
corals, hydras

CTENOPHORA
comb jellies, flat worms,
ribbon worms, round worms, etc.

BRYOZOA
moss animals

PLANT KINGDOM

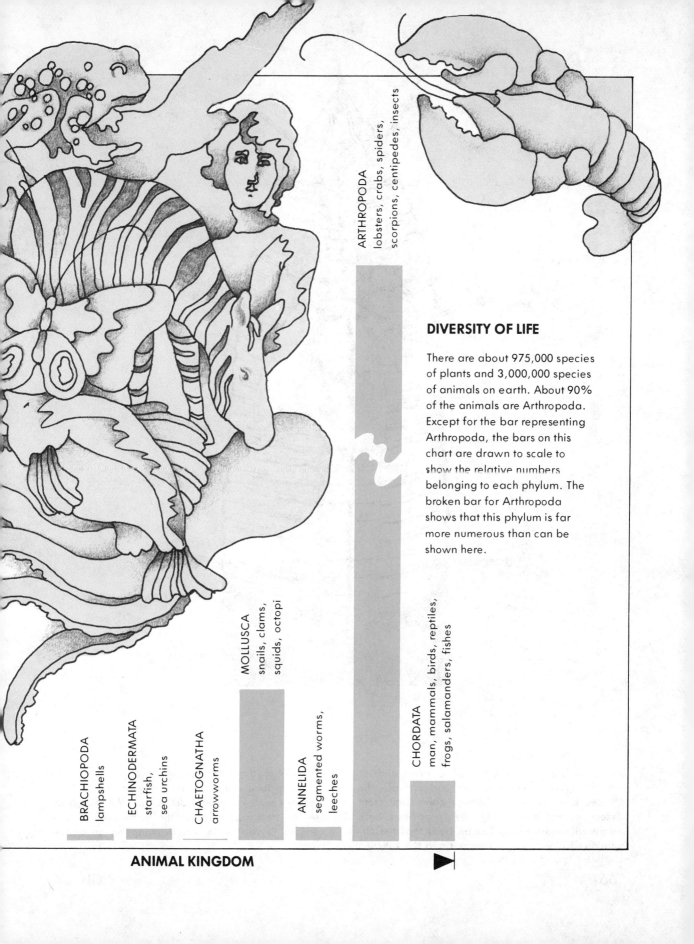

DIVERSITY OF LIFE

There are about 975,000 species of plants and 3,000,000 species of animals on earth. About 90% of the animals are Arthropoda. Except for the bar representing Arthropoda, the bars on this chart are drawn to scale to show the relative numbers belonging to each phylum. The broken bar for Arthropoda shows that this phylum is far more numerous than can be shown here.

ARTHROPODA
lobsters, crabs, spiders, scorpions, centipedes, insects

MOLLUSCA
snails, clams, squids, octopi

CHORDATA
man, mammals, birds, reptiles, frogs, salamanders, fishes

BRACHIOPODA
lampshells

ECHINODERMATA
starfish, sea urchins

CHAETOGNATHA
arrowworms

ANNELIDA
segmented worms, leeches

ANIMAL KINGDOM

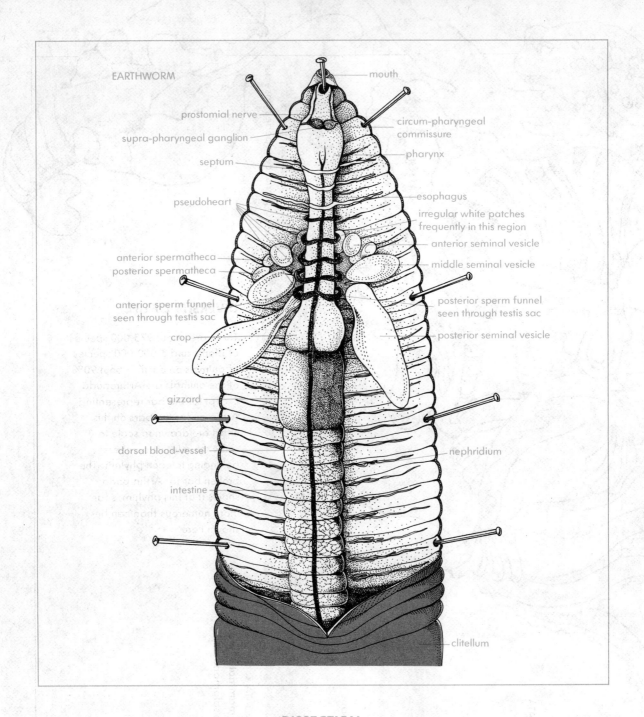

EARTHWORM

mouth

prostomial nerve

supra-pharyngeal ganglion

septum

pseudoheart

anterior spermatheca
posterior spermatheca

anterior sperm funnel
seen through testis sac

crop

gizzard

dorsal blood-vessel

intestine

circum-pharyngeal
commissure

pharynx

esophagus

irregular white patches
frequently in this region

anterior seminal vesicle

middle seminal vesicle

posterior sperm funnel
seen through testis sac

posterior seminal vesicle

nephridium

clitellum

DISSECTION

Dissection is a necessary tool of learning and re-search in biology and medicine. For example, the doctor's knowledge of anatomy came first from dissection, and it was only when physicians were permitted to dissect the human body that the cir-culation of blood was discovered and the function of bodily organs was understood. Students are re-quired to take courses in anatomy, including lab-oratory courses involving dissection. Manuals give step-by-step instruction on the techniques of dis-section, illustrated in this drawing of an earth-worm.

from the numerous fossil remains found in rocks. Today there are only about 200 living species.

Phylum Mollusca: Chitons, Snails, Clams, Tooth Shells, Squids, Octopuses, Nautiluses

There are well over 150,000 species found all over the world in oceans and freshwater and on land. They consist of many species we use as food and contain species that are pests in gardens. Many have beautiful shells and produce valuable pearls.

Phylum Annelida: Segmented Worms, Sandworms, Earthworms, Leeches

The earthworms are beneficial to man because they turn over and enrich immeasurable tons of farming soil each year. There are about 8,000 species in the phylum.

Phylum Arthropoda: Crustaceans, Spiders, King Crabs, Lobsters, Centipedes, Millipedes, Insects

All these animals have an exoskeleton (a skeleton worn on the outside), and their limbs are jointed. They exist even in the polar regions and the deepest parts of the seas and large lakes. Each class in the phylum is worth studying by itself; insects alone are estimated to contain more than 2 million species. The entire phylum contains close to 3 million species.

Phylum Echinodermata: Sea Lilies, Starfishes, Sea Urchins, Sea Cucumbers

These are animals with spiny skin occurring in all marine waters from pole to pole and from depths to shallows. There are probably more than 5,500 species.

Flame scallop, or file clam, from the waters of the Florida Keys. These bivalves swim with dance-like motions. Their long, reddish-orange tentacles are really sensory organs.

Dragonfly. Damselflies fold their wings while resting; dragonflies spread theirs, as shown here. Dragonflies and damselflies are separate suborders —not male and female of the same species.

American or common egret. Seen throughout most of the U.S. this magnificent, snowy-white heron stands more than three feet tall. It is the emblem of the National Audubon Society.

Phylum Chordata: Tunicates, Lancelets, Lampreys, Sharks, Bony Fishes, Amphibians, Reptiles, Birds, Mammals

This phylum contains all animals with a notochord, a bony spinal column, or both. There is a Super Class, Pisces, which includes all the fishes, and another Super Class, Tetrapoda, which includes all land vertebrates (even though, like the whales and dolphins, some have readapted to the seas). The Super Class Tetrapoda is subdivided as follows:

Class Amphibia: salamanders, frogs, toads

Class Reptilia: alligators, crocodiles, dinosaurs, turtles, lizards, snakes.

Class Aves: birds, from ostriches and penguins to canaries

Class Mammalia: mammals, including marsupials, such as opossums and kangaroos; and placentals, such as lions, tigers, cattle, elephants, rodents, monkeys, whales, horses, and man

We know more about these last four classes than we do about all the other plants and animals, because they are generally large enough to be visible and, by having a backbone, and paired limbs and eyes, are most like us. There are almost 9,000 birds and about 7,000 mammals already named and catalogued; there are about 60,000 species in the Phylum Chordata.

Young sea lion. Sea lions—mammals that have returned to the sea to live—have front and hind limbs that function as flippers. California, or Galapagos, sea lions are often on view in large aquariums.

Green frog. This frog lives throughout the Eastern U.S. Like all amphibians, green frogs are cold-blooded and, like most, they breed in water and live near water throughout the year.

THE ECOSYSTEM

The relationships among living things, and among living things and their environments, make up a complex study known as ecology. Ecologists think of three different concepts in relation to their studies: population, biotic community, and ecosystem. The population is all the individuals of every species that live in one area—all the plants, all the animals, all the humans, all the snakes. All these different populations form a biotic community. All the living things plus their environment make up what we call an ecosystem.

Natural ecosystems are incredibly complex: they include every living thing from the tiniest bacteria and viruses to the largest animals and giant trees; further, they include all the physical and chemical forces that act upon the area— air, water, wind, weathering, soil erosion, chemical changes in rocks, and so on. Still, all these components can be placed in five basic categories, examples of which are shown in the illustrations on this and the next pages.

First, there must be energy for any of the living things in the ecosystem to survive. The primary source of this energy is the sun; energy moves through the ecosystem along pathways known as food chains. Food chains depend initially on the ability of green plants to convert the sun's energy to energy forms that can be used by animals. Only green plants can convert the solar energy into food energy, which is essential to the survival of all life on earth.

Green plants, then, are the second important component of the ecosystem—producer organisms. These organisms carry this name because they produce, through photosynthesis, the food on which all the other organisms depend. They convert the solar energy to complex chemical compounds that either form the plant body itself or are stored in various ways (seeds and nuts, fruit, etc.).

All the animals in the community, as well as certain nongreen plants, are consumer organisms. They must acquire their energy secondhand from the green plants, for animals have no way of converting solar energy into a form they can use. Primary consumers take their energy directly from the plants; they are herbivores such as deer, rabbits, chipmunks, squirrels, many insects, seed-eating birds, and others. The carnivores, or meat-eating animals, are secondary consumers because they derive

Oxygen and carbon dioxide exchange. Plants take in carbon dioxide from the air and soil, and give off oxygen. Animals breathe in oxygen and give off carbon dioxide. Plants actually use small amounts of oxygen in their life processes, especially for photosynthesis.

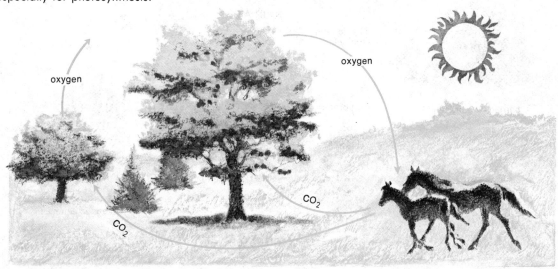

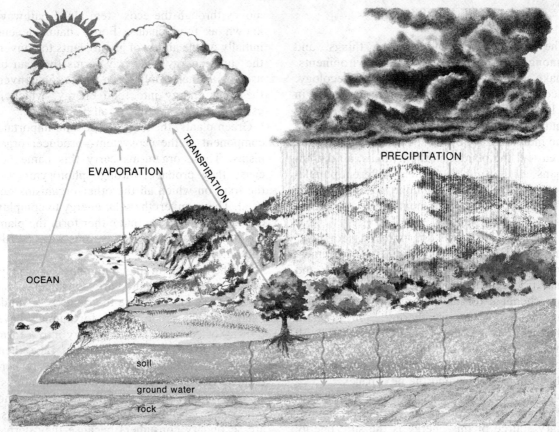

EVAPORATION

TRANSPIRATION

PRECIPITATION

OCEAN

soil

ground water

rock

Water cycle (*above*). Every drop of the earth's moisture circulates in a vast cycle for use by all forms of life.

Nitrogen cycle (*below*). All life requires nitrogen, but most forms cannot use it in its gaseous form. It is converted to nitrate compounds before certain plants use it to make protein.

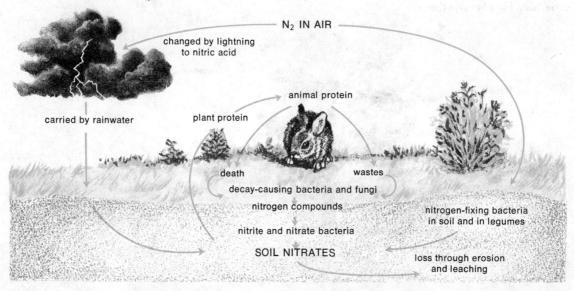

N_2 IN AIR

changed by lightning to nitric acid

carried by rainwater

animal protein

plant protein

death

wastes

decay-causing bacteria and fungi

nitrogen compounds

nitrite and nitrate bacteria

nitrogen-fixing bacteria in soil and in legumes

SOIL NITRATES

loss through erosion and leaching

BIOLOGY

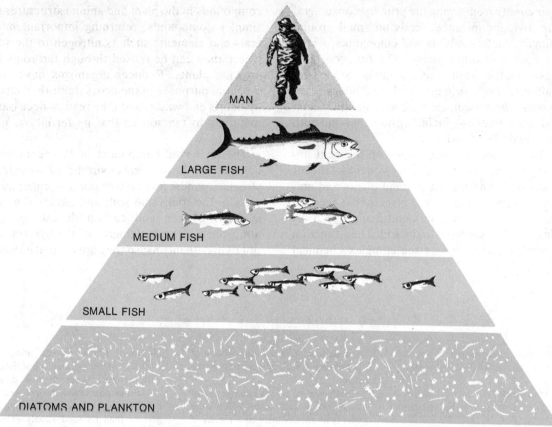

Energy pyramid (*above*). Tiny plants are eaten by many small fish; the fish are eaten, in turn, by fewer big fish; a top carnivore, such as man, eats a big fish.

Mineral cycle (*below*). A natural ecosystem depends on a stable (sometimes minute) supply of water, gases, and minerals circulating through the system.

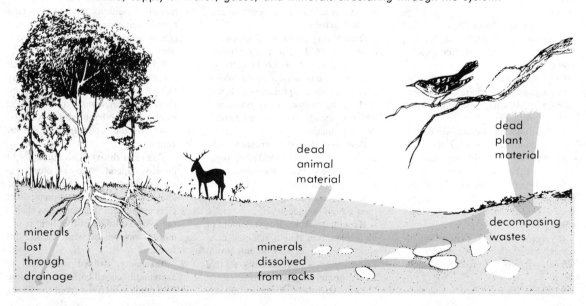

their energy from eating the primary consumers. The owl, for instance, feeds on small ground animals, such as rabbits and chipmunks, which eat grass and other plants. The fox, too, eats these smaller plant-eating animals. Some animals are both primary and secondary consumers; some birds eat both seeds and insects, and many animals—including humans—eat both meat and plant foods.

Other living creatures make up the next important component of the ecosystem—reducer organisms. These are the small plants and animals, bacteria, fungi, and insects that feed on the bodies of dead plants and animals and return their constituents to the soil. Their function is vital, for they reduce the complex chemical compounds in the plant and animal structures to simpler compounds, returning important minerals and elements such as nitrogen to the soil where they can be reused through the roots of growing plants. Reducer organisms have two essential purposes in the ecosystem: they clean up debris and waste, and they restore necessary materials to the soil so that its fertility is not drained.

The final vital component of the ecosystem comes from the physical environment—water in streams, ponds, and underground storage; minerals in the rocks and soil; and essential gases such as oxygen and carbon dioxide in the atmosphere. These elements of the system are not living organisms; so they are termed *abiotic*.

LAWS, THEORIES AND HYPOTHESES

Aerobic respiration: Oxygen consuming metabolism of glucose or other foods.

Allen's rule: Within a species, protruding parts tend to be shorter in cold climates.

Anaerobic respiration: Cellular metabolism in the absence of oxygen.

Antibiosis: One organism taking the like of another to preserve its own.

Asexual reproduction: Reproducing without fusion of two nuclei from different cells.

Code, genetic: Theory that hereditary information is carried in the sequence of bases in deoxyribonucleic acid (DNA).

Coloration, adaptive: The theory that organisms acquire in some manner a blending coloration with their environment.

Competition law of evolution: If two species compete strongly, the frequent but not inevitable outcome is that one of them becomes extinct.

Convergent evolution: Development of resemblance between organisms whose ancestors were less alike.

Divergent evolution: Divergence of resemblance between organisms whose ancestors were very much alike.

Eugenics theory: Theory that human genetics offers the possibility of improving the characteristics of the race.

Euthenics theory: A counterpart of eugenics which emphasizes the effects of environment as a means of improving humans by making fuller use of their potentiality.

Geotropic response: "earth turning response." The growth of roots downward is a positive response in plants. Growth of the shoot of plants upward is said to be a negative geotropic response.

Germ theory of disease: Recognition in the late 1870s that many ailments were the result of bacterial infections.

Heredity, transforming principle: A chemical extract (presumably DNA) from a bacterium (*Pneumococcus*) which is capable of carrying hereditary information.

Homology theory: Correspondence between structures of different organisms is due to their inheritance from the same ancestral line. Such structures may be dissimilar in spite of their common ancestry.

Hypothesis, defined: A statement of an explanation that a scientist considers possible. It may be only an informed guess which is usually testable by experimental observation.

Law, scientific: A theory or explanation which proves adequate over a long period and is consistent with the most recent scientific data.

Malthus population theory: Reproductive power of a population is much greater than its food supply. Thus, the food supply will become limiting at some point and serve as a check on the increase in population. First stated by the Englishman, Thomas Malthus in 1798.

Natural selection: The theory that natural conditions tend to eliminate certain variations in a species and render other variations advantageous over a long period of time.

Polyclimax hypothesis: A belief that several "climax communities" may exist in an area. That is, one community of organisms may be limited by climate, another by soil conditions, others by the topography of the region, etc.

Skin color theory: The skin color of humans depends partly on blood pigments, partly on its light scattering characteristics, and partly on pigment cells in the skin. Pigmentation that is not lost in ultraviolet-free light is primarily responsible for racial differences.

Taxonomy, defined: The field of systematic classification or naming. The name is derived from the Greek word *taxis* which means arrangement.

Theory, defined: Constant successful testing of a hypothesis leads to its acceptance as a theory. It may be impossible, for various reasons, to prove the explanation completely, but it also is impossible to disprove any point, so the explanation is called a theory.

Weber's law: A statement of the relationship between our ability to detect an increase or decrease in the intensity of a sensation, especially light detection, and the increase or decrease in the strength of a stimulus.

GLOSSARY OF BIOLOGICAL TERMS

A

abdomen, *n.* in vertebrates, the belly region that contains the viscera; in anthropods, the posterior region of the body.

abductor, *n.* a muscle that draws a part of the body away from the median line or normal position.

absorption, *n.* process of taking up water and solutions by cells or tissues.

accretion, *n.* growth in size, especially by addition or accumulation.

acromegaly, *n.* a permanent enlargement of the bones of the head, hands, and feet, caused by abnormal activity of the pituitary gland.

adaptation, *n.* the means by which an organism fits itself to live and reproduce in a particular environment.

adaptive, *adj.* enzymes formed when their specific substrates are available.

adductor, *n.* a muscle that moves or pulls a part of the body toward the median axis.

adrenalin, *n.* a hormone produced by the adrenal glands; a drug containing this hormone, used to raise blood pressure, stop bleeding, etc.

adsorption, *n.* process by which molecules of one substance attach themselves to the surface of another substance.

aerobic, *adj.* refers to organisms that can live and grow only where free oxygen is present.

aggregate fruit, *n.* fruit composed of a number of small, simple fruits, resulting from one flower, such as a blackberry.

albinism, *n.* the condition in animals or persons lacking normal coloration; albinos have a white skin, whitish hair, and pink eyes.

albumen, *n.* the white of an egg; the nutritive protein substance in germinating plant and animal cells.

algae, *n. pl.* a group of plants, one-celled, colonial, or many-celled, containing chlorophyll and having no true root, stem, or leaf: algae are found in water or damp places.

allele, *n.* one of a pair of genes affecting inheritance.

amitosis, *n.* simple cell division, without structural change in the nucleus.

amnion, *n.* the membrane surrounding the embryos of mammals, birds, and reptiles.

amoeba, *n.* a protozoon in which the shape is subject to constant alterations due to formation and retraction of pseudopodia.

Amphibia, *n. pl.* a class of vertebrates, including frogs, toads, newts, and salamanders, that usually begin life in the water as tadpoles with gills and later develop lungs: they are cold-blooded and scaleless.

anabolism, *n.* refers to the constructive phase of metabolism, during which complex substances are synthesized.

anaerobic, *adj.* indicates the absence of free oxygen.

anatomy, *n.* the science of the structure of plants and animals; the structure of an organism or body.

anemia, *n.* condition caused by deficiency of hemoglobin in the blood.

annual, *n.* a plant that lives only one year or season.

annual ring, *n.* the ring of wood resulting from one year's growth in a root or stem, as viewed in a cross section.

antenna, *n.* a movable sense organ located on the heads of various anthropods.

antibiotic, *n.* a substance produced by a living organism which will kill, or inhibit the growth of, a parasitic organism.

antibody, *n.* a substance produced by an organism to counteract the effect of a foreign substance, usually a protein.

antigen, *n.* a substance which stimulates the production of antibodies when introduced into the body of an organism.

antitoxin, *n.* an antibody, formed to act against a specific toxin.

aorta, *n.* the main artery of the body, carrying blood from the left ventricle of the heart to all parts except the lungs.

appendage, *n.* any subordinate or external organ or part, as a leg or tail.

aquatic, *adj.* growing or living in or upon water.

arboreal, *adj.* of or like a tree; living in trees or adapted for living in trees.

artery, *n.* vessel which carries blood away from the heart.

arthropod, *n.* any member of a large group of invertebrate animals with jointed legs and a segmented body, as the crustaceans, arachnids, insects, and myriapods.

asexual, *adj.* refers to reproduction without the union of male and female germ cells.

assimilation, *n.* the conversion of digested products into protoplasm by an organism.

asymmetry, *n.* lack of symmetry; in animals, the condition in which their opposite sides are not alike.

atavism, *n.* resemblance to a remote ancestor in some characteristic which nearer ancestors do not have; reversion to a primitive type.

atrophy, *n.* a wasting away or failure to grow of an organ, etc., because of insufficient nutrition.

auditory, *adj.* of hearing or the sense of hearing.

auricle, *n.* either one of the heart's two chambers which receive blood from the veins.

bacillus, *n.* a rod-like bacterium.

backbone, *n.* the column of bones (vertebrae) along the center of the back; spine.

back-cross, *v.t.* to mate a cross or hybrid to a member of one of the parental stocks.

back-mutation, *n.* reversion of a mutant gene to its original state.

bacteriology, *n.* the science dealing with bacteria.

benthos, *n.* the flora and fauna found at the bottom of the sea.

biennial, *n.* a plant that lasts two years, usually producing flowers and seed the second year.

bilateral symmetry, *n.* refers to the arrangement of body parts in which right and left halves are mirror images of each other.

bile, *n.* the bitter, greenish fluid secreted by the liver and found in the gall bladder: it helps in digestion.

binary fission, *n.* a process by which an organism divides into two approximately equal parts; hence, a form of asexual reproduction.

biochemistry, *n.* the chemistry of living organisms.

biology, *n.* the science that deals with the origin, history, physical characteristics, habits, etc., of plants and animals: it includes botany, zoology, and their subdivisions.

brain, *n.* the large anterior end of the central nervous system.

buccal, *adj.* of the cheek or cheeks; of the mouth.

bulb, *n.* an underground bud that sends down roots and has a very short stem covered with leafy scales, as in a lily, onion, etc.

callus, *n.* a growth forming over a cut or wounded area on a plant stem.

cambium, *n.* located between xylem and phloem, this is a layer of meristematic cells.

cancer, *n.* the name given to a group of diseases that are characterized by uncontrolled cellular growth.

capillaries, *n. pl.* small, thin-walled blood vessels connecting arteries and veins. Exchanges between the blood and the cells of the body take place through the walls of the capillaries.

catabolism, *n.* the breaking down of larger molecules into smaller ones; hence, destructive metabolism.

cell, *n.* a small unit of protoplasm, usually with a nucleus and an enclosing membrane: all plants and animals are made up of one or more cells.

cellulose, *n.* a complex carbohydrate which is the chief component of the wall of the plant cell.

cephalic, *adj.* of the head, or skull, or cranium; in, on, near, or toward the head.

cerebellum, *n.* a part of the brain immediately in front of the medulla which regulates complex muscular movements.

cerebrum, *n.* the anterior part of the brain, large and lobed which functions in learning, memory, and conscious sensations.

chemosynthesis, *n.* a process of food manufacturing carried on by certain bacteria; in this process, the bacteria use energy released by the oxidation of inorganic compounds.

chlorophyll, *n.* the green coloring matter of plants; in the presence of sunlight it converts carbon dioxide and water into carbohydrates.

chromosomes, *n. pl.* composed of chromatin and located in the nucleus, these bodies contain the genes.

cilia, *n. pl.* small hair-like bits of protoplasm which move in unison to move cells or particles over its surface.

cloaca, *n.* the chamber into which the kidney ducts, the genital ducts, and the intestine all empty.

clone, *n.* a group of cells all descended from a single common ancestor.

coagulation, *n.* curdling or clotting; the changing from a liquid to a viscous or solid state by chemical reaction.

cocoon, *n.* the silky case which the larvae of certain insects spin about themselves to shelter them during the pupa stage.

colony, *n.* a group of contiguous cells, usually derived from a single ancestor, growing on a solid surface.

conjunctiva, *n.* the mucous membrane lining the inner surface of the eyelids and covering the front part of the eyeball.

cornea, *n.* the transparent outer coat of the eyeball, covering the iris and pupil.

corolla, *n.* the petals, or inner leaves, of a flower.

cortex, *n.* the bark or rind of a plant.

cross-pollination, *n.* the process of transferring pollen from the anther of one flower to the stigma of another.

cyst, *n.* the inactive stage of some organisms when they are enclosed in a wall or sac.

cytology, *n.* the branch of biology dealing with the structure, function, pathology, and life history of cells.

dactyl, *n.* a finger or toe.

decay, *n.* refers to the breakdown of organic materials which involves microorganisms.

dermis, *n.* the layer of skin just below the epidermis; derma.

diagnosis, *n.* discrimination of a physiological or pathological condition by its distinctive signs.

dialysis, *n.* separation of dissolved crystalloids and colloids through semipermeable membrane, crystalloids passing more readily.

differentiation, *n.* refers to the specialization of cells and tissues during development for the purpose of performing particular functions.

digestion, *n.* the conversion of insoluble food substances into soluble substances which may be absorbed.

dioecious, *adj.* having the male reproductive organs in one individual and the female organs in another; in the gametophyte, having eggs and sperms produced on different plants.

disease, *n.* a particular destructive process in an organism; specific illness or departure from health.

diuretic, *a.* increasing the secretion of urine. *n.* any agent causing diuresis.

diurnal, *a.* opening during the day only; active in the day-time.

DNA (Dioxyribonucleic Acid), *n.* the genetic material of all cells.

dominant, *adj.* in genetics, designating or of that one of any pair of opposite Mendelian characters which, when factors for both are present in the germ plasm, dominates over the other and appears in the organism; opposite of the recessive.

dormancy, *n.* state of sleep or inactivity, as in buds during winter or the embryos of seeds when stored.

E

ecology, *n.* the branch of biology that deals with the relations between living organisms and their environment.

ectoplasm, *n.* the outer layer of the cytoplasm of a cell.

embryo, *n.* an animal in the earliest stages of its development in the uterus.

embryology, *n.* the branch of biology dealing with the formation and development of embryos.

endemic, *adj.* prevalent in or restricted to a certain locality or group.

endocrine, *adj.* refers to any gland that produces one or more internal secretions that are carried by the blood or lymph to some part whose functions they regulate.

entomology, *n.* that part of zoology which deals with insects.

enzyme, *n.* an organic substance produced in plant and animal cells, causing changes in other substances by catalytic action.

epidermis, *n.* the outermost layer of the skin in vertebrates; the outermost layer of cells covering seed plants and ferns; the outer layer of the shells of many mollusks.

epithelium, *n.* cellular, membrane-like tissue that covers surfaces, forms glands, and lines most cavities of the body.

esophagus, *n.* the passage for food from the pharynx to the stomach; gullet.

estrogen, *n.* any of several estrus-producing compounds.

expiration, *n.* the act of emitting air from lungs; emission of carbon dioxide by plants and animals.

F

facet, *n.* a division of the compound eye.

fauna, *n.* the animals of a specified region or time.

femur, *n.* the thighbone.

fermentation, *n.* the breakdown of complex molecules in organic compounds, caused by the influence of a ferment.

fertilization, *n.* the process of making the female reproductive cell fruitful by introducing the male germ cell; the egg nucleus and sperm nucleus together form a zygote.

fetus, *n.* the unborn young of an animal while still in the uterus or egg, especially in its later stages.

fission, *n.* a form of asexual reproduction in which the parent organism divides into two or more parts, each becoming an independent individual.

flagellum, *n.* a whiplike part serving as an organ of locomotion in bacteria and certain cells.

floriculture, *n.* the cultivation of flowers or ornamental plants.

fungus, *n.* any of a group of plants, including mildews, molds, mushrooms, etc., that have no leaves, flowers, or green color and reproduce by means of spores.

G

gamete, *n.* a reproductive cell that can unite with another similar one to form the cell that develops into a new individual.

ganglion, *n.* a mass of nerve cells serving as a center from which nerve impulses are transmitted.

gastric, *adj.* of, in, or near the stomach.

gene, *n.* any of the elements in the chromosome by which hereditary characters are transmitted and determined.

genetics, *n. pl.* the branch of biology that deals with heredity and variation in similar or related animals and plants.

genus, *n.* a classification of plants or animals with common distinguishing characteristics: a genus is the main subdivision of a family and includes one or more species.

geotropism, *n.* movement or growth of a living organism in response to the force of gravity, either toward the center of the earth or away from the center of the earth.

germination, *n.* the process by which a seed begins to sprout and grow.

gestation, *n.* the period during which mammals carry their young in the uterus during pregnancy.

gland, *n.* any organ that separates certain elements from the blood and secretes them in the form of a substance for the body to use, as adrenalin, or throw off, as urine.

grain, *n.* a small, hard seed or seed-like fruit, especially that of any cereal plant, as wheat, rice, corn, etc.; the arrangement of fibers, layers, or particles of wood, leather, stone, etc.

gustatory, *a.* pertaining to sense of taste.

gymnosperm, *n.* any of a large class of plants producing seeds not enclosed in a seed case or ovary, as certain evergreens.

H

habitat, *n.* native environment; the place where a person or thing is ordinarily found.

haploid state, *n.* state of having only one set of chromosomes, as in spores or gametes.

hemoglobin, *n.* the red coloring matter of the red blood corpuscles: it carries oxygen from the lungs to the tissues, and carbon dioxide from the tissues to the lungs.

hemophilia, *n.* a hereditary condition in which the blood fails to clot quickly enough, causing prolonged uncontrollable bleeding from even the smallest cut.

herb, *n.* any seed plant whose stem withers away annually, as distinguished from a tree or shrub whose woody stem lives from year to year.

heredity, *n.* the transmission from parent to offspring of certain characteristics; tendency of offspring to resemble parents or ancestors.

histamine, *n.* an amine discharged by the tissues in allergic reactions: it dilates blood vessels, stimulates gastric secretion, etc.

histology, *n.* the branch of biology concerned with the microscopic study of the structure of tissues.

homeostasis, *n.* the balance of nature; maintenance of equilibrium between organism and environment; the constancy of the internal environment of the body, as in birds and mammals.

hormone, *n.* a chemical substance formed in some organ of the body, as the ovary, adrenal glands, etc., and carried to another organ or tissue, where it has a specific effect; a similar substance in plants.

horticulture, *n.* the art or science of growing flowers, fruit, and vegetables.

hybrid, *n.* the offspring of two animals or plants of different species, etc.

hypertrophy, *n.* excessive growth due to increase in size of cells.

hypopituitarism, *n.* deficiency of pituitary gland, resulting in a type of infantilism.

I

ichthyology, *n.* the study of fishes.

immunity, *n.* resistance to a specified disease or toxic substance.

implant, *n.* an organ or part transplanted to an abnormal position; a graft.

inbreeding, *n.* breeding through a succession of parents belonging to the same stock, or very nearly related.

ingestion, *n.* the process of taking food into the body for digestion.

inoculate, *v.t.* to implant bacteria, etc., into soil suitable for their growth.

instinct, *n.* an inborn tendency to behave in a way characteristic of a species: natural, unacquired response to stimuli.

insulin, *n.* a secretion of the pancreas which helps the body use sugar and other carbohydrates.

interbreed, *v.* to cross different varieties of plants or animals.

intestines, *n. pl.* the lower part of the alimentary canal, extending from the stomach to the anus and consisting of a convoluted upper part (the small intestine) and a lower part of greater diameter (the large intestine).

invertebrate, *n.* any animal without a backbone (vertebral column).

J

jugular, *adj.* refers to the neck or throat; *n.* either of two large veins in the neck carrying blood back from the head to the heart.

K

kidney, *n.* either of a pair of glandular organs in vertebrates, which separate water and waste products from the blood and excrete them as urine through the bladder.

L

larva, *n.* an insect in the earliest stage after hatching, before it is changed into a pupa; the early form of any animal that changes structurally when it becomes an adult, as the tadpole.

latex, *n.* a milky liquid in certain plants and trees, as the rubber tree, milkweed, etc.: it is the basis of various products, notably rubber.

layering, *n.* the process of partly covering a living plant with earth so that it may take root.

lichen, *n.* any of a group of mosslike plants consisting of algae and fungi growing in close association in patches on rocks and tree trunks.

liverwort, *n.* any of a group of green, red, purple, or yellow-brown plants resembling the mosses.

luminescence, *n.* any giving off of light caused by the absorption of radiant or corpuscular energy and not by incandescence; any cold light.

lymph, *n.* a clear, yellowish, alkaline fluid found in the lymphatic vessels of the body; it resembles blood plasma but contains colorless corpuscles.

M

maggot, *n.* a wormlike insect larva, as the legless larva of the housefly.

mandible, *n.* the jaw, especially the lower jaw; either part of a bird's beak; either of the pair of outermost, biting jaws of an insect or other anthropod.

meiosis, *n.* the nuclear changes in the maturation of germ cells, in the process of which the chromosome number is reduced from diploid to haploid.

membrane, *n.* a thin, soft, pliable layer of animal or plant tissue that covers or lines an organ or part.

mesophyte, *n.* a plant which grows best in a moderately moist environment, neither very wet nor very dry.

messenger RNA (mRNA), RNA that serves as a template for protein synthesis.

metabolism, *n.* the continuous processes in living organisms and cells, comprising those by which food is built up into protoplasm and those by which protoplasm is broken down into simpler substances or waste matter, with the release of energy for all vital functions.

metamorphosis, *n.* a change in form or function as a result of development; e.g., the physical transformation undergone by various animals after the embryonic state, as of the tadpole to the frog.

Metazoa, *n. pl.* the large zoological division made up of all animals whose bodies are composed of many cells.

mildew, *n.* a fungus that attacks various plants or appears on damp cloth, paper, etc., as a furry, whitish coating.

mitosis, *n.* the indirect method of cell division, in which the nuclear chromatin is formed into a long thread which in turn breaks into chromosomes that are split lengthwise.

mold, *n.* a furry growth on the surface of organic matter, caused by fungi, especially in the presence of dampness or decay; any fungus producing such a growth.

molt, *v.i.* to shed the hair, outer skin, horns, etc., prior to replacement by a new growth, as birds, reptiles, etc.

morphology, *n.* the branch of biology dealing with the form and structure of animals and plants.

mucous membrane, *n.* a mucus-secreting membrane lining body cavities and canals, as the mouth, etc., connecting with the external air.

mutant, *n.* an animal or plant with inheritable characteristics that differ from those of the parents.

mutation, *n.* a sudden variation in some inheritable characteristic of an animal or plant; an individual resulting from such variation.

N

nerve, *n.* any of the cordlike fibers carrying impulses between the body organs and the central nervous system.

neuron, *n.* the structural and functional unit of the nervous system, consisting of the nerve cell body and all its processes.

nucleus, *n.* the central, spherical mass of protoplasm in most plant and animal cells, necessary to growth, reproduction, etc.

nutrition, *n.* the series of processes by which an organism takes in and assimilates food for promoting growth and repairing tissue.

O

ocular, *adj.* of, for, or like the eye; by eyesight.

olfactory, *adj.* refers to the sense of smell.

ophthalmic, *adj.* of or connected with the eyes.

optic nerves, *n. pl.* nerves running from the brain to the eyes.

ovary, *n.* the female reproductive gland, in which ova are formed; in plants, the organ which produces ovules.

oviduct, *n.* a duct or tube through which the ova pass from the ovary to the uterus or to the outside.

oviparous, *adj.* producing eggs which hatch after leaving the body.

ovulation, *n.* the process of producing ova and discharging ova from the ovary.

P

pancreas, *n.* a large, elongated gland that secretes an alkaline digestive juice into the small intestine: the pancreas of a calf, etc., when used as food is called sweetbread.

parasite, *n.* a plant or animal that lives on or within another from which it derives sustenance.

parathyroid, *adj.* designating or of any of four small glands located on or embedded in the thyroid gland: their secretions increase the calcium content of the blood.

parthenogenesis, *n.* reproduction by the development of an unfertilized ovum, seed, or spore, as in certain insects, algae, etc.

pasteurization, *n.* a method of destroying or checking bacteria in milk and some other liquids by heating the liquid to 142°–145° for thirty minutes.

pathogenic, *adj.* causing disease.

pathology, *n.* the study of the nature of disease, especially with the structural and functional changes caused by disease; in botany, deals with the diseases of organisms.

penicillin, *n.* a powerful antibiotic obtained from the green mold penicillium.

perennial, *n.* a plant with a life cycle of more than two years.

peristalsis, *n.* the wave-like muscular contractions and dilations of the walls of the alimentary canal and certain other hollow organs, that move the contents onward.

petal, *n.* any of the component parts, or leaves, of a corolla.

phagocyte, *n.* any leucocyte that ingests and destroys other cells, bacteria, etc., in the blood and tissues.

photosynthesis, *n.* the formation of carbohydrates in plants from water and carbon dioxide, by the action of sunlight on the chlorophyll.

phototropism, *n.* tropism toward or away from light.

phylum, *n.* any of the broad, basic divisions of the plant or animal kingdom.

physiology, *n.* the branch of biology dealing with the functions and vital processes of living organisms or their parts and organs.

pigment, *n.* any coloring matter in the cells and tissues of plants or animals.

pistil, *n.* the seed-bearing organ of a flower, consisting of the ovary, stigma, and style.

pith, *n.* the soft, spongy tissue in the center of certain plant stems.

plankton, *n.* the microscopic animal and plant life found floating in bodies of water, used as food by larger organisms such as fish.

plasma, *n.* the fluid part of blood without the corpuscles; also the fluid part of lymph or intramuscular liquid.

pollen, *n.* the yellow, powderlike male sex cells on the stamens of a flower.

pollination, *n.* the process of placing pollen on the upper tip of the pistil, or from the microsporangium to the gymnosperm's pollen chamber.

primordial, *adj.* existing at or from the beginning; primitive; fundamental; original.

protein, *n.* any of a class of complex nitrogenous substances occurring in all animal and vegetable matter and essential to the diet of animals.

protoplasm, *n.* a semi-fluid, viscous, translucent colloid, the essential living matter of all animal and plant cells.

protozoan, *n.* any of a number of one-celled animals, usually microscopic, belonging to the lowest division of the animal kingdom.

pseudopodium, *n.* a temporary projection of the protoplasm of certain protozoa, serving as a means of moving about or for taking in food.

pupa, *n.* an insect in the stage between the larval and adult forms.

Q

quadruped, *n.* an animal, especially a mammal, with four feet.

R

recessive, *adj.* refers to that one of any pair of opposite Mendelian characters which, when factors for both are present, remains latent.

reflex, *n.* an involuntary action or automatic response to a stimulus which may or may not cause a conscious sensation.

regeneration, *n.* the growing of a new part to replace one that is injured or lost.

respiration, *n.* the processes by which a living organism or cell takes in oxygen, distributes and utilizes it in oxidation, and gives off products, especially carbon dioxide.

retina, *n.* the innermost coat of the back part of the eyeball, on which the image is formed by the lens.

rhizome, *n.* a horizontal, rootlike stem under or along the ground, which usually sends out roots from its lower surface and leafy shoots from its upper surface.

RNA (Ribonucleic Acid), *n.* a polymer of ribonucleotides.

ruminant, *n.* any of a group of four-footed, hoofed, even-toed, and cud-chewing mammals, such as cattle, sheep, goats, deer, etc.

saprophyte, *n.* any organism that lives on decaying organic matter, as some fungi and bacteria.

scion, *n.* a shoot or bud of a plant, used for grafting.

secretion, *n.* the separation and elaboration of a substance from the blood or sap.

self-pollination, *n.* the process by which a flower is fertilized by its own pollen.

serology, *n.* the science dealing with the properties or use of serums.

serum, *n.* any watery animal fluid, especially blood serum, the yellowish fluid which separates from the clot when blood coagulates.

sinus, *n.* a cavity, hollow, etc.; specifically, any of the air cavities in the skull opening into the nasal cavities; a channel for venous blood; or a narrow channel leading from a pus-filled cavity.

species, *n.* a single, distinct kind of plant or animal, having certain distinguishing characteristics: a biological classification.

spore, *n.* a small reproductive body, usually a single cell, produced by mosses, ferns, etc., and capable of giving rise to a new individual.

streptomycin, *n.* an antibiotic drug similar to penicillin, obtained from certain molds and used in treating various diseases.

striated, *adj.* grooved, streaked with fine lines.

symbiosis, *n.* the living together of two dissimilar organisms in a close association that is advantageous to both.

taxonomy, *n.* the science of classification; classification of animals and plants into phyla, species, etc.

tendon, *n.* any of the inelastic cords of tough, fibrous connective tissue by which muscles are attached to bones or other parts; a sinew.

tendril, *n.* a threadlike part of a climbing plant, serving to support it by clinging to an object.

tentacle, *n.* a long, slender, flexible growth about the head or mouth of some invertebrates, used to feel, grasp, propel, etc.

thyroid, *n.* the thyroid gland; a large ductless gland near the trachea, secreting the hormone thyroxine, which regulates growth; malfunctioning of this gland can cause goiter.

tissue, *n.* the substance of an organic body or organ, consisting of cells and intercellular material.

toxin, *n.* any of various poisonous compounds produced by some microorganisms and causing certain diseases; any of various similar poisons secreted by plants and animals.

transpiration, *n.* the process by which vapor and moisture pass through tissue and other permeable substances, especially the pores of the skin or the surface of plant leaves; the giving off of vapor and moisture.

tropism, *n.* the tendency of a plant or animal to move or turn in response to an external stimulus, as light, either by attraction or repulsion.

tuber, *n.* a short, thickened, fleshy part of an underground stem, as a potato.

umbilical cord, *n.* a cordlike structure connecting a fetus with the placenta of the mother and serving to convey food to, and remove waste from the fetus.

ungulate, *adj.* having hoofs; of or belonging to the group of mammals having hoofs.

ureter, *n.* a duct or tube that carries urine from a kidney to the bladder or cloaca.

urethra, *n.* the canal through which urine is discharged from the bladder in most mammals.

uterus, *n.* a hollow, muscular organ of female mammals in which the ovum is deposited and the embryo and fetus are developed and protected; womb.

variety, *n.* a group having characteristics of its own within a species.

vaso-motor nerves, *n. pl.* nerves that regulate the expansion and contraction of blood vessels.

vein, *n.* any of the bundles of vascular tissue forming the framework of a leaf blade.

ventricle, *n.* either of the two lower chambers of the heart which receive blood from the auricles and pump it into the arteries.

viruses, *n. pl.* infectious disease-causing agents, smaller than bacteria, which always require intact host cells for replication and which contain either DNA or RNA as their genetic component.

viscera, *n. pl.* the internal organs of the body, such as the heart, lungs, liver, intestines, etc.

vitamin, *n.* any of a number of complex organic substances found variously in foods and essential for the normal functioning of the body.

viviparous, *adj.* bearing living young instead of laying eggs: most mammals are viviparous.

weed, *n.* any undesired, uncultivated plant that grows in profusion so as to crowd out a desired crop, etc.

wilting, *adj.* the process of becoming limp because of the loss of water from the cells.

xerophyte, *n.* a plant that thrives in a hot, dry climate.

xylem, *n.* the woody tissue of a plant, especially, in higher forms, the firm part that conducts moisture.

zoogeography, *n.* the science dealing with the geographical distribution of animals.

zoology, *n.* the branch of biology dealing with the classification of animals and the study of animal life.

zygote, *n.* the result of the union of the male and female sex cells. The zygote therefore has a diploid number of chromosomes.

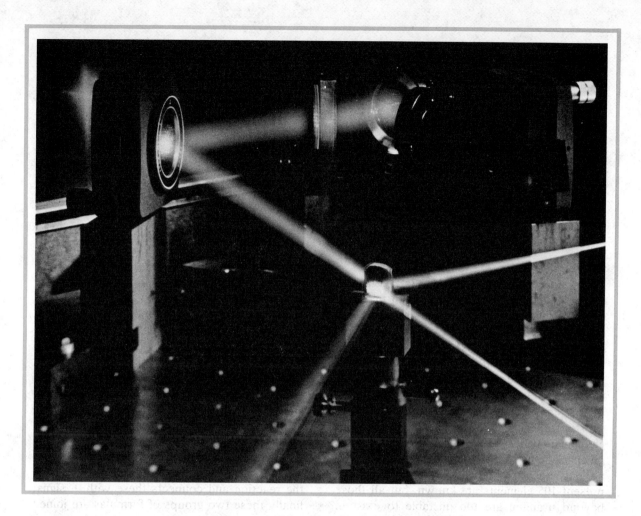

CHEMISTRY AND PHYSICS

The growth of population in all parts of our planet has made us aware of the need for full exploitation of our natural resources without damaging the environment we share. Two areas of study important to achieving this goal are chemistry and physics. As these sciences develop, the line of demarcation between them becomes ever fainter, and modern scientists must know a great deal about both subjects to move toward solving the problems we face.

Because of the importance of science in today's world, even laymen must strive for a degree of understanding. Citizens may not specialize in science but they must understand what scientists are doing. Scientists, in turn, must try to keep laymen informed. No matter what your own career may be, you will find interest in the following discussion of science.

Chemistry

When studying samples of matter, a chemist finds that most are *mixtures* that can be separated by physical means into various *compounds,* which in turn can be broken down into *elements*. The elements themselves can be broken down into subatomic particles but, in general, the chemist's concern does not go beyond the elements.

An element is the simplest kind of chemical substance. The smallest possible particle of an element is called an *atom,* and all atoms of a given element have the same basic structure, although they may differ slightly in weight. At present 105 elements are known, but all those beyond uranium are too unstable to exist in nature. The 105 known elements are the building blocks of the entire universe.

A compound is formed by the chemical union of two or more elements or from two or more atoms of the same element. The smallest possible particle of a compound is called a *molecule.* New compounds can also be formed by the chemical reaction of other compounds. It is obvious that the number of compounds is very much greater than the number of elements. In fact, the number of compounds that can be made is so large as to be practically infinite.

Each element has been assigned a symbol consisting of either one or two letters, often the first letter or first two letters of its name. This makes it easier for the chemist to write formulas and equations. For example, the symbol for hydrogen is H, for oxygen it is O, for calcium it is Ca, but for sodium it is Na, from *natrium*. The formula of a compound shows the different elements it contains and the number of atoms of each element per molecule. For example, the formula for common salt, sodium chloride, is written NaCl, to indicate that the molecule contains one sodium atom and one chlorine atom. The formula for water is written H_2O, because water has two hydrogen atoms and one oxygen atom. To write a chemical reaction, the chemist first writes the formulas for the atoms or molecules that react and connects them with + signs; next he writes the formulas for the atoms or molecules that are formed by the reaction and connects these with + signs; finally these two groups of formulas are joined with an = sign or an arrow, thus forming a *chemical equation.*

A simple example would be the formation of sodium chloride from sodium and chlorine. Since a molecule of chlorine gas consists of two atoms, the equation is $2Na + Cl_2 = 2NaCl$. This says that two atoms of sodium react with one molecule of chlorine and produce two molecules of sodium chloride. In other words, the chemical equation must be *balanced,* so that all atoms appearing on one side of the equation also appear on the other, although in different combinations.

An example of a slightly more complicated chemical reaction is the formation of aluminum sulfate, $Al_2(SO_4)_3$, from aluminum hydroxide, $Al(OH)_3$, and sulfuric acid, H_2SO_4.

$$2Al(OH)_3 + 3H_2SO_4 = Al_2(SO_4)_3 + 6H_2O$$

This equation says that two molecules of aluminum hydroxide react with three molecules of sulfuric acid to produce one molecule of aluminum sulfate and six molecules of water. Note that each atom that appears on the left also appears on the right. Note also that certain combinations, namely OH and SO_4, have been grouped in parentheses. These are called *radicals,* which are combinations of atoms that frequently act as a unit in chemical reactions. In a way, they behave almost like elements, since they can be recombined as a unit but are seldom created or destroyed. This is obviously true of the SO_4 radical in the above equation, but it is also true, although less obvious, of the OH radical, since the formula of H_2O is more correctly written HOH.

THE THREE STATES OF MATTER

Nearly every element or compound can exist in any one of three states, as a solid, a liquid, or a gas. A familiar example is water, which in the solid state is called ice or snow, in the liquid state is called water, and in the gaseous state is called steam or water vapor.

The physical state of any substance depends on the temperature and pressure. At atmospheric pressure, the temperature at which the solid form changes to the liquid is called the *melting point.* The temperature at which the *vapor pressure* of the liquid, that is, the pressure of the gaseous state of the substance in equilibrium with the liquid state, becomes equal to atmospheric pressure is called the *boiling point.*

Gases. A *gas* has no boundary surface. It will take the shape of and expand to fill any container in which it is placed. Gases respond readily to changes in pressure and temperature. The volume of the gas molecules is usually only a small fraction of the total space they occupy.

Liquids. In a *liquid,* the molecules are free to move about but not to separate from one another. A liquid will take the shape of the container in which it is placed, but it will not expand to fill the entire space available. The volume of

A substance is classified as a solid, liquid, or gas according to how easily its molecules move about in relation to one another. Molecules of a solid are fixed to each other in a definite pattern. Molecules of a liquid are free to move but not to separate. Molecules of a gas are unattached and free to move about.

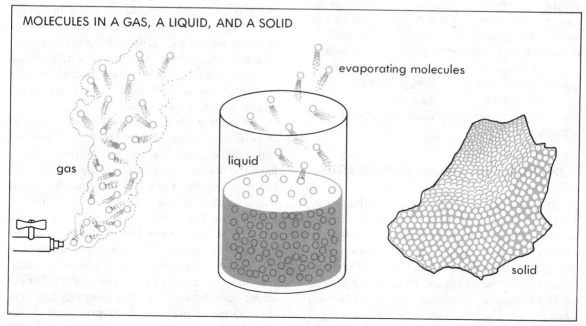

MOLECULES IN A GAS, A LIQUID, AND A SOLID

gas

liquid

evaporating molecules

solid

Chemical laboratory. Here at Du Pont's Experimental Station, Wilmington, Delaware, a chemist synthesizes organic compounds for use in studying reactions of plants and animals.

a liquid is changed only slightly by changes in temperature and pressure.

Solids. A *solid* retains its shape and resists forces tending to change its shape. It has high tensile and shear strength; that is, it is not as easy to pull apart as a liquid. The molecules of some solids, such as metals, are arranged in definite patterns called crystals. Other solids, such as chalk, are not crystalline but amorphous. Some substances that appear to be solids are really liquids of very high viscosity; that is, they flow very slowly. Glass is such a substance.

PHYSICAL AND CHEMICAL CHANGES

A *chemical change* always results in the formation of one or more new substances or compounds. Otherwise, the change is a *physical change*. Boiling water to produce steam does not cause a chemical change, because the molecules of both the steam and water are H_2O. The rusting of iron is a familiar example of chemical change, because the iron reacts with oxygen

from the air to produce a new substance, ferric oxide.

Very often, both physical and chemical changes take place at the same time.

ATOMIC STRUCTURE

The idea that matter can only be divided so far before coming to a particle, called an atom, which cannot be divided any further was first proposed by the Greek philosopher, Democritus, about 400 B.C. But it was not until 2200 years later that the idea was accepted fully and became the basis for modern chemistry and much of physics. In 1803, John Dalton, an English chemist, reformulated the atomic theory and showed that it explains a great deal about the chemical properties of substances. Since then, the atomic theory has become as firmly established as any theory can be.

By now, it is not only known that the atom exists, but a great deal is known about its structure. In 1897, the English physicist, J. J. Thompson, showed that atoms can be made to give up negatively charged particles, which he called *electrons*. Since all atoms are electrically neutral, this means they must contain as many positive charges as they do the negatively charged electrons. Another English physicist, Ernest Rutherford, proposed the theory that the atom consists of a nucleus with a positive charge with enough electrons rotating around it to balance the charge. This was modified by the Danish physicist Niels Bohr in 1913 to give the atomic model we use today.

The nucleus of the atom is known to consist of positively charged particles called *protons* and neutral particles called *neutrons,* which have the same *mass* (or amount of matter) as the protons. Orbiting the nucleus, somewhat as the planets orbit the sun, are electrons equal in number to the protons. The electrons have much less mass than the protons. Although nearly all the mass of the atom is in the nucleus, the nucleus is extremely small. The whole atom, including the electrons, is about 100,000 times larger than the nucleus. This means that most of the volume of the atom is empty space. If the

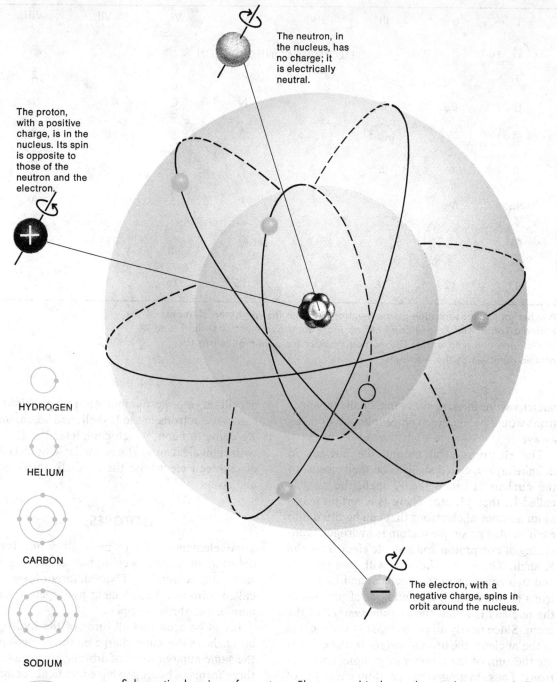

The neutron, in the nucleus, has no charge; it is electrically neutral.

The proton, with a positive charge, is in the nucleus. Its spin is opposite to those of the neutron and the electron.

The electron, with a negative charge, spins in orbit around the nucleus.

HYDROGEN

HELIUM

CARBON

SODIUM

POTASSIUM

Schematic drawing of an atom. Electrons orbit the nucleus in layers, or shells. Hydrogen, for instance, has only one electron, which is in the first shell. It combines with another element either by losing its electron (leaving a bare proton) or by sharing an electron from the other element (completing the K shell). Helium has two electrons in its outer shell. Because that shell is filled, helium does not combine easily with other elements. All outer shells are chemically complete when they contain eight electrons, although they may hold more. In heavier atoms all shells contain some electrons.

CHEMISTRY AND PHYSICS

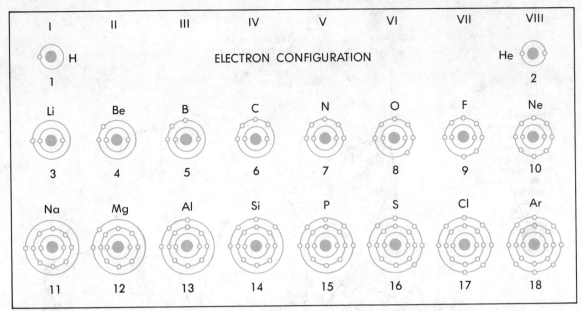

A schematic representation of the electrons for the first eighteen elements of the Periodic Table. The K shell can hold no more than two electrons; the L and M shells each can hold eight. The numbers under the schematics are the atomic numbers of the elements.

nucleus were the size of a tennis ball, the electrons would be, on the average, about two miles away.

The electrons orbit around the nucleus in definite layers, called shells. The shell closest to the nucleus is called the K shell, the next is called L, then M, etc. There is a certain maximum number of electrons that can be fitted into each shell. The simplest atom is hydrogen, consisting of one proton and a single electron in the K shell. The next is helium, with two protons and two neutrons in the nucleus, and two electrons in the K shell. The number of protons in the nucleus is called the *atomic number* of the atom. Since nearly all of the mass of the atom is in the nucleus, the *atomic weight* is close to being the sum of the number of protons and neutrons. Thus, hydrogen has an atomic number of 1 and an atomic weight of 1; helium has an atomic number of 2 and an atomic weight of 4.

The K shell is filled when it has two electrons, so the next atom, lithium, atomic number 3, must put one electron into the L shell. Since lithium has four neutrons and three protons, its atomic weight is close to 7. The next element,

beryllium, atomic number 4, atomic weight 9, has two electrons in the L shell, and so on, until we come to neon, which completes the L shell with eight electrons. The M shell can hold a total of eighteen electrons; the N shell, thirty-two; and so on.

ISOTOPES

Most elements exist in more than one form, differing in atomic weight but all having the same atomic number. These different forms are called *isotopes*. The element hydrogen, for example, has three isotopes.

It can be seen that all three of the hydrogen atoms have the same charge on the nucleus and the same number (one) of orbiting electrons. All three forms of hydrogen have identical chemical properties.

Many isotopes, especially those made in the laboratory, are unstable and undergo radioactive decay. This is true, for example, of tritium. This makes some isotopes very useful as tracers in chemical reactions and other processes.

CHEMISTRY AND PHYSICS

Radiocarbon dating is a valuable technique for finding out the age of objects containing carbon, such as wood, cloth, or paper. All such organic objects start out with a certain proportion of radioactive carbon 14, produced by the action of cosmic rays on carbon dioxide in the atmosphere. This carbon 14 slowly disappears, owing to radioactive decay. By determining the proportion of carbon 14 to the total carbon content, we can calculate the age of the object.

TABLE OF ATOMIC WEIGHTS

For many chemical calculations, it is important to know the atomic weights of the various elements. These are the weights relative to a standard, usually the most abundant isotope of carbon, which is assigned a value of 12. The table of atomic weights (page 186) shows that most of these values are close to whole numbers. One reason they are not whole numbers is that most of the elements have isotopes, and the atomic weight is an average of the isotopes in the proportions in which they occur in nature.

The three hydrogen isotopes. Some elements, such as aluminum, have only one isotope; most have more. About fifty isotopes are radioactive, losing particles to become isotopes of other elements.

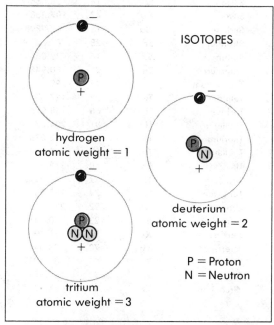

ISOTOPES

hydrogen
atomic weight = 1

deuterium
atomic weight = 2

tritium
atomic weight = 3

P = Proton
N = Neutron

THE PERIODIC TABLE

Early in the nineteenth century, chemists noted that the elements seemed to fall into several groups, with certain elements showing definite family resemblances. The Russian chemist, Mendeleev, published the first successful periodic table of the elements in 1869. He showed that if the elements were arranged in the approximate order of increasing atomic weight, the elements showed a periodic change in properties from metallic to nonmetallic. The rows of the periodic table begin with the strongly metallic elements on the left; as we move across the rows, we see that the non-metals are on the far right. We now know that the order is actually one of increasing *atomic number*. The vertical rows are called *families* or *groups*. The members of each family or group have the same number of electrons in their outer shells. (The Periodic Table appears on pages 188–189.)

CHEMICAL REACTIONS

Role of Electrons in Chemical Reactions

In nearly all chemical reactions, only the electrons in the outermost shell are involved. A chemical reaction consists of the transfer of one or more electrons from one atom to another, or a sharing of electrons between two atoms. Atoms react in such a way as to reach a state of greatest stability, which, for the great majority of atoms, means ending up with eight electrons in the outer shell. It does not matter that the outer shell is capable of holding many more; the chemical demands of the atom are satisfied by eight. The atoms in the first period of the periodic table are exceptions to this rule. For H, Li, Be, and B, an outer shell of two electrons is usually achieved.

An illustration of a reaction in which an electron is transferred from one atom to another is the reaction of sodium and chlorine to produce sodium chloride.

The Na has transferred its one outer electron to the chlorine, which has seven. This leaves each atom with an outer shell of eight. The loss of an electron leaves the Na with a positive

Name	Symbol	Atomic Number	Atomic Weight	Name	Symbol	Atomic Number	Atomic Weight
Actinium	Ac	89	227	Mercury	Hg	80	200.59
Aluminum	Al	13	26.9815	Molybdenum	Mo	42	95.94
Americium	Am	95	243	Neodymium	Nd	60	144.24
Antimony	Sb	51	121.75	Neon	Ne	10	20.179
Argon	Ar	18	39.948	Neptunium	Np	93	237
Arsenic	As	33	74.9216	Nickel	Ni	28	58.71
Astatine	At	85	210	Niobium	Nb	41	92.906
Barium	Ba	56	137.34	Nitrogen	N	7	14.0067
Berkelium	Bk	97	247	Nobelium	No	102	255
Beryllium	Be	4	9.0122	Osmium	Os	76	190.2
Bismuth	Bi	83	208.980	Oxygen	O	8	15.9994
Boron	B	5	10.811	Palladium	Pd	46	106.4
Bromine	Br	35	79.904	Phosphorus	P	15	30.9738
Cadmium	Cd	48	112.40	Platinum	Pt	78	195.09
Calcium	Ca	20	40.08	Plutonium	Pu	94	244
Californium	Cf	98	251	Polonium	Po	84	210
Carbon	C	6	12.01115	Potassium	K	19	39.102
Cerium	Ce	58	140.12	Praseodymium	Pr	59	140.9077
Cesium	Cs	55	132.9055	Promethium	Pm	61	147
Chlorine	Cl	17	35.453	Protactinium	Pa	91	231
Chromium	Cr	24	51.996	Radium	Ra	88	226.0254
Cobalt	Co	27	58.9332	Radon	Rn	86	222
Copper	Cu	29	63.546	Rhenium	Re	75	186.2
Curium	Cm	96	247	Rhodium	Rh	45	102.9055
Dysprosium	Dy	66	162.50	Rubidium	Rb	37	85.47
Einsteinium	Es	99	254	Ruthenium	Ru	44	101.07
Erbium	Er	68	167.26	Samarium	Sm	62	150.35
Europium	Eu	63	151.96	Scandium	Sc	21	44.956
Fermium	Fm	100	257	Selenium	Se	34	78.96
Fluorine	F	9	18.9984	Silicon	Si	14	28.086
Francium	Fr	87	223	Silver	Ag	47	107.868
Gadolinium	Gd	64	157.25	Sodium	Na	11	22.9898
Gallium	Ga	31	69.72	Strontium	Sr	38	87.62
Germanium	Ge	32	72.59	Sulfur	S	16	32.064
Gold	Au	79	196.967	Tantalum	Ta	73	180.948
Hafnium	Hf	72	178.49	Technetium	Tc	43	99
Helium	He	2	4.0026	Tellurium	Te	52	127.60
Holmium	Ho	67	164.930	Terbium	Tb	65	158.9254
Hydrogen	H	1	1.00797	Thallium	Tl	81	204.37
Indium	In	49	114.82	Thorium	Th	90	232.038
Iodine	I	53	126.9045	Thulium	Tm	69	168.934
Iridium	Ir	77	192.2	Tin	Sn	50	118.69
Iron	Fe	26	55.847	Titanium	Ti	22	47.90
Krypton	Kr	36	83.80	Tungsten	W	74	183.85
Lanthanum	La	57	138.91	Uranium	U	92	238.03
Lawrencium	Lw	103	256	Vanadium	V	23	50.9414
Lead	Pb	82	207.19	Xenon	Xe	54	131.30
Lithium	Li	3	6.941	Ytterbium	Yb	70	173.04
Lutetium	Lu	71	174.97	Yttrium	Y	39	88.9059
Magnesium	Mg	12	24.305	Zinc	Zn	30	65.37
Manganese	Mn	25	54.9380	Zirconium	Zr	40	91.22
Mendelevium	Md	101	258				

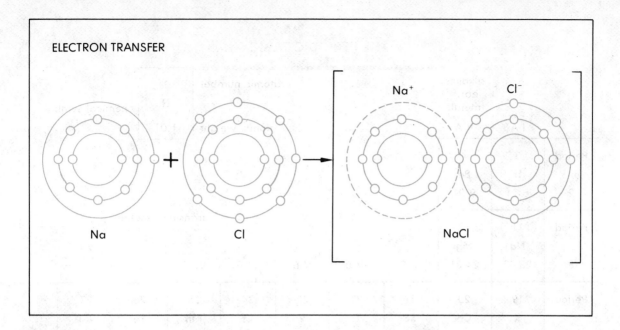

ELECTRON TRANSFER

Na   Cl   Na⁺   Cl⁻   NaCl

charge; the gain of the electron gives the chlorine a negative charge. That is, both become *ions,* which are atoms or radicals with electric charges. The attraction between the oppositely charged ions is the bond that holds the two atoms together. This type of bond is called an *ionic bond.*

Another way of completing the outer shell is for two or more atoms to share their electrons so that each has the desired eight without an actual transfer. This is called a *covalent bond.* For example, two atoms of chlorine react to form a covalent bond producing chlorine gas, Cl_2.

Only the outer rings are shown in the illustration. The great majority of chemical compounds have covalent rather than ionic bonds.

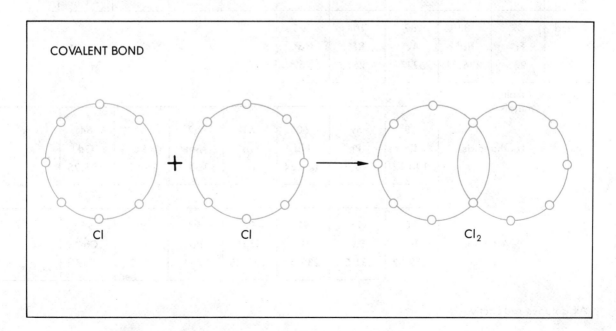

COVALENT BOND

Cl   Cl   Cl₂

THE PERIODIC TABLE

			atomic number — 1
			H — chemical symbol
			atomic weight — 1.01

alkaline earth metals

	I A	II A							
Period 2	3 **Li** 6.94	4 **Be** 9.01							
Period 3	11 **Na** 23.00	12 **Mg** 24.31	III B	IV B	V B	VI B	VII B		VIII
Period 4	19 **K** 39.10	20 **Ca** 40.08	21 **Sc** 44.96	22 **Ti** 47.90	23 **V** 50.94	24 **Cr** 52.00	25 **Mn** 54.94	26 **Fe** 55.85	27 **Co** 58.93
Period 5	37 **Rb** 85.47	38 **Sr** 87.62	39 **Y** 88.91	40 **Zr** 91.22	41 **Nb** 92.91	42 **Mo** 95.94	43 **Tc*** 98.91	44 **Ru** 101.07	45 **Rh** 102.91
Period 6	55 **Cs** 132.91	56 **Ba** 137.34	57 **La** 138.91	72 **Hf** 178.49	73 **Ta** 180.95	74 **W** 183.85	75 **Re** 186.2	76 **Os** 190.2	77 **Ir** 192.2
Period 7	87 **Fr*** 223	88 **Ra*** 226.02	89 **Ac*** 227	104 **Rf*** 261	105 **Ha*** 262				

transition metals

alkali metals

Lanthanoids	58 **Ce** 140.12	59 **Pr** 140.91	60 **Nd** 144.24	61 **Pm*** 147	62 **Sm** 150.4	63 **Eu** 151.96	64 **Gd** 157.25
Actinoids	90 **Th*** 232.03	91 **Pa*** 231.04	92 **U*** 238.03	93 **Np*** 237.05	94 **Pu*** 244	95 **Am*** 243	96 **Cm*** 247

* All isotopes radioactive

					non-metals				rare gases
				III A	IV A	V A	VI A	VII A	2 **He** 4.00
				5 **B** 10.81	6 **C** 12.01	7 **N** 14.01	8 **O** 16.00	9 **F** 19.00	10 **Ne** 20.18
		I B	II B	13 **Al** 26.98	14 **Si** 28.09	15 **P** 30.97	16 **S** 32.06	17 **Cl** 35.45	18 **Ar** 39.95
	28 **Ni** 58.71	29 **Cu** 63.55	30 **Zn** 65.37	31 **Ga** 69.72	32 **Ge** 72.59	33 **As** 74.92	34 **Se** 78.96	35 **Br** 79.90	36 **Kr** 83.80
	46 **Pd** 106.4	47 **Ag** 107.87	48 **Cd** 112.40	49 **In** 114.82	50 **Sn** 118.69	51 **Sb** 121.75	52 **Te** 127.60	53 **I** 126.90	54 **Xe** 131.30
	78 **Pt** 195.09	79 **Au** 196.97	80 **Hg** 200.59	81 **Tl** 204.37	82 **Pb** 207.2	83 **Bi** 208.98	84 **Po*** 210	85 **At*** 210	86 **Rn*** 222

other metals

65 **Tb** 158.93	66 **Dy** 162.50	67 **Ho** 164.93	68 **Er** 167.26	69 **Tm** 168.93	70 **Yb** 173.04	71 **Lu** 174.97
97 **Bk*** 247	98 **Cf*** 251	99 **Es*** 254	100 **Fm*** 257	101 **Md*** 258	102 **No*** 255	103 **Lw*** 256

Valence

The number of electrons an element gains or loses in a reaction is called the *valence* of that element. An element that loses electrons is said to have a positive valence; one that gains electrons has a negative valence. The valence is written as a superscript above the symbol of the element, on the right-hand side. For example, calcium has a valence of +2, since it loses two electrons in reactions and may be written Ca^{+2} or Ca^{++}. Most of the metallic elements, which are those on the left side of the periodic table, have only a single valence; that is, Na is always +1, Mg is +2, Al is +3. Most of the nonmetallic elements, however, have variable valences, which can be positive or negative, meaning that sometimes they gain electrons and sometimes they lose electrons. For example, nitrogen can have valences of −3, +1, +2, +3, +4, or +5.

In writing the formula of a molecule, the positive and negative valences must be equal. Thus, magnesium is +2 and chlorine is −1; therefore, magnesium chloride must be $Mg\ Cl_2$. Since Al is +3, aluminum chloride is $Al\ Cl_3$.

Oxidation-Reduction

This is a basic type of chemical reaction. A substance is said to be *oxidized* when it loses electrons; a substance that is *reduced* gains electrons. These two processes always go on simultaneously. When one substance is oxidized, something else must be reduced. In the reaction between Na and Cl, Na is oxidized and Cl is reduced. The rusting of iron, forming ferric oxide, Fe_2O_3, is a familiar example of oxidation, with the iron being oxidized and oxygen, from air, being reduced. It is because oxygen is such a common oxidizing agent that the whole process was named "oxidation."

Some Reactions in Inorganic Chemistry

Inorganic chemistry deals with the reactions of all the elements with the exception of carbon.

Most inorganic compounds can be classed as *acids, bases,* and *salts.* An *acid* is a compound that is able to give up a hydrogen ion to some other compound. The compound that receives the hydrogen ion is called a *base.* The product of the reaction between an acid and a base, other than water, is called a *salt;* the reaction itself is called *neutralization.* An example of neutralization is the reaction of hydrochloric acid and sodium hydroxide to form sodium chloride and water:

$$HCl + NaOH = NaCl + H_2O$$

Most inorganic compounds, when dissolved in water, form *ions;* that is, they separate into positive and negative parts, the process being called *ionization.* For example, sulfuric acid, H_2SO_4, when dissolved in water ionizes as follows:

$$H_2SO_4 = 2H^+ + SO_{4-}$$

Double Decomposition. This is another type of inorganic reaction in which two compounds interchange their positive and negative parts. An example is the reaction of sodium chloride with silver nitrate:

$$NaCl + AgNO_3 = AgCl + NaNO_3$$

ORGANIC CHEMISTRY

The chemistry of carbon is unique and is considered as a separate branch of chemistry, organic chemistry. It is called organic because until 1828 chemists believed that the familiar carbon compounds such as ethyl alcohol, acetic acid, sugars, and so on, could only be produced by living, that is, organized creatures. In 1828, however, the German chemist Wohler succeeded in making urea, a typical "organic" compound, from ammonium cyanate, a typical inorganic compound. Chemists came to accept the idea that organic chemistry is simply the chemistry of carbon compounds.

Carbon is unique because its atoms have the ability to link together to form chains almost limitless in size. This is probably the result of the position of carbon in the middle of the first period in the periodic table. Carbon has four electrons in its outer shell, and these are available for covalent sharing with hydrogen, oxygen, nitrogen, sulfur, chlorine, and other elements, but especially with other carbon atoms. This means that a practically unlimited number of compounds is possible.

To illustrate the way carbon forms compounds by sharing its electrons, let us show the compound methane, the main component of natural gas. Showing only the electrons in the outermost shell, the structure is

$$
\begin{array}{c}
\text{H} \\
\cdot\cdot \\
\text{H} : \text{C} : \text{H} \\
\cdot\cdot \\
\text{H}
\end{array}
$$

The carbon atom shares its four electrons with four H atoms, each of which contributes one to the sharing. The result is that the carbon atom completes its outer shell with eight electrons, and each hydrogen atom completes its shell with two electrons.

Methane is the first member of a series of compounds called *saturated hydrocarbons* or *alkanes*. Petroleum is largely a mixture of many saturated hydrocarbons. These compounds all contain only hydrogen and carbon, and the carbons are linked to each other by *single bonds* only, meaning that each carbon, in sharing with another carbon, contributes only one electron to the bond. The next member of this series is called ethane, C_2H_6, and has the following structure:

$$
\begin{array}{c}
\text{H}\ \ \text{H} \\
\cdot\cdot\ \ \cdot\cdot \\
\text{H} : \text{C} : \text{C} : \text{H} \\
\cdot\cdot\ \ \cdot\cdot \\
\text{H}\ \ \text{H}
\end{array}
$$

The next member, propane, C_3H_8, has three carbons in a row, and so on.

Unsaturated Compounds

It is possible for a carbon atom to share two or even three of its electrons with another carbon. The resulting compounds are called *unsaturated*. The simplest unsaturated compound is ethylene, C_2H_4. It has the following structure:

$$
\begin{array}{c}
\text{H}\ \ \text{H} \\
\cdot\cdot\ \ \cdot\cdot \\
\text{H} : \text{C} \vdots \text{C} : \text{H}
\end{array}
$$

Each carbon has contributed two electrons to the shared bond with the other carbon, producing what is called a *double bond*. Ethylene is the first member of a series of hydrocarbons called *olefins* or *alkenes*, each of which contains one carbon pair with a double bond. The next member is propylene, C_3H_6.

Compounds also exist where two carbons share three electrons each, forming a *triple bond*. The simplest compound in this series is acetylene, C_2H_2, whose structure is

$$
\text{H} : \text{C} \vdots \text{C} : \text{H}
$$

This is the first member of a series of hydrocarbons called *acetylenes* or *alkynes*. The next member is methylacetylene or propyne, C_3H_4.

Representing the Structure of Organic Compounds

Organic chemists generally represent a pair of electrons, which is a single bond, by a short dash. A double bond is shown by two parallel dashes, and a triple bond is shown by three. In this way, methane is shown as

$$
\begin{array}{c}
\text{H} \\
| \\
\text{H} - \text{C} - \text{H} \\
| \\
\text{H}
\end{array}
$$

Ethylene is

$$
\begin{array}{c}
\text{H}\ \ \text{H} \\
|\ \ \ | \\
\text{H} - \text{C} = \text{C} - \text{H}
\end{array}
$$

And acetylene is

$$
\text{H} - \text{C} \equiv \text{C} - \text{H}.
$$

GLOSSARY OF TERMS USED IN CHEMISTRY

acid. A compound which is able to donate a hydrogen ion to other compounds. In water, it produces hydrogen ions.

atom. The smallest possible structural unit of an element.

atomic number. The number of protons in the nucleus of an atom, or the number of electrons an atom possesses.

atomic weight. The weight of an atom compared with carbon 12, which has been assigned a weight of 12.

base. A compound capable of receiving a hydrogen ion from an acid.

boiling point. The temperature at which the vapor pressure of a liquid is equal to the atmospheric pressure.

chemical change. The formation of new compounds.

chemistry. The science that deals with the composition of matter and with changes in this composition.

compound. A substance consisting of two or more atoms joined by chemical bonds.

covalent bond. A chemical bond between two atoms in which electrons are shared.

crystal. A substance having an ordered arrangement of atoms or groups of atoms. These are mostly solids, but liquid crystals also exist.

double decomposition. In inorganic chemistry, an exchange of positive and negative parts between two ionized compounds.

electron. A negatively charged particle that orbits the nucleus of an atom.

element. A substance composed of atoms, all of which have the same atomic number and the same chemical properties.

inorganic chemistry. The branch of chemistry that deals with elements other than carbon.

ion. An atom or group of atoms bearing an electric charge.

ionic bond. A chemical bond in which two atoms or groups of atoms are held together by opposite electric charges.

ionization. The breakup of a compound in solution into ions.

isotope. A form of an element differing from other forms in atomic weight but not in atomic number or chemical properties.

melting point. The temperature at which a solid turns to a liquid or vice versa.

mixture. Aggregate of two or more substances not chemically united.

molecule. A group of atoms held together by chemical bonds.

neutralization. The reaction of an acid with a base to form a salt.

neutron. A nuclear particle having the same mass as the proton but zero electric charge.

organic chemistry. The chemistry of carbon compounds.

oxidation. Loss of electrons in a chemical reaction, or a reaction with oxygen.

proton. A nuclear particle with the same mass as the neutron but with a positive electric charge.

radical. A group of atoms that usually react as a unit in chemical reactions.

radiocarbon dating. The determination of the ratio of carbon 14 to carbon 12 as a means of determining the age of objects.

reduction. A chemical reaction in which electrons are gained.

salt. The product, other than water, of the reaction between an acid and a base.

unsaturated hydrocarbons. Organic compounds that have double or triple carbon-carbon bonds.

valence. A number that shows the combining power of an element or radical, usually the number of electrons gained, lost, or shared.

vapor pressure. The pressure of the gas phase of a liquid when the two phases are in equilibrium.

Physics

Both chemistry and physics deal with matter and energy and the way they change and interact. The chemist, however, deals mostly with the changes that matter can undergo. The physicist is more interested in the various forms of energy and how they change into one another, as well as in the nature of matter and how matter and energy are related.

FUNDAMENTAL CONCEPTS OF PHYSICS

Mass and Weight. *Mass* is the amount of matter in an object. The mass of a book would be the same no matter where it was in the universe. *Weight* is the pull of gravity on a given mass. The book would weigh only 1/6 of its earth weight on the moon, because the moon has 1/6 of the earth's gravitational pull.

Force. *Force* causes the motion of things to change in speed or direction. A force can also prevent change in motion when another force is acting. A book resting on a table is acted on by the force of gravity, but the table exerts an equal upward force on the book, preventing it from moving.

Work. A force is said to do work when it moves a body in the direction of the force. The work done is the product of the force and the distance moved.

$$W = F \times d$$

where W is work, F is force, and d is distance.

Energy. This is the ability to do work. Energy is converted into work when it is used to produce motion.

Power. The rate at which work is done is called *power*.

$$P = \frac{W}{t}$$

where P is power, W is work, and t is time.

Momentum. This is the mass of a moving object multiplied by its velocity.

$$P = mv$$

where P is momentum, m is mass, and v is velocity.

NEWTON'S LAWS OF MOTION

In 1687, Sir Isaac Newton published three fundamental laws that describe the motion of bodies.

The First Law. A body in motion in a straight line tends to stay in motion in a straight line until acted upon by an outside force; a body at rest tends to stay at rest until acted upon by an outside force.

The Second Law. When an unbalanced force acts on a body, the body will accelerate in the direction of the force, and the magnitude of the acceleration will be proportional to the force and inversely proportional to the mass of the body.

$$a = \frac{F}{m}$$

where a is acceleration, F is force, and m is mass.

The Third Law. For every action, there is an equal and opposite reaction. A space rocket takes off because the gas it propels downward reacts to push the rocket upward. The action and reaction occur at the same time and on different bodies.

THE LAW OF CONSERVATION OF ENERGY

This law states that energy can neither be created nor destroyed but only changed in form. This is also known as the *First Law of Thermodynamics*. In nuclear reactions, mass is converted to energy, in accordance with the well-known Einstein equation

$$E = mc^2$$

where E is the energy produced, m is the mass and c is the velocity of light.

If matter is really a special form of energy, the conservation law still holds.

THE LAW OF CONSERVATION OF MOMENTUM

This law states that in any interaction of bodies, the total momentum of the interacting bodies does not change. Momentum is defined by the relation

$$P = mv$$

where P is momentum, m is mass, v is velocity, and where p and v have the same direction.

For example, if a stationary billiard ball is struck by a moving ball of the same mass, the velocity of the moving ball must be shared between them. If the second ball stops dead, the first must move off with a velocity equal to the second before the collision.

HEAT

Molecules are in a state of perpetual motion, which manifests itself as a form of energy we call *heat*, measured as temperature. In the Fahrenheit scale, the temperature of melting ice is called 32 degrees or 32° and that of boiling water is called 212°. In the Celsius (formerly called the Centigrade) scale, the melting and boiling points of water are called 0° and 100°. The Celsius scale is used in scientific work and is gradually displacing the Fahrenheit scale for all temperature measurements. Another scale of scientific importance is the absolute, or Kelvin, scale. This scale is based on the idea that there is a temperature, absolute zero, at which molecular motion ceases entirely. Absolute zero has

Common temperature scales. For the Celsius and Fahrenheit scales, the reference points are freezing and boiling points of water; for the Kelvin scale, absolute zero.

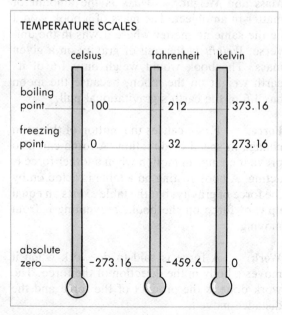

TEMPERATURE SCALES

	celsius	fahrenheit	kelvin
boiling point	100	212	373.16
freezing point	0	32	273.16
absolute zero	-273.16	-459.6	0

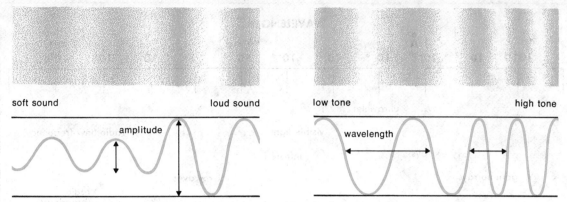

soft sound   loud sound   low tone   high tone

amplitude   wavelength

Sound waves. The loudness of sound is determined by the height of the wave, which is the distance between its crest and trough. This distance is the amplitude of the sound wave. The distance from one wave to the next, which determines the pitch of sound, is the wavelength.

been calculated to be 273.16° below zero Celsius. To convert degrees Celsius to degrees absolute, add 273.16.

Heat and Work

Heat is the least efficient form of energy because of the random nature of the molecular vibrations. To get work out of randomly moving molecules, we must induce them to move predominantly in one direction. A typical heat engine, such as a steam engine, does this by providing a heat sink, or condenser, at a lower temperature than the steam. The efficiency of a heat engine is proportional to this temperature difference and is given by the expression

$$\frac{T1 - T2}{T1}$$

where $T1$ is the absolute temperature of the hot gas or vapor and $T2$ is the temperature of the sink or condenser.

WAVE MOTION

Energy is often transmitted in the form of *waves,* that is, back and forth or up and down vibrations. The energy of a wave travels, but the medium in which the vibrations take place only vibrates or oscillates. There are two main types of waves. In *transverse* waves, the vibrations are perpendicular to the direction of the wave. In *longitudinal* waves, the vibrations are parallel to the wave direction. The *frequency* of a wave motion is the number of cycles of a wave motion per unit of time.

Sound

Sound is a longitudinal vibration of a medium at frequencies that the human ear can detect. The medium can be a gas, a liquid, or a solid. When a tuning fork is struck, it starts to vibrate at a frequency that depends on the size of the fork and the material it is made of. This vibration sets the air molecules around the tuning fork vibrating back and forth at the same frequency. When the energy reaches us, our eardrums vibrate too; and we hear a tone.

ELECTROMAGNETIC WAVES

These are transverse vibrations; that is, the oscillations are perpendicular to the direction of the wave. Light is a small part of a very large range, or spectrum, of transverse waves called *electromagnetic waves* because they combine electrical and magnetic properties. The electromagnetic spectrum is divided into regions according to *wavelength,* that is, the distance between the crests of two adjacent waves. In order

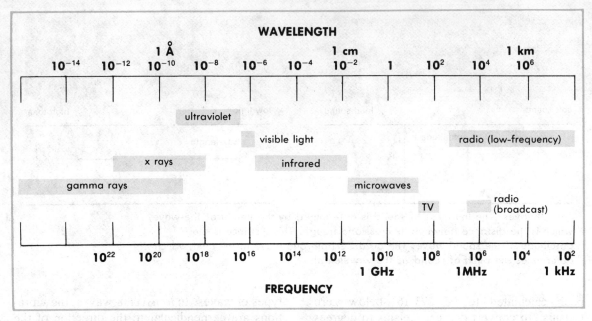

Spectrum of electromagnetic waves. Wavelength is measured in meters, and frequency in hertz, which equals one cycle per second. Visible light, an electromagnetic wave, occupies a small portion of the spectrum.

of increasing wavelength, the division is into gamma rays, X rays, ultraviolet rays, visible light, infrared rays, microwaves, and radio waves. Each region merges gradually into the next. The energy of a wave is

$$E = hV$$

where V is the *frequency*, that is, the number of vibrations per second, and h is a number called *Planck's constant.*

Many determinations have been made of the speed of light, which is the same as the speed of all the other electromagnetic waves. The value accepted today is 2.99793×10^8 meters per second. This is the speed in a vacuum. In a denser medium, such as glass, the speed is less. This enables us to bend and focus light with lenses, making photography, microscopes, and telescopes possible. By the use of prisms, we can even separate light into its various wavelengths.

The high accuracy of the figure we have for the speed of light makes it possible to measure the distance of objects such as the moon by *radar.* Radar is an instrument that bounces microwaves off an object and measures the time for the echo to return. Knowing the speed of light, the distance to the object can be calculated.

Radar is also used by highway police to get an instantaneous reading of the speed of an automobile by taking into account the *Doppler effect.* If an object emitting a tone is receding from us, the pitch is lower than from the object at rest; that is, the wavelength is increased. If the object is moving toward us, the wavelength is decreased. From the increase or decrease of the wavelength of the radar waves bounced off a moving car, the police can read the speed. The Doppler effect also tells us that the universe is expanding, since light from distant galaxies shows known spectra that are shifted toward longer wavelengths, indicating that the galaxies are receding from us.

The *laser* is a device that amplifies focused light waves and concentrates them in a narrow, very intense beam. The emitted light, called *coherent light,* does not spread much and so does not lose intensity. It can deliver great energy to a small area and holds great promise for future applications.

CHEMISTRY AND PHYSICS

Niels Bohr (1885–1962). Winner of 1922 Nobel Prize for physics, Bohr showed how atoms radiate and absorb energy. This Danish physicist was director of the Institute of Theoretical Physics, Copenhagen. On a visit to the United States, 1938–39, he warned scientists here that German scientists had been conducting experiments that led him to believe that the uranium atom could be split.

MODERN PHYSICS

Relativity

Until the beginning of this century, many scientists believed that Newton's laws of motion and law of gravity offered a satisfactory basis for explaining the physical world. In 1905, Albert Einstein published his theory of special relativity, which showed that Newton's laws were really special cases of more general laws. This theory has changed our concepts of space, time, mass, and energy. It makes two basic assumptions: (1) The measured value of the speed of light in a vacuum is always the same no matter how fast the observer or light source is moving; and (2) absolute speed cannot be measured, only speed relative to some other object. The results that follow these assumptions, although they appear to contradict common sense, are in complete agreement with experimental results. The theory predicts that, to an observer at rest, a moving object will appear shorter and more massive than the same object at rest, and a moving clock will appear to be going more slowly. These effects, which are significant only at speeds approaching light, have been confirmed by experiment. The famous equation for the equivalency of mass and energy

$$E = mc^2$$

where E is energy, m is mass, and c is the speed of light,

also comes out of the special theory of relativity.

Quantum Theory

Newton believed that light consists of particles, while the Dutch physicist Huygens and others felt light was a wave. Today both views are believed correct: radiation has the properties both of particles and waves, depending on the kind of experiment we do. The German physicist, Max Planck, studying radiation from so-called black bodies, concluded that his results could only be explained if energy were produced in separate packets, which he called *quanta*. A *quantum* of light is called a *photon*. The energy of a quantum is

$$E = hV$$

where V is the frequency of the radiation and h is a constant called Planck's constant.

Einstein soon showed that the *photoelectric effect,* which is the release of electrons by metals when irradiated by light, can only be explained in terms of the quantum theory.

The Principle of Uncertainty

Newton believed that if we knew the exact position and momentum (that is, mass multiplied by velocity) of a particle at some instant, it should be possible to calculate where the particle would be at any time in the future. In 1927, the German physicist Heisenberg showed this is not so, by proving that it is impossible to determine both the exact position and speed of any particle at the same time, since the act of measuring disturbs the particle and introduces an error into our measurements. This is called the *principle of uncertainty* and has led to a new way of describing the behavior of atomic particles, called *quantum* or *wave mechanics.*

Nuclear Physics

Radioactivity. The French physicist Becquerel discovered in 1896 that uranium gives off radiation, which fogs photographic film. Soon after, Marie and Pierre Curie isolated two new radioactive elements, polonium and radium. It has since been found that all elements above atomic number 83 are naturally radioactive. The radioactivity of a sample decreases continually with time, and the rate of decrease is different for each element. The rate of radioactive decay is usually expressed as the *half-life,* the time required for half the atoms to decompose. The half-life ranges from a fraction of a second for some isotopes to billions of years for others. For example, uranium of atomic weight 238 (U^{238}) has a half-life of 4.5 billion years.

Radioactivity originates in the nucleus of the atom. There are three types of radioactive de-

SOME NUCLEAR PARTICLES

particle family	particle	mass	charge	average lifetime in seconds
Photon	Photon	0	0	Stable
Graviton	Graviton	0	0	Stable
Electron	Electron	1	−1	Stable
	Electron neutrino	0	0	Stable
Muon	Muon neutrino	206.77	−1	2.20×10^{-6}
		0	0	Stable
Meson	Pions	273.2	+1	2.2×10^{-8}
		264.2	0	1.8×10^{-16}
	Kaons	966.3	+1	1.1×10^{-8}
		974.6	0	6.0×10^{-11}; 3.7×10^{-8}
Baryon	Proton	1836.12	+1	Stable
	Neutron	1838.65	0	1.013×10^3
	Lambda	2182.8	0	2.62×10^{-10}
	Sigma	2327.6	+1	7.9×10^{-11}
		2333.5	0	10^{-20}
		2342.6	−1	1.6×10^{-10}

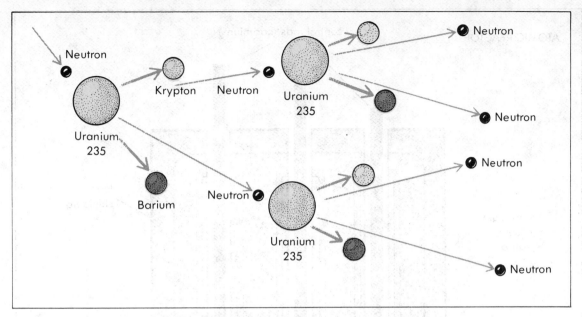

A chain reaction is required to produce an atomic explosion. When a neutron splits a uranium atom, two neutrons are released. These, in turn, split two uranium atoms, which release four neutrons, and so on in ever-expanding and accelerating reaction. If the amount of uranium is large enough, an explosion occurs.

cay. The nucleus can emit a *gamma ray*, which is an electromagnetic wave of very high frequency. It can also emit an *alpha particle*, which is the nucleus of a helium atom containing two protons and two neutrons. Since the loss of protons means a decrease in the atomic number (the number of protons in the nucleus) and since the atomic number determines the chemistry of the atom, the result is the formation of a new element. When radium loses an alpha particle, for example, the products are helium and radon.

The third type of radiation is the *beta particle*, which is an electron. Since it has a charge of −1, its loss increases the positive charge on the nucleus by 1, producing a new element. We can imagine a neutron losing an electron and becoming a proton.

Transmutation of the Elements.   If the atomic nucleus can be struck with some kind of projectile, it is possible that it will undergo a change in charge, thereby changing the nature of the element. In 1918, Rutherford bombarded nitrogen with alpha particles (helium nuclei) and found that oxygen was produced.

Nuclear Fission.   In 1939, the German physicists Hahn and Strassman discovered that if U^{235} (an isotope of uranium of atomic weight 235) is bombarded with neutrons, U^{236} is formed. This isotope is unstable and splits into several fragments in a process called *nuclear fission*. The fission process releases enormous amounts of energy, because there is some conversion of mass to energy. As previously noted, the relativity theory says that when a mass, m, is converted to energy, the energy is

$$E = mc^2$$

where c is the speed of light.

Since c^2 is a very large number, E is great even for small values of m. The fission process requires a neutron to start it, but the fission that follows produces many neutrons. If these are captured by other U^{235} atoms, a chain reaction can occur, producing an instantaneous explosion. This requires a certain *critical mass* of uranium, since otherwise the neutrons will escape. This is the principle of the fission bomb.

To use the fission reaction to produce nuclear power, it is necessary to have a controlled

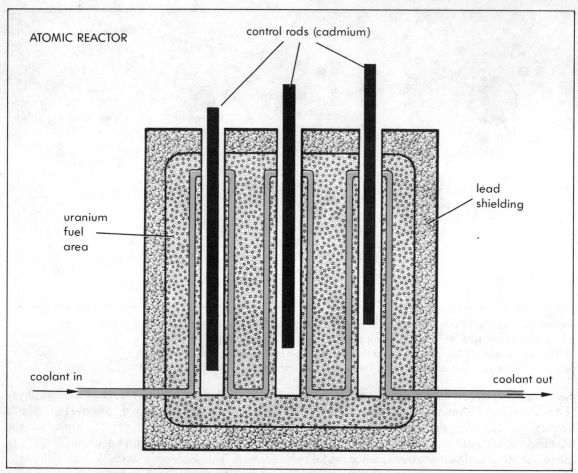

ATOMIC REACTOR

control rods (cadmium)

lead shielding

uranium fuel area

coolant in

coolant out

An atomic pile employs rods of a neutron-absorbing material. The rods capture free neutrons, slow the reaction, and maintain a steady reaction rate.

reaction, produced by constructing a uranium-graphite pile into which cadmium rods are inserted. Cadmium is a good absorber of neutrons, so the reaction can be slowed down simply by pushing the rods further into the pile. The huge amounts of heat produced are used to drive electric generators.

Nuclear Fusion.   Another way to release very large amounts of energy is by fusing the nuclei of certain light atoms to form heavier ones. In this process, there is a conversion of mass to energy. This *fusion reaction* is the source of the energy of the sun. In the sun, four H atoms are fused to make He. To start this reaction requires temperatures that are difficult to attain in a controlled way. We have suc-

ceeded in making hydrogen, or fusion, bombs by using nuclear fission bombs to attain the necessary temperatures. If we could achieve a controlled fusion reaction, the energy worries of mankind would be over.

Fundamental Structure of Matter.   Until recently, the atom was thought to consist only of protons, neutrons, and electrons. Physicists and engineers now have constructed accelerators capable of raising the velocity of particles such as protons to nearly the speed of light. When these particles smash into an atomic nucleus, many types of new particles are produced. The new particles thus discovered have a wide range of properties and no satisfactory theory accounts completely for them.

CHEMISTRY AND PHYSICS

GLOSSARY OF TERMS USED IN PHYSICS

absolute temperature scale. Also called the Kelvin scale, it is based on the idea of a temperature, absolute zero, at which all molecular motion stops. Absolute zero is 273.16° Celsius. To convert degrees Celsius to degrees absolute, add 273.16 to the Celsius temperature.

acceleration. Rate of change of velocity with time.

alpha particle. The nucleus of a helium atom, consisting of two protons and two neutrons.

beta rays. Electrons emitted by atomic nuclei in certain radioactive transformations.

black body radiation. The type of radiation emitted when a perfectly absorbing body is heated.

celsius temperature scale. Based on the temperature of melted ice (assigned a value of 0°) and boiling water (assigned a value of 100°). The interval is divided into 100 degrees.

critical mass. The mass of uranium or other material in a fission nuclear bomb required for a chain reaction at a constant rate.

Doppler effect. The change in wavelength that results when the source producing the waves is moving with respect to the receiver.

energy. The ability to perform work.

electromagnetic waves. Systems of varying electrical and magnetic fields, regenerating each other and traveling through space as a wave.

Fahrenheit scale of temperature. In this scale, melting ice is assigned a value of 32° and boiling water 212°. The interval is divided into 180 degrees.

force. That which causes acceleration or distortion of shape.

frequency. The number of cycles of a wave motion per unit time.

gamma ray. Electromagnetic radiation of very short wavelength resulting from the radioactive decomposition of atoms.

gravitation. A force between two masses which is directly proportional to the product of their masses and inversely proportional to the square of the distance between them.

half-life. The time it takes for half of the atoms of a radioactive element to become transformed as a result of radioactive decay.

heat. Energy transferred from one place to another, owing to temperature difference.

inertia. The property of an object that makes it resist change in its velocity.

infrared radiation. Electromagnetic radiation of longer wavelength than visible light, with a maximum wavelength of 10^{-4}m.

longitudinal waves. Waves in which the oscillation of the moving particles is parallel to the wave direction.

mass. The amount of matter in a body. It is a measure of the inertia of the object.

microwaves. The portion of the electromagnetic spectrum between infrared and radio frequencies.

momentum. The mass of an object multiplied by its velocity.

nuclear fission. The splitting of heavy nuclei caused by absorption of neutrons.

nuclear fusion. The creation of atomic nuclei by the fusion of lighter nuclei.

nuclear physics. Study of changes in atomic nuclei.

nuclear reaction. A change in an atomic nucleus caused by combination with elemental particles such as neutrons or other nuclei.

phase. The time relation of two cyclic motions. Two motions are in phase if they reach their peaks simultaneously.

photon. A quantum of light or other electromagnetic radiation.

photoelectric effect. Emission of electrons by an object as the result of irradiation by light.

pitch. The frequency of a sound wave.

Planck's constant. The ratio between the energy and frequency of a photon.

power. The rate at which work is done.

principle of uncertainty. The theory that it is impossible to measure both the exact position and exact velocity of an atomic particle at the same time.

quantum. The smallest unit of quantized energy, that is, energy which can only have certain integral values. For electromagnetic energy, the quantum is called a photon.

radar. A device for detecting distant objects by reflection of microwaves.

radioactivity. The spontaneous breakdown of atomic nuclei.

relativity. The principle that all frames of reference are equivalent for the description of physical events.

sound waves. Longitudinal vibrations of audible frequency.

spectrum. A continuous series of wavelengths.

temperature. The property of an object by which it can transfer heat to another object.

transmutation. A change of one element into another as the result of a nuclear event.

transverse waves. Waves in which the particles move perpendicularly to the direction of the wave.

ultraviolet. The portion of the electromagnetic spectrum lying between X rays and visible light.

wave. A cyclic disturbance traveling through a medium.

wavelength. The distance between adjacent peaks of a wave.

work. The product of a force and the displacement of the object in the direction of the force.

X rays. The portion of the electromagnetic spectrum between gamma rays and the ultraviolet.

SOME IMPORTANT LAWS OF CHEMISTRY AND PHYSICS

Avogadro's Law. All gases at a given temperature and pressure contain the same number of molecules per unit volume.

Boyle's Law for Gases. At a constant temperature, the volume of a gas is inversely proportional to the pressure.

Charles's Law for Gases. At a fixed pressure the volume of a gas is directly proportional to the absolute temperature.

Conservation of Matter and Energy. In any change, the sum of the amount of matter and the amount of energy remains constant.

Conservation of Momentum. For any collision, the total momentum (mass multiplied by velocity) of all the bodies involved remains unchanged.

Force Between Two Charged Bodies (Coulomb's Law). The force is proportional to the product of the charges and inversely proportional to the square of the distance between them.

Gravitational Law. The gravitational force between two bodies is directly proportional to the product of their masses and inversely proportional to the square of the distance between their centers.

Hooke's Law. Within the elastic limits of any body, the strain produced is proportional to the stress applied.

Le Chatelier's Principle. If stress is applied to a system at equilibrium, the system reacts so as to undo the effects of the stress.

Newton's Laws of Motion

I. A body continues in a state of rest or in uniform straight line motion unless acted upon by an outside force.

II. The change in motion of a body is proportional to the force applied.

III. To every action, there is an equal and opposite reaction.

Ohm's Law. Electric current is equal to the ratio of voltage and resistance.

Periodic Law of the Elements. The elements, when arranged in order of increasing atomic numbers, show periodic variations in chemical and physical properties.

Thermodynamics, Laws of

I. When work is transformed into heat or vice versa, the amount of work is always equivalent to the amount of heat.

II. It is impossible by any continuous self-sustaining process for heat to be transferred from a colder to a hotter body.

Energy in Today's World

A technological society such as the United States consumes large amounts of energy. The availability and safety of energy sources are increasingly being seen as major problems.

SOURCES OF ENERGY WE USE TODAY

In the United States, our main source of energy is *fossil fuels,* such as oil, coal, and natural gas. These account for 90 percent of our energy consumption. Water power is about 5 percent and nuclear energy is another 5 percent. The main problem with the use of fossil fuels is that the world's supply is limited, it is not renewable, and we are using it so fast that it will be gone in about 200 years. Already, the United States must import billions of dollars worth of expensive foreign oil because our once-large domestic supplies are nearly exhausted. Also, these fuels, especially coal, present serious environmental and pollution problems.

NEW SOURCES OF ENERGY

Nuclear Energy. The fission reaction, in which atoms of uranium or thorium are split by the absorption of neutrons, produces very large amounts of energy, millions of times as much as the same weight of coal. Electric power plants using the fission reaction are expected to provide about 50 percent of our electricity by the year 2000. We have enough uranium to supply our energy needs for several hundred years. However, there are serious drawbacks to the use of fission:

1. Thermal pollution. The power plants produce a great deal of waste heat that must go into the atmosphere and water systems. The result of this discharge of waste heat may be an appreciable warming of the climate, with unpredictable results.
2. Disposal of radioactive wastes. The wastes will remain radioactive for thousands of years. How to dispose of them without polluting the environment is a serious problem.
3. Possibility of an accident releasing radioactive materials.

The fusion reaction, in which hydrogen nuclei are fused to produce helium, also releases immense amounts of energy, and uses a source of energy which is available in vast amounts. A controlled fusion reaction has not yet been developed.

Solar Energy. If we could use as little as 0.1 percent of the energy we daily receive from the sun, we would need no other energy supply. The main problem in utilizing solar energy is collecting it, which would require enormous installations. The cost of the electricity thus produced would be three or four times what we pay now. Solar heating and cooling of homes

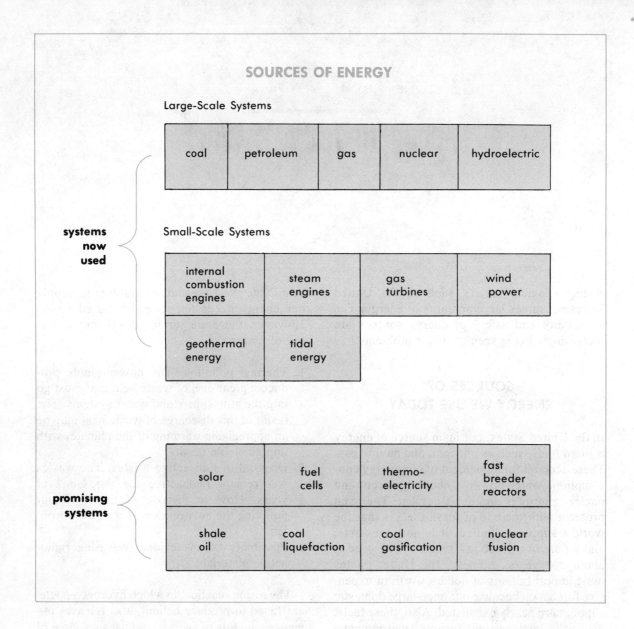

SOURCES OF ENERGY

Large-Scale Systems

coal	petroleum	gas	nuclear	hydroelectric

systems now used

Small-Scale Systems

internal combustion engines	steam engines	gas turbines	wind power
geothermal energy	tidal energy		

promising systems

solar	fuel cells	thermo-electricity	fast breeder reactors
shale oil	coal liquefaction	coal gasification	nuclear fusion

are feasible and should, in time, significantly reduce the need for other energy sources for this use.

Geothermal Energy. Because of the presence of radioactive elements, the interior of the earth is very hot. About twenty-five miles down, for example, the temperature is about 1000°C. Hot rock, underground hot water, and steam are a large potential source of energy. However, underground hot water sources usually are heavily polluted with sulfur compounds and minerals. The use of heated rock to heat water, which would be circulated through the rock, offers the possibility of large amounts of energy, but development of such plants would require a massive investment of money.

Tidal Power. In some parts of the world, such as Nova Scotia, tides rise to great heights. This daily movement of water could be used to generate power which would be useful in particular areas.

SOCIAL SCIENCE

Anthropology, economics, geography, psychology, and sociology are treated in the following pages. These subjects have interested men and women for many years, but knowledge of them has expanded so rapidly that many social science courses taught in school today did not exist a generation ago. This rapid growth has been stimulated by discoveries about the early history of man, concern about how to use our natural resources wisely, and problems of individuals and nations in getting along with one another.

To help you learn more about social science, this section explains its significant developments and provides interesting biographical information on the men and women who have made outstanding contributions. If you have not yet given serious thought to studying social science, this information may help you develop an interest in this vital field.

Anthropology

Anthropology is that field of the social sciences which seeks to describe and interpret the development of man since his appearance on earth, and his relation to his cultural development. It is sometimes considered also to be one of the behavioral sciences, since it is the study of the individual in his culture and of differences between cultures. This study of man (*anthropos* is the Greek word for man), dealing with all aspects of culture, is being altered daily because man is constantly gaining new knowledge, new concepts, and new technology. The Samoan culture that Margaret Mead described 50 years ago, for example, no longer exists. It was destroyed by tourists and modern technology, surviving only in Professor Mead's work.

Many of the methods of investigation used by anthropologists are the same as those used in the natural sciences. The anthropologist shares the most common sources of data, however, with the other social scientists. These sources are direct observations, interviews, records, and statistics assembled in the field.

An anthropologist may use a *historical* approach, as in a study of a single ethnic or social group. Or he may choose to use a *comparative* approach to test whether a characteristic is indigenous (originating in a particular region) or is shared by two or more cultures.

Physical anthropology studies man as a biological being. Other branches of the science depend on the work of physical anthropologists in producing facts. Physical anthropologists determine, for example, the predominant hair and eye color of groups or races. By comparing skulls and other bones found at ancient sites of human life, they establish the structure of early man. In such work physical anthropology shows itself closely related to the biological science of anatomy. Without this basic research, the other branches of anthropology would have far less information to use.

Cultural anthropology places man in a culture. Culture is a term upon which no two anthropologists entirely agree. A simple definition is "man's way of adjusting to his environment." Aspects about this man-in-a-culture studied by the cultural anthropologist are his land or territory; his way of living on that land (solving his food problems; his tools), his enemies; his beliefs; his creative expressions, such as art or dance; his relationships with others (the structure of his family life and community).

Archaeology. Archaeology is a subdivision of cultural anthropology. It is the study of the ancient evidence of man's culture. It has a historical viewpoint. It seeks to describe the cultures of the distant past. By skillful digging and by careful examination of all the surviving artifacts, archaeologists can reconstruct the physical and social features of an ancient family, town, or even race.

Techniques of finding promising places in which to dig are highly sophisticated. Aerial photography is used to help identify a site that might be productive. Geographers and mapmakers are consulted and historical records, which often give clues, are scrutinized minutely by researchers. The Bible, for example, has proven a reliable source for clues to sites.

Equally useful to archaeology is knowing *how* to dig. The earliest archaeologists were often travelers seeking treasures for museums. They hired gangs of laborers and dug as fast as they could. Today a site is laid open with all the care of a surgeon performing a delicate operation. The entire site is carefully photographed, surveyed, plotted, and divided into small areas. Every scoop of earth is examined, and even the smallest piece of charred wood, pottery, or metal is marked as to where it was found.

Two remarkably accurate methods of dating artifacts have been developed. The first, dating by means of pottery, began in 1890 through an insight by the Near Eastern archaeologist Sir Flinders Petrie. At the mound known as Tell el-Hesi (possibly the Biblical Eglon), Petrie discovered "at one stroke a series of all the varieties of pottery over a thousand years." He called pottery the "essential alphabet of archaeology." Artifacts made of other materials, such as wood, cloth, and skin, decay. Metal corrodes and was not commonly used by ancient people because of its cost. Pottery, however, is made of clay, and clay survives fire, storms, and time. Clay jugs (amphoras) for wine and olive oil have survived from ancient times even at the bottom of the ocean, relics of sunken ships. All kinds of household utensils made of clay (bowls, oil lamps, water jugs, etc.) are found wherever people lived in community, most of the utensils broken into pieces (shards) and thrown into the town dump—all of it valuable evidence of an ancient way of life. Today the system of dating by pottery, based on relationships between all kinds of ancient pottery and known historical dates, is almost an exact science.

The second method of dating, recently developed, is known as Radiocarbon 14 dating. It depends on the predictable rate of decay of the radioactivity of this isotope. All living organic matter has a known amount of radioactivity in its carbon content. When a plant or an animal dies, its radioactivity begins to diminish. The rate of decay can be calculated (though it is sometimes subject to interference by contamination from an extraneous natural source). A scientist can measure the amount of radioactivity remaining in the carbon-containing sample of a plant or animal and then calculate the number of years that have elapsed since the plant or animal died.

SIGNIFICANT FIGURES IN ANTHROPOLOGY

Lewis Henry Morgan (1818–1881). By training a lawyer, Morgan came to be known as the father of American anthropology because of his life-long work and writings on American Indian tribes. In 1847, the Senecas gave him honorary membership in their tribe, and in 1851, his book, *The League of the Iroquois* was published, the first scientific account of the life of an Indian tribe. *Houses and House* (1881) sets forth the relationship between the domestic architecture and the social organization of North and Central American Indians.

Heinrich Schliemann (1822–1890). Born of poor German parents, Schliemann was virtually self-educated, yet by age 25 spoke seven languages in addition to German. A successful international businessman before he was 30, he

Self-trained archaeologist Heinrich Schliemann. He rediscovered the ancient city of Troy and also found remains of even older cities.

Margaret Mead. The anthropologist's works include *People and Places,* a landmark description of the techniques of her field.

joined the gold rush in California and made a fortune. He retired, traveled extensively, studied ancient and modern Greek, and became an enthusiastic and knowledgeable searcher for ancient Greek city sites. Becoming convinced that the Troy of Homer's *Iliad* was to be found under the mound at Hisarlik in Asia Minor (Turkey), he used his wealth to begin excavations in 1871. After two years he wrote a report and turned to excavating the tombs of Mycenean kings. He returned to Troy for further investigations in 1876 and again in 1882–1883 and 1890 with Wilhelm Dörpfeld, a careful, methodical technician who complemented Schliemann's more romantic approach. Schliemann receives credit for uncovering and distinguishing the successive layers of the cities built atop each other on the single site at Hisarlik. But it was Dörpfeld who, after Schliemann's death in 1890, determined that Homer's Troy was layer VI (later corrected to VIIA) from the bottom, and not II, as Schliemann had believed. Yet Schliemann and his discoveries awakened the world to the potentialities and the excitement of archaeology. Today the interest in tracing the history of ancient civilizations is greater than ever.

Sir Edward Burnett Tylor (1832–1917). Tylor is considered by some to be the first great name in anthropology. Born and educated in England, he traveled in the United States and in Mexico and wrote *Researches into the Early History of Mankind* (1865). His best known book is *Primitive Culture,* and his greatest contribution to the study of man and culture was his analysis of religion as behavior motivated by value. He explained to the western world the belief of millions of sub-Saharan Africans in what he called *animism,* the belief that natural objects and phenomena, and even the universe, possess souls.

Franz Boas (1858–1942). Born in Germany, Boas came to the United States in 1886. He became an inspiring teacher of anthropology at Columbia and Clark universities. His work in the culture of early man quickly made him one of the world's leading authorities on the races of man. He was exacting in his collection of scientific data and a titan in his field, and three of the most prominent figures in modern anthropology were his students.

Alfred Kroeber (1876–1960). Known as the "anthropologist's anthropologist," Kroeber founded and taught in the Department of Anthropology at the University of California at Berkeley. Although he focused on Indian tribes of North and South America, his coverage of the general fields of ethnology, social organization, linguistics, and archaeology, was enormous.

Ruth Benedict (1887–1948). Benedict was an English teacher turned anthropologist. Kroeber called her *Patterns of Culture* (1934) a milestone in the development of anthropology. Margaret Mead said that Benedict's work was "based on scholarly knowledge of the sources, combined with first-hand experience of American Indian tribes."

William Foxwell Albright (1891–1971). Born in Chile of American missionary parents, Albright contributed to the study of anthropology through his studies in archaeology and religion in Palestine. He systematized the pottery-dating

SOCIAL SCIENCE

Mary and Louis S. B. Leakey assemble Zinjanthropus skull near Olduvai Gorge, Tanzania. At Fort Ternan, Kenya, the Leakeys uncovered animal bones many millions of years old. Some were from extinct ancestors of the modern giraffe, elephant, and ostrich.

method for biblical sites begun by Petrie. His role as a teacher of scores of younger biblical archaeologists, at Johns Hopkins University and at the American School for Oriental Research in Jerusalem, advanced all biblical studies significantly.

Margaret Mead (1901–   ).   Across 45 years, Mead carried out studies of cultures of remote peoples. Research in Samoa in 1925–26 produced *Coming of Age in Samoa*, describing the development of an adolescent girl in a Polynesian society. Her *New Guinea Journal* was produced for television in 1968. Called by Rebecca West "a genius of the prophetic sort," Margaret Mead considers herself a specialist in "the conditioning of the social personalities of both sexes."

Louis Leakey (1903–1972).   The British anthropologist Leakey, born in Kenya, became the leading authority on the ancient peoples of East Africa. A major contributor to the study of prehistoric man, his work at Olduvai Gorge was monumental. The Gorge is probably the most

important prehistoric site anywhere in the world. There, the skull of the earliest toolmaking man was found, and in 1967 Leakey found fossil remains of the earliest known manlike creature. Leakey and his wife trained many Kenyans who became outstanding fossil finders. Thus, Leakey's work is carried on today to advance our knowledge of the prehistoric past.

Zinjanthropus skull, found in Olduvai Gorge, Tanzania, is 1,750,000 years old.

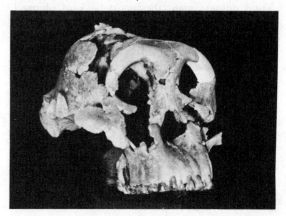

GLOSSARY OF ANTHROPOLOGICAL TERMS

acculturation. Changes in one culture as a result of contact with one or more other cultures. Sometimes the groups exchange cultural elements more or less equally; more often acculturation refers to a primitive society slowly adapting to, and becoming at least partly assimilated by, a more advanced society. American Indians, for example, have taken over most, but not all, of the cultural traits of the white, West European invaders. *Applied anthropology* often refers to the study of how to achieve deliberate cultural change, such as the successful introduction of complex farm equipment to a primitive society that does not know how to use or care for such machinery.

age set or **age grade.** Groups of persons whose age determines their role, or activity, in society. The age span usually is several years, for example, the teen-age period in American society. Sometimes the age span may be only one year or a subdivision of an age set, such as the high school class of 1978. An age set usually progresses together through the various roles of a society, as does a generation in a particular society. There are usually well-defined obligations of one age set to another, as, for example, a freshman class showing deference to senior class, or seniors assuming the obligation of tutoring freshmen.

animism. A belief that all living things, such as trees, animals, and birds; and all inanimate things, such as rivers and mountains; possess an innate soul, spirit, or force. Many primitive peoples throughout the world believe that "spirits" live in objects, that these spirits may be "good" or "bad" and that, since they may sometimes transfer from object to object or even enter into and possess men, they must be kept pleased. Some anthropologists hold that modern religions derive in part from these ancient beliefs. In philosophy animism refers to a belief in a vital source, principle, or spirit separate from material things and governing all behavior.

clan. A group of persons claiming descent from a common ancestor. The relationship between the members of the clan is defined as either patrilineal (related through the male line of descent) or matrilineal (related through the female line of descent). The members of most clans feel themselves closely related and require their members to marry outside their clan to avoid incest. Many clans are named after a totem, which offers their members protection. Scottish clans have accepted membership through both male and female relationships, and marriage within clans has been customary

culture. All human activity, sometimes called patterns of behavior or ways of life, that are transmitted from one generation to the next. The essence of culture consists of traditional ideas and their values. It consists also of human achievements in every field and of activities in language, art, government, war, religion, family, and education. Scientists who study the culture of both past and present are called *anthropologists;* those who study the cultures of today are called *sociologists*. Culture is generally considered a human phenomenon, because animals cannot store up and transmit the knowledge they gain from daily experience. The term *culture* has been adopted by ethologists (scientists who study the behavior of animals). All human societies have their distinctive cultures, which show common elements, such as religion, social structure, economic organization, and regulation of food, clothing, shelter, and weapons. *Cultural traits* are distinctive ways of behaving, such as marriage practices of monogamy or polygamy. A *cultural complex* or *pattern* is a group of cultural traits dependent on each other, such as the aspect of American Indian culture that depended on the hunting of buffalo. It is believed that all cultures pass through an evolutionary sequence, but that all stages may not appear in the history of every culture. The evolutionary stages of cultures are usually described as the hunting-gathering society, the food-producing society, and the urban or city-state society.

diffusion. The historical process by which cultural similarities spread to various societies. Three processes of diffusion are recognized: (1) *Primary diffusion* (also known as *cultural dispersion*) occurs when migrating peoples carry their cultures to other societies. (2) *Secondary diffusion* occurs when one society borrows directly from another. (3) *Stimulus diffusion* occurs when the strength of an idea causes change. Cultural similarities may also develop from *invention*, which is the only way of producing change in an original direction. Invention includes the creation of new ideas as well as things.

ethnocentrism. The view that one's own group or society is superior to all others. Ethnocentrism usually expresses itself in hostility against other groups, resulting in discrimination and violence. Ethnocentric behavior is usually rewarded; nonconformity is punished, often severely.

ethnology, ethnography. The anthropological study of the origins, growth, and change of culture in primitive societies, which have simple political, economic, and technological development. Early ethnological studies described culture in terms of the historical processes of migration and acculturation; but, in order to correct undemonstrable assumptions about the behavior of ancient people, modern ethnologists compare ancient and modern cultures, using rigorous scientific method. *Ethnology* is not to be confused with *ethology*, the study of *animal* behavior.

folkways and **mores.** Habits or customs common to a society are its folkways: common courtesies or fashions, for example. If a person violates a folkway, he is usually punished, perhaps by shunning or exclusion. *Mores* are folkways that are considered essential to a society's welfare or survival: matters of sexual conduct, family responsibilities, religious practices, for example. Violations of mores are often violations of law and produce shock, horror, and moral indigna-

tion. They result in severe penalties of the perpetrator. Crimes such as theft, murder, or desecration are violations of mores, since they involve the sanctity of property, the value of life, and the inviolability of religious or national symbols.

matriarchy and **patriarchy.** A society tracing descent through the female or a society in which women are the leaders is a matriarchy. Patriarchy refers to a society that traces descent through the male or in which males are the leaders.

society. A group of individuals living together as members of a community.

taboo. A restriction or prohibition placed against an act, object, place, or word which, if violated, will result in punishment. Taboos derive from a belief that certain personal or social situations or acts are inherently dangerous, such as improper behavior in shrines and temples, participation in such ritually unclean events as childbirth or death, or contact with persons and things associated with sacred persons, like kings, priests, or high officialdom. In primitive societies taboos are often placed against persons, places, or things that are thought to have special powers. Violation of a taboo is believed to unleash hostility upon the community. Violators are severely punished and a rite of purification is usually performed by priests. In Judaism prohibitions against unclean or sacred things are taboos.

Economics

HOW ECONOMIC SYSTEMS WORK

To satisfy its material needs, a society must answer basic questions: *What* to produce? *How* to produce? *How* much to produce? *Who* is to produce it? *For whom? Who* decides all these things? How the society solves these problems determines the type of economic system it will have.

There are two principal economic systems functioning in the world today: capitalism and

socialism. Socialism exists in various forms, the most widespread being communism.

Capitalism

Capitalism has been the principal economic system in the West for about four centuries. It is based on the free interaction between owners of capital (factories, machinery) and nonowners who sell their services (labor) to the owners. Theoretically, owners may produce whatever

Sign in supermarket suggests coffee prices can be driven down if consumers buy less, thus creating a surplus. In a free market a surplus of goods will cause prices to drop, and a scarcity will cause prices to rise.

they wish, in the manner and quantity they wish. Workers may sell their services at their price, and they sell these services when and to whom they wish. In this system every commodity and service has its price, the worker's price being the wage rate, established by agreement with the owner. The prices charged by owners and labor are affected by supply and demand. For example, if there are fewer pianos on the market than people who want them, there is a scarcity and the price rises. Manufacturers will produce more pianos, since profits are rising with the prices. As more pianos become available, the price goes down and the manufacturer slows production.

Theoretically, the same situation holds in labor and land markets. If lumberjacks become scarce, their price (wage) goes up and job opportunities in lumbering increase. As more lumberjacks become available, their wage goes down and young men look for work in a less crowded field. Or, in land use, if peanuts bring a better price than cotton, farmers will choose to grow peanuts.

So, in a capitalist society—in a free economic system—this complex mechanism of supply and demand and the resulting fluctuations in costs and prices automatically decide the basic questions of *What? How?* and *For Whom?*

What? The kind and quantity of goods produced depend on what consumers buy with money received for services and wages. Since manufacturers profit on bought goods only, the manufacturers make only what will sell.

How? Competition determines production methods. The more technology used and the less paid for labor, the lower the market price and, all other factors remaining equal, the greater the profit. At the same time, producers must maintain the attractiveness of their product in the marketplace, either through superior quality or attractive presentation.

For Whom? Since supply and demand in large part determine the amount of money available to the wage-earner, they also determine the amount most consumers have available to spend. In this way, goods are distributed and the cycle completed.

212

The Growth of Capitalism. Adam Smith, in his book *The Wealth of Nations* (1776), stated that if every individual could pursue his own economic interest without interference—particularly from government—a harmonious, free, perfectly competitive economy would automatically result, with maximum production and well-being for all. Centuries before Smith described his ideal system (a hands-off policy known as *laissez-faire*) a capitalism of commerce and trade developed from the huge British woolen cloth industry. From the Middle Ages through the eighteenth century, this mercantilism flourished, fed by increasing long-distance trade, growth of commercial towns and the middle class, and New World wealth. The invention of the flying shuttle and the spinning jenny revolutionized the industry. Production was moved from homes to factories. Further inventions—the steam engine, cotton gin, and sewing machine—further eliminated the old ways. The new ways spread to the United States and Europe, and the Industrial Revolution was under way. By the mid-nineteenth century, the golden age of capitalism had arrived.

Smith's *laissez-faire* philosophy of totally free competition prevailed. There were free trade, the gold standard, colonialism, and political support for the businessman. Capitalists, continually amassing capital, eventually dominated labor. Among the results were long working hours, deplorable working conditions, child labor, and other abuses.

Late last century a depression deeply involved capitalists. Antiquated management, marketing, and accounting methods, as well as a shortage of working capital forced consolidation of small companies into giant corporations, able to sell stock and quickly raise money. Monopolies and cartels were formed which regulated prices, destroying competition. "Big business" of this kind meant that perfect competition as Smith had envisioned it no longer existed. There were no controls to keep prices fair, no checks to preserve a pure capitalistic economy responsive to the needs of the people.

The labor movement emerged as a reaction to this situation; later, an increasing governmental role developed. Legislation, such as the Sherman Antitrust Act, worked to break up the enormous monopolies that controlled markets and spawned injustices. With the stock market crash of 1929, *laissez-faire* ended and, in the United States, pure capitalism suffered the Great Depression of the 1930s. The extensive social legislation of the New Deal of Franklin Roosevelt's administration resulted. Meanwhile socialism found supporters. Although communism did not spread to the West at the time Russia adopted it, it challenged capitalism as a socially just economic system.

Today, pure capitalism is nonexistent. What

THE BUDGET DOLLAR

SOURCES OF INCOME

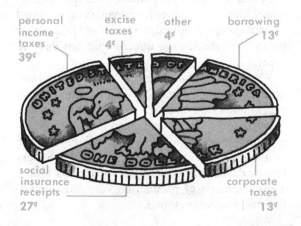

personal income taxes 39¢

excise taxes 4¢

other 4¢

borrowing 13¢

social insurance receipts 27¢

corporate taxes 13¢

EXPENDITURES

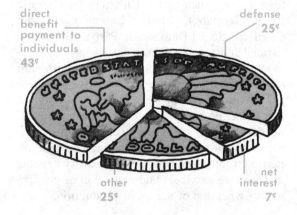

direct benefit payment to individuals 43¢

defense 25¢

other 25¢

net interest 7¢

has emerged and now is called capitalism is a mixed economy, a regulated free-enterprise system containing both private ownership and government control and influence. In short, capitalism survives mixed with a form of socialism in such nations as the United States, Great Britain, West Germany, and Japan.

Socialism

Socialism, in various forms, offers the most obvious alternative to capitalism. Pure socialism holds that all property belongs to the community, and that production, allocation of labor, distribution, and exchange of goods should be government-controlled. Ideally, each community member gives "according to his ability" and receives "according to his work or deed." (Some theorists prefer "according to his need.") Socialism attempts to structure economic equality for all.

Early socialism was most deeply influenced by Sir Thomas More's *Utopia* (1516), the name of an imaginary island exhibiting political, legal, and economic perfection. Followers of the Utopian ideal believe the natural human order requires communal ownership of property, which results in natural harmony. In the attempt to reinstate such natural order, some Utopians founded socialistic groups, hoping others would found more, thus drawing population from the capitalistic environment. Their expectation was the eventual federation of these groups for the purpose of dominating economic life. They proved impractical and failed.

The socialism most acceptable to the West is evidenced in the leading Western European reform parties such as the Christian Democratic Party (Germany), Britain's Labour Party, and Sweden's Social Democratic Party—all labeled "social democrats." These parties have in common such economic policies as government ownership of productive capital in areas where private enterprise will not, cannot, or should not enter; economic planning for production of needed, though not profit-producing commodities; taxation to redistribute income and inherited wealth; generous social security benefits and welfare services; and extension of government ownership of means of production.

Many forms of socialism have arisen—Christian socialism, guild socialism, Fabianism (evolutionary socialism), and state and Marxian socialism (communism).

Communism

The most radical socialist system, communism, is based on the teachings of Karl Marx, who published his book *Communist Manifesto* in 1848. As in other socialist systems, property is owned by the community, and goods are distributed, ideally, according to need.

The three basic economic problems are solved by the Soviet Union as follows. (Other communist nations—particularly China—differ in some degree from the Soviet system.)

What? The Soviet nation owns nearly all the capital (means of production such as factories, land, mines), and economic planners determine what is to be produced. At this time the nation appears to favor industry that increases capital, builds up the economy, and aids the stockpiles of defense products; consumer goods are of secondary importance and often scarce.

How? The state-owned facilities are run by managers who are loyal and sympathetic members of the Communist Party. For their services the managers receive good pay and special privileges. The state assigns to each manager a quota of goods to produce. If the quota is met, a manager may receive a bonus or special commendation; if it is not met, the manager may be demoted or otherwise punished. Consequently, under this arrangement, managers may hoard goods, keep production low, or find other means of establishing quotas that are easy to meet.

Workers may be assigned to an industry and not be completely free to try out employment in other industries or other parts of the country. They receive wages and incentive pay; piecework pay is common. Communications between industries in various regions is sometimes lacking, and know-how may not be passed along. Thus, methods of production vary from primitive to highly developed.

For Whom? In theory, goods in a communist economy are distributed according to need. In the Soviet Union, the security of the state is cared for before individual needs are met. Social and political stratifications influence the distribution of commodities.

On the other hand, education does not require money. Children of the poor who distinguish themselves in the state examinations may be selected for college or university. The highly educated, particularly college professors, rank high socially; they may be given ownership of a car, a country cottage, or a well-equipped laboratory.

Money has limited value. Many goods, such as certain kinds of housing, are not purchasable; the state distributes them on a political basis. The government imposes such heavy taxes on certain products that the average Russian cannot afford them.

The Growth of Communism. The founders of modern communism, Karl Marx and Friedrich Engels, formulated the theory known as "scientific socialism." They held that history reveals that human society passes through stages of economic production. The first is the primitive, communal state in which the means of production (land, tools, etc.) are communally owned. In the second, third, and fourth states—slavery, feudalism, and capitalism—a few own the means of production; the masses, working for the few, are exploited. (Later communist theorists do not consider capitalism a necessary stage.) The inequality causes conflict (class struggle). Eventually the existing owner class is replaced by the industrial working class, and once again the means of production are owned by the community. After this stage no new class arises to exploit the masses.

After the publication of *Communist Manifesto,* many European socialist parties embraced communist views, but would not or could not operate outside the Western democratic framework. In Russia, however, no democratic framework existed, only a peasant class severely abused by its rulers. Among the many Russian Marxists was Vladimir Lenin, who was committed to establishing a proletarian dictatorship by force. He and his followers organized a group of revolutionaries, called the Bolsheviks, who seized power in 1917. After the revolution came three years of war between the Reds (Bolsheviks) and the Whites (upper classes), from which the Reds emerged the victors and the Communist Party was established. In the 1930s Joseph Stalin collectivized agriculture and nationalized industry.

Communism is now a worldwide movement fostered by communist parties everywhere, parties modeled after the Communist Party of the Soviet Union. Today the Communist Party dominates not only the Soviet Union, but also China, the Eastern European satellite nations, Cuba, and several Asian and African nations.

SIGNIFICANT FIGURES IN ECONOMICS

Thomas Gresham (1519?–1579). An English merchant and financier, Gresham is remembered today chiefly for Gresham's Law, which states that debased or mutilated money tends to drive from circulation sound, or good, money. It is an economic principle based on the tendency of people to hoard: they keep what is good and pass along what is bad. After World War I, for example, so much paper money was printed that coin disappeared from circulation. Gresham was not the first to state the principle. Medieval merchants knew well that clipped coins circulated first.

Adam Smith (1723–1790). The founder of classical economics and the advocate of *laissez-faire* policies, Scottish economist Smith formulated the basic tenets of capitalism. Believing that people know what is best for themselves and that the profit motive is sufficient to supply the necessary goods at competitive prices, Smith stood squarely against government controls and monopolistic practices. He argued for free trade and free markets. His famous five-volume treatise *Inquiry into the Nature and Causes of the Wealth of Nations* (1776), the first fully developed theory of political economics, states that the value of a product derives from the labor that produces it; and that

Adam Smith, eighteenth-century economist. During the American revolution Smith said England would profit as much from trade with free states as from her colonial possessions.

Thomas R. Malthus, early student of population dynamics. He counseled against social reforms, claiming that reform encouraged population growth among the poor.

labor itself, not land or money, is the true source of a nation's wealth. *The Wealth of Nations,* one of the most influential books ever written, had an enormous impact on the policies of West European and American governments. To this day, Adam Smith remains a widely respected figure in economics.

Thomas Robert Malthus (1766–1834). An English economist best known for his theory that a population increases more rapidly than the food supply that supports it, Malthus concluded that starvation, disease, and war are unavoidable checks on population growth. Malthusians exercised strong influence on classical economists, especially David Ricardo, but they were generally refuted by modern economists, who pointed to abundant food supplies created by scientific agricultural techniques. In recent years, however, some ecological studies of the dynamics of populations in natural systems have lent support to Malthus's basic assumption. Certain conservationists now point to increasing population as the most serious threat to natural resources and world stability.

David Ricardo (1772–1823). An English classical economist, Ricardo believed that as soon as wages rise above the subsistence level, the population increases to the point where competition forces wages down again, a theory that in part derives from Malthusian doctrine. Ricardo's most famous book is the *Principles of Political Economy and Taxation* (1817), in which he credits the value of a product to the labor that produces it and states that a landowner's rent is a gift from nature. His theory of value greatly influenced Karl Marx, who based his economic theories on it; and Henry George (1839–1897), the American reformer, who held that all men have an equal right to the use of land. Ricardo was a strong advocate of free trade, believing that if no restrictions were placed on trade, each country would soon produce what was most advantageous to it. One of the first scientific social scientists, Ricardo greatly influenced the methods of later economists. Ricardo, with Adam Smith and J. S. Mill, counseled the doctrine of laissez-faire. This approach was consistent with the new emphasis on individualism and competition.

216

Karl Marx, founder of communism. His ideas have had a profound effect on intellectual thought and political affairs right up to the present in all countries of the world.

Karl Marx (1818–1883). The German philosopher Marx formulated the political-economic theories of modern socialism and communism. Rooted in a philosophical system called dialectical materialism, which states that all reality is material and that all change is the result of a conflict between opposites, Marxism holds that history proceeds from a continuous class struggle between labor and capital for power and wealth. Based on the assumption that in *laissez-faire* capitalism labor does not receive full value for its work and that profits remain in the hands of the capitalist, Marxism predicts that ever more severe economic depressions will periodically occur, causing ever more bitter social unrest and the inevitable collapse of capitalism, at which point the working class will assume political control over industry. With his collaborator Friedrich Engels (1820–1895) Marx issued *The Communist Manifesto* (1848), which urged the workers of the world to revolt against the capitalists and to seize political power. Marx's famous work, *Das Kapital* (1867–1894), completed by Engels, which has had immense influence throughout the world, is a critical study of classical *laissez-faire* capitalism. It enlarges upon Marx's dialectical materialism as postulated in the *Manifesto* and argues for state control of all industry. Modern communism, especially as it is practiced in the Soviet Union and East Europe, derives from Marx-Engel's formulation of international socialism-communism. Modern capitalism, however, with its mixed economies and welfare policies, has thus far disproved Marx's predictions of continuous class struggle and of the inevitable collapse of the capitalist state.

John Maynard Keynes (1883–1946). An exceptionally influential British economist of the first half of the twentieth century, Keynes began his career as a classical economist committed to free trade and unrestrained monetary policies. He severely criticized the reparations and nationalistic economic policies adopted by the Allies at Versailles after World War I and gained fame by correctly predicting they would bring Europe to ruin. Keynes came to believe later that governments should spend huge sums of money on public works in order to maintain full employment and increase purchasing power. He also supported government intervention in monetary policies. Both positions were designed to lessen the impact of economic depressions. During the Great Depression of the 1930s, many of Keynes's ideas were adopted by President Franklin D. Roosevelt in his New Deal. After World War II several West European nations adopted a program of full employment, thus eliminating one of the chief criticisms Marxism levels at capitalistic society. Keynes's major work is *The General Theory of Employment, Interest and Money* (1936).

Ernest Friedrich Schumacher (1911–1977). Former head of the British Coal Board, Schumacher became known as an economist studying the direction in which the multinational megasystems of our world culture must go in the twenty-first century. His books *Small is Beautiful* (1973) and *Guide for the Perplexed* (1977) suggest, as a partial solution, an "intermediate technology," which turns from size and speed in our economic endeavors to an evaluation of the direction and purpose of human progress.

SOCIAL SCIENCE

GLOSSARY OF TERMS IN ECONOMICS

balance of payments. The difference between a nation's imports and exports of goods, services, gold, capital, etc., over a given period (usually one year). If a nation's balance of payments is adverse—if there are more imports than exports —it may eventually affect the stability of the nation's currency. Balance of trade differs from balance of payments in that it excludes capital and service transactions and gold shipments.

capital, capitalism. In general, wealth, whether in money or property, owned and used to produce more money (interest) or something of value. In classical economics, capital is one of the three major factors of production, the others being land and labor. In business, capital is the money and credit needed to start and operate an enterprise, or the total wealth or assets of a firm, including such assets as securities, trademarks, patents, good will, etc. A distinction is frequently made between *fixed* capital, funds used for fixed assets (buildings, machinery, land, timber preserves, and the like), and *working* capital, funds needed to carry on business. Capital can also refer to the excess of assets over liability, that is, the net worth of an enterprise.

capital goods. Machines and tools used in the production of other goods.

capitalist. An owner of capital; an advocate of capitalism.

caveat emptor. Latin: "let the buyer beware," a merchandising maxim summarizing the common-law rule that the buyer must examine, judge, and test his purchase to see that he is getting the quantity and quality expected. *Caveat venditor* (Latin: "let the seller beware") is a merchandising maxim placing responsibility on the seller for any defects or deficiencies in items sold.

class struggle. In Marxian thought, the constant struggle for political and economic power waged between capitalists and workers.

commodities. Articles of trade or commerce, such as wheat, tin, and lumber; products as distinguished from services (insurance, dentistry, dry cleaning).

consumer. A person who buys and uses a commodity or service.

consumer goods. Products designed to satisfy people's needs and wants (shoes, clothing, golf balls) and not to produce other goods (for example, shoe machinery).

deflation. A general fall in the level of prices of goods and services that, in effect, increases the value of money. Though beneficial to creditors and to those with fixed incomes and large savings (whose money thereafter can purchase more in real terms), deflation usually brings about increased unemployment of both labor and capital.

distribution. The process by which commodities reach consumers, including warehousing, selling, shipping, and advertising.

entrepreneur. An entrepreneur is a person who organizes and manages a business; he also assumes the risks and takes the profits, if any.

goods. Articles of trade; wares, merchandise.

gross national product. The total output of goods and services of a country, stated at market prices for a given year. In the United States, as defined by the Department of Commerce, the GNP is the total market value of the goods and services produced by the nation's economy, before deduction of depreciation charges and other allowances for capital consumption.

inflation. A persistent general upward movement of prices for commodities and factors of production.

interest. The charge made for the loan of money. It is usually a percentage of the principal, the amount borrowed.

macroeconomics. The study of the economy as a whole; economic studies or analyses that consider aggregates of individuals or groups of commodities, such as total consumption, employment, or income. See *microeconomics*.

market economy. Virtually identical with the concept of free enterprise. In a market economy the basic decisions as to what should be produced and at what prices are determined in the marketplace, unhampered by government direction or control.

marketing. All business activities directed toward selling goods to the consumer; especially, market research, inventory control, selling, advertising, and promotion.

marketplace. The commercial world, viewed as an arena in which ideas and goods compete for recognition.

Marxism. Marxist doctrine may be summarized as follows: 1. The state has historically been a device of the dominant class for exploiting the masses. 2. Historical change has been brought about in the past mainly through the class struggle. 3. The capitalist system contains the seeds of its own decay. 4. The proletariat will topple capitalism as capitalism brought down feudalism. 5. The relatively short period of the dictatorship of the proletariat will be followed by an ushering in of a truly socialist order and a classless state.

mercantilism. An economic system that prevailed in Europe from the end of the Middle Ages to the start of the Industrial Revolution about 1750. Kings and their advisors placed emphasis on increasing state holdings in precious metals (gold and silver) and on trade that would bring bullion to their treasuries. All efforts were directed toward maintaining or increasing this flow inward, especially through overseas trade ventures in America and the Orient. Mercantilism eventually led to such constricting policies as royal or state monopolies and bans on emigration and the exporting of machinery.

microeconomics. The economic study or analysis of small groups of people, individuals, and industries.

nationalization. To nationalize is to bring some business (for example, a coal industry) under the direct control or ownership of the nation in which it lies or operates—either with or without compensation to the owners.

profit. Receipts from sales, less costs.

proletariat. The class without property, dependent for support of life on wages; the working class.

stock exchange. An organized market where members buy and sell listed securities according to established rules. The primary purpose of the stock market is to bring together all buyers and sellers and increase the marketability of the securities listed on that exchange.

supply and demand. Buyers seek to obtain goods at the lowest price obtainable; sellers of those goods seek to get as high a price as possible. The seller represents supply; the buyer, demand. Ultimately from this tension a point of equilibrium in the market is reached.

tax. A compulsory payment levied on citizens by their government for its own maintenance and for other expenditures for the common good. An *income tax* is a graduated tax based on income, usually providing exemptions for low-income groups. It was adopted in the United States in 1913 by the 16th Amendment to the Constitution. An *excise tax* is a tax imposed on the manufacture, sale, or consumption of a particular commodity, or on the use of a particular service. Federal excise taxes are levied, for example, on gasoline, cigarettes, and alcoholic beverages. Other forms of taxes levied on individuals and corporations include *inheritance taxes* imposed on the value of the property received by the heirs of a deceased person; *sales taxes* based on a percentage of the selling price; *customs duties* on imports and sometimes on exports; and special taxes for *social security* and *unemployment compensation*.

wealth. From the viewpoint of the economist, wealth is everything having economic value measurable in price.

Geography

Geography is a descriptive science. What it describes is the surface of the earth, in just about every imaginable way: its character, division into continents and countries, elevations, climates, soils, and plant and animal life and distribution. It also asks questions about men living on this earth: Where are they, and how many? How is man using the land in various places? What industries has man created, and where? This insatiable curiosity, this desire to know the earth we live on, extends to all the diverse features of the earth's surface.

Geography's concerns have another dimension: How have these geographic features come to be what they are? And how have they influenced, how do they now influence, the distribution of man and the kinds of things with which he busies himself?

Another characteristic of geography is that it is not interested in single separable items. In this respect geography is unique among the systematic sciences. It takes as its focus the regions, nations, continents, and other unit areas that form a complex in which all the individual elements that comprise geography are combined and are interacting.

Geography differs from the other social sciences in having a long history. Man has apparently always been interested in what the other side of the mountain looks like. In the sixth century B.C. Hecateus wrote his *Description of the Earth,* and in the fifth century B.C. Herodotus, the Greek known today as the father of both history and geography, compared his own people with the Persians and with peoples living near the Aegean Sea. Strabo, another Greek, traveled widely in Asia, Africa, and Europe at the beginning of the Christian Era, collecting material for his geographic writings. Ptolemy, a famous Egyptian astronomer, mathe-

matician, and geographer, was the first to treat geography systematically. About 150 A.D. Ptolemy attempted to gather all that was known about the earth's surface and wrote an eight-volume *Geographical Outline* that was used until the great age of exploration (fifteenth century) made his theories obsolete.

Geography is an integrating, or synthesizing, science. It serves as a bridge between the physical sciences and the social sciences. The data gathered and organized from the physical world are factual. Uses made of these data, and the interpretations placed on them, may have physical, economic, or social implications. Geography's standard methods of data collecting, such as mapping, census taking, and field observation, are coupled today with aerial photography and computer techniques that open up unending possibilities for description and analysis for widely varying needs among the other disciplines, as well as for geography itself.

Five approaches to geographic study are available:

(1) The physical or earth science approach studies the earth as a sphere—its waters, its atmosphere, earth-sun relations, plant and animal life, rocks, and minerals. The study of our earth's weather and climate is called meteor-

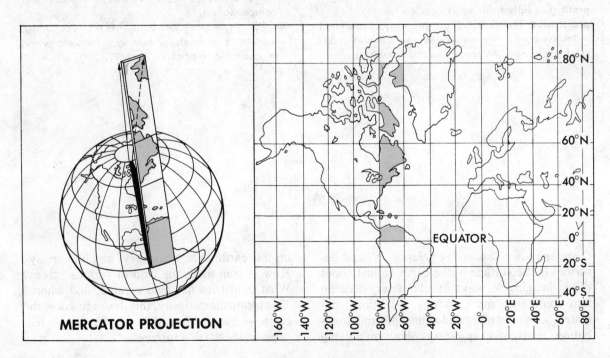

MERCATOR PROJECTION

ology or climatology. Current attempts to control amounts of rainfall depend on the skill of the meteorologist. The study of the ocean's tides, waves, and currents is called oceanography. Recently an oceanographic team from the United States joined a team from the Soviet Union in an international project researching the ocean in Antarctica.

(2) The regional approach studies a geographical area by regions. The regions may be selected on the basis of similarities of physical features, or on the basis of a notable cultural or technological level, or on political territorial boundaries. Area studies may be local, national, or global. They may deal with problems particular to a region or common to several regions. For example, a survey of rainfall patterns in the Middle East could be made which could then be compared with rainfall in Egypt and other North African nations, to the economic advantage of all states in the region.

(3) The spatial approach examines how man fits into the physical space he occupies. It is concerned with the location of places, such as the proper location of a new city (as with Brasilia, Brazil's modern capital city) or a new major port facility. It also deals with the geometry of the earth's surface. The preparation of maps and the design of appropriate map projections are called cartography. More than one hundred different projections have been worked out mathematically, using combinations of three basic types of projection: orthographic, cylindrical, and conic. Using an equal-area projection, usually of the conic or polyconic type, a student can compare areas of wheat production all over the world. The topographic maps put out by the U. S. Geological Survey showing the elevation and configuration of land areas are also of this type. The true shapes of land and water are best shown by the method of cylindrical projection. The famous Mercator maps, of cylindrical projection, were made specifically for navigation. There are many other kinds of maps that show the importance of cartography to modern research, for example, earthquake distribution; ocean currents; humid or dry continental regions; and rainy, equatorial regions.

(4) The man-land, or cultural, approach is interested in how man has used his environment and with man's attitude toward the land. Many different kinds of land use are studied. Agricultural, forest, mining, manufacturing, residential, and recreational are some uses that concern the cultural geographer. Problems such as the population explosion, the production of sufficient

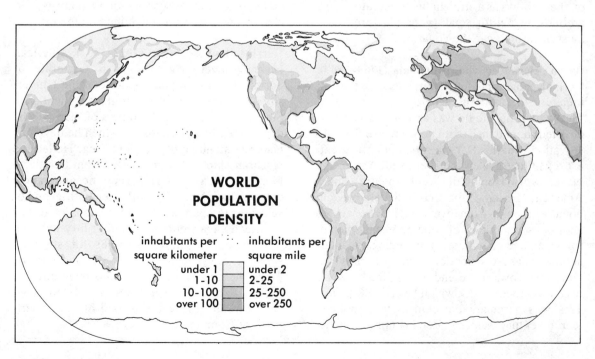

WORLD POPULATION DENSITY

inhabitants per square kilometer	inhabitants per square mile
under 1	under 2
1-10	2-25
10-100	25-250
over 100	over 250

food for the undernourished peoples of the world, and new sources or new methods of conserving existing sources of energy are among those the modern geographer can help to solve. (5) The historical approach adds the dimension of time to the study of the earth: how has change in the physical features of an area across a period of time affected its social or cultural or economic development? A good example is the Sinai desert, portions of which were once fertile under Nabatean methods of water husbanding and irrigation two thousand years ago, a knowledge lost to successor civilizations, but now being reintroduced by Israeli geographers and engineers.

SIGNIFICANT FIGURES IN GEOGRAPHY

Gerardus Mercator (1512–1594). Belgian mathematician and geographer, is the father of modern mapmaking. The Mercator projection, first used in 1569, transposes an area of the curved earth's surface to a flat surface. It shows meridians and parallels of latitude cutting each other at right angles. Mercator maps were a huge aid to navigators because a course drawn on them shows as a straight line. Mercator maps are most useful for small geographic areas and most accurate near the equator.

Baron Alexander von Humboldt (1769–1859). German geographer and naturalist, gave the first impetus to modern geographical research. Throughout his life he was an untiring traveler, devoted to, and insistent upon, precise field observation. Charles Darwin called him the greatest scientific traveler that ever lived. Among the places von Humboldt went to are South America, Mexico, Cuba, and India. He brought home with him from every region he visited enormous quantities of topographical, meteorological, and climatic data, including soil characteristics and distribution of animal and vegetable life. Toward the end of his life, he wrote his encyclopedic work which he called *Kosmos*. This was a remarkable contribution to nineteenth-century science, documenting and describing every known characteristic of the physical earth and the heavens, and driving home to readers the interrelation of all natural phenomena.

Matthew Fontaine Maury (1806–1873). American naval officer, founded modern oceanography. In his work charting ocean currents, he described the Gulf Stream as "a river in the ocean." A leader in systematizing observations at sea, he initiated international cooperation in studying the ocean. Although his theories and his methods did not meet with the approval of all American scientists of his day, he gained considerable recognition during his lifetime and even more following his death for his work in oceanography.

George B. Cressy (1896–1963). An outstanding American geographer, noted for his field investigations in the Far East, most especially in China. While teaching at the University of Shanghai, 1923–1929, he compiled the data for the book that made him famous, *China's Geographic Foundations*. Later he published additional studies in Asiatic geography. Cressey stands as a modern representative of the tradition begun by Humboldt of opening up vast new areas to accurate research, sound analysis, and clear reporting to the scientific community.

Harris Bates Stewart, Jr. (1922–   ). American oceanographer who earned a doctorate at Scripps Oceanographic Institute of the University of California in 1956. From his student days Stewart has felt that the future of man will be determined by the degree to which he develops his understanding of the global sea. He led the research ship *Explorer* in 1960 from Seattle to Norfolk, Virginia, gathering oceanographic data, including profiles of the sea bottom and of seawater temperatures, a continuous record of the earth's magnetic field, and at fifty different oceanographic stations samples for study of salinity, oxygen, and inorganic phosphorus. Since the mid 1960s Stewart has been director of the Atlantic Oceanographic and Meteorological Laboratories for the United States Department of Commerce.

MAPS AND MAP READING

Maps have been drawn and used by man since he began to explore the earth's surface. Now, as he reaches out into space with sophisticated telescopes and photographic equipment, he has made maps of space too. The making of maps is called *cartography;* the people who draw them are called *cartographers.*

Globes and Maps

Since the earth is round, we get the truest picture of it by drawing our maps on *globes.* Globes are interesting to study because they provide a picture of the entire earth. However, their usefulness is limited: they are cumbersome,

The antique map above bears a crude resemblance to the shape of Eurasia, but the 15th century map below is more a work of imagination than cartography.

TYPES OF PROJECTIONS

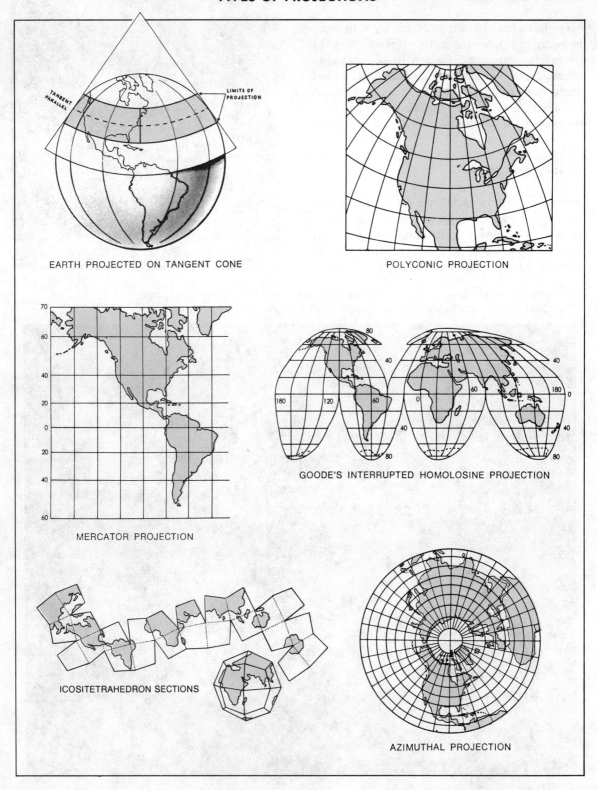

EARTH PROJECTED ON TANGENT CONE

POLYCONIC PROJECTION

MERCATOR PROJECTION

GOODE'S INTERRUPTED HOMOLOSINE PROJECTION

ICOSITETRAHEDRON SECTIONS

AZIMUTHAL PROJECTION

SOCIAL SCIENCE

bulky, and expensive. More importantly, because globes are usually quite small, they offer little room for information.

For these reasons, maps are used most of the time. Maps are flat pictures of the world or an area of it. They are relatively inexpensive and can be folded, hung on a wall, or bound in a book, called an *atlas*. To use maps well, there are certain facts about them that you should know.

The Grid. If you look at a globe of the earth, you will notice crisscross lines on it. The lines that go around the globe parallel to the equator are called *parallels,* or lines of *latitude.* Those that go up and down from the North to the South Pole are called *meridians,* or lines of *longitude.* These lines intersect to form a grid.

The grid is a system invented by navigators and scholars hundreds of years ago. With it you can locate any place on earth accurately if you know its latitude (how many degrees it is from the equator) and longitude (how many degrees it is from the prime meridian). For example, Nashville, Tennessee, is 36.10 degrees north and 86.48 degrees west. With this information you can easily find Nashville on a map of the United States. Washington, D.C., is 38.50 degrees north and 77.00 degrees west. Find the latitude and longitude of your town.

All reliable maps and globes have parallels and meridians marked on them. They are particularly useful to navigators on ships and airplanes, who use the grid as an absolute reference when calculating their course.

Map Projections

To understand map projections, think of the earth as an orange. Imagine that you can peel off a section of the earth's crust (the skin of an orange). Then imagine that you try to flatten the section you have peeled off. If you do this correctly, you will soon find out that the section cannot be flattened without tearing it at the edges, or distorting it in some way. This is the fundamental problem of representing the earth —a sphere—on a flat surface. How can we flatten out something that is round?

Through the years cartographers have had to face the problem of transferring the information on the globe to a flat surface with the least distortion. The solution they have developed for doing this is called *map projection.* The term comes from the cartographer's attempt to project the grid from the globe to the flat surface. While no single projection is better than all others, certain projections are better than others for showing specific things or meeting specific objectives.

The *Mercator projection* was devised by the great mapmaker Gerhard Mercator (1512–1594). It is a rectangle on which all parallels and meridians cross each other at right angles. Therefore, any straight line shows compass direction, which is very helpful to navigators. The drawback of the Mercator projection is that it greatly distorts land areas around the poles and in the higher latitudes, such as Greenland, making them appear much larger than they really are.

The *conic projection* has straight or slightly curved meridians that converge at the poles (or an imaginary area beyond the poles). It has arc-shaped parallels. Shape and distances are most accurate along the straight or nearly straight meridians. Distortions increase as the meridians begin to curve. The conic projection is most often used for area or large-scale maps, especially in the United States. A popular variation is the *polyconic projection.*

In *azimuthal projections,* one point on the globe, usually the equator or one of the poles, is selected as center. All lines that radiate from the center give true direction relative to the point that is chosen. Because distortion occurs along the outer edges, azimuthal projection is a poor method for mapping the world, but especially useful for mapping hemispheres.

For the most accurate picture of the world, we use *interrupted projections,* such as Goode's projection. Although there is some distortion along the outer edges, interrupted projections are truest in size and space relationships.

Detailed maps now are made by aerial photography. During World War II, this process was accomplished by combat aircraft flying at a known altitude above earth. Now scientists are able to place their cameras aboard rockets and satellites to cover vast areas.

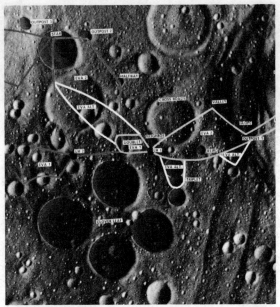

Apollo 13 landing site on the moon. This photograph provides the basis for a map of the Fra Mauro region, showing the routes the astronauts planned to use in their explorations.

Two geologists at Mission Control Center, Houston, Texas, use maps and aerial photographs to follow the activity of Apollo 15 astronauts on the surface of the moon.

Map Reading

Maps give an immense amount of information about the area of the earth they cover. They show such things as topography (physical features), vegetation, population distribution, economic and social conditions, climate, and even something about the history of the area. But no single map can do all these things. It would be too crowded to be useful, so different kinds of maps give different kinds of information. Probably the most popular and useful are transportation maps used for travel by sea (charts), by air (aeronautical maps), and by land (road maps). Relief maps, using raised surfaces, are helpful in showing topography.

Legends. Somewhere on every good map there is a legend, which tells what information the cartographer intends to show. It also tells the area the map covers, its projection, its scale, and the symbols used to convey information. In short, the legend tells how to use the map.

One of the most important things on the legend is the scale. It is the ratio of distances on the map to actual distances on the earth. Scale can be expressed in many ways. A *verbal scale* gives the relationship in words: *1 inch equals 100 miles.* A *graphic scale* gives the ratio on a line or bar. Most of the scales on road maps are graphic scales. There are also *representative fraction scales,* which show how many units on the map equal one unit on the earth. 1:10,000 or 1/1,000,000.

The legend also identifies the *symbols* used in the map. For example, the capital of a country or a state may be distinguished from other cities by use of a star inside a dot. Border lines are usually broken, while rivers are marked with solid lines of varying widths. On road maps, highways, state roads, and country roads are marked with solid lines, which may also be of different colors or widths. Railroad tracks may be shown as solid lines with cross-hatches, and so on.

One of the most important map symbols is *color.* Color is especially important on topographic maps to show elevation. Also found on topographical maps are *contour lines,* which connect areas of equal elevation.

Electronic map room. Scientists of the Water Resources Team of the U.S. Geological Survey in Phoenix, Arizona, can feed data into wall-size, computerized maps for use anywhere in the world. Here the scientists are wiring sections used to portray water tables.

Coordinates. One of the most important uses for a transportation map, of course, is to locate specific places. Many such maps have *letter-number coordinates,* which help you determine a particular location. If you have a road map handy, open it up and spread it out so that you can refer to it as you read about letter-number coordinates.

To use a system of coordinates, look up the place you want to find in the index, located somewhere on the map (or in front or back of an atlas). Note the letter and number that follow the entry: G6, for example. Then look at the top of the map, where you will find a series of letters; locate the letter G. On the side of the map you will find a series of numbers; look there for the number 6. Then draw an imaginary line across the map at the number, and another up and down at the letter. Near where the lines intersect, you will find the place you seek. Now try to find a few other places on your own. (Notice that the principle for locating these places with coordinates is very similar to that used for locating places by means of parallels and meridians.)

Mapping the Ocean Floor

We now know that the rapidly growing population of our planet requires full utilization of all available resources. As we look for new means of attending to the pressing needs of people everywhere, our attention turns to the riches of the oceans. There is every indication that these great bodies of water can supply minerals, food, and sources of power.

Accurate mapping of the ocean floor is vital to this search for resources. A device used for mapping is the echo-sounder, which measures the depth of the ocean by recording the time it takes for a sound to travel to the bottom and return as an echo. Echo-sounders have established that beneath the waters there are great valleys, called submarine canyons. In addition there are ocean trenches as much as seven miles deep. This knowledge of the ocean is important because it can help locate places where the resources are likely to be found. Once mapping is complete, full exploration and utilization of ocean resources can begin. With our maps we can mine these riches for the benefit of all.

GLOSSARY OF TERMS USED IN GEOGRAPHY

Prefixes

archaeo-. From Greek, meaning *old*.

bio-. From Greek, meaning *life*.

cosmo-. From Greek, meaning *world* or *universe*.

demo-. From Greek, meaning *people*.

geo-. From Greek, meaning *Earth*.

hydro-. From Greek, meaning *water*.

meteor-. From two Greek words, meaning *raised in the air* or *beyond*.

morpho-. From the Greek, meaning *form* or *structure*.

pedo-. From Greek meaning *soil* (a confusing geographic combining form, since there are two other *ped-* prefixes: *ped-* meaning *foot*, from Latin; and *ped-* meaning *child*, from Greek.

peri-. From Greek, meaning *around*.

zoö-. From Greek, meaning *animal*.

Suffixes

-gen. From Greek, meaning *produced*.

-graph. From Greek, meaning *draw, write, record*.

-logy. From Greek, meaning *word* or *speech*; by extension, *study* or *science*.

-nomy. From Greek, meaning *law, arrangement*.

---

biogeography. One of three major fields of geography, with two branches: plant geography and zoögraphy.

cartography. The making of maps. The word includes all phases of production: construction of projections, design, compilation, drafting, and reproduction. A person so engaged is a *cartographer*.

climate. The climate of a locality or region is the composite of temperature, barometric pressure, precipitation, sunshine, winds, humidity, etc. over an extended period of time and averaged to give characteristic conditions. *Weather* includes the same elements as *climate*, but implies a more particular time and place, especially a much shorter time-range. *Climatology* is the branch of geography that deals with climates. A person so engaged is a climatologist. See also *meteorology*.

cosmography. The description, mapping, or representation of the main features of the universe.

demography. A branch of human geography dealing with vital statistics.

erosion. A process in which the surface of the Earth is worn away (eroded) by the action of water, glacial ice, wind, etc.

geomorphology. A branch of physical geography, dealing with landforms in their origins, development, and characteristics.

glaciation. The effect of the action of glaciers on a place.

human geography. A major field of geography, dealing with social, historical, political, and economic factors. Its focus is wholly on human beings on Earth, now and in past times.

hydrology. A branch of physical geography dealing with the distribution, uses, and effects of water, both above and below ground.

landform. Any noteworthy feature—a hill, a valley, a plain—caused naturally by erosion, sediment, glaciation, etc.

meridian. A great circle drawn from any point on Earth that passes through both poles. Any such great circle will form an angle of intersection with the virtually-standard zero meridian of Greenwich, England, and with the equator.

meteorology. Virtually the same as climatology, but today more closely associated with weather and weather predictions.

morphology. A biological term meaning the study of form and structure—in the case of geography, the study of the form and structure of the surface of Earth. The more precise word is *geomorphology*.

plant geography. A branch of *biogeography*, dealing with the plant communities existing in distinctive habitats. There are two approaches: the study of plants in relation to their environment (plant ecology); and floristic geography, the study of single species and how they are distributed and controlled.

soil geography. The science of soils, their nature, characteristics, distribution, uses, etc. Also called *pedogeography* and *pedology*.

topography. The mapping or charting of the physical details of a relatively small area, often including a detailed description of distinguishing features.

zoögeography. The science dealing with the distribution of animals and the causes and effects of such distribution, including a consideration of environmental factors.

Psychology

Psychology is the study of the human mind and behavior, including man's understanding of himself. Psychology is the chief area of the social sciences in which understanding of human behavior, within and among individuals, is the primary concern. The two words "human" and "behavior" are equally important.

Psychology has its foundation in human anatomy and the biological functioning of the senses. In this connection, it is significant that a psychiatrist—a person qualified to treat mental disorders—must possess a doctorate in medicine to practice his or her specialty.

Psychology emphasizes the scientific method and the widely accepted procedures of science in experimentation. But direct experimentation in human behavior is not always possible; it is easier to experiment on animals. Much research that can later be helpful in understanding human behavior is done, therefore, with lower animals; for example, rats and pigeons are often used to test theories of learning. Nevertheless, psychologists persistently look for *human* data and for cause-and-effect relationships that can be observed scientifically.

The Psyche legend of Greek mythology from which psychology takes its name is an indication that man has from very early times looked for an explanation of his own actions. (Psyche was the beautiful girl who personified the soul and was loved by Eros.) Yet it was not until 1879, when William Wundt established in Leipzig the first psychological laboratory, that there was a truly scientific approach to human behavior.

At about the same time that the study of psychology was established in Europe, remarkable growth in the field took place in the United States. Toward the end of the nineteenth century, departments of psychology were established at many of the large universities, each having a prominent leader of a particular aspect of the discipline.

William James is considered by some to be the father of American psychology. His book *Principles of Psychology* (1890) became a standard textbook. Known as a pragmatic philosopher, he was the first Harvard Professor of Psychology, from 1889 to 1897. G. Stanley Hall studied first at Harvard, then in Germany, and returned to Johns Hopkins University where he established the first American research laboratory in the 1880s. J. McKeen Cattell, whose area of investigation was visual perception, headed a new Department of Psychology at the University of Pennsylvania in 1888. E. B. Titchener in 1892 came from England to Cornell University, where he worked on the theory that human consciousness could be divided into elements on the basis of sensation, images, and feelings.

By the early twentieth century, interest in psychological studies had developed significantly both in Europe and in America. Distinct schools had emerged within the discipline, for example, the psychoanalysts, the experimentalists, the behaviorists, the gestaltists, and the humanists. Key figures in these fields became focal points for research students as well as for critics.

SIGNIFICANT FIGURES IN PSYCHOLOGY

Sigmund Freud (1856–1939).   The founder and towering figure in psychoanalysis. Freud was born in Moravia into a middle-class Jewish family. He began his psychological studies with the use of hypnosis in the treatment of hysteria (1895). He developed theories of the subconscious and of personality which were regarded as revolutionary. His method of treating mental and emotional illness, by interpreting the dreams of his patients to uncover their repressions, was called psychoanalysis. Freud's theories were not understood in this country until he visited here in 1909. His *General Introduction to Psychoanalysis* appeared in 1910 and was in its seventeenth edition by 1927. Freud's last major contribution to psychoanalytic theory (1923) was the dual concept of the ego, or conscious part of the personality that controls behavior; and the id, or that subconscious part of the psyche associated with instinctual impulses. A controversial figure, he died in London where he had fled from Hitler's Germany. Few men of any age have influenced so many areas of learn-

Sigmund Freud, founder of psychoanalysis. Freud lectured and wrote a great deal to explain his ideas. By the time Freud died, he had influenced all of the modern world.

ing—literature, anthropology, art—outside their own disciplines. As we approach the end of this century, psychologists are reconsidering and modifying Freudian teachings.

Carl Jung (1875–1961).   Early in his career Jung, a native of Switzerland, was a Freudian psychologist. In 1916 he published *The Theory of Psychoanalysis,* his own theory of the unconscious as an undeveloped rather than a repressed segment of personality. Over this interpretation he broke with Freud and adopted his own theory of analytical psychology. His *Analytical Psychology* (1935) emphasized present conflicts as causes of personality disorders, taking into account evolutionary and cultural influences. Jung was the first to describe "introvert" and "extrovert" personalities. He was interested in a great many related fields—the human psyche, religion, mythology, the occult—even flying saucers!

Ivan Pavlov (1848–1936).   World famous for his work in experimental psychology, Pavlov is noted for his studies of conditioned reflexes, first published in 1926. He received the Nobel Prize in Physiology and Medicine in 1904.

Edward Lee Thorndike (1874–1949).   Another psychologist who did extensive research on animal behavior was Thorndike, best known as a leading educational psychologist. A student of William James at Harvard, Thorndike's research on animal intelligence required that he keep close watch on his subjects, chickens. Since his landlady objected to his having chickens in his room, he continued his experimentation elsewhere and described his findings in *Animal Intelligence* (1911). His techniques of animal experimentation and his methods of psychological measurement were important steps forward in American psychological studies before World War I. From his work with animals he drew conclusions about human behavior and applied them to the field of educational psychology. Well known for his methods in the statistical measurement of intelligence, he later experimented extensively in the elements of human learning, and his many publications became required reading for students in the field.

B. F. Skinner (1904–   ). The objective methods of observation of human behavior used by the behaviorists were popular with many and disliked by some psychologists. Critics of Skinner and his theory of "operant conditioning" consider its mechanistic approach dehumanizing. The "Skinner box," based on the principle of reward to reinforce learning, was a teaching machine invented by Skinner. His own daughter spent two years in an "air-crib" he devised as the ideal environment for the nurture of infants. A Harvard Professor of Psychology, Skinner is also the author of *Walden Two.*

Max Wertheimer (1886–1943). In the 1920s and 1930s a new movement, gestalt psychology, developed. The word "gestalt" comes from the German word meaning "shape" or "form," and its major contribution to the psychology of perception is the concept that man responds not to individual stimuli but to a whole image. Among the founders of the gestalt movement working in the United States was Wertheimer, a refugee from Hitler's Germany. Wertheimer was considered by Albert Einstein to be a genius. Kurt Lewin (1890–1947), also a German refugee and a gestaltist, is better known as a pioneer in social psychology. His work was in group dynamics, and he is famous for a study comparing authoritarian and democratic group behavior. He helped to establish the Research Center for Group Dynamics which is now located at the University of Michigan.

Jean Piaget (1896–   ). In the 1940s and 1950s interest increased in the specialized field of child psychology. Piaget, the remarkable Swiss psychologist, has combined philosophy and biology with psychology in his approach to learning. He has observed and tested thousands of children and interviewed nearly as many in order to determine how they view the complex world adults know. His writings have been translated into six languages. His most recent work is *Memory and Intelligence* (1974).

Fritz Redl (1902–   ). Another humanistic psychologist who has contributed to the study of children's problems with a positive approach is Australian-born Redl. He prefers the concept of "mental health" to that of "mental illness," looking for supportive experiences through which emotionally disturbed children can improve. Redl belongs to a strong modern trend among psychologists toward a humanistic psychology offering an optimistic view of man.

Rollo May (1909–   ), American teacher and psychologist, and **Ronald Laing (1927–   ),** Scottish-born British psychoanalyst, are of this school of "third-force" psychologists who prefer, while not being uncritical of modern society, to make a positive affirmation of the individual in the world. Instead of projecting a determinist attitude that man must accept whatever happens, May contends that by adopting a positive attitude, the individual can change what happens within himself and around him. Laing, who has done much in the field of schizophrenia, has questioned many of the current concepts of what is normal behavior. He suggests that the so-called aberrations of the emotionally ill may be justifiable responses to conditions found throughout society rather than truly abnormal behavior.

Jean Piaget, child psychologist. His understanding of the intellectual growth of children has greatly influenced today's students of child development as well as today's teachers.

GLOSSARY OF PSYCHOLOGICAL TERMS

amnesia. Condition in which memory is partially or totally lost.

behaviorism. The psychological doctrine that emphasizes the primary value of objective study of actual responses. The extreme behaviorist eliminates all consideration of the conscious or unconscious.

conditioned reflex. A psychological process in which a particular response results from a stimulus totally different from the stimulus that usually brings forth that response. The classic example is Ivan Pavlov's dog experiment, in which the ring of a bell elicited salivation by the animal, due to the repeated simultaneous offering of meat and the bell sound.

conditioning. Modification or development of a behavior response or pattern.

determinism. The doctrine that all facts or events result from pre-existent causes, one of the basic assumptions of psychoanalysis. This doctrine is particularly pertinent to Freud's understanding of the dream.

dream. A succession of hallucinatory images, ideas and sensations, mentally occurring during sleep or just before going to sleep or awakening.

dream interpretation. An attempt to understand the content of dreams, sometimes by means of free association of ideas. In psychoanalysis, followers of Freud maintain that dreams are a mixture of sensory experiences during sleep, involved with experiences and dreads of the waking life of that day or earlier, plus repressed wishes or thoughts from the unconscious.

extrovert. An individual who is primarily interested in people, activities, and situations outside himself.

gestalt. An integrated whole, form, pattern, configuration, in contrast to a simple summation of units within the whole.

gestalt theory. A psychological theory that arose in Germany early in this century as a reaction against the analytical method. It maintained that all experiences are presented in integrated patterns which are more than the sum of parts or elements—that wholeness is a feature of the experience also. Therefore, the response of an individual cannot be analyzed, since it is a response to a whole pattern, not only a sum of particular responses to elements in the situation. It started as a theory of perception, but has expanded to include investigations of learning and other fields of mental life.

hypnosis. A sleep-like condition, usually induced by another person, in which the individual is influenced to a degree by suggestions from the hypnotist, with whom the hypnotized person continues in rapport. In some cases, hypnotism brings out of the unconscious certain facts or impressions that have been buried in the unconscious.

intelligence quotient. A number arrived at by taking the mental age of an individual (as determined by intelligence tests), multiplying it by one hundred, and dividing that resulting figure by the chronological age of the individual. The final figure is held to indicate the relative level of mental ability.

introspection. Examination of, and reflection upon, the content of one's own mind.

introvert. An individual who is primarily concerned with his own mental life and experiences.

manic-depressive. A term describing a category of functional psychoses, characterized by the alternation of elation and depression. There is a marked hereditary factor in manic-depressive disease, and some connection with body form. A large proportion of cases exhibit pyknic structure (rounded, obese body with large body cavities). The disease is far more frequent in females than in males.

paranoia. A rare, chronic mental disorder in which the individual suffers delusions of grandeur or, more frequently, delusions of hostility and persecution. The individual then shows extreme distrust and suspicion of others.

personality. The integrated, distinctive organization of the physical, mental, moral, and social qualities of an individual as shown in social relationships. The personality appears as a whole structure comprising natural and acquired drives, motivations, habits, complexes, impulses, and compulsions, feelings and strivings, opinions, beliefs, and ideals.

psyche. The mentality of an individual. A substitute term for mind, spirit, soul. In classical myth, Psyche was the personification of the human soul.

psychiatrist. One who treats mental and nervous disorders. A medical degree is a prerequisite for practice. An older term for psychiatrist is "alienist."

psychiatry. The science or practice of treating mental and emotional disorders.

psychoanalysis. A method, developed by Freud, of dealing with mental and nervous disorders. It involves consideration of all aspects of the mental life of the patient, particularly emphasizing the content and processes of the unconscious. It employs an elaborate method of examination and treatment, based on the use of free association. The patient may be given a list of stimulus words, to each of which he must respond with the first word that occurs to him. Rapidity of the response as well as its content is of importance to the examiner. Free association may also take the form of a "train of thought" experiment, in which the patient is given one stimulus word and is then encouraged to give continuously the ideas that come to mind. This is essentially the method of the psychoanalyst (often called "analyst" as "analysis" is the popular term for psychoanalysis).

psychology. The area of biological science that is concerned with the phenomena of human life and behavior. It deals with the origins, growth, and manifestations of conscious and unconscious processes, using available methods appropriate to the particular field of study. Main branches of psychology are abnormal, animal, child, genetic, industrial, and social. General divisions of psychological methods are analytic, behavioristic, gestalt, introspective, and statistical. A psychologist has knowledge of psychology in general, or in a special area of the science. In England and the United States, the expert is marked by status in a recognized psychological association or society.

psychopath. Unstable individual, emotionally unreliable to a nearly pathological degree, but showing no specific mental disorder.

psychosis. A disordered or diseased mental condition.

schizophrenia. The most frequent and serious form of functional psychosis, this mental disease evidences dissociation (splitting or schism) between functions of feeling (emotion) and functions of thinking. A psychosis is called "functional" because it is a mental disease with no discoverable physical cause. Post-mortem examination shows no differences between the nervous systems of schizophrenics and those of healthy individuals. There are several subtypes of the disease, but simple schizophrenia has definite symptoms: a lack of emotional attachment to persons or things; a lack of interest in everyday, normal things, or in friends, or in what is going on around the patient; an absence of ambition or initiative. Apathy and indifference mark the schizophrenic: nothing seems worthy of effort. The result is a vegetative existence of eating, sleeping, and excreting, with no enthusiasm for even these functions.

self. The personality regarded as an agent, aware of its own continuing identity.

subconscious. A descriptive term for processes of the same sort as conscious processes, but of which the conscious is unaware. It is used frequently instead of unconscious.

Sociology

A simple definition of sociology is difficult because it is seen differently by different schools of sociologists. Important in the word is the Latin word *socius,* meaning a companion, an associate, a comrade or ally. Some sociologists stress the relationships, the ties that bind two, or even hundreds of thousands of people. Others prefer to focus on what happens to one person in his relations with others.

But sociology, as it is now usually conceived, has broader areas of concern, such as society as an organism with its social institutions, which it sets out to study in terms of their development, structure, and functions. So a widely accepted definition of sociology is "the science of society, social institutions, and social relationships," which seems at the same time to have lost the concept of "companion." However, to counteract this, it appears that concern for the individual is increasing in institutions and government. The welfare recipient, the senior citizen, the consumer—all are considered individually instead of being squeezed into a group mold.

Sociology can be understood more easily if looked at from several perspectives. A student might see sociology as a field of study covering the way we live—our lives, our customs, our institutions, everything that makes up the culture of a group. He might study the personality of a group or the processes of interaction within the group. Within this framework he might cover such subjects as the nature of group processes, the origin and growth of the community, social planning, and crime in the community.

Another perspective might be taken by a sociological researcher. His interest might be in the methods of sociology, and his concern would be whether to use objective or subjective approaches. An objective approach is one that is clearly described, step by step, so as to be easily duplicated by another researcher. Census data, community surveys, questionnaire inquiries, and statistical collection fall into this category. The subjective approach is one that is not able to be duplicated by another investigator. The case study, the life-history of an individual, the participant-observer technique—all of which depend to a great degree on the judgment and insight of the investigator—are examples of subjective methods.

The student, the teacher, and the researcher might all think of sociology as a point of view. Each might examine his own treatment of the science. If he aligns himself with the *scientific* group, he dedicates himself to a search for truth at any cost, deals with facts, and makes impersonal evaluations. If he prefers to be known as a sociologist with a *humanistic* view, he is committed to areas of science that demand value judgments and some sense of responsibility for the improvement of individual human life.

SIGNIFICANT FIGURES IN SOCIOLOGY

Auguste Comte (1798–1857) of France gave the science of sociology its name. Although he was primarily a philosopher and mathematician, he made vast contributions to the knowledge of social phenomena. His own view was that the crown of his labors was establishing the science of sociology. Comte believed that sociology could contribute substantially to the well-being and harmony of society.

Herbert Spencer (1820–1903) in England attempted to explain in *Synthetic Philosophy* (1860–1867) his theory that two processes are at work in all sociocultural phenomena. One process was a gradual development from the simplest forms to the more complex, and the other a concurrent process of dissolution from the complex to the simple. He tried to apply these two principles to all areas of study: biology, psychology, politics, and society in particular. In his theory of development, he was a prophet of Darwinian evolution. He hypothesized that our ideas adapt to ever-new challenges, so man's mind and morals continually improve. He explained his theory in *Principles of Sociology*.

Emile Durkheim (1858–1917), perhaps the greatest of French sociologists, made important contributions to modern theories of sociology. His pioneer study of suicide (1897) is considered a classic of theoretical research. He conceived of sociology as the collective mind of society and regarded the institution as the basic unit of society. Though he regarded statistics as a vital part of research and believed in the "nonrational" element of sociology, he was very aware of the impact of philosophy on the study of society.

Max Weber (1864–1920), a German, was interested in understanding values and norms of behavior and in the explanation of cause-and-effect relationships. In the interpretation of social institutions, he tackled such areas as the place of religion in social change and the role of discipline as a process of socialization.

SOCIAL SCIENCE

Max Weber, influential sociologist. He opposed Marxism, seeing that events have many causes, such as religion and strong leadership, rather than economic factors alone.

David Riesman (1909–) is well-known for his book *The Lonely Crowd,* a study of the social and psychological factors in the modern gregarious American. Though not by training a professional in the field, he has been described as a sociologist with style, a moralist with a new vocabulary, and a writer with remarkable insight. Riesman is a social critic who likes to probe the dark corners of contemporary society.

Daniel Bell (1919–), Professor of Sociology at Harvard since 1969 after ten years at Columbia, personifies the strong bond between the modern sociologist and modern education. Bell views the American university as a politico-social institution where the knowledge of scholarly inquiry and learning relate avenues of investigation to each other. He sees the modern student in need of an understanding of himself in a historical context, ideally possessing an "integrated mind responsive to its own ultimate concerns and aware of its own human capabilities."

GLOSSARY OF SOCIOLOGICAL TERMS

aristocracy. In sociology those most esteemed by others as having social and sometimes political dominance.

attitude. An established tendency, somehow acquired, to react positively toward or negatively against a person or thing. To some, an attitude is a mental state, to others a feeling or emotion. The words "manner," "disposition," and "feeling" all approach "attitude" as used in sociology. Attitude comes forth in approaching or withdrawing types of behavior, but often remains latent and unexpressed.

behavior. The way a person acts under given circumstances

bureaucracy. A graded hierarchy of nonelective officials. A bureaucracy is characterized by specialization of functions, excessive adherence to regulations, and consequent lack of flexibility and individual initiative. A bureaucrat is not disturbed by paperwork and red tape, is almost unremovable, and would rather pass responsibility and decision-making one step up on the ladder of authority than make a decision. A bureaucracy tends to proliferate on its own.

Bureaucracies are known not only in the executive branches of government; they flourish in large businesses, labor unions, the military establishment, and large social organizations.

class. A category by which persons may be classified. Also a body of persons considered to have certain social, economic, educational, or other characteristics in common: the professional class, the wage-earning class, etc. The possible categories are many: by age, occupation, wealth, etc.

crime. An overt act against society's rules, as encoded in the criminal law of the state: lawbreaking.

culture. The distinctive ways of living of a particular group or society at a given time. Culture consists of the traditions, customs, ethics, attitudes, taboos, language, government, science, skills, art, etc. of the group, which are transmitted from generation to generation. Culture is not static, since its aspects are constantly amplified, modified, or changed through contact and communication with others.

delinquency. Failure or neglect of an individual to

perform a duty or obey the law. The word is most often used to define offenses (anti-social behavior, law-breaking) by minors (persons under 18 years, generally).

deviance. Behavior that departs from an acceptable standard or norm. The person so behaving is known as a deviant or deviate.

elite. A select, favored, or aristocratic group, formerly selected by birth, nowadays by ability to succeed and acquire great influence in corporate or national affairs, military organizations, and wherever power resides. Only rarely are members of an elite identified and elevated by reason of aptitude tests.

ethnic. The adjective from Greek, *ethnos*, nation, people. An ethnic trait, for example, is one belonging to, shared by, or distinctive of people belonging to a particular race, language division, or other large group.

family. A fundamental social institution of husbands and wives, living together in a socially-sanctioned, more or less lasting relationship with their children and having recognized rights and responsibilities. The usual types of marriage found around the world have been monogamy, polygamy, polyandry, and group marriage.

ghetto. Refers chiefly to a portion of a city in which members of a minority group live because of social pressures and various forms of discrimination.

institution. For sociologists, the important definition is the one designating as an institution any well-established and integrated pattern of behavior through which social control is exerted and which meets the needs or desires of the society. Marriage and the family are institutions in this sense.

minority group. A subgroup within a larger group, such as a nation or a society. A minority normally has its own ties—racial, cultural, or religious. Even in a democracy, a minority group often suffers through the operation of the principle of majority rule, which precludes their proportionate representation and often leads to discrimination.

norm. A standard, a criterion for judging the character or conduct of an individual, or the performance of a societal form or function. A typical pattern, a model, the average. Norms are socially sanctioned modes of behavior, generally recognized rules.

prejudice. An attitude—normally negative, but also at times positive—usually emotional at root and based on inadequate evidence and experience. Prejudice may be directed toward individuals, groups, races, or nationalities; toward particular traits of any of these; and toward ideas or institutions. In recent years, racial and religious prejudices have been much-discussed forms of prejudice.

race. A biological term for a subdivision of a species, including the human species. One theory about the distribution of races holds that original men broke up and became localized in separated areas of the earth and that these basic groups also subdivided and relocated. Hence a wide variety of races, each distinguishable, each with a common ancestor. However, racial affiliation cannot now be determined by genealogy, as was attempted in the books of the Old Testament. But each of these races, due chiefly (it is thought) to environmental factors, developed distinctive traits. Today a Caucasian, therefore, is a person who shows typical Caucasoid traits. The concept of race can be abused with harmful effects, as occurred under Hitler in Nazi Germany when the term "Aryan" (a cultural, linguistic term) was used ideologically as a racial term.

segregation. The practice of separating or setting apart from the main group of society; also the state of being segregated.

social change. A comprehensive term designating the outcome of all kinds of social oscillations affecting the social pattern, form, or scene generally. Social change may be good, bad, or indifferent, permanent or temporary.

social stratification. The horizontal division of society into various groups on different levels (strata) in terms of ancestry, social standing, wealth, profession, race, education, and the like.

society. An organized, large-scale group living as members of a community according to cultural, political, and religious norms. A society is a functioning organism, marked by self-maintenance, self-perpetuation, and complex human relationships. Generally speaking, it has its own territory. A viable society is more likely, under stress, to quiver, bend, and adapt than to break down entirely.

sociology. The study of the origin, development, organization, and functioning of human society; the science of the fundamental laws of social relations, institutions, etc.

LANGUAGE AND LITERATURE

No education is complete without thorough study of the magic of great thoughts conveyed through literature. From long before the time of William Shakespeare, men and women in all civilized countries have expressed their best insights in works of poetry and prose. For these reasons, the following pages review the masterpieces of world literature and present information on the lives of the gifted people who produced them.

To assist you further in your personal development, a Dictionary of English Usage is provided as a guide for improved writing and speech. Consult this dictionary whenever you are uncertain about how to use a particular word or phrase. By increasing the precision of your language, you will improve your ability to express yourself clearly and effectively.

World Literature

This section gives you a handy reference guide to the many types of literature and to important books in world literature, along with plot summaries of Shakespeare's plays.

It also gives you suggestions for improving your own writing—whether it is a composition for class or a piece of writing you want to try on your own.

MAJOR FORMS IN LITERATURE

Autobiography. An autobiography is the life history of a person written by himself. The *Confessions* of St. Augustine (late fourth and early fifth centuries) is probably the world's greatest spiritual autobiography. Cellini's *Autobiography of Benvenuto Cellini* is a vivid picture of the Italian Renaissance and some of its outstanding personages, as well as of the great artist. Rousseau's *Confessions,* published in 1782, was the first great introspective autobiography. Among the most famous modern autobiographies are Benjamin Franklin's *Autobiography* (1868), Leo Tolstoy's *Confessions* (1882), Helen Keller's *The Story of My Life* (1902), Henry Adams's *The Education of Henry Adams* (1906), Edward Bok's *Americanization of Edward Bok* (1920), Mark Twain's *Autobiography* (1922), and the *Autobiography of Lincoln Steffens* (1931).

Biography. A biography is the history of the life of a person. Modern biography tries to record the development of a personality, to portray individuals as they really were.

In early times biography was often written for political or moral purposes. In the first century A.D. Plutarch wrote his *Parallel Lives,* comparing the careers of a score of Romans with the same number of Greeks, pair by pair; and countless later writers (Shakespeare among them) drew on this work for facts and characterization. Tacitus, the great historian, wrote a life of his father-in-law Agricola that is a classic; and Suetonius's *Lives of the Caesars* (written about A.D. 120) is gossipy and full of scandal. These are samples of what is called "antique biography," written to emphasize certain moral qualities or to teach a political lesson.

Biography in English begins in the sixteenth century with William Roper's *Life of Sir Thomas More* and George Cavendish's *Life of Cardinal Wolsey.* In the seventeenth century Izaak Walton wrote the *Lives* of Donne, Hooker, Herbert, and others that are the forerunners of modern personal biography. James Boswell's *Life of Samuel Johnson* (1791), considered one of the great biographies of all time, was based on Boswell's lifelong firsthand records of Johnson's sayings, habits, and everyday activities. Johnson himself wrote a series of *Lives of the Poets.*

In modern biography the English writer Lytton Strachey initiated the debunking tradition, taking public figures down from their pedestals. In *Eminent Victorians* (1918) and *Queen Vic-*

toria (1921) he portrayed the real person behind the popular public image, although many critics think he went out of his way to emphasize negative traits. Gamaliel Bradford's *American Portraits* (1920) were the first of many spiritual portraits that he called *psychographs*.

Other outstanding modern biographies are André Maurois' *Ariel* (1923), the life of Shelley; Hervey Allen's *Israfel* (1926), a life of Edgar Allan Poe; Carl Sandburg's series on Lincoln, *The Prairie Years* (1926) and *The War Years* (1939); and Ernest Jones's *Life and Works of Sigmund Freud* (1953–55).

Some fictionalized biographies, such as Irving Stone's *Lust for Life* (1934), about Vincent van Gogh, and *The Agony and the Ecstasy* (1961), about Michelangelo, have been highly popular, as have historical biographies dealing with the relationship of two public figures such as *Nicholas and Alexandra* (1967) by Robert K. Massie, and *Eleanor and Franklin* (1971) by Joseph P. Lash. A unique American tradition is the campaign biography written for a presidential candidate. The first was written by Nathaniel Hawthorne for Franklin Pierce.

Blank Verse.   Blank verse is unrhymed iambic pentameter, the most common metrical form in English dramatic and epic poetry. Iambic pentameter has five metrical feet to a line, each having one unstressed syllable followed by one stressed syllable. It was first used by Henry Howard, Earl of Surrey, in his translations from the *Aeneid* in the sixteenth century. The first English drama written in blank verse was Sackville and Norton's tragedy *Gorboduc* in 1561–62. Christopher Marlowe made masterly use of the form in his tragedy *Tamburlaine* (1589), while in the next decade it was Shakespeare who perfected it.

Diary.   A diary is a daily record of personal, informal activities. The diaries of historical figures are helpful to historians in reconstructing past events, and often provide intimate details of motives and manners that are not found in official records.

The most famous diary in the English language is that of Samuel Pepys (1633–1703), who recorded the manners and foibles of London in the 1660s.

Carl Sandburg (1878–1967), American poet, known as "the poet of industrial America." His biography of Abraham Lincoln won a Pulitzer Prize.

Perhaps the most famous diary of modern times is that of Anne Frank (1929–1945), a Dutch-Jewish girl who spent many months hiding from the Nazis occupying Amsterdam. Other famous diaries have been those of the Englishmen John Evelyn (1620–1706) and Jonathan Swift (1667–1745); and of the two Frenchmen Edmond de Goncourt (1822–1896) and his brother Jules de Goncourt (1830–1870).

Drama.   A drama is a literary composition in prose or verse which represents life and character through action and dialogue and is intended for performance by actors on a stage. The word "drama" is from a Greek word meaning action.

The drama apparently originated in Greece where, from the fifth century B.C., plays were part of religious festivals. The great Greek tragedians—Aeschylus (*Oresteia* trilogy, *Prometheus Bound*), Sophocles (*Oedipus Rex, Antigone*), and Euripides (*Medea, Suppliants*) —developed a pure form of poetic tragedy which has set the standard for all later tragic dramatists. The Greeks invented comedy too, with the bawdy, topical plays of Aristophanes (*The Birds*) and the witty works of Menander.

A few centuries later, Roman comedy writers Plautus and Terence and, still later, the tragedian Seneca drew heavily on these Greek models, but their own contributions had considerable later influence.

Drama declined until the late Middle Ages, when the Church began to use plays for religious instruction. Mystery plays, which were based on liturgy and the Bible, became a popular feature of religious feasts in the eleventh century, as did the fourteenth-century mystery plays, which dramatized incidents from the lives of the saints. Another type of religious drama, the allegorical morality play (*Everyman*) appeared in the fifteenth century, teaching by means of abstract personification of virtue and vice.

Classical influences during the Renaissance stimulated the revival of secular drama throughout Europe. In England, the pre-Shakespearean scene featured the lively early comedies of Nicholas Udall (*Ralph Roister Doister*, c. 1553) and William Stevenson (*Gammer Gurton's Needle*, 1556); the Senecan tragedies of Sackville and Norton (*Gorboduc*, 1561–62) and Thomas Kyd (*Spanish Tragedy*, c. 1587); and the verse drama of Shakespeare's most distinguished predecessor, Christopher Marlowe (*Doctor Faustus*, 1588; *The Jew of Malta*, c. 1592).

Then came William Shakespeare, the acknowledged genius of world drama, whose history plays, comedies, and tragedies brought life in all its variety to the stage. Tyrants, barmaids, fairies, gravediggers, fools, princes, witches, and drunkards are presented with equal vitality in dramas whose matchless poetry and timeless themes still hold audiences today. *Richard III, A Midsummer Night's Dream, As You Like It, Hamlet, Macbeth, King Lear,* and *The Tempest* are among those most frequently performed.

The wry comedies of Shakespeare's friend and rival Ben Jonson, the middle-class farces of Thomas Middleton, and the tragedies of John Webster were the most important plays prior to the closing of the theaters under Cromwell's Puritan government (1653–58). The Restoration of Charles II (1660) ushered in a revival with the fine comedies and tragedies of the poet John Dryden (*All for Love,* 1677) and the comedies of manners of William Congreve (*The Way of the World,* 1700). The eighteenth century was dominated by the realistic comedies of Oliver Goldsmith (*She Stoops to Conquer,* 1773) and the witty and still popular plays of Richard Brinsley Sheridan (*The Rivals,* 1775; *The School for Scandal,* 1777).

Meanwhile, Continental drama flourished. In Spain, the seventeenth-century Golden Age of Literature began with the prolific founder of Spanish drama, Lope de Vega, whose successor, the more intellectual Pedro Calderón de la Barca (*Life Is a Dream,* c. 1636), influenced European dramatists throughout the Romantic period. France of the seventeenth century was dominated by the great writers of classical tragedy Pierre Corneille (*Le Cid,* 1637) and Jean Racine (*Phèdre,* 1677) and by the supremely witty and irreverent Molière (*The Misanthrope,* 1666; *Tartuffe,* 1669). Germany's dramatists of the Enlightenment and the Romantic period include Lessing (*Nathan the Wise,* 1779), Schiller (*The Robbers,* 1781; *Don Carlos,* 1787), and Goethe (*Faust,* 1808, 1838). In Russia, Nikolai Gogol satirized small-town corruption in that country's first notable drama, *The Inspector General* (1836). The later master of Russian drama, Anton Chekhov, set his upperclass protagonists against a background of social change in such famous plays as *The Seagull* (1896) and *The Cherry Orchard* (1903). A starkly naturalistic play, *The Lower Depths* (1902), was written by Maxim Gorki.

With the powerful psychological and ideological drama of the Norwegian Henrik Ibsen, modern drama began. His themes and techniques in such plays as *Rosmersholm* (1866), *Peer Gynt* (1867), *A Doll's House* (1879), and *Ghosts* (1881) outraged his audiences but profoundly influenced other dramatists. Other giants were to follow. Sweden's August Strindberg wrote painful psychological dramas (*Dance of Death,* 1901) and dipped into surrealism (*A Dream Play,* 1902). Irish-born George Bernard Shaw produced challenging and brilliantly iconoclastic plays on a wide range of subjects, including the still popular *Man and Superman* (1903), *Major Barbara* (1907), *Pygmalion* (1913), and *Saint Joan*

(1923). During the same period, a number of other important playwrights emerged from the Irish literary renaissance: William Butler Yeats (*Kathleen ni Houlihan,* 1902), John Millington Synge (*Riders to the Sea, The Playboy of the Western World,* both 1907), and, somewhat later, Sean O'Casey (*Juno and the Paycock,* 1924; *The Plough and the Stars,* 1926).

After World War I, three major playwrights appeared: Italy's Luigi Pirandello, Germany's Bertolt Brecht, and America's Eugene O'Neill. Pirandello's symbolistic and psychological plays, such as the celebrated *Six Characters in Search of an Author* (1921), reflect the cynicism and disillusion of Europeans in the postwar period. Brecht's taut and innovative ideological dramas—such as *Man Is Man* (1927), *Mother Courage* (1939), and *Caucasian Chalk Circle* (1944–45)—sought to engage the minds rather than the emotions of his audience, using techniques he called "epic theater." O'Neill broke new ground in the United States with passionate, experimental works such as *Desire Under the Elms* (1924), *Mourning Becomes Electra* (1931), and *Long Day's Journey into Night*

Virginia Woolf (1882–1941), English novelist and essayist, whose work is known for its introspective quality. Her best works are *To the Lighthouse, Jacob's Room, A Room of One's Own,* and *Mrs. Dalloway.*

(1956). Elmer Rice and Clifford Odets also produced important plays during this period.

During World War II, Tennessee Williams and Arthur Miller set troubled protagonists against their social environments. Williams's *The Glass Menagerie* (1944) and *A Streetcar Named Desire* (1947) and Miller's *Death of a Salesman* (1949) have become American classics.

The postwar period brought new experiments. The "theater of the absurd," influenced by the philosophies of Sartre and Camus, developed in France under the leadership of Samuel Beckett (*Waiting for Godot,* 1952), Jean Genêt (*The Blacks,* 1958), and Eugène Ionesco (*The Chairs,* 1951; *Rhinoceros,* 1959). Absurdists stressed character interrelationships, questioned life's meaning, and portrayed deep anguish and despair. The movement's impact was felt in England in the work of Harold Pinter (*The Caretaker,* 1960) and in the United States, where Edward Albee took a lighter approach, slamming home social criticism through mockery and shock tactics (*The American Dream,* 1961; *Who's Afraid of Virginia Woolf?,* 1962; *A Delicate Balance,* 1966). A new wave of realistic social drama began in England with "angry young man" John Osborne's *Look Back in Anger* (1956) and Arnold Wesker's *Chicken Soup with Barley* (1958). England's Robert Bolt, Germany's Peter Weiss, and the United States' Jack Gelber, among many others, give promise for the future.

Epic. An epic is a long narrative poem celebrating the deeds of heroes of history or of legend. The ancient Greek *Iliad* and *Odyssey* of Homer typify the ancient epic. Vergil's *Aeneid* is a famous ancient Roman epic. Out of Iceland came the great epic fragments of the *Elder Edda,* but the Old English *Beowulf* stands out as the most perfect and important epic in all Teutonic literature, although the German *Nibelungenlied* is perhaps more widely known. The *Chanson de Roland* is the greatest epic of France; *Cantar de Mío Cid* is Spain's. There have been no great epics since Milton's *Paradise Lost.*

Essay. An essay is a short literary composition, usually in prose, telling the writer's thoughts and reflections on a subject. There are three kinds of essays: the formal, polished essay on a specific subject; the purely technical and scientific exposition; and the personal essay.

The term "essay" was first used by the French writer Michel de Montaigne in 1571; he chose the word *essais* to designate his writings as attempts, trials, or experiments. The first of Montaigne's *Essays* came out in 1580. They were a new kind of writing, dealing with any subject or idea that came to the author's mind. They were brief or rambling, full of interruptions and personal moods and opinions on life and men, formless yet bound together by the personality of the author.

Francis Bacon was the first of the English essayists. He published a volume of ten essays in 1597. Abraham Cowley, who wrote *Discourses by Way of Essays* (1668), is often called the father of the English essay. The *Tatler* and *Spectator* papers (1709–14) of Addison and Steele are witty and opinionated commentary. The *Essays of Elia* (1820–23) by Charles Lamb are delightful examples of the leisurely personal essay; Macaulay's essays, in contrast, are impersonal and informative. Later important English essayists include Matthew Arnold, John Ruskin, Thomas Carlyle, Virginia Woolf, Alice Meynell, G. K. Chesterton, and George Orwell.

The essay is uniquely suited to expressing the writer's personal view of life, as shown in the writings of Emerson and Thoreau. Other American essayists have written gently humorous or satirical pieces, like those of James Thurber or E. B. White; or have written about science and nature from a personal viewpoint, like Rachel Carson, Joseph Wood Krutch, and Loren Eiseley.

Free Verse.   Free verse is verse that is rhythmical without formal meter, stanza, or rhyme. The French term *vers libre,* meaning "free verse," was adopted by a modern school of poets in Europe and America who sought to liberate poetry from conventional metrical rules. Among the early exponents of the school were Amy Lowell, Carl Sandburg, Ezra Pound, and T. S. Eliot, and it became the characteristic poetic idiom of the twentieth century.

Charlotte Brontë (1816–55), English novelist whose greatest work is *Jane Eyre*. In her early work, Charlotte collaborated with her sister Emily, best known for the novel *Wuthering Heights*.

Free verse is not exactly new and it is not exactly free. The King James version of the Bible—a metrical English based on an Oriental poetry form without meter and rhyme but with parallelism and powerful figures of speech—and Walt Whitman's *Leaves of Grass* are early and influential examples of free verse. Its wide modern acceptance is based on the need to adapt poetry to the natural rhythms of speech.

Lyric Poetry.   Lyric poetry is the most emotional and musical of the divisions of poetry. A lyric always expresses subjective feeling, the personal hopes and joys, sorrows and fantasies of the author; narrative and dramatic poems, by contrast, tell a story. A lyric is always comparatively short because great emotion cannot long be sustained. It is usually composed of several stanzas. Sonnets are lyrics, as are madrigals, odes, hymns, elegies, and the like.

The word *lyric* comes from the Greek *lyra*, an ancient musical instrument of the harp type; lyrics were originally intended to be sung to the accompaniment of the lyre. Most modern lyrics are written only as confessions of inner experience, meant to be read.

Narrative-Dramatic Poetry.   This is a kind of poetry that tells a story by recounting and describing events, actions, and personalities; lyric poetry, by contrast, briefly expresses a subjective emotion. Narratives are frequently long, even book-length.

Narrative poetry is probably the oldest form of poetic expression, stretching back to ancient epics, sagas, and ballads, and to the medieval metrical romance. The dramatic monologue uses theatrical techniques in its storytelling. Verse dramas are also sometimes considered dramatic poetry. See also *Epic.*

Novel.   The novel is a sustained, fictional prose narrative of considerable length which traditionally contains a realistic portrayal of life, full-bodied characters, and an individual point of view. The novel developed from the heroic epic and courtly romances of the Middle Ages; another notable precursor was the Italian *novella,* found in its most polished form in Boccaccio's fourteenth-century story collection *The Decameron.* In Spain, two outstanding and widely imitated forerunners of the novel were the chivalric romance *Amadís de Gaula* (c. 1508) and the picaresque tale *Lazarillo de Tormes* (1554), the latter an episodic story of a rogue hero. Cervantes's classic *Don Quixote* (1605, 1615) shows the influence of both: it mocks the excesses of chivalric stories while presenting a realistic picture of Spanish life.

In England, Lyly's *Euphues* (1578), a stilted, artificial courtly romance, found many imitators; the best were Thomas Lodge (*Rosalind,* 1590) and Sir Philip Sidney (*Arcadia,* 1590). Thomas Nash imitated the Spanish picaresque tale in *The Unfortunate Traveller* (1594). John Bunyan's *Pilgrim's Progress* (1678, 1684), though also episodic in plot, was an allegory of remarkable power. In the eighteenth century, the English novel developed rapidly, with deepened character portrayals, definite moral (or immoral) ideas, and unified—as opposed to episodic—plots. Defoe's *Robinson Crusoe* (1719) and *Moll Flanders* (1722) were outstanding forerunners of Samuel Richardson's *Pamela* (1740). Henry Fielding developed the novel's comic potential in *Joseph Andrews* (1742), his

satire of *Pamela,* and gave the picaresque story a new structural firmness in *Tom Jones* (1749). Other outstanding novelists followed, among them Tobias Smollett, Laurence Sterne, and Oliver Goldsmith. Horace Walpole's Gothic novel *The Castle of Otranto* (1764) inspired others, notably Ann Radcliffe, to write tales of castles and demons.

The nineteenth-century English novel began with the craftsmanship, accurate social picture, and finely drawn characters of Jane Austen (*Pride and Prejudice,* 1813) and gained new life and dimensions in the vivid works of Charles Dickens (*Oliver Twist,* 1837–39; *David Copperfield,* 1849–50; *A Tale of Two Cities,* 1859). A new realism and social consciousness also appeared in Thackeray's monumental *Vanity Fair* (1847–48). Emily and Charlotte Brontë's passionate novels and the brilliant regional and philosophical works of Thomas Hardy rounded out an exceptionally rich century for the English novel.

Major novels in eighteenth-century France included a picaresque tale by Le Sage (*Gil Blas,* 1715) and the love tragedies of Abbé Prévost (*Manon Lescaut,* 1731) and Rousseau (*La Nouvelle Héloïse,* 1761). In the nineteenth century appeared Stendhal's social panorama, *The Red and Black* (1831); Dumas *père*'s adventure tale, *The Three Musketeers* (1844); Flaubert's realistic, carefully structured *Madame Bovary* (1857); and Zola's scientific studies of character and environment in such novels as *Nana* (1880), the first works of Naturalism. Goethe had written his fine novels *The Sorrows of Young Werther* (1774) and *The Apprenticeship of Wilhelm Meister* (1795–96) in Germany. And in Russia the nineteenth century produced several masterpieces of modern fiction: Pushkin's vivid tale of a peasant revolt, *The Captain's Daughter* (1836); Gogol's satire of provincial Russia, *Dead Souls* (1842); Tolstoy's monumental saga, *War and Peace* (1869) and the sensitive *Anna Karenina* (1875–77); Turgenev's timeless *Fathers and Sons* (1862); and Dostoevski's profound and passionate *Crime and Punishment* (1866) and *The Brothers Karamazov* (1880).

In the United States, James Fenimore Cooper's frontier stories and Nathaniel Hawthorne's

Ernest Hemingway (1898–1961), American novelist and Nobel laureate whose style influenced two generations of writers. His best works are *A Farewell to Arms* and *The Sun Also Rises*.

Saul Bellow (1915–   ), Quebec-born American novelist and Nobel laureate whose works include *Humboldt's Gift, Henderson the Rain King, The Adventures of Augie March*, and *Herzog*.

studies of religious repression paved the way for two authors who broke new ground: Herman Melville, whose classic *Moby-Dick* (1851) combined rich symbolism and ideology with gripping realism; and Mark Twain, whose *Tom Sawyer* (1876) and *Huckleberry Finn* (1884) inspired more accurate dialogue and action in works that followed. At the turn of the century, the Anglo-American Henry James (*The Portrait of a Lady*, 1881; *The Ambassadors*, 1903; *The Golden Bowl*, 1904) foreshadowed the twentieth-century novel with his technical brilliance, symbolism, and concentration on psychological motivations.

Many experiments in the twentieth century have extended the novel's resources; perhaps most influential have been the stream-of-consciousness techniques of James Joyce and Virginia Woolf; the clipped, objective dialogue and narration of Ernest Hemingway; the nightmarish dream-novels of Franz Kafka; and the innovative anti-novel initiated by Samuel Beckett. Outside the United States, the century's outstanding novelists have been Germany's Mann, Grass, and Böll, relentless examiners of their

society; France's Proust, Camus, and Beckett, men of different gifts; the Soviet Union's Sholokhov, Ehrenburg, Pasternak, and Solzhenitsyn, chroniclers and critics of Soviet society; Italy's Silone, Pavese, and Moravia, a few of their country's brilliant postwar neo-realists; and England's Galsworthy, Orwell, Golding, Tolkien, and Burgess, whose works span the century.

In the United States, giants such as Hemingway, Fitzgerald, Faulkner, and Steinbeck stand beside the naturalists Dreiser and Caldwell, social satirist Sinclair Lewis, and Dos Passos, Farrell, Salinger, Mailer, and Algren. Ethnic interest began with such outstanding writers on the black experience as Wright, Ellison, Baldwin, and Brown, and continued with the Jewish chroniclers Bellow, Malamud, and Roth. Such novelists as Barth, Vonnegut, Styron, and Gardner give promise for the future.

Short Story. A short story is a brief, fictional prose composition usually involving a limited number of characters in a single illuminating incident or seeking an intense effect through the

LANGUAGE AND LITERATURE

William Faulkner (1897–1962), American novelist and Nobel laureate. His greatest works are *Light in August, Sanctuary, As I Lay Dying,* and *The Sound and the Fury.*

accumulation of impressions. In the West, the Romantic movement brought early examples of the form with the stories of E. T. A. Hoffmann and J. L. Tieck in Germany and those of Irving, Poe, and Hawthorne in the United States. In Russia, Pushkin's tales of country gentry and privileged classes and Gogol's sympathetic studies of simple people laid the groundwork for the sophisticated stories of Turgenev and the brilliant and moving peasant tales of Chekhov. Flaubert and de Maupassant wrote stories of polished craftsmanship in France, while tales in the nineteenth-century United States varied widely, from the gentle humor of local colorists Harte and Twain to the witty surprises of O. Henry. Short stories remain as individual in style, purpose, and construction as their writers, and twentieth-century short story lovers may dip into such diverse authors as Maugham, Kafka, Hemingway, Joyce, Babel, Faulkner, Porter, Capote, Salinger, and Updike.

Sonnet.   A sonnet is a poem of 14 lines in iambic pentameter arranged in accordance with a prescribed rhyming scheme. There are two leading forms, the Italian (or Petrarchan) and the English (or Shakespearean) though many English poets have used other rhyme schemes. They differ chiefly in that the Italian sonnet uses the first eight lines (the octet) to expose the theme, and the six remaining lines (the sestet) to resolve its conflicts; its rhyme scheme is *abba abba cdecde* or *cdcdcd*. The Shakespearean sonnet is often divided into three quatrains that supply examples, and ends with a summary rhymed couplet.

EXAMPLE OF ITALIAN SONNET

a Earth has not anything to show more fair;
b Dull would he be of soul who could pass by
b A sight so touching in its majesty.
a This City now doth, like a garment, wear
a The beauty of the Morning; silent, bare,
b Ships, towers, domes, theaters, and temples lie
b Open unto the fields, and to the sky;
a All bright and glittering in the smokeless air.

c Never did sun more beautifully steep
d In his first splendor, valley, rock or hill;
c Ne'er saw I, never felt, a calm so deep!
d The river glideth at his own sweet will:
c Dear God! The very houses seem asleep;
d And all that mighty heart is lying still.
Wordsworth, "On Westminster Bridge"

EXAMPLE OF ENGLISH SONNET

a Let me not to the marriage of true minds
b Admit impediments. Love is not love
a Which alters when it alteration finds,
b Or bends with the remover to remove.

c Oh no! it is an ever-fixéd mark,
d That looks on tempests and is never shaken;
c It is the star to every wandering bark,
d Whose worth's unknown, although his height be taken.

e Love's not Time's fool, though rosy lips and cheeks
f Within his bending sickle's compass come;
e Love alters not with his brief hours and weeks,
f But bears it out even to the edge of doom.

g If this be error and upon me proved,
g I never writ, nor no man ever loved.
Shakespeare, Sonnet 116

LITERARY MASTERPIECES
OLD AND NEW

Aeneid. The *Aeneid* is a Latin epic poem by the Roman poet Vergil and is dated 19 B.C.; it is the classic work telling of the founding of Rome by the Trojan hero Aeneas. It narrates Aeneas's wanderings before he reaches the seven hills of Rome, his love and abandonment of Dido, Queen of Carthage, his descent into hell, his war against a rival, Turnus, and his marriage to Lavinia, which promised continuation of his lineage. It closely follows Homer's great epic *The Iliad.*

Animal Farm. This is an anti-Utopian novel by British author George Orwell (Eric Blair), published in 1945, and written in the form of a beast fable. A group of animals overthrow their human masters and set up a communal society. Events in the animal Utopia closely parallel events in the Soviet Union, and the majority of animals are more cruelly victimized by their new masters than they were by the old. The chief animal villain, the pig Napoleon, is easily recognized as Stalin.

Arthurian Legend. The cycle of verse and prose tales concerning the mythical King Arthur of Britain and his knights of the Round Table forms the Arthurian legend. The legend provided one of the principal themes of medieval romance throughout Europe. The Arthur of romance is of marvelous birth. He is conceived by Queen Igraine when his father Uther Pendragon magically disguises himself as Igraine's husband. Arthur is marked for kingship as a young boy when he proves to be the only one who can remove the sword Excalibur from a stone in which it is imbedded. This is interpreted as a sign of the true king. (In a common variant, Arthur receives Excalibur from the mysterious Lady of the Lake who hands it up to him through the water.) Arthur marries Guinevere and establishes his court at Camelot, where he is advised by the wizard Merlin, and where he gathers at his Round Table the flower of knighthood. The adventures and love affairs of the various knights constitute the bulk of the legend. Finally, the adulterous love of Arthur's

favorite knight Lancelot and his queen Guinevere leads to the disintegration of the fellowship of the Round Table. Arthur's treacherous nephew Mordred attempts to usurp his throne. Though Arthur kills Mordred in battle, he is severely wounded. In some versions he dies and is buried in Glastonbury, England. In others, Sir Bedivere throws Excalibur into the lake. The Lady's hand reaches out to receive it. A barge appears and carries Arthur to the isle of Avalon, from which he is expected to return some day, healed of his wounds.

The legends are of Celtic origin and have a complicated history. There is some evidence that Arthur was a historical figure, a Celtic chieftain of the sixth century, who repelled an invasion of Saxons into Welsh territory. The earliest stories about Arthur are Welsh and emphasize his magic helpers (or hinderers), Merlin and his sister Morgan le Fay.

Arthur was given a place in history as a conqueror of Europe by the monkish chronicler Geoffrey of Monmouth in his largely fictitious *History of the Kings of Britain,* written in Latin in the twelfth century. In the fifteenth century the English prose *Morte D'Arthur* by Sir Thomas Malory fixed the legend in its traditional form. Modern versions include Alfred Tennyson's poems *Idylls of the King* and the novel *The Once and Future King* by T. H. White.

Babbitt. *Babbitt* is a novel by American writer Sinclair Lewis and was published in 1922. Its hero, George Babbitt, a small town businessman and town booster, whose horizons are limited to Zenith, the "greatest little city in the world," gave his name to an emergent social type. Although Babbitt comes to vaguely realize that the narrow aspirations of Zenith are not the whole of life, he is never able to act on this idea.

Beowulf. *Beowulf* is an Anglo-Saxon epic poem written about A.D. 1000 and is based on a mixture of legendary and historical events that took place in sixth-century Scandinavia. It is the oldest epic in a European vernacular.

The poem opens in Denmark at the court of King Hrothgar. For twelve years the monster Grendel has walked into Hrothgar's great mead hall, Heorot, and devoured as many as thirty warriors in one night. Then, unexpectedly, the young hero Beowulf, a prince of the Geats of southern Sweden, arrives from across the sea to aid Hrothgar. He wrestles with Grendel and tears off his arm, and Grendel flees to his den to die. The next night Grendel's mother, the water-hog, comes to avenge her son and devours another warrior. Beowulf follows her to the bottom of the sea and, after a terrible underwater fight, kills her and cuts off the head of Grendel's corpse. The Danes celebrate their delivery with great rejoicing in the mead hall and with speeches recalling heroic deeds of the past. Beowulf returns to his own people, laden with rich gifts.

Years later Beowulf becomes king of the Geats and rules for fifty years until a fearful dragon comes to lay waste his land. The old king, with eleven companions, sets out to destroy the dragon. At the sight of the fire-breathing monster his companions, except for the loyal Wiglaf, flee. The aged Beowulf fights against odds and kills the dragon but receives his own death wound in the combat. His grieving people place his body on a great funeral pyre and bury the dragon's treasure with his ashes.

Billy Budd.   *Billy Budd* is a short novel by American writer Herman Melville, published in 1925. It is a parable of the eternal conflict between good and evil and the limits of human justice. Unjustly accused of mutiny by the evil Claggart, the sailor Billy Budd, a model of natural innocence, kills Claggart and accepts his punishment—death.

Bourgeois Gentilhomme, Le ("The Would-Be Gentleman").   This is a play by the French dramatist Molière (Jean Baptiste Poquelin). It was performed in 1670 and is a satire on hypocrisy. M. Jourdain, a tradesman, aspires to be a gentleman by taking training in superficial courtesies. Fortunately, his inherent but more genuinely appealing vulgarity makes him impervious to the transformation.

Bridge of San Luis Rey, The.   This novel by American writer Thornton Wilder, published in 1927, reviews the lives of five people, strangers to one another, who are killed in the collapse of a Peruvian bridge, raising the question of whether their deaths were coincidental or part of a divine plan.

Brothers Karamazov, The.   This novel has often been considered the masterpiece of the Russian novelist Feodor Dostoevski and was published in 1879–80. It deals with the murder of a corrupt landowner Karamazov and the reactions of his three sons. The eldest, Dmitri, a wild, impulsive, hard-drinking ex-soldier, a rival of his father for the favors of the fair Grushenka, is unjustly accused of the crime. The second son, Ivan, a proud and cold intellectual incapable of love, feels guilty of the intellectual crime of despising his father and wishing him dead. The youngest son, Alyosha, is a figure of saintlike innocence, capable of undivided love. In addition to being a suspenseful story of crime and mystery, the work explores Dostoevski's religious and social ideas. The atheism and despair of Ivan are weighed against the faith of Alyosha, but there is no easy choice between them. The novel introduces a multitude of characters, divided in heart and lacerated in feeling, whose motivations Dostoevski probes remorselessly.

Candide.   *Candide* is a satirical novel by the French author Voltaire, published in 1759, and is directed against the notion that "everything happens for the best in this best of all possible worlds." The plot, thick with farcical misadventures (most of the incidents having some precedent in history), is concerned with the sometimes divided fortunes of Candide, his beloved Cunegonde, and his tutor Dr. Pangloss, who is the embodiment of optimism. In the end, somewhat reluctantly married to Cunegonde, Candide settles down to grow vegetables.

Canterbury Tales, The.   This is a collection of tales, mostly in verse, by Geoffrey Chaucer, and is both his masterpiece and one of the great works in English literature. The tales were written between about 1387 and 1400, the year of Chaucer's death. They tell of the poet joining a company of pilgrims on their way to Canterbury to visit the shrine of St. Thomas Becket.

To while away the journey, their host, Harry Bailey, suggests that each pilgrim tell two stories going, and two coming back: the pilgrim judged to have told the best tale is to get a free dinner. Chaucer completed twenty-four of the tales, from chivalric romance to folk tale to sermon to bawdy fable. The pilgrims, who come from all walks of life, are vividly described by Chaucer, and within the framework of the pilgrimage he brilliantly develops their personalities.

Catcher in the Rye, The. This novel by American author J. D. Salinger, published in 1951, concerns youth's disenchantment with a hostile adult world. It is cast as a long monologue spoken by Holden Caulfield, who has run away from his prep school, preferring to head for New York rather than go home. In spite of his external sophistication, Holden maintains an incorruptible innocence during a weekend of disillusioning experiences.

Chanson De Roland ("The Song of Roland"). This is an Old French *chanson de geste*. It recounts the fight of Roland, the most famous of Charlemagne's paladins, against the Saracens. The *Chanson* tells how Roland's army was ambushed at the pass of Roncesvalles in 778. Although hopelessly outnumbered, Roland was too proud to sound his horn for help, and he and his companions fought until every man was killed. At last, fatally wounded, Roland sounded his horn for help, and Charlemagne, thirty leagues away, came and destroyed the Saracens.

Cherry Orchard, The. This play by the great Russian playwright Anton Chekhov, first performed in 1904, mirrored Russian society at the end of the nineteenth century, when a long-rooted feudal system was giving way to social and economic change. The cherry orchard on the estates of the once wealthy Ranevskis, representing all that was idyllic in the past, must now be sold from under them. The Ranevskis are too inert to do much to help themselves, and in this they are contrasted with the practical Lopakhin, son of a former serf on the estate, who buys the cherry orchard, planning to cut down the trees and build houses.

Christmas Carol, A. This story of Christmas by Charles Dickens was published in 1843. Old Ebenezer Scrooge, a "clutching, covetous old sinner" and Tiny Tim, the crippled child of Bob Cratchit, Scrooge's downtrodden clerk, are two of the main characters. It is the story of Scrooge's regeneration: fantastic visitations by three spirits of Christmas (the ghosts of Christmas Past, Christmas Present, and Christmas Yet to Come) changed him from an unfeeling money-lover to a benevolent human being who sends a turkey to the Cratchit family to make their Christmas merry.

Cid, Song of the, or *Cantar (or Poema) de mío Cid.* This is a twelfth-century heroic poem considered the first masterpiece of Spanish literature. It celebrates El Cid, Ruy (or Rodrigo) Díaz de Vivar, the great national hero of Spain of the eleventh century; he was a historical figure whom the poem and later ballads gave almost legendary stature. *Le Cid* (1637), by the French classical playwright Pierre Corneille, is the first great tragedy in modern French.

Crime and Punishment. This masterly novel by the Russian writer Feodor Dostoevski, published in 1866, develops the theme of redemption through suffering. The penniless student Raskolnikov believes that his natural superiority places him above the moral law of common men. He finds good reasons for committing for gain two brutal murders, and the novel furnishes an examination of these reasons, which, one by one, are proved to be insupportable. Conscience will not permit Raskolnikov to use the money obtained through his crime, and his anguish slowly leads him to confess and embrace the consequent punishment—hard labor in Siberia—which is the gateway to his redemption.

Cry, the Beloved Country. This moving novel by the South African writer Alan Paton, published in 1948, deals with the tragedies, both personal and national, that flow from racial persecution. The central character, Stephen Kumalo, a Zulu clergyman, finds that in Johannesburg his sister has been forced to become a prostitute while his son is a murderer.

Cyrano de Bergerac. A romantic drama by French playwright Edmond Rostand, *Cyrano de Bergerac* was first performed in 1897. Loosely based on the historical Savinien de Cyrano, the title role is a poet and swordsman who is disfigured by a long nose. He acts as a go-between for his close friend and the woman whom both love—Cyrano secretly. In the end he dies, but not before knowing that she understood and responded to his love for her.

David Copperfield. This novel by British writer Charles Dickens, published in 1849–50, is a sentimental story of an orphan's struggles. It deals with the sufferings of young David after his mother's death, and with cruel treatment by his stepfather, schoolmasters, and employers. The hypocritical Uriah Heep is one of the book's many memorable characters. David finds friends, too—his aunt Betsy Trotwood, the optimistic Mr. Micawber, and the kite-flying Mr. Dick—and matures through their kindness to become a successful writer.

Death of a Salesman. A play by American writer Arthur Miller, first performed in 1949, this is the modern tragedy of an ordinary man, Willie Loman, an aging traveling salesman. Faced with loss of his livelihood, and the failure of his sons whom he has inculcated with his values of achieving success through being "well-liked," Willie is bewildered by his fate. Unable to understand why this familiar American dream worked for others but not for himself, Willie commits suicide in a final, pathetic effort to rescue his family through his insurance money.

Decline and Fall of the Roman Empire, The History of the. British historian Edward Gibbon's classic work, published in 1776–88, considers the fall of Rome and traces the dissolution of the Empire over more than a thousand years. Gibbon attributes the decline of Rome primarily to the corruption of classical Greco-Roman rational ideals by the emotional appeal of Christianity and other Eastern religions.

Divine Comedy, The. A long allegorical poem written about 1307–21 by the Italian poet Dante Alighieri. This work has been considered the supreme literary achievement of the Middle Ages. It expresses the poet's vision of the divine plan for justice in this world and the next. Dante originally called it *The Comedy,* because it begins in sorrow and ends happily, and also because it was written in Italian at a time when serious works were written in Latin. "Divine" was added to the title in the sixteenth century.

The first book, *Inferno,* begins with a prologue. In the middle of his life, the poet finds himself stranded in a dark wood (the world of sin and error). Unable to escape, he is helped by the intervention of his idealized beloved Beatrice (divine grace), who has been dead for ten years and is now in heaven. The Roman poet Vergil (the highest representative of human reason and pagan ethics) guides Dante out of the wood by a roundabout journey through the Afterlife. On Good Friday in the year 1300, they enter Hell, descending through nine circles in which the sinners become increasingly more infamous and their torments more hideous. There Dante sees well-known historical figures, princes, popes, and personal enemies, all vividly characterized. The lowest circle is reserved

Charles Dickens (1812–1870), English novelist. He created many memorable characters, including Oliver Twist, Ebenezer Scrooge, and Uriah Heep, whose names have become well known.

The Swedish film and stage actress Liv Ullman was highly acclaimed for her 1977 portrayal of the rebellious Nora in Ibsen's *A Doll's House*.

for traitors such as Judas Iscariot, Cassius, and Brutus.

In the second book, *Purgatorio,* Vergil leads Dante through Purgatory, where he is purged of his sins, as far as the gates of Paradise. As that is as far as human reason can go, Vergil leaves and Beatrice guides Dante through the nine ascending circles of Paradise. In the tenth circle, St. Bernard becomes his guide, and Dante briefly experiences a vision of the Eternal Light, Divine Wisdom, or God.

The number three, symbolizing the Trinity, is used throughout as a structural principle. Thus, the work is divided into three books, each having thirty-three cantos. The cantos are written in *terza rima,* a three-line verse form invented by Dante specifically for this work.

Doll's House, A.   This play by Norwegian dramatist Henrik Ibsen, first performed in 1879, supports women's rights. Nora Helmer, a spoiled housewife, thoughtlessly forges a check to save her husband from financial ruin. When she is scolded for this childish deed, rather than praised for her resourcefulness, Nora suddenly realizes that she is not a responsible partner, but merely a decorative ornament in his life.

Tired of being a doll, Nora leaves her husband and family to become a real person.

Don Quixote de la Mancha, The Ingenious Gentleman.   This picaresque novel, published in two parts in 1605 and 1615, is the masterpiece of the Spanish writer Miguel de Cervantes. It was a satire of the romances of chivalry popular in Cervantes's day.

An impoverished old gentleman, Alonzo Quixano, infatuated with knight-errantry, changes his name to Don Quixote de la Mancha and with an uncouth peasant, Sancho Panza, as his squire, embarks on a series of misadventures. His valorous deeds, such as tilting at windmills that he believes to be giants, are inspired by a peasant girl whom he believes to be the Lady Dulcinea. Ironically, he dies thinking he has been a failure, although in his pursuit of his illusory ideals he has shown far greater nobility than his sane, materialistic contemporaries.

Don Quixote has had a lasting influence on Western literature, and Sancho Panza ranks with the great comic characters of all time. It is the greatest prose work of Spanish literature, and its episodic structure influenced novel form for nearly 200 years.

Fathers and Sons.   A novel by Russian author Ivan Turgenev, published in 1862, this work is memorable for the character Bazarov, who became the representative type of the new generation of "nihilists" (cultural and political anarchists). An analysis of Russian society on the eve of the emancipation of the serfs, the work focuses on the contrasting values of Kirsanov, an aristocratic landowner, his son Arkady, a liberal freethinker, and Arkady's radical friend Bazarov, who in spite of his frightening contempt for the culture of the past, is portrayed sympathetically.

Faust.   Faust, a figure in numerous legends and literary works, is based on the few facts known of the life of a sixteenth-century charlatan and magician. Faust is archetypical of the overreacher, one with an insatiable desire for power and knowledge.

The Tragical History of Doctor Faustus, a play by English dramatist Christopher Marlowe (published in 1604), is one of the most famous dramatizations of the legend. It is based on the *Faustbuch,* published in 1587 at Frankfurt am Main by Johann Spies. The play is in the morality tradition and anti-Papist. Faustus, a good and learned man, sells his soul to Mephistopheles (the devil), practices necromancy, and plays tricks on the Pope. When payment is due, he despairs and is taken to hell.

Faust, a dramatic poem by German writer Johann Wolfgang von Goethe (published in two parts in 1808 and 1832) is another famous version of the legend. Faust is tempted by the devil and although he sins seriously, he remains aware of truth and goodness and is saved.

Finnegan's Wake.   This novel by Irish writer James Joyce, published in 1939, is a stream-of-consciousness experiment in form and meaning. Drawing on seventeen languages, it attempts to give coherence to all human experience and, through the dreams of Humphrey Chimpden Earwicker, to find the universal myth.

Forsyte Saga, The.   This is a series of novels by British writer John Galsworthy. *The Man of Property* (1906), *In Chancery* (1920), and *To Let* (1921) were collected in *The Forsyte Saga* (1922). The history of the Forsyte family was continued in *The White Monkey* (1924), *The Silver Spoon* (1926), and *Swan Song* (1928) which were collected in *A Modern Comedy* (1929).

The underlying theme of this social chronicle of the changes in manners and morals from Victorian England to the post-World War I period is the conflict beauty creates in men's lives.

For Whom the Bell Tolls.   This novel by the American novelist Ernest Hemingway, published in 1940, is a tragic story of courage and compassion. Its hero, Robert Jordan, an American who volunteers in the Spanish Civil War, grows beyond a cold concern for his military objective and dies with the awareness that his struggle was for all men.

Great Expectations.   A novel by Charles Dickens, published in 1861, this is the story of Pip, a village boy who longs for riches and social station, and suddenly receives from an

James Joyce (1882–1941), Irish novelist, whose innovative style allows great psychological detail. His major works are *A Portrait of the Artist as a Young Man, Ulysses,* and *Finnegans Wake.*

unknown source wealth and the chance for an education. His "great expectations" lead him to attempt to act like a fine gentleman, but when they disappear he returns to a sense of real values.

Great Gatsby, The.   This novel by F. Scott Fitzgerald, published in 1925 and generally regarded as his greatest completed work, is set in New York and is a searing exposure of the desperate boredom and spiritual bankruptcy of the Jazz Age, and of the thoughtless cruelty of great wealth. Its violent plot is concerned with the efforts of Jay Gatsby, a wealthy racketeer who poses as a businessman to win his idealized love, the spoiled and wealthy Daisy, cousin of Nick Carraway, the story's narrator. Not only does Gatsby fail, he dies alone and deserted even by the hangers-on who had flocked to his lavish parties.

Gulliver's Travels.   This is a satire by Jonathan Swift, published in 1726, which tells of Lemuel Gulliver's voyages to imaginary lands: Book I, to the island of Lilliput, where he finds himself a giant prisoner of a race of people six inches tall, but every bit as vain and pompous as the people of his homeland; Book II, to Brobdingnag, the land of the giants, where he suffers the indignities of being swallowed and burped up by a squalling infant, and being carried away by a puppy; Book III, to various countries, chief of which is the floating island of Laputa, the Cloud Cuckooland of eccentric scholars; and Book IV, to the country of the Houyhnhnms, a land where horses with an intelligence superior to that of mankind carry on an ideal government, despite the fact that they share their island with an inferior race of Yahoos who cannot participate in it.

Huckleberry Finn, The Adventure of. A novel by American writer Mark Twain (Samuel Langhorne Clemens), this is generally considered his masterpiece. The story, told in the vernacular of Huck, a true child of nature, deals with his daring act of helping Jim, a runaway slave, to escape. Huck and Jim, floating down the Mississippi on a raft, enjoy a peace and freedom and mutual respect that is a sharp contrast to the meanness of society in the river

Mark Twain (Samuel Langhorne Clemens, 1835–1910), American novelist, essayist, and humorist. His great novels include *The Adventures of Huckleberry Finn* and *The Adventures of Tom Sawyer*.

towns where they stop. Twain uses the irony of Huck's innocent view of life to criticize the barbarity of "sivilization."

Human Comedy, The. This is the name given to the novels of the French writer Honoré de Balzac. Balzac intended to portray the private dramas of all aspects of French life—Paris and the provinces—the worlds of peasants, soldiers, businessmen, and fashionable society. The first of the series, *Les Chouans,* a historical novel, appeared in 1830. The last two works, *Cousin Bette* and *Cousin Pons,* appeared in 1847–48. Though Balzac did not live to complete his ambitious project, he covered an enormous range of subjects and environments. His description and psychology were realistic; he was fascinated by money, success, and failure, and their effects on character. *Eugénie Grandet* (1833) is the story of the daughter of a miser, who lives the penurious life of a household drudge until middle age when her father's death makes her an heiress and she gives her money to the poor. Perhaps his most famous work is *Père Goriot* (1835), the story of a bourgeois father who sacrifices his fortune and his life to the ambitions of his two snobbish daughters.

Iceman Cometh, The. This tragedy by American playwright Eugene O'Neill, produced in 1946, is often considered his greatest work. Through an intricate network of religious symbolism, O'Neill tells the story of a man's death brought about by loss of hope.

Iliad. The *Iliad* is a Greek epic poem by Homer. A recitative poem in the ancient bardic tradition, it was orally composed in about the ninth century B.C. and first transcribed in the sixth century B.C.

It is a heroic account of the Greek victory in the Trojan War. Started by the elopement of Paris and Helen (the wife of Menelaus, the Greek commander and brother of King Agamemnon), the war enlists all of the Greek and Trojan heroes, including Achilles, Odysseus, Hector, and Troilus, and most of the gods. The conflict is decided by Zeus, who gives victory to the Greeks.

Generally considered the greatest literary work of western civilization, the *Iliad* is the starting point for virtually every epic of Greco-Roman literature—for instance, the *Odyssey* and the *Aeneid*—and the model for every later epic in the classical tradition.

Jane Eyre.   This novel by British writer Charlotte Brontë, published in 1847, deals with the love of a modest and plain but intelligent governess and her ill-tempered, discourteous employer Rochester. The impediment to their love, and the cause of Rochester's moodiness, is an insane wife he has kept hidden in the house. When Jane learns of the wife's existence, she leaves. Later, when the wife is killed and Rochester is blinded in a fire, the lovers are reunited.

Leatherstocking Tales.   These novels of early frontier life by James Fenimore Cooper all have the same hero, the scout Leatherstocking or Natty Bumppo, who combines knowledge of the woods with Yankee ingenuity. The series contains *The Pioneers* (1823), *The Last of the Mohicans* (1826), *The Prairie* (1827), *The Pathfinder* (1840), and *The Deerslayer* (1841). These books remained popular throughout Europe long after their reputation declined in the United States.

Leaves of Grass.   This is the collection of poems by Walt Whitman on which his reputation stands. When it was first published in 1855, it attracted little attention, but it was expanded and revised throughout Whitman's lifetime. In this work Whitman assumes the stance of a national bard. He celebrates himself ("Song of Myself") and his country. He celebrates democracy, fellowship, the love of men, and the love of men and women. He celebrates the eternal cycle of birth and death ("Out of the Cradle Endlessly Rocking"). Readers were originally shocked by the poet's conceit, his prophetic tone, and his egalitarian acceptance of all aspects of life. His irregular verse form, the forerunner of free verse, was also considered unpoetic. Today this work is considered the embodiment of American Romantic nationalism.

Life on the Mississippi.   This autobiographical story by Mark Twain, published in 1883, depicts his life as a pilot up and down the great river before the Civil War.

Long Day's Journey into Night.   A domestic tragedy by Eugene O'Neill, this is the most personal and intimate of all his works. Written about 1941, it was not performed until 1956, after the author's death. The play embodies all the bitterness and ambivalence of the author's feelings toward his family. It is set in a country house in the year 1912. The characters—the four members of the Tyrone family—are patterned on O'Neill's family. The father is a famous actor, the mother a drug addict who lives on memories of her innocent Catholic girlhood. The elder son is an alcoholic, and the younger son (O'Neill), while struggling to break away to a new life, learns he is stricken with tuberculosis.

Look Homeward, Angel.   This first novel by Thomas Wolfe, published in 1929, is of the type called in German a *Kunstlerroman*, a novel of an artist's development. Its autobiographical

The 1956 production of *Long Day's Journey into Night*, starring Florence Eldridge and Frederic March, established the story of the tragic Tyrone family as Eugene O'Neill's masterpiece.

hero Eugene Gant, a physical giant and precocious genius, loves and hates his home town of Altamont (Asheville, North Carolina), struggles against the limited horizons of his family, receives vague indications of immortality from a few sympathetic people, and finally sets out on a quest for fame and fortune as a writer.

Lord Jim. This novel by Joseph Conrad, written in 1900, deals with a young English seaman who impulsively abandons his sinking ship carrying Muslim pilgrims. Unable to understand or to reconcile this ignoble act with his own self-image, Jim cannot face returning home. He lives out his life among the South Sea Island natives, whose love and admiration for him are expressed in their nickname *Tuan* (Lord) Jim. But luck is against Jim. Unwittingly he betrays his native friends and meets death at their hands, a fate that finally resolves his guilt.

Lord of the Rings, The. This trilogy of fantasy novels with allegorical overtones was written by the English scholar J. R. R. Tolkien. It consists of *The Fellowship of the Ring* (1954), *The Two Towers* (1954), and *The Return of the King* (1955). It deals with the long and often grim and terrible quest of the Hobbits to destroy the magic ring they possess in order to keep it from falling into the hands of evil powers.

The trilogy carries on a story first introduced in Tolkein's *The Hobbit* (1937), a fantasy written for children. Tolkien, a scholar of Old English and Old Norse literature, drew on old legends for the setting and atmosphere of "Middle-earth."

Madame Bovary. A novel by French writer Gustave Flaubert, published in 1856, *Madame Bovary* censures romanticism in its portrayal of a provincial wife, Emma Bovary, who finds life married to a dull country doctor a great disappointment. Emma magnifies routine flirtations with neighboring men into grand passions, neglects her home, and spends money recklessly on affairs. Rejected by her young lover, she commits suicide. Her unsuspecting husband dies of grief. Their only child goes to the workhouse.

Misanthrope, Le. This comedy by the French playwright Molière, was first produced at the Palais-Royal, Paris, in 1666. This brilliant drawing-room comedy explores the character of the supercritical Alceste, who can find fault with everyone except himself—though always "for their own good." The play was immediately successful and has remained popular for more than 300 years.

Misérables, Les. This novel by Victor Hugo was published in 1862. The title means "the wretched ones." Jean Valjean, the hero, is an ex-convict who has been sentenced to the gallows for stealing a loaf of bread. The generous sympathy of a bishop who befriends him after he is released changes Valjean's character. He becomes a successful businessman and mayor of his town, but he is hounded by Javert, a detective, and when his notoriety as an ex-convict threatens the happiness of Cosette (daughter of a woman Valjean befriended), Valjean disappears. Cosette and her lover Marius, learning of Valjean's self-sacrifice, search for him and find him as he is dying.

Moby-Dick. A novel by American author Herman Melville (1851), *Moby-Dick* is considered by many to be the finest American novel ever written. This tale of Captain Ahab's search for the great white whale that has crippled him is rich in symbolism and philosophical overtones. At the same time, the book is an exciting narrative and a precise description of the New England whaling industry of the time. The narrator, Ishmael, is the only survivor of the mad quest.

Nineteen Eighty-Four. This novel written in 1949 by the English satirist George Orwell offers a prophetic forecast of the future under totalitarian rule. It is a terrifying projection of life in the superstate watched over by Big Brother, where no one dares to trust another, and each lives in dread that his secret thoughts ("thought crimes") may be revealed on his face ("face crime").

Odyssey, The. This is Homer's epic of Odysseus, a king of Ithaca and one of the foremost of the Greek chiefs in the Trojan War.

Odysseus thwarted the sirens' song by stopping the ears of his sailors and having himself bound to the mast. He thus avoided shipwreck and was able to continue his journey home.

The *Odyssey* describes the ten years of wandering and hardship Odysseus encountered on his voyage home from the war. He touched upon the shores of the Lotus Eaters in Africa. He escaped death from the one-eyed Cyclops Polyphemus by his courageous trickery, blinding the giant and concealing himself beneath one of the Cyclops's sheep as they crowded out of the cave. He remained one year with Circe, the enchantress, and seven years with the ocean nymph Calypso on her island. He braved the dangers of Scylla and Charybdis and heard the sirens sing while he was bound to the mast, thus escaping them. He was shipwrecked on the shores of Phaeacia and there cared for by Nausicaa and her father, who gave him ships to continue his voyage home.

At last he reached Ithaca disguised as a beggar, to find his wife Penelope surrounded by a host of insolent suitors, each coveting the kingdom. With the aid of his son Telemachus and his faithful herdsman Eumaeus he slew them all and reigned another good sixteen years.

Old Man and the Sea, The.   This is a novel by Ernest Hemingway, published in 1952. It deals with the struggles of an old Cuban fisherman to protect a huge fish, his first catch in many weeks, from sharks. The old man fights gallantly for two days but the sharks win in the end. Because of its theme of the dignity and irony of primal struggle, the book was hailed as a return of Hemingway's original, simple heroic code.

Oliver Twist.   A novel by British writer Charles Dickens, published serially from 1837 to 1839, this is a melodramatic tale of poverty and the London underworld. Oliver, an unknown waif, escapes from a workhouse only to fall into the hands of Fagin, the master of a den of thieves. Fagin forces Oliver to break into a house. Oliver is caught by his intended victims who recognize at once that he is no common criminal. Through their kindly interest, Oliver discovers his true parentage; Fagin and his crew are brought before the law, and Oliver is adopted by a wealthy gentleman.

One Day in the Life of Ivan Denisevich.   This novel by Russian writer Alexander Solzhenitsyn, published in 1962, describes a typical "good" day in the life of a prisoner in a Soviet concentration camp in Siberia. Ivan counts the day good because he manages to conceal a little extra food for himself, because he incurs no unusual punishment for misconduct, and because he avoids the dreaded sentence to solitary confinement in a freezing cell that befalls one of his fellow prisoners.

Our Town.   An elegiac play by the American writer Thornton Wilder, performed first in 1938, *Our Town* deals with the cycle of life in a New England town called Grovers Corners, but meant to be Everytown. A narrator comments on the town's activities and leading citizens. A girl and young man fall in love and marry. The young wife dies in childbirth and is buried among her fellow townsmen in the local cemetery.

Paradise Lost.   This epic peom in blank verse by John Milton, was published in 1667. Its purpose is "to justify the ways of God to man." It relates how some of the angels revolted against God and were cast out of Heaven into Hell. They decide to revenge themselves upon the Almighty by invading the earth and leading man to sin. Satan, chief of the fallen angels, corrupts Adam and Eve, the first human beings, and brings about their expulsion from Paradise. *Paradise Lost* is regarded as the greatest epic in the English language. A sequel, *Paradise Regained* (1671), deals with the theme of redemption.

Pickwick Papers, The.   This is a story by Charles Dickens, issued in parts in 1836–37. It is made up of a series of adventures of Samuel Pickwick, Esq., founder and president of the Pickwick Club, his valet Sam Weller, and other companions. The work brought fame to Dickens at the age of twenty-four.

Pilgrim's Progress, The.   An allegory by the English preacher John Bunyan, the first part of which was issued in 1678, *The Pilgrim's Progress* describes the adventures of its hero, Christian, on his way from the City of Destruction to the Celestial City. He fights with Apollyon, looks on Vanity Fair, passes the castle of Giant Despair, and, after these and many other trials, reaches the Delectable Mountains and crosses the Black River to the Shining Gate. Its plain, direct style was welcomed by the common people and was as popular in New England as in the author's own country.

Playboy of the Western World, The.   This play by the Irish dramatist John Millington Synge, performed in 1907, is about a young country lad, Christie Mahon, who thinks he has killed his father and, horrified, flees his home. But he is received as though he were a hero, bold and brave, and the flattering attentions bring about a complete change in his naturally timid personality. Christie's moment of glory is over when his father turns up alive. The play is greatly admired for the richness of its language, and is still remembered for the outrage with which its early performances in Ireland and America were greeted, resulting in the "Playboy Riots" in Dublin, New York, and Philadelphia.

Pride and Prejudice.   This was the first novel by Jane Austen, written in 1796 (when she was twenty-one years old) and published in 1813. The scene is laid in the English countryside,

and the plot concerns the Bennett family's attempts to find suitable husbands for three daughters. The intimate drawing of the book's middle-class characters is done with humor and charm. Prejudice is represented by Elizabeth Bennett; Pride, by Mr. Darcy, her wealthy suitor. As Darcy overcomes his pride, Elizabeth overcomes her prejudice, and the two are married at last, giving this comedy of manners a happy ending.

Raisin in the Sun, A.   This play by Lorraine Hansberry, produced in 1959, was the first play by a black writer dealing specifically with everyday problems of blacks to win both popular and critical acclaim. It received the New York Drama Critics Award for the best play of the season. It concerns an ordinary Chicago family's struggles to make a living and retain their dignity. The title is from a poem by the black poet Langston Hughes. In the play a determined mother fights to keep her children's dreams from drying up like "a raisin in the sun."

Red Badge of Courage, The.   A novel by Stephen Crane, published in 1895 when the author was about twenty-four years old, *The Red Badge of Courage* is a study of a man's feelings in battle, written by one who had never been in a battle. Henry Fleming, a raw country boy, enlists at the outset of the Civil War. The book describes his mental states as he waits for action, his panic under fire, and his final conquest of cowardice through identification with his comrades. It is one of the first books to treat battle realistically rather than as a theater for displays of gallantry.

Return of the Native, The.   The sixth novel of Thomas Hardy, *The Return of the Native* was published in 1878. The time is "between 1840 and 1850"; the scene is Egdon Heath in Hardy's Wessex country. The "native" is Clym Yeobright, who has been in Paris but, wishing to lead a less selfish life, returns to the village in which he was born and there plans to open a school and improve local conditions. His decision disappoints his mother's hopes for a brilliant future for him, and she is more alarmed when he falls in love with Eustacia Vye, an

Thomas Hardy (1840–1928), British novelist and poet. His best-known novels are *The Return of the Native, Far from the Madding Crowd, Tess of the d'Urbervilles,* and *Jude the Obscure.*

exotic, restless, and dissatisfied girl, with whom he leads a troubled existence. An aura of fateful tragedy broods over their relationship. Clym's mother meets an accidental death, Eustacia drowns herself, and Clym, his sight impaired, finds his vocation as an itinerant open-air preacher and lecturer.

Riders to the Sea.   This one-act play by John Millington Synge, first performed in Dublin in 1904, was one of the finest achievements of the Irish literary renaissance. A starkly tragic play, it pictures a day like any other day in an Aran Island fishing village. But it is the day when the old woman Maurya, who has lost four sons at sea, sees her youngest son Bartley brought home drowned.

School for Scandal, The.   This play by the Irish-born English dramatist Richard Brinsley Sheridan, first performed in 1777, was critical of contemporary manners. Its satire is essentially moral, however, not social, being directed against hypocrisy and pretense. Its complicated plot, played out against a background of fashionable trivia, is concerned with exposing Joseph Surface's duplicity in trying to win the considerable fortune of Maria, ward to Sir Peter Teazle, by making advances to Sir Peter's much younger, inexperienced wife from the country. In the end, Joseph is found out; his generous-natured cousin Charles is rewarded and wins Maria's hand; and Lady Teazle, having been taught a lesson about life's real values, is reconciled with her husband. The play, one of the most popular in the English language, is often revived.

Silent Don, The.   Written by Soviet novelist Mikhail Sholokhov, this historical chronicle tells of the Don Cossacks and of one in particular, Gregor Melekhov, during World War I, the Russian Revolution, and the ensuing civil war. *The Silent Don* (also translated as *The Quiet Don*) was originally published in four volumes between 1928 and 1940 and was translated into English as two volumes, *And Quiet Flows the Don* (1934) and *The Don Flows Home to the Sea* (1940).

Stranger, The (*L'Etranger*).   This novel by the Algerian-born French philosopher Albert Camus, published in 1942, embodies the author's belief that life in the modern world is "absurd," or meaningless. It views man as a "stranger" in the world, and is about a man named Meursault, who is unable to find any reason for living or to experience any kind of emotional reaction, even to harrowing events. Faced with death, however, he discovers that the simple fact of life itself is enough to justify existence.

Streetcar Named Desire, A.   This play by the American author Tennessee Williams, performed in 1947, was awarded a Pulitzer Prize. The play concerns Blanche Dubois, an aging, unstable Southern belle who comes to stay with her sister, Stella. Her refined behavior and coquettish manner provoke a conflict with her earthy brother-in-law, Stanley Kowalski. The title sums up the theme of the play, which is set in the French Quarter of New Orleans, where a streetcar named "Desire" shares its track with one named "Cemetery."

Tom Jones.   Properly called *The History of Tom Jones, a Foundling,* this comic romance by Henry Fielding, one of the founders of the English novel, was published in 1749. It relates the adventures of high-spirited, impulsive, and generous Tom, who, despite many discreditable escapades, at last wins the confidence of his foster father, Squire Allworthy, and the love of beautiful Sophia Western. The novel is remarkable for its vitality and sweeping picture of eighteenth-century London and country life.

Tom Sawyer, The Adventures of. This classic of small-town American boyhood written by Mark Twain in 1876 was based on his memories of growing up in Hannibal, Missouri. Tom, an imaginative boy who is fond of adventure stories, finds himself involved in a real life adventure when he and his friend Huck Finn witness a murder committed by Injun Joe. The terrified boys run away, but return in time to prevent an innocent man from being condemned for the crime.

Turn of the Screw, The. This novel-length ghost story by Henry James was published in 1898. A young governess goes to an isolated country house to take care of two charming children, Miles and Flora. She sometimes sees a strange man and woman on the grounds whose descriptions match those of the former valet and governess, who are both dead. She gradually realizes that the children, thought outwardly angelic, are possessed by these evil ghosts. Her attempts to free them end in tragedy.

Ulysses. *Ulysses,* a novel by the Irish writer James Joyce, first published in 1922, has become a landmark of psychological and naturalistic fiction. The story takes place in Dublin in one day, June 16, 1904. The ordinary events of that day experienced by the leading characters—the autobiographical Stephen Dedalus; Leopold Bloom, a Jewish advertising salesman; his wife Molly Bloom, the eternal daughter of Eve—are carefully recorded. Joyce uses the method of free-association interior monologue and sometimes interpolates a variety of other styles that are brilliant literary parodies.

Utopia. A humanistic treatise in two parts, written in Latin by the English statesman Sir Thomas More, *Utopia* was published in 1516. It presents a critique of contemporary social and political ills and offers a solution to them in the description of Utopia, an ideal island society where reason governs and no one grasps for power. The island has given its name (literally meaning "no place") to all such ideal societies.

Vanity Fair. This novel by William Makepeace Thackeray, first published in 1847–48, satirizes social customs of early nineteenth-century England and Europe, introducing an unprincipled charmer, Becky Sharp. This book is considered a classic because of its vivid portraits of the scheming Becky and the meekly good Amelia Sedley.

Walden. This essay published in 1854 by the American philosopher-writer Henry David Thoreau celebrates man's individuality and oneness with nature. *Walden* chronicles the author's experiences while living in the woods near Walden Pond in 1845–47.

War and Peace. An epic novel by Russian novelist Leo Tolstoy, published in 1864–69, *War and Peace* gives a view of all of Russian society at the beginning of the nineteenth century, focusing on the Napoleonic Wars. It expresses an optimistic view of life in spite of the presence of evil, which can be successfully resisted by love and family happiness.

Waste Land, The. This poem by Anglo-American writer T. S. Eliot, published in 1922, reflects the pessimism of alienated artists after World War I. An allegory of the barrenness of western civilization, it follows the Fisher King's journey through the "wasteland" of modern life.

Wuthering Heights. The one novel by Emily Brontë, published in 1847, *Wuthering Heights* is a somber tale of love and vengeance. Its central character is the orphaned Heathcliff, whose thwarted love for Catherine Earnshaw leads him to take revenge on her and her family.

WILLIAM SHAKESPEARE (1564–1616)

William Shakespeare was born in Stratford-on-Avon; his father was a tanner and a councilman. Shakespeare attended grammar school in Stratford-on-Avon and married Anne Hathaway there in 1582. They had three children.

Shakespeare became an apprentice in London's famous Globe Theater and later acted and wrote his plays for the Globe. While little is known about Shakespeare's life—questions have even been raised concerning whether he wrote all the plays attributed to him—this much we can say: his dramatic skill, memorable characters, and superb poetry have established Shakespeare as the greatest writer in the English language. Besides his plays, every well-read adult must sooner or later dip into Shakespeare's sonnets and discover there further proof of his genius.

When we consider that not a single day goes by without productions of Shakespeare's plays somewhere in the world, it is clear that those great plays hold fascination for everyone. Every actor has the ambition of playing Hamlet, Macbeth, Othello, and King Lear; every actress wants to portray Ophelia, Lady Macbeth, Desdemona, and Cordelia. But these are only the great tragic roles. There are many other equally challenging roles for actors and actresses with a comic bent. And those of us who cannot hope to play Shakespeare can find the richness of Shakespeare's language and the wisdom of his insights by settling into a comfortable chair and acting the plays alone in our imaginations.

SHAKESPEARE'S PLAYS

Comedies

The Comedy of Errors (1590).   Two brothers both named Antipholus, "the one so like the other as could not be distinguished," and their servants named Dromio, "male twins, both alike," are separated in infancy during a shipwreck. Bachelors Antipholus and Dromio of Syracuse, searching for their brothers, enter Ephesus, where they meet two women who claim to be their wives. Going home with them,

William Shakespeare (1564–1616), English poet and playwright, considered the greatest writer of the Western world. His many tragedies, histories, and comedies are performed everywhere.

Antipholus and Dromio enter into a comedy of errors, in which merchants, wives, and servants mistake the pair with their twins until the confusion finally clears up and all are sorted out.

The Taming of the Shrew (1593).   This play within a play concerns Katharina, a beautiful but harsh-tongued and obstinate girl no one wants to marry. Petruchio agrees to marry Katharina, and her father Baptista of Padua allows his younger daughter Bianca to be courted by Gremio, Hortensio, and Lucentio. Lucentio wins Bianca's hand. Petruchio, on his own wedding day, arrives late at church dressed like a madman, swears throughout the service, and leaves Padua immediately with Katharina before the wedding reception. In Verona Petruchio tames Katharina by torturing her with mock kindness: her food is not good enough to eat, her bed not fit to sleep in, her clothes unfit to wear. Katharina, for the sake of peace, gives in and returns to Padua a model wife, amazing the henpecked husband of once-gentle Bianca by lecturing on the duties of a wife to her husband.

The Two Gentlemen of Verona (1594). Fickle Proteus woos Julia in Verona, while constant Valentine falls in love with Silvia, daughter of the Duke of Milan. Proteus is ordered to Milan. After pledging undying love to Julia, Proteus proceeds to the court where he also falls in love with Silvia and reveals to the Duke Valentine's plan to elope with Silvia. Valentine is banished from the court and becomes the leader of a group of outlaws in a nearby forest. Proteus, with the help of a page named Sebastian, really Julia in disguise, bids openly for Silvia's hand in marriage. Silvia flees in search of Valentine but is caught by Proteus who tries to force his attentions upon her. Caught by Valentine, Proteus begs and receives forgiveness. The Duke has a change of heart and allows Valentine and Silvia to be reunited as Julia, her true identity disclosed, is joined with Proteus.

A Midsummer Night's Dream (1595). Egeus, father of Hermia, promises her to Demetrius despite her love for Lysander. Athenian Duke Theseus supports Egeus's decision, so Hermia and Lysander plan to meet in the woods and elope. Helena, in love with Demetrius, reveals Hermia's plan to Demetrius and he sets out to search for the lovers. In the woods, various tradesmen rehearse a play of which Peter Quince is the director and vain Nick Bottom is the star. The play is to be presented in honor of the Duke's marriage with the Amazon Queen Hippolyta. The woods are enchanted by fairies who have come to bless the royal wedding. Oberon, who is the fairy king, and the mischievous sprite Puck play outrageous tricks on everybody until Theseus and Egeus arrive. The various spells are undone, and the various couples are sorted out and happily married.

Love's Labour's Lost (1596). Ferdinand, King of Navarre, and three of his lords have sworn to study and fast, out of the sight of women, for three years. Arrival of the Princess of France and three of her ladies obliges the four men to disregard their vows for state reasons. They soon fall in love with the ladies and begin to woo them. The courting is interrupted by news of the death of the Princess's father, and the Princess imposes a year's wait on the courtship as the play ends.

The Merchant of Venice (1597). The Venetian Jewish moneylender Shylock demands a pound of flesh of Antonio if Antonio fails to repay a loan Shylock has made to Antonio's friend Bassanio. While Bassanio is at Belmont winning the hand of Portia by correctly choosing one of three chests, as stipulated in her father's will, Shylock's daughter Jessica flees Venice with her father's money and her lover Lorenzo. Antonio's message to Bassanio, warning him that the debt has fallen due, causes Bassanio to rush to court. Shylock refuses late payment of the money due him, ignores pleas of mercy, and demands his payment in the form of a pound of flesh taken from around the heart. Portia disguises herself as a lawyer and grants Shylock's request, but warns him that the death of Antonio that may result will leave Shylock open to charges of threatening the life of a Venetian citizen. Shylock is ordered to give up his money to Antonio and to the state. By Antonio's wish, Shylock is permitted to give the money to Jessica.

As You Like It (1598). Rosalind is expelled from court by her uncle Frederick, usurper of her father's throne. Disguised as Ganymede, a country lad, she travels with her cousin Celia to the Forest of Arden, where her secret love, Orlando, has joined the followers of her exiled father, Duke Senior. Ganymede pretends to help Orlando rid himself of his infatuation by encouraging him to make love to her as though she were Rosalind. Orlando is on his way to one of their lovers' meetings when he kills a lion and saves the life of his wicked brother Oliver, who has actually come to kill Orlando. Oliver is full of remorse and asks Ganymede's forgiveness for the delay and falls in love with Celia. The couples are married as Duke Senior regains his lands from the penitent Frederick.

Much Ado About Nothing (1599). Claudio is in love with Hero, daughter of the Governor of Messina. His own wedding date set, Claudio arranges for his friend Benedick and Hero's cousin Beatrice to fall in love. Don John, seeking revenge on his brother Don Pedro, Prince of Arragon, attempts to wreck the marriage of Claudio, Pedro's favorite. Claudio witnesses a clandestine meeting between Hero's maid and one of Don John's men. Thinking Hero unfaithful, Claudio disgraces her at church, provoking Benedick to challenge Claudio to a duel. The crisis ends happily when Hero's presumed lover confesses the plot, and Claudio agrees to marry one of Hero's cousins to gain forgiveness. At last, Claudio and Hero are married, along with Benedick and Beatrice.

Twelfth Night, or What You Will (1600).

Viola, disguised as a boy and employed in Illyria by Duke Orsino to serve as messenger in his courtship of Olivia, finds herself in love with the Duke. Malvolio, Olivia's steward, complains continually of the sloth of the two knights, Sir Toby Belch, who is Olivia's uncle, and Sir Toby's hanger-on Sir Andrew Aguecheek. Finally the knights trick the steward into humiliating circumstances and lock him up as mad. Viola's twin brother, Sebastian, presumed drowned in a shipwreck, appears in Illyria and is mistaken for the King's page and married by Olivia. Confused and furious at first, the Duke readily marries Viola after she removes her disguise and tells him of her love.

The Merry Wives of Windsor (1600).

Sir John Falstaff writes identical letters to the wives of Windsor gentlemen Ford and Page, professing his love. The honest wives pretend to offer encouragement but plan revenge on the knight. The Pages' daugher Anne meanwhile is courted by Dr. Caius, Slender, and her favorite, Fenton. Falstaff is humiliated in his first visit to Mistress Ford when the basket of dirty clothes in which he hides from Ford is dumped into a muddy ditch. On his second visit, he disguises himself as a woman whom Ford hates. Falstaff is beaten for his trouble. The wives and their husbands humiliate Falstaff a third time when mock fairies pinch and burn him while Anne elopes with Fenton.

All's Well That Ends Well (1603).

When Count Bertram departs for the King's court, he is followed by the maid Helena, who is the secret admirer of the count. Helena administers to the sick King a cure inherited from her father. Recovered, the King gives Helena a ring and grants her Bertram as a husband. Displeased, Count Bertram sends the low-born Helena to his mother, flees to Florence, and promises to be her true husband when she can get his ring and bear his child. Helena travels to Florence, changes place with a local maid in Bertram's bed, and switches his ring with hers. Believing Helena dead, Bertram returns home. The King sees Helena's ring on the count's hand and demands an explanation. Helena appears and confesses the plot. Claiming that she has fulfilled both parts of Bertram's requirements, Helena gains him as a true husband.

Measure for Measure (1604).

Lord Angelo is ruling in the absence of the Duke of Vienna. To observe the justice of Lord Angelo's rule, the Duke disguises himself as Friar Ludovick and returns to move among his people. Just at that time, Angelo has revived capital punishment for immoral behavior. Unable to marry his beloved Juliet, young Claudio is unjustly seized and sentenced to immediate execution. Claudio's sister Isabella leaves her nunnery to plead for mercy from Angelo, who offers her brother's life in exchange for her honor. Indignant, Isabella refuses but, at Ludovick's direction, consents and is replaced by Mariana, who once was betrothed to Angelo. Later, Angelo orders the execution of Claudio, but the prison official disobeys. The Duke of Vienna removes his disguise and confronts Angelo. The Duke then pardons Angelo, who marries Mariana while the Duke marries Isabella and Claudio marries Juliet.

Cymbeline (1609).

Imogen, daughter of British King Cymbeline, is secretly married to Posthumus. Imogen's stepmother reveals the secret marriage to Cymbeline, who banishes Posthumus. In Italy Posthumus enters into a bet with Iachimo that Imogen will remain faithful. The bet involves a diamond ring that Imogen had given Posthumus. By trickery Iachimo enters Imogen's bedchamber and brings evidence to Posthumus of his wife's infidelity. Posthumus orders Imogen's murder, but Imogen is spared. Dressed as a man, she flees to a forest and is befriended by Belarius and two sons of Cymbeline stolen in their infancy by

Belarius. A Roman army invades Britain, and Imogen becomes the page of the Roman general. Cymbeline is captured in battle with the Romans and then rescued. Posthumus, who has returned from Italy to fight for Cymbeline, surrenders himself for execution as punishment for having returned. Iachimo discloses his trickery in the bet, and the couple is reunited.

The Winter's Tale (1610). Leontes, King of Sicily, mistakenly suspects his wife Hermione of infidelity with Polixenes, King of Bohemia. A plot to poison Polixenes fails, but Hermione is imprisoned. Hermione bears a daughter, and the King orders Antigonus, a Sicilian lord, to leave the baby to die on a desert shore. Hermione dies of grief, and Leontes is filled with remorse. Antigonus has left the baby in Bohemia and is himself killed by a bear. The baby Perdita is brought up by a shepherd and falls in love with Florizel, son of King Polixenes. Polixenes discovers the love affair, and Florizel, Perdita, and the old shepherd flee to Leontes's court. The identity of Perdita is revealed, to Leontes's joy. A statue of Hermione turns out to be the living Hermione hidden from Leontes. Polixenes, learning that Perdita is the daughter of Leontes, is happy to have his son marry her.

The Tempest (1611). Prospero, Duke of Milan, has been ousted from his throne by Antonio, his brother. Set adrift on the sea with his daughter Miranda, Prospero finds his way to an island, the place of banishment of the witch Sycorax. Prospero releases Ariel and other spirits imprisoned by Sycorax, and they now obey Prospero's orders. The sole inhabitant of the island, the witch's son Caliban, also obeys Prospero's orders. Prospero lives on the island with Miranda for twelve years, when a ship carrying Antonio and the King of Naples and his son Ferdinand is wrecked on the island. Everyone is rescued, but Ferdinand is separated from the others and thought to be dead. In turn, Ferdinand believes all the others are dead. Ferdinand and Miranda fall in love. Acting under Prospero's orders, Ariel terrorizes Antonio and the King of Naples. The King repents his past cruelty and reconciles with Prospero and restores him to his throne in place of the frightened Antonio. Leaving Caliban behind, all the other mortals prepare to leave the island.

Histories

The First Part of King Henry the Sixth (1590). A messenger from France reports the Dauphin crowned king as Henry V is buried. The defense of France is complicated by quarreling between Duke of Gloucester and the Bishop of Winchester, representing the Lancaster "Red Rose" and the York "White Rose." Joan of Arc takes and loses Orleans, regains Burgundy's force, but dies at the stake, betrayed by her own people. Richard Plantagenet presses his claim to the throne after Mortimer reveals that Richard's father, the Earl of Cambridge, is not a traitor. Richard is named Duke of York. Henry VI goes to France for his coronation and accepts a truce. He promises to marry Armagnac's daughter, but is persuaded by Suffolk of Lancaster to marry Margaret of Anjou instead.

The Second Part of King Henry the Sixth (1591). The opponents of Humphrey, Duke of Gloucester, plot to oust him as a result of his criticism of territorial concessions to the French included in Henry's marriage settlement. Ambitious Margaret, Henry's queen, manages to arrange banishment of the Duchess of Gloucester. The Duke, who resigns office to follow his wife, is imprisoned and murdered. To appease Commons, the Duke of Suffolk, who is the Queen's favorite, is exiled and later killed. York, having urged rebel Jack Cade to agitate in London, leads troops against an Irish rebellion and threatens rebellion in England unless the Duke of Somerset is imprisoned. Forces of Lancaster later fight and lose to forces of York, with the Duke of York's deformed son killing the Duke of Somerset. The King and Queen flee, with York in pursuit.

The Third Part of King Henry the Sixth (1592). Henry decides to will the throne to the Duke of York instead of to his own son, much to the displeasure of Queen Margaret. A battle between York's and Margaret's forces ends in York's death. Warwick deserts Henry and joins Edward and Richard, sons of the Duke of York.

They defeat the Queen and put Edward on the throne. Henry, deposed, is imprisoned in the Tower of London, and King Edward marries Lady Elizabeth Grey instead of the French Lady Bona. Warwick and the French join Margaret in restoring Henry to the throne. Henry soon is in the Tower again, but Margaret's forces are defeated by Edward at Tewkesbury. King Edward's brother Richard, Duke of Gloucester, kills Henry in the Tower. Edward and Elizabeth reign while Richard, his eye on the throne, falsely pledges his loyalty.

The Tragedy of King Richard the Third (1593). The deformed Richard, Duke of Gloucester, plots to secure the throne. By manipulating his brother, sickly King Edward IV, Richard causes the death of another brother, the Duke of Clarence. Edward dies, and Richard sends Edward's two sons to the Tower, presumably to await coronation, while Richard arranges to be crowned King of England. King Richard then murders the two young princes and plans to kill his wife in order to marry his niece Elizabeth, who is sought after by the Lancastrian Earl of Richmond. Richmond's forces march on London. Richard is slain, and Richmond accepts the crown. He plans to marry Elizabeth and join forever the houses of Lancaster and York.

The Life and Death of King John (1594). The French and English fight over the claim of young Arthur to the British throne. The battle ends in a stand-off, with peace made by marriage of the French Dauphin Philip to King John's niece. Fighting begins again when Rome orders France to support its spurned appointee to Canterbury. John yields and Rome forgives, but Philip marches on, claiming the British throne for himself. Arthur is captured and accidentally killed. The English nobles accuse John of murder and join the French armies. Learning they are only pawns in the struggle, they return as John dies of poison, the Dauphin retreats, and Prince Henry prepares to ascend the throne.

The Tragedy of King Richard the Second (1595). The Duke of York warns Richard of the dangers of his policy of confiscation of the lands of the

dying John of Gaunt, and Richard departs for Ireland. Gaunt's son and heir Henry Bolingbroke, exiled as a result of a quarrel with the Duke of Norfolk, seeks revenge by invading England. When Richard returns from Ireland, Bolingbroke seizes him, forces Richard's abdication, and imprisons Richard in Pomfret Castle. Loyal York foils Aumerle's plot against Henry IV. Sir Pierce, hoping to please his King, murders Richard and is banished by Henry, who pledges a Holy Land pilgrimage to gain forgiveness.

The First Part of King Henry the Fourth (1597). Henry Percy, called Hotspur, refuses the King's demand for prisoners taken in recent wars. The ensuing battle against Henry's forces aligns Percy, Douglas, and Prince Hal against Henry. Prince Hal and his friend Falstaff have been carousing together and accosting travelers on the King's highway. Hal kills Hotspur in the battle of Shrewsbury, but Falstaff, who has come upon the body, pretends to have killed him.

The Second Part of King Henry the Fourth (1598). Mowbray, Hastings, and the Archbishop of York war against Henry. Pressed with debts and charged with recruiting soldiers, Falstaff examines the men Justices Shallow and Silence present. He picks the ones who fail to bribe him. On the battlefield, Prince John deceives the rebel leaders into dismissing their troops and surrendering. Contrary to his promise, John orders them executed. Prince Hal visits the dying king, dreads the anxiety a crown entails, and promises his father he will mend his ways. During the coronation, Falstaff's familiar greetings incense Henry V, who orders his old friend banished.

The Life of King Henry the Fifth (1599). England's claim by hereditary right from Edward III to certain French dukedoms evokes an insulting reply from the Dauphin. Henry vows to invade France. A French assassination plot is uncovered, and Hal has the traitorous lords pass their own sentences of execution. Falstaff dies in London, and his comrades join the battles in France, during which Nym and

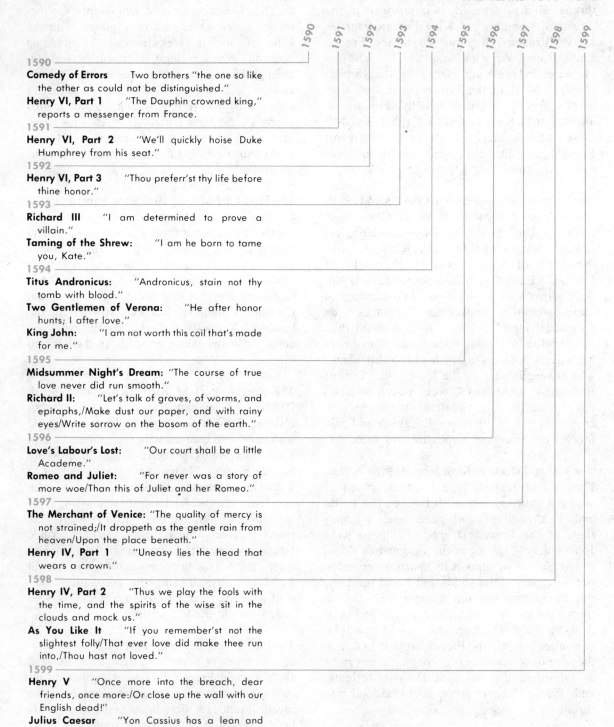

1590 ─────────────

Comedy of Errors   Two brothers "the one so like the other as could not be distinguished."

Henry VI, Part 1   "The Dauphin crowned king," reports a messenger from France.

1591 ─────────────

Henry VI, Part 2   "We'll quickly hoise Duke Humphrey from his seat."

1592 ─────────────

Henry VI, Part 3   "Thou preferr'st thy life before thine honor."

1593 ─────────────

Richard III   "I am determined to prove a villain."

Taming of the Shrew: "I am he born to tame you, Kate."

1594 ─────────────

Titus Andronicus: "Andronicus, stain not thy tomb with blood."

Two Gentlemen of Verona: "He after honor hunts; I after love."

King John: "I am not worth this coil that's made for me."

1595 ─────────────

Midsummer Night's Dream: "The course of true love never did run smooth."

Richard II: "Let's talk of graves, of worms, and epitaphs,/Make dust our paper, and with rainy eyes/Write sorrow on the bosom of the earth."

1596 ─────────────

Love's Labour's Lost: "Our court shall be a little Academe."

Romeo and Juliet: "For never was a story of more woe/Than this of Juliet and her Romeo."

1597 ─────────────

The Merchant of Venice: "The quality of mercy is not strained;/It droppeth as the gentle rain from heaven/Upon the place beneath."

Henry IV, Part 1   "Uneasy lies the head that wears a crown."

1598 ─────────────

Henry IV, Part 2   "Thus we play the fools with the time, and the spirits of the wise sit in the clouds and mock us."

As You Like It   "If you remember'st not the slightest folly/That ever love did make thee run into,/Thou hast not loved."

1599 ─────────────

Henry V   "Once more into the breach, dear friends, once more:/Or close up the wall with our English dead!"

Julius Caesar   "Yon Cassius has a lean and hungry look;/He thinks too much: such men are dangerous."

Much Ado about Nothing   "In mine eye she is the sweetest lady that ever I look'd on."

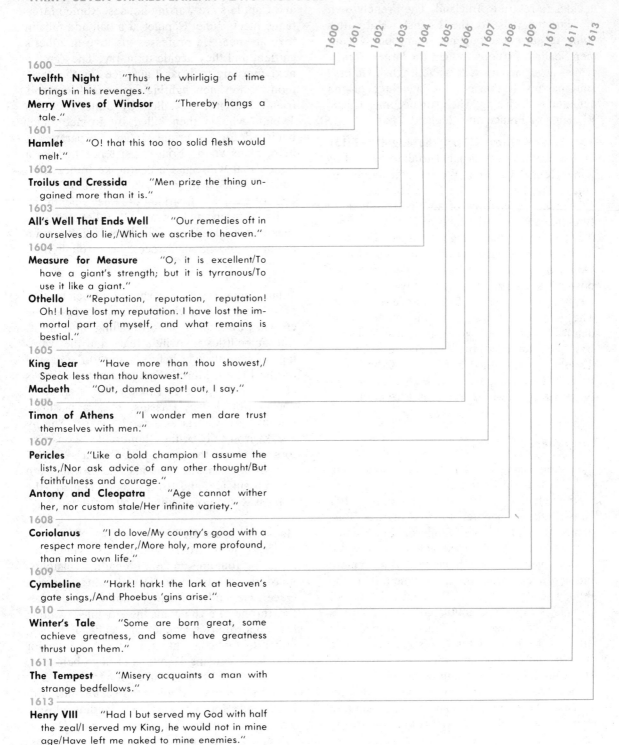

1600

Twelfth Night   "Thus the whirligig of time brings in his revenges."

Merry Wives of Windsor   "Thereby hangs a tale."

1601

Hamlet   "O! that this too too solid flesh would melt."

1602

Troilus and Cressida   "Men prize the thing un-gained more than it is."

1603

All's Well That Ends Well   "Our remedies oft in ourselves do lie,/Which we ascribe to heaven."

1604

Measure for Measure   "O, it is excellent/To have a giant's strength; but it is tyrranous/To use it like a giant."

Othello   "Reputation, reputation, reputation! Oh! I have lost my reputation. I have lost the im-mortal part of myself, and what remains is bestial."

1605

King Lear   "Have more than thou showest,/Speak less than thou knowest."

Macbeth   "Out, damned spot! out, I say."

1606

Timon of Athens   "I wonder men dare trust themselves with men."

1607

Pericles   "Like a bold champion I assume the lists,/Nor ask advice of any other thought/But faithfulness and courage."

Antony and Cleopatra   "Age cannot wither her, nor custom stale/Her infinite variety."

1608

Coriolanus   "I do love/My country's good with a respect more tender,/More holy, more profound, than mine own life."

1609

Cymbeline   "Hark! hark! the lark at heaven's gate sings,/And Phoebus 'gins arise."

1610

Winter's Tale   "Some are born great, some achieve greatness, and some have greatness thrust upon them."

1611

The Tempest   "Misery acquaints a man with strange bedfellows."

1613

Henry VIII   "Had I but served my God with half the zeal/I served my King, he would not in mine age/Have left me naked to mine enemies."

LANGUAGE AND LITERATURE

265

Bardolph are hanged and a frightened Pistol decides to return to England. The French town of Harfleur falls to the English. Hal, after going disguised among his weary but valiant men, leads his troops to fight the larger French armies at Agincourt, a decisive English victory. Hal marries Katherine, the daughter of the defeated French king. Their son becomes Henry VI, King of France and England.

The Life of King Henry the Eighth (1613). Queen Katherine is brought to divorce trial by King Henry. Cardinal Wolsey, the conniving churchman fresh from his false accusation and subsequent execution of the noble Duke of Buckingham, tries the faithful Katherine, once the widow of the King's brother, but then opposes the King's marriage to Anne Bullen (Anne Boleyn), who is a Protestant. Wolsey's power wanes as the King discovers his great wealth, and he dies under sentence of treason. The King's marriage to Anne precedes the death of Katherine, whose marriage to Henry has been annulled by Archbishop Cranmer. Though accused as a heretic, Cranmer is defended by King Henry and then made godfather of the newborn Princess Elizabeth.

Tragedies

Titus Andronicus (1594).   The Roman General Titus sacrifices the eldest son of Tamora, captive Queen of the defeated Goths. After Titus's eldest daughter Lavinia marries Bassianus instead of the Emperor Saturninus, Tamora becomes Empress and is empowered to gain revenge. Through the designs of Tamora and her lover Aaron, the Moor who fathers the child she later bears, Bassianus is killed. Lavinia is raped and mutilated, two of Titus's sons are executed, and Titus is duped into cutting off a hand. Titus feigns madness while his last son Lucius, in exile, raises an army. The army advances, prompting Saturninus and Tamora to seek a parley at Titus's house. Titus kills Tamora's sons and serves them as a dish for the royal couple. Titus kills Lavinia to end her shame and stabs Tamora. Saturninus kills Titus, but is killed by Lucius, who then becomes Emperor and executes Aaron.

Romeo and Juliet (1596).   The Montagues and Capulets are warring houses. Romeo Montague meets Juliet Capulet at a ball and falls in love at once. He professes his love in Juliet's garden, and they decide to marry. They go the next morning to Friar Laurence for the ceremony. Soon, new fighting occurs and Romeo's friend Mercutio is killed by Juliet's cousin Tybalt, who is then killed by Romeo, later banished for his crime. Juliet, desperate for help, plans at the Friar's insistence to take a potion that will cause a death-like trance from which Romeo will rescue her. Romeo fails to hear of the plan. Learning of Juliet's death, he visits the tomb and kills himself. Juliet awakens, sees Romeo dead, and kills herself. Filled with remorse, the families reconcile through their common grief.

Julius Caesar (1599).   During the celebration of Julius Caesar's victory, Caesar refuses the crown three times before falling into a fit. Caesar belittles his wife's fears and the warnings of a soothsayer before going to the capital on the Ides of March. Brutus, convinced he is acting for the good of Rome, joins a group of conspirators led by Cassius. They assassinate Caesar. At Caesar's funeral, Mark Antony speaks ironically of the "honorable" conspirators and teases the crowd with Caesar's "will." A civil war ensues. Cassius and Brutus both commit suicide, and Brutus is proclaimed "the noblest Roman of them all" by Antony.

Hamlet Prince of Denmark (1601).   Hamlet's father's ghost orders Hamlet to avenge his father's "foul and unnatural death." Claudius, murderer of the dead Danish king, marries Queen Gertrude, Hamlet's mother, and takes the throne. Feigning madness while awaiting his opportunity, Hamlet misleads Polonius, father of Ophelia, into thinking that love for Ophelia is causing Hamlet's strange behavior. Hamlet enlists the aid of an itinerant band of actors to recreate a poisoning scene and, with his friend Horatio, watches Claudius closely during the performance. Gertrude calls Hamlet to her chamber, where he rashly stabs eavesdropping Polonius. Subsequently, Hamlet causes Ophelia, mad from grief, to drown herself. Claudius attempts to remove Hamlet to England, but fails. He plots with Polonius's son Laertes to fence with Hamlet and wound him with a poisoned foil. Hamlet is mortally wounded, Laertes and Claudius are killed, and Gertrude dies after drinking a cup of poison intended for Hamlet.

The History of Troilus and Cressida (1602). Young Cressida pretends indifference to her uncle Pandarus's proposal to match her with Troilus, youngest son of King Priam of Troy. Outside the city walls, Greek Ulysses complains to his generals of a lack of unified effort to regain Greek Helena from her abductor Paris. When the Trojan champion Hector challenges to single combat the best Greek, Ulysses tries to arouse Achilles to arms by choosing Ajax. The plan fails. Hector, surprised by the choice of Ajax, calls a truce. Deeply in love, Cressida promises eternal fidelity to Troilus before being sent to the Greek camp, where she joins her father and takes Diomedes as her lover. In a final battle, Achilles' best friend is killed by Hector who, while unarmed, is killed by Achilles, his body being dragged away by Achilles' horse. Troilus leaves the stage cursing Pandarus, who then delivers an epilogue.

Othello the Moor of Venice (1604). Desdemona, bride of Othello, is entrusted to the care of Iago while Othello rushes to defend Cyprus from a Turkish invasion, which soon is ended by a storm. Iago, insulted by Othello's preference for Cassio as top lieutenant, plots revenge and enlists the aid of Roderigo in disgracing Cassio and making Othello jealous. Roderigo's brawl with Cassio gains the first objective, and Desdemona's handkerchief, obtained by unsuspecting Emilia and placed by her husband Iago in Cassio's possession, gains the second. Obsessed by jealousy, Othello kills his wife, takes his own life, and leaves Iago, murderer of Emilia, to be punished for his treachery.

King Lear (1605). Lear's loving daughter Cordelia refuses to follow her sisters Goneril and Regan in flattery of their father. The Earl of Kent is banished for defending Cordelia, and the King of France accepts disinherited Cor-

Globe Theatre, Southwark, London, was built 1599, burned 1613 during a performance of *Henry VIII*, and was rebuilt in 1614. Shakespeare acted at the Globe and saw his plays produced there.

delia as his wife, as Lear leaves his kingdom divided between his two other daughters. Suddenly stripped of his remaining rights, Lear goes mad from knowledge of his error and wanders out in a storm accompanied by his fool. He rails against the ingratitude of children. Aided by Goneril and Regan, Edmund causes his father, the Earl of Gloucester, to be blinded for aiding Lear. Kent sends Lear to Cordelia's care in Dover, while Gloucester's true son Edgar tends his father. Victorious over the invading French, Edmund executes Cordelia and causes Lear to die of grief. With Gloucester dead, Regan killed by Goneril who commits suicide, and Edmund executed, England is rebuilt by Edgar and Kent.

Macbeth (1605). The victorious generals Banquo and Macbeth are met by witches, who prophesy that Macbeth is to be thane of Cawdor and king. Macbeth travels to Duncan and finds that the first prophecy has come true. Lady Macbeth presses her husband to make the second prophecy true by killing Duncan during his visit, but Macbeth is reluctant. After he does murder Duncan, Banquo, and Macduff's child and wife, Macbeth rules tyrannically while Lady Macbeth goes mad from the sins of too much blood. Another visit to the witches assures Macbeth that "none of woman born" shall harm him. He returns home satisfied that he is safe. After Lady Macbeth's suicide, Macbeth resolutely faces Macduff, who was delivered by Caesarian section. Macbeth is killed, and Duncan's son Malcolm succeeds Macbeth as King of Scotland.

The Life of Timon of Athens (1606). Flattering opportunists surround wealthy, gullible Timon of Athens and divide his dwindling fortune. Bankrupt Timon confidently but futilely requests loans from the men he considers his friends, and he subsequently invites them to one last feast, at which he serves nothing but water. Cursing all men, particularly Athenians, Timon retreats to a cave where he accidentally finds gold, which he gives to thieves to further their profession and to a dissident general to destroy Athens. The attack frightens the Athenian senators who, seeking Timon's military leadership, are told to hang themselves. The general is appeased as Timon dies. His tomb is found by the seashore, with an epitaph expressing his hatred of mankind.

Pericles Prince of Tyre (1607). Pericles has guessed the infamy of Antiochus, Emperor of Greece. As a consequence, his life is threatened, and he leaves his government in the hands of Helicanus and sails from Tyre. After a shipwreck on the coast of Pentapolis, Pericles, the lone survivor, contends successfully for the hand of Thaisa, daughter of King Simonides. Helicanus, the minister left in charge of Tyre, informs Pericles that Antiochus has died and the people of Tyre want him to return as king. Pericles and Thaisa set out for Tyre by sea. Thaisa gives birth to a daughter, but Thaisa in a deep faint appears dead and is buried in a chest at sea. The chest comes ashore at Ephesus, where Thaisa is restored to life. Thinking Pericles dead, she becomes a priestess in the Temple of Diana. Pericles takes his daughter Marina to Tarsus and leaves her with the governor and his wife. When Marina grows up, the governor's wife, Dionyza, grows jealous of

the girl's accomplishments and plots to kill her. Marina is carried off by pirates and sold into a brothel. Her purity and piety win the attention of Lysimachus, governor of Mitylene, who secures her release. Pericles, in mourning for his daughter, finds her in Mitylene. Directed in a dream to go to the Temple of Diana, he finds Thaisa. Marina marries Lysimachus, and Dionyza and her husband are burned to punish them for their planned crime.

Antony and Cleopatra (1607). Antony, torn between reason and passion for Cleopatra, realizes he is losing respect and position in Rome. He reconciles with his fellow rulers, Lepidus and Octavius, and marries Octavius's sister. Cleopatra, enraged, knows Antony will return to her one day because Octavius's sister is unattractive. The situation degenerates until Antony and Octavius do battle at Actium. Antony loses that battle and another in Egypt and returns to Rome. Cleopatra attempts to woo him back by sending word that she is dead. Griefstricken Antony kills himself. Cleopatra also commits suicide.

Coriolanus (1608). The jealous Roman tribunes Sicinius and Junius Brutus complain of the pride of Marcius, commander of the troops of the city fighting against Corioli and its warrior Aufidius. Corioli is taken, Aufidius is routed, and Marcius is hailed "Coriolanus" for his bravery. Coriolanus is elected Roman Consul, but Sicinius and Junius Brutus arouse the plebeians to protest the election. They hope that Coriolanus's contempt for the rabble will result in his banishment. Joining with Aufidius, Coriolanus subdues Rome and returns to Corioli, where Aufidius accuses Coriolanus of treason and plots his assassination. The Roman is killed. Repentant Aufidius mourns the death of the noble soldier and helps bear away the body.

A Dictionary of English Usage

A

a, an. *A* and *an* are forms of the indefinite article used to refer to one person, place, abstraction, or other "thing" within a class named by a following noun—they do not indicate *which* one. Since the forms carry the notion of "one," they are used only before singular nouns.

The form *an* is used before any word beginning with a vowel sound, and sometimes before a word beginning with an *h* sound, if the first syllable of that word is not stressed. The form *a* (usually pronounced ə—see the dictionary pronunciation key) is used before words beginning with a consonant sound, with the possible exception already noted. Some words spelled with an initial vowel letter, of course, are pronounced with a beginning consonant sound. Examples: *a universe, a history, a historian; an early riser, an honor.*

It is considered to be more formal and more literary to say *this kind of book* or *that sort of egg* rather than *this kind of a book* or *that sort of an egg.* The indefinite article after *kind of* and *sort of* is not uncommon in colloquial use.

abbreviations. Courtesy dictates that abbreviations should not be used unless they are explained or are likely to be understood without explanation. Technical writing and discussion make use of numerous abbreviations established within the specialty; many abbreviations (such as *Mr., A.M.,* and *P.M.*) are so common that avoiding them would be thought eccentric. Excessive use of abbreviations, however, is generally unpleasant, especially when they are slangy. Except for items such as have already been referred to, abbreviations are regarded as more informal than full forms. Such terms as *prof, exam, math* (produced by "clipping" words) are characteristic of student jargon generally appropriate only in very informal use among students themselves.

about, almost. *About* in the sense of "almost" is informal usage in such phrases as *about done, about through, about dead.*

absolute(ly), positive(ly). Indiscriminate use of these words as intensives is common. Careful speakers and writers, being aware of the traditional meanings of the terms, usually confine them to expressions in which they may be taken literally, such as *I am absolutely certain; I heard his positive denial.*

accept, except. These words in speech are usually distinguished by the pronunciation of their first syllables; in correct writing, they are always distinguished by spelling. *Accept* means to take willingly what is offered, to agree to (a proposal), or to believe (an explanation or a doctrine). *Except* is either a verb or a preposition. As a verb, it means to exclude (*I except him from my generalization*), to omit, or to object (a lawyer may *except to a witness*). As a preposition, *except* means "leaving out" (*John is kind to everybody except himself*).

accidentally, incidentally. Note that the

present spelling of these words adds -ly to the adjective forms *accidental* and *incidental*.

across. The pronunciation *acrost* (with a final *t* sound) is not Standard English. The expression *over across* is sometimes heard in colloquial use; it is avoided in formal speech and writing.

adapt, adopt. *Adapt* means to change something to make it suitable for a new use. One may adapt oneself to different circumstances. A novel may be adapted for the stage. *Adopt* means to decide upon (a plan), to choose to treat someone as a close relative, or to vote to accept a motion or resolution.

advice, advise. An adviser gives advice. *Advice* is a noun; *advise* is a verb.

affect, effect. Though these words are often pronounced alike, they *can* be differentiated in speech. They *must* be distinguished in spelling. *Affect* is usually a verb meaning to like, to pretend, or to influence or change something in some way. Less commonly, it is a noun meaning "a feeling or emotion."

Effect is a verb meaning to accomplish (something), or it is a noun meaning "result" or "what is accomplished." Examples: *The principal effected changes in the school, but I didn't like the effects.*

aggravate. The original meaning of *aggravate* was "to add weight to." Colloquially, it is often used to mean "irritate," as in "His way of speaking aggravated me." In formal speech or writing, *aggravate* is used only to mean "to make worse," as in "The difficulty was aggravated by misunderstanding."

ain't. *Ain't* was originally a contraction of *am not* (compare *can't*, which in some regions is pronounced *cain't*). Well over a hundred years ago, it came to be widely used also as a contraction for *are not* and even for *is not* and *have* or *has not*. Perhaps because of the indiscriminate use, *ain't* fell into disfavor among many careful speakers. It is not used now in published writing, except in representation of speech. The expression is pretty generally regarded by educated people (even by some who use it) as nonstandard, uncultivated speech.

all ready, already. *All ready* means "completely ready" (*I was all ready for the picnic*) or it means that all of what has been referred to is ready (*The boys were all ready to shout*). *Already* is an abverbial expression meaning "by or before a particular time": *The sun was already up when I awoke.* Though often pronounced alike, these expressions should not be confused in writing.

all right. Although there would be logical justification for a spelling form *alright,* it is not firmly established among our conventions of writing. It sometimes appears in advertising and in very informal writing, but never in the sense "completely right" or "everyone right."

all the farther, as far as. In the sense of "as far as," *all the farther* (*That's all the farther he can walk*) is a regional expression, though in regions where it is current, it may be used by educated people. It is *not* characteristic of literary English.

all together, altogether. This is another pair of expressions often pronounced alike but kept distinct in spelling. *Altogether* means "entirely," as in "Harry was altogether too late." The two separate words can have other words put between them: *The family were all together,* or *All the family were together.*

allude, elude. To allude to something is to refer to it; usually, the verb carries the idea of indirectness in referring: *The poet subtly alluded to King Arthur.* Note that the verb *allude* is regularly followed by the particle *to.*

To elude something or somebody is to evade or escape: *The suspect eluded the police.*

allusion, illusion, delusion. An allusion is a reference, either direct or implied: *The poet made an allusion to King Arthur.* An illusion is a mistaken notion, either serious or harmless: *What you thought you saw the magician do was an illusion.* A delusion (from the verb *delude*) is a serious deception: *Hitler's fatal delusion was that he was infallible.*

almost, most. In speech, *almost* is often shortened to *most,* and the shortened form is sometimes written with an initial apostrophe: *They had done 'most everything necessary.* But *almost* is still the standard form of written English.

already. *See* ALL READY.

alright. *See* ALL RIGHT.

although, though. As subordinating conjunctions, these two words are equivalent. *Although* is generally felt to be a little more formal than *though*. *Altho* and *tho* as simplified spellings have some uses, but they are seldom allowed in formal writing.

The colloquial use of *though* in place of the sentence-connector *however* (*I thought, though, that he would never get here*) is not generally considered suitable for writing.

altogether. *See* ALL TOGETHER.

among, between. *Among* is used when referring to more than two persons or things: *The prize money was distributed among three winners*. *Between* is historically related to the word *twain*, which in turn comes from *two*. Some people prefer to confine use of *between* to references to only two persons or things, but many excellent speakers and writers do not follow this practice.

amongst. This is a legitimate variant of *among*, but it is not in common use in the United States.

amount, number. Measurement of what is named by a mass noun or abstract noun is reported as an amount; number refers to the counting of units: *a certain amount of courage, a large amount of money, a large number of pennies*.

an. *See* A.

and. Like other coordinating and correlative conjunctions, *and* is sometimes used by good writers and speakers as the first word in a sentence felt to be coordinate with the sentence immediately preceding it.

Such an expression as "Come and visit us" is generally considered more informal than "Come to visit us."

and/or. Useful as this expression might be, most cultivated speakers and writers feel it should be confined to legal or commercial writing. It is accurate but awkward.

and so. The connective idea carried by this pair of words can usually be carried by either one of them alone. Frequent use of *and so* (as in *It rained, and so we came home*) is generally avoided by adults.

anticlimactic. Note the spelling of this adjective, which means "characterized by arrangement that does not culminate in a climax." It has nothing to do with *climate*.

anyway. In Standard English, this adverb never takes a final *-s*. *Anyways* is heard only in dialects that have not generally been turned to literary use.

anywhere, everywhere, nowhere, somewhere. None of these words takes a final *-s* in Standard English. These words are widely felt to be more appropriate in writing than are the related colloquial terms, *anyplace, everyplace, noplace, someplace*.

appraise, apprise. *Appraise* means to judge or estimate the value of something. *Apprise* means notify or inform about: *We apprised him of his duty to appraise the property*.

apt, liable, likely. These words are sometimes treated colloquially as equivalents, the first two being given the sense of "likely." The basic meaning of *apt* is "fitted" or "naturally suited" for something or to do something. The basic meaning of *liable* is "legally bound" or "responsible" for something. Meanings from these basic ones have brought the uses of *apt* and *liable* nearer to that of *likely*, but many writers carefully avoid interchanging the three words.

aren't I? Some people have the curious notion that this is an elegant expression to be used in avoiding *ain't I?* Many other people find *aren't I?* particularly distasteful. The alternative to both, of course, is *am I not?*

around, 'round. *Around* in the senses of "about" or "nearby" is colloquial: *Let's start around ten o'clock. The book is around here someplace*. The preposition or adverb *around* is often shortened in speech by suppression of the first syllable. When such shortening is represented in writing, an apostrophe should be used to indicate the omitted syllable: *'round*, as in *the other way 'round*.

as. The use of *as* in the sense of "because" or "since" is often ambiguous: *We were bored, because we knew what he would say* is better than *We were bored, as we knew what he would say*.

assay, essay. As verbs, these words mean, respectively, to test or evaluate and to attempt. As nouns, *assay* means "the result of testing or evaluation," and *essay* means "the result of an attempt." A specialized meaning of *essay* is "a piece of writing resulting from a person's attempting to express his observations and ideas on a particular subject."

astronomy, astrology. The distinction between these two words involves the distinction between a science of celestial bodies (astronomy) and a pseudoscience that purports to deal with the influence of the stars (astrology). Long ago, astrology was widely regarded as a science.

at. The use of *at* in such expressions as *Where are we at?* is colloquial in some regions. It is not characteristic of literary English.

athlete, athletics. In cultivated circles, a pronunciation of these words that puts a vowel sound after *ath-* calls attention to itself and is usually disapproved.

awful(ly). These expressions (adjective and adverb) have lost their original force through overuse in speech and informal writing. If you intend to identify something as producing awe, you will usually need to select different terms. *See* COUNTER WORDS.

awhile, a while. *Awhile* is an adverb. After a preposition, *a while* should be used: *Help me for a while.* Similarly, we use the noun and article in *The lesson will take a while.* The original meaning of *while* is "time."

B

back. Since the prefix in words like *return* or *replace* means "again" or "back," it seems like unnecessary repetition to say such things as *returned back,* but you may say *returned again* to indicate a second return.

backward(s), forward(s), inward(s), outward(s), onward(s), toward(s). As adverbs, these words may or may not have a final *s,* though the forms without *s* are more common in this country. As adjectives, they never have a final *s. The backward boy walked forward,* or *. . . forwards.*

bad, badly. *Bad* is the adjective, *badly* the adverb. There is no rational justification for saying *The flower smells sweetly* or *I feel badly* (when the meaning is that you feel either sick or sorry). The first of these examples would be taken by most cultivated people as a sign of grammatical ignorance, but expressions like the second are quite often used by people who ought to know better. The adverb form is required only to qualify the nonlinking senses of verbs of feeling, taste, and smell.

barely. *See* DOUBLE NEGATIVE.

because. *See* DUE TO and REASON IS BECAUSE.

began, begun. These are, respectively, the standard past tense and past participial forms of the verb *begin*. Right now, *I begin;* yesterday *I began; I have begun. Begin* or *begun* as simple past tense forms are localisms.

beside(s). As a preposition in the sense of "at the side of" or "next to," we normally use *beside* (without the final *s): I walked beside him.* As an adverb or a preposition carrying other senses, the forms with or without the final *s* are interchangeable.

better, best. *See* HAD BETTER, BEST.

between. *Between* as a preposition takes objective forms of personal pronouns as objects to follow it, no matter what words intervene. Correct: *between him and me, between the repulsive old man and me. See* AMONG.

biannual, biennial, bimonthly, biweekly. The only one of these words that is always understood is *biennial,* which means "every two years." The prefix *bi-* has reference, of course, to *two.* Do *biannual, bimonthly,* and *biweekly* mean "once every two years, months, or weeks" or "twice every year, month, or week?" Since they have been used in both senses, concern for clarity suggests avoiding them in use unless the context explains the intended meaning.

borrow, lend. One borrows *from* someone and lends *to* someone: *John borrowed from Jane the book he had asked me to lend him.*

boughten. The Standard English form of the past participle of *buy* is *bought.*

bunch. *Bunch* is applied to things like radishes; when applied to things for which we have other established group names, *bunch* is usually confined to informal speech. We say *group of girls, flock of sheep,* etc.

burst, bust. The verb *bust* originated as a dialect form of *burst. Bust* (with its past tense and past participial form *busted*) was long felt to be slang, and it still is in the sense of "hit hard" (*Ed busted Jed on the nose*). The past participle is colloquial when it is made to mean "moneyless."

but. For use of *but* as the first word in a sentence, *see* AND.

C

calculate, reckon. In general Standard English, both these words mean "to compute" or "to arrive at a conclusion after careful consideration." In regional dialects they came to be indiscriminately used for such verbs as *think, suppose, expect*. They are not so used in literary English.

Calvary, cavalry. *Calvary* is a proper noun—the name of the place where Christ was crucified. *Cavalry* refers to soldiers on horseback. Note the difference in pronunciation.

came. The past tense form of *come* in Standard English is *came: He came yesterday*.

can, may. In formal writing, a distinction is usually made between *can* and *may*. *Can* is not allowed to refer to permission to do something, or to the mere possibility of an act or occurrence. The special use of *may* to refer to permission (*May I have a cookie?*) is a convenient one, and is widely admired. But since the power to act is often dependent on permission to act, *can* is often used informally to express both ability and permission to act (*Can I take the car tonight, Father?*).

cannot (can't) hardly, barely. *See* DOUBLE NEGATIVE.

can't. *See* CONTRACTIONS.

capital, capitol. The form spelled with *-ol* refers only to the temple of Jupiter in Rome or to a building set apart as the seat of government. For all other uses, the spelling requires *-al*.

case. *See* CIRCUMLOCUTION.

catalog, catalogue. Both spellings are established. Perhaps it is a good rule to prefer the simplest spelling of a word that is allowable.

censor, censure, censer. A *censor* is a person who undertakes to control public morals (nowadays, usually by prohibiting certain kinds of expression in literature and visual art). *Censure* is "blame" or "condemnation." *To censure* someone is to blame or condemn him. A *censer* is a vessel in which incense is burned; it is used in certain religious rituals.

circumlocution. Being concise is usually a virtue in speaking and writing. The opposite of conciseness is circumlocution, talking around a subject before getting to the point. Some words seem to invite circumlocution; one such is *case*. "In case I can't come . . ." is less direct than "If I can't come. . . ." "In all except a few cases, our winters are mild" could well be replaced by the more concise "Our winters are almost always mild."

cite, site, sight. *Cite* is a verb, meaning to mention specifically as an example, illustration, or authority (*He cited the Constitution to support his argument*). *Site* is a noun meaning "a location" (*We live on the site of an ancient Indian village*). *Sight* may be a noun meaning "a view," "the capacity for seeing," or "an aiming device on a gun"; it may also be a verb with such meanings as "to observe" or "to take aim."

climactic, climatic. These are both adjectives, but the first is related to *climax*, the second to *climate*. *See* ANTICLIMACTIC.

comprehensible, comprehensive. *Comprehensible* means "capable of being understood" (*The explanation was comprehensible*). *Comprehensive* means "complete" (*The explanation was comprehensive*).

connote, denote. To denote means to express a specific, literal meaning. To connote is to suggest meanings that are incidental, dependent on associations, touching the emotions. Words that denote the same thing may connote quite different meanings. To use a standard example, your house is your home, but *home* suggests a set of associations that *house* does not. It is also true that a word which has a single denotation may have quite varied connotations. We can suppose that *snow* has different connotations for people in Newfoundland from those it has for people in Florida.

consensus. Note the spelling of this word; it is not related to *census*. A consensus is a general agreement: *Though a few members still disapproved, the convention reached a consensus in favor of the proposed action.*

continual(ly), continuous(ly). A traditional distinction between these words applies *continual* and *continually* to a succession of repeated events (such as continual showers), while it applies *continuous* and *continuously* to what is unbroken or uninterrupted (as in *continuous traffic*).

contractions. Contractions of verbal auxiliaries and of the negator *not* are thoroughly established in English. Examples: *can't, I'm, he's, we've, she'd.* They tend to be avoided in formal writing, but even there forms such as *can't, won't,* and *couldn't* are often appropriate. *Could've, would've, should've,* though common in speech, normally appear only in informal writing.

could of, would of, should of. These spellings are usually taken to be signs of ignorance or carelessness. Correct forms: could have, would have, should have.

council, counsel. The first is a noun meaning "a deliberative assembly" (*The Boy Scouts held a Council*); the second is either a noun meaning "advice" or a verb meaning "to advise." Neither word should be confused with *consul,* an official who represents his government in a foreign country.

counter words. Words that have been so long used indiscriminately to express approval or disapproval that they now carry only general, not specific, meanings are called *counter words.* The label calls attention to the ease with which we pick up words like *awful, cute, lovely, lousy, marvelous, nice, terrible, terrific,* and use them without bothering to preserve distinctions they were once capable of making. Such words have lost their denotations, and even their connotations may be vague. Though useful in informal speech, counter words are avoided in careful expression.

cute. *See* COUNTER WORDS.

credible, credulous, creditable. A statement is *credible* if it is believable. A person is *credulous* if he tends to believe what he is told, even though it is nonsense. We say something is *creditable* when it is worthy of being praised— that is, of being given credit.

criterion, criteria. *Criterion* (meaning "a standard or test for judging something") is a Greek word whose Greek plural is *criteria.* We may also give it the English plural *criterions.* To use *criteria* as if it were a singular noun is to display ignorance.

curriculum, curricula. The Latin plural of the noun *curriculum* is *curricula. Curriculums* is a respectable English plural of the same word.

dairy, diary. A dairy has to do with milk or the cows that produce it. A diary is a daily record of some kind.

dangling modifier. A modifier is said to be "dangling" when no word that it can properly modify is supplied. Such dangling modifiers usually appear at the beginnings of sentences. The prepositional phrase dangles in *At the age of three, John's father died.* Of course, we know that a father did not die at the age of three, but for a moment we are aware that the syntax of the sentence suggests just that—and so we smile. Dangling modifiers that are likely to elicit such a reaction ought to be avoided.

Most frequently, dangling modifiers are participial or gerund phrases that open sentences. Example: *Coming into the room, my eyes fell upon the dresser.* That sentence is also momentarily humorous, but not all dangling modifiers invite misinterpretation. If we say, "On looking further into the subject, the problems seem more and more complex," nobody is likely to be misled. The rule should be to avoid dangling modifiers that call attention to themselves or that might really be misunderstood.

darling. *See* COUNTER WORDS.

datum, data. *Data* is the Latin plural of *datum.* It should take a plural verb as well as the modifier *these.* In common speech and in much informal writing, however, it is treated as a singular collective noun. *Datum* is rarely used in any kind of expression.

definite(ly). This adjective and adverb seem to be on their way to becoming counter words used simply to gain emphasis. *See* COUNTER WORDS.

delusion. *See* ALLUSION.

denote. *See* CONNOTE.

dialog, dialogue. Either spelling is correct; *dialogue* is probably more common.

diary. *See* DAIRY.

did, done. The past tense of *do* is *did: He did it yesterday. Done* is the past participle: *He has done it many times.*

different from, than, to. *Different than* is common in speech and informal writing: *The work today is different than it was yesterday.* In formal writing, many people carefully use *from* after *different*: *The work is different from what it was yesterday. Different to* is an established British usage.

disinterested, uninterested. Careful speakers and writers are likely to use *disinterested* only to mean "impartial" or "unbiased." *Uninterested* means "indifferent" or "without interest." The useful distinction is not always preserved, even by good writers.

dived, dove. Both these past tense forms of *dive* are current; the regular inflection (*dived*) has more prestige as the finite past, and it is the only standard form of the past participle: *He has dived.*

doesn't, don't. *Don't* is plural. Say *He doesn't; they don't.*

double possessive. *A friend of John's* illustrates, with its preposition *of* and its inflected possessive, what is called a double possessive. This is a usage that is thoroughly established.

double negative. Speakers of English use at least three types of double negatives. If one says "It is not unlikely that John will come," there is some likelihood that John will come. This type of double negative is in standard use; indeed, it has a kind of literary flavor.

If one says "I don't have no money," anyone who knows English will understand an emphatic statement about your finances. Two such negatives do *not* make a positive, no matter what happens in mathematical multiplication. But, though such double negatives were in standard use 600 years ago, they have long been banished from literary English.

A third type of double negative is that in which a negator is associated with such weakly negative adverbs as *hardly, barely,* or *scarcely,* as in *I can't hardly hear you.* Those also are banned from literary English, though they are more widely heard in speech than are those identified in the last paragraph. Avoid these double negatives to avoid possibility of criticism.

dreamed, dreamt. Both these forms are established as the past tense of *dream.*

drink, drank, drunk. These are the principal parts of the verb in general Standard English, although there is a great deal of regional varia-tion in speech. The adjective *drunken* is standard when it comes before the noun it modifies (as in *a drunken sailor*).

drowned. This is the correct form of the finite past tense and the past participle of the verb *drown.* Don't say or write *drownded.*

due to. Many people (even some who do not follow their own prescription) insist that *due to* should always be used in the sense of "attributable to," never in the sense of "because of" or "as a result of." The traditional rule would allow "His weariness was due to iron-poor blood," but not "He was tired, due to iron-poor blood." The tradition is weakening, but it is by no means obsolete.

E

each and every. This phrase has a special use in legal documents, and it once was an emphatic expression. It is now a cliché.

easy. There are some expressions in colloquial English in which *easy* is an adverb: *take it easy, easy come, easy go.* Elsewhere, the adverbial form is *easily: We can say that easily.*

economic, economical. Both these forms are adjectives, but one applies to general matters of finance and livelihood (*economic aid, economic planning*), the other to specific instances of thrift (*economical shopping*). The adverb related to both the adjectives is *economically.*

effect. *See* AFFECT.

egoism, egotism. *Egoism* is a term applied to self-centeredness or to the conviction that one's own personal interests ought always to be served. Though *egotism* is sometimes made to mean the same thing, it usually connotes boasting and much talk about oneself.

elegy, eulogy. An elegy is a formal composition (usually in words or music) mourning the death of someone or the passing away of things or conditions that have been admired. A eulogy is formal praise of somebody or something.

else's. *Anybody else's, everyone else's,* and similar "group genitives" are current in present-day English. *Anybody's else* is an expression once thought to be elegant; such constructions now seem stiff.

emigrant, immigrant. These words can be readily distinguished if one recognizes that the first is formed with the Latin prefix *ex-* meaning "from" or "out of" while the second carries the prefix *in-,* meaning "in" or "into." One *emigrates* from a country and *immigrates* into another. The same person, of course, does the *emigrating* and the *immigrating;* the difference is in the point of reference.

enthuse. Many people object to making a verb *enthuse* out of the adjective *enthusiastic.*

epic, epoch. An epic is a particular kind of long poem about a hero (or heroes); as an adjective, *epic* refers to a quality thought to be like one found in an epic. The noun, of course, is also loosely applied to what people want to represent as extraordinary, as in advertisements announcing "an epic" when a store is initiating a sale. An epoch, on the other hand, is an historical period of time—an important one having distinct and special characteristics.

especial(ly), special(ly). In some contexts, these words are interchangeable. In others, careful writers are likely to use *especially* when the meaning is "principally," "particularly," or "most importantly," but *specially* when the meaning is "uniquely." Examples: *The car was specially built as a racer. Jack was especially fond of fried chicken.*

etc. This abbreviation stands for the Latin *et cetera,* meaning "and others." It is a sign of ignorance to write "and etc." or to say "and et cetera." Use of the abbreviation is often justified, but its availability is a temptation to be vague or unspecific.

except. *See* ACCEPT.

expect. In literary English, *expect* means "to look forward to" or to assume something as proper or likely. As a synonym for *think, suppose,* or *guess,* the use of *expect* is colloquial only.

F

fact that. This expression is often used to no good purpose. *It is a fact that he overslept* may be more directly stated, *He overslept,* or *I know he overslept.* Due to the fact that . . . is characteristically weaker than *because. See* CIRCUMLOCUTION.

famous, infamous. Whereas *famous* means literally "widely known," it may suggest an admirable reason for the fame. *Infamous* means "widely known for something considered reprehensible." *Hitler is infamous.*

farther, further. Some people carefully confine *farther* to refer to physical distance, using *further* to refer to additional ideas, thoughts, and other immaterial things. The distinction, however, is not required in good usage. There is no *fartherer* in Standard English. *See also* ALL THE FARTHER.

faze. This verb, which means "to disturb" or "to disconcert," is more common in speech than in writing. It should not be confused with *phase,* which has a completely different meaning.

feel. *See* BAD, BADLY.

fewer, less. *Fewer* is applied to count nouns, *less* to mass nouns. *Fewer people were present, and they spent less time in discussion.*

fine. *See* COUNTER WORDS.

fix. This word in various contexts can mean so many things that objections to what seems its overuse have often been voiced. More formal synonyms are available to express most of its meanings. In the sense of "getting ready," as in "She's fixing to go shopping," the verb is regional. The noun meaning "a predicament," as in "He was in a fix," is colloquial only.

flammable, inflammable. Both these words mean "easy to set afire." The negative of *flammable* is *nonflammable.*

flaunt, flout. The long-established meaning of *flaunt* is "to display boldly what some people may disapprove." To *flout* someone or something is to treat him or it with contempt. The distinction between these two words is a clear and useful one.

fly, flee. Birds *fly;* criminals *flee.* But figuratively, fugitives are also said to *fly* from their pursuers. *Flew* and *flown,* the finite past and the past participle of *fly,* however, are seldom applied to fugitives. The verb *flee* has only one past tense form, *fled.*

folk, folks. Both these forms are plural. *Folk* usually refers to culturally associated common people in the aggregate, as in *mountain folk* or *folk song.*

formally, formerly. The first is the adverb built on *formal;* the second is the adverb built on *former*. They should not be confused in pronunciation or spelling.

former, latter. These terms apply properly to a pair of items. When there are more than two items in a series, we can use *first* and *last*.

formulae, formulas. These are, respectively, the Latin plural and the English plural of *formula*. The former is usually found in technical writing. *Formulas* is a thoroughly respectable form.

forward(s). *See* BACKWARD(s).

funny. Since this word can mean either "odd" or "humorous," it can raise a problem of interpretation. Besides, it is overworked in informal speech. *See* COUNTER WORD. In literary English it is seldom used in the sense of "peculiar."

further. *See* FARTHER.

G

get. *Get* (with its other forms, *got* and *gotten*) has acquired dozens of meanings. Often, a more specific verb is more forceful. Both *got* and *gotten* are used as the past participle.

go, went, gone. These are the principal parts of the verb *go*. In Standard English, *went* is never used as the past participle.

good, well. *Well* may be either an adjective (meaning "in good health") or an adverb describing how something is done (*She sang well*). In Standard English, *good* is usually an adjective. One says something sounds, smells, or tastes *good*. *I feel good* usually indicates that the person speaking is happy or in good spirits, while *I feel well* implies that he is not ill. *See* BAD, BADLY.

got, gotten. *Got* is usually preferred to *gotten* as the past participle. *See* GET.

grand. *See* COUNTER WORDS.

guess. As a synonym for *suppose* or *assume*, this verb is colloquial only. *See* EXPECT.

H

had better (best). These expressions have long been established in English and are appropriate in speech and writing. Example: *You had better come early.*

had of, had've. Neither of these expressions is used in Standard English; the first is doubly inept, for it is a misspelling of the second. Say "I wish I had worked harder," not "I wish I had've worked harder."

had ought. Neither this expression nor its negative (*hadn't ought*) is Standard English.

hanged, hung. The second of these forms is more widely used as both finite past tense form and past participle of the verb *hang*. Some people avoid the use of *hung* in reference to death by hanging; other equally reputable speakers and writers do not.

hardly. *See* DOUBLE NEGATIVE.

have got. Use of this expression (as in *We've got to go* or *They had got the debt paid off*) is certainly more common in informal speech than in writing. When not overused, the construction is respectable.

healthful, healthy. Some writers make a useful distinction between these two adjectives, assigning to *healthful* the meaning "health giving" and to *healthy* the meaning "in good health."

height. This standard spelling suggests the standard pronunciation. In older English, a pronunciation and spelling ending in *-th* was fairly frequent.

I

if, whether. It is less formal to say, "I don't know if he intends to come" than to say, "I don't know whether he intends to come or not." Both constructions are well established.

illusion. *See* ALLUSION.

imply, infer. A useful distinction is made by careful speakers and writers who employ *imply* only to mean "suggest" or "state indirectly" and *infer* to mean "draw a conclusion from evidence." The evidence for an inference can be either verbal or of some other sort. It is possible to say, "The speaker did not *imply* what the hearers *inferred*."

ingenious, ingenuous. *Ingenious* means "skilful, clever, inventive." *Ingenuous* means "innocent, guileless, or unsophisticated."

in regard to. *See* REGARD.

incidentally. *See* ACCIDENTALLY.

incredible, incredulous. *See* CREDIBLE.

infer. *See* IMPLY.

inflammable. *See* FLAMMABLE.

inside, inside of. Since both mean the same thing, the former is more economical. It is also more frequently used in writing.

interesting. This word is overused, with the result that it has lost specific meaning. *See* COUNTER WORDS.

invitation, invite. In Standard English, *invite* is a verb only. Its use as an equivalent for the noun *invitation* originated as slang.

inward(s). *See* BACKWARD(S).

irregardless. *Regardless* has a negative suffix and does not need a negative prefix. One sometimes hears *irregardless* in speech, but it is nonstandard.

it says. Such an expression as "It says in the paper . . ." is colloquial. The more formal and literary expression would be "The paper says. . . ."

its, it's. *Its* is the possessive form of *it*. *It's* is a contraction of *it is*.

J

judicial, judicious. *Judicial* is properly used to describe behavior or procedure related to or befitting a judge or court of law. *Judicious* is an adjective applied to carefully considered and wise conduct that has required a decision.

judgment, judgement. Both these spellings are established. The first is the more common in the United States.

K

kind of, sort of. These phrases are often preceded by *this* or *that*, *these* or *those*. A problem of grammatical agreement arises when the phrases are followed by a plural noun. In easy conversation, speakers have long said such things as "These *kind of* machines." Careful speakers, on the other hand, have generally made a virtue of saying "This *kind* (or *sort*) *of* machines" or "These *kinds* (or *sorts*) *of* machines." In formal writing, the demonstrative always agrees in number with the grammatical number of *kind* or *sort: this kind, these kinds.*

L

laboratory. Note the correct spelling of this word.

latter. *See* FORMER.

lay. *See* LIE.

lead. This may be a verb whose past tense form is *led*. It may also be a noun referring to a kind of metal.

learn, teach. We *learn* many things that nobody specifically *teaches* us. The past tense form of *learn* (*learned*) has two pronunciations. It is usually given one syllable, but when it is made to describe a person extraordinarily well educated (*a learned person*), it has the older pronunciation in which the *-ed* is made a separate second syllable.

leave, let. In Standard English, *leave* never has the meaning "allow." The verb that carries such a meaning is *let: Let us go. Leave*, of course, is also a noun (as in *a soldier's leave*). An older meaning of *let* was "to hinder," or (as a noun) "prevention." These older meanings are preserved in the expression "without let or hindrance" and in the tennis term, "a let ball."

lend, loan. It may be useful to confine *loan* to use as a noun referring to what is (or might be) lent. In England, the distinction between *lend* as a verb and *loan* as a noun is preserved among educated speakers; in the United States it is not as carefully preserved.

less, lesser. These are both comparative forms of *little*. *Lesser* is less commonly used, and it is generally confined to comparisons involving judgment of importance (as in *the lesser of two evils*). *See also* FEWER.

let. *See* LEAVE.

liable. *See* APT.

lie, lay. As a verb meaning "to be untruthful," *lie* has the past tense form *lied*. When *lie* means "to recline," its past tense is *lay* and its past participle is *lain*. These are the forms careful speakers and writers use as intransitives. The transitive verb *lay,* meaning "to place" something or "to cause to lie," has the past tense form *laid*. It is possible, of course, to say, "The hens *laid* well," for this expression is derived from "The hens *laid* eggs. . . ."

lief. This archaic word is seldom seen in

literary writing nowadays, but in speech it may be heard in such expressions as "I would (or had) as lief come as not."

like, as (if). *Like* is rarely used as a conjunction in formal writing, and it almost never appears in a position where *as if* would fit. In speech and informal writing, however, it is not uncommon in the meaning of either "as" or "as if." This usage is disliked by many educated people who insist that *like,* when not a verb, should be confined to use as a preposition, as in *The marines fought like tigers.* Unfortunately, consciousness of objections to use of *like* in such a sentence as "Do like I do" has misled some speakers into avoiding the word and producing such ridiculous statements as "The marines fought as tigers." Here the meaning could be "in the form of tigers."

likely. *See* APT.

loan. *See* LEND.

look bad. *See* BAD.

lovely, lousy. *See* COUNTER WORDS.

lying. This is the present participle of *lie* in both its meanings. *See* LIE.

M

mad. The basic meaning of *mad* is "insane" or "mentally deranged." Use of *mad* as an equivalent of *angry* or *annoyed* is colloquial.

majority, plurality. When applied to votes, *majority* means "more than half." In the same context, *plurality* means "the largest number cast for a particular candidate." If more than two candidates run for an office, it is obvious that one may win a plurality of the votes without winning a majority of them. In other contexts, *majority* is often a pretentious word that could be replaced by *most. Majority,* of course, has other meanings that are explained in the dictionary entry.

may. *See* CAN.

median. This word should not be confused with *medium,* though the two words are related in origin and meaning. *Median* means "middle." It may refer, for example, to the strip that separates the traffic on an expressway, or it may refer to the middle number in a series. The plural of *median* is *medians.*

medium. This word has several distinct mean-

ings; see the dictionary entry. It is often applied to that which makes something else possible, as in *Television is a medium of communication.* The Latin plural of *medium* is *media;* the established English plural is *mediums.*

mighty. The use of *mighty* as an adjective qualifier (*He is mighty good at golf*) is colloquial.

moral, morale. *Morale* is a noun only, and it refers to the way people feel (whether in good spirits or not). *Moral* may be either an adjective or a noun, but it is concerned with what is right or wrong (ethically). It is possible for people to have high *morale* and low *morals.*

most. *See* ALMOST.

myself. Sometimes, speakers feel it is less self-assertive to use *myself* rather than *I* or *me.* There is no good reason for such expressions as "They asked John and *myself* to come," or "My mother and *myself* were given the responsibility."

N

native, citizen. You are a native of the place where you were born; you are a citizen of the country or political subdivision where you have legal rights and duties of citizenship.

never, not. The indiscriminate use of *never* to mean simply *not* is colloquial. *Never* means, literally, "not at any time." Colloquial: "I was late this morning, because Mother never woke me up."

nice. *See* COUNTER WORDS.

none is, none are. Although *none* is a compound made from *no* and *one,* the word long ago ceased being only a singular. The grammatical number of the verb used with it depends, as it does with collective nouns, on the meaning ascribed to it.

not un-. *See* DOUBLE NEGATIVE.

notable, notorious. *Notable* is an adjective that is at least neutral; *notorious* describes something or somebody well known for qualities that are unpleasant or are disapproved. *See* FAMOUS.

nowheres. *See* ANYWHERE.

number. *See* AMOUNT.

numbers. It is customary to use figures for numbers in addresses, dates, page references, and official names such as *Public School 31.* Naturally, figures are used in lists of numbers, statistics, and mathematics texts. In ordinary writing that is at all formal, numbers are spelled out at the beginning of a sentence, and consistency in practice elsewhere is maintained. Many writers make a practice of spelling out any numbers that take only two words (*ninety-nine,* but *101*). Small numbers are generally spelled out, but some writers use figures for all beyond ten.

O

O, oh. When used as part of a vocative expression, *O* is always capitalized and is not separated by punctuation from the name of what is called on ("Where is thy sting, O Death?"). *Oh* is capitalized only at the beginning of a sentence and is often followed by a comma or exclamation point ("Oh, Harry! Come here, won't you?").

of. *See* COULD OF *and* INSIDE.

off from, off of. *Off* and *of* were originally simply the stressed and unstressed forms of the same word; as adverbs, they could carry the meaning of "away from." Many people still feel *off from* and *off of* are redundant expressions. In formal writing *from* or *off* are used by themselves.

oh. *See* O.

O.K., OK, okay, okeh. This expression is America's contribution to international communication. Known and used almost everywhere in the world as an indication of approval or correctness, it is still not generally used in formal writing. When it is represented in writing, any of the forms noted here may be used, and some others as well.

on, onto, on to. The prepositions *on* and *onto* sometimes mean the same thing: *She got on* (or *onto*) *the streetcar.* But in some contexts, *onto* indicates direction of movement, whereas *on* does not: *He stood on* (not *onto*) *the desk and then climbed onto the bookcase. Onto* should not be confused in spelling with the adverb *on* plus the preposition *to* as in *Go on to the next lesson.*

on, upon. These prepositions usually have the same meaning, but *upon* seems more formal.

on account of. It is slangy to use *on account of* as a substitute for *because,* as in "He broke the date with Jane *on account of* she annoyed him."

one. Use of *one* as an indefinite pronoun meaning "a person" is not characteristic of easy speech or informal writing, where the same notion is often expressed by the indefinite *you.* When *one* is used in the sense described here, custom in the United States allows reference to it by means of *he* and *himself: One finds it difficult to understand himself.* Some writers of formal English, however, make a virtue of referring to it only with *one, one's* and *oneself: When one loses one's temper, one has only oneself to blame.*

only. Intonation in speech almost always indicates clearly what *only* should be taken to modify. In writing, it is important to place *only* in a position where it is not likely to be misinterpreted. A sign, THIS ELEVATOR ONLY FOR DELIVERIES, could mean that only one elevator was available for deliveries, or that "this elevator" was to be used only for deliveries, nothing else. Normally, putting *only* just before the word it modifies prevents ambiguity: *Only I gave her flowers. I gave her only flowers* (or . . . *flowers only*).

onto. *See* ON.

onward(s). *See* BACKWARD(S).

ought. *See* HAD OUGHT.

ourn, yourn. *Like theirn, hisn,* and *hern,* these forms were invented on analogy with *mine* and *thine,* but only *mine* and *thine* are Standard English. The other forms are found in some regional dialects.

outside of. *See* INSIDE.

outward(s). *See* BACKWARD(S).

P

participle. *See* DANGLING MODIFIER.

pass. The spelling of the past tense and past participle of this verb is *passed.* Though the noun, adverb, adjective, and preposition *past* are pronounced in exactly the same way, a distinction in spelling is expected. Example: *The past president passed the house, thinking of days gone past.*

pay. The past tense of *pay* is *paid*, except in nautical contexts where a line may be described as being *payed out.*

per, percent, percentage. *Per* is a preposition (as in *per diem, per year,* and *per student*) that has a technical or statistical connotation. What it says usually can be said more simply (*a day,* etc.). But the term *percent* (note the spelling) is indispensable. This word is represented by the graphic symbol % only when it follows a specific figure (as in *40%*)—and even in such a position is often spelled out. *Percentage* is the term often, but not always, used when a figure is not specified (as in *an impressive percentage*).

perfect, perfectly. *See* COUNTER WORDS.

persecute, prosecute. To persecute someone is to cause that person to suffer unjustly. To prosecute someone is to take legal action against that person for the purpose of securing justice. If someone carries on a course of action, that person can also be said to be prosecuting it; a nation is said to prosecute a war.

personal, personnel. These words should not be confused in spelling or pronunciation. The second is used only to refer impersonally to employees or people on the staff of an organization of some kind.

perspective, prospective. *Perspective* has to do with ways of seeing things or ways of understanding something: *A school seems very different from the perspective of a student than from the perspective of a teacher. Prospective* is usually an adjective meaning "possible in the future": *Ted is a prospective member of the literary society.*

phenomenon. This is a singular form. The Greek plural is *phenomena;* there is also an established English plural: *phenomenons. Phenomena* is not properly used as a singular form. Compare *criterion, criteria.*

plenty. It is colloquial to use *plenty* to modify an adjective (as in *He was plenty good*). The omission of the preposition *of* in such expressions as *plenty of time* is nonstandard.

plurality. *See* MAJORITY.

politics. Like many other nouns that end in *-ics, politics* was originally a plural form but may now also be used as a singular.

positive(ly). *See* ABSOLUTE(LY).

practicable, practical, practically. A plan is practicable if it is capable of being put into practice. It is practical if it is sensible, if it works, or if it seems likely to work advantageously. *Practically* is, of course, the adverb made from *practical,* and it usually carries its original meaning in formal speech and writing. In informal speech and writing, it is often made to mean "almost" or "nearly": *He was practically a moron.* Some people object to this use.

practice, practise. The first of these spellings is more common in the United States.

precede, proceed, procedure. Note the conventional spelling of the second syllable in these words.

precedence, precedents. *Precedence* may be pronounced with the heaviest stress on either the first or the second syllable. It means "priority in rank or order." *Precedents* is the plural of *precedent;* both forms take the heaviest stress on the first syllable. A *precedent* is an action or event that has already occurred.

predominant, predominate. Do not confuse the adjective *predominant* with the verb *predominate.*

preposition at the end of a clause. Prepositions often appear at the ends of clauses and sentences in Standard English. To put them there frequently may give an unwanted flavor of the colloquial or very informal. But to torture a sentence in order to avoid such placement of a preposition can produce a ridiculous construction, as Winston Churchill pointed out when he remarked, "This is the kind of arrant nonsense up with which I will not put."

prescribe, proscribe. To *prescribe* is to require or strongly advise; a doctor *prescribes* medicine or a course of action. To *proscribe* something is to prohibit it, and when a governmental authority banishes or condemns a person to drastic penalties, it may be said to have *proscribed* him.

pretty. Though *pretty* was originally simply an adjective, in colloquial English it is now too often used as an unneeded qualifier of adjectives and adverbs. In formal writing, avoid such expressions as, "The book is pretty good, and I read it pretty carefully."

principal, principle. The basic meaning of *principal* is that of an adjective meaning "most important"; but like its synonym *chief,* it has also become a noun through omission of words that it might modify. We now speak of the principal of a school, or of a sum of money as principal (in contrast to the interest it may draw). *Principle* is always a noun.

procedure, proceed. *See* PRECEDE.

prophecy, prophesy. If someone *prophesies*, that person produces a *prophecy*. The *s* marks the verb; the *c* marks the noun.

proved, proven. Both forms are used as the past participle of the verb *prove*. The form ending in *n* is less frequent, except when it modifies a noun: *a proven evil*.

Q

quantity. Uncountable things, such as milk, sand, and lumber, are measured as quantities; countable things should not be referred to as quantities. We say, "There are many people here," but not "There is a large quantity of people here."

quick(ly). *See* SLOW(LY).

quote, quotation. A quotation is something that is actually quoted. It is illogical to say that a piece of literature contains many quotations, when the meaning is that people have drawn many quotations from it. *Quote* has traditionally been a verb; its use as a shortening of the noun *quotation* is colloquial, and is not appropriate in formal writing.

R

rarely ever, seldom ever. These are colloquial expressions. In more formal (and economical) use, *ever* is omitted.

rather. *See* HAD BETTER.

reason is because. Instead of using this expression, it is more logical to say *the reason is that* . . . . Often, it is more direct to say that something happened because . . . , rather than *The reason it happened is that* . . . .

reckon. *See* CALCULATE.

regard. *As regards, in regard to,* and *with regard to* are established expressions in Standard English; *in regards to* or *with regards to* are not.

respectfully, respectively. *Respectfully* de-

scribes courteous behavior. *Respectively* means "considering each of two or more items or persons individually and in the order named." Correct: *John respectfully apologized to his father, his mother, and his teacher, respectively.*

Rev., Reverend. Many people consider it disrespectful to refer to a clergyman as *Reverend* or *the Reverend* without using his name. Still others regard it as proper only to use *Reverend* (or in writing, the abbreviation *Rev.*) with a following *Mr.* or with a given name: *Rev. Mr. Smith* or *the Rev. John Smith.*

rhyme, rime, rhythm. The spellings *rhyme* and *rime* are equally well established. There is only one conventional spelling of *rhythm*.

'round. *See* AROUND.

run. The past tense form of this verb is *ran*: *The rabbit ran away.* The past participle is *run*: *The rabbit has run away.*

S

sacrilegious. This adjective is associated with the noun *sacrilege* rather than with *religious*. Note the spelling carefully.

said, same. These words, when used in legal papers, may mean "exactly the person or thing that has been identified earlier." Except in legal contexts, use of these words in such a sense is generally frowned on.

scarcely. *See* DOUBLE NEGATIVE.

see, saw, seen. These are the standard principal parts of the verb *see*. Correct: *I see today; I saw yesterday; I have seen.*

seldom ever. *See* RARELY EVER.

-self. *See* MYSELF.

set, sit. *Sit* is usually an intransitive verb. Its past tense form is *sat*. *Set* originally meant "to cause to sit," and in many of its uses that is still what it means. This usually transitive verb is *set* in both the present and the past tense. Its occasional intransitive uses are illustrated by *The sun sets in the west* and *A hen sets on eggs.*

shall, will. The distinction between these words when referring to the future is usually only that *shall* is more formal (and less frequently used). In questions involving a first person pronoun as subject, however, *shall* is meaningfully used where there is a choice to be made, *will* where no choice is in question. *Shall we go through Atlanta on the way to Miami?* implies that we might go to Miami by at least two routes. *Will we go through Atlanta?* merely asks whether the route decided on will take us through Atlanta.

should, would. *Should* has more regularly than *shall* retained the sense of expressing obligation; it also expresses probability (*We should be able to finish the job by noon*). *Would* expresses habitual past action and polite requests (*He would often ask, "Would you please close the door?"*). Both *should* and *would* are used in conditional clauses; in them, *should* often connotes greater uncertainty (compare *If she should come, I could leave* and *If she would come, I could leave*). Where the two words are interchangeable, *should* seems the more formal.

should of. *See* COULD OF.

sight. *See* CITE.

sing. In formal English, *sang* is the past tense form of *sing,* while *sung* is its past participle only. Occasionally in informal writing, *sung* may be used as the past tense form. Such an expression as *She has sang* is never used.

sink. Both *sank* and *sunk* are used as the past tense form of this verb. The past participle is *sunk,* unless the form *sunken* is used to modify a noun (*a sunken ship*).

sit. *See* SET.

site. *See* CITE.

slow(ly). Both *slow* and *slowly* are adverbs. There are, of course, some expressions in which only *slowly* would be used. We would not say, "He slow climbed the hill." *Slow* is also an adjective.

so. In informal speech and writing *so* is sometimes used as a qualifier approximately equivalent to *very.* Such usage can easily become tiresome.

somewhere. *See* ANYWHERE.

sort of. *See* KIND OF.

special(ly). *See* ESPECIAL(LY).

specie, species. *Specie* means "money in the form of coins"; the word has no plural form. *Species,* a term meaning "a distinct kind" of something, is used either as a singular or plural noun.

split infinitive. To split an infinitive (as in *He failed to fully understand the problem*) is in itself neither a virtue nor a vice. Accuracy and clarity in expression of meaning, or rhythm appropriate to style are the considerations that do or do not justify placing an adverbial modifier between *to* (the sign of the infinitive) and the verb form it introduces.

splendid. *See* COUNTER WORDS.

stationary, stationery. The first of these words is an adjective that means "unchanging" or "not moving." The second is a noun referring to writing materials. Note the spellings.

statistics. In Standard English, the normal form of this word usually has a final *s. Statistics* is always treated as a plural except when the word names a branch of study: *Statistics is a kind of applied mathematics.*

stratum. The Latin plural of this word is *strata;* the English plural is *stratums.* Both forms are established in English.

such. Use of *such* as a mere qualifier (as in *I had such a good time!*) is colloquial.

sure(ly). Use of *sure* as an adverb ("Are you going?" "*Sure.*") is colloquial only.

swim. The past tense form of this verb is *swam;* the past participle is *swum.*

T

teach. *See* LEARN.

terrible, terrific. *See* COUNTER WORDS.

that there. *See* THIS (THESE) HERE.

the fact that. *See* FACT THAT.

theirselves. *Themselves,* not *theirselves,* is the standard form.

them kinds, them there. These are nonstandard expressions. The standard substitute for the first is *those kinds,* for the second, simply *those.*

there is, there are. In expression with any degree of formality, agreement of verb and true subject is generally expected: *There are lots of things to do.* An exception is made when the subject is a compound in which the first element is singular: *There is ham and eggs for breakfast.*

this (these) here, that (those) there. These expressions are nonstandard when used as modifiers of nouns.

though (tho). *See* ALTHOUGH.

those (these) kind. *See* KIND OF.

thru. This simplified spelling of *through* is almost never used in formal writing.

thusly. This form is not used. *Thus* is correct.

till, until. These words may be used interchangeably. There is no need to write *'til*. Note that *till* has two *l*'s, *until* only one.

to. *See* SPLIT INFINITIVE.

toward(s). *See* BACKWARD(S).

transpire. The original meaning of *transpire* was "to exhale." Many people feel that using it to mean "to happen" is pretentious.

try and, try to. *See* AND.

U

uninterested. *See* DISINTERESTED.

United States. The name of our nation is nowadays normally singular, although political orators sometimes speak of *these United States*.

unless. To substitute *without* for *unless* is nonstandard usage.

until. *See* TILL.

used. Be careful in spelling not to drop the *d* in this past tense of *use*.

V

venal, venial. *Venal* describes corruption or corruptibility as a result of greed for money or other material gain. *Venial* means "forgivable." A *venial* sin is not a deadly sin.

very. Like other qualifiers of adjectives and adverbs, *very* has lost much of its force through overuse. Sometimes the omission of the qualifier produces a stronger expression than does its use.

virtue, virtuosity. *Virtue* refers to merit of any sort. *Virtuosity* refers to an artist's technical skill.

W

wait for, wait on. With the meaning "to serve," *wait on* is in general English use (*She was hired to wait on tables*). In the sense of "wait for" (*We haven't time to wait on Fred*) *wait on* is colloquial.

'way, away. In informal speech, *away* is often shortened by omission of the first syllable. Such usage is not common in writing, but when it occurs, it should be represented by *'way* (*We saw him 'way down the road*).

well. *See* GOOD. In speech, *well* is often overused as an attention-claimer or mere time-filler (*Well . . . well, I don't know*).

went. *See* GO.

whether. *See* IF.

while. *See* AWHILE.

whilst. In England, but not in the United States, *whilst* is common as an alternative to the conjunction *while*.

whose, who's. *Whose* is the possessive form of *who, which,* or *that*. It should not be confused with *who's*, the contraction of *who is*.

will. *See* SHALL.

with regard. *See* REGARD.

without. *See* UNLESS.

would. *See* SHOULD. *See also* COULD OF.

Y

you. *See* ONE.

you all. As a plural of *you*, this is a regional colloquialism.

you and I. *You and I* (*he*) (*she*) may be correctly used only in subjective positions (*You and I can do the job*). As an object of the verb (*He called you and me*) or as an object of a preposition (*We will choose between you and him*), only an objective form can be properly coordinated with *you*.

your, you're. In writing, the possessive *your* should not be confused with *you're*, which is a contraction of *you are*.

WRITING AND RESEARCHING

As students advance through school, they discover that their teachers assign more and more papers based on library research. What teachers are asking for is thorough study of published information as well as your own consideration of the meaning and significance of what you find. Thus, a research paper becomes a matter of applying your experience and ideas to what you find and then expressing your conclusions in an interesting, carefully thought-out form. In preparing such a paper you, of course, have to conform to the requirements of standard bibliographic format.

The following pages supply all the information you will need about how to conduct library research efficiently, when and how to take notes, and how to prepare initial and final drafts of a paper, including footnotes and bibliography.

Using the Library

RESEARCH SKILLS

Anyone who hopes to do well in high school and college must be able to write a good research paper. Such papers may be as simple as describing a simple machine or experiment—a homemade radio, a doorbell, a barometer, the hatching of chickens, a bacterial culture, the analysis of pond water, or the germination of beans. They may deal with library research on a historical figure or event, interviews with city officials, a study of welfare procedures, the need for improved health services in a rural area, or the use of leisure time by people residing in a housing project. They may require analysis of a book, a play, or the career of a literary figure.

As you advance in your educational career, you will take on research tasks of ever-increasing complexity. The reports you write will themselves become more and more complex. Once you have left school, you will find that the most attractive careers demand that you continue to conduct research of one type or another and that you continue to write research reports.

A research paper demonstrates your ability to think and write coherently. It teaches you how to study and shows you where your abilities and talents lie. If you can master the techniques of research and research writing, you will help yourself advance smoothly through your years of schooling and gain a respected position in professional life.

KINDS OF LIBRARIES

Libraries are of three general types. A *technical* library is usually devoted to a specialized subject and is intended for use in a particular field. Thus, there are engineering libraries, medical libraries, science libraries, etc. A *circulating* library has as its primary function circulating books to many types of readers. Most public libraries are classified as circulating libraries. A *reference* library is a work place for scholars and students who seek to study and learn.

A reference library seeks to be as complete as possible in all fields of study. Such a library contains an enormous number of books. Some of them are available for use only in the library. A small number are usually available for overnight use outside the library. It is important for you to become familiar with the types of books your library contains, where they are located, and how they are to be used.

THE CARD CATALOGUE

The *main reference room* of a library normally contains the card catalogue—an index by author, title, and subject to every book in the library. The main reference room also contains a selection of basic reference books that are consulted so frequently that they are kept on shelves in the room for the use of everyone who qualifies as a student or scholar. The call desk—at which librarians issue books when they are brought up from the stacks in answer to requests from readers—is also located in the main reference room. The stacks are the shelf areas of the library in which are kept most of the books of the library. The librarian in charge of the reference collection is stationed at the call desk.

The card catalogue is the key to the library's collection. This alphabetical file of index cards lists all the books the library contains and is arranged, as has been said, by author, title, and subject. You will have to use this catalogue many times throughout your school career and in your adult life, if you pursue a professional career, so be sure to familiarize yourself with the information the typical card contains. The following discussion shows how a card gets into the catalogue and what the card contains.

When a library receives a book, the book goes to a cataloguer, who examines it, makes out a card that contains the author's name and birth date (if the author is deceased, it also contains the death date), the title of the book, the publisher, place and date of publication, the number of pages, and the size of the book in centimeters. The card also contains such information as whether the book includes maps, plates, illustrations, or a bibliography (a listing of books on related subjects).

The cataloguer also determines the subject covered by the book and gives it a classmark. The classmark in most libraries is based either on the Dewey decimal system or the Library of Congress system. Both these systems are described later in this section. The classmark carried by a book determines where it will be placed on the library shelves, and the card carries this same classmark. By arranging books carrying closely related classmarks near one another, readers who have access to the stacks can easily find books on the same subject. The clerks who search the stacks for books know just where to go to find a book a reader requests. At the bottom of the card, the cataloguer lists the subject entries that will help readers locate books on a particular subject when specific titles and authors for books on that subject are not known to the reader. Separate cards are made out for the author, the title, and the subject headings. These cards are

Main reading room, Library of Congress, Washington, D.C. The library has one or more copies of every book or publication copyrighted in the United States.

then inserted alphabetically into the card catalogue, and the book is made available to readers.

The Main Entry Card. The main entry card is filed alphabetically by author, or title if there is no author. In some cases, the issuing body is considered the main entry. Thus, Ibsen, as the author of a play, is a main entry. The Government of Japan may be a main entry. The United Nations General Assembly may be a main entry. A work having so many authors or collaborators that it can be filed only by title, such as *The New York Times* or the *Encyclopedia Americana*, would be found under those titles as main entries. The simplest way to locate a book in a card catalogue is to look for it under the main entry.

Secondary Entry Cards. Secondary entry cards are added to the card file to help readers who do not know the main entry. The principal secondary entries are for subject, joint author or authors, editor, illustrator, translator, or compiler. Thus, even if you did not know that Leonard Lurie was the author of *The Impeachment of Richard Nixon,* you would be able to

The card catalogue is the key to a library's resources. Efficient use of the catalogue saves time in research. Make careful notes of all the information you need.

find the card for that book under the subject heading "Nixon, Richard M." Secondary entry cards are invaluable in helping readers use a library's collection. When you are doing research on a topic, you should familiarize yourself with all possible subject entries to help you find books that will be useful for your work. The librarians in your library can help you.

Tracings.   Tracings are also useful in locating books that will help you when you are doing research. A tracing is the information on the bottom of a catalogue card that indicates to the cataloguer the entries that should be added to the main card entry. Students must learn to use these tracings, because they help direct the reader to books on the same subject being researched or to related subjects. You can think of tracings as keys to the subject headings in the card catalogue.

LOCATING BOOKS YOU NEED

When you are working in a large library, you must be organized as you go about your research. Consult the card catalogue in a logical manner—alphabetically by author, title, or subject. Skipping about from one part of the catalogue to another wastes time and may cause you to overlook books you might otherwise have found. If you know an author's name, look first under author. It is the easiest entry to find in a card catalogue. If you cannot find a book under the author's name but you know the title, check quickly for that. Remember, though, that titles that are not distinctive are generally not catalogued, so do not waste time searching first for a title. If you know neither the author nor the title, search for the book under the subject. Be sure to get the correct subject. Don't waste time guessing at the subject. Get it right the first time.

Once you have located the card for the book you want, fill out a *call slip* with the author, title, and classmark. You will find the classmark in the upper left-hand or right-hand corner of the card.

Classification Systems.   Classmarks are designated either under the Dewey decimal system or the Library of Congress system in most libraries you will use. The Dewey decimal system classifies books under ten categories.

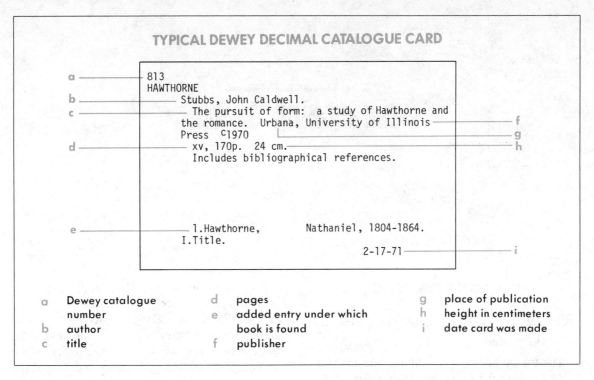

TYPICAL DEWEY DECIMAL CATALOGUE CARD

```
a ──────── 813
           HAWTHORNE
b ──────────────── Stubbs, John Caldwell.
c ──────────── The pursuit of form:  a study of Hawthorne and
           the romance.  Urbana, University of Illinois ──── f
           Press  C1970                                       g
d ────────────── xv, 170p.  24 cm. ────────────────────────── h
           Includes bibliographical references.



e ──────────── 1.Hawthorne,      Nathaniel, 1804-1864.
           I.Title.
                                 2-17-71 ──────────────────── i
```

a   Dewey catalogue   d   pages   g   place of publication
    number   e   added entry under which   h   height in centimeters
b   author   book is found   i   date card was made
c   title   f   publisher

000 General Works
100 Philosophy
200 Religion
300 Sociology
400 Philology
500 Natural Science
600 Useful Arts
700 Fine Arts
800 Literature
900 History and Biography

N Fine Arts
P Language and Literature
Q Science
R Medicine
S Agriculture
T Technology
U Military Science
V Naval Science
Z Library Science, Bibliography

The Library of Congress system uses the letters of the alphabet to divide information into twenty categories. The letters I, O, W, X, and Y are not used; the letters E and F are both used for American history.

A General Works
B Philosophy, Religion
C History
D Foreign History
E, F American History
G Geography, Anthropology
H Social Sciences
J Political Science
K Law
L Education
M Music

Microfilm.   Microfilm is a miniature photographic copy of a book, newspaper, or magazine. Use of microfilming helps a library conserve shelf space. It also makes available to libraries copies of books or other works that can no longer be bought. You may find that books you are seeking are available in microfilm.

The librarian will show you how to use the microfilm reader. Once you have set the machine up for use and adjusted it to your needs, you will find it easy to use. It is almost as convenient to use as a book. The one drawback is that you cannot flip between pages as easily as you can with a printed work. In the case of a newspaper or magazine item you are looking for, you must try to make sure you have the correct page reference.

Researching a Topic

CHOOSING THE TOPIC

There are three rules for choosing a topic for research:

1. The topic must be a reasonable one for you.
2. The topic must be interesting for you.
3. Your instructor must approve the topic.

A reasonable topic for you is one on which you have some prior knowledge. If you were to undertake an analysis of various types of energy and knew nothing about coal, gas, oil, and nuclear technology, you would be faced with so big a job that you might not be able to complete your research in the time available. In addition you must know, before you spend too much time on the job, whether your library has enough information to satisfy your needs. If you will not be able to find what you need, there is no point in setting out to do the research.

The question of whether you find a topic interesting is quite important. You will research and write best those papers that are interesting to you. All the steps involved in doing a research paper become a source of pleasure instead of a source of unhappiness. You work endlessly and tirelessly when you enjoy a topic; you fatigue quickly when you hate what you are doing. This means that you must not choose the first topic that comes to mind. Search for a topic until you find one that will hold your attention. The best topic of all is one that you find fascinating.

The question of whether your instructor approves your choice of topic must not be overlooked. When considering a topic you have submitted for instructor approval, the instructor will consider your ability to do the paper, based on your background and the availability of the material you will need. Instructors know the resources of their school libraries and know the abilities of each student. Be guided by your instructors' wishes. They have your interests in mind. They want you to study topics that are worthy of your time, topics on which they can assist you, topics that will teach you how to do research.

In some courses your instructors will suggest subjects for consideration by all members of the class. They may even schedule individual conferences to help each student find a suitable subject. But most instructors will not offer to help students find the specific topics they will research.

Three Useful Definitions

Subject. A broad area for research.
Topic. Field within a subject on which specific research will be undertaken.
Theme. The central statement that can be made after research of a topic is concluded. The theme is a statement to be supported by the research paper.

WRITING AND RESEARCHING

When students suggest topics they have found after preliminary research of a subject, most instructors will be pleased to discuss the merits of one or more possible topics. They will not consider the theme established after full research until the research paper is completed and submitted.

PRELIMINARY RESEARCH

This part of the work is performed with three goals in mind:

1. To select the topic to be developed fully.
2. To locate as many research sources as possible.
3. To verify that the research can be performed.

During this part of the work, there is no point in reading carefully. All you want to do is discover your useful sources, sources that establish whether or not you can meet your three goals.

In performing preliminary research for a history paper, for example, you may be interested in a particular country, period, or phase of development. Perhaps you are interested in Great Britain, the colonial period, or the industrial revolution. Can you see that all these subjects are too large for a research paper? What you need is a topic within one of these subjects that you can handle in the time you have available.

Can you narrow them down? Perhaps you might think of doing a paper on the effect of England's isolation from the Continent on English history during the nineteenth century. Perhaps you could write on the relation between England's colonial policy and her commercial development. What about the impact of the Corn Laws on England? You might find a paper in such a topic.

These suggestions are not made to direct you toward a specific topic for writing; they are intended, rather, to help stimulate your thinking on whatever subject interests you. If you are going to write for a literature course, to take another example, you may find that you can arrive at a topic by selecting a period of literature that interests you. From there you could

Before a paper is complete, every item in the bibliography must be checked for accuracy and completeness. This may mean one additional library session.

move your thinking into a specific school of writers who worked during that period. It is easy enough to see that you could then narrow your thinking down to a comparison of the work of two writers, the work of a single writer, one work by that writer, or even one aspect of that one work. Or you can compare and contrast several works, considering them on the basis of a common idea, character, or attitude.

As you can see, then, you can get your thinking down to a topic you can handle, and you must do so before you begin actual work on the research for your paper. Once you have made a tentative selection, you will find that there is more work to be done before you can be certain you have selected a topic you can handle. The topic may have to be limited further in order to be able to complete your work in the time available, and you must be certain that your library can provide the books and articles you will need.

In general, however, the best technique for finding a suitable topic is to proceed from the general to the specific. Your first step in your library research is to read general articles on your topic in one of the major encyclopedias—

the *Encyclopaedia Britannica* or the *Encyclopedia Americana*. These reference works will give you an introduction to your subject and a short, selective bibliography identifying the most important authors and works in the field. The second step after that is the search in the library card catalogue.

DEVELOPING A WORKING BIBLIOGRAPHY

Your working bibliography for a paper is the list of books and articles you think will provide the background information you will need for your paper. This bibliography comes from your reading of encyclopedia articles, books, and other articles as well as from your search of the library card catalogue. The best way to record entries in your working bibliography is to use a single index card or slip of paper for each source you think you will use. Every time you find a *book* that may be helpful, make out a card or slip with the following information:

- Author's full name
- Title of the work
- Place and date of publication

Every time you find an article that may be helpful, make out a card or slip with the following information:

- Title of the article
- Name of the journal
- Volume number
- Inclusive pages of the article

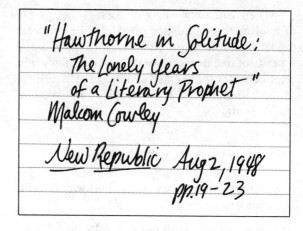

Be sure to make out a card for every source even if the source does not end up being used in the paper. A working bibliography shows all useful sources consulted, whether or not specific material is taken from them. If you keep your working bibliography up-to-date and complete, you will not have to do any last-minute scrambling to locate sources you have read.

TAKING NOTES ON READING

Once you have selected your topic and you have read some general works on it, you can begin to break down your topic into its natural subdivisions. For example, in writing a paper about the Nixon-Kissinger China policy, you will probably want to consider the following:

- United States attitude toward China from 1948 until Nixon became president in 1968
- Support for the Nationalist Chinese in the United States Senate
- The ping-pong door-opener
- The Nixon trip to China
- Events leading toward recognition by the United Nations

If your topic breaks into logical subdivisions in this way—and you will find logical subdivisions in any good topic you choose—it will be helpful to number each of the subdivisions and list them on a sheet of paper. As you find material relating to any of your subdivisions, you can key your notes on the reading you do to the specific subdivision to which they relate. Your sheet of paper containing the subdivisions of your topic will be consulted when you write specific notes.

It is best to write notes on large index cards—5 X 8 inches—so that you will have enough room in which to write. If necessary, use more than one card for each source you consult, but then be sure to number the cards in sequence so that you can use them easily when you write your paper. As you encounter material you wish to note, make out a card for the source, giving the following information:

- Number of subdivision
- Author, title, and page number(s) of source
- Notes

You will find that if you have subdivided your topic logically, the subdivisions of your topic will become the section headings of your paper. You will also be able to check on the logic of your subdivisions when you outline your paper.

As you work in the library, check your notes frequently to see that you are getting information that will be useful and to be sure that you have taken the information correctly. You must also check your notes to make certain you are getting the information you need for all parts of the topic you have chosen. If you find that information on a certain part of your topic is not coming to light, you may have to alter your topic to reflect that availability of information. In the Nixon-Kissinger topic, for example, you may find that your library lacks information on "the ping-pong door-opener." If that is so, you may want to eliminate this incident as a major portion of your topic.

As you start work on any day, look ahead at all the subdivisions for which you need information. In that way, you can make certain you recognize pertinent information when you come upon it. You may be reading about the Nixon trip to China and come upon material relating to the ping-pong match or one of the other subdivisions. If you are aware of your needs, you will be alert to such windfalls. If you are not, you may miss out on a good chance to collect information you need.

As you work in a particular source, be sure to get all the information you need in a single sitting. There is no point in putting down a book until you have milked it dry. You don't want to

STUDENT'S NOTES FOR HAWTHORNE PAPER

I. Malcom Cowley, "Hawthorne in Solitude,"
    New Republic, Aug. 2, 1948

- Time in isolation important to development as writer
- Led to emphasis on psychological realism
- While others traveled the world, Hawthorne looked inside himself for material

"During his years of solitude Hawthorne learned more about the art and the trade of writing than others learned in the marketplace." (p. 19)

waste time finding a book a second time when you could have done all your work in it in one session. The job of locating and checking out sources eats up your time in a library.

Before stopping work on any day, look back over your notes to see that you can read them all. If you cannot be sure you have taken all your notes correctly, you can look back at your sources to check for errors. If you wait until weeks later to correct errors, you may never be able to find your sources again. Libraries are in constant use, and the books or journals you want may be in use by others. Check dates for accuracy. Check names for spelling. Check quoted material to see that you have transcribed every word exactly.

Your last step before leaving the library is to schedule your next visit to the library and decide what you will be doing during that visit.

THREE TYPES OF READING NOTES

The notes you will take on your research fall into three categories:

- Direct quotation
- Paraphrase
- Comment

Direct quotation is the correct form for a particular note when a source has stated an idea so concisely that you cannot improve it further, or when any change in the way the idea is stated will impair its literary quality.

Paraphrasing is the preferred type of note-taking when you can state an idea or present information more concisely or clearly than the author has supplied it.

Commentary in note-taking represents your own reaction or response to something you read in one of your sources. You may be reading the report of a journalist on the Nixon-Kissinger China policy and find that, in your opinion, the journalist has given less than fair treatment to the subject. If that is so, then you note your characterization of the journalist's work.

In summary, then, you may quote directly, paraphrase, or comment. The choice is dictated by the nature of what you are reading and your

Microfilm copies of newspapers, books, and documents speed research once you master use of the reader. Learn to use this resource if your library has microfilm equipment.

response to it. Keep in mind as you work that you are selecting material and developing your thoughts for the single purpose of writing a good research report. As you work along in your reading, read all your notes over and over again to see what you are getting and what you are thinking. A good research paper depends on careful thought about what you find. It is not merely a long account of a trip through a library.

While you may have started your research on a topic with a particular attitude toward your topic, the things you read may begin to alter your thinking. Do not ignore—do not be afraid of—contradictory material. Learn to argue logically with evidence that goes against your beliefs; learn to change your beliefs when you cannot find evidence to sustain your beliefs. Your final paper must not ignore contradictory material, so your notes must include that material. If you skirt the truth as you research, your final paper will also skirt the truth. A good research paper presents the facts and the arguments needed to reach a reasonable conclusion.

A visit to the stacks will tell you quickly whether the books you need are available. In many libraries students must obtain special permission—stack privileges—to enter the stacks.

PRIMARY AND SECONDARY SOURCES

The sources you will use as you do research fall into two categories:
- Primary sources
- Secondary sources

Primary sources are first-hand records of events. They may be newspaper accounts written at the time when the events occurred. They may be autobiographies of the participants, diaries of the participants, letters of the participants. They may also be reports of experiments in scientific research.

Secondary sources evaluate, criticize, relate, or otherwise deal with primary source information. Such sources include the work of historians writing about past events, the work of commentators with no first-hand knowledge of the events they deal with, and the like.

Both primary and secondary sources of information have to be evaluated by you when you are doing research. Primary sources must be evaluated for their validity, for the intelligence and experience of the observer, and the accuracy of the report. People who participate in an event may not be qualified either by background or objectivity to tell you what really happened. Indeed, they may even set out to present a point of view that casts them in a favorable light. (Can you imagine what researchers will have to go through some day in writing an account of the Nixon impeachment? Think of all the books that have been, are being, and will be written by the various players in that drama—all professing to tell the truth, the whole truth, and nothing but the truth.)

Secondary sources require even greater evaluation. The interpretations of events presented may be biased, inaccurate, or incompetent; on the other hand, they may be incisive, accurate, and invaluable. How can you evaluate your sources? The fact is that unless you have first-hand knowledge of your research topic—that is, unless you participated in the events you are researching—you will not be able to evaluate sources with certainty until you become highly qualified in the subject.

Yet there are guidelines for judging the reliability of a source:

1. Evaluate the publisher of the information. In most cases, publishers are responsible for the validity of the works they publish. The most reliable publishers are

   - University presses of major academic institutions
   - Major commercial publishing houses
   - Scholarly societies

   You may be sure that such publishers care a great deal about what they publish and take great pains to see that they publish honest information. (Of course, they also make mistakes, but these mistakes are usually pointed out quickly in print.)
2. Find out who the author is and what position the author holds. Use such sources as the *Dictionary of American Biography, Who's Who in America,* or the *Dictionary of National Biography* (for British authors).

A WARNING TO THE BEGINNING RESEARCHER

No matter how interesting you find a text you are using, don't spend valuable time reading anything that does not pertain to the topic you are researching. It is easy to get lost in an interesting book that provides valuable information—but information that does not contribute to your job of research. Save that reading for another time, a time after you have finished your paper.

Such reading during the precious weeks you have for completing a paper robs you of the time you need.

Check the information on the title page of a book or the biographical footnote in a journal article. An author's affiliation or accomplishments will normally be listed there.

3. Consult your teacher, who will usually be able to help you validate a source.

Getting Down to Writing

You have selected a subject, narrowed that subject down to a specific topic, constructed a working bibliography, subdivided your topic logically, read through all your sources, taken appropriate notes on your sources—direct quotes, paraphrase, and commentary—and taken care to the best of your ability that all your sources, both primary and secondary, are as reliable as research of your own plus the help of your teacher can determine. Much time has passed. If you are on schedule, you now have ample time for outlining—the necessary first step in writing a research paper.

THE OUTLINE

Before writing any work of substantial content and length, you would do well to construct a careful outline. In most of the courses you will take that require a research paper, you will be required to submit an outline before preparing your paper. The outline tells you that you really have something to say, that you have thought it through totally, and that your writing can proceed in an orderly fashion. By organizing your thoughts in an outline, you make your writing easier. Above all, by organizing your thoughts in an outline, you make your reader's task easier.

The procedure for developing an outline is not difficult. While an outline can take various forms, it should contain three essential elements:

- Theme statement
- Main ideas and supporting elements
- Documentation sources

The *theme statement* is the central thought that has emerged from your research. It summarizes in brief form the entire paper you will write. Everything else in your paper will support your theme statement in some way: by expansion for emphasis, by explanation, by documentation, or by example.

The *main ideas* of your paper are the most important statements the paper makes in support of the theme statement. The *supporting elements* are the most important details the paper provides in support of the main ideas. If you think of the theme statement of a paper as the backbone of the paper, the main ideas are the most important remaining elements of the skeleton of the paper. The supporting elements are the organs of the body. Altogether, these parts of the paper become an entire, completely developed research paper.

The *documentation sources* are the books, articles, and other important sources of information you have found during your research to substantiate what you will present in your paper. They are included in the outline in order to make your job of organizing and writing your paper as simple as possible. If you have keyed all of your 5 X 8 note cards to the main elements of your paper, you will be able to arrange them in the same order in which you will write the parts of your paper.

WRITING THE THEME STATEMENT AND OUTLINE

In order to write a one-sentence summary of your thinking, you should ask yourself what you have found and concluded about your topic. Have you examined the relationship between historic trends in two countries? What have you found? The answer is the *theme state-*

Accurate, detailed note-taking at the library creates the record of research you will need in thinking through and writing your research papers.

ment of your paper. Have you examined the development of a writer from early works to full maturity? What have you found? The answer is the *theme statement* of your paper.

Let us take an example. You have been studying the life of Nathaniel Hawthorne. Your working bibliography numbered almost forty different sources. As you worked through all that material, you were struck by the influence of Hawthorne's understanding of his family history on his subsequent development as a writer. You learned that one ancestor of Hawthorne's was instrumental in arranging cruel punishment of Quakers in the town of Salem, Massachusetts; another sat as a judge in the trials of women accused of witchcraft. You also learned that Hawthorne was an avid reader of colonial history and that he was interested in the psychology of the Puritan. You saw that Hawthorne's tales and romances were concerned with the struggle between Puritan philosophy and more humane instincts.

As a result of all your reading—both in secondary sources of biography and criticism of the author's work and in primary sources (Hawthorne's work)—you have written the following theme statement:

> Already inclined toward introspection by nature and experience, Nathaniel Hawthorne spent twelve years after college in virtual isolation, writing and rewriting his *Twice-Told Tales* and forming the style that characterized all his literary output throughout his career.

Once you have written this theme statement, you have set the tone and approach for your entire paper. Now you have the job of writing the rest of the outline and keying to it all the documentation sources you will use as you write. Here is one outline you might arrive at; it is presented without the sources of documentation you might use. Note that this is a *topical outline*.

Title   That Lonely Hawthorne Chamber
  I. Introduction
 II. Early Childhood
     A. The early years
     B. Death of father
        1. Effect on Hawthorne
        2. Self-imposed isolation of Hawthorne's mother
        3. Life with relatives
III. New England School Days
     A. Education
     B. Foot injury and subsequent two-year isolation
     C. Life in Maine
 IV. Bowdoin College Days
     A. Education
     B. Companions
     C. Decision to become a writer
  V. The Lonely Chamber—Learning to Write
     A. Twelve years of isolation
        1. Critics—favorable and unfavorable
        2. Writing apprenticeship
     B. Anguishing through his Puritan ancestry
     C. Emergence from the Lonely Chamber
 VI. Themes in Hawthorne's works showing early influences
     A. Isolation of mankind
     B. Evils of Puritanism
VII. Conclusion

This outline is just one example of the ways in which you can approach the organization of a research paper. In general, there are four types of research papers: historical, biographical, literary, and analytical.

A *historical* paper can be developed chronologically, or it can be developed by first thoroughly analyzing all the important events of an era and then discussing related side issues. A *biographical* paper can also be organized in both these ways. Your choice of organization will depend on how you have viewed the life of your subject. The emphasis to be placed on events will determine the order of presentation you select. In a *literary* paper you may decide to trace a certain theme in the work of one or more authors. In developing your ideas in such a paper, it is most common to select only the major works of the authors for analysis. If you choose to study both major and minor works, you would probably work through the major works first and then finish up with the minor works. You could also treat the works chronologically. If you are dealing with the images in the work of a particular author, you would probably deal with the central images first and then go on to the related images. In either case, your paper would be strengthened by pertinent examples of the images with which you deal. In an *analytical* paper dealing with a problem or event, you would treat the central issues first before going on to related side issues. Thus, if you were dealing with a particularly stressful time in the history of a country, you would work first through the most important aspects of the situation before covering the less important problems.

It would be helpful for you to see an example of a *sentence outline*. The paper is intended for a course in anthropology or ancient history.

Theme Statement   Burial rites among the ancient Greeks, the Egyptians, and the Anglo-Saxons differed in detail, but all three groups used cremation and interment, and the Egyptians and Anglo-Saxons both practiced burial at sea.
Title   Ancient Burial Rites
  I. Ancient Greeks usually burned their dead heroes.

A. The *Iliad* recounts the cremation of Hector and Patroclus.
B. Frequently the ashes of the dead were placed in urns.
C. Other sections of the *Iliad* suggest interment.
   1. Erection of a barrow for Patroclus.
   2. Other evidence of the existence of barrows.
II. Egyptians interred their leaders.
A. Pyramids are seen in the Nile valley.
B. Archaeologists have found burial ships.
III. Anglo-Saxons practiced interment, cremation, and ship burial.
A. There is evidence of interment in *Beowulf*.
B. In the same poem, Beowulf is burned on a huge pyre.
C. The Sutton Hoo find reveals the existence of ship burial.
IV. Conclusion.

This outline is by country. The same paper could have been organized just as well by type of burial:

I. Ship burial
II. Interment
III. Cremation

As the writer, you have the choice of type of organization for the paper you research and write. In every case, however, your teacher has the right to approve or disapprove the outline you construct.

WRITING THE PAPER

Once you have completed a satisfactory outline for your paper, you are ready to begin writing. Understand, however, that your outline is there to help you move along logically from the first sentence of your paper until the last. If you find at any point that the outline you have developed does not meet your needs, you are free to restructure it. As you gain experience in researching and writing, you will find that your outlines tend to become more realistic and more helpful. It is only through using outlines that

writers learn to write them. Anyone who has not written a paper of some length and substance cannot expect that early attempts at writing outlines will produce good outlines every time.

Some writers like to write out a first draft of a paper as quickly as they can, paying no particular attention to *how* they express themselves but concentrating instead on *what* they are saying. Others perfect each sentence as they go along. A good outline has the special advantage of keeping you abreast of everything you want to say. Since there is no chance you will lose your train of thought, you can pay special attention to your choice of words, sentence structure, and paragraph development.

When you get ready to write, all you need are the tools of your trade: outline, dictionary, notes, pen and paper, and a handbook of composition. Writers vary in selecting the part of the paper to be written first. Some choose to begin with the section they most enjoy writing, while others—and this is the more generally preferred method—start with the opening paragraph and continue writing until they reach the end of the paper. No matter which way you begin, be sure that you have firmly in mind the theme statement your paper will support. Everything you write is designed to establish the truth of that statement.

Complete the first draft of your paper before you begin any revision. Even if you try to polish your writing as you work along, you will find some need for revision after you have finished, so it is better to finish the first draft and then get on with needed rewriting. As you work through your first draft, you may want to use certain short cuts that experienced writers use.

One helpful short cut is pasting or stapling note cards into your first draft when the note cards carry material you will want to quote word for word. Why bother to copy quotations verbatim when you are only working on a first draft? First of all, copying takes time. Secondly, copying may mean making mistakes.

Another helpful short cut is to set a goal for each session of writing. If you set a reasonable goal for each session of writing, you will find that you can complete that unit of writing in the time allotted. You then can take a break from your writing, do other school tasks, or set another goal for the next period of time and get on with your work.

A third short cut you will find helpful is to look back at material you have already covered in your first draft before setting to work on the next part. Looking back in this way helps you pick up the thread of your discussion and reacquaints you with the thoughts you are about to pursue.

A fourth short cut is to examine your outline to see just what you are going to cover in each period of writing. The outline helps you if you use it in this way. It also tells you just which portion of your notes you will be using in that period.

WRITING THE FINAL DRAFT

Once you have completed your first draft, it would be well for you to take a break from writing. You cannot do a good job of examining your work for mistakes immediately after you have finished it. Coming back to the first draft after a period of time enables you to view your work objectively. Go through your paper with pen in hand to make any changes you think necessary. Do this work in more than one pass. The first pass should concern itself with the general flow of information and ideas. Is the logic just what you want? Would a reader be convinced by your argument? Is all the information present that is needed to convince the reader? Does your ordering of the material meet the reader's needs? In this first pass, then, you should find errors of omission, of incompleteness, of poor arrangement.

In the second pass, you should read as an English teacher or editor might. Is every word spelled correctly? Is the punctuation sound? Does each word say what it is supposed to say? Is the paragraph structure clear? Is your introduction truly an introduction? Is your conclusion truly a conclusion? Do your paragraphs have topic sentences? Are your verbs as vivid as they can be? Do all your verbs agree in number and person with their subjects? Are all necessary footnotes in place? Is your bibliography complete and in correct form?

When you are satisfied that you have met all these requirements in the first draft, you are ready to make your final draft. Prepare this draft as carefully as you can. If you are typing your paper—and this is by far the most widely accepted form for a research paper—look back over every page when you finish it and before you remove it from your typewriter. See that you have typewritten everything correctly.

Prepare your final drafts of your bibliography and cover sheet, observing the rules established in your school, and you are ready to submit your paper.

FOOTNOTES AND BIBLIOGRAPHY

Every statement or idea that is not your own must be footnoted, so your reader knows where it came from. You need a citation for

- *Concepts quoted or paraphrased from another source*
- *Facts or opinions found in another source*
- *Ideas that have been of primary importance in shaping your concepts*

If you *never neglect to cite* a source, you will never have trouble in footnoting research papers. It is better to cite too frequently than to take a chance on neglecting to cite a source you have used.

You may place your citations either in footnotes at the bottom of a page or within the text. You must consult your teacher to find where to place your citations. Readers prefer to have citations placed within the text, as shown in this example:

> In her most influential work (*A Vindication of the Rights of Woman* [1792]) Mary Godwin made an eloquent plea for equality.

The same reference could be made in a footnote at the bottom of the page. It then would require a number at the end of the sentence to which the footnote is keyed, with the same number used in the footnote. These numbers go from 1 to the highest number needed for a footnote in

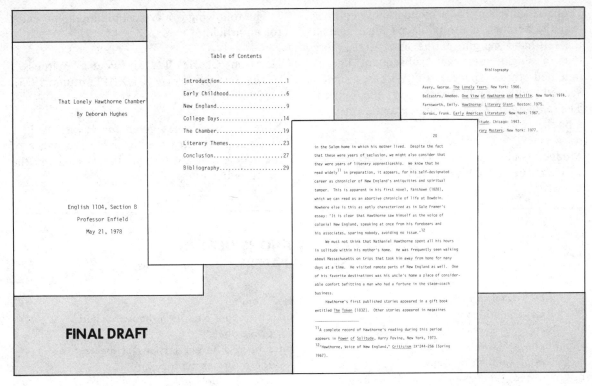

FINAL DRAFT

the paper. Note that the number in the text appears after—without a space between it and the word—and slightly above the word (a half-line on the typewriter).[8]

In footnoting a book, write the following items in the order and form indicated:

1. Author's name in normal order, followed by a comma. Give the name in full unless the author is known by initials.
2. Title of the work, underlined, followed by a comma unless immediately followed by a parenthesis.
3. Place and date of publication, enclosed in parentheses, with the place of publication followed by a comma.
4. Page reference in Arabic numbers. If you are referring to a single page, place the abbreviation "p." before the page number; to more than one page, the abbreviation "pp."

In footnoting an article, you will need the same entries as above, with the addition of the

book or journal in which the article was found. A sample of each type of footnote is supplied for your reference:

Article in a book

[17] Percy Bysshe Shelley, "A Defence of Poetry," *Criticism: The Foundation of Modern Literary Judgment,* eds. Mark Shorer, Josephine Miles, and Gordon McKenzie (New York, 1948), p. 456.

Article in a journal

[18] Ronald Singer, "Emerging Man in Africa," *Natural History,* LXXI (November 1962), 12.

Note the inclusion of the volume number of the journal. Note also the omission of the "p." for page.

The bibliography for a research paper is an alphabetical listing by author's last name of every work cited in the text of the paper or in the footnotes. A bibliography may also include works that aided you in thinking through your paper even though you never cited those works. Be careful not to pad your bibliography by including works you have not read or that were not helpful to you.

---

[8] Mary Wollstonecraft Godwin, *A Vindication of the Rights of Woman* (London, 1792).

The requirement for a bibliographic entry is that the author's name is placed flush against the left-hand margin. If the entry runs more than a single line, each subsequent line is indented three spaces. Entries are single-spaced, with double spaces between entries. The following is a typical bibliographic entry for a book:

Mudge, Isadore Gilbert. *Guide to Reference Books*. 6th ed. Chicago, 1936.

The following is a typical bibliographic entry for an article:

Harrison, Charles T. "The Poet as Witness," *The Sewanee Review*, LXIII (Autumn 1955), 539–550.

Note that the pages given for an article in a bibliographic entry are the inclusive pages of the article and not the number of pages in the entire publication.

COMMON ABBREVIATIONS USED IN RESEARCH PAPERS

c., ca. (circa): about
cf. (confer): compare
cm.: centimeter
ed.: editor, edition, edited by
et al. (et alii): and others
et seq. (et sequens): and the following
f., ff.: the following page(s)
fig.: figure
ibid. (ibidem): in the same place
il., illus.: illustration, illustrated by
loc. cit. (loco citato): in the place cited
MS, MSS: manuscript(s)
n.d.: no date given
n.s.: new series

No.: number
op. cit. (opere citato): in the work cited
p., pp.: page(s)
passim: in different sections of the text; no page or pages cited
q. v. (quod vide): which see
rev.: revised, revised by
s.: series
sic: thus, used in brackets to indicate an apparent error was found thus in the original
sup.: supplement(s)
tr.: translation, translated by
vol., vols.: volume(s)

MANAGING YOUR MONEY

No responsible person can ignore the practical, everyday side of life. All of us must learn to cope with problems of managing income and expenditure. Anyone who does not take these matters seriously lives a life of worry and uncertainty. For these reasons, the following pages deal first with learning to handle and invest your money. Learn these lessons well. The next topic is an explanation of insurance matters, so important today. You then will find valuable information on how to prepare a job resume, a necessary task in getting many types of jobs. Finally, for those who aspire to owning their own businesses, the section closes with information on how to launch a business successfully. Because so many young business ventures fail, the information on this subject cannot be overlooked. Pay special attention to the advice given.

Handling Your Money

No matter how much money you make, without budgeting you can find yourself on a depressing financial treadmill. Millions of Americans spend what they make, borrow as much more as they can, and live out their lives unhappily, trying constantly to keep up with current expenses and debt repayments—simply because they do not plan ahead.

All budgets, whether they are based on your estimates of personal income and expenses, those of a business, or those of the United States government, are similarly organized. Budgets consist of estimates of how much you will earn (usually over a period of a year), how much you will spend over the same period, and whether or not anything will be left over for savings and other investments in the future.

You should figure your budget for each year and refigure it at least every six months to account for major changes in income or expenses that were not clear at the beginning of the year; this would include such things as a raise in pay or change in job on the income side, and such things as a raise in rent or unexpected medical costs on the expense side.

Within each year's figures, you will want to do a personal "cash flow" estimate, much as businesses do in trying to estimate how much cash will come in each year—and when it will be needed. This is important in your budgeting, because some kinds of expenses—like taxes—occur at regular intervals and must be provided for in advance.

A good way to go about budgeting is as follows:

1. Figure your expected income for the year. Let us assume you *take home* $150 per week. That would be $7,800 per year, or $650 per month. That amount is what you have available to spend on *current* expenses. You should not rely on borrowing to meet current expenses. Borrowing should be reserved for such things as houses, education, and other investments in the future.

2. Figure your *fixed expenses* for the year. They will probably include housing, personal and property insurance, automobile insurance and estimated automobile maintenance, loan repayments (if you have any loans outstanding), and property taxes (if you own property).

3. Estimate your *variable expenses* for the year —those expenses over which you have some day-to-day control. They will include such items as food, clothing, personal care items, gasoline, and recreation. Include an estimate of some kinds of costs that are variable, but not really under your control—such as medical and dental costs.

Total your anticipated yearly expenses and subtract them from your anticipated yearly income. If you have some money left, consider putting some of it into a savings account for a "rainy day"; those days always come. If, on the other hand, you find yourself estimating more outgo than income, you will need to go back and start thinking about ways of supplementing income or cutting expenses—or both.

After you have completed the process of figuring the yearly budget, take all the figures you have developed and lay them out on a monthly calendar. It might look something like this:

	Jan	Feb	March	April	May	June	July	Aug	Sept	Oct	Nov	Dec
Income	650	650	650	650	650	650	650	650	650	650	650	650
Expenses	550	550	950	550	850	550	550	750	550	550	550	550
Remainder	100	100	(300)	100	(200)	100	100	(100)	100	100	100	100
Cumulative surplus or deficiency	100	200	(100)	0	(200)	(100)	0	(100)	0	100	200	300

This example shows a surplus of $100 in January, rising to $200 in February. But expenses in March are $300 higher than income (the figures in parentheses are deficits). It could be due to the need to pay some large fixed bill, such as car insurance. That means $100 extra has to be found somewhere in March—from savings, from borrowing, or from supplementary income. The need for more dollars happens also in May, June, and August, but the cumulative year-end total is plus $300. That's "rainy day" money, which can be used to satisfy cash needs in the year ahead.

BANK ACCOUNTS

Savings Accounts. All cash beyond current needs should be put into a savings account. Any banker will be happy to open one for you in about fifteen minutes—even with a starting deposit of as little as five to ten dollars. Your cash will then collect interest, usually from the day it is deposited. And the very existence of your savings account is evidence that you are a responsible person. That can be helpful in securing a loan or any other form of credit.

Checking Accounts. A checking account is a "must." Without one, there is no practical way of handling your money efficiently. Most bills

should be paid by check, for convenience and also because the checks themselves, once cancelled, become evidence that payment has been made.

Banks in many areas offer checking accounts that require little or no minimum deposit and that charge very little for each check used.

When you have a checking account, you must be careful to keep it in good order. A check drawn against insufficient funds will be returned by your bank; this can be a serious matter for your credit rating and sometimes can cause an unpleasant situation between you and the person to whom you have given the check. Sometimes trouble with the law is another consequence of writing a "bad check." The lesson is clear: never knowingly issue a check when you do not have the funds to cover it in your account—even when you think you will surely have enough to cover it the next day.

Handling Your Checkbook. Your checking account can cause you other kinds of problems if you do not keep it carefully. There is nothing quite so destructive of good financial planning as to realize you do not have the hundreds of dollars you thought you had.

Here are a few simple rules to follow in handling your checkbook:

1. Never write a check without immediately filling out the check stub in your book. Note the amount of the check, to whom it was written, the date of the check, and what it was for.
2. Try to avoid checks made out to "cash." If you must make a check out to "cash," be sure to note what it was for at the lower left

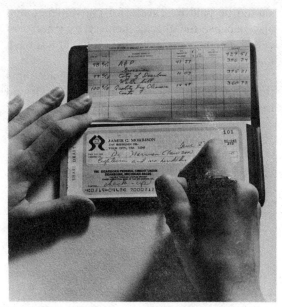

Typical personal check. It is good practice to note on a check the purpose for which it is drawn and to record the full details of every check drawn. Checks can be lost.

corner of the front of the check. Many banks provide checks that include a line for such memos.

3. Do not postdate a check, that is, date it ahead of the present date. Banks will not accept postdated checks. People usually postdate checks because they do not have enough money to cover them at the time the checks are written; if the account still has insufficient funds when the check is presented for payment, the result is a "bounced" check.

4. Record all deposits as carefully as you record checks. Banks make mistakes, and all too often deposits are mishandled. Keep your deposit slips as evidence of deposits made.

5. Carefully examine your monthly bank statements and all cancelled checks. You want to know that all deposits were recorded, that all checks cashed against your account were your checks and have your valid signature on them, and that certain checks are still uncashed. Compare your checkbook with your bank statement for errors on your part or theirs.

6. Always be careful to balance your checkbook on a day-to-day basis. "Balancing" your checkbook is simply a matter of putting in all deposits, subtracting all checks from the total cash in the account as you write the checks, and comparing your checkbook with your bank statement.

BORROWING MONEY

Several things must be remembered when you go out to borrow money:

1. Money borrowed must be paid back—promptly and completely. A borrower who fails to repay or who repays slowly has a hard time borrowing again. A borrower who pays back on time and in full develops a good credit rating and can borrow again.
2. Lenders—banks, loan companies, merchants—belong to credit checking organizations that are able to review your records of payment to others.
3. Interest must be paid on loans, so that you always pay back more than you borrow. The amount of interest charged by different kinds of lenders varies a good deal.
4. Lenders base decisions on whether or not to lend you money on your previous credit record, on your current money situation, on your overall assets, and on evaluation of your character. That is why it is important to have a record of borrowing and paying back, even if you borrow small amounts.

It is a good idea to open a savings or checking account (or both) in a bank you think you may want to borrow from one day. And it is important to have money in those accounts when you attempt to borrow—which means not waiting to request a loan until you are out of money. Successful borrowing often depends on advance planning—the kind of budgeting, for example, that we previously discussed.

It is also a good idea, when you walk into a bank to borrow money, to be dressed neatly. Lenders often base personal loan decisions on a little evidence of financial responsibility and a lot of personal character estimates.

KINDS OF LENDERS AND LOANS

Banks. Two kinds of loans are most commonly made by banks:

1. Loans for a specific time, and often for a specific purpose, such as:
   a. Personal loans on the basis of your signature, involving a promise by you to repay over a period of time—usually one to three years, with repayments monthly. You state how you plan to spend the money as part of the loan application.
   b. Automobile purchase loans, in which repayment is promised by you and backed by the value of the car. If you don't pay, the bank gets the car—but you will still have to pay for any balance still due after the car has been repossessed and sold at auction.
   c. Education loans to students, which are often guaranteed by federal and state funds. Such loans carry very low rates of interest and long terms of repayment.

2. The line of credit, in which the bank extends you credit up to a stated amount. You may use the credit or not, or use it for whatever purposes you wish. As you repay, usually a small percentage of the total amount owed monthly, your credit "revolves"; that is, it moves upward toward the top limit available again. For example, when a bank issues you a credit card (VISA, Mastercharge) with a credit limit of $500, the bank has given you a line of credit of $500. Personal lines of credit often go as high as $5,000, sometimes higher. Business lines of credit can go much higher.

Interest rates vary greatly for different kinds of loans and lenders. Always ask the lender what the *real rate of interest* is on a loan you are asking for. You will generally find that loans secured by collateral (real things, like cars and homes and certain kinds of stocks and bonds) carry the lowest real interest rates. Personal loans, loans made just on your own signature (promise to pay), are more expensive. Lines of credit are usually most expensive.

Credit cards make it possible to avoid carrying large amounts of cash, but you must remember that any charge made with one of these cards means a debt to be repaid.

Merchants. When you buy a refrigerator, open a charge account at a department store, or finance a car directly with the seller, you are borrowing money. The merchant who sells you the refrigerator is really lending you the purchase price of the refrigerator and charging you interest, just as if you had borrowed money from a bank and paid for the refrigerator in cash.

Interest charges tend to be as high on these kinds of purchases as on lines of credit. You are usually better off financing major purchases with lower cost bank loans or cash.

Loan Companies. Millions of Americans borrow money from loan companies, often because they feel they cannot get bank loans, but sometimes because they do not realize that loan company interest charges are higher than bank interest charges.

Always try to borrow from a bank before going to a loan company. If you must use a loan company, borrow as little as possible and for as short a term as possible. The interest charges can be a heavy financial drain.

Investing Your Money

In considering what to do with any money you have that may be available for investment, there are some fundamental facts to understand and there are questions to ask yourself.

It is basic to the nature of our economy that available money must either be invested or it will lose value. Inflation is a long-term, constant, irreversible trend. Look at an 1898 Sears Roebuck catalogue and you will see prices that seem astonishingly low. But it is not that the prices are low—the dollar then bought a great deal more than it buys today. Therefore, if you have a hundred dollars and put the money away in your attic or under your bed, you are guaranteeing that in ten to fifteen years it will have lost half its value or more and will buy only what fifty cents or less will buy today.

It is equally basic that the higher the interest rate promised on an investment, the riskier the investment. If an investment looks too good to be true, the chances are a hundred to one that it really is too good to be true. There are thousands of professional investment advisors and large investors looking for investment opportunities all the time, which means that interest rates will always continue to reflect the relative attractiveness and safety of the investment.

Here are some questions that apply to any investment you may want to make.

1. How much of a risk are you willing to take? If the money you are investing is vital to you —money that is intended for education, housing, retirement, or other long-term goals—then you must not invest it in anything risky. That rules out adventuring in any but the safest stocks and bonds of large corporations, and points you mainly toward savings accounts, government bonds, and similar low-interest, high-safety investments.

2. Can you invest and leave the money alone, or is it possible that you may need to use the money for something else soon? If the answer is that you cannot just leave the money alone, then you cannot think of such long-term investments as land. Land may be hard to sell just when you need to sell it. You will probably prefer investments that can be turned easily into cash.

3. Do you know what you are investing in or are you just taking the word of somebody else? The country is full of unhappy former high-flying stock market investors who did not understand what they were investing in and lost their money when the stock market went bad in the late sixties and early seventies.

KINDS OF INVESTMENTS

Savings Accounts. These are old-fashioned and safe. They yield modest but respectable rates of interest, ranging from about five and one-half percent at commercial banks for ordinary accounts to as much as eight percent at some savings institutions for long-term accounts.

Buying and selling stock

There are two types of markets in which stock is traded: the securities exchange and the over-the-counter market. The most widely used and best known are the security exchanges, particularly the New York Stock Exchange on Wall Street, called the "Big Board." To have its stock traded on an exchange, that is, to be "listed," a company must meet specifications: it must have issued a certain number of shares, have a minimum number of stockholders, and have a specified dollar value. If a company cannot or does not want to have its stock listed on an exchange, that company has "unlisted" stocks, traded over the counter.

Buying and selling stock is easy. Simply telephone a stockbroker. He will make it possible for you to do business with someone you have never met and probably never will, someone who may live thousands of miles away.

Let's say that Peter, who lives in San Francisco, decides he wants to buy 100 shares of Consolidated Gas, Inc., a stock listed on the Big Board. He has checked his newspaper and found that it was selling for $20 at the time the market closed the day before.

Peter simply dials his broker to see what the price is at the moment. (There is no fixed price for stock, as there is for a loaf of bread at the supermarket.) His broker responds: "20 to a quarter." This means that the figure at which people are willing to buy is $20, and the figure at which they will sell is $20.25. Thus when Peter agrees to buy 100 shares at the market price, all he knows is that the price will be the best possible between $20 and $20.25.

Meanwhile, Paul, who lives in New Orleans, decides he wants to sell 100 shares of Consolidated Gas to pay for his new car. He calls his broker, who gives him the same quote: "$20 to a quarter." As he places the order to sell, he too makes a commitment to sell at whatever the market price is at the instant of sale.

The brokerage firm acting for Paul contacts its representative in the New York Stock Exchange, who tells the firm's floor trader to sell the 100 shares. The trader goes to the trading post on the floor of the exchange where Consolidated Gas is traded. (Each trading post, which is similar to a booth in a bazaar, has a specialist who auctions off a few kinds of stock.) There he may meet the trader who represents Peter's firm.

Each broker is committed to try to get the best price he can for his clients. Peter's trader could pay $20.25 a share, but instead tries to get the price down a little by bidding 20⅛. Paul's trader could sell the stock at $20, but instead, considering 20⅛ a good price, snaps up the offer by replying: "Sold at 20⅛."

Thus two men have made a $2,012.50 deal without ever having met each other. Of course, they must each pay a commission to the broker.

The following chart is typical of how stocks are listed in daily newspapers.

1		2	3	4		5	6	7	8	9
12—Month High	Low	Stock	Div	Yld %	PE Ratio	Sales 100s	High	Low	Last	Chg.
18⅞	16½	GiantP	1.20	7.0	4	x22	17¼	16¾	17¼	+ ⅝
12¾	5½	GntYell	.15e	1.3	19	119	11½	11¼	11⅜	− ¼
5⅞	4½	Glasrock		..	..	1	4⅞	4⅞	4⅞	.....
20¾	15⅝	Glatfltr	.98	5.2	6	14	19	18¾	19	+ ¼
17	10⅜	Glnmr	.50	4.2	6	27	12	11⅝	12	+ ⅝
16⅝	11⅛	Globeln	.70	5.7	5	1	12¼	12¼	12¼	+ ⅛
21⅜	6⅞	GloucstE		..	238	1	21⅜	21⅜	21⅜	.....
3⅝	2	Glover	.10e	3.2	..	7	3⅛	3⅛	3⅛	+ ⅛
4½	3½	Gldblatt	.20	5.7	9	32	3½	3½	3½	.....
15	10⅛	GoldnCyc		..	42	5	12¾	12⅝	12⅝	− ⅜
19¾	9⅜	GoldnW	.85e	4.4	6	43	19⅜	18⅜	19¼	+1
1½	⅝	Goldfield		..	..	16	1	⅞	1	+1-16
3	1½	GoodLS		..	13	3	2¾	2¾	2¾	.....
8⅞	2¼	Gdrich wt		..	..	5	2⅜	2¼	2⅜	+ ⅛
24¼	19¾	GormR	1	4.5	8	104	22⅜	22	22	− ¼
8½	5¼	GrandAu	.30	4.3	12	56	7	6¾	7	+ ⅜
9	6⅝	GrndCtl	.40	4.9	5	13	8¼	8⅛	8⅛	+ ⅛
13	7¾	GrangrA		..	9	16	11¾	11⅜	11⅝	− ⅛
7½	5⅜	GtAmInd		..	4	4	6½	6⅜	6½	.....

1. Highest and lowest prices paid for the stock during the year.
2. Abbreviated name of the company.
3. Amount of quarterly dividend paid on each share.
4. Price-earnings ratio.
5. Sales in 100s.
6. Highest price for the day.
7. Lowest price for the day.
8. Price for which the stock sold in the last transaction of the day.
9. Change in the closing price that day compared with the previous business day.

Government Bonds and Other Federal Government Investments. Normally, these yield low interest but are extremely safe ways of saving and investing your surplus cash. But beware of state and municipal bonds—some are safe but many are not, as cities and states run into financial trouble in many parts of the country.

Corporate Bonds. These tend to yield more interest than savings accounts and government investments, but are somewhat riskier.

Corporate Stocks. Corporate stocks can be good investments, depending on the corporation, the condition of the economy, and other factors. Or they can be bad investments, as so many have found out in recent years. Look be-fore you leap, and if you decide to invest in the stock market, do so by buying stocks listed on a major exchange, preferably the stocks of major and well-established American corporations. Ask your local banker, accountant, or lawyer to recommend a stockbroker; then ask the stockbroker which companies you ought to invest in; then get as much information as you can before risking your money.

Commodities, Commodity Futures, and Collectables. Commodities, commodity futures, and collectables like art and silver plate are best left for professional investors. There is always some new investment game around, the "surefire way to make a million dollars" that is only sure to lose your money.

Insurance

There are types of insurance for just about all the risks people face. The following are the main forms of insurance common in our country at this time:

Unemployment Insurance. This form of insurance has been increasingly widespread since the Great Depression of the 1930s. It guarantees a person some period of income after he or she has lost a job through no fault of the individual. (You have to work for some months in order to qualify for payments.) Unemployment insurance funds are supported by contributions from both employers and employees. It is important to employees that their employers withhold unemployment insurance and other withholding taxes from their paychecks, so that laid-off employees are sure of getting their unemployment payments if they are unable to find new jobs immediately.

Social Security. It is called "old age and survivor's insurance" and is usually payable on reaching the age of sixty-five, although under some circumstances it can be payable earlier. Social Security is administered by the federal government and funded by contributions from employers, employees, and the self-employed.

Workmen's Compensation. When someone is hurt on, or because of, his or her job, this kind of insurance pays some of the medical and other disability-connected bills. It is funded by payments from employers, employees, and the self-employed.

Life Insurance. Life insurance is mostly death insurance. Its main function is to provide cash for your loved ones after you die. There are three principal kinds of life insurance:

1. Life insurance that pays a specified amount if you die, and which also accumulates a savings account from the yearly premiums you pay to keep up the insurance. This is called whole life insurance, and the savings account portion is called cash surrender value, meaning the amount you are paid if you cancel the insurance after paying premiums on it for some years. Whole life insurance is usually bought by individuals. Premium payment rates are usually fixed at the time of purchase and remain the same for as long as the insurance is kept in force.
2. Life insurance that pays a specified amount if you die, but has no savings account feature. Premium payments are much lower than those for whole life insurance. This is usually called term insurance, because it typically runs for several years at one premium rate, and then for the next several years at a somewhat higher premium rate. It is the form of life insurance most often used by employers and associations when supplying group insurance to employees and members.
3. Life insurance that is basically a savings account, but which has a death insurance feature, called annuities. Typically, you pay a relatively high premium on an annuity and build up a substantial savings account. If you die before the annuity savings account has fully built up for payment to you, then your beneficiaries get the full amount of the annuity, as if you had lived to collect it.

Hospital and Surgical Insurance.   Insurance that usually pays hospital room, board, and associated charges, as well as all or part of in-hospital surgical charges from doctors and other medical professionals. Such insurance is sometimes privately purchased, sometimes provided by employers as a part of job-connected benefits.

Major Medical Insurance.   Insurance that takes over where hospital and surgical insurance leaves off. It is catastrophe insurance to provide for cases in which hospital and surgical insurance pays for a stated amount of hospital bills and then runs out, while the expense of hospitalization continues. It is often provided as a part of job-connected benefits, but many people buy their own personal policies besides, since company plans usually terminate when employment ends. Major medical insurance requires a physical examination before a private company will insure you, and it is possible to leave a job, lose your major medical coverage, and not be well enough to qualify for new coverage—which can be a financial disaster if you encounter a major health problem.

Salary Continuance Insurance.   Medical insurance of all kinds is inadequate to cover one of the main costs of illness—the loss of salary or wages. Therefore, some people buy insurance policies that will pay them a specific amount each week for a number of months or years if they are unable to work.

Fire Insurance.   If you own a home, you will need to have fire insurance on the house and its contents if you want to get a mortgage. The holder of the mortgage will probably require you to keep that insurance in force. If you live in rental housing, fire insurance protection is equally important. Fire insurance payments rarely cover the full value of property lost, but are often enough to enable you to rebuild, purchase new belongings, and get a fresh start.

Automobile Insurance.   Most states require automobile insurance coverage if you own a car. Even if it is not required, you should consider it a necessity, as the main function of auto insurance is to cover injury to people—yourself and those involved with you in any accident. Its secondary function is to protect against property loss.

Wills.   In a sense, making a will is a kind of insurance—that your loved ones will not want for the necessities of life because you were negligent. Without a valid will, whatever you leave behind can be tied up in the courts for months and even years, while much that should go to your heirs will instead go to cover legal costs. If you do not have a will and have a family, go to a lawyer and have one drawn up.

Going into Business

Millions of Americans go into business at some time in their lives. Some do well. Most do not and are out of business after a short time—savings gone, back at work for someone else, wondering where they went wrong. In our country it is quite natural for people to want to go into business. It is undesirable to do so without full preparation.

Here are some questions to ask yourself before you make the decision to go into business:

1. Are you the right kind of person to go into business? It means long hours, probably low pay for a long time and many worries you would not have if you were working for someone else. Do you want to be in business badly enough to cope with all that?
2. Do you have any experience in the kind of business you want to go into? It is economic suicide to go into a business you know nothing about. The country is full of good cooks who thought they could run restaurants but didn't know the restaurant business. If you want to go into a business, study it and work for someone else for as long as it takes to learn what you need to know.
3. Do you have enough money? If not, can you get enough without endangering your whole future? In fact, do you really know how much money you will need to do it right? You will need savings and often loans from family and friends besides. You will probably need a friendly banker, with whom you should discuss the whole business before

you go into it. A sound banker's advice may be invaluable when considering a business, and a banker who has thought well of you is an excellent source of loans.
4. Have you carefully studied the town, the neighborhood, and the street where you mean to go into business? Will you be locating in an up-and-coming area? Are others nearby, in similar businesses, doing well?
5. If you're buying a going business, have you had a competent accountant, one who is experienced in buying and selling businesses, look over every aspect of the proposed purchase? Are you satisfied that you understand every aspect of the proposed transaction yourself?
6. Have you had a lawyer examine the necessary licenses, titles, zoning approvals, and the like, to ensure against potentially crippling legal problems?
7. Have you made adequate arrangements with your suppliers before getting started?
8. Have you made detailed plans for advertising, pricing, buying—all the specifics of the business?

If the answers to these basic questions are all a resounding "yes," then you may indeed be able to go into business.

HOW TO ORGANIZE

There are three major ways in which a business can be owned and organized: individual proprietorship, partnership, and corporation.

Proprietorship. If the owner of the business is one individual who has invested capital in it, it is an individual proprietorship. Anybody can go into this kind of business. No legal agreements or documents are required. All profits belong to the owner (who must pay taxes on them when paying personal income tax), and all losses are the owner's responsibility. The question of loss is one of the biggest drawbacks of the single proprietorship: the owner has unlimited liability; that is, if the business fails, creditors may sue and take all personal possessions—savings, house, automobile, etc.

In number, individual proprietorships dominate American business. There are virtually millions of small enterprises that do less than $100 worth of business a day, started by people who have only a few thousand dollars of capital. Unfortunately, only a few succeed, for if there are no initial profits (and usually there are none), the business is finished whenever the capital is used up—unless, of course, more capital can be borrowed or gotten in some other way. Borrowing venture capital is very difficult, as banks would rather not risk lending money to unproven enterprises.

Partnership. If ownership in a business is divided between two or more persons who put up the capital, take the risks, and divide the profits, it is a partnership. In most partnership agreements, each partner agrees to provide some of the work. If, for example, Bob puts up $20,000 and Ted puts up $60,000 to start the Ace Deodorant Co., and both agree to work for the firm, Bob might receive $5,000 a year for his services and one-third of the profits, while Ted would receive $15,000 a year and two-thirds of the profits.

One of the best ways for a single proprietor in financial trouble to find money is to find a partner. For example, Helen, who started Prima Deodorants five years before, might ask Bob to invest his $20,000 in her company. The partnership agreement may be the same, but Helen puts up her factory, inventory, know how, good will, and so on, all worth $60,000.

As in proprietorships, there is unlimited liability in partnerships—no protection from creditors if the business goes bankrupt. In fact, each person is liable to the full extent of his fortune for *all* debts contracted by the partnership. So if a partnership goes under, all partners are expected to pay the debts according to the percentage of their interest, but if they cannot, those with the smaller percentages still are liable for what the other partners owe. If Bob and Ted's Ace Deodorant Co. goes bankrupt, Bob is liable for one-third of the debts and Ted for two-thirds. But if after Ted sells his jewelry, home, automobiles, and all of his personal effects, he cannot pay his portion, then Bob is responsible for the debt, even if he must sell all his personal effects to cover it.

Another disadvantage to the partnership is that each time a partner enters or leaves the firm, a new agreement must be drawn up. Thus, as companies grow and more partners are admitted (and there may be one hundred or so), the ritual of drawing up the new agreements becomes cumbersome and time-consuming.

Either one of these disadvantages may be reason enough to look into the advantages of the corporation.

Corporation. A corporation is an association of individuals that by law is considered a separate entity or "person" with a life of its own apart from that of its members. It has rights and duties, just like individuals. It can own property. It is liable for its debts. It may enter into contracts. It can be sued, but it is entitled to "due process" and "equal protection" under the law.

To incorporate, a business must receive a charter from the state in which it is located or has an office. The ownership is then divided into shares of stock, each having an initial stated value, called "par value." Individuals share in the ownership according to the number of shares they hold. They also get to share in the management of the company with their vote (usually each share gives its owner one vote) and to receive some of the corporate earnings in the form of dividends.

There are several advantages to the corporation, which account for the fact that today nearly all but the smallest businesses in the United States are incorporated. The most important is "limited liability." After the investor

A good business letter is short and to the point. It conserves the time of reader and writer. Here is a typical letter, with explanatory notes.

```
                                    Smith Homewares
                                    22 Willow Way
                                    Grand Rapids, Michigan 30405
                                    Tel: 999-666-1212
                                                                        ——— a

                                                    June 10, 1978        ——— b


Mr. John E. Alexander
Vice President                                                           ——— c
Alexander Home Products, Inc.
2222 Cadillac Street
Detroit, Michigan 30303

Dear Mr. Alexander:

Thank you for your letter of June 1, explaining your policy on _____  ——— d
quantity orders of your Jiffy-Alexander electric can openers.

            four dozen openers.  We understand that by ordering    _____ ——— e
            we will qualify for your 10% discount.

            local representative call me so that we can arrange     _____ ——— f
            ation of your complete microwave oven line.  Tuesday
            nings are best for me.

                            Sincerely,                                   ——— g

                            Mary Smith

                            Mary Smith                                    ——— h
                            President
```

```
        Smith Homewares
        22 Willow Way
        Grand Rapids, Michigan 30405




                Mr. John E. Alexander
                Vice President
                Alexander Home Products, Inc.
                2222 Cadillac Street
                Detroit, Michigan 30303
```

a This is a company letterhead, which supplies the recipient of the letter with the name, address, and telephone number of the business. It is usually a printed form, on which the letter is typed.

b Always include the date of the letter.

c Full name of the individual to whom the letter is sent, full title, and full address of the company, including zip code. If the person addressed is a woman, it is often best to use Ms., rather than Miss or Mrs., unless you know the individual prefers Miss or Mrs.

This is also the way the outside of the envelope will be typed.

d The first paragraph refers clearly to previous correspondence, by date and subject.

e The second paragraph orders a specific amount of merchandise and clearly states Mary Smith's understanding of the terms of the order.

f The third paragraph makes a new and specific request, and states a preferred time.

g "Sincerely" is one preferred form. "Sincerely yours" or "Yours sincerely" is also acceptable. More personal forms, like "Cordially," are used when people know each other well. "Very truly yours" is formal and suggests a lawyer's letter rather than a business letter.

h The sender's name is always typed under the signature. Many signatures are hard to read, and some are impossible.

```
                          JOHN A. SMITH
                          222 North Adams Street
a                         Stamford, Connecticut  10222
                          Tel: 201-222-333

b   Objective             To obtain a job in outside selling.

c   Work                  Automobile salesman
    Experience            Merlyn Agency
                          105 Dean Street
    7/75-6/77             Stamford, Connecticut  10242
                          Reported to Mr. Jack Jones, Sales Manager.

                          In this Ford agency, I sold the entire Ford line.
                          Received Ford Certificate of Achievement for 1977.

    6/74-8/74             Salesman
                          Stone's Bargain Mart
                          633 17th Street
                          Stamford, Connecticut  10242

d                         I worked as a clothing salesman at Stone's,
                          both in the summer and part-time during the school year.

    Education             Associate in Arts degree
    1973-75               Fairfield Community College
                          100 First Avenue
                          Norwalk, Connecticut  10444

e                         Major:   Distribution
                          Clubs:   Vice-President Distribution Club 1975
                          Sports:  Captain of intramural basketball team

    1969-73               Andrews High School
                          111 Second Street
                          Stamford, Connecticut  10333

                          Honors:   Honor Roll every year
                          Clubs:    Automobile, Rifle and Archery Clubs
                          Sports:   Varsity basketball, Rifle team

f   Special               My major skills are in selling and marketing.  I have
    Skills                trained, and feel that I have developed considerable
                          skill in many aspects of selling in two years of
                          successful selling experience.

    Personal              Born August 1, 1953, Stamford, Connecticut.
                          Parents both living.  Father owns garage.

g   References            Available on request.
```

a Full information here, including zip code and telephone area code.

b Try to make your job objective as clear and specific as you can.

c Your work experience includes where you worked and what you did. In this instance, it includes evidence that you did it well—the Certificate of Achievement. You will often want to include the name of someone who can be called upon to verify the information given—in this instance, Jack Jones.

d By all means put in summer and part-time jobs. They tell a prospective employer that you have been working, have held jobs, have some "get up and go."

e Include honors, clubs, sports—anything that will show you are a bright, active, and successful person.

f Focus on skills that show you to be well suited for the kind of job you want.

g Family information helps an employer understand that you are a stable person and come from a stable background.

A good resume tells prospective employers:

Who you are and where you can be reached.

What sort of job you are looking for.

What your previous work experience has been.

What your education has been and where it was secured.

What special skills you have to offer.

What special interests you have that may indicate you would be a good person for the job.

Something of your personal history.

pays for a share of stock, his risk-taking is over. The investor-owner need not worry about losing his personal fortune if the venture fails; all he can possibly lose is his original investment. Because stock owners are legally protected, the corporation in need of capital finds it relatively easy to float and sell new stock.

The profits of a corporation are taxed as a separate entity at a high rate. In addition, owners of stock pay a personal income tax on the dividends they receive. In recent years, corporate profits have been taxed more than 50 percent. Although there are tax loopholes that corporations can take advantage of, the small corporation often finds it hard to survive with heavy tax burdens.

Protecting Yourself As A Consumer

People who buy goods and services have much more protection than they did as recently as twenty years ago. The old rule, "Let the buyer beware," has given way to "Let the buyer be careful—but there are laws to protect you if you're not as careful as you ought to be."

Here are some of the most important consumer protection basics:

1. You are protected against deceptive and incomplete labeling of many products by a series of laws enacted in the sixties and seventies. If you buy a product on the basis of a description you later feel was false, you have the right to complain to the seller, to the manufacturer, to the local Better Business Bureau, to any local consumer protection organizations, to the Federal Trade Commission, or Bureau of Consumer Protection in Washington, and to request a refund.
2. Lenders are required by the Truth in Lending Law to state the real rate of interest on all loans.
3. Employers cannot fire you simply because your wages have been garnisheed (to garnishee is to take an amount out of every pay-

check by court order to satisfy debts). And only a small portion of your wages can be garnisheed at all.
4. There are a number of protections in connection with automobile sales, including prohibition of such fraudulent practices as turning back the odometer of a used car before selling it.

Read labels carefully. These two look similar but tell different stories. The sauce with real meat weighs one ounce less than the other.

GLOSSARY OF MONEY AND BUSINESS TERMS

accounting. The science of organizing, classifying, and summarizing business records. An accountant determines the method used to keep the books and evaluates the financial condition of an enterprise.

annuity. Insurance policy paying a fixed sum per year after recipient of proceeds of policy reaches a specified age.

appreciation. Increase in value. Often used to describe a rise in the value of land, houses, or other substantial property.

appraisal. Formal estimate of the value of property of any kind, usually by a certified professional appraiser.

assets. The property or resources of a business, that is, the value of the things the business owns or has owed to it in contrast to the liabilities or amounts owed to others. The excess of assets over liabilities is called net worth.

audit. Careful, thorough independent verification of accounting figures, usually by a professional accountant.

balance sheet. A statement of the assets (carried on the left-hand side of the balance sheet) and liabilities (carried on the right side) of a business at a particular time, derived from a double-entry bookkeeping system after the books have been closed and the accounts summarized. The purpose of a balance sheet is to show the financial status and the net worth of the company.

bankruptcy. Court proceeding in which businesses or individuals are declared unable to meet their debts. The court then either (1) takes over any business or personal assets that can by law be taken and distributes them proportionally among the creditors; or (2) tries to help a business work out its problems under court supervision, forcing creditors to wait for payment until the business can operate successfully.

bill of lading. Document that lists all goods in a shipment, as certified by a shipping company.

bond. A device used by corporations, individuals, or governments to borrow money. It is basically an IOU or promissory note, usually issued in multiples of $1000 (though $50 or $100 bonds are not uncommon); the corporation promises to pay the bondholder a stated amount of interest for a specified length of time and to repay the loan on the expiration date. A bondholder is not the same as a shareholder of a corporation; a bondholder is a creditor, while a shareholder is a part owner.

broker. Anyone who buys and sells for others, usually for a percentage of the value of the goods sold.

bookkeeping. The keeping of systematic, concise, and convenient records of the financial transactions of a company. Unlike the accountant, who analyzes the financial records of a business, the bookkeeper simply maintains the accounting records, or books, of a business. The most modern system of bookkeeping is the double-entry system, which requires two entries for each transaction—one a debit and the other a credit. Single-entry bookkeeping is an easier method, practical only for very small businesses; only one entry is made for each transaction.

capital. In general, wealth, whether in money or property, owned and used to produce more money (interest) or something of value. In business, capital is the money and credit needed to start and operate an enterprise or the total wealth or assets of a firm, including such intangible assets as securities, trademarks, patents, good will, etc.

A distinction is frequently made between fixed capital, funds used for fixed assets (buildings, machinery, land, timber preserves, and the like), and working capital, funds needed to carry on business. Capital can also refer to the excess of assets over liability, the net worth of an enterprise.

cash flow. Amount of money moving through a business in a given time, including all cash received and all cash spent. A *cash flow statement* shows all sources of cash received and all amounts of cash spent in any period.

caveat emptor (Latin, "let the buyer beware"). A merchandising maxim summarizing the common-law rule that the buyer must examine, judge, and test his purchase to see that he is getting the quantity and quality expected. *Caveat venditor* (Latin, "let the seller beware") is a merchandising maxim placing responsibility on the seller for any defects or deficiencies in items sold.

collective bargaining. Process of labor contract negotiation between employers and employees.

contract. Legally binding agreement, in writing, signed by those making the agreement.

co-signer. One who guarantees that a loan made to someone else will be repaid, by signing the note between lender and borrower.

deflation. A general fall in the level of prices of goods and services that, in effect, increases the value of money. Though beneficial to creditors and to those with fixed incomes and large savings (whose money can purchase more in real terms), deflation usually brings about increased unemployment of both labor and capital.

dividend. A specified amount of money paid (usually every quarter) to the stockholders of a corporation for each share of stock they hold. The payment is made to distribute the profits of the corporation; its amount is determined by the board of directors.

fiscal year. A corporation accounting year. It can be any period of twelve consecutive months (not necessarily the calendar year) chosen for annual financial reporting.

gross national product. The total output of goods and services of a country, stated at market prices for a given year. In the United States, as defined by the Department of Commerce, the GNP is the total market value of the goods and services produced by the nation's economy, before deduction of depreciation charges and other allowances for capital consumption.

income statement. A summary of the income and expenses of a business, showing the revenues, expenses, and net profit or net loss during the period (usually one year) covered by the report. An income statement is also sometimes called an operating statement or a profit and loss statement.

inflation. Persistent general upward movement of the prices for commodities and factors of production. An inflationary spiral occurs when prices rise; wages and salaries rise to compensate for the higher cost of living; prices and wages rise again and again.

interest. The charge made for the loan of money. It is usually a percentage of the principal, the amount borrowed.

liabilities. The debts of a business or an individual.

over the counter. A market for securities not listed with securities exchanges; transactions are made directly between dealers (usually by telephone) who act as principals or brokers for customers. Stocks so traded are called over-the-counter stocks.

price/earnings ratio. The current market price of a share of stock divided by its most recently stated yearly profits. For example, a stock selling for $10.00 per share, with profits of $1.00 per year, has a price/earnings ratio of 10:1.

stock. A share in the ownership of a corporation. When stock is purchased, the buyer is really investing his money in the corporation and becomes its part owner, with the right to share in the profits through dividends and usually to exercise some control over the corporation's policies through the election of directors.

There are two kinds of stock, common and preferred. Preferred has preference over other stocks of the same company with regard to dividend payments and distribution of assets if the company liquidates. Common stock does not have prior claim on dividends and assets in case of liquidation, but usually it is the only class of stock with voting rights in the management of the company.

statute of limitations. Law fixing the time beyond which no legal action can be taken. This varies according to the kind of action, with a range of three to seven years on most kinds of commercial matters.

stock exchange. An organized market where members buy and sell listed securities according to established rules. The primary purpose of the stock market is to bring together all buyers and sellers and increase the marketability of the securities listed on that exchange.

VOCATIONAL ARTS

Teaching the practical things we like to do for ourselves has long been one of the tasks of American education. Courses in woodworking, metal trades, automotive repair, and the like are taught widely today in high schools and adult schools. If you have an interest or skill in one of these trades or in secretarial work or cosmetology, you will find much practical information in the following pages.

In practicing any one of these skills, you must always plan before you begin work, know as much as possible about the materials and equipment you will use, and sharpen your dexterity and technique until you achieve full proficiency. You may find, as so many others have, that pursuing one of these areas as a hobby may become so satisfying that you will want to turn it into your life work.

Industrial Arts

An industrial society needs imaginative designers and skilled technicians, but it also needs a great number of persons who understand how things work. Such a society—the United States, for example—needs men and women who know what all the tools of manufacturing are, who understand the materials used in manufacturing, and who can think in terms of processes, products, and all the activities related to the production of goods to satisfy consumer demand.

For these reasons, career education in the industrial arts no longer runs on narrow tracks. Instead it stresses occupational clusters. One such cluster is that of materials—wood, metal, and plastics—and the manufacture of products made from them. Anyone who wishes to become skilled in this or any other area should prepare for jobs requiring *a cluster of related skills and knowledge*. With such a background, a skilled worker can roll with the punches that come from the replacement of tools—and jobs—because of technological advance.

WORKING WITH WOOD, METAL, AND PLASTICS

An important fact to understand in working with wood, metal, and plastics is that the concepts of the production processes are similar. The operations of cutting, forming, shaping, assembling, and finishing are practically identical throughout industry. Understanding that this and similar principles can be transferred to any

material is fundamental to a student's progress.

The information in this section begins with a discussion of the raw materials and goes on to the fundamental techniques, basic tools and machines, and final finishing methods.

Woods

There are four basic types: *hardwoods, softwoods, plywood,* and *hardboard*. Hardwoods come from deciduous, or broadleaf, trees; softwoods, from coniferous, or evergreen, trees. Plywood is made from thin layers of wood glued face to face. Hardboard is made from softwood pulp compressed into boards.

Hardwoods.   Hardwoods are more durable than other types of wood. One of their chief uses is in making furniture. They tend to be more expensive than other types of wood. The principal hardwoods are:

- *Mahogany,* a reddish-brown, fine-grained wood widely used for cabinet making. It resists swelling and warping and has low shrinkage. Mahogany is strong yet easy to work, and its grain produces a number of different figures, depending on how it is cut.
- *Teak,* a heavy, durable wood, extremely resistant to decay. Teak has very little shrinkage and resists warping. It is used in boat construction, especially for decks; its moisture-resistant qualities have made it popular for household items such as trays and bowls.

- *Oak,* a durable wood, excellent for bending, turning, and shaping. Although oak does not absorb moisture, its resistance to shrinkage, swelling, and warping is not high. White oak has a high resistance to decay. Oak is used for furniture, floors, and interior trim, as well as for barrels and handles.
- *Maple,* a fine-textured, strong wood, with good shaping qualities and good shock resistance. Moderate resistance to shrinking, swelling, and warping. Maple is used for floors and furniture and for chopping blocks.
- *Walnut,* a strong, fine-textured wood, easier to work and more resistant to shrinkage, swelling, and warping than oak or maple. Resistant to decay. Used in furniture and cabinet work, in paneling, and for gunstocks.
- *Cherry,* a close-grained wood, resistant to warping. Cherry is prized for furniture and cabinet work because it ages well and tends to turn red.
- *Hickory* includes true hickory and pecan hickory. True hickory is a hard, heavy, strong wood, highly resistant to shock; its most important use is in tool handles. Pecan wood does not have this quality, but its texture makes it useful for furniture and paneling.
- *Elm,* a hard, heavy, strong, shock-resistant wood, not particularly resistant to shrinkage, swelling, warping, or decay. Chiefly used for boxes, crates, and furniture.
- *Ash,* a heavy, stiff, tough wood. White ash is used to make baseball bats and long handles for tools. Other types of ash are used for furniture and interiors.

Other furniture hardwoods include beech; birch, which bends well; and rosewood, a fragrant wood that takes a high polish and is used in musical instruments, veneers, inlay work, carved casket boxes, and similar items.

Softwoods. Softwoods tend to be knottier than hardwoods, and softwood lumber tends to be rough or split at the ends. Principal softwoods are:

- *Redwood,* a medium-hard wood that is exceptionally resistant to decay, rot, moisture, shrinkage, swelling, and warping. These qualities make it suitable for such uses as lawn furniture, siding, and fencing.
- *Cedar,* an easy-to-work wood; resistant to shrinkage, swelling, warping, and decay. Eastern red cedar is quite hard, suitable for fenceposts; its reddish color and its fragrance also make it suitable for chests and closet linings, since its fragrance repels moths.
- *Fir* includes true fir and Douglas fir. True fir is a soft, light wood that takes a good finish but has little resistance to decay. It is widely used for shipping containers and interior trim. Douglas fir is strong, stiff, and rather hard. It is widely used for frames, windows, and doors.
- *Spruce,* a strong, light wood, somewhat harder than fir and similar uses.
- *Pine,* a soft, light wood, resistant to shrinkage, swelling, and warping. Most species are easy to work; the chief exception is the Southern yellow pine, which is harder than other pines. Pine is used in building construction, shelving, and similar applications.

Wood frame for a new house. Sheathing, often of plywood, is placed over the framing members. Since plywood resists twisting and bending, it adds strength. In this use, plywood saves installation time and cost and provides a good nailing surface when adding roofing and siding.

WOODWORKING TOOLS

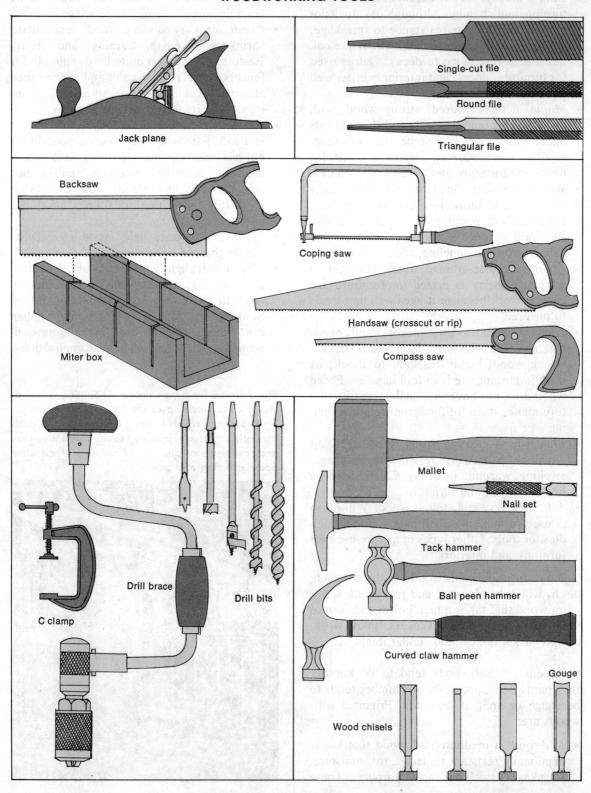

Jack plane

Single-cut file

Round file

Triangular file

Backsaw

Coping saw

Miter box

Handsaw (crosscut or rip)

Compass saw

C clamp

Drill brace

Drill bits

Mallet

Nail set

Tack hammer

Ball peen hammer

Curved claw hammer

Wood chisels

Gouge

Plywoods. Plywoods are made from thin sheets of wood glued face to face. An odd number of sheets is always used, and the grains run in alternate directions. If the center, or core, is a solid piece of wood rather than a number of veneers, it is called lumber-core plywood. Plywoods can be made of hardwood, softwood, or a combination of both, depending on the intended use. Combinations have a softwood core and a hardwood surface.

Hardboards. Hardboards come in many different varieties, depending on the manufacturing process and the intended use. Hardboard may be either smooth on one side and rough on the other (called S1S, smooth 1 side) or smooth on both sides (S2S, smooth 2 sides). The smooth surface may be enameled or plastic-laminated. The board may be tempered, or treated with oils and resins to make it moisture resistant; this process darkens the board. It may be perforated (pegboard). If the hardboard is made with wood chips and the chips are visible in the edge, it is called particleboard. This may be single- or three-layer, or it may be extruded, with a fuzzy surface (beaverboard).

Grading Lumber. Lumber is commonly classified as either select or common; *select* is of high quality with few or no defects, suitable for finishing, while *common* has defects and is more suitable for construction. Common lumber is graded numerically, from 1 to 5, with 1 the best quality. Select lumber may be graded as:

- B and better, *also called 1 and 2 clear, which is the best, with small imperfections if any.*
- C select, *which may have small knots or similar imperfections.*
- D select, *which has larger imperfections that can be painted over.*

Plywood is graded according to face quality, strength, and intended use. The quality of the face and back is indicated by two letters, one for face and one for back: N is the best grade, followed by A, B, C, and D. Strength is indicated by a group number, which actually grades the plywood according to the type of wood used in its manufacture. Group 1 is the strongest, followed by Groups 2 through 5. Plywood is also graded as Interior or Exterior, depending on the glue used in manufacture; exterior, made with waterproof glue, may be used for marine and outdoor applications.

Other grading terms used for wood are:

- F.A.S., *firsts and seconds.*
- K.D., *kiln dried.*
- R.W. and L., *random widths and lengths.*

Measuring Lumber. Lumber is sold in standard widths and thicknesses—1″ x 2″, 2″ x 4″, 6″ x 6″, and so on. These numbers represent the *nominal* size, that is, the size of the board as it comes from the sawmill. As the board dries out during the seasoning process, it shrinks; so the *actual* size of the board will be a little less than the nominal size. Nominal size does not apply to the length of a board; that is, an 8-foot 2″ x 4″ will actually be 8 feet long.

The greatest amount of shrinkage takes place along the circumference of the annual growth rings—that is, along the grain lines that you see in the end of a board. Boards are either *plain-sawed* (cut tangentially to the rings, with the end grain running from edge to edge) or *quarter-sawed* (cut radially from the log, with the end grain running from top to bottom). With softwoods, plain-sawed is referred to as *flat-grain,* and quarter-sawed as *edge-grain.*

Lumber is usually ordered by the *board foot,* which is a unit of measure equal to a 1″ x 12″ that is 1 foot long. To determine the number of board feet in a board, multiply the nominal thickness and width in inches by the length in feet and divide by 12. For example, an 8-foot 2″ x 4″ contains:

$$\frac{2 \times 4 \times 8}{12} = 5\frac{1}{3} \text{ board feet.}$$

Molding, interior trim, dowels, and similar items are sold not by the board foot but by the *linear foot,* which is simply the length in feet. Plywood and hardboard are sold by the panel in various standard sizes and widths.

KINDS OF WOOD JOINTS

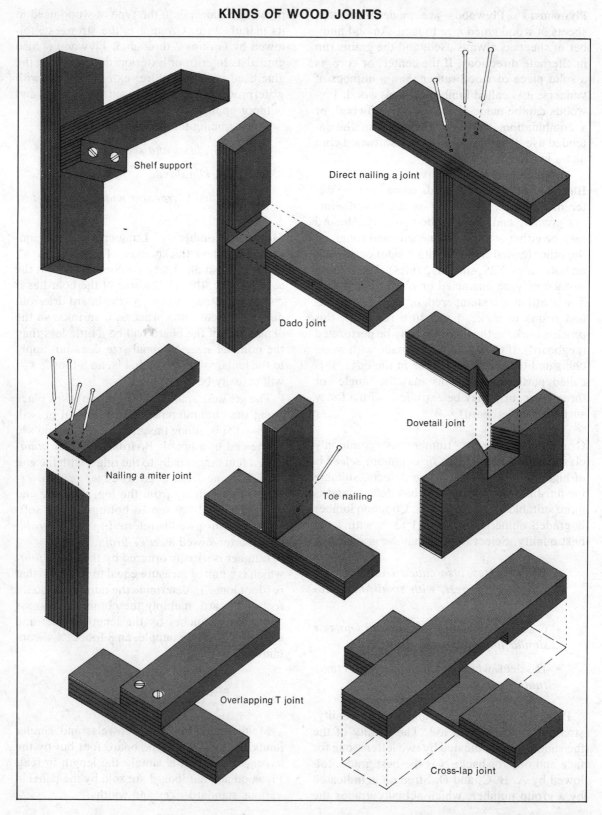

Shelf support

Direct nailing a joint

Dado joint

Dovetail joint

Nailing a miter joint

Toe nailing

Overlapping T joint

Cross-lap joint

Fastening and Joining Wood. There are three main methods of fastening wood: with nails, with screws, and with adhesives. When extra strength is required, adhesives and screws are often used together.

Nails are the quickest and easiest form of fastener. They are sized according to length, which can be given in inches or by penny size, a measure based on what was once the price (in English pence) for a hundred nails of that size. Penny sizes go from 2d (2-penny) to 60d. A 2d nail is 1 inch long; from there, each higher penny number represents another $\frac{1}{4}$ inch in length, up to 10d (3-inch). From there, sizes run as follows:

$$12d = 3\frac{1}{4}'' \qquad 40d = 5''$$
$$16d = 3\frac{1}{2}'' \qquad 50d = 5\frac{3}{8}''$$
$$20d = 4'' \qquad 60d = 6''$$
$$30d = 4\frac{1}{2}''$$

Nails are usually driven through the thinner piece of wood into the thicker piece. The nail should be three times as long as the thickness of the thinner piece. Various types of nails are made for different purposes, finishes, and materials.

There are two main varieties of *screws*— slotted and Phillips. The three head types are roundhead, oval head, and flathead; the last two must be countersunk. Screws are sized by length in inches and by diameter, which is given by gauge number. Gauge numbers run from 0 $\left(\text{about } \frac{1}{16}''\right)$ to 24 $\left(\text{about } \frac{3}{8}''\right)$, with 2 through 16 gauge being the commonest.

Nails and screws will split wood if you are not careful. Hardwoods, such as oak and maple, split more easily than softwoods, but hardwoods also hold nails better than softwoods. When working with hardwoods, drill a clearance hole through the thinner piece as well as a pilot hole into the thicker piece.

So many different types of *adhesives* are available today that it is impossible to list them. They have different applications, bonding strengths, and prices, and these factors will determine which one you choose for the job. Epoxy adhesives, for example, will glue almost

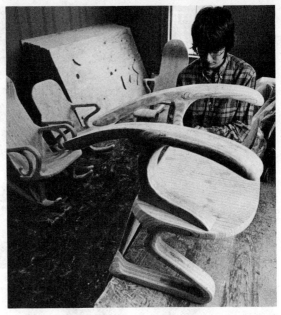

Working wood. Shaping wood to take advantage of its grain and sanding it carefully to bring out its beauty are important in producing fine furniture.

any two materials together in a permanent bond, but they cost much more than other glues.

Working Wood. The common methods of working wood include cutting, drilling, planing, filing, sanding, gouging (with chisels), and carving. In addition, there are other methods, which include the following:

- *Routing,* or cutting slots, grooves, or edgings with a router.
- *Jointing,* or planing with a high-speed power tool called a jointer.
- *Shaping,* which is similar to routing, except that the tool is stationary and the wood is guided around the cutter, which cuts wood off the edge.
- *Turning,* which involves spinning the wood in a lathe and using various chisels and gouges to form cylindrical shapes.
- *Bending,* which is usually done with the help of hot water or steam. Some woods, especially birch or oak, take to bending better than others. Some types of plywood also bend well; because of this they are widely used in boatbuilding.

Industrial arts skills. Students receive instruction in many trades and skills that will be useful in their careers and hobbies. No matter what your interest, you will do well to acquire manual skills.

VOCATIONAL ARTS

Finishing Wood. The first step in finishing wood is to make a smooth finishing surface. Nail holes, dents, gouges, and splits must be filled with stick shellac or wood dough and sanded. The entire surface is then sanded, vacuumed to remove the dust, and wiped down with a rag moistened with turpentine.

Most of the sanding can be done with power sanding machines, but a final hand-sanding will be necessary for a high-quality finish. Sandpaper is available in grades from very coarse to very fine; different manufacturers use different grading number systems. The most common abrasive materials are aluminum oxide, garnet, emery, flint, and silicon carbide.

Since finishing materials tend to darken wood, *bleaching* is often necessary to obtain a light-colored finish. Wood bleach lifts the grain, so the wood must be sanded after the bleach dries. After sanding, it is important to neutralize the wood with a vinegar-water solution.

If the wood is an open-pore type, it should be treated with a wood *filler* after sanding and bleaching. Open-pore woods include oak, rosewood, walnut, teak, and mahogany. Closed-pore woods such as pine, cherry, maple, or birch usually do not need a filler. Fillers are brushed on, allowed to stand, then wiped to fill the pores.

Stains are used to alter the color of wood and to bring out the grain. It is not necessary to stain the wood; if you want to emphasize the grain, however, use a light-colored stain. Oil stains must be wiped off, not allowed to dry, or else they will hide the wood. Water and alcohol stains are wiped or sprayed on and allowed to soak into the wood. Water stains, like bleaches, raise the grain, so the wood must be sanded after it dries. Water stains may also cause swelling and warping.

Open-pored woods and woods that have been oil-stained are best treated with a *sealer* before the final finish is applied. Shellac is the most common sealer. A coat of shellac will prevent the oil stain from bleeding into the final finish, or prevent the final finish from being absorbed into the wood while drying. Other sealers besides shellac are available, and some come mixed with a stain. These should be used for exterior applications, since shellac cracks under moisture.

Shellac can also be used as a final finish. It is easy to use but is sensitive to moisture and has a limited shelf life—about six months at most. Old shellac will not dry, so test it on a scrap of wood. Shellac in usable condition should dry in an hour.

Lacquers and *varnishes* are commonly confused. The confusion in terms stems from the introduction of other types such as the polyurethane finishes, which some manufacturers call lacquers and others varnishes.

Both lacquer and varnish must be applied thinly; they can be applied to bare wood. Spar varnishes have ingredients that enable them to stand up to salt water. Polyurethane finishes dry well in a humid atmosphere, in contrast to other varnishes and lacquers, which harden well in dry air.

Almost all finishes will darken the wood to some degree. To determine in advance what color your wood will be with a certain finish, brush the finish onto a piece of glass, applying as many coats as you intend to use; then place the glass over the wood. Be sure to observe it under the kind of light that will usually shine on the finished piece—daylight, fluorescent light, or whatever.

Your final finish can be protected with paste wax, which is available in colors as well as clear. Wax can be used to cover an uneven staining job or a partial refinishing.

A hand-rubbed oil finish takes more work than other methods, but it gives wood a luster unmatched by any other method. Boiled linseed oil is thinned with turpentine, using a ratio of one-half (1:1) to two-thirds (2:1) oil, depending on how dark you want your finish. The wood surface must be bare and thoroughly sanded, dusted, and dried. Brush on the oil until no more will penetrate; then wipe off the excess. Rub with a cloth pad, pressing hard enough to generate heat with the friction caused by the heel of your hand; the heat sets the oil. Allow the wood to dry warm for two days; then repeat the hand-rubbing process four or five times. The effort it takes to produce a truly professional finish is worthwhile.

Metals

Metals are classified as either ferrous or nonferrous. Ferrous metals contain iron; nonferrous metals do not. Ferrous metals have by far the widest application because of their strength and relatively low cost. Aluminum, though more abundant than iron, is much more expensive to extract.

Ferrous Metals.   All ferrous metals are made from iron, which is extracted from iron ore. Molten iron from a blast furnace pours into molds where it hardens into 100-pound bars, called pigs. This *pig iron* may be remelted and poured into molds to form parts for machines, stoves, etc. *Cast iron,* as this is known, is hard and strong, resists corrosion, and can be machined, but is relatively brittle. Pig iron that has been remelted and purified becomes *wrought iron,* which is tough, ductile, and malleable. Wrought iron is formed by heating in a forge and hammering into shape. Because it has no stiffness or spring, it has been replaced in many applications by steel.

Steel is a refined form of iron. It is classified according to carbon content. *Low carbon steel,* also called mild or machine steel, is similar to wrought iron in its qualities; it is used for screws, nails, chains, and some machine parts. *Medium carbon steel* is used for bolts and hand tools. *High carbon steel,* also called tool steel, is used for machine tools, springs, and ball bearings. The properties of a type of steel can be changed by applying various heat treatments. This is important in the case of tool steel, since a tool that has lost its cutting edge can be sharpened and rehardened. Steel may also be improved for a particular purpose by alloying it. The best-known steel alloy is *stainless steel,* steel with nickel or chromium added.

Nonferrous Metals.   Nonferrous metals include all metals that do not contain iron. Some nonferrous metals, such as uranium and bismuth, have little or no application in metalworking. Others, such as platinum and silver, are used primarily in such fields as jewelry and electronics. In metalworking, the principal nonferrous metals include these:

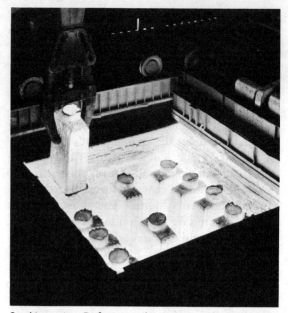

Soaking pits. Before steel ingots can be rolled, they must be heated evenly to a temperature of about 2200° F. The gas furnaces that do the heating are called soaking pits.

- *Aluminum,* a light, soft metal in its pure state. Aluminum is alloyed with other metals to give it strength. It is naturally resistant to corrosion and has high strength at low temperatures.
- *Copper,* a tough, malleable, ductile, long-wearing metal with a high conductivity for both heat and electricity.
- *Gold,* a heavy precious metal, highly malleable and ductile, but too soft in its pure state to have much use except as gold leaf. For jewelry, gold is usually alloyed with copper or silver to harden and strengthen it.
- *Lead,* a heavy, soft metal, highly resistant to corrosion and impervious to radiation. Lead is an important ingredient in solder; its resistance to corrosion makes it important in lining and sheathing.
- *Magnesium,* the lightest of the structural metals. Pure magnesium burns easily and produces enormous heat; therefore, it is usually alloyed with other metals to make it less flammable.
- *Nickel,* a magnetic metal, resistant to corrosion; its most important use is in alloys with iron to make stainless steel.

Temper mill. To impart the proper stiffness and flatness, workmen feed steel sheets into a temper mill, which can process 4,120 feet an hour or more.

- *Tin,* an important metal in alloys, solder, and coatings. Tin coatings protect other metal surfaces from oxidation, as in the plated steel used for tin cans.
- *Titanium,* an exceptionally corrosion-resistant metal, lighter and stronger than steel.
- *Zinc,* a malleable, ductile metal, resistant to corrosion. It is used in outdoor applications such as gutters and flashings, but its chief use is in coating ferrous metals in the process known as galvanizing.

Alloys. There are numerous alloys with different properties, which can be altered by even a slight change in the proportion of metals alloyed. The most common alloys are:

- *Brass,* an alloy of copper and zinc, sometimes hardened with a little tin. Used in plumbing, screws, and hardware.
- *Bronze,* a copper and tin alloy; harder than brass. Used in springs, screens, and statues.
- *Pewter,* a tin-based alloy which may contain lead, antimony, copper, zinc, or a combination of those metals. Pewter was once widely used for dishes and household utensils; if

pewter is to be used for bowls, pitchers, and the like, it should contain no lead.

Tools. *Layout tools* are used to mark a pattern on metal before cutting. After the surface has been coated with layout dye or a copper sulfate solution, the pattern is marked with a scriber, or metalworker's pencil. A steel rule, protractor, try square, and combination bevel are used to mark straight lines and angles accurately. A divider is used to lay out circles and arcs; it is also useful for measuring or transcribing distances.

Files are one of the most important tools in metalworking. They come in different lengths, cross-sectional shapes, cuts, and degrees of coarseness. Three grades of coarseness are commonly available: bastard, second cut, and smooth cut. Some types also come in "coarse" and "dead smooth" grades. The longer the file, the larger the teeth; even though two different-length files are rated smooth cut, the longer one will be coarser.

The teeth of a file may be single cut, double cut, or curved-tooth. Double cut is used for rough work, single cut for finishing. A curved-tooth file is used for finish work on surfaces and on soft metals. Files must be cleaned frequently with a wire brush.

Cutting tools include hacksaws, fly cutters for cutting holes in sheet metal, and various metal cutters such as tin snips. Hacksaw blades should be mounted with the teeth pointing away from the handle so as to cut on the push stroke. Jigsaws also have special blades designed to cut sheet metal; these are especially useful for scroll work. Other important tools for metal work are *taps* and *dies.* Taps are used to cut threads inside a hole, dies are used to cut threads outside a pipe or rod. There are various types of threads, but the most important are the National Form, either NC (coarse) or NF (fine). Threads are sized according to the diameter of the thread and the number of threads per inch.

Sharpening Tools. Cutting tools should be kept sharp. When they are not in use, protect their cutting edges in some way, such as by hanging them on a rack. When you sharpen them on a grinder, be careful not to let them get

METALWORKING TOOLS

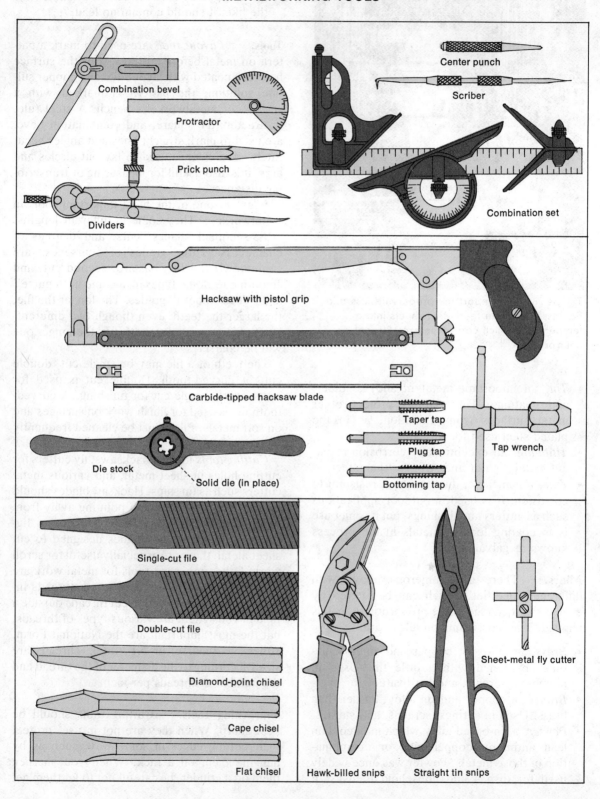

Combination bevel

Protractor

Prick punch

Dividers

Center punch

Scriber

Combination set

Hacksaw with pistol grip

Carbide-tipped hacksaw blade

Taper tap

Plug tap

Bottoming tap

Tap wrench

Die stock

Solid die (in place)

Single-cut file

Double-cut file

Diamond-point chisel

Cape chisel

Flat chisel

Sheet-metal fly cutter

Hawk-billed snips

Straight tin snips

hot from the grinding, or they will lose their hardness and their ability to hold an edge. After a while, however, any tool that is repeatedly sharpened will lose its hardness. The tool must then be rehardened and retempered.

To harden steel, heat it to about 1500°F. This is most easily done by heating the edge with a blowtorch until it glows bright red. Then quench the metal by dipping it in water or oil. Since hardened steel is brittle, you must then temper it; reheat it and quench it again. The proper temperature depends on the use of the tool; wood chisels should be heated dark brown, cold chisels purple, screwdrivers blue.

Working Metal. Metal is supplied in sheets, in rods, and in bars, which may be square, hexagonal, or octagonal. It is also supplied in the form of wire, tubing, and pipe.

The basic methods of working metal are cutting, drilling, threading, bending, and hammering. Special processes include:

- *Tooling,* making a raised surface on metal foil. Tooling is usually done with special tools by pressing on the reverse side of the foil.
- *Raising,* making a raised surface on sheet metal by hammering on the reverse side into a form, usually made of wood.
- *Planishing,* hammering sheet metal over a stake or other solid surface.
- *Roll forming,* making a cylinder out of sheet metal.
- *Braking,* forming an angle bend in sheet metal, usually by clamping it and hammering the bend over an edge of some kind.
- *Spinning,* turning sheet metal over a form on a lathe.
- *Annealing.* With ferrous metals, annealing is used to soften hardened steel. The process consists of heating the metal and allowing it to cool slowly—in lime, or ashes, or a hot oven that has been turned off. With nonferrous metals, annealing is used to soften metals that have hardened from being worked too much. In this case, it consists of heating and quenching (cooling rapidly in water).
- *Case hardening* is a special way of hardening ferrous metal that impregnates the surface metal with carbon. The metal object is packed in a carbonizing material, such as charcoal; it is heated red in an oven for several hours, cooled slowly, then hardened and tempered.

Metal Shaping. Shaping includes processes used to change the size or shape of metal without cutting or filing. Shaping processes are used to produce metal for use by the metalworker, as well as to make metal parts. The processes include casting, forging, rolling, pressing, and extrusion.

Casting, in which molten metal is poured into a mold and allowed to harden, is one of the oldest forms of metal shaping. In sand casting, a wood or metal pattern is made in the shape of the desired product. Sand is packed around the pattern, which is removed, leaving the mold. Molten metal is poured into the mold and allowed to harden, after which the sand is broken away from the casting. This process leaves a rough surface on the casting; a smooth surface can be obtained by using a mixture of sand and resin as the mold medium in the process called shell molding.

Permanent molds are reusable and can be removed without breaking after the casting has cooled. If a solid part is not required, some of the molten metal can be poured off after a shell has formed inside the mold. The resulting hollow casting is called a slush casting.

Lost-wax, or investment-mold, casting produces precision castings needing no machining. It is used to cast statues as well as parts from alloys that are difficult to machine. A wax pattern of the part to be cast is placed in a box or flask, which is then filled with liquefied refractory plaster. The mold is then baked in an oven; the plaster hardens and the wax melts out. Liquid metal is poured into the cavity left by the wax and left to cool, after which the mold is broken away.

In die casting, molten metal is injected into a die by a machine, which maintains pressure until the casting cools. Centrifugal casting takes place in a rapidly rotating mold; centrifugal force produces parts with greater accuracy and improved physical properties.

Forging is another shaping process. Metal is heated and hammered by hand to the desired

Metal working. Using a hammer and chisels, a craftsman hammers a metal bar to desired specifications. Most of this type of work is now done by machine.

shape. Parts may be drop-forged in a press with a machine hammer and anvil; dies for each part are mounted in dovetails cut in the hammer and anvil.

Rolling is the process that produces most metal for the metalworker. Metal is passed between two rolls rotating in opposite directions. Depending on how the rolls are shaped, metal can be produced in a variety of forms—bars, plates, rods, sheets, slabs, and strips. If the metal is heated during rolling it is hot-rolled; otherwise, it is cold-rolled.

Pressing involves shaping flat metal in a press with matched dies. In the *extrusion* process, metal is put under pressure to make it plastic so it will flow through a die in a continuous length.

Joining Metal. Probably the oldest method of joining metal is forge welding. When heated sufficiently, certain kinds of metal, such as wrought iron, become soft enough so that two heated pieces can be hammered and made to flow together. Forge welding has largely been replaced by other methods, of which the most important for the metalworker are soldering, riveting, and welding.

Soldering is one of the easiest methods of joining metal, although not as strong as other methods. It is used to join wire for electrical conductivity; to join sheet metal parts in making an impervious bond, such as that needed in sheathings and linings; to join metal parts where the joint must be strong but not permanent, as in plumbing; and similar applications.

A soldering iron must be properly tinned in order to solder well. A corroded tip should be filed down to bright, smooth metal before tinning; if the tip is dirty but not corroded, it should be cleaned with an abrasive. Heat the iron and then melt solder onto the tip and allow it to flow, covering the tip. If the solder does not adhere well, cool the iron and clean it again, taking care not to touch the cleaned tip, since the oils on your skin will prevent the tip from tinning.

Each different metal requires a certain kind of flux for soldering. Rosin-core solder can be used for jobs such as wiring; the rosin acts as a flux. After the surfaces to be soldered have been cleaned (again, do not touch a cleaned surface), apply the proper flux and heat the surfaces until they are hot enough so that solder will melt and flow when touched to the metal. Never melt the solder on the iron, or your joint will not hold. A much stronger joint can be obtained by using hard solder, but this requires much greater heat than a soldering iron can supply. A blowtorch is generally used.

Another form of soldering is sweat soldering. The parts to be joined are both heated and tinned separately, then clamped together and reheated to melt the solder and form the joint.

Welding is the other joining method involving heat. In forge welding, the parts are heated and hammered together. More important now is fusion welding, in which the metal parts are heated hot enough to flow together without forging. *Gas welding* and *arc welding* are the methods most often used in metalworking. In gas welding, heat is generated by the combustion of gases, and the flame is applied to the areas to be joined until they melt together. Often additional metal, as from welding rods, is used to fill the space at the joint. The usual apparatus is an oxyacetylene torch, in which oxygen and acetylene are combined and burned. The acetylene is turned on and the torch is lit; then oxy-

Weld shop. The welder protects his eyes from the blinding light and sparks by wearing a transparent mask. Welding has replaced riveting in the construction of most machines.

gen is fed in until the torch flame burns with two colors.

Arc welding includes a number of processes in which an electric arc is established between an electrode and the parts to be welded. Depending on whether the electrodes are carbon or metal, the processes are known as carbon-arc or metal-arc welding. Power for an arc welder may be supplied by normal AC current or by a DC generator. DC welding can produce a higher heat and so is used in welding heavy metal. The electric arc of an arc welder produces a blinding light; for this reason, an eye shield must always be worn. This safety precaution is essential for protection of the welder, whose vision would otherwise be damaged.

Welding has almost completely replaced *riveting* in commercial applications such as construction and shipbuilding, but riveting is still a useful method of joining, especially since it requires no heat. The exception is the boiler rivet, which is heated so that it can be headed while hot. For sheet metal work, however, rivets are headed with a rivet set.

Before riveting, make sure you have removed the burr raised by the drill or metal punch you used for the rivet holes. Rivets are sized by length and shank diameter, except for small sheet-metal rivets, which are sized by the weight of 1,000 rivets of a given size. In order to form a proper head, the shank must project through the rivet holes and protrude on the other side to a distance equal to 1½ times the diameter of the shank. (For countersunk rivets, the stem allowance should be the same as the diameter.) Using a rivet set, flatten the joint by hammering on the rivet set with the shank in the deep hole; then start the head with the hammer and finish heading with the hollow of the rivet set.

One advantage of rivets is that they can be removed. The head can be struck off with a chisel, or the rivet can be drilled out.

Other methods of joining metal are bolting, screwing, and bonding with adhesives. Sheet-metal screws are self-tapping and need only be screwed in after the top hole has been widened enough so that the threads do not tap the top hole. Epoxy adhesives are especially suitable for bonding metal.

Finishing Metal. The most important finishing processes are cleaning and polishing. When these are completed, the surface is sometimes decorated by means of various processes, such as enameling, etching, peening (hammering with the ball end of a ball peen hammer), chasing (indenting with a hammer and tools), or matting (punching designs in the surface).

Cleaning is often done by a process called *pickling,* in which the metal is dipped in a solution of sulfuric acid, then washed. When making a pickling solution, remember the acid solution rule: ALWAYS ADD THE ACID TO THE WATER, NEVER THE OTHER WAY. Mixing acid with water generates a great deal of heat; pouring water into acid can boil the solution so quickly that it spatters all over you. When using the pickling solution, be careful not to breathe the fumes from the acid.

Metals are usually polished with emery, silicon carbide, or aluminum oxide. The final abrasive can be steel wool; the final polishing can be done with a buffing wheel. If you use a buffing compound, be sure your buffer has a dust collector so you won't inhale the buffing wheel lint and compound.

Plastics

There are thousands of varieties of plastics, made from about forty basic plastic resins. Plastics are generally classified as either *thermoset* or *thermoplastic*. Thermoset plastics harden under heat and pressure; they cannot be remelted and molded into a different shape. Thermoplastics melt in heat and harden when cooled; they can be remelted and remolded. Some plastic resins can be made in both thermoset and thermoplastic varieties.

Working, Shaping, and Joining Plastics. Plastics can be worked and shaped by almost any of the methods used for wood or metal, using the same tools. In addition, thermoplastics can be bent or molded by application of heat. Furthermore, plastics can be dyed so that the color is uniform throughout the plastic. This gives them an advantage over wood and metal, which can only be colored on the surface. Plastics can be finished like wood and even made to resemble different wood grains and textures.

Plastics are joined in the same ways as wood and metal: screws and bolts, welding, and adhesives. Thermoset plastics cannot be welded. Each type of plastic requires an adhesive with certain qualities. Some adhesives, like epoxy,

Making plastic film. An operator checks a film bubble in the Saran Wrap factory, located in Midland, Michigan. This plastic product finds many uses in food packaging.

are appropriate for most plastics, but do not assume an adhesive will work; read the label on the adhesive. Transparent plastics can be welded so that the seam is also transparent.

TERMS USED IN THE MANUFACTURING/CONSTRUCTION INDUSTRY

building codes. Laws and regulations that apply to a specific town, city, or region. The purpose is to provide minimum standards for safe designs, kinds and uses of materials, and methods of construction for new and existing buildings.

frame construction. Construction method in which the structural parts are of wood or dependent on a wood frame for support.

manufacturing. The process of taking raw materials and turning them into useful ware.

mass production. A technique used to produce a large volume of standardized products. Highly specialized machines are arranged to match the product flow. Materials and parts are moved by conveyors, chutes, and pipes.

post and beam construction. Method of construction in which large framing members replace joists, studs, and rafters. Because of their larger

size, the members can be spaced farther apart.

prefabrication. The making of parts and subassemblies in manufacturing plants and then transporting them to a building site for final assembly.

process engineering. The selection of processes and procedures to be used in manufacturing a product.

production control. Concerned with the flow of material and parts through the various processing and assembly areas. Its purpose is to make the most efficient use of people, power, and equipment.

product engineering. The area of engineering that converts the design sketches, drawings, and models into working drawings and specifications.

quality control. The process of insuring that quality standards are maintained in manufacturing.

ELECTRICITY AND AUTOMOTIVE ENGINEERING

Electricity can be obtained from a large variety of sources: hydroelectric generators, gas generators, nuclear power plants, and solar energy cells. The uses of electricity are many and various—light, heat, and the operation of machinery are but a few. But no matter what its source, no matter what its ultimate use, electricity obeys the same fundamental rules. Once these are understood, it is possible to deal with electricity in all its applications.

In the case of automotive engineering, the challenge is to find new ways to generate the mechanical power to move vehicles economically, safely, and without damaging the environment.

Electricity

Electricity, in the form of electrons, can be harnessed to serve many useful purposes because it will flow through a conductor, creating an electrical current. Electronics, on the other hand, deals with free-moving electrons in nonconductors, such as a gas or a vacuum; in semiconductors; and in conductors.

Electrical current is easily understood if one thinks of it as a flow similar to that of water in a pipe. The force of the water that comes out of a faucet depends on three factors: the amount of water flowing through the pipe; the amount of pressure at the other end that is forcing the water to flow through the pipe; and the size and shape of the pipe—that is, the resistance the water encounters. In an electrical current, the amount of electricity (that is, the number of electrons) that flows through a conductor is measured in *amperes*. An ampere can be defined as a certain number of electrons (6.242 quintillion, to be exact) flowing past a certain point in a conductor in one second.

There is no such thing as a perfect conductor: all conductors interfere to some degree with the flow of electrons through them. The best conductors are metals; gold and silver are theoretically the best, while aluminum and copper are the most practical. The best nonconductors, or

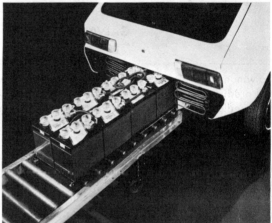

Copper Electric Town Car. This prototype cruises at 40 mph and has a top speed of 55 mph. Its batteries slide out the rear of the car for recharging.

insulators, are wood, ceramics, rubber, and most plastics. The property of interfering with the flow of electrons is called *resistance,* and it is measured in *ohms*.

The pressure forcing the electrons through the conductor is called electromotive force; it depends on the property of electricity that an excess negative charge in one place will move if possible through a conductor to a place where there is an excess positive charge, just as water seeks its own level through gravity flow. The electromotive force is measured in *volts*. A volt is defined as the electromotive force necessary to move a current of 1 ampere through a conductor where 1 watt ($^1/_{746}$ of a horsepower) of

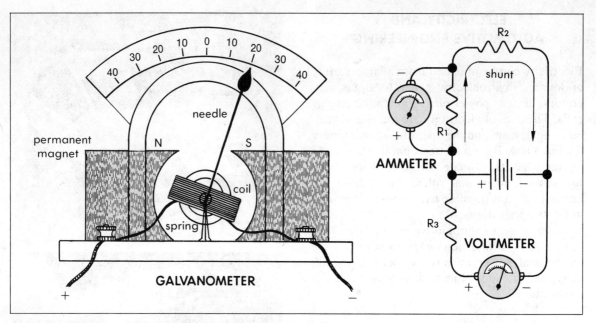

Galvanometer detects a small amount of electricity. The current through the coil produces a magnetic field that is repelled by the magnet's field, causing the needle to deflect. In an ammeter, which measures current, the detector is modified to shunt most of the current past it.

power is expended in overcoming the conductor's resistance. The amount of resistance in this conductor is then 1 ohm. The relationship between current, pressure, and resistance is basic to a good understanding of electricity. It is expressed in a series of equations known as Ohm's Law, where I stands for current, E for pressure, and R for resistance.

$$I = \frac{E}{R} \quad \left(\text{amperes} = \frac{\text{volts}}{\text{ohms}}\right)$$

$$E = IR \quad (\text{volts} = \text{amperes} \times \text{ohms})$$

$$R = \frac{E}{I} \quad \left(\text{ohms} = \frac{\text{volts}}{\text{amperes}}\right)$$

Current and pressure are measured with an *ammeter* and *voltmeter* respectively. To measure a current, an ammeter must offer no more resistance than the conductor does; thus, it must have high conductivity and low resistance. A voltmeter, on the other hand, measures the pressure difference between two points; therefore, it must have sufficiently high resistance to draw virtually no current. Once the current and pressure have been measured, resistance can easily be calculated according to Ohm's Law.

Electrical power is measured in *watts;* one watt is the power represented by a current of 1 ampere under a pressure of 1 volt. This can be represented by a set of equations similar to Ohm's Law, where P is power in watts.

$$I = \frac{P}{E} \quad \left(\text{amperes} = \frac{\text{watts}}{\text{volts}}\right)$$

$$P = IE \quad (\text{watts} = \text{amperes} \times \text{volts})$$

$$E = \frac{P}{I} \quad \left(\text{volts} = \frac{\text{watts}}{\text{amperes}}\right)$$

Furthermore,

$$P = I^2R \quad (\text{watts} = \text{amperes}^2 \times \text{ohms})$$

$$P = \frac{E^2}{R} \quad \left(\text{watts} = \frac{\text{volts}^2}{\text{ohms}}\right)$$

Circuits. Electricity as it is used in lighting, appliances, and other practical applications flows in a *circuit*—from the source to the appliance and back to the source. If two appliances are on the same circuit, they may be connected

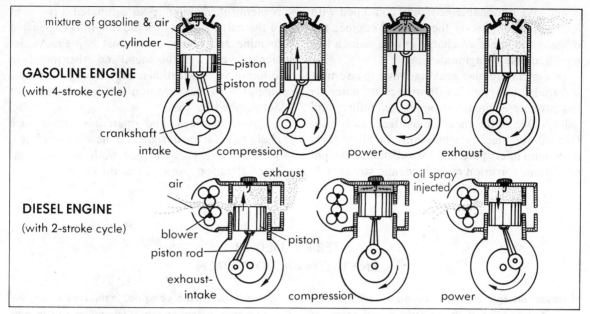

GASOLINE ENGINE
(with 4-stroke cycle)

mixture of gasoline & air
cylinder
piston
piston rod
crankshaft
intake   compression   power   exhaust

DIESEL ENGINE
(with 2-stroke cycle)

air
exhaust
oil spray injected
blower
piston
piston rod
exhaust-intake   compression   power

Gasoline and diesel engines are the chief types of internal combustion
engines. In the gasoline engine, a mixture of gasoline and air is exploded
by a spark. In the diesel air is first compressed to raise it to a high temperature
before oil is injected, causing an explosion.

either in *series*—so that current flows first through one, then through the other, then back to the source—or *parallel*—so that the current flows to and from each appliance through separate wires, so it is not necessary to turn on both appliances to complete the circuit.

For a *series circuit,* the following rules apply:

The current is the same in all parts of the circuit.

The total resistance is the sum of the resistance of the separate parts.

The total voltage is the sum of the voltages across the separate parts.

For a *parallel circuit,* the following rules apply:

The total current is the sum of the currents flowing through the separate parts.

The voltage is the same across all parts of the circuit.

The total resistance is equal to the total voltage divided by the total current.

Automotive Engineering

Engineering and design in the automotive field are changing radically because of anti-pollution laws and the energy crisis. The federal government has already caused a change in automobile engineering by emphasizing safety standards; anti-pollution legislation is causing a similar change. Fear of a national fuel shortage will probably result in an even greater change in the next few years.

Each of these new requirements—safer cars, cleaner air, less energy consumption—creates problems for the designer, the manufacturer, and the mechanic. Safer cars are heavier and burn more fuel; anti-pollution devices increase fuel consumption—but fuel must be conserved. Detroit auto makers are finding it nearly impossible to meet anti-pollution requirements; in the future, they will have to make their cars more economical and still hold down prices.

A number of new power sources are being studied—steam, electricity, gas turbines—but the internal combustion engine is still the only important type used in automobiles. Two new types have recently been developed, both of which give reasonable economy combined with low pollution. One is the Wankel engine; the other is the stratified-charge engine, which is a modified piston-engine design.

Designers are also seeking ways to use new materials that weigh less than present materials but provide adequate strength, reliability, and safety. One of the metals most frequently substituted for steel is aluminum. In alloy form aluminum offers potential for substantial weight reduction, corrosion resistance, and strength. It is plentiful, making up an estimated 8 per cent of the earth's crust. Yet aluminum is expensive to mine and refine, so its cost is high. As designers work with this metal and other metals in automotive applications, they have to exercise ingenuity to make certain that benefits are not outweighed by cost.

Power sources and materials, then, are challenges facing designers of new automobiles. There is every confidence both will be met, given time for research and development.

TERMS USED IN ENERGY/TRANSPORTATION

chemical energy. Energy generated and stored in the combination of the molecules and atoms of various substances. It is the energy of life and growth. An example of this is the way plants use light from the sun.

diesel engines. Diesel engines have about the same mechanical parts as gasoline engines except for the spark plugs. The gas is ignited by rapid compression. They are more economical than gasoline engines and are used in heavy trucks, buses, etc.

energy. The capacity or ability to do work. It can be studied under six major classifications:

    heat energy
    radiant energy
    nuclear energy
    chemical energy
    electrical energy
    mechanical energy

gasoline engines. Engines that produce power by the expansion of the gasoline as it is ignited by a spark plug in a closed cylinder. The piston is connected to a crankshaft which is connected by the power train to the wheels.

geothermal power. Power that uses the so-called dry steam reservoirs formed when a supply of underground water flows into fractured hot rocks. Wells are drilled into these reservoirs, and the steam is piped into a generating station.

heat energy. Speed of molecular action in a substance.

internal combustion engine. In this type of engine, the energy that makes the engine run is generated by burning fuel inside the engine itself: gasoline engines, diesel engines, jet and rocket engines, and gas turbines.

jet engines. Jet engines have a reaction engine that takes in air from the outside as an oxidizer to burn fuel and ejects a jet of hot gases backward to create a thrust.

kinetic energy. Energy in motion: the spinning wheel or swinging hammer.

mechanical energy. Energy resulting from the motion of objects and masses. It can be observed in a moving train, swinging lever, or turning wheel. Mechanical energy is transmitted from one place to another by gears, belts, and pulleys.

nuclear energy. Originates in the forces that hold the nucleus of an atom together. To release these forces, the nucleus is split apart by a chain reaction. This reaction is called nuclear fission and results in the production of tremendous amounts of heat. This heat is used to generate steam for turbines that drive electrical generators.

potential energy. Energy at rest: the force of water behind a dam or the heat energy stored in coal and oil.

radiant energy. A wave motion: x rays, ultraviolet, visible light, infrared, heat, radio waves, radar, microwave, and several others.

GRAPHIC ARTS

Graphic Arts is concerned with creating and producing visible images on varied surfaces. The production phases include design and layout, composition, photo conversion, image carriers, image transfer, and finishing and binding. These production classifications apply to the six basic reproduction processes used today to transfer images from one material to another: (1) planography or lithography; (2) letterpress or relief; (3) stencil or screen; (4) gravure or intaglio; (5) photographic; and (6) electrostatic.

Lithography

Lithography, or planography, is the art of printing from a flat surface. It is a process based upon the principle that oil (ink) and water (aqueous solution) will not readily mix. Offset-lithography is the most important method used in the United States today. Typical examples of work done by offset-lithography include newspapers, books, magazines, and commercial circulars and brochures.

Offset lithography, because it uses a rubber roller, easily prints on papers having rough textures. It is rapidly replacing older methods of printing.

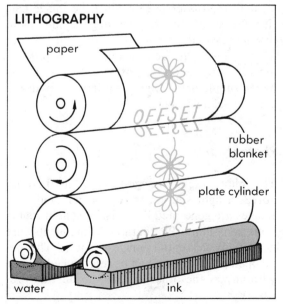

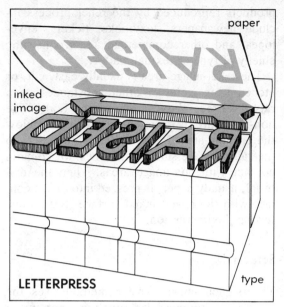

Letterpress printing, though losing popularity, is taught in schools, which often have small letterpresses. Students set type by hand, but type is cast by machine in print shops.

An image of words or pictures is placed photographically on a flat surface, usually a thin metal plate. The plate is then attached to a cylinder on an offset press containing ink and water rollers. When the plate cylinder is rotated, the water rollers transfer an aqueous solution onto the entire plate surface. The non-image areas are moistened; but the plate image area is not, as it is grease-receptive, which repels the water. Then the ink rollers cover the entire plate surface, with the water repelling the ink and the grease-receptive image area accepting the ink. The inked plate-image is transferred or offset on a rubber blanket to the stock being printed upon.

Letterpress

Letterpress printing, also known as relief, requires a three-dimensional ink carrier which is on a raised surface. The raised surface transfers the ink directly to the stock surface by contact pressure. Letterpress printing is the oldest method of transferring images and the second largest process used in the industry. Common products reproduced by the relief process include newspapers, textbooks, tickets, envelopes, and other commercial items consisting chiefly of type or textual matter.

The relief-image area is usually cast, cut, or etched from metal or other substances on a raised surface above a supporting body. The non-image area is recessed—that is, it lies below the printing area. Ink is applied with rollers to the raised image surface and does not come in contact with non-image areas. Then the material, usually paper, is pressed into direct contact with the raised inked surface, thus transferring the impression.

Screen

This stencil image-transfer method uses the principle of forcing ink through an open-image area. Industry commonly refers to this process as screen printing or silk-screen printing. Screen printing can be used to produce large images with heavy ink deposits on nearly any solid surface, material, or shape. Posters, billboards, felt pennants, glass containers, toys, electrical

Silk-screen printing can be used on nearly any kind of surface, such as wood, plastic, cloth, glass, and paper. It is often used to reproduce works of fine art.

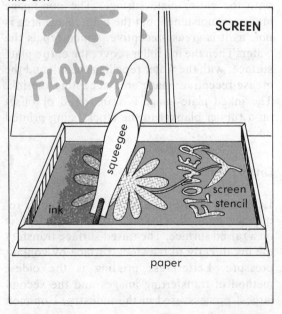

circuits, plastics, and decals effectively employ this flexible stenciling method.

The printing stencil is a paper- or ink-resistant material in which an image has been removed by one of several methods, such as hand-cutting or by photomechanical means. The stencil is attached to a tightly stretched image-carrier that consists of an open-weave fabric, such as silk, nylon, polyester, or stainless steel screen attached over a frame. Ink is poured into the screen frame and forced through the open-image areas of the stencil with a rubber blade or squeegee. Masking materials block out the unwanted, or non-printing, areas. The ink flows through openings in the fabric under pressure from the squeegee and is transferred onto the surface of the stock or objects being printed.

Gravure

Gravure, or intaglio, printing refers to images reproduced from recessed areas. The image is usually etched or cut into a steel or copper plate by mechanical or chemical methods. After the image has been engraved below the plate surface, fluid ink is deposited over the entire image-carrier (the plate), filling the recessed areas. The non-image areas of the plate surface are wiped or scraped clean from ink with a dull blade. Then the stock or paper being printed upon is pressed against the image carrier. Pressure is exerted, causing the fluid ink in the depressions of the plate image to transfer to the paper. Products of this type of printing include paper money, postage stamps, newspaper supplements, and a variety of food and candy packaging labels.

Photography

The photographic image-transfer method involves a light source, image carrier, and film. Images are generated by registering light reflections on film. Photographic chemicals are needed to make the images visible. The developed pictures can then be reproduced for use with any of the other printing production processes.

A camera is loaded with film. When the lens in the camera opens, light reflected from the object being photographed enters the camera and strikes the film. During the production process, a negative image results from the film being developed in photographic chemicals.

The film is then used to make negative enlargements. These negatives are placed in an enlarger between a light source and lens. Light is projected onto the surface of light-sensitive paper. The positive image projected onto the paper becomes visible after being chemically developed. Any number of pictures can be reproduced from a single negative.

Xerography

Xerography, electrostatic printing, works on the principle that particles having opposite electrical charges, positive or negative, will attract each other. Unlike other printing methods, xerography uses no ink, pressure, or chemicals for transferring images on paper or other surfaces. Instead, a fine powder known as toner is used with photoconductive materials, and the electrical attraction creates duplicate images.

Xerography is considered an office-copying process for limited numbers of copies. However, this electrostatic printing technique has been used commercially to print on various surfaces where pressure on the surface must be kept to a minimum.

Plates made of an electrically conductive material, such as sheet metal or foil, are used in the production stage to transfer the images from paper. The image to be printed is then projected onto the positively charged plate. An exposure to the original image is made the same way as with photographic film. Where light hits the plate, the electrostatic charge discharges; where light is withheld, the charge remains.

When the negatively-charged toner is sprinkled over the material being printed, it is attracted to the positively-charged image areas and falls away from the nonprinting area. After the powder adheres to the image areas, it is heated, causing the toner to fuse to the printed surface.

Photographic printing produces a negative that can be used either to make a positive photographic print or a printing plate for offset, letterpress, or gravure. In xerography the image transfer is achieved by electric attraction and repulsion. Since xerography is quick, it is used in offices.

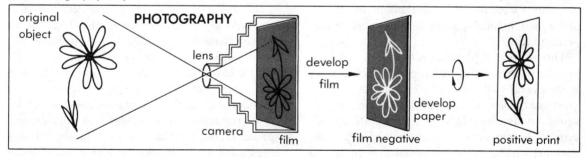

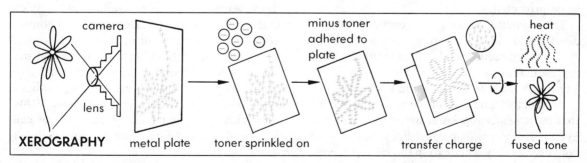

Graphics

Graphics refers to the many different ways information is communicated by drawings. The field of technical graphics is so large and complex that draftsmen usually specialize in one type or area. Common classifications of technical drawings include multiview, pictorial, schematic, and architectural.

Multiview. A multiview drawing is one of the most useful systems employed by draftsmen. Also called orthographic projection in the trade, a multiview drawing shows two or more views of an object in true representation. The orthographic projection represents the separate view of a three-dimensional object on a two-dimensional surface. Every detail of size and shape is precisely drawn on a single flat sheet of paper showing the length, depth, and height of the object. Three views are usually drawn, with the top view always placed above the front view. The right side-view normally appears to the right of the front view.

Pictorial. A pictorial drawing shows two or three surfaces of an object in a single view. It shows objects as they would appear if photographed. Assembled and exploded pictorial drawings are used to show how parts of machines and other devices are put together. They are widely used by the general public in service and repair manuals, sales catalogs, and do-it-yourself kits.

Three types of pictorial projections are used in industry: isometric, oblique, and perspective, with several subtypes under each of these three groupings. Each of the three-dimensional representations is dependent upon the relative position of the object, the observer, and the plane upon which the image of the object is imagined to be projected.

The isometric pictorial presentation is most often used in engineering, when accurate sketches are needed. Oblique three-dimensional representation is used when quick work is desired with the true shape of the front features.

Perspective pictorial drawings are the ones that most nearly represent what is seen by the eye or camera, with parallel lines that tend to converge as they recede from the viewer's eyes.

Schematic. A schematic drawing represents the parts of a system by diagrams and graphic symbols. It is frequently used in the electronics field to show electrical and electronic circuits. Component specifications and their connecting elements such as wires, printed circuits, and parts lists are included in master production drawing.

An engineer originates the technical information found in a schematic diagram in the form of a rough sketch. The draftsman transposes the rough sketch into the standard drafting layout with the complete component designations, accurate notes, and related clarifying information. These elements of a schematic diagram are usually combined with other types of drawing to provide a comprehensive and useful package.

Architectural. Architectural drafting is used in preparing drawings for the construction of houses and commercial buildings. It involves the same basic principles as other types of technical drawings, with special methods of representation and symbols necessary to show a large building on a small scale. These drawings usually show building details, including floor plans, various structural elevations, plumbing and electrical information, and a pictorial rendering.

The design of a house or commercial building is usually developed to an architect's scale varying from the normal ¼″ = 1′0 to some details requiring a full-size reproduction on paper. The basic drawings or set of working drawings will contain all the dimensional relationships considered essential to communicate the details for construction. A floor plan is a fully-dimensioned layout of each floor, including all features such as walls, doors, and window locations. Also, a floor plan contains a complete graphic description of electrical and plumbing symbols. Compass directions and overall dimensions of the building locations are on site, or plot, plans. Foundation/basement plans indicate concrete specifications, footing outlines, and openings for doors and windows. Structural elevations and framing plans show ceiling, walls, and roofing details for each exterior elevation.

TYPES OF
TECHNICAL DRAWINGS

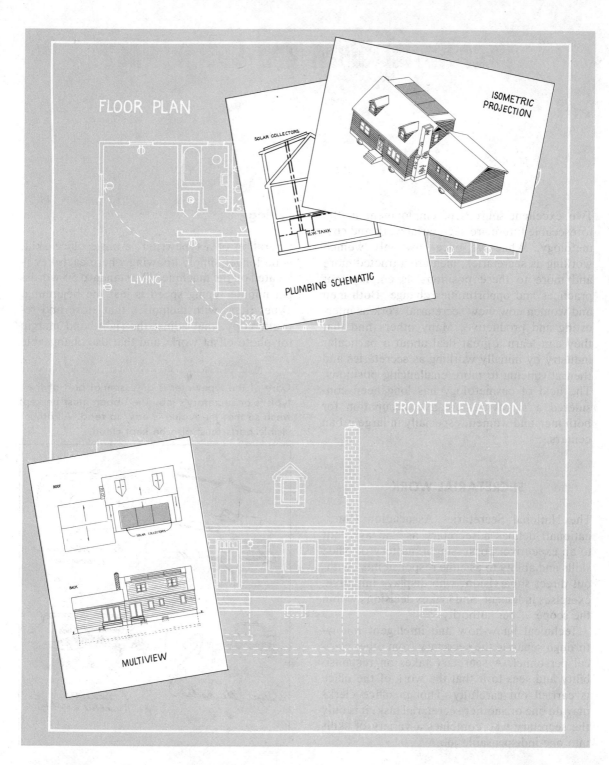

FLOOR PLAN

LIVING

SOLAR COLLECTORS

H.W. TANK

PLUMBING SCHEMATIC

ISOMETRIC
PROJECTION

FRONT ELEVATION

ROOF

SOLAR COLLECTORS

BACK

MULTIVIEW

Secretarial Work and Cosmetology

Two excellent sources of employment in the foreseeable future are secretarial work and cosmetology. While we once saw only women working as secretaries, men are attracted more and more to these positions as employment practices and opportunities change. Both men and women now view secretarial work as interesting and productive. Many others find that they can learn a great deal about a particular industry by initially working as secretaries and then advancing to more challenging positions. The field of cosmetology has long been considered a satisfying, creative occupation for both men and women, especially in large urban centers.

SECRETARIAL WORK

The National Secretaries Association (International) defines a secretary as "an assistant to an executive, possessing a mastery of office skills and ability to assume responsibility, without direct supervision, who displays initiative, exercises judgment, and makes decisions within the scope of her authority."

Technical know-how and intelligent follow-through separate the secretary from other clerical personnel. A secretary takes on responsibility and sees to it that the work of the office is carried out carefully. Though office clerks may do one or another secretarial task, it is only the secretary who combines a variety of skills into one indispensable job.

Typing

Operation of a typewriter, a basic office skill, is no longer simply knowing where each key is located on the machine. The standard 50-words-per-minute typing speed is just the beginning. Typewriters with memories that store and retrieve copy, that adjust the right-hand margin for photo-offset work, and that use changeable

Care of the typewriter is an essential part of the typist's or secretary's job. The ribbon must be kept fresh so that the typing is easy to read. All other visible parts must also be kept clean.

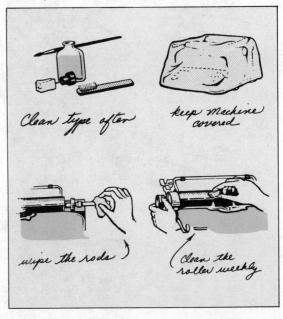

Clean type often

keep machine covered

wipe the rods

Clean the roller weekly

type faces are only a few of the specialized kinds of machines available today.

Anyone aspiring to a secretarial position must be able to transfer typing skills to whatever machine, manual or electric, the employer uses. Training on the job for these specialties is today the general practice, but basic knowledge of the machine, combined with speed and accuracy, is an essential foundation for a career as a secretary.

Acquiring skill in using a typewriter is one of the best investments you can make in building a career. No matter how automated typewriting becomes as technology advances, you can always count on industry, business, and government to value precision and speed in typing. So be certain that you never neglect this skill. Typing is a good first career step.

Dictation

The two standard methods of shorthand are Gregg and Pitman, named after the men who devised these systems of individual symbols that take the place of a group of letters.

A secretary is expected to take dictation at the rate of 100 to 120 words per minute.

Today various dictating machines are saving time for both executive and secretary. These machines permit dictation anywhere: at home, on a plane, in a car, as well as in the office. This frees the busy secretary to do other tasks.

Many of these machines are similar to small tape recorders, with additional devices to permit operation by the secretary. Whatever the system in a particular office, the secretary is expected to be able to adapt quickly.

The secretary must know how to transcribe dictation in the proper office style. The three most popular styles are: *blocked* form, *semi-blocked* form, and *full-blocked* form.

In the *blocked* form, the lines of the inside address and the lines of the body of the letter begin at the left margin. Both the date and closing begin at or near the center. The *semi-blocked* form is essentially the same as the blocked, but the first line of each paragraph is indented. In the *full-blocked* form, all the lines, including the date, begin at the left margin.

Filing

Keeping track of necessary papers in an easy-to-retrieve fashion is the essential reason for filing. Various systems are used, depending on the nature of the business, the preference of the employer, and the scope of a secretary's authority. In most large offices, a file clerk is employed for this specific purpose, but the secretary is ultimately responsible.

Correspondence

A secretary often must dictate or compose correspondence reflecting the thoughts of an executive on any matter in a clear, concise fashion. By being able to turn routine mail over to a secretary in this manner, an executive saves time for matters in which personal decisions are required. It also adds variety, interest, and stimulation to the secretary's job.

Part of handling correspondence may involve routing it through office channels, and keeping track of its progress so it may be returned to the

Office workers keep records, type correspondence, file papers, and answer the telephone. A smoothly run office, essential to nearly any business, depends on important office skills.

files when it has been read by those who must know its contents. Any successful office must keep a careful record of all correspondence and inter-office memorandums.

The Telephone

Answering the telephone is an important responsibility. The competent secretary is aware that an important client may be on the line. Using tact and judgment, the secretary decides which calls are put through, which callers are to be politely shunted elsewhere, and what the company policy is in any given situation.

On all calls the secretary has pencil ready to record the name and affiliation of the caller. If an executive is not taking calls at the time or is out of the office, the secretary should always so inform the caller and fill in a standard form for taking messages. This message note includes the time of day, where the caller can be reached, whether the call is to be returned, and any message the caller cares to leave.

Telephone calls must be answered courteously and messages taken accurately. This is a typical form used by many secretaries. A carbon is made for a permanent record.

phone

for _____
date _____ time _____
mr. _____
of _____
phone_____
message_____
_____
_____
operator_____

Most companies have a policy on how a phone call is to be answered. Whatever the policy, a secretary's telephone manners must be beyond reproach, whether answering or making calls.

Office Equipment

A secretary may not be called upon to use the many new office machines now available but must take care to learn how they operate. Most manufacturers of this equipment have training sessions; the secretary should take advantage of them and be ready to train other workers in use of the machines.

Copiers are the most common addition to office equipment. Frequently companies use them instead of making carbon copies. Inter-office communications systems are sometimes part of the telephone equipment and sometimes are separate units. Their efficient operation is essential to a secretary's job. In addition, especially in a small office, many secretaries are called upon to operate bookkeeping machines, calculators, and other accounting aids.

As new devices are brought on the market, an alert secretary will study their use with an eye to their possible application.

Other Responsibilities

The range and scope of secretarial positions can be as wide as the types of businesses that employ them. Some secretaries are called upon to write reports. Others may be asked to do statistical research. Most serve as receptionists for their employers, handling visitors with tact and discretion in order to help conserve executive time.

In a small firm, handling petty cash is usually the responsibility of a secretary, who must be accurate in keeping records, making sure each voucher is signed.

Arranging appointments, making travel plans, and coordinating office meetings are all part of the general responsibility of the secretary. In addition, the secretary may supervise the work of other clerical employees.

Professional Standing

Many employers are seeking secretaries with more to offer than the basic typing and shorthand skills. In addition to the standard business courses, whether taught at a secretarial school or taken in conjunction with other studies, some college training is desirable. In fact, some colleges are now offering special programs for those interested in becoming secretaries. Typing and shorthand skills alone qualify one to be only a stenographer. Further training should include economics, human relations, business administration, accounting, and business law.

A secretary may aspire to professional standing by attempting to pass the Certified Professional Secretary examination administered by the Institute for Certifying Secretaries, which is a department of the National Secretaries Association (International).

The qualifications for taking this test include certain educational standards, in addition to professional experience. The examination is based usually upon the many different types of secretarial work, with emphasis on judgment, understanding, and administrative skills gained through experience as well as on techniques of dealing with people, exercising decision-making abilities, understanding business law, accounting, and numerous other criteria. The examination takes two days and is divided into sections. Those who do not pass the entire test the first time can try again at a later date. Those who do win certification have tangible evidence of their professional standing.

Specialties

In addition to the general business community, there are many special jobs for secretaries with the right training. Five of the possibilities are legal, medical, technical, bilingual and executive positions—all of them well paid.

Legal secretaries are employed in law firms and legal departments of many large corporations. They help prepare briefs, in addition to standard secretarial responsibilities. They must know legal procedure, court functions, litigation procedures, and legal terminology.

EMPLOYMENT OF CLERICAL WORKERS
BY OCCUPATION

workers (1974)
in millions

	0	1	2	3	4
secretaries and stenographers					
bookkeepers					
typists					
cashiers					
receptionists					
store clerks and storekeepers					
shipping and receiving clerks					
statistical clerks					
file clerks					
postal clerks					
office machine operators					

A *medical secretary* may work for an individual doctor, a group of doctors, or a research facility, an insurance company, a hospital, or a publisher of medical textbooks. A medical secretary must have a good medical vocabulary, be able to prepare case histories, do medical reports, deal with people who are ill, and often handle a doctor's billing.

A *technical secretary* may assist an engineer or scientist in drafting reports and research proposals. A scientific background and knowledge of the special terminology involved are essential.

A *bilingual secretary* is called upon to conduct her regular job fluently in at least one other language and have a knowledge of the business customs of the country whose language he or she speaks.

An *executive secretary* is truly an executive, having great responsibility. Demonstrated management ability is essential, as he or she must often direct the activities of others. An executive secretary must also be able to organize many commitments and responsibilities and have a thorough understanding of business affairs.

TERMS USED IN SECRETARIAL WORK

agenda. List of the points to be covered at a business meeting.

appointments book. Permanent chronological record of appointments, meetings, and conferences.

audit. Examination of a financial document or record and the material to support its conclusions, by someone trained in bookkeeping.

balance sheet. Financial document showing a company's profit and loss, prepared at a specific date.

board of directors. Officially elected group that controls a corporation.

diary. Daily record of any data deemed vital to an executive and often kept up to date by a secretary.

enclosures. Any items included with a letter.

expense account. Record kept by an employee to explain out-of-pocket expenditures on the company's behalf.

fair copy. Exact replica of any document with all corrections made on it.

minutes of meeting. Record of what happened at a meeting. Some are verbatim reports, others the essence of what was said.

organization chart. The position and title of each executive in a company.

petty cash. A fund from which small cash expenses are paid.

reference initials. The secretary's initials, typed in lower case, after the executive's capitalized initials at the bottom of a letter.

tickler file. Record kept by a secretary to remind a staff of tasks that must be performed on specific dates.

COSMETOLOGY AND BEAUTY CULTURE

Art and science both have a role to play in the field of cosmetology—the enhancement of beauty through the care and treatment of the skin, hair, and nails.

The desirability of an artistic touch in a beautician is obvious; the need for an understanding of some chemistry, anatomy, bacteriology, and sanitation becomes apparent when a prospective beautician thinks about mixing hair dyes, for example, or giving facials, sterilizing equipment, and preventing infection.

Today an estimated 500,000 Americans are employed as hairdressers and cosmeticians. Though most of them are women, male workers in the field are becoming more numerous.

Training and Licensing

All states require a cosmetologist to be licensed. The general qualifications usually include a tenth grade education, good overall health, an age minimum of at least sixteen years, and training in either a public or private beauty school. A few states allow apprentice training.

A full-time day student can usually graduate in from six months to a year; a night school pupil will take longer. Some public vocational schools offer instruction in beauty culture and also provide academic courses leading to a high school diploma.

The actual course of study provided in a school will include lectures, demonstrations, and practical work. The training includes such subjects as hygiene, sanitation, applied chemistry, anatomy, applied electricity, and business organization as well as cosmetology. At first, beginning students work on mannequins and then on each other. As they progress, they may be allowed to work on customers who patronize the school's own salon.

The licensing examination is usually both written and practical. Some states also require an oral report to accompany the practical demonstration. Most states will recognize a license issued by another state. Each state's Board of Beauty Culture can supply a list of its specific requirements.

If you intend to become licensed in cosmetology, take care that you learn all textbook subjects as well as all practical aspects of the program. Read the section "How to Study" provided in the Young People's Edition for help in improving your study habits.

JOBS IN EDUCATION FOR COSMETOLOGISTS	
public vocational schools	department head guidance counselor teacher (cosmetology) substitute teacher
private beauty schools	school owner director supervisor or dean teacher (cosmetology)
outside of beauty culture schools	state board member state board inspector manufacturer's educational director guest artists

SALON JOBS			
salon owner or concessionaire			
salon supervisor			
permanent wave technician	hair stylist	wig stylist	hair straightening specialist
	hair coloring technician	scalp and hair specialist	
facial expert	make-up artist	manicurist	receptionist

Special Skills

In addition to the courses taught in every school of beauty culture, certain personal traits are important.

Physical stamina is necessary, because most beauticians stand on their feet for long periods of time. Good color vision is essential for hair dyeing. Dexterity cannot be overlooked as a requirement for everything from applying nail polish to rolling up slippery curlers during a permanent wave.

Other desirable traits are an ability to follow a customer's instructions as well as a willingness to deal with people in a friendly, but professional, manner. Being able to explain the choice of a particular procedure to a customer in easy-to-understand language helps make a beautician's job easier and can increase earnings.

In any occupation there is a considerable difference between the earnings of people who deal well with the public and those who do not. By improving your skill in dealing with people, you help yourself.

High school class in beauty culture. In addition to learning basic skills, students must know what products are safe and effective for their clients. School training and work under careful supervision are required before a cosmetologist can be considered fully competent to operate independently.

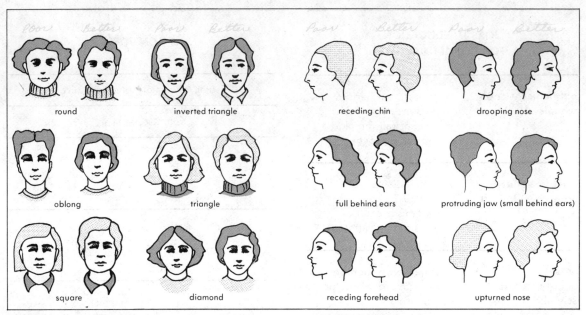

Shapes of heads. Hair styles should be selected to emphasize clients' good points and play down less attractive features. As the stylist works, full attention must be paid to a client's wishes without producing an undesirable overall effect.

Hair

By far the largest part of a cosmetologist's work is concerned with the care, appearance, and health of the customer's hair.

The choice of the proper shampoo is generally left to the beautician, who may be asked to explain to a customer why a special product is indicated for a particular condition, such as bleached, dyed, or overly permanented hair.

The hairdresser is trained to give special scalp treatments for such problems as dandruff, excess oil, or dryness.

Among the tasks requiring both special skill and artistic ability is cutting and styling, often called setting. A customer wants to know which style is flattering, as well as which will work best with her particular texture and color of hair. Whether to use a pair of scissors or a razor is usually dictated by the style chosen, as well as by the preference of either the stylist or the customer. The texture of the hair and the shape of the face may also influence the decision on style.

Current fashion also is an important factor in cutting and styling. Beauticians are often looked upon by their customers as experts in the fashion field, and are relied upon to provide up-to-date hairstyles.

Next to cutting and setting, the giving of a permanent wave and hair-straightening are the major parts of a hairdresser's job. Since most effects of a permanent last for months, the beautician must be well aware of the chemistry of the products used and whether a heat or cold method is better. Other factors to be considered are the condition of the customer's hair, whether it has been previously dyed or bleached, whether it is naturally white or very thin, and whether it is to be worn long or short.

Knowing how to alter hair color by a temporary rinse or more permanently with dyes or bleach is also an important part of a beautician's work. Here, too, the chemistry of the products to be used and the skin tone of the customer are important.

One of the newer aspects of a beauty operator's job comes from the popularity of wigs and hairpieces. As more and more women start working, they rely increasingly on wigs and hairpieces to help maintain their appearance. Keeping wigs clean and appropriately styled is one of the more recent additions to beauty culture.

Skin

Coming to the aid of a customer who seeks help with minor skin problems or general care also falls to the cosmetician.

Facials are used, either as masks or packs to beautify skin, shrink enlarged pores, temporarily improve circulation, remove dead skin, regulate the oil balance, slow wrinkling, and deep clean. The complex task of selecting which lotion, cream, or pack will do the best job is the responsibility of the well-trained beautician.

Cosmeticians know how to select make-up that is most flattering to specific skin tones and textures. Testing for the proper shade of powder, for instance, is done on the forearm, just above the wrist. A dry skin will need a cream base to retain the makeup, while an oily skin will do best with a heavier powder.

Cosmetics can also play a role in improving some skin conditions, and it is the cosmetician who must be able to make the appropriate suggestions to an inquiring patron. Included in skin care is the removal of superfluous hair. Some of the methods at the beautician's disposal are abrasion, shaving, chemical pastes, tweezing, and waxing. The method to be used depends on the amount of unwanted hair, where it is growing, how sensitive the customer's skin may be, and whether allergies are a factor. Usually a test patch is done to be sure the method chosen will not cause a rash.

Nails

Generally the beautician will also give manicures, though in larger establishments a manicurist may be employed. The shape of the nails and the condition of the hands are the first consideration in giving a manicure.

Nails and finger tips are classified into three types. The **artistic** is relatively long and narrow. The free edge of the nail is often well over the finger tip. The **square** is rather short and broad,

with a nearly flat nail. The free edge is well back from the tip. The **spatulate** is narrower at the base than at the free edge. The way the nail is shaped should conform to its classification.

The nails and finger tips are cleansed, and old polish is removed. Any stains or rough spots must be gently removed or smoothed. The nails must be filed carefully, going only toward the tips to avoid splitting.

Buffing the nails requires the use of an instrument with a removable chamois. Care must be taken since vigorous rubbing can generate unpleasant heat.

When trimming cuticles, the nipper must be used with caution to avoid cutting live tissue. The skin on the hands and fingers is softened with lotion and often a hand massage follows.

Any hangnails, ingrown nails, or furrows must be gently treated before polish can be applied.

Though certain colors are more fashionable at one time or another, no manicurist should urge the use of a special shade that may seem inappropriate to the particular customer.

Sanitation and Hygiene

Since cosmetology is a personal service, all rules of sanitation and hygiene must be observed.

State laws generally govern such matters as adequate ventilation, water supply, sewage disposal, cleaning of loose hair from floors, scrubbing sinks and counters, and sterilization of brushes, combs, towels, etc.

All bottles and jars of any creams, lotions, or solutions should be clearly labeled and kept covered at all times. All creams and lotions should be removed from their containers with disposable spatulas.

Short-cuts must never be taken when sterilizing equipment. The manufacturers' instructions must be followed precisely to avoid the transmission of disease. While these suggestions should be taken for granted by all of us who are involved in any activity that can result in passing germs from one person to another, they are of special importance for someone who works in a shop or owns a shop in which personal care is offered to the public.

HAZARDS

Though every precaution may be taken, there are certain hazards in the cosmetology field that must be noted.

Skin irritations are common from prolonged exposure to permanent wave solutions, tints, and dyes. Operators with allergies or sensitivities must take extra care. Frequent washing with special soaps and the regular use of hand lotion will help control this, as will the use of protective gloves.

Other problems for beauticians are **varicose veins** and related foot and leg disorders. The selection of comfortable, well-fitting shoes is a necessity. There will be times when style must be sacrificed for health, since an operator with aching feet cannot work efficiently.

Cuts can frequently appear during the course of giving a manicure, or from broken glass or apparatus. Immediate treatment to control bleeding and reduce the likelihood of infection is required.

Burns are not uncommon in a beauty shop. Sterilizing equipment, hot curling irons, or permanent waving apparatus are all potentially dangerous.

Electric shock can result from a defective connection or from touching a piece of electrical equipment with wet hands.

Damage suits are also a hazard for anyone working in the personal service field. Claims of malpractice, negligence, or failure to render proper service are possible. Each salon should seek adequate insurance to cover these claims, and each operator must understand the coverage.

TERMS USED IN COSMETOLOGY

alkalis. Often found in chemical water softeners. They have a harsh effect on the skin and can discolor the hair if too much is used.

antiseptic. Substance that stops the growth of bacteria.

back-combing. A way of combing the hair from almost the end toward the head to give it a fuller appearance.

bleaching action. Chemical alteration to lighter shades of the coloring matter in all kinds of animal fibers.

bulb of hair. Part of the covering of the hair shaft within the follicle.

chignon. Knot or roll of hair worn close to the head.

coiffure. The way the hair is arranged.

cortex of hair. Main part of the hair shaft which contains the pigment.

depilatory. Chemical agent used to remove unwanted hair.

emollient creams. Creams used to lubricate the skin, as during a massage.

feathering. A way of cutting the hair so that the strands are of different length; used either to thin a very heavy head of hair or to make it lie closer to the head.

lanolin. Fatty substance frequently used in cosmetics, soaps, creams, ointments, etc. It comes from the wool of sheep.

mantle. The flap of skin adjacent to the sides of the nail.

matrix of nail. The lighter colored crescent at the base of the nail.

medulla of hair. The center core of each strand of hair that contains the pigment.

pedicare. Cosmetic treatment of the feet, with special emphasis on the toe nails.

sebaceous glands. Oil glands found all over the skin except on the palms and soles. It is their secretion that keeps the skin soft.

seborrhea oleosa. Excessively oily skin or scalp. It is a very common defect.

split ends of hair. Occurs when the cortex of the hair shaft is splintered at its end, giving the hair a ragged, dry look.

PLANNING YOUR FUTURE

As students progress through school, they look forward to useful and satisfying careers. Some of them have a clear idea of what they one day will do, but many others do not. With the help of parents and school counselors, they seek information about possible careers and the types of preparation required. The important thing for you to remember in your own search is that many, varied jobs are available if you know where to look and how to prepare yourself.

To help in your search, the following pages present career information based on the latest statistics collected by the United States government. As you read, you will find that opportunities are available in fields you may never have considered. You will also find out just how you should prepare yourself to take advantage of the opportunities.

Choosing Your Career

Take time in your school years to make plans for the field in which you will possibly make your living as an adult.

Doing this is good sense these days. Unemployment among young people just out of high school and college has run almost twice as high as unemployment among all American workers through the late 1970s. *Young men and women who start their working years without planning ahead have to look longest for jobs.*

More women have gone to work in recent years—even women raising families—in part because of higher and higher living costs. More than 40 million American women now hold jobs. That's about half of all women over 16.

What you do in your education will count in many ways, large and small, in your future career. And your education in turn should be planned for the kind of career you select.

You can easily see how different kinds of education would lead you to different careers in the three career charts that follow. The charts are based on authoritative findings of the United States Department of Labor.

These charts give you wide samplings of careers that stand open to you: first, with a high-school diploma; second, with special training after high school, often just one or two years' study at a community college; third, with a college education, normally taking four years to complete.

You can see several other important things from these charts. For example, a four-year college education is not essential to you as preparation for a good career. College graduates do have higher average incomes than other workers, but some college graduates have lower incomes than other persons who entered their careers after high school, or after special training following high school.

Be especially sure to notice in the charts that careers differ in their employment prospects. Some careers provide almost certain job prospects if you do well in training for them. Other careers—usually ones widely viewed as glamorous—involve stiff competition for jobs.

When deciding between two careers, you might weigh such matters as your preference for income and your dedication to a life work.

If you think you might want a career that requires a college education, read carefully the closing section on "College Opportunities Today." Even financial limitations need not keep you from college.

A final thought before you read the information that follows: In the United States, the chance to go to school never ends. High schools and colleges today accept students of all ages in programs of continuing education. Thus, you may always resume your education if you interrupt your studies. It is never too late to gain additional education, whether it is to advance your career or satisfy your personal needs or goals.

Occupation	Qualifications and Training	Employment Trends to 1985
Airline Stewards and Stewardesses	Must be young, attractive, poised, resourceful; must meet certain physical standards.	Very rapid growth as aircraft increase in number and size. Many additional openings also will occur as attendants transfer to other occupations. Continued fuel shortages may reduce employment opportunities.
Automobile Mechanics	Most general mechanics learn their skills in 3-to-4-years' experience on the job.	Plentiful job opportunities with more automobiles and pollution-control devices to be maintained.
Bank Tellers	Trained on the job. Applicants with clerical experience preferred. Must be able to meet bonding standards.	Rapid employment growth as banks expand their services. Favorable opportunities for part-time work during peak business hours.
Barbers	State license required, usually granted for graduation from a State-approved school; often, must also pass a physical exam, be at least 16 (or 18), and have finished at least the eighth grade.	Short-run decline in job opportunities; barbers who specialize in hairstyling meet more success than conventional barbers.

These mechanics are adjusting the pollution control system of a new car.
Bank tellers work in pleasant surroundings similar to any modern office.

Occupation	Qualifications and Training	Employment Trends to 1985
Broadcast Technicians	Must pass written examination for Federal Communications Commission Radio-telephone First Class Operator License for most jobs. Courses in math, science, and electronics useful. Technical school or college training advantageous.	Slow growth, with most openings resulting from deaths and retirements. Some openings will occur as new radio and television stations open, but labor-saving devices will limit demand.
Bus Drivers (Intercity)	One year's driving experience, good hearing and eyesight required; must be at least 21. Usually must have a chauffeur's license.	Little or no change in employment is expected, but hundreds of job openings will become available yearly from retirements.
Business Machine Serviceworkers	Usually trained on the job or in manufacturers' training schools. Basic knowledge of electricity and electronics advantageous.	Very rapid increase. Opportunities particularly good for those who have training in electronics.
Carpenters	Many carpenters learn on the job; others are trained in 4-year apprenticeships entered at 17.	Generally good job opportunities, but job openings may vary greatly from year to year with swings in construction activity.
Cashiers	Some high-school business courses and after-school store experience helpful.	Abundant openings due to the large size and high turnover of this occupation; after some years, slower growth due to computerized check-out systems.
Construction Machinery Operators	Many learn through informal training and experience, but 3-year apprenticeship recommended.	Rapid increase as more bulldozers, cranes, and other heavy machines are used in construction work.

Television cameramen provide coverage of events like this half-time ceremony.
Carpenters are essential in home building and other construction jobs.

PLANNING YOUR FUTURE

Cooks and Chefs	Many learn as helpers on the job; others enter the field after food-preparation courses in or after high school.	Unusually good opportunities with continued growth in restaurants and in eating out.
Dental Laboratory Technicians	Training may be obtained on the job, in vocational high school, or in junior college. Manual dexterity needed.	Very good prospects for experienced technicians. Very favorable opportunities for recent graduates of approved training programs.
Dispensing Opticians and Optical Mechanics	Training may be obtained on the job, in apprenticeship, in vocational school, or junior college.	Very rapid increase due to growth in demand for prescription lenses.
Electricians (Construction)	A 4-year apprenticeship recommended, but many learn trade through job experience.	Rapid increase as construction expands and more electric outlets, switches, and wiring are needed for appliances, air-conditioning systems, electronic data processing equipment, and electrical control devices.
Firefighters	Must be at least 21 and in good physical condition. Must pass a written intelligence test.	Rapid growth as fire departments enlarge their staffs and paid firefighters replace volunteers. Keen competition for jobs in large cities.
Hotel Front Office Clerks	Clerical skills, including typing and bookkeeping, helpful.	Rapid employment growth as the number of hotels, motels, and motor hotels increases.

There are many job openings for retail salesworkers. More physically demanding careers include construction and firefighting.

Occupation	Qualifications and Training	Employment Trends to 1985
Hotel Managers and Assistants	Increasing emphasis on college education, though successful hotel experience is generally chief requirement.	Very good prospects, especially for those who have degrees in hotel administration.
Insurance Agents and Brokers	College training is helpful but not essential. Courses in accounting, economics, and insurance useful. All agents and most brokers must obtain State licenses.	Moderate growth. Despite an expected increase in sales volume, selling will remain keenly competitive.
Machinists	A 4-year apprenticeship is best way to learn trade, but many learn on the job.	Moderate employment growth due to rising demand for machined goods such as automobiles, household appliances, and industrial products.
Masons (Cement and Concrete Finishers)	Skills learned either in 2-year or 3-year apprenticeships or on the job.	Good growth prospects with increasing use of concrete as a building material, but possibly subject to variations.
Models	Modeling school training usually preferred. Courses in art, speech, drama, fashion design, dancing, and salesmanship also useful.	Moderate increase, but competition for available jobs will be keen.
Police Officers	Generally must be 21 and U.S. citizen. Local civil service regulations usually govern appointment.	Increased demand for protective services should create very good employment opportunities; specialized training will become increasingly important.

Many machinists learn their trade at a community college like this one. Typists can find varied and interesting work in small, informal offices.

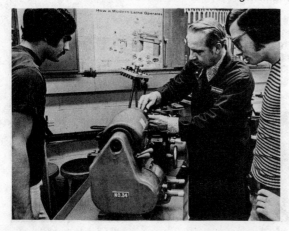

PLANNING YOUR FUTURE

Occupation	Qualifications and Training	Employment Trends to 1985
Salesworkers in Retail Stores	High school graduation preferred but not always required.	Many openings for either full-time work, or for part-time work on weekends or in peak seasons.
Stenographers and Secretaries	High school courses in typing and shorthand or post-high school course in business subjects helpful.	The increasing use of dictating machines will limit opportunities for office stenographers. Excellent prospects for secretaries and shorthand reporters.
Taxi Drivers	Usually calls for a chauffeur's driving license, a local cab driver's license, and often at least age 21 (for insurance).	High turn-over in this field should create constant job openings; offers opportunities for part-time or temporary work.
Telephone and PBX Installers and Repairers	Phone companies give special courses and on-the-job training.	Increase due to growing demand for phones and (by companies) for private branch exchange (PBX) and automatic switching (CENTREX) systems.
Typists	Must meet certain requirements of accuracy and speed (generally 40 to 50 words a minute).	Rapid employment growth with good opportunities for competent typists, especially those familiar with automatic typewriters.
Waiters and Waitresses	At least 2 or 3 years of high school are often preferred; skill in simple calculating is helpful.	Plentiful opportunities expected, due to overall growth in the field and its high turn-over.

Clothing stores are always looking for personable, qualified salespeople.
Restaurants offer opportunities for those skilled in the art of serving.

Occupation	Qualifications and Training	Employment Trends to 1985
Actors and Actresses	Formal training in drama courses useful; college degree increasingly necessary. Experience, however, is sometimes chief requirement. Talent necessary.	Overcrowding in the acting field is expected to persist, resulting in keen competition. Moreover, many actors are employed for only a part of the year.
Airplane Mechanics	Most train in FAA-approved mechanics' schools. Large airlines train a few in 3- or 4-year apprenticeship programs. A license from the FAA is frequently required.	Although employment is expected to increase about as fast as the average for all occupations, opportunities in various areas of aviation will differ. Good opportunities in general aviation; keen competition for airline jobs; opportunities in the federal Government dependent upon defense spending.
Commercial Artists	Usually 2 or 3 years of art school. Vocational high school helpful. Artistic talent necessary.	Talented and well-trained commercial artists may face competition for employment and advancement in most kinds of work. Those with only average ability and little specialized training will encounter keen competition and have limited advancement opportunities.

Highly qualified airline mechanics are essential to air travel safety. Well-trained computer operators can work in varied and interesting positions.

PLANNING YOUR FUTURE

Occupation	Qualifications and Training	Employment Trends to 1985
Computer Operating Personnel	Training usually provided on the job. For console operator, some college training may be preferred.	Employment of keypunch operators is expected to decline because of advances in other data entry techniques and equipment. Employment of console and auxiliary equipment operators should grow faster than the average for all occupations, in response to the expanding usage of computer hardware, especially terminals.
Computer Programmers	Educational requirements vary by type of organization. The Federal Government and organizations that use computers for science and engineering require college graduates; graduate degrees may be needed for some positions. Employers who use computers to process business records do not require college degrees but prefer technical training beyond high school.	Employment is expected to grow faster than the average for all occupations, as computer usage expands, particularly in medical, educational, and data processing services. Best opportunities for programmers with some training in systems analysis.
Cosmetologists	License required. Usually applicant must be at least 16 and have completed at least 10th grade and a State-approved cosmetology course. In some states, an apprenticeship may be substituted for the cosmetology course.	Employment is expected to grow about as fast as the average for all occupations, in response to the rise in demand for beauty shop services. Good opportunities for both newcomers and experienced cosmetologists, including those seeking part-time work.

Only trained operators can run high-speed computers. Commercial artists find employment in many areas of advertising and publishing.

PLANNING YOUR FUTURE

Occupation	Qualifications and Training	Employment Trends to 1985
Dancers	Training begins between ages 7 and 12, usually at a professional dancing school. Talent essential.	Those seeking professional careers in dance are likely to face keen competition, despite an expected faster than average rate of employment growth. Teaching offers the best opportunities.
Dental Assistants	Post-high-school courses in dental assisting preferred. Some learn on the job.	Employment is expected to grow faster than the average for all occupations, in response to the increasing use of assistants by dentists. Excellent opportunities, especially for graduates of approved programs. Favorable outlook for part-time work.
Dental Hygienists	License necessary. Graduation from 2-year dental hygiene school required.	Employment is expected to grow much faster than the average for all occupations, in response to the increasing use of hygienists by dentists. Very good prospects for graduates of approved programs.
Drafters	Technical training usually required in a junior college, technical institute, or vocational school; also 3- or 4-year apprenticeship.	Employment is expected to increase faster than the average for all occupations, as more drafters will be needed as support personnel for a growing number of scientists and engineers. Best opportunities for holders of associate degrees in drafting.

Dental hygienists, foresters, dancers . . . opportunities for employment in our economy are varied and interesting.

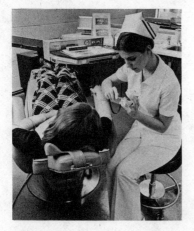  

PLANNING YOUR FUTURE

Occupation	Qualifications and Training	Employment Trends to 1985
Electroencephalographic (EEG) Technicians	Most qualify through on-the-job training, but formal training in colleges, universities, and hospitals is available.	Employment is expected to grow faster than the average for all occupations.
Engineering and Science Technicians	Technical training after high school usually required. Many train on the job.	Employment is expected to grow faster than the average for all occupations, as a result of industrial expansion and an increasingly important role for technicians in research and development. Favorable employment opportunities, particularly for graduates of post-secondary school technician training programs.
Forestry Technicians	One or 2 years' training after high school or experience such as planting trees and fighting fires.	Employment is expected to increase faster than the average for all occupations. However, due to the anticipated large number of qualified applicants, even those with specialized post-high school training may face competition.
Funeral Directors and Embalmers	Twenty-one is generally the minimum age required by law. All states require embalmers to be licensed. Graduation from a mortuary science school and 1–2 year apprenticeship required.	Little change in employment is expected. Nevertheless, prospects are good for mortuary school graduates due to openings created by replacement needs.

Science technicians can begin working at the apprentice level. Skilled technicians assist engineers in creating new technology for advanced equipment.

Interior Decorators

Usually a 3-year course at a recognized art school or institute, or a 4-year college course with a major in interior design or decoration.

Competition for beginning jobs. Best opportunities for talented college graduates who majored in interior design and graduates of professional schools of interior design. Those with less talent or without formal training are likely to face increasingly keen competition.

Library Technicians and Assistants

Formal post-high school training for library technicians preferred. Some learn on the job.

Employment is expected to grow faster than the average for all occupations. Best opportunities in large public and college and university libraries, particularly for graduates of academic programs.

Medical Assistants

Most receive training in a physician's office. Training may be obtained in vocational high schools or institutes and in junior colleges.

Employment is expected to increase faster than the average for all occupations in response to the growth in the number of physicians. Excellent opportunities, particularly for graduates of accredited junior college programs.

Medical Record Technicians and Clerks

Most employers prefer technicians who are graduates of college or hospital-based programs lasting 10 months to 2 years. High school diploma and on-the-job training are usually adequate for clerks.

Very good outlook for clerks due to the anticipated expansion in medical facilities and recordkeeping. Favorable prospects for technicians with at least an associate degree; those with less education may face strong competition.

A medical assistant may monitor electrocardiographs. Violinists often pursue teaching careers in addition to performing.

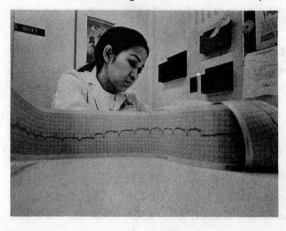

PLANNING YOUR FUTURE

Occupation	Qualifications and Training	Employment Trends to 1985
Musicians	Training through private study or in a college or conservatory. For teaching in public schools, a 4-year course in a college or conservatory and a State certificate usually required. Musical talent necessary.	All but the highest caliber of symphonic players are likely to face keen competition. Better prospects for those qualified as teachers as well as musicians than for those qualified as performers only.
Optometric Assistants	Vocational or technical school programs are becoming more important. However, most train on the job.	Employment is expected to grow much faster than the average for all occupations, in response to greater demand for eye-care services. Excellent opportunities for those who have completed formal training programs.
Photographers	Generally 2 or 3 years of on-the-job training. For some specializations, post-high school training is needed.	Employment is expected to grow about as fast as the average for all occupations. Good opportunities in technical fields such as scientific and industrial photography. Portrait and commercial photographers are likely to face keen competition.
Physical Therapist Assistants and Aides	Most qualify through on-the-job training. Others learn their job in vocational, technical, or adult education programs or in junior colleges.	Employment is expected to grow much faster than the average for all occupations, resulting in excellent opportunities for both assistants and aides.

Optometric assistants and physical therapists enjoy rewarding work in the medical field. Most photographers find practical training a necessity.

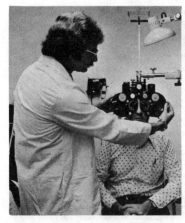

Radiologic (X-Ray) Technologists

Usually a 2-year post-high school training program. Bachelor's degree important for teaching or administration.

Despite faster than average employment growth as X-ray equipment is increasingly used to diagnose and treat diseases, graduates of approved programs may face competition for choice positions. Part-time workers will find the best opportunities in physicians' offices and clinics.

Registered Nurses

Three types of training available: diploma programs (3 years) mainly in hospitals; associate degree programs (2 years) in junior and community colleges; and baccalaureate degree programs (4–5 years) in colleges or universities. License required for practice.

Favorable opportunities, especially for nurses with graduate education seeking positions as teachers and administrators. Particular demand in some southern states and many inner-city locations.

Respiratory Therapy Workers

Although training may be obtained on the job, junior college programs are stressed.

Employment is expected to grow much faster than the average for all occupations, owing primarily to the many new uses for respiratory therapy.

Singers

Training through private lessons in a conservatory or in a college. To teach music in public school, a B.A. in music education and a State certificate are required. Musical talent necessary.

Keenly competitive field, despite an expected faster than average rate of employment growth. Some opportunities will arise from the expanded use of TV satellites, cable TV, and wider use of video cassettes, but the best prospects are in teaching.

Registered nurses are in demand for both hospital and teaching positions.
X-ray technologists play an important role in the diagnostic process.

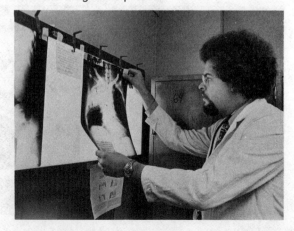

PLANNING YOUR FUTURE

Occupation	Qualifications and Training	Employment Trends to 1985
Surveyors	Usually special training following high school plus training on the job. Some specialties require a college degree.	Employment is expected to increase much faster than the average for all occupations, in response to the rapid development of urban areas. Best opportunities for those with post-secondary school training in surveying.
Technicians for Operating Rooms	Training may be obtained on the job in hospitals, vocational schools, junior colleges, or in "medic" programs of the Armed Forces.	Employment is expected to grow faster than the average for all occupations, as operating room technicians increasingly assume more of the routine nursing tasks in the operating room.
Television and Radio Service Technicians	Technical or vocational school training, correspondence courses plus training on the job, or military service courses. Some learn entirely on the job.	Employment is expected to increase faster than the average for all occupations, in response to the growing number of radios, television sets, phonographs, tape recorders, and other home entertainment products.
Workers in Occupational Safety and Health	Graduates of 2-year occupational safety or health curriculums hired as technicians. Continuing education important.	Employment is expected to increase faster than the average for all occupations, as growing concern for occupational safety and health and consumer safety continues to generate programs and jobs.

One rapidly expanding medical field is respiratory therapy. Professional singers find work where they can as performers or teachers.

Occupation	Qualifications and Training	Employment Trends to 1985
Accountants	College degree may be required for better jobs; junior college, business school, or correspondence course training acceptable for some jobs.	Very good opportunities. Because of the growing complexity of business accounting requirements, college graduates, particularly those who had part-time accounting experience while in school, will be in greater demand than other applicants. Those trained in computer techniques also will be preferred.
Announcers, Radio and Television	College education plus several years' experience minimum for network broadcasting. Must have a good voice and a good command of English. Small stations sometimes employ vocational or high school graduates.	Despite average employment growth as new radio and television stations are licensed and as more cable television stations begin their own programming, applicants are likely to face keen competition. Better opportunities in radio than in television.
Architects	License required. May be earned by a 5-year bachelor of architecture degree program followed by 3 years' experience, or a master's program followed by 2 years' experience.	Favorable opportunities. Employment is expected to increase much faster than the average for all occupations, as a result of the growth of nonresidential construction.

This woman disk jockey discovered that there are more jobs in radio than in TV.
Landscape architects are called in on both small and large projects.

PLANNING YOUR FUTURE

Bank Officers

Management trainees should have a business administration major. Courses in accounting, economics, commercial law, political science, and statistics also valuable.

Employment is expected to grow faster than the average for all occupations, as the increasing use of computers and the expansion of banking services require more officers to provide sound management. Many opportunities for college graduates as management trainees with good growth potential.

Chemists

Bachelor's degree with major in chemistry is minimum; graduate training usually necessary in research and teaching.

Good opportunities for graduates at all degree levels. Increased demand for plastics, man-made fibers, drugs, and fertilizers in addition to activities in health care, pollution control, and energy will contribute to the need for additional chemists.

Dentists

Four years in dental college preceded by 2 to 4 years of predental college work. All states require a license.

Employment is expected to grow faster than the average for all occupations, as dental services increase in response to the expansion of prepayment arrangements. Excellent opportunities for qualified dentists make this a sound career choice.

The chemist's advanced degrees are needed for work in this specialized field.
Education and work experience are needed for a career as a bank officer.

Engineers

Bachelor's degree in engineering generally preferred, although experience as a technician may sometimes be substituted for a degree. Graduate training usually required for teaching and research.

Employment is expected to grow faster than the average for all occupations. Very good opportunities for engineering school graduates as supply is likely to fall short of demand. Many openings also will be filled by upgraded technicians and graduates in related fields.

Geologists

Bachelor's degree in geology or a related field adequate for many jobs. Advanced degree helpful for advancement.

Good employment opportunities for bachelor's degree holders. Employment is expected to increase faster than the average for all occupations because of the continued rise in demand for petroleum and minerals.

Lawyers

Usually 4 years of college followed by 3 years of law school. Must be admitted to bar for court practice.

A continued increase in the number of law school graduates is expected to create keen competition for salaried positions. Prospects for establishing a new practice probably will be best in small towns and expanding suburban areas.

Librarians

Completion of a 1-year master's degree program in library science. A Ph.D degree is advantageous for teaching and advancement to top administrative positions.

Applicants are likely to face competition for choice positions. Best opportunities for new graduates in public and special libraries.

Geologist Harrison Schmitt was the first scientist on the moon. Well-trained librarians are necessary to keep both public and university libraries in order.

Occupation	Qualifications and Training	Employment Trends to 1985
Meteorologists	Bachelor's degree in meteorology or related field. Graduate degree necessary for research and teaching.	Favorable opportunities in industry, weather consulting firms, radio and television, and government
Pharmacists	Usually 3 or 4 years of professional study in a college of pharmacy following 2 years college. License necessary.	Employment is expected to grow about as fast as the average for all occupations, due to the establishment of new pharmacies and more extensive use of pharmacists in hospitals and clinics. Very good outlook as the number of job openings is expected to exceed the number of pharmacy school graduates.
Physical Therapists	A bachelor's degree from a school of physical therapy and a license.	Employment is expected to grow much faster than the average for all occupations, due to an expansion of rehabilitation programs and facilities. Favorable opportunities for new graduates, particularly in suburban and rural areas.
Physicians	Requires licensing after 4 years of medical school preceded by 4 years of college in almost all cases. Nationwide, less than half the college graduates applying to medical school are accepted.	Very good employment outlook. Particular demand in primary care areas such as general practice, pediatrics, and internal medicine, especially in rural sections of the country.

A medical career demands extensive training but it is a very rewarding field. Pharmacists work with physicians to provide adequate health care.

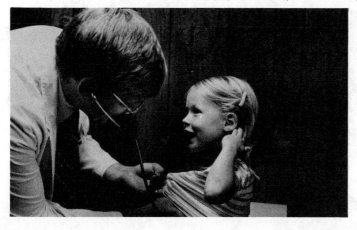

Occupation	Qualifications and Training	Employment Trends to 1985
Reporters, Newspaper	Talented writers with little or no formal training are sometimes hired, but most newspapers consider only those with a college education. Graduate work increasingly important.	Favorable opportunities for those with exceptional writing talent and the ability to handle highly specialized scientific and technical subjects. Best prospects on weekly or daily newspapers in small towns and suburban areas.
Social Workers	Bachelor's degree generally the minimum. Master's degree in social work required for some positions.	Employment is expected to increase faster than the average for all occupations.
Teachers: Kindergarten, Elementary and Secondary School	Teaching certificate necessary in public schools and in some parochial and private schools. Certification usually requires a bachelor's degree and education courses. Master's degree sometimes required.	Competition expected through the mid-1980s. If patterns of entry and reentry continue, the number of persons qualified to teach will exceed the number of openings. A recent survey found teacher supply least adequate in mathematics, natural and physical sciences, industrial arts, special education, and some vocational-technical subjects.
Veterinarians	Licensing required after 4 years' study in a school of veterinary medicine, entered almost always only after 4 years of college. Nationwide, less than one-fifth of all college graduates applying to veterinary school are admitted.	Favorable employment opportunities as a result of growth in the pet population and the numbers of livestock and poultry, and an increase in veterinary research.

Meteorologists help protect our society from large-scale disasters. Teachers guide their students step-by-step through the learning process.

PLANNING YOUR FUTURE

College Opportunities Today

"*Should* I go to college?" That's an important question you may already have asked yourself. But first, you need to know the answer to a different question: "*Can* I go to college—if I want to?"

Yes, you can go to college.

Money is probably the main factor you think might keep you from college. Surveys have found that studious young Americans from all but the richest families see lack of money as their main barrier to college.

You may have heard, for example, that a year at college today costs an average of $4,000 or as much as $7,500 and up at the most expensive colleges—from $16,000 to $30,000 in all for a traditional four-year college education.

But you should also know that a great deal of financial aid is available to students who need it. Financial aid for college students now totals *twelve billion dollars a year.*

You should realize too that there are many ways of getting a college education for as little as a few hundred dollars a year in tuition.

Taken together, these billions in aid plus the many low-cost options for college add up to a wealth of opportunities to get a college education you can afford.

If you have the talent, the academic background, and the drive to undertake the years of effort demanded by college studies, nothing should be permitted to hold you back. The rewards of college study go far beyond increased earning power. College gives us an opportunity to gain the cultural background that enriches our entire lives and those of our families.

TO GO TO COLLEGE

The opportunities available today make it possible for almost any ambitious, hard-working high school graduate to get a college education, regardless of his or her financial situation.

Still, college is neither essential nor desirable for every high school graduate. It would probably be wise for you to decide *against* college in circumstances like these:

1. You feel impatient at the thought of college studies; you're bored with school, bookwork, and classes.
2. By the time of your high school graduation, you will have carried out plans that effectively prepare you to make a good living, perhaps as

   - secretary or stenographer
   - dental assistant
   - auto mechanic
   - radio-TV service expert
   - union apprentice to a carpenter, electrician, or plumber
   - police officer
   - member of the U.S. Postal Service or Armed Forces
   - employee of a successful small business (maybe a family business or farm) that you have already begun to learn and may some day run as your own.

HOW MUCH COLLEGE FOR YOU?

If you do plan on a career that requires education and training beyond high school, you need not think only of the traditional four-year college education.

Whether your schooling after high school runs less than a year or eight years and more depends on the kind of career you select.

For example, young men and young women can qualify as ambulance personnel—Emergency Medical Technicians—after only a few months' training. Or they can qualify as regular hospital nurses (Licensed Practical Nurses, LPNs) earning a good salary after just a year's training. Increasing numbers of men today do become nurses.

To become a physician or senior scientist, on the other hand, would take four years of college followed by four years of study (or more) for the doctor's degree at a medical school or university.

Two years of college at a low-cost community college have proven to be a choice widely popular among young people today. Two-year occupational programs at such colleges prepare graduates for a variety of interesting, well-paid careers. Two-year transfer programs at these colleges prepare many other graduates for transfer to four-year colleges and completion of work for the bachelor's degree.

FINANCING COLLEGE BY KEEPING COSTS LOW

One way to make college financially feasible for you is to take advantage of many available opportunities to further your education at low cost.

Community colleges throughout the country provide such opportunities. Their average cost for tuition and fees in 1978 was $389.

State colleges and universities offering a four-year college education represent your next lowest-cost choice. Their tuition and fees in 1978 averaged $621.

If you could live at home and commute to a community college, state college, or state university, the costs of tuition and fees would represent your largest single direct outlay for college.

FINANCING COLLEGE WITH FINANCIAL AID

As noted before, billions in financial aid are offered to you and other college students whose needs may run far beyond what their families can afford. This aid could even enable you to go to one of the most expensive colleges in the country, if you qualify for admission.

Your high school guidance office probably has full information about this aid. You can also find out about it by writing or visiting colleges that interest you.

As a quick checklist of major sources you should explore, here are the principal forms of aid available in the United States today and the total annual amount in aid each provides:

- Basic Educational Opportunity Grant Program (Federal, no interest); 2.1 billion dollars

- National Direct Student Loan Program (Federal, 3% interest); 310 million dollars

- Guaranteed Student Loan Program (Federal and State, 7% interest); 954 million dollars

- State grant, scholarship, and loan programs; 810 million dollars

- Scholarships, loans, and aid jobs provided by the colleges themselves; 1 billion dollars

- Scholarship programs of companies, unions, civic groups, foundations, and other private organizations; 55 million dollars

Here's a closing wish for you—good planning! It's even better for you than good luck.